OIL EXPLOITATION AND HUMAN
IN NIGERIA'S OIL PRODUCIN(

OIL EXPLOITATION AND HUMAN RIGHTS VIOLATIONS IN NIGERIA'S OIL PRODUCING COMMUNITIES

Olubayo OLUDURO

intersentia

Cambridge – Antwerp – Portland

Intersentia Publishing Ltd.
Trinity House | Cambridge Business Park | Cowley Road
Cambridge | CB4 0WZ | United Kingdom
tel.: +44 1223 393 753 | email: mail@intersentia.co.uk

Distribution for the UK:
NBN International
Airport Business Centre, 10 Thornbury Road
Plymouth, PL6 7PP
United Kingdom
Tel: +44 1752 202 301 | Fax: +44 1752 202 331
Email: orders@nbninternational.com

Distribution for the USA and Canada:
International Specialized Book Services
920 NE 58th Ave Suite 300
Portland, OR 97213
USA
Tel.: +1 800 944 6190 (toll free)
Email: info@isbs.com

Distribution for Austria:
Neuer Wissenschaftlicher Verlag
Argentinierstraße 42/6
1040 Wien
Austria
Tel.: +43 1 535 61 03 24
Email: office@nwv.at

Distribution for other countries:
Intersentia Publishing nv
Groenstraat 31
2640 Mortsel
Belgium
Tel.: +32 3 680 15 50
Email: mail@intersentia.be

Oil Exploitation and Human Rights Violations in Nigeria's Oil Producing Communities
Olubayo Oluduro

©   2014 Intersentia
Cambridge – Antwerp – Portland
www.intersentia.com | www.intersentia.co.uk

Cover illustration: Danny Juchtmans

ISBN 978-1-78068-131-3
D/2014/7849/25
NUR 828

*This work is dedicated to my father, the late Justin Akinyemi,
for instilling in me the virtue of hard work,
doggedness, and love of God and men.*

ACKNOWLEDGEMENTS

The desire to reach the pinnacle of one's chosen profession has made me be more resolute than ever in seeking knowledge and towards this end, the successful completion of my PhD Programme.

I am particularly indebted to Prof. Dr. Luc Lavrysen, my Promotor, who diligently and painstakingly went through the work and for his insightful and helpful comments. His thoroughness, amiable disposition, useful suggestions and queries greatly facilitated the timely completion of this work. In spite of his tight schedule, he was always there to attend to me whenever the need arose. I also owe a debt of gratitude to other members of my Guidance Committee, Prof. Dr. Eva Brems, Prof. Dr. An Cliquet and Prof. Dr. Tom Vander Beken for their guidance and unflinching support, without which this work would not have been accomplished. I also want to express my profound gratitude and thanks to Prof. Dr. Delphine Misonne and Prof. M.T. Ladan for their incisive comments and useful suggestions on this work. Special thanks also to the Public Law Department administrative staff, especially Yvan De Maeseneire, for his assistance throughout the programme.

I also want to thank the individuals and organizations, such as ERA, SERAC, the National Human Rights Commission, the ECOWAS Court, NESREA and others too numerous to mention, for the materials provided and for the support given to me during my fieldwork.

There is no gainsaying the fact that the kind of peace, love and care I experienced on the home front contributed tremendously to the successful completion of this work. In this regard, I would like to stress the understanding and unflinching support of my amiable, loving and charming wife Bolaji Oluduro, my children, Temitayo, Oluwafolakemi, Oluwaseun, Oluwanifemi and Olumide through all my absences from home during the course of the programme. I will forever remain grateful to my mother, Mrs. Kehinde Oluduro, for all her contributions, support and prayers. She is indeed a true mother.

I want to specially thank my University, Adekunle Ajasin University, Akungba-Akoko, Ondo State, Nigeria for granting me study leave to embark on this programme and for all the financial assistance. Special thanks go to the Vice-Chancellor, Prof. Femi Mimiko, the immediate past Vice-Chancellor, Prof. Dr. (Med) Philip Abiodun, former Ag. Vice-Chancellor, Prof. Oladele Awobuluyi and all the entire staff and management of Adekunle Ajasin University for all their support. I am particularly indebted to the Education Trust Fund, Abuja for financial assistance/funding throughout the period of this programme.

I also wish to place on record my sincere appreciation to Prof. 'Yomi Dinakin, the pioneering Dean of the Faculty of Law, Adekunle Ajasin University, Akungba-Akoko, for his unflinching support and motivation throughout this Programme. I am also grateful to Prof. 'Yemi Akinseye-George, the immediate past Dean of the Faculty of Law, Adekunle Ajasin University for his inspiration and advice which no doubt contributed to the timely completion of this programme. My profound gratitude goes to my brother, Olubisi Oluduro who has always been a motivating factor in my quest to acquire more knowledge. I also want to thank the other members of my family, Mrs. Agoi Grace, Mr. M.A. Oluduro, Mrs. M.M. Olasunkanmi, Mr. G.O. Oluduro, Bunmi Akinbode, Kemi Oluduro, Tope Raymond, Blessing Oluduro, Ojo Oluduro, Anthony Oluduro, Rose Oluduro, and other members too numerous to mention. My gratitude goes to my able friend Chief Magistrate M.A. Akinsanya for being there for me. I really thank you for your support and encouragement. I must also not fail to mention the contribution of O.J. Jejelola, the Ag. Dean, Faculty of Law, Adekunle Ajasin University, Tajudeen Ibraheem, A.M Owoyemi, Olugbenga Oke-Samuel, S.F. Ojomu, E.N. Olowokere, Lolade Olateru-Olagbegi, Bola Adewusi, Victor Ayeni, all of the Faculty of Law, Adekunle Ajasin University, Akungba Akoko. I am highly indebted to Dr. Rhuks T. Ako, Dr. Femi Adekoya, Prof. A.O. Popoola, Dr. A.A. Idowu, Dr. Dayo Akomolede, Ag. Dean, Faculty of Law, Ekiti State University, Nigeria, Mr. Joseph Ayodele, Pastor & Pastor (Mrs.) Afolabi, Pastor Ayo Fasusi, Anthony Adeyemi, Prof. Ademola Abass, Dr. Ebenezer Durojaye, Saint Peters, Dr. T.F. Yerima, Dr. Adefi Olong, Dr. R.K. Salman, L.O. Alimi, Dr. Muhammed Akanbi, Sunday Olorundahunsi, Chief Registrar of the Supreme Court of Nigeria, Mr. Dayo Abe, Mr. B.J. Lawani, Mrs. Olabisi Ayankogbe, Dr. David Efevwerhan, Laurens Lavrysen, Prof. Kaniye Ebeku, Dr. Cyril Obi, Dr. Engobo Emeseh, Shola Omotola, Bede Nwete, Dr. Busuyi Mekusi, Cosmos Fasole, Hon. Olotu Fatai, Charles Okhavhe, Femi Lawal, Bimbo Lawal, Bernard Awomuse, Makia Randolf Musongo, Genesis Chevure, Jestinah Chevure, Helen Etta, Oceana, Tarila Ebiede, Mr. & Mrs. Lasisi Sanyafunmi, Mr. Asunloye Isaac Olusola, the Chief Academic Planning Officer, Adekunle Ajasin University, F.T. Olorunmaye, Dr. E.F. Ogunbodede, Dr. Lanre Adeyemi, Dr. Adeleke Salami, Japheth Aremo, E. Mbang Akpambang, Dr. I.O. Babatunde, for their immense contribution to the success of this programme. To my friends and colleagues in the department, Wen Xiang, Jesse Lambrecht, Roel Meeus, Nicky Broeckhoven, Tania Van Laer, I say thank you all.

Finally, I would like to thank everyone whom I have come across on my way and has contributed one way or the other to the successful completion of this programme, who are too numerous to mention herein.

CONTENTS

SELECTED ABBREVIATIONS

AAU Law Journal	Ambrose Alli University Law Journal
ACJ	African Court of Justice
ADR	Alternative Dispute Resolution
Afr. Hum. Rts. L.J.	African Human Rights Law Journal
African J. Legal Stud.	African Journal of Legal Studies
AIDS	Acquired Immunodeficiency Syndrome
Am. J. Int'l L.	American Journal of International Law
Am. U. Int'l L. Rev.	American University International Law Review
Am. U. J. Int'l L. & Pol'y	American University Journal of International Law and Policy
Ann. Surv. Int'l & Comp. L.	Annual Survey of International and Comparative Law
Annu. Rev. Environ. Resour.	Annual Review of Environment and Resources
Ariz. J. Int'l & Comp. L.	Arizona Journal of International and Comparative Law
ASICL	African Society of International & Comparative Law
ASME	American Society of Mechanical Engineer
ATCA	Alien Tort Claims Act
ATS	Alien Tort Statute
AU	African Union
Bcf	Billion cubic feet
Berkeley J. Int'l L.	Berkeley Journal of International Law
BoRs	Bill of Rights
Brooklyn J. Int'l L.	Brooklyn Journal of International Law
B.U. Int'l. L.J.	Boston University International Law Journal
CBD	Convention on Biological Diversity
CDHR	Committee for the Defence of Human Rights
CEDAW	Committee on the Elimination of Discrimination against Women
CERCLA	Comprehensive Environmental Response, Compensation, and Liability Act
CESCR	Committee on Economic, Social and Cultural Rights
CFRN	Constitution of the Federal Republic of Nigeria

Colo. J. Int'l Env.L. & Pol'y	Colorado Journal of International Environmental Law and Policy
Colum. J. Envtl. L.	Columbia Journal of Environmental Law
Colum. J. Transnat'l L.	Columbia Journal of Transnational Law
Comp. Media L.J.	Comparative Media Law Journal
Cornell L. Rev.	Cornell Law Review
Corp. Soc. Responsib. Environ. Mgmt.	Corporate Social Responsibility and Environmental Management
COSEND	Consolidated Council on Social and Economic Development of Coastal States of the Niger Delta
CSO	Civil Society Organisation
DDR	Disarmament, Demobilization and Reintegration
Denv. J. Int'l L. & Pol'y	Denver Journal of International Law and Policy
DPR	Directorate of Petroleum Resources
ECHR	European Court on Human Rights
ECJ	European Court of Justice
ECOWAS	Economic Community of West African States
EEZ	Exclusive Economic Zone
EFCC	Economic and Financial Crimes Commission
EGASPIN	Environmental Guidelines and Standards for the Petroleum Industries in Nigeria
EIA	Environmental Impact Assessment
EITI	Extractive Industries Transparency Initiative
Emory Int'l L. Rev.	Emory International Law Review
ERA	Environmental Rights Action
ESCR	Economic, Social and Cultural Rights
EU	European Union
FEPA	Federal Environmental Protection Agency
FNC	forum non conveniens
FOI	Freedom of Information
Fordham Envtl. L. Rev.	Fordham Environmental Law Review
Fordham Int'l L.J.	Fordham International Law Journal
FREP	Fundamental Rights (Enforcement Procedure)
FWLR	Federation Weekly Law Report
GC	Global Compact
Georgetown Int'l Envtl. Law Review	Georgetown International Environmental Law Review
Geo. Wash. Int'l L. Rev	George Washington International Law Review
GRBPL	Gravitas Review of Business and Property Law
Harv. Hum. Rts. J.	Harvard Human Rights Journal
Harv. Int'l L.J	Harvard International Law Journal
Hastings Int'l & Comp. L. Rev.	Hastings International and Comparative Law Review

Hastings W. Nw. J. Envtl. L. & Pol'y	Hastings West-Northwest Journal of Environmental Law and Policy
HIV	Human Immunodefiency Virus
Hous. J. Int'l L.	Houston Journal of International Law
HRW	Human Rights Watch
Hum. Rts. Q.	Human Rights Quarterly
IACHR	Inter American Courts of Human Rights
ICC	International Chamber of Commerce
ICJ	International Court of Justice
ICPC	Independent Corrupt Practices & Other Related Offences Commission
IDEA	Institute for Democracy and Electoral Assistance
Indian J. Int'l L.	Indian Journal of International Law
INGO	International Non-Governmental Organisation
Int'l. Energy L. & Tax'n Rev.	International Energy Law and Taxation Review
IOC	International Oil Companies
IOE	International Organization of Employers
IPIECA	International Petroleum Industry Environmental Conservation Association
IUCN	International Union for Conservation of Nature
IWGIA	International Work Group for Indigenous Affairs
J. Consum Policy	Journal of Consumer Policy
J. Energy Nat. Resources L.	Journal of Energy and Natural Resources Law
J. Envtl. L.	Journal of Environmental Law
J. Hum. Ecol.	Journal of Human Ecology
J. Hum. Rts. L. & Prac.	Journal of Human Rights Law and Practice
J.L. & Com.	Journal of Law and Commerce
J.P.P.L.	Journal of Private and Property Law
J. Transnat'l L. Pol'y	Journal of Transnational Law and Policy
JV	Joint Venture
ICCPR	International Covenant on Civil and Political Rights
ICESCR	International Covenant on Economic, Social and Cultural Rights
ILO	International Labour Organization
LASU	Lagos State University
LFN	Laws of the Federation of Nigeria
LGA	Local Government Area
Loy. L.A. Int'l & Comp. L.J.	Loyola of Los Angeles International and Comparative Law Journal
Loy. L.A. L. Rev.	Loyola of Los Angeles Law Review
LUA	Land Use Act

McGill Int'l J. Sust. Dev. L. & Pol'y	McGill International Journal of Sustainable Development Law and Policy
Melb. J. Int'l L.	Melbourne Journal of International Law
MEND	Movement for the Emancipation of the Niger Delta
Michigan J. Int'l L.	Michigan Journal of International Law
Mich. St. J. Int. L.	Michigan State Journal of International Law
Minn. J. Global Trade	Minnesota Journal of Global Trade
MMR	Maternal Mortality Ratio
MNC	Multinational Corporations
MNOC	Multinational Oil Corporations
MOSOP	Movement for the Survival of Ogoni People
MqJICEL	Macquarie Journal of International and Comparative Environmental Law
NAPIMS	National Petroleum Investment Management Services
N.C.J. Int'l. & Com. Reg.	North Carolina Journal of International Law and Commercial Regulation
NCP	National Contact Point
NDBDA	Niger Delta Basin Development Authority
NDDB	Niger Delta Development Board
NDDC	Niger Delta Development Commission
NDRDMP	Niger Delta Regional Development Master Plan
NEITI	Nigeria's Extractive Industries Transparency Initiative
NESREA	National Environmental Standards and Regulations Enforcement Agency
Newc L.R.	Newcastle Law Review
NGOs	Non-Governmental Organisations
NHRC	National Human Rights Commission
NHRI	National Human Rights Institution
NIALS	Nigerian Institute of Advanced Legal Studies
Nig. J. of Contemp. L.	Nigerian Journal of Contemporary Law
NJC	National Judicial Council
NNOC	Nigerian National Oil Corporation
NNPC	Nigerian National Petroleum Corporation
NOSDRA	National Oil Spill Detection and Response Agency (Establishment) Act
NUJS Law Review	National University of Juridical Sciences Law Review
Nw. J. Int'l Human Rights	Northwestern Journal of International Human Rights
NWLR	Nigerian Weekly Law Report

N.Y.U. J. Int'l. & Pol.	New York University Journal of International Law and Politics
OCSLA	Outer Continental Shelf Lands Act
OD	Operational Directive
OECD	Organization for Economic Co-operation and Development
OHCHR	Office of the High Commissioner of Human Rights
Okla. City U. L. Rev.	Okla. City University Law Review
OML	Oil Mining Lease
OMPADEC	Oil Mineral Producing Areas Development Commission
OP	Operational Policy
OPA	Oil Pollution Act
OPEC	Organization of Petroleum Exporting Countries
OPL	Oil Prospecting License
Pace Envtl. L. R.	Pace Environmental Law Review
PIB	Petroleum Industry Bill
PIC	Prior Informed Consent
PP	Public Participation
PSC	Production Sharing Contract
Queen's L.J	Queen's Law Journal
RECIEL	Review of European Community and International Environmental Law
Rev. Afr. Comm'n Hum. Peoples' Rts.	Review of African Commission on Human and Peoples' Rights
RICO	Racketeer Influenced and Corrupt Organizations Act
RSC	Risk Service Contract
SERAC	Social and Economic Rights Action Center
SERAP	Socio-Economic Rights and Accountability Project
SPDC	Shell Petroleum Development Company
SRSG	Special Representative of the Secretary-General
Stan. Env'l L.J.	Stanford Environmental Law Journal
Stan. J. Int'l L.	Stanford Journal of International Law
Stud Tribes Tribals	Studies of Tribes and Tribals
Suffolk Transnat'l L. Rev.	Suffolk Transnational Law Review
Syr. J. Int.l & Comm.	Syracuse Journal of International Law & Commerce
Tex. Int'l L. J.	Texas International Law Journal
The Geo. Wash. Int'l L. Rev.	The George Washington International Law Review
TNCs	Transnational Corporations
Transnat'l L. & Contemp. Probs.	Transnational Law and Contemporary Problems
Tul. Envtl. L.J.	Tulane Environmental Law Journal

TVPA	Torture Victim Protection Act
UCLA J. Envtl. L. & Pol'y	UCLA Journal of Environmental Law and Policy
UDHR	Universal Declaration of Human Rights
UK	United Kingdom
U. Miami Inter-Am. L. Rev.	University of Miami Inter-American Law Review
U. Miami Int'l & Comp. L. Rev	University of Miami International and Comparative Law Review
UN	United Nations
UNCAC	United Nations Convention against Corruption
UNCLOS	United Nations Convention on Law of the Sea
UNCTAD	United Nations Conference on Trade and Development
UNDP	United Nations Development Programme
UNEP	United Nations Environment Programme
UNICEF	United Nations International Children Educational Fund
US	United States
Va. J. Int'l L.	Virginia Journal of International Law
Vand. J. Transnat'l L.	Vanderbilt Journal of Transnational Law
VPs	Voluntary Principles
VPSHR	Voluntary Principles on Security and Human Rights
WHO	World Health Organization
Wis. Envtl. L.J.	Wisconsin Environmental Law Journal
Yale Hum. Rts. & Dev. L.J.	Yale Human Rights and Development Law Journal
Yale J. Int'l L.	Yale Journal of International Law
Yale L.J.	Yale Law Journal
ZaöRV	Zeitschrift für ausländisches öffentliches Recht und Völkerrecht

TABLE OF CASES

LIST OF SELECTED INTERVIEWEES

GOVERNMENT INSTITUTIONS, DEPARTMENTS AND AGENCIES

National Human Rights Commission
Ministry of Environment, Abuja
National Environmental Standards and Regulations Enforcement Agency (NESREA)

NGOS AND CIVIL SOCIETY GROUPS

Environmental Rights Action (ERA)
The Social and Economic Rights Action Centre (SERAC)
Environment and Justice Initiative

NAMED PRIVATE INDIVIDUALS

Chima Ubani – Environmental Rights Action
Murphy Akiri – Environmental Rights Action
Chief Abidi Mayoku – Ubeji Community Leader
Paul Eneuntowose Keku – National Public Relation Officer (PRO), Ubeji Community
James Okoro – Member, Ubeji Community of Elders
Jonah Gbemre – Youth and Representative, Iwherekan Community
Prof. 'Yemi Akinseye-George – former Special Assistant to the Hon. Attorney-General of Federation and Minister of Justice and Human Rights Expert.
Olugbenga Oke-Samuel – Activist and Environmentalist
Dr. R.K. Salman – Human Rights Activist

INTRODUCTION

ABSTRACT

This work is a critical examination of the various human rights violations and environmental damage associated with oil exploitation in the oil producing communities of Nigeria, and the role and responsibilities of the major multinational companies (MNCs) in respect of those violations. It examines the various categories of human rights that are vulnerable to the activities of oil multinational companies and stresses that human rights cannot be secured in a degraded or polluted environment. It assesses the existing human rights instruments, legislation and enactments regulating the exploration of oil in Nigeria, their effectiveness in the protection of the rights of the people living in the oil producing areas and highlights areas that need to be reformed in the light of the experience of other countries.

The work examines the various legal frameworks regulating oil exploitation in Nigeria to discover whether the laws as they exist are effective, adequate, accessible and justiciable to promote adequate safeguard for the protection of the rights of the people in the oil producing areas. Examples of such laws include the Land Use Act 1978 which vested all land in the State; the Petroleum Act of 1969 which vested the ownership of oil in the Federal Government; and section 20 of the 1999 Constitution of the Federal Republic of Nigeria (CFRN) which provides that the 'State shall protect and improve the environment and safeguard the water, air and land, forest and wildlife of Nigeria'. It also considers the issue of enforcement of the laws relating to environmental protection in Nigeria.

The work further aims at investigating whether in spite of the long years of agitation by activists and scholars for legal accountability of Non-State Actors for their human rights violations, positive results have been achieved towards establishing such frameworks at the national level. This work discusses the effectiveness of solutions created at the international level in the form of codes of conduct and norms to regulate the activities of the oil MNCs in improving the situations especially in developing countries, like Nigeria where these MNCs operate. It also explores the various avenues that can be used to assert responsibility for corporate human rights violations and how best to impose responsibility for these violations in view of the unwillingness, indifference or inability of the Nigerian Government to protect the human rights of the people in these communities.

The work contends that the strengthening of the monitoring roles of some
international bodies/institutions, the strengthening of certain procedural rights
of the people, and the empowerment of the civil society/NGOs will be the best
options for regulating the oil MNCs so as to ensure adequate protection of the
rights of the people in the oil producing communities in Nigeria.

BACKGROUND TO THE STUDY

The oil and gas industry carries out its activities in some of the most challenging
places in the world and faces complex human-rights related issues in many of
those locations.[1] They are often implicated in human rights violations and
environmental injustice, and this generally worsened a bad situation in developing
countries. The activities of these multinational corporations seriously destroy self-
sustaining ecosystems and also undermine the peoples' ability to meet their basic
needs, which include food, clothing, shelter, safe drinking water, health and clean
environment and above all, their quality of life. As a result of this, human rights,
peace and sustainable development are sacrificed by the economic interests of the
MNCs and the host country.

Nigeria with a population of over 140 million[2] is the world's 12th largest oil
producer and the eighth-largest oil exporter.[3] It is Africa's largest oil producer
with the bulk of its exports going to the United States.[4] Among the sub-Saharan
African countries, Nigeria is the largest source of EU oil imports.[5] Nigeria's
proven oil reserves as at January 2006 stood at 35.9 billion barrels, which is equal
to 32% of total African and 3% of world proven reserves.[6] It also has proven gas
reserves of 5.2 trillion m³, which is equal to 36% of total African and 2.9% of
world proven reserves.[7] Nigeria's intensive oil sector accounts for nearly 40% of
the Gross Domestic Product (GDP), but declined steadily to an average of 14.71%

---

[1] See Richard Sykes, Oil and Gas Industry Efforts on Behalf of Human Rights and Sustainable
     Development, at www.spe.org/twa/print/archives/2008/2008v4n2/twa2008_v4n2_Pillars.pdf
     [accessed 3 March 2009].
[2] The population of Nigeria was estimated to be 140, 003, 542 million in the 2006 census
     figure. See Nigeria 2006 Census Figures, Office of the National Bureau of Statistics, at www.
     nigerianstat.gov.ng/Connections/pop2006.pdf [accessed 3 March 2010].
[3] BBC News, Nigeria and China sign $23bn deal for three refineries, 14 May 2010, at www.bbc.
     co.uk/news/10116945 [accessed 7 February 2012].
[4] P. O. Oviasuyi and Jim Uwadiae, The Dilemma of Niger-Delta Region as Oil Producing States
     of Nigeria, Journal of Peace, Conflict and Development, Issue 16, pp.110–126 at 111 (2010).
[5] Baumüller, Heike et al., The Effects of Oil Companies' Activities on the Environment, Health
     and Development in Africa, being a Study conducted for the Directorate-General for External
     Policies of the EU Parliament, August 2011, p.11 at www.chathamhouse.org/sites/default/
     files/0811ep_report_0.pdf [accessed 7 February 2012].
[6] Atlas on Regional Integration in West Africa Economy Series, Oil and Gas, ECOWAS-SWAC/
     OECD, April 2007, p.10, at www.oecd.org/dataoecd/28/34/38798400.pdf [accessed 7 February
     2012].
[7] Ibid.

of the country's total export between 2006 and 2011;[8] and contributed about 80% of budgetary revenues that all tiers of government heavily depend on.[9] In 2006, the Nigerian Government estimated it is earning about $36 billion each year from the extensive petroleum Industry.[10] Notwithstanding the several billion of dollars generated from oil exploration, the Niger Delta, which is the oil and gas rich wetland in the Southern part of Nigeria and which firmly, established Nigeria 'as a major world producer of oil,' has mainly encountered the negative effects of this oil exploitation. With over 50 years of oil exploitation, vast stretches of the region have poor water quality, pollution and disruption and degradation of farmlands and fishing ports, destruction of wildlife and biodiversity, loss of fertile soil, without them having been afforded adequate compensation or a planned mitigation policy for the areas affected.[11] The response of the people in this region in the form of protests and campaigns against the activities of the oil multinational companies (MNCs) have resulted in violations of their civil and political rights and economic, social and cultural rights[12] in form of extra-judicial executions, arbitrary detentions, unlawful restrictions on their rights to freedom of expression, association and assembly by the security agents mostly with the connivance and active support of the oil MNCs. The return of Nigeria to democratic rule in 1999 raised expectations of the oil producing communities that an end would be put to the militarization of the region and a human rights regime ushered in. However, the human rights abuses in the region continue and the situation remain unchanged despite the transition from military to civilian regime. While these violations remain, the local inhabitants of the region are yet to get an appropriate means and procedure of seeking redress against the oil MNCs whose activities are the root cause of these abuses. The rigid adherence of courts in Nigeria to common law principles in many of the actions in respect of oil-related matters, and the inability of parties to get adequate remedies under those common law principles are an important feature of this research. Such an understanding of the impacts of oil exploration activities on the human rights of

---

8   National Bureau of Statistics, *Review of the Nigerian Economy in 2011 & Economic Outlook for 2012-2015*, May 2012, p.8, at www.nigerianstat.gov.ng/ [accessed 7 February 2012].

9   Uwafiokun Idemudia, 'Assessing corporate-community involvement strategies in the Nigerian oil industry: An empirical analysis,' *Resource Policy* 34 (2009) p.135.

10   Asume Isaac Osuoka, *Oil and Gas Revenues and Development Challenges for the Niger Delta and Nigeria*, being a paper presented at the Expert Group Meeting on the Use of Non-Renewable Resources for Sustainable Local Development, Organized by the UN Department of Economic and Social Affairs, Friday 21 Sept., 2007, UN Headquarters, New York, at www.un.org/esa/sustdev/sdissues/institutional_arrangements/egm2007/presentations/isaacOsuoka.pdf [accessed 5 May 2010].

11   See generally, Michael Watts, "Sweet and Sour," in Michael Watts (ed) (2008), *Curse of the Black Gold: 50 Years of Oil in the Niger Delta*, powerHouse Books, Brooklyn, NY, pp.36–61; Niger Delta Human Development Report (2006), United Nations Development Programme (UNDP), Abuja, Nigeria.

12   See Oputa Report, Vol. 3, pp.28–66 at www.nigerianmuse.com/nigeriawatch/oputa/Oputa VolumeThree.pdf [accessed 22 April 2010].

the local inhabitants of the region and the examination of the ways of dealing with them are central to the search for durable peace in this conflict-ridden region.

IMPORTANCE AND RELEVANCE OF THE RESEARCH

Given the strategic importance of oil in the Nigerian economy and in the world, a lot has been written on the Nigerian oil Industry and on oil exploration in the Niger Delta region, which is the oil producing region in Nigeria. The literature reviews the Niger Delta issue from different perspectives ranging from the political economy of oil,[13] multinational companies and conflicts in Niger Delta,[14] a criminological approach to solving the Niger Delta crisis,[15] socio-anthropological perspective of oil exploration, environmental and human rights issues relating to oil,[16] and most recently, about the Niger Delta people in International Law.[17] Many of the existing reports and studies on human rights and the environment in the Niger Delta, include The Price of Oil (1999) by the Human Rights Watch; the Amnesty International Reports 'Nigeria: Are Human Rights in the Pipeline? (2004); 'Nigeria Ten Years on: Injustice and Violence haunt the oil Delta' (2005); 'Nigeria: Petroleum, pollution and poverty in the Niger Delta' (2009); and the annual reports of Nigeria-based NGOs such as Environmental Rights Action (ERA) 'Gas flaring in Nigeria (2005) – and the Constitutional Rights Project (CRP) – 'Land, Oil and Human Rights in Nigeria's Delta Region' (1999). These studies and reports recognize the obligation of the Nigerian Government to protect the environment as well as to pay some attention to the rights that are affected by oil exploration in the Niger Delta. None of them have considered, as will be done in this work, the current failure of international solutions in the forms of voluntary codes and international norms to regulate the MNCs, particularly in the Niger Delta, as well as the impact that the strengthening of

---

[13] Soala, Ariweriokuma, (2009), The Political Economy of Oil and Gas in Africa: The Case of Nigeria, Routledge, London & New York; U. Ekpo (2004), The Niger Delta and Oil Politics, International Energy Communications Limited Publications, Lagos; Steve Azaiki, (2006), Oil, Politics and Blood: The Niger Delta Story, Y-Books; Augustine Ikein, (1991), The Impact of Oil on a Developing Country: The Case of Nigeria, Evans Brothers Nigeria Ltd., Ibadan; Sarah Ahmad Khan (1994), Nigeria: The Political Economy of Oil, Oxford University Press, USA; B.O. Okaba (2005), Petroleum Industry and the Paradox of Rural Poverty in the Niger Delta, Ethiope Publishers, Benin City.

[14] Kenneth Omeje (2006), High Stakes and Stakeholders: Oil Conflict and Security in Nigeria, Ashgate Publishing Ltd., England; Cyril Obi and Siri Aas Rustad (eds) (2011), Oil and Insurgency in the Niger Delta: Managing the Complex Politics of Petro-Violence, The Nordic Africa Institute, Zed Books, London/New York.

[15] See Kekong Bisong (2009), Restorative Justice for Niger Delta, Maklu Publishers, Antwerpen.

[16] Oronto Douglas and Okonta I. (2001), Where Vultures Feast, Sierra Club San Francisco; Muhammed T. Ladan (2007), Biodiversity, Environmental Litigation, Human Rights and Access to Justice: A Case Study of Nigeria, Faith Printers and Publishers, Zaria.

[17] Kaniye Ebeku (2006), Oil and the Niger Delta in International Law. Resource Rights, Environmental and Equity Issues, Rudiger Koppe Verlag, Germany.

some international institutions and NGOs can make towards the regulation of the oil multinationals for the prevention of human rights abuses associated with environmental harm in the Niger Delta. Besides, none of these works has discussed in-depth how the human rights concept of environmental protection as contained in the Constitution and the African regional system can be used by victims of environmental harm to seek redress in the courts of law. This study therefore seeks to fill that gap.

Also, the work shall specifically answer the research questions posed below as they are yet to be specifically addressed by the previous literatures on this area.

AIMS AND OBJECTIVES OF THE STUDY

The basic aims of this work are to examine the level of human rights violations and environmental damage associated with oil exploitation in the oil producing areas of Nigeria, and the role and responsibilities of the oil multinational companies in respect of those violations. Hence, the objectives of the study are to:

(a) appraise the legal framework regulating oil exploitation in Nigeria and the extent to which these laws protects the inhabitants of the oil producing communities in Nigeria (Niger Delta) from adverse impacts of oil activities;
(b) examine the impacts of oil exploitation on the human rights of the people in the Niger Delta region;
(c) determine the effectiveness of solutions created at the international level in the form of voluntary codes and legal norms to regulate the activities of the oil multinationals companies, particularly those in the oil producing areas of Nigeria, and
(d) determine ways in which the activities of oil multinational corporations can be better regulated to ensure better protection of the rights of the people in the oil producing areas.

RESEARCH QUESTIONS

This research seeks to examine the effectiveness or otherwise of the legal framework in place in Nigeria in the oil industry for the protection of the human rights of the local inhabitants of the oil-producing communities and how some existing institutions can be strengthened to offer adequate protections. The research work is aimed at answering the following questions:

1. How adequate is the legal framework in place in Nigeria to regulate oil exploitation in a sustainable manner?

2. How effective, accessible or justiciable are the extant laws and regulations in the promotion of adequate safeguards for the protection of the rights of the people in the oil-producing areas and how best can they be improved upon?
3. Why the deplorable environmental situations exemplified by the Ogoni campaign for economic and social rights still remain in the Niger Delta region?
4. How best can some of the agencies and existing institutions be strengthened to afford adequate protection of the rights of the oil-producing communities in Nigeria?
5. How can the oil multinational companies operating in these communities meet their responsibilities in terms of international standards and principles regulating activities of oil companies in the host and neighbouring communities?

METHODOLOGY

The study relies on primary and secondary sources of information. The primary sources are the Constitution, national legislation, judicial decisions, regional and international instruments. Secondary sources of information were sourced from textbooks, journal articles, periodicals, newspapers, magazines, dissertations/theses, conference papers/working papers, internet documents, previous research findings, government records, records of non-governmental organizations and oil companies.

Another method also adopted in this work is fieldwork conducted in Nigeria in order to obtain the necessary data and relevant information from the local inhabitants of the oil-producing communities, the oil MNCs, relevant government agencies, academic experts in human rights and the civil society. The use of interviews as a basic method of data gathering is no longer limited to social science researchers as it is now a universal mode of systematic inquiry.[18] The researcher benefited from the assistance provided by the Environmental Rights Action (ERA), a non-governmental organisation through the provision of one of its staff to accompany the researcher to some of the affected communities. Several of these communities had a lot of respect for ERA which they claimed had assisted and was still assisting the communities in matters of environment and human rights. The closeness and the intimacy of the ERA to the host communities of Niger Delta greatly enhanced the easy accessibility of the researcher to these communities and strengthened the confidence of these communities in the researcher. The researcher engaged in face-to-face unstructured interviewing

---

[18]   Andrea Fontana and James H. Frey, "The Interview: From Structured Questions to Negotiated Text", in Norman K. Denzin and Yvonna S. Lincoln (eds) (2003), *Collecting and Interpreting Qualitative Materials*, California, Sage Publications, Inc., p.63.

in the form of open questions, though sometimes minimally controlled to avoid derailment out of the subject matter of the research, in view of the fact that 'flying words and worthy words'[19] are a necessary condition for assessing how successful an interview is. The adoption of unstructured interviews in the form of a natural conversation that is skillfully guided by the researcher gives the researcher the latitude to ask any question, in the form and order determined by him, and the opportunity to prompt, probe and ask supplementary questions from the interviewees as the occasion warrants.[20] The responses received from the interviewees[21] and information from other relevant sources formed the basis of the recommendations and conclusions of this work. The researcher usually commenced the interview with self introduction, followed by carefully informing them about the research and its purpose, which is academic, and adding the fact that the findings from the data collected could serve as a means to bring an end to the problems faced by the host communities in the oil rich region of Nigeria, and all other communities with the same problem, among others. This also saved the researcher from the demand for payment by some of the interviewees (local inhabitants of the region) who thought that the research was been supported by the government or international bodies, and so, wanted their own share. Equally, the interviewees were assured of the confidentiality of the information supplied in the course of the interview and given the choice of remaining anonymous.

The researcher's knowledge of the theme of the research assisted a lot regarding the questions to ask, their relevance of it to the research questions and in making on-the-spot decisions on the sequence to follow and how deeply to engage the interviewee on an issue. In other words, making an on-the-spot decision on how to get the best – in terms of breadth or depth – out of a particular situation.[22] The researcher also took into account the mood, general demeanour and the body-language of the interviewees, observing when they were tired, bored, or irritated or offended so as to determine when and how to adjust to the interviewees' conduct. These matters affected the interviewees, particularly the Niger Delta peoples' frankness, openness and trust in the research. However, as a result of the perceived fear of the negative consequences that might attend their voicing feelings concerning the impacts of the oil exploratory activities on their human rights and environment, many of the interviewees, particularly the local inhabitants of the Niger Delta, pleaded for anonymity. The researcher sought and got the permission of the interviewees to record the interviews and to take notes. Hence, the researcher combined note-taking, audio recording and photographs in capturing the interviewees' opinion and views on issues relating to the subject

---

[19]   Corrine Glesne (1999), *Becoming Qualitative Researchers: An Introduction,* Longman Inc., New York, p.81.
[20]   John D. Drewer (2000), *Ethnography,* Open University Press, Buckingham, p.66.
[21]   See Appendix A for the list of the interviewees.
[22]   Jennifer Mason (2002), *Qualitative Researching,* Sage Publications Ltd., London, Thousand Oaks, New Delhi, pp.72–73.

of the research. The advantage of this is that these data-recording methods
complement each other as what one of the recording instruments is unable to
capture, the other captures, and helps to overcome the problem of equipment
failure. During the fieldwork with some of the NGOs, NHRC, ECOWAS Court,
and some government departments, the researcher was given some documents
and case reports that were useful to the research. The NGOs, particularly ERA
and SERAC gave the researcher some of their publications that are relevant to
the research, and which are relied upon in this work. With the exception of a few
individuals, the views expressed cannot be traced to particular interviewees.[23]
The researcher during the fieldwork visited some of the host communities in
the Niger Delta region, the Nigerian NHRC, the ECOWAS Court, some NGOs
offices, some Environmental and human rights activists, and other stakeholders.
This provided the opportunity for the researcher to come in direct contact with
these people and to engage them on the subject of the research. In order to focus
on the issues and the geographical areas that are relevant to the research, the
researcher in selecting the people to be interviewed, adopted purposeful,[24] rather
than the random sampling. This enabled the researcher to focus on actors and
communities considered relevant to the research questions and the situation been
investigated, which random sampling might not have been able to achieve.

In order to verify the information supplied during the interviews, the
information were always crosschecked against other relevant sources. During the
course of the interviews, some of the interviewees, particularly the communities
agreed to have the names of their communities mentioned. The researcher was
however faced with a lot of difficulties in getting information from government
departments as a result of government bureaucracy and an unwillingness on the
part of the officials to grant interviews or to disclose information. Consequently,
some of the interviewees, particularly in the government employ, gave
information on the basis of anonymity, while some provided certain information
on the strength that their names will not be made public in view of risk to their
jobs. Hence, this research faced limitations of response of the oil MNCs, not
covering all the oil producing communities, and not giving the real names of the
interviewees.

The study adopts the rights-based approach. Apart from the fact that it is
based on a legal foundation of universal entitlement, a rights-based approach
provides a basis to hold relevant actors accountable and can generate law and

---

[23]   Charles Olufemi Adekoya, Poverty: Legal and Constitutional Implications for Human Rights
        Enforcement in Nigeria, being a Doctoral Dissertation in the Faculty of Law, University of
        Ghent, Belgium, 2008–2009, p.9.

[24]   According to Patton: 'The logic and power of purposeful sampling lies in selecting *informa-
        tion-rich* cases for study in depth. Information-rich cases are those from which one can learn a
        great deal about issues of central importance to the purpose of the research ...' See M. Patton
        (1990), *Qualitative evaluation and research methods*, Sage Publications, Newbury Park, CA,
        p.169.

policy reform.[25] This approach will serve as a means to analyze the rights of the people that are vulnerable to the activities of the oil multinational companies, the potential impacts of these activities on their rights and also as a basis for holding the relevant actors responsible.

The importance of a rights-based approach in relation to the oil-producing communities of Nigeria is the appreciation of the fundamental basis of the procedural rights, giving the people a basis to demand information concerning environmental matters affecting them, to participate in decision-making as a matter of right, rather than to be passive on environmental matters affecting them, and where government fails to comply with laws, it can legally be held to account by the people. As noted by UNICEF, 'a rights-based approach seeks to raise levels of accountability in the development process by identifying 'rights holders' and corresponding 'duty bearers' and to enhance the capacities of those duty bearers to meet their obligations.'[26] A rights-based approach requires the development of laws, administrative procedures, and practices and mechanisms to ensure the fulfilment of entitlements, as well as opportunities to address denials and violations. Reversing the violations of human rights of the people in this region demands determined efforts from all stakeholders particularly with respect to the adoption of approaches that can help to meet these great challenges. It is in this respect that a rights-based approach which requires the development of laws, administrative procedures, and practices and mechanisms to ensure the fulfilment of entitlements, as well as opportunities to address denials and violations[27] recommends itself.

SCOPE AND STRUCTURE OF THE STUDY

The main focus of the work is Nigeria. However, since the subject of oil exploitation and its attendant human rights violations are not unique to Nigeria, it is useful to examine the impact of oil exploitation on the human rights of people living in

---

[25]   See Centre on Housing Rights and Eviction (COHRE) (2008), *A rights-based review of the legal and policy framework of the Ghanaian water and sanitation sector*, Geneva, Switzerland p.1, at www.cohre.org/sites/default/files/rights-based_review_of_ghanaian_watsan_sector_dec_2008.pdf [accessed 3 March 2010].

[26]   United Nations Educational, Scientific and Cultural Organization (UNESCO) (2007), *A Human Rights-Based Approach to EDUCATION FOR ALL: A framework for the realization of children's right to education and rights within education* (UNICEF New York 2007), p.11, at http://unesdoc.unesco.org/images/0015/001548/154861e.pdf [accessed 3 March 2010].

[27]   *Ibid.* Indeed, the five inter-connected principles, which have been internationally recognised by the UN as forming the core of human-rights based approach are: 1. Express application of the international human rights framework; 2. Empowerment; 3. Participation; 4. Nondiscrimination and prioritisation of vulnerable groups; and 5. Accountability- See Amnesty International (Irish Section), *Our Rights, Our Future. Human Rights Based Approaches in Ireland: Principles, Policies and Practice*, p.6 at www.ihrnetwork.org/files/IHRN-AI%20HRBA%20Ireland%20Sept05%20FINAL.pdf [accessed 3 March 2010].

the oil communities in other areas of the World to enable us to learn from their experiences and examples. Examples are provided from developed countries as well as developing countries.

The study is divided into seven chapters. Chapter One deals with the introduction of the work, the historical development of oil and gas in Nigeria, the location and history of the oil-producing communities of the Niger Delta, the evolution of State participation in oil exploitation, and examines the multinational and indigenous oil companies operating in the Niger Delta.

Chapter Two discusses the status of the Niger Delta people in the Nigerian State. The question of ownership of land and natural resources (oil) within the context of domestic and international law are also examined. It looks at the legal regime of resource control in Nigeria and determines whether a change in ownership of oil or a review in the revenue allocation formular in favour of the oil-producing communities will help in resolving the environmental crisis in the Niger Delta region.

Chapter Three examines the legal/institutional framework for oil operations in Nigeria and discusses the adequacy or otherwise of these laws in the protection of the rights of the people living in the oil-producing areas. Some of the challenges to effective regulation of environmental practices of MNCs in Nigeria are also dealt with. The chapter further examines State responses to environmental insecurity in the Niger Delta, in the form of developmental programmes and initiatives embarked upon by the Government, and comments on the effectiveness or otherwise of these development initiatives in engendering peace in the region.

The fourth chapter considers the relationship between environmental degradation and human rights, the constitutional recognition of environmental rights in Nigeria, the categories of human rights that are vulnerable to the activities of oil multinational companies and the impact of oil exploitation on the human rights of the oil-producing communities in Nigeria. It examines the doctrine of State responsibility as a means of holding private actors (MNCs) accountable for human rights, and the desirability or otherwise of extending human rights obligations to private actors. The chapter also discusses the various initiatives in the form of codes of conduct that have been developed to regulate the activities of MNCs. It looks at their advantages and shortcomings and calls for a legally binding instrument for corporate environmental accountability. Initiatives taken by some other jurisdictions to regulate the activities of MNCs are also considered. Finally, the chapter examines the U.S. transnational human rights litigation in the form of the Alien Tort Claims Act (ATCA) and its relevance to environmental and human rights claims to the Niger Delta People.

Chapter Five discusses the impact of corruption in the oil sector on human rights in Nigeria, the challenges and prospects of combating corruption in Nigeria and what role the human rights approach could play in solving oil-related litigations in the Niger Delta.

Chapter Six examines the issue of corporate environmental accountability through a process of institution building. Essentially, it examines how the strengthening of procedural rights; and some existing institutions like the National Human Rights Commission, the African Commission, the African Court on Human and Peoples' Rights and the African Court of Justice, and the ECOWAS Court can help to regulate the MNCs so as to improve the human rights of the people in the oil-producing communities in Nigeria. The prospects and challenges of empowering the civil society groups and NGOs towards effective participation in the regulatory process of the MNCs in Nigeria are also discussed.

Chapter Seven is the concluding chapter. It contains the main contributions of this work to knowledge and makes recommendations for tackling the challenges identified in this research. The chapter also contains suggestions for future research, acknowledges the limitations of the research and discusses the implications of the research for legislation, policy and practice.

CHAPTER ONE

HISTORY AND DEVELOPMENT OF OIL EXPLOITATION IN NIGERIA

1.1 THE NIGER DELTA: ITS GEOGRAPHY, PEOPLE AND CULTURE

The Niger Delta region has been a flash point in the Africa's most populous nation, Nigeria.[28] Nigeria has a population estimated at 140 million people – nearly one quarter of sub-Saharan Africa's population, and with over 250 dialectical ethnic groups speaking near 400 languages. The three major tribes are Hausa-Fulanis in the North, Yorubas in the West and the Ibos in the East. The Ijaws of the South are the fourth largest ethnic group and are a majority in the Niger Delta region along with the Urhobos, Isokos, Ibibios, Itsekiris, Ukwanis, Ogonis and other minority groups.[29]

However, it is difficult to define the areas that legitimately constitute the "Niger Delta". Some people define the Niger Delta in terms of its ethnography, as the region occupied principally by the Ijaw peoples, together with a variety of smaller ethnic groups, including the Itsekiri, the Urhobo and Isoko peoples in the western parts of the Delta. This definition, it has been argued, does not produce a territory with precisely defined boundaries, as the Ijaw people are to be found in areas far beyond the Delta whilst there are other ethnic groups inhabiting the interior extremities of the Delta.[30]

---

[28] Nigeria became independent from Britain on 1st October, 1960 with just 3 regions, each dominated by a single ethno-linguistic group. In 1976, there were 19 States and by 1996, this number had increased to 36 States with a Federal Capital Territory at Abuja. The number of Local Government Areas (LGAs), a unit created in 1979 by the Federal Military Government, has risen from 300 when established to 774 today. Section 3 (1) and Part 1 of the First Schedule of the 1999 Constitution of the Federal Republic of Nigeria listed the States in Nigeria while section 3(6) and the second column of Part I of the First Schedule listing the Local Government Areas.

[29] Akpobibibo Onduku, The Lingering Crisis in the Niger Delta: Field Work Report, at www.peacestudiesjournal.org.uk/docs/oilconflict.PDF [accessed 23 December 2010].

[30] Steve Azaiki (2007), *Inequities in Nigerian Politics: The Niger Delta, Resource Control, Under Development and Youth Restiveness*, Y-Books, Ibadan, p.23; Earth Rights Institute, *Niger Delta Fund Initiative: Political definition of N-Delta*, at www.earthrights.net/nigeria/news/definition.html [accessed 10 March 2009].

It can alternatively be defined in political terms as the South-South geopolitical zone of Nigeria, comprising six of Nigeria's thirty-six States, namely, Akwa-Ibom, Bayelsa, Cross-River, Edo, Delta and Rivers, as these States are seen as the main centre of Nigeria's oil industry. Some scholars have, however, disagreed with this definition. Those critical of a political definition based on administrative structure have argued that the Niger Delta should be defined geographically as a triangle, with its apex between Ndoni and Aboh, descending eastwards to the Qua Iboe River at Eket and westwards to the Benin River with its base along the Atlantic Coast between the Bights of Benin and Biafra.[31] This definition appears to agree with the position of other writers who have contended that "East of the Benin River lies the delta of the Niger, a land of myriad channels, creeks, and mangrove swamps".[32]

In a study of the pre-colonial history of the Niger Delta, Alagoa, E.J classifies a specific area of the region as the core, the western and eastern Niger Delta.[33] The geographical basis of the classification is the grouping of the pre-colonial States that lie within the delta of the River Niger. This definition seems acceptable to those who make a distinction between the "core" and "peripheral" Niger Delta in the composition of States in present-day Nigeria.[34] They contend that the core Niger Delta States are Rivers, Bayelsa, Delta and some parts of Akwa-Ibom and Imo States,[35] and this excludes Edo and Cross River States. Indeed, the Sir Henry Willink Commission appointed by the British Secretary of State on 26 September

---

[31]   The Daily Champion (Lagos/Nigeria), Wednesday 8 August 2001, p.13, quoted in Programme on Ethnic and Federal Studies (PEFS) (2004), *The Niger Delta Question: Background to Constitutional Reform*, Monograph New Series No. 8, Department of Political Science, University of Ibadan, Ibadan, p.10.

[32]   Philip Curtin, Steve Feierman, Leonard Thompson and Jan Vansina (1981), *African History*, Longman Group Limited, London, p.244. Orluwene adopted the geographical definition of the Niger Delta as comprising Delta, Bayelsa, Rivers, Akwa Ibom and Cross River State, that is, the core Niger Delta known to cover the former British colonial division of Ahoada, Brass, Degema, Opobo, Ogoni, Western Ijaw and Warri- Ozioma B. Orluwene, "Elite Networks and Conflicts in the Niger Delta Region", in *International Conference on The Nigerian State, Oil Industry and the Niger Delta*, Conference Proceedings, organized by the Department of Political Science, Niger Delta University, Wilberforce Island, Bayelsa State, Nigeria, Harey Publications Company, 2008, pp.349–350; B.O. Okaba (2005), *Petroleum Industry and the Paradox of Rural Poverty in the Niger Delta*. Ethiope Publishers, Benin City, p.4. See also T.T. Tamuno, "The Geographical Niger Delta (GND)", *International Conference on The Nigerian State, Oil Industry and the Niger Delta*, op. cit., pp.916–917.

[33]   E.J. Alagoa, "The Niger Delta States and their Neighbours to 1800", in J.F.A. Ajayi and Michael Crowder (eds), *History of West Africa*, (1976) Volume One, Longman Group Limited, London, p.331.

[34]   See Programme on Ethnic and Federal Studies (PEFS) (2004), *The Niger Delta Question: Background to Constitutional Reform*, op. cit., p.10.

[35]   IDEA (2002), *Democracy in Nigeria: Continuing Dialogue for Nation Building*, Lagos/Nigeria, p.15; Michael Watts, *Sweet and Sour*, Niger Delta Economies of Violence Working Paper No. 18, 2008, available at www.ie.ufrj.br/datacenterie/pdfs/download/seminariopped.pdf [accessed 3 March 2010], where Watts state that the core states of the Niger Delta – Bayelsa, Rivers, Delta and Akwa Ibom – cover 45,000 sq. kms, account for half of the regional population and for more than three-quarters of on-shore oil production.

1957 defined and recommended as follows: "We were impressed, in both the Western and Eastern Regions, with the special position of the people, mainly Ijaw, in the swampy country along the coast between Opobo and the mouth of the Benin River". We suggest that constitutionally, it would be necessary to include on the concurrent legislative list a new subject, which might be "The Development of Special Areas"[36] so that it would be the joint responsibility of both the Federal and the State Governments to develop these areas. The Willink Commission definition and some of the geographical definitions would exclude several parts of what is presently being known as Niger Delta.

Noting the disagreement in the definition of the Niger Delta, Okechukwu Ibeanu[37] argued that at least four definitions of Niger Delta can be discerned from the various definitions given by scholars, and these he classified into: Maximal socio-political, Minimal socio-political, Maximal geographical and Minimal geographical. According to him:

> "The *maximal socio-economic* definition of the Niger Delta is the definition adopted by the Federal Government of Nigeria through the Niger Delta Development Commission, its principal intervention agency in the Niger Delta. This definition identifies the Niger Delta as corresponding to the geographical area of the nine States namely, Abia, Akwa-Ibom, Bayelsa, Cross-River, Delta, Edo, Imo, Ondo and Rivers... The 'core states' argument yields the *minimal socio-political* definition of the Niger Delta, which limits the region to the States of the so-called South-South zone... The South-South zone consists of the States of Akwa-Ibom, Bayelsa, Cross-River, Delta, Edo and Rivers...Within this minimalist definition, a distinction is often made between the "core Niger Delta" and the "peripheral Niger Delta". The "core Niger Delta States" consist of Bayelsa, Delta and Rivers States, while the "peripheral Niger States" are Akwa-Ibom, Cross-River and Edo. In effect, while the maximal sociopolitical definition is based on petroleum resources alone, the minimalist definition is linked to States consisting mainly of ethnic minorities that are located totally or partly in the Niger Delta Basin.
>
> The *maximal geographical* definition of the Niger Delta fixes it as the areas of southern Nigeria with river systems linked to the River Niger as it drains into the Atlantic Ocean at the Bights of Benin and Biafra. This area will fall roughly between Benin River in the Southwest and the Cross-River in the Southeast, and then northwards to River Anambra. This definition is justified by the systemic nature of the ecology of the area and the interrelated and organic nature of social conditions and, therefore, social problems. On the other hand, the *minimal geographical* definition of the Delta locates it as the 70,000 square kilometers of low-lying swampy terrain and multiple channels through which the River Niger empties into the Atlantic Ocean. It stretches about 100 kilometers inland. Consequently, it has

---

36   The Willink, Commission Report, Section 3: Special Areas, Paragraph 26, Chapter 14.
37   Okechukwu Ibeanu, *Civil Society and Conflict Management in the Niger Delta: Scoping Gaps for Policy and Advocacy*, CLEEN Foundation Publication, p.17 at www.cleen.org [accessed 3 March 2010].

*been fixed as a triangle with its apex North around Ndoni or Aboh, descending
downwards and westwards to Benin River estuary and eastwards to the Imo River
estuary. Its base is the continental shelf along the Atlantic."*[38]

These conflicting definitions of Niger Delta, which developed after the
ascendancy of oil boom era in Nigeria, have been attributed by one source to
economic and political reasons. The source emphasised that in the colonial and
early independence periods, the Niger Delta was more or less conterminous with
Ahoada, Degema, Opobo, Ogoni, Brass, Western Ijaw and the Warri Divisions,
and the agitation in this region before the oil ascendancy had always been for the
creation of a distinct political region so as to allay their fears of being dominated
by the majority ethnic groups.[39] It noted that:

> *"In recent decades, the definition of the Niger Delta has been bedevilled by politics.
> This was not so before the ascendancy of crude oil in the Nigerian economy…But
> since the oil boom era of the early 1970s, the definition of the Niger Delta, which has
> tended to connote some proprietary rights over the oil wealth, has become highly
> politicised. Political boundaries suddenly have assumed great significance because
> of their importance in determining which States and local governments fall among
> the 'oil producing areas' of Nigeria with all its implications for revenue sharing. At
> various times in the recent political history of Nigeria, squabbles over the oil wealth
> have led to agitation for boundary adjustments between States and for the creation
> of local governments even within the States in the delta region."*[40]

For practical purposes, the Niger Delta region is defined in this study as
comprising the area covered by the natural delta of the Niger River and the areas
to the east and west, which also produce oil. The natural limits of the Niger River
Delta can be defined by its geology and hydrology. Its approximate northern
boundaries are located close to the bifurcation of the Niger River at Aboh, while
the Western and Eastern boundaries are around the Benin River and the Imo
River, respectively. The area covers approximately 25,900 square kilometers.[41]
The broader Niger Delta region, which includes all oil-producing areas and
others considered relevant for reasons of administrative convenience, political
expedience and development objectives, extends the land area to 75,000 square
kilometers. It is this definition that is used by the NDDC and the Niger Delta

---

[38]   *Ibid*, pp.17–18 (bold mine). Ibeanu therefore concluded that officially, the Niger Delta consists
      of the nine States of Abia, Akwa-Ibom, Bayelsa, Cross-River, Delta, Edo, Imo, Ondo and Rivers
      and ethnically, it consists of the Ijaw, Urhobo, Efik, Ibibio, Ogoni, Edo, Yoruba (mainly Itsekiri
      and Ilaje) and the Igbo.

[39]   Niger Delta Environmental Survey (1997), vol. 1, 7.

[40]   *Ibid.*

[41]   Niger Delta Human Development Report (2006), UNDP Publication, p.19.

Human Development Report.[42] It will include all the "core" and "peripheral" states,[43] and so agrees with the classification of the Niger Delta in geopolitical terms as the South-South zone. Defined in this way, the Niger Delta consists of nine States (Abia, Akwa Ibom, Bayelsa, Cross River, Delta, Edo, Imo, Ondo and Rivers),[44] with 185 local government areas. This definition accords with Michael Watts'[45] description of the Niger Delta of Nigeria as a vast sedimentary and oil-rich basin of some 70,000 sq. kms and composed officially of nine states (Abia, Akwa-Ibom, Rivers, Bayelsa, Delta, Imo, Cross River, Ondo and Edo), 185 local government areas (LGAs) and a population of roughly 28 millions. According to him, the Niger delta hosts a massive oil infrastructure – 606 fields (40% off shore), 5,284 wells, 7,000 kilometers of pipelines, ten export terminals, 275 flow stations, ten gas plants, four refineries and a world class six-train liquefied natural gas (LNG) installation on Bonny Island – that is more or less ungovernable.

This definition is adopted for the purpose of this study, because these nine States contain the oil wells which the country exploits for self-sustenance. The Niger Delta is thus a geopolitical territory in which the oil-producing communities are mainly located.

---

[42]   *Ibid.* See also Iruonagbe T. Charles, "The Niger Delta Crisis: Challenges and Prospects for Peace and Stability", *International Conference on The Nigerian State, Oil Industry and the Niger Delta, op. cit.,* p.637.

[43]   See IDEA (2002), *op. cit.,* p.15.

[44]   The Niger Delta Development Commission Act No. 2 of 1999 which set up the Niger Delta Development Commission (NDDC) to handle the environmental problems in the Niger Delta, listed in section 30, which is the interpretation section, the nine States (Abia, Akwa Ibom, Bayelsa, Cross River, Delta, Edo, Imo, Ondo and Rivers). The section goes on to add that any other State in Nigeria which produces oil may be a member State. No clear cut distinction is made between "Niger Delta" and "Oil Producing States" by the Act. This economic delineation of the region therefore refers to all the contiguous oil-producing States, and it is this description that is used in federal legal documents such as the NDDC Act. See Rhuks T. Ako, *et al,* Resolving Legislative Lapses through Contemporary Environmental Protection Paradigms- A Case of Nigeria's Niger Delta Region, *Indian Journal of International Law,* Vol. 47, No. 3, p.432 (2007).

[45]   Michael Watts, *Petro-Insurgency or Criminal Syndicate? Conflict, Violence and Political Disorder in the Niger Delta,* Niger Delta Economies of Violence Working Paper No. 16, 2008, at http://geography.berkeley.edu/ProjectsResources/ND%20Website/NigerDelta/WP/16-Watts. pdf. [accessed 3 March 2010]. The widely publicised land mass of Niger Delta (70,000 square kilometres) is only a geographic estimation. Politically, the region is much larger: the nine states that make up the Niger Delta occupy surface area of about 112,110 square kilometres (**Abia State** 4,877, **Akwa Ibom** 6,806, **Bayelsa** 11,007, **Cross River** 21,930, **Delta** 17,163, **Edo** 19,698, **Imo** 5,165, **Ondo** 15,086, **Rivers** 10,378) – 12% of Nigeria's territory. Today, out of over 606 oil fields in the Niger Delta, 60% of them are onshore while 40% are offshore- See Niger Delta Development Commission (NDDC) 2004. Niger Delta Regional Development Master Plan: Summary of Draft Report. September, p.2; Social Development Integrated Centre (Social Action) (2009), *Carry Go,* Citizens Report on State and Local Government Budgets in the Niger Delta 2008, Published by Niger Delta Citizens and Budget Platform, at http://saction.org/ebook/carry%20 go-full%20report.pdf [accessed 5 May 2010]. Wilson Akpan, *Oil, People and the Environment: Understanding Land-Related Controversies in Nigeria's Oil Region,* at www.codesria. org/Links/conferences/general_assembly11/papers/akpan.pdf [accessed 3 March 2010]; Uwafiokun Idemudia, Assessing corporate-community involvement strategies in the Nigerian oil industry: An empirical analysis, *Resources Policy* 34, 133–141, 135 (2009).

1.1.1 NIGER DELTA PEOPLE AND POPULATION

The region has five linguistic and cultural groups – Ijaw, Yoruba, Edo, Igbo and Cross River with each having numerous sub-groups.[46] The Ijaws, which are the largest and are said to have the longest settlement history are the most complex linguistically. They have numerous clans each of which has some linguistic and cultural distinctiveness. This group, which occupies virtually the whole of Bayelsa State, is also found in Rivers, Akwa Ibom, Delta, Edo and Ondo States.[47]

The communities affiliated to the Edo can be found from Degema and Engenni in Rivers State to the Urhobo, Isoko, Erowha and Okpo in Delta State. The Itsekiri have linguistic affiliation with the Yoruba, but have oral traditions which trace a closer relationship with the Edo.[48] Among the Edo group, the Urhobo is the largest.

In the Cross River region there are Ogba, Abua, Odua; Ogoni and others in Rivers States; the Obolo/Andoni in both Rivers and Akwa Ibom States; and the Ibeno, Ibibio, Oron and others in Akwa Ibom.[49] The Ibibio is the largest of these groups. Of these, Ogoni is the most well known, especially internationally, presumably because of its agitation for resource control and autonomy. The ethno-cultural complexity of the Niger Delta region is clearly illustrated by the fact that even a small ethnic group like the Ogoni (about 500,000 people), is made up of at least four cultural groups: the Khana, Gokama, Tai and Eleme.[50]

The main Yoruba groups are the Itsekiri of Delta State, and the Ilaje and Ikale of Ondo State. The communities deriving from the Igbo include Ika and Ukwuani in Delta State; Ndoni, Egbema, Ogba, Ikwerre and Ekpeye of River States; Ohaji and Oguta of Imo State and Asa in Abia State.[51] Each of these categories embrace a large number of ethnic/linguistic communities some of which extend beyond the boundaries of the Niger Delta.[52] This probably explains why the categorization of the Niger Delta States has widened to include the Cross River, Edo, Imo, Abia and

---

[46]   See Constitutional Rights Project (CRP) (1999), *Land, Oil and Human Rights in Nigeria's Delta Region*, CRP, Lagos, p.7; Niger Delta Human Development Report, *op. cit.*, p.21.

[47]   See Niger Delta Human Development Report, *Ibid*, p.21.

[48]   Constitutional Rights Project (CRP) (1999), *Land, Oil and Human Rights in Nigeria's Delta Region*, *op. cit.*, p.7.

[49]   *Ibid*, p.8.

[50]   See Niger Delta Human Development Report, *op. cit.*, p.22.

[51]   Constitutional Rights Project (CRP) (1999), *Land, Oil and Human Rights in Nigeria's Delta Region*, *op. cit.*, pp.7–8; T.T. Tamuno, "The Geographical Niger Delta (GND)", *International Conference on The Nigerian State, Oil Industry and the Niger Delta, op. cit.*, pp.926–927; Etiosa Uyigue and Matthew Agho, *Coping with Climate Change and Environmental Degradation in the Niger Delta of Southern Nigeria*, Community Research and Development Centre (CREDC) Nigeria (2007), at http://priceofoil.org/wp-content/uploads/2007/06/07.06.11%20 -%20Climate_Niger_Delta.pdf [accessed 5 July 2009]; Olayiwola Owolabi and Iwebunor Okwechime, Oil and Security in Nigeria: The Niger Delta Crisis, *Africa Development*, Vol. XXXII, No. 1, pp.1–40, 11 (2007).

[52]   SPDC Nigerian Annual Report (1998), People and the Environment, p.3.

Ondo States. Thus, in its present form, the Niger Delta covers the South-East and South-West geopolitical zones of Nigeria.[53]

Population: It is not an easy task to give exact up-to-date population figures for African countries due to unreliable statistical data. However, going by the 2006 census, the total population of all the nine States of the Niger Delta was 31,224,577 as shown in Table 1:1 below. This was made up of 16,092,797 males and 15,131,780 females. There are indications of a predominance of males in the population of the Delta unlike the 1991 census figures which showed an almost equal number of men and women in the Niger Delta. This trend may not be unconnected to the influx of migrant males from other parts of Nigeria.[54] The Niger Delta population is projected to rise to 39.2 million by 2015 and 45.7 million by 2020.[55]

Table 1:1. Total population of all the nine States of the Niger Delta

S/N	State	Male (million)	Female (million)	Total
1	Abia	1,434,193	1,399,806	2,833,999
2	Akwa Ibom	2,044,510	1,875,698	3,920,208
3	Bayelsa	902,648	800,710	1,703,358
4	Cross River	1,492,465	1,396,501	2,888,966
5	Delta	2,074,306	2,024,085	4,098,391
6	Edo	1,640,461	1,577,871	3,218,332
7	Imo	2,032,286	1,902,613	3,934,899
8	Ondo	1,761,263	1,679,761	3,441,024
9	Rivers	2,710,665	2,474,735	5,185,400
Total		16,092,797	15,131,780	31,224,577

Source: Nigerian News census 2006, at www.nigeriannews.com/census/census2006.htm [accessed 6 June 2009].

The land and human population density are important in relation to development pressures in this region. With a population of about 32 million (24% of Nigeria's total population), it has one of the highest population densities (265 people/ km²) in the country.[56] The population distribution within each State is uneven, most especially in the core Niger Delta States, where the fragmented, swampy, landscape constrains human settlements. The population is youthful: 62 per cent are below 30 years of age, while 36 per cent are between 30 and 69, and just 2 per cent aged

---

[53] Ibaba S. Ibaba, Oil and Political Consciousness in the Niger Delta, *Nigerian Journal of Oil and Politics* (Special Edition), Vol. 2, No. 1, p.80 (2002).
[54] World Bank Report, *Niger Delta Social and Conflict Analysis*, Sustainable Development Department Africa Region, May, 2008, at http://siteresources.worldbank.org/EXTSOCIAL DEV/Resources/ [accessed 3 March 2010].
[55] See Niger Delta Human Development Report, *op. cit.*, p.24; Okechukwu Ibeanu, *Civil Society and Conflict Management in the Niger Delta: Scoping Gaps for Policy and Advocacy, op. cit.*, p.19.
[56] Social Development Integrated Centre (Social Action) (2009), *Carry Go*, Citizens Report on State and Local Government Budgets in the Niger Delta 2008, *op. cit.*

70 and above. The age structure of the population has important implications for
development planning, making social investment a crucial need.[57]

1.1.2 CULTURE

The culture of a people depicts its way of life. It is the total sum of the material and
intellectual equipment whereby its members satisfy their biological and social
needs and adapt themselves to the environment.[58] The Niger Delta comprises
several ethnic groupings with diverse cultural and traditional institutions. It
was reported by the early European visitors that the region celebrated its marine
inheritance through masquerades, regattas, fishing festivals, etc.

The people of Niger Delta have many myths about God, the Supreme Being,
gods or minor deities, spirits and ancestors. They believe in divination, life after
death and reincarnation, destiny, witchcraft, magic and sorcery, strongly holding
the view that the spiritual sphere directs the events of the material world.[59] The
names given to their children reveal God's supreme qualities and attributes. For
instance, *Oghene* or *Orise* – the Omnipotent God; *Chukwu* – God Almighty, etc.
The core Niger Delta sees God as a Supreme Being that created all things, and
should not be confused with the gods and ancestors who are just intermediaries.
The Itsekiri in Western Delta believe in, and worship the souls of the dead, called
Ebura. They do this by pouring libation and making meat and food offerings to
ancestors.[60] The Itsekiri also worship the following principal gods (*umales*): *Erikpe*
(prophylactic); *Ugbokua* (has to do with war); *Adda* (protective and destructive);
Umalokun, Agbiniji, Birikimo, etc. They offer various sacrifices ranging from
human beings and animals to drinks. The Ndoni of the eastern Niger Delta believe
in the worship of gods and goddesses whom they believe offer them protection,
fortune, peace, etc. Among these are *Ndoni Alishi* – the goddess of trade, fortune
and peace; *Abni* – the earth deity; *Eze Agamab* – the god of vengeance, etc. The
Kalabari/Ijaw people of the eastern Delta believe in and worship a national deity
called *Owoame Akaso* who is normally consulted in the selection of a king.
Alagoa, E.J., has this to say:

> *"The national god was of most direct relevance to the life of each "Ibe" or delta.
> This god was usually connected with the founding ancestor and was worshipped
> in various parts of the Ijaw area including the Supreme Being, God. The major
> communities of Kalabari like Abonnema, Bakana, Buguma that sprang up from*

---

57   World Bank Report, *Niger Delta Social and Conflict Analysis, op. cit.*; Niger Delta Human
      Development Report (2006), *op. cit.*, p.52.
58   Ralph Piddington (1950), *An Introduction to Social Anthropology*, Oliver and Boyd, London,
      p.3.
59   Steve Azaiki, *Inequities in Nigerian Politics: The Niger Delta, Resource Control, Underdevelop-
      ment and Youth Restiveness, op. cit.*, p.47.
60   William A. Moore, (1970), *History of Itsekiri*, Frank Cass & Co. Ltd., London, pp.214–215.

Elem Kalabari believe in and worship a national deity called Owoame Akaso. They believe that this deity guided and guarded their founding fathers to their settlement. During conflicts or disputes especially in the selection of a king, Akaso is normally consulted to choose the right person. The Ogonis, in turn, believe and worship Soa – the earth goddess whom they believe is responsible for soil fertility and good harvest. They also believe in and worship other minor deities like Gbenebega, Ban Gokana, Ban Mkpobu, etc."[61]

The Central Ijaw people also believe in and worship gods and goddesses. In terms of war, they consult and worship *Egbesu* or war god. They also worship *Beni-Otu*, or water deity and other gods.

1.1.3 OCCUPATIONS

To a large extent, the geographical location of the Niger Delta and its resources determine the traditional primary occupations of the people: fishing and farming. Forestry was introduced as the third major economic activity in the region during the colonial days. We also have secondary occupations which include local industries like gin distillation, textile weaving, boat carving, etc.; and tertiary occupations like trade and commerce, transportation, etc.

1.1.3.1 Primary Occupations

Fishing: The main ecosystem, which aids the fishing activities, includes inshore waters, brackish waters, mangrove swamp, fresh water swamps, flooded plains as well as rivers. Various studies have indicated that the region is home to various kinds of fish such as Bony fish, crabs and lobsters, oysters, periwinkles, squids, sharks, rays, scats, shrimps, etc. Powell[62] in his study of freshwater fish species concludes that the Niger Delta has more species of freshwater fish (197) than any other coastal system in West Africa. Also, the Niger Delta Wetland Centre (NDWC) has identified 16 fish species that are endemic to the region, and another 29 that are near-endemic.[63]

---

[61] Quoted in Steve Azaiki, *Inequities in Nigeria Politics: The Niger Delta, Resource Control, Underdevelopment and Youth Restiveness, op. cit.*, pp.51–52.

[62] C.B. Powell (1993), *Sites and species of Conservation Interest in Central Axis of the Niger Delta (Section C)*, report submitted to the Natural Resources Conservation Council of Nigeria, Biodiversity Unit, Rivers State University of Science and Technology, Port Harcourt, Nigeria, quoted in Collins N.C. Ugochukwu and Jurgen Ertel, Negative Impacts of Oil Exploration on Biodiversity Management in the Niger Delta Area of Nigeria, *Impact Assessment and Project Appraisal*, 26(2), 141–145 (2008).

[63] NDWC, Niger Delta Environmental Survey (1997), Environmental and Socio-economic Characteristics, second phase of field report, Vol. 1, Environmental Resource Manager Limited, quoted in Collins N.C. Ugochukwu and Jurgen Ertel, *Ibid*.

Agriculture: The following are some of the agricultural activities going on in this region:

(a) food crops: yam, cassava, rice, cowpea, maize, potato, melon, cocoyam;
(b) tree crops: rubber, palm oil, raffia palm, cashew, mango;
(c) livestock: goats, pigs, fish, rabbits.

1.1.3.2 Secondary Occupations

Local Industry: Gin Distillation: This owes its origin to indigenous technology. It involves tapping raffia palms for wine and its distillation as gin, otherwise called *kai-kai, ogogoro, koun-uru, akpeteshi*, etc. This local gin is used traditionally for pouring libation to ancestors and gods in almost all the communities in the Southern zone of Nigeria.[64]

Textiles: This region is noted for the manufacturing of textiles. They use the vertical cotton loom in the manufacturing of *akwete* cloth which is extensively used by the Western Deltans of Urhobo, Kwale, Itsekiri and the Ika-Ibo for traditional ceremonies.

Boat Carving: As a result of the riverine nature of the area, the people in this region provide substantial services in barge and tug-boat construction so providing means of transportation. They also engage in ship repairs. They use trees like Bolo (Mammea africana) for this purpose.

1.1.4 TRADE AND COMMERCE

This region has been a centre for trade for ages. The major trading posts were Bonny, Okirika, Nembe and Elem Kalabari. These posts served as a trading post during the Trans-Atlantic slave trade. Following the abolition of the slave trade, the palm oil and palm kernel trades replaced the slave trade, and the palm produce was shipped overseas from the seaports of Port Harcourt, Onne, Warri, Sapele and Burutu. This trade in palm oil and kernel soon earned the Niger Delta its name as the "Oil Rivers".[65] This large demand for palm produce led to widespread cultivation of palm trees in the region. The other products traded were earthenware produced by the Itsekiri, the Ijaw exchanging their salt for fish with Nembe Fishermen, and the Apo people of the central freshwater Delta specializing in the building of canoes, etc. All these increased trade between the coastal people and their counterparts in the hinterland, and led to inter-marriage and cross-cultural affiliations.

---

[64]   Steve Azaiki, *Inequities in Nigeria Politics: The Niger Delta, Resource Control, Underdevelopment and Youth Restiveness, op. cit.*, pp.40–41.
[65]   *Ibid*, p.43.

It is interesting to note that today, agriculture, fishing and forestry account for about 44 per cent of employment in this region.[66] Since the ascendancy of the oil industry, most of these economic activities have declined. Rubber plantations that once covered and dominated large portions of land in Edo and Delta were abandoned and allowed to revert to bush with the arrival of the oil boom. However, since the 1990s, efforts are now being made by the Government to resuscitate the economic activities that once formed the major source of earnings in this region.

1.1.5 ECOLOGY

The ecology of the Niger Delta includes the following:

(i) brackish or saline mangrove swamp belt separated from the sea by sand beach ridges for most of the coastline;
(ii) fresh water, permanent and seasonal swamp forests; and
(iii) dry land rain forests.[67]

The World Bank[68] has identified four types of ecological zones: **freshwater swamp forests** covers about 11,700 km^2 of the Niger Delta and lie in the hinterland away from the mangrove. Of all the ecological zones, it is the most heterogeneous with different species of flora and fauna; **mangroves** which occupy a total area of 10,240 km^2 and are characterized by regular salt-water inundation. It accommodates the most important flora and fauna and creeks, which are kept open by tidal action and flooding, flow throughout the forests. The mangrove forest of Nigeria is the third largest in the world and the largest in Africa with over 60% of this found in the Niger Delta.[69] The mangrove swamp with its interlocking branches of trees, constitute foliage which has reduced considerably, the penetration of sunlight to the ground. It is the most economically rich among the four ecological zones, vital to the fishing industry and the local economy of the region; **lowland rainforests**

---

[66]   See Niger Delta Human Development Report, *op. cit.*, p.25.
[67]   Ibaba S. Ibaba, Oil and Political Consciousness in the Niger Delta, *op. cit.*, p.80; Nwankwoala H., Coastal Aquifers of Nigeria: An Overview of its Management and Sustainability Considerations, *Journal of Applied Technology in Environmental Sanitation*, 1 (4): 371–380, at 373 (2011).
[68]   World Bank (1995), Defining an Environmental Development Strategy for the Niger Delta, World Bank, Washington DC., quoted in Collins N.C. Ugochukwu and Jurgen Ertel, Negative Impacts of Oil Exploration on Biodiversity Management in the Niger Delta Area of Nigeria, *op. cit.*, pp.141–145. For more discussion on the ecology of the Niger Delta, see Kaniye Ebeku (2006), *Oil and the Niger Delta in International Law. Resource Rights, Environmental and Equity Issues*, Rudiger Koppe Verlag, Germany, pp.127–129.
[69]   Human Rights Watch (1999), *The Price of Oil: Corporate Responsibility and Human Rights Violations in Nigeria's Oil Producing Communities*, New York; Gabriel Eweje, Environmental Costs and Responsibilities Resulting from Oil Exploitation in Developing Countries: The Case of the Niger Delta of Nigeria, 69 *Journal of Business Ethics* 27–56, 34 (2006).

which cover around 7,400 km^2 of the region and represents the non-riverine or upland areas; **barrier island forest** also called 'beach ridge island,' which is the smallest of these four zones in the Niger Delta and consists of the freshwater forest found between the coastal beaches and the estuarine mangroves. Describing the ecological situation of the Niger Delta region, Etiosa Uyigue and Matthew Agho state that:

> *"About 2,370 square kilometers of the Niger Delta area consists of rivers, creeks and estuaries and while stagnant swamp covers about 8600 square kilometers. The delta, with mangrove swamps spanning about 1900 square kilometers has the largest mangrove swamps in Africa, (Awosika, 1995). The region falls within the tropical rain forest zone. The ecosystem of the area is highly diverse and supportive of numerous species of terrestrial and aquatic flora and fauna and human life."[70]*

The Niger Delta is blessed with flora and fauna with which no other area in Nigeria can compare. The Niger Delta region alone holds 60–80% of all Nigerian plant and animal species.[71]

The extensive forests in the region harbour a rich diversity of wildlife, including mammals, reptiles, insects, birds, and many more. For example, the mangrove forests harbour the mona monkey, speckle-throated otter, and marsh mongoose; and the freshwater swamp is home to the black squirrel and antelopes, as well as species of monkeys and apes including the chimpanzee. We also have elephants in this zone.[72] As a result of the environmental degradation that daily occurs in the region, most of these species are no longer widely distributed in viable populations, and are now classified as vulnerable, threatened, or endangered.[73] This is confirmed from a statement by Shell in one of its publications: 'Having once been described as having one of the richest biodiversity aggregations in Nigeria, remote sensing imagery has shown that forest and water-ways of the entire Niger Delta are under threat of irrecoverable damage.'[74]

---

[70]   Etiosa Uyigue and Matthew Agho, Etiosa Uyigue and Matthew Agho, *Coping with Climate Change and Environmental Degradation in the Niger Delta of Southern Nigeria, op. cit.*; L.F. Awosika (1995), Impacts of global climate change and sea level rise on coastal resources and energy development in Nigeria, in J.C. Umolu (ed), Global Climate Change: Impact on Energy Development, DAMTECH Nigeria Limited, Nigeria.

[71]   N.J. Ashton-Jones and Oronto N.D. (1994), *Report to Statoil (Nigeria) Ltd.: Baseline Ecological Survey of the Niger Delta*, Pro-Natura International, Lagos, p.29, quoted in Kaniye Ebeku (2006), *Oil and the Niger Delta in International Law. Resource Rights, Environmental and Equity Issues, op. cit.*, p.130.

[72]   See Kaniye Ebeku, *Ibid*, p.131.

[73]   See Collins N.C. Ugochukwu and Jurgen Ertel, *op. cit.*, p.143.

[74]   Quoted in Alfred Ilenre, "The Case of Shell-Nigeria", in Rudolf Traub-Merz/Douglas Yates (eds) (2004), *Oil Policy in the Gulf of Guinea. Security and Conflict, Economic Growth, Social Development*, International Conference Friedrich-Ebert-Stiftung Proceedings, p.155.

1.2   A BRIEF HISTORY OF NIGERIAN OIL AND GAS

The search for oil in Nigeria began as far back as 1908, when a German business interest formed the Nigerian Bitumen Company to undertake exploration for bitumen in the coastal areas of Araromi in the present day Ilaje local government area of Ondo State. This activity was hindered by the outbreak of the First World War in 1914. In 1937, Shell D' Arcy, the forerunner of the present day Shell Petroleum Development Company, was granted by the English colonial government sole concessionary rights throughout Nigeria in the exploration of crude oil.[75] The company began its search for oil at its operational base at Ihuo, ten miles northeast of Owerri, Imo State. Again, the outbreak of another war, World War II, disrupted the operations of this company but by around 1946, the company restarted its geological and geophysical investigations and it was discovered that the oil-yielding structure was centered in the Niger Delta.[76] It is important to note that Shell were joined this time by British Petroleum (the British then state-owned oil company), thereby establishing what was generally known as the Shell-BP.[77] Its deep exploration well was drilled in 1951 at Ihuo, to the depth of 11, 228 feet, but yielded no success. The determined investigative work by Shell-BP drew the attention of other mineral oil companies to Nigerian crude oil. One of these companies was Mobil Exploration Nigeria Limited and it was granted an exploration licence in 1955 to cover an estimated area of about 281,782 m².[78] Mobil also acquired oil exploration licences relinquished by Shell-BP as well as for off-shore areas of South Eastern Nigeria. Thus, before 1955, only Shell-BP held concessions in Nigeria but by 1960, this had increased. The first oil-well in Nigeria where a commercial quantity was first found was drilled at Oloibiri in present day Bayelsa State in 1956. As a result of absence of competition, Shell during this period was able to explore at its leisure 15,000 square miles in the Niger Delta,

---

[75]   This was done by the promulgation of the Minerals Oil Ordinance No. 17 of 1914 (amended in 1925, 1950 and 1958) which gave an oil exploration monopoly in Nigeria to British firms. To further consolidate the monopolistic interest of Shell D' Arcy, the colonial government again promulgated the Minerals Ordinance of 1945, which provides that:
"*The entire property and control of all minerals and mineral oil, in, under, or upon any land in Nigeria, and of all rivers, streams, and watercourses throughout Nigeria, is and shall be vested in the **crown**".*

[76]   Victor Ojakorotu, *Oil Minorities and Politics of Exclusion in the Niger Delta of Nigeria,* at www. sidos.ch/method/rc28/abstracts/victor%20Ojakorotu.pdf. [accessed 3 March 2010].

[77]   G. Etikerentse (1985), *Nigerian Petroleum Law,* 1ˢᵗ ed., Macmillan, London, p.1; Patrick D. Okonmah, Right to a Clean Environment: The Case for the People of Oil-Producing Communities in the Nigerian Delta, *Journal of African Law,* Vol. 41, No. 1, p.44 (1997). See also, F.O. Ayodele-akaakar, *Appraising the Oil & Gas Laws: A Search for Enduring Legislation for the Niger Delta Region,* at www.jsd- africa.com/Jsda/Fallwinter2001/articlespdf/ARC%20 20APPRAISING%20THE%20OIL%20and%20Gas.pdf [accessed 23 November 2009].

[78]   See Victor Ojakorotu, *Oil Minorities and Politics of Exclusion in the Niger Delta of Nigeria, op. cit.*

which it converted into oil mining leases.[79] As noted by Jide Osuntokun, Shell D'
Arcy operated:

> *"... under Mineral Oil Ordinance No. 17 of 1914 and its amendments of 1925 and*
> *1950, which allowed only companies registered in Britain or any of its protectorates*
> *the right to prospect for oil in Nigeria, and further provided that the principal offi-*
> *cers of such companies must be British subjects. Between 1938 and 1941, Shell BP*
> *undertook preliminary geological reconnaissance. After (a five-year interruption)*
> *by World War II, it intensified and followed up this activity with geophysical surveys*
> *in the 1946–51 period. In 1951, Shell BP drilled its Wildcat well ... In 1956, it made*
> *the first commercial discovery at Oloibiri in Rivers State".[80]*

Other well followed at Afam, a year later, and at Ebutu and Bomu (both in Ogoni
land in the Niger Delta) in 1958. This was followed by the construction of pipelines
from Oloibiri to Port Harcourt to facilitate export. The export of the first cargo of
crude oil took place on 17 February, 1958 at the production level of 5,000 barrels
per day.

Meanwhile, in 1959, the sole concession right over the whole country, earlier granted to Shell, was reviewed and exploration rights were extended to other
foreign companies. This was in line with the policy of increasing the pace of exploration, while at the same time ensuring that the country was not too dependent
on one company or nation.[81] Shell therefore relinquished about 50 per cent of
its Niger Delta concession, but retained the potentially most successful parts or
the most promising areas. Tenneco, an American Company arrived in Nigeria in
April 1960, and granted a concession along the Western Coast.

By the time Nigeria achieved its independence in October 1960, intense
exploration activities were already in place, and policies that would lead to major
economic and political changes in the oil sector were formulated. In line with this,
exploration companies outside Britain and the United States of America (USA)
were invited to establish presences and explore in Nigeria. Oil was becoming
a vital energy fuel, and Nigeria's production had more than tripled from 5,000

---

[79]   Patrick D. Okonmah, Right to a Clean Environment: The Case for the People of Oil-Producing
       Communities in the Nigerian Delta, *op. cit.*, p.44; Yinka Omorogbe, The Legal Framework for
       the Production of Petroleum in Nigeria, 5 *J. Energy Nat. Resources L.* 273–291(1987). Schatzl
       notes that: 'The opportunity of exercising an autonomous strategy throughout two decades in
       the realm of concession politics brought about the result that this company today possesses
       the optimal concession site in the country. Its monopolistic position in the past with respect
       to licence selection affords Shell-BP both now and in the future a position of dominance in the
       development of the mineral oil industry'. See L.H. Schätzl (1969), *Petroleum in Nigeria*, Oxford
       University Press, p. 3, quoted in Patrick D. Okonmah, *Ibid*, p.44.
[80]   Jide Osuntokun, Oil and Nigerian Development, *Development Outlook* 1, No. 3, 40 (1986).
[81]   N.K. Obasi, *Foreign Participation in the Nigerian Oil and Gas Industry*, at www.waado.org/
       Environment/OilExploration/oilcompanies_ history_obasi.htm [accessed 3 March 2010]. The
       sole concessionary rights granted to Shell-BP by the 1914 Minerals Ordinance were repealed
       by virtue of section 2 of the Mineral Oils (Amendment) Act, 1958.

barrels per day in 1958, to 17,000 barrels per day in 1960.[82] This encouraging oil-production potential attracted a number of international oil companies into Nigeria, and within the first five years of independence no less than nine international oil Companies had become active in the country, namely: Shell BP, Mobil, Tenneco, Texaco, Gulf (now Chevron), Safrap (now Elf), Agip, Philip and Esso. These companies were soon joined, in the late 1960s by Japan Petroleum, Occidental, Deminex, Union Oil, Niger Petroleum and Niger Oil Resources. The climax of that era was the formation of the Nigerian National Oil Corporation (NNOC), the predecessor of the Nigerian National Petroleum Corporation (NNPC), and the admission of Nigeria in OPEC, the Organization of Petroleum Exporting Countries in July 1971.[83] During this period, oil production had moved from 17,000 barrels per day (bpd) in 1960 to 45,000 bpd in 1966 and later to 1million bpd in 1970, shortly after the Nigerian civil war. With the rapid increase in production, the revenue accruing to the government also increased. From 1971, the Nigerian government gradually entered into joint venture agreements with several multinational oil companies engaged in the exploration and production of oil in the country and acquired shareholdings in these ventures.

The history of oil in Nigeria would not be complete without referring also to the correlating search for gas. The history of Natural Gas production started in 1958 with the commencement of crude oil production from Oloibiri and Afam and increased from 45 million cubic meters (mcm) in 1958 to 481 mcm in 1962. It was in 1963 that gas production began commercially, when 5 per cent of gross production was marketed.[84] The greatest increases in the gross production of natural gas, as with those in crude oil, occurred in the 1970s. Since 1988, Nigeria has been in another period of gas growth, largely due to increasing exploration expenditure and crude oil discoveries by oil companies.[85] Indeed, oil production levels determine the amount of Associated Gas (AG) produced, and this affects the amount of flaring. The rate and level of connection was summarised in a June 2001 speech by SPDC's current Chief Executive, Basil Omiyi,[86] saying that, 'on the average, about 1000 standard cubic feet (scf), of gas is produced in Nigeria with every barrel of oil. Therefore, with oil production of some 2.2 million barrels per day, about 2.2 billion scf of associated gas is produced everyday'.

From the available records, it appears that almost all the AG in the first 20 years of the industry in Nigeria was flared. For example, 2.1 billion cubic feet per day (bcf/d) or 92 per cent was flared in 1981. This barely declined during

---

[82]   See N.K. Obasi, *Ibid.*

[83]   *Ibid.*

[84]   L.H. Schätzl, *op. cit.*, p.223.

[85]   Emejuru Chukwucheta ThankGod, *A Critical Appraisal of the Legal Framework for the Protection of the Environment Against Oil and Gas Pollution in Nigeria*, M. Phil. Thesis Submitted to Obafemi Awolowo University, Ile-Ife, Nigeria, August 2006, pp.7–8.

[86]   Quoted in Environmental Rights Action/Friends of the Earth Nigeria/Climate Justice Programme Report (2005), *Gas Flaring in Nigeria: A Human Rights, Environmental and Economic Monstrosity*, p.10.

the 1980s, standing at about 88 per cent in 1989.[87] It appears to have reached about 2.6 bcf/d in the late 1990s, including venting, but by then, this was about 75% of all gas production.[88] In 2001, Nigeria emerged as the world's number one flarer and venter – 16.8 billion cubic metre per year (bcm/y) on both absolute and proportionate terms, based on the OPEC figures for that year.[89] A recent satellite imagery study by the World Bank in collaboration with the US National Oceanic and Atmospheric Administration (NOAA) estimated the total world flaring volume in 2006 at 168 bcm.[90] The data, however, showed Russia displaced Nigeria as the top gas flarer in the world with 50.7 bcm as against Nigeria with 23 bcm, thus rating Nigeria second in the World. Nigeria accounted for about 13% of global flaring.[91] The Nigerian amount is, however, more than the third and fourth countries combined,[92] and almost four times higher than the nearest African country, Algeria, which is recorded as having flared and vented 5.5 bcm.[93] Over 2.5 billion cubic feet of crude associated gas is flared in Nigeria every day and this equals 40 per cent of all of Africa's natural gas consumption in 2001.[94] In economic terms, it translates into a loss of $2.5 billion[95] in Government revenues and $72 billion for the period 1970–2006.[96] While 99 per cent of associated gas is used or re-injected into the ground in the United States and Western Europe,[97] a staggering 76 per cent of associated gas is flared in Nigeria[98] by the same multinational oil companies.

---

[87]   *Ibid.*

[88]   *Ibid.*

[89]   *Ibid*, p.12.

[90]   National Oceanic and Atmospheric Administration (NOAA) Final Report to the World Bank, 'A Twelve Year Record of National and Global Gas Flaring Volumes Estimated Using Satellite Data,' 30 May 2007, at http://siteresources.worldbank.org/INTGGFR/Resources/DMSP_flares_20070530_b-sm.pdf [accessed 3 March 2010].

[91]   Environmental Rights Action/Friends of the Earth Nigeria/Climate Justice Programme Report (2005), *Gas Flaring in Nigeria: A Human Rights, Environmental and Economic Monstrosity, op. cit.*

[92]   Third highest was Iran (11.4 bcm) and fourth was Iraq (8.1 bcm).

[93]   National Oceanic and Atmospheric Administration (NOAA) Final Report to the World Bank, *op. cit.*

[94]   Adekunbi Ero, Gone with the Wind, *TELL* (Special Edition), 50 years of Oil in Nigeria, Feb. 18, 2008, p.59.

[95]   *Ibid* .

[96]   Environmental Rights Action/Friends of the Earth Nigeria, *Fact Sheet: Harmful Gas Flaring in Nigeria*, November 2008, at www.foe.org/pdf/GasFlaringNigeria_FS.pdf [accessed 16 February 2010].

[97]   Shell Guilty Campaign: Oil Change International, Friends of the Earth (International, Europe, U.S. and The Netherlands), PLATFORM, and Greenpeace UK (2009), *Shell's Big Dirty Secret: Insight into the world's most carbon intensive oil company and the legacy of CEO Jeroen van der Veer*, at www.foeeurope.org/corporates/Extractives/shellbigdirtysecret_June09.pdf [accessed 13 March 2011].

[98]   Michael Watts, Petro-violence: Community, Extraction, and Political Ecology,' being a paper prepared for the Workshop on Environment and Violence, University of California, Berkeley, 24–26 September, 1998.

With the seventh largest gas reserves in the world,[99] available statistics reveal that Nigeria's gas reserve is currently estimated at about 120 trillion cubic feet (tcf).[100] The country's gas reserve production ratio is also estimated at about 125 years compared to crude oil, which is less than 30 years.[101] It was once observed that Nigeria is: '... a gas province with a bit of oil in it ... In oil equivalent terms, we have discovered more gas than oil, even though we have not began looking for gas yet'.[102] This implies that Nigeria is even more endowed with natural gas than crude oil, which is an indication that the sector will for a long period of time continue to dominate the economic sphere of the country.

The question then is: Why have the oil multinational companies continued to flare the vast reserve of gas rather than utilizing it for domestic power generation and for other economic purposes? Several factors have been blamed for the continuous flaring of gas in Nigeria, among which include lack of necessary technology for the gathering and conserving the gas flared,[103] low gas demand in the domestic and regional markets, low level of environmental consciousness of the consequences of gas flaring, failure of the Government to meet its financial contribution under the existing joint venture agreements to the cost of any gas injection facility, lack of a clearly defined long-term vision for the gas sector, lack of a robust fiscal, legal, contractual and regulatory framework and institutions to deal with foreign investors.[104] Aside from the economic loss to Nigeria, the adverse human and environmental consequences of the discharge of enormous carbon dioxide, methane and other gases into the atmosphere daily such as global warming, acid deposition and climate change are grave. Experiences of countries like Saudi Arabia, Algeria, and Norway in flaring reduction and gas utilization should serve as a pointer to the Nigerian Government that it is indeed possible for such routine flaring to cease. For example, in Saudi Arabia, 'gas flaring emissions fell from 38 billion cubic meters per year in the early 1980s to a mere 120 million cubic meters per year in 2004',[105] with the associated gas providing the basis of a successful petrochemicals industry. This has now made Saudi Arabia one of the world's largest producers of urea – a widely used agricultural fertilizer. In

---

[99]   Baumüller, Heike *et al.*, *op. cit.*, p.11.
[100] See Udoma Udo Udoma, Incentives for the Gas Ventures in Nigeria, *MPJFIL* Vol. 2 No.3, p.1 (1998), quoted in Peter Terkaa Akper, "Socio-Political Issues in Oil and Gas Exploitation in Political and Economic Reform in Nigeria", in I.A. Ayua and Guobadia D.A (eds) (2001), Political Reform and Economic Recovery in Nigeria, NIALS Publication, p.522.
[101] *Ibid.*
[102] See Nigerian Environment Study/Action Team (1991), *Nigeria's Threatened Environment. A National Profile*, p.45.
[103] Garba I. Malumfashi, Phase-Out of Gas Flaring in Nigeria By 2008: The Prospects of a Multi-Win Project (Review of the Regulatory, Environmental and Socio-Economic Issues), *Petroleum Training Journal* Vol. 4 No. 2, p.102 (2007).
[104] Soala Ariweriokuma (2009), *The Political Economy of Oil and Gas in Africa: The Case of Nigeria*, Routledge London and New York, p.178.
[105] Rashad Kaldany, *Global Gas Flaring Reduction: A Time for Action!*, being a Keynote Speech at the Global Forum on Flaring & Gas Utilization Paris, December 13th, 2006, at www.world-bank.org/html/fpd/ggfrforum06/kadany.pdf [accessed 16 February 2010].

Norway, a clear and detailed gas flaring and venting policy, careful evaluation of
the development plan as well as the cooperation of the Norwegian Government
with oil companies contributed to the successful Norwegian Gas Utilization
Policy.[106] A lot can be achieved through gas flaring reduction, this includes
but is not limited to: 'lowering CO2 emissions while opening new economic
opportunities through gas utilization, and at the same time enhancing energy
security by increasing available supplies',[107] engendering peace and stability in the
Niger Delta region, and the nation at large.

It can be seen therefore that oil production in Nigeria has come a long way.
The importance of oil in Nigeria's political economy has increased considerably.
As earlier mentioned, Nigeria, currently is the eighth largest oil exporting
country in the world with oil revenue accounting for about 80 per cent of the
total government revenue (from 70% of total government revenue in 1970), 95%
of foreign exchange earnings (from one per cent of Nigeria's export earnings in
1958), 40% contribution of Gross Domestic Product (GDP) and four per cent of
employment![108]

Given the above fact, it might be expected that the Niger Delta region (oil is
yet to be found in any other area in Nigeria aside from the Niger Delta region)
whose land generates this enormous wealth would derive substantial benefits
in terms of development. The ensuing chapters will examine to what extent the
Niger Delta communities have been able to benefit from the enormous resources
of their land in terms of provision of infrastructural facilities and institutions like
education, health, water supply; and how far their human rights and environment
have been protected by the oil MNCs operating in the region.

1.3 MULTINATIONAL OIL COMPANIES OPERATING IN THE NIGER DELTA REGION

Multinational oil companies are the major players in the oil and gas sector in
Nigeria and are credited with the pioneering efforts that brought about the chains
of events that shaped the oil industry in the country. The evolutionary process
that has brought Nigeria to its present position may have been delayed for decades
without the tremendous investment of multinational oil companies into the
industry.[109]

---

[106]   Gulzhan Nurakhmet, *Gas Flaring and Venting: What can Kazakhstan Learn from the
        Norwegian Experience?*, at www.dundee.ac.uk/cepmlp/car/html/CAR10_ARTICLE14.PDF
        [accessed 16 February 2010]. It was reported that in 2004, only 0.16 per cent of the total annual
        AG from oil production was flared in Norway because approval of the development plan is
        contingent upon provision for gas reinjection, gas export or other AG utilization schemes.
[107]   *Ibid.*
[108]   See TELL (Special Edition), 50 Years of Oil in Nigeria, Feb. 18, 2008 p.33.
[109]   See Steve Azaiki (2007), *Oil, Gas and Life in Nigeria*, Y-Books Publishers, Ibadan, p.46; See
        also United Nations Conference on Trade and Development UNCTAD/CALAG African Oil

Today six of these multinational oil companies operating in the Niger Delta have become giants in the industry. They are Shell Petroleum Development Company (SPDC), Chevron, Mobil, Agip, Total Fina Elf, and Texaco. These companies operate internationally and have technical knowledge with strong financial base. Their activities in Nigeria usually relate to upstream operations and these six companies alone hold up to 98% of Nigeria's oil blocks, reserves, and operating assets.[110] These companies have enabled the oil sector in Nigeria to record an exploration success rate that places her among the highest in the World.

1.3.1   SHELL PETROLEUM DEVELOPMENT COMPANY

Shell, whose predecessor Shell D'Arcy was a pioneer of oil exploration in the country, is today the leading oil company in Nigeria. It changed its name from Shell BP Petroleum Company of Nigeria Limited to Shell Petroleum Development Company of Nigeria on 1 August 1979. The company is unarguably the dominant and also the oldest player in the field. Its accomplishments include:[111]

- *"Becoming the first multinational company to be incorporated (1937) and licensed (1939).*
- *Discovering and drilling Nigeria's first commercial oil field in Oloibiri.*
- *Becoming the first to produce and export crude oil from Nigeria (1958).*
- *Producing 6,000 barrels of oil per day in 1958, it now produces about one million barrels per day and more than 700 million scf/d of gas from its oil fields.*
- *Producing the largest quantities of oil and gas in Nigeria.*
- *Producing nearly half of Nigeria's oil and 95% of its commercial gas.*
- *Covering the largest Oil Mining Lease area with 31,000 square kilometers, which contain over 50% of the country's oil and gas reserves*
- *Operating more than 90 oil fields*
- *Discovering and drilling Nigeria's first commercial deep water well."*

The Company operates at present a total of 44 onshore oil mining licences covering 31,000 km², which contain over 50% of the country's oil and gas reserves. It further operates the NNPC/Shell/Elf/Agip joint venture in which NNPC holds 55%, Shell 30%, Elf 10% and Agip 5%.[112] The scale of the company's operations is massive, involving an infrastructure of 6,200 kilometers of pipelines, more than 1,000 oil producing wells, 87 flow stations, eight gas plants and two large

---

and Gas Services Sector Survey Volume 1- Nigeria Creating Local Linkages by Empowering Indigenous Entrepreneurs UNCTAD/DITC/COM/2005/6, United Nations Publications New York and Geneva, 2006.

[110]   Steve Azaiki, *Ibid.*
[111]   *Ibid* pp.47–48.
[112]   *Ibid* p.48

terminals at Forcados and Bonny, spread throughout the Niger Delta.[113] Shell
has some 4,000 staff, ninety-five per cent of whom are Nigerians. In addition,
the company has another 8,000 contract staff, again mostly Nigerians, and it is
estimated that another 20,000 people are employed by contractors working for
SPDC.[114]

Shell has interests in five companies in Nigeria, *viz*: Shell Petroleum Develop-
ment Company of Nigeria Ltd. (SPDC), Shell Nigeria Gas (SNG), Shell Nigeria
Exploration and Production Company (SNEPCO), Nigeria Liquefied Natural Gas
Ltd. (NLNG), and Shell Nigeria Oil Products (SNOP).[115] Shell's major significant
involvement in Nigeria's gas industry is its investment in the Nigeria Liquefied
Natural Gas (NLNG) project in Bonny, Rivers State. The joint venture partners in
the project are NNPC with a 49% stake; Shell, the Managing Partner with 25.6%,
Elf, with 15% and Agip, with 10.4%.

1.3.2 EXXON/MOBIL

Mobil Exploration Nigeria Incorporated started its operations in Nigeria in 1955
as an affiliate of Mobil Corporation. It changed to Mobil Producing Nigeria in
June 1969. In December, 1999, there was a merger between ESSO Exploration,
Mobil Producing Nigeria Limited, Mobil Oil Nigeria Plc, and Mobil Producing
Nigeria Unlimited. In reality, this merger was between two major oil giants that
operate upstream activities – Exxon Corporation and Mobil Corporation. By this
merger, Exxon Mobil today has a presence in more than 200 countries and employs
over 123,000 workers.[116] Today in Nigeria Exxon Mobil's two subsidiaries, Mobil
Producing Nigeria Unlimited and Esso Exploration and Production Nigeria
Limited, are influential exploration and production companies.[117] Mobil received
its first offshore Oil Prospecting Licences (OPLS) in 1961, drilled its first wild cat
in 1963 and made its first discovery in 1964. It began production in 1970. It has
over 400 employees in Nigeria overseeing assets of some $145 million and annual
sales of petroleum products of more than six million barrels a year.[118] Following
its commencement of crude oil production in 1970, the Nigerian Government
acquired a 35% participation in operation of the company. This was increased

---

[113]   N.K. Obasi, *op. cit.*
[114]   *Ibid.*
[115]   Shell Petroleum Development Company of Nigeria Limited, "Should Oil Companies Directly
        Finance Development Projects for Local Communities? The Case of Shell-Nigeria", Rudolf
        Traub-Merz/Douglas Yates (eds) (2004), *Oil Policy in the Gulf of Guinea. Security and Conflict,
        Economic Growth, Social Development*, International Conference Friedrich-Ebert-Stiftung
        Proceedings, p.145.
[116]   Steve Azaiki, *Oil, Gas and Life in Nigeria, op. cit.*, p.51.
[117]   *Ibid.*
[118]   N.K. Obasi, *op. cit.*

to 55% in 1974 and to 60% in 1979 and this remains the same today.[119] Mobil is the second largest oil producer in Nigeria behind Shell, operating 88 offshore platforms.[120]

1.3.3 CHEVRON NIGERIA LIMITED

Chevron Nigeria Limited started its exploration and production activities in Nigeria as Gulf Oil Company (Nigeria) in December 1961, when it got its first oil prospecting licence from the Federal Government. The receipt of another prospecting license in June 1962 consolidated the company's interests over a concession area measuring 5,000 square kilometers offshore and about 2,500 square kilometers onshore in the Niger Delta.[121] The company, on 8 December 1963, discovered Nigeria's first successful offshore field, christened 'OKAN' meaning 'one' in the Itsekiri language, spoken by the local people of the nearby onshore area. The company commenced export on 1 April 1965, shipping Nigeria's first consignment of offshore crude to the world market.

On 1 April, 1973, the Federal Government, through the then Nigerian National Oil Corporation (NNOC), now NNPC acquired a 35% stake in the company. This stake increased to 60% with Chevron holding 40%. When Gulf Oil Corporation and Chevron Corporation merged their global operations in 1984, Gulf in Nigeria effectively became a subsidiary of Chevron. The name changed to Chevron Nigeria Limited in July 1991.[122] By the end of 1998, the Chevron/NNPC joint venture had recorded a total average production of 418,000 barrels of oil per day.

One important landmark development in Chevron's participation in the Nigerian petroleum industry is the West African Gas Pipeline (WAGP) project. Under this project, gas is to be pumped from Nigeria's Escravos area in Delta State to the West African countries of Benin, Togo and Ghana.[123] A memorandum of understanding for this project was signed on 11 August, 1999 between the Governments of Nigeria, Benin, Togo and Ghana and a consortium of six companies – Chevron, Shell, Nigerian National Petroleum Corporation, Ghana National Petroleum Corporation, Societe Beninoise de Gaz and Societe Togoleise de Gaz,[124] Chevron being the largest shareholder with a 36.7 per cent interest. Chevron has recently announced the commencement of crude oil production from the Agbami off-shore field. First oil from the field was achieved in May 2008 and by early 2009 total crude oil production averaged 170,000 barrels per day (116,000 net) and is projected to increase to 250,000 barrels of crude oil and

[119]   Steve Azaiki, *Oil, Gas and Life in Nigeria, op. cit.*, p.52.
[120]   *Ibid.*
[121]   N.K. Obasi, *op. cit.*
[122]   *Ibid.*
[123]   *Ibid.*
[124]   *Ibid.*

natural gas liquids per day by the end of 2009. The field, discovered in 1998, is
the largest deep water discovery in Nigeria and is estimated to hold potentially
recoverable volumes of 900 million barrels.[125] Chevron is the operator and has a
68.2 per cent share under the unit agreement. Other partners are NNPC, Famfa
Oil Limited, Petrobras and Statoil.

1.3.4 TEXACO OVERSEAS (NIGERIA) PETROLEUM COMPANY UNLIMITED

Texaco Overseas (Nigeria) Petroleum Company Unlimited emerged under the
umbrella of Amoseas (Texaco and Chevron) in 1961, and since then, it has been
busy making steady progress in exploration and production of oil. It started
producing oil in 1970, and today produces approximately 55,000 barrels of crude
oil per day, through six offshore production facilities. It operates six fields in
the shallow waters offshore Bayelsa State, which together produce nearly 70,000
barrels of oil per day.[126] It operates a joint venture with the Nigerian National
Petroleum Company (NNPC). The percentage equity shares are as follows: NNPC
(60%), Texaco (20%) and Chevron (20%). The Company has a total workforce of
nearly 300 employees, 95 per cent of whom are Nigerian nationals.

Texaco is a leader in deepwater activities, currently holding Offshore
Prospecting Licence (OPL) interests in five deepwater blocks (Blocks 213, 215,
216, 217 and 218) through its subsidiary Star Deep Water Petroleum Limited.[127]
In early 1999, Texaco and its partners Famfa and Braspetro announced a major
discovery, Agbami, in the deep waters 70 miles off the coast in the central Niger
Delta. Testing of the Agbami 2 appraisal well revealed that the Agbami structure
is a giant discovery with potential recoverable reserves in excess of one billion
oil-equivalent barrels. The Agbami discovery ranks among the largest single well
finds to date in deepwater West Africa.[128] The structure spans an area of 45,000
acres, and the company's share of the production from this source is expected to
exceed 50 percent.

Texaco has continued to engage in a lot of community development projects
in its area of operation particularly in Bayelsa and Delta States.

---

[125]   See The Nation, Friday, August 1, 2008, p.33.
[126]   Nigeria. Crude Oil Exploration and Production, at www.nnpcgroup.com/aboutus.htm.
        [accessed 5 July 2009].
[127]   Steve Azaiki, *Oil, Gas and Life in Nigeria, op. cit.*, p.56.
[128]   Nigeria. Crude Oil Exploration and Production , *op. cit.*

1.3.5 TOTAL FINA ELF

Total Fina Elf is the fifth largest oil and gas multinational company in the world. Elf Petroleum Nigeria Limited was incorporated as Safrap in 1962 and belonged then to the family of Elf Aquitaine Group. In its 41 years of operation, the company has recorded progressive growth:[129]

- *"In the early 1960s it discovered Obagi, one of the Nigeria's major oil fields. So far it has produced more than 500 million barrels.*
- *In the 1970s, it was engaged in the development of the fields in the swamp areas of OML 57.*
- *In the 1980s, important oil fields were discovered in the offshore OMLs 99,100, and 102;*
- *In the 1990s, production started in earnest from the offshore discoveries (OMLs 100 and 102);*
- *In the 1990s, and beyond, Elf Petroleum has been recording remarkable success in deep offshore activities. It is involved in four joint venture partnerships, and is the operator of two of the four."*

Elf Petroleum Nigeria Limited holds 40% equity of the four onshore blocks and four offshore blocks in its joint venture with NNPC, with the latter holding 60%. It holds a 15% interest in the Nigerian LNG joint venture company in partnership with the NNPC (49%), Shell (25.6%) and Agip (10.4%). Its latest expansion of the Bonny Island LNG plant will have a significant impact in the drive to eliminate gas flaring in the Niger Delta region of Nigeria.[130]

1.3.6 NIGERIAN AGIP OIL COMPANY LIMITED

Nigerian Agip Oil Company Limited belongs to the ENI Agip Division. Following its incorporation in 1962, it was granted an Oil Prospecting Licence for four blocks covering an area of 5,313 km². In 1965, it signed a Joint Operating Agreement with Philips. Its successful exploratory activities, and the discovery of oil in Ebocha in 1965, led to the conversion of OPL 34 to an Oil Mining Licence in 1967.[131] It started production in 1970. Nigerian Agip signed a participation agreement with the Federal Government (represented by NNPC) and with Philips Oil Company Nigeria Limited in 1971; and the equity shares were split in 1979 between the

---

[129] Steve Azaiki, *Oil, Gas and Life in Nigeria, op. cit.,* pp.56–57.
[130] Nigeria: Constitution of two new gas liquefaction trains, at http:// www.total.com/en/press/ press_ releases/pr_2002/020327_Nigeria_construction_1240.htm. [accessed 5 July 2009].
[131] Steve Azaiki, *Oil, Gas and Life in Nigeria, op. cit.,* p.58.

NNPC (60%), Agip (20%) and Philips (20%).[132] In 2002, its production levels stood at 200,000 barrels per day (from 25,000 barrels per day in 1977).[133]

By acquiring 5% participating interest in the NNPC-Shell joint venture, the company is now one of the largest oil-producing conglomerates in Nigeria. It also holds 10% equity in the NNPC-Shell-Elf-Agip joint venture in the Liquefied Natural Gas project.[134] Two subsidiaries of ENI-Agip Nigerian (Agip Exploration Limited incorporated in 1966 and Agip Energy and Natural Resources Nigeria Limited incorporated in 1980) are deeply involved in exploration and production activities in Nigeria. Operation statistics reveal that in the past 42 years, Agip has drilled 328 wells (99 of them exploratory), with a success rate of 54%. Out of 46 fields discovered, 26 were put into production, and it has commissioned two gas recycling plants, Obiafu/Obirikom and Kwale/Okpai, in 1985 and 1987 respectively.[135]

There are other multinational companies that are also, but in a small way, exploring for oil in the Niger Delta. For example, we have Pan Ocean Corporation which started its production of crude oil in 1976, Statoil incorporated in 1992 and began drilling activities in Nigeria in 1995, and Conoco incorporated in Nigeria in 1991.

1.4   INDIGENOUS OIL AND GAS COMPANIES

For several years, the multinational companies had a near total monopoly of the oil sector in Nigeria. The dominance of the multinational companies has continued recently. The indigenous explorers and producers joined the industry to bring about some semblance of "Nigerianization".[136] In 1990, the Federal government, however offered some blocks in the Niger Delta and Benin basins, on concessionary terms, to a number of indigenous oil companies in order to encourage and stimulate local participation in the oil and gas sector. Prominent indigenous companies that have been licensed include Dubri Oil Limited, Consolidated Oil Limited, Yinka Folawiyo Petroleum Company Limited, Allied Energy Resources, Amni International Petroleum Development Company Limited, Atlas Petroleum International Limited, Summit Oil International, International Petrol Energy Company, Express Petroleum and Gas Company Limited, Noreast Petroleum, and International Oil Nigeria Limited. By the late 1990s, many of these companies had moved into production including Atlas, Amni, Cavendish, Moni Pulo, Conoil, Dubril, Express and Peak Petroleum.

---

[132]   *Ibid.*
[133]   *Ibid.*
[134]   *Ibid,* pp.58–59.
[135]   *Ibid.*
[136]   *Ibid,* pp.61–62.

These indigenous oil companies are faced with some problems, among which are lack of technical expertise and problems of raising enough capital outlay for oil exploration and production. With the Government's policy being to allow as much as 40% equity participation in indigenous oil companies by foreigners, the hope of achieving the objective appears bright. It would achieve the objective of solving the problem of funding in the highly capital intensive industry, and boosting the technological know-how of the local firms.[137] This would fully equip the firms for the active participation, alongside foreign companies, in the development of newly allocated deep, and ultra-deep, offshore blocks, thus increasing oil-related activities in the Niger Delta and raising the nation's crude oil reserves and daily production capacity from an estimated 37.2 billion barrels and 2.5 million bpd as of the end of 2011 to 40 billion barrels and 4.0 million bpd, respectively in the next few years.[138]

In 1992, the Nigerian Association of Indigenous Petroleum Explorers and Producers was formed by these indigenous oil companies. It has since positioned itself to implement the Government's agenda of increasing local content in the industry and reducing foreign domination over the industry by encouraging new entrants and working towards acquiring advance technology and technical expertise.[139] They are breaking new grounds, and are presently recording production figures of 150,000 barrels per day (which amounts to 5% of national production).

In the area of gas, the major company is the Nigeria Liquefied Natural Gas Ltd. (NLNG). This operation is the Nigeria's largest gas project. Trains 1 and 2 of the Nigeria LNG project at Bonny Island were completed in September 1999, and Nigeria (LNG) is the vehicle developing the project and is owned by NNPC (49%), Shell (25.6%), Total (15%) and Agip (10.4%).[140] The first two trains have the capacity to process 252.4 bcf of gas annually. The third train began operations in November 2002 and increased the projects' capacity by 131 bcf of gas. Currently, NLNG has six trains and a production capacity of 22 million metric tons per year (1.1 Tcf), and a seventh train is under construction to boost the capacity of the facility by 8 million metric tons per year.[141]

---

[137] Udeme Ekpo (2004), *The Niger Delta and Oil Politics*, International Energy Communications Ltd. Publishers, Lagos, p.15.

[138] *Ibid*; U.S. Energy Information Administration, *Nigeria,* at www.eia.gov/countries/analysis-briefs/Nigeria/nigeria.pdf [accessed 15 February 2013].

[139] *Ibid*, p.63.

[140] See *Nigeria Energy Report*, Norton Rose, June 2003, at www.nortonrose.com/knowledge/publications/pdf [accessed 3 March 2010].

[141] *Ibid*; U.S. Energy Information Administration, *Nigeria,* at www.eia.gov/countries/analysis-briefs/Nigeria/nigeria.pdf [accessed 15 February 2013].

1.5 THE EVOLUTION OF STATE PARTICIPATION IN THE OIL INDUSTRY

The oil industry in Nigeria was initially completely dominated and controlled by foreign oil companies. The development of the sector has been governed by several economic policy principles such as those related to licences and leases signed with foreign oil companies. The Mineral Oil Act 1914 was passed to "regulate the right to search for, win and work mineral oils". It specified that "the power conferred upon the Governor-General to grant licences and leases for mineral oils shall be exercised subject to the condition that no lease or licence shall be granted except to a British subject or to a British Company". This was the position of the law until the change introduced into the law by section 2 of the Mineral Oils (Amendment) Act 1958 that allowed for entry into the industry by non-British companies. This accounts for the dominant position occupied and still maintained by Shell in the industry.[142] As a follow up, the Petroleum Decree No. 51 of 1969 was promulgated to repeal the entire colonial 1914 Mineral Oil Act. This decree vested the ownership and control of petroleum in the State Government. The Decree also introduced changes such as the reduction in duration of leases from thirty years to twenty years; the Nigerianization of the vital organs of the oil industry; and the establishment of governmental control over oil operations.[143] This remains the basis for the regulatory system in operation today.

The first major step by the Government to get involved in the oil sector was the establishment, in 1971, of the Nigerian National Oil Corporation (NNOC), the forerunner to the Nigerian National Petroleum Corporation (NNPC). The NNOC's brief was to "participate in all aspects of petroleum including exploration, production, refining, marketing, transportation, and distribution". In July 1971, Nigeria joined the Organization of Petroleum Exporting Countries (OPEC). It is important to stress that right from its establishment in 1960, OPEC attempted to redefine the relationship between the oil companies and the oil-producing countries. By 1968, a break-through was effected, when it was resolved that the oil-producing countries should enter into participation agreements with the oil companies.[144] The Nigerian State therefore attempted to articulate in practical terms OPEC's resolution on participation with the formation of NNOC in 1971.[145] Nigeria pioneered a trend in that particular year, that is 1971, as it took

---

[142] Godfrey Etikerentse, "Oil and Gas Exploration in Nigeria: Challenges for the 21st Century", in I.A. Ayua and Guobadia D.A. (eds.) (2001), *Political Reform and Economic Recovery in Nigeria*, *op. cit.*, p. 494.

[143] Augustine A. Ikein (1990), *The Impact of Oil on a Developing Country: The Case of Nigeria*, Evans Brothers (Nigeria Publishers) Ltd, Ibadan, pp.2–3.

[144] Kayode Soremekun and Ebenezer Obadare, "Politics of Oil Corporations in Post Colonial Nigeria", in Omotoye Olorode *et al.* (eds) (1998), *Ken Saro-Wiwa and the Crises of the Nigerian State*, Committee for the Defence of Human Rights (CDHR) Publications, Lagos, p.41.

[145] See Kayode Soremekun, Nigeria Petroleum Policy and External Relations, Unpublished PhD Thesis Submitted to the Department of International Relations, University of Ife, 1984.

up equity shares in the holdings of Nigerian Oil Company (33.33%) and in Safrap, the Nigerian arm of the French Company Elf (35%). After Nigeria joined OPEC, NNOC acquired 35% stakes in Shell BP, Gulf, and Mobil, on 1 April 1973. Also, in 1973, it entered into a production-sharing agreement with Ashland oil. On 1 April 1974, stakes in Elf, Agip/Phillips, Shell BP, Gulf, and Mobil were increased to 55% and, on 1 May 1975, the NNOC acquired 55% of Texaco's operations in Nigeria.[146]

Apart from the fact that NNOC had limited powers as a public corporation, it faced from its inception the problem of attempting to manage a highly complex industry without adequate technical and financial resources. These problems were dramatically illustrated several times during its subsequent history as it could not fully achieve the objectives for which it was set up. The Ministry of Petroleum Resources continued to perform regulatory functions. On 1 April 1977, just about six years after it had been set up, the NNOC was reconstituted as the Nigerian National Petroleum Corporation (NNPC) as a result of the merger of the NNOC and the Nigerian Ministry of Petroleum Resources.[147] One of the reasons for the change may not be unconnected with its operating failures, of the 1970s, which became publicly known at the time of the 1980 Crude Oil Sales Tribunal investigations. This investigation revealed that, for instance, from 1975 to 1978, the NNOC and NNPC had failed to collect some 182.95 million barrels of their equity share of oil being produced by Shell, Mobil, and Gulf with potential revenue estimated to be in excess of $2 billion.[148] An additional revelation was that, until forced to do so by the Tribunal, NNOC had not produced audited accounts from 1975 onward.[149]

In line with the objectives of the Government's 1977 indigenization Decree, the NNPC succeeded in raising the Government's equity participation significantly on 1 July 1979, when its stakes in the Nigerian businesses of the following companies were raised to 60 percent: Elf, Gulf, Mobil, Texaco, and Pan Ocean. NNPC's stake in the Shell venture was raised to 80 per cent on 1 August 1979, after BP lost its 20 per cent stake following disagreements with the Nigerian government

---

[146]   Nigerian National Petroleum Corporation, at www.nnpcgroup.com/ep.htm. [accessed 3 March 2010].

[147]   The NNPC was created by Decree No. 33 of 1977, as a successor to the NNOC, itself created in 1971 as the first major effort to "indigenize" the oil industry, in response to the OPEC call for member States to participate more actively in oil operations. NNPC is responsible for production, transportation, refining, and marketing of oil and petroleum products. In 1986, the Petroleum Inspectorate, responsible for regulation and policy formulation, was detached from NNPC and given instead to the Department of Petroleum Resources; while preferable to the previous situation, in which NNPC regulated itself, the inspectorate still lacks independence. See Human Rights Watch (HRW) (1999), *The Price of Oil: Corporate Responsibility and Human Rights Violations in Nigeria's Oil Producing Communities*, New York, p.27; Sarah Ahmad Khan (1994), *Nigeria: The Political Economy of Oil*, Oxford University Press, USA, pp.22–28.

[148]   See Nigerian National Petroleum Corporation, at www.nnpcgroup.com/ep.htm. [accessed 3 March 2010].

[149]   *Ibid.*

over South Africa. But this has since reduced. The NNPC operates both as a
regulatory body, as an operator and as a vehicle for Government's investments
in the industry through its subsidiaries.[150] In 1988, NNPC, the biggest State-
owned company south of the Sahara, formally became a commercial, integrated
oil company (operating both in the upstream and downstream sectors) whose
products attracted internationally competitive prices.[151] With the establishment
of the NNPC, the traditional concessions granted to international oil companies
were abolished and replaced by the joint venture agreements (JV), production
sharing arrangements (PSC) and service or risk contracts, respectively.[152]

Joint Ventures: The main onshore exploration and production activities carried
out today by foreign oil companies in Nigeria are in joint ventures with the NNPC,
the State oil company. In a 'joint venture' the operator (TNOCs) the joint venture
partner (NNPC) and in rare cases other foreign investors share the operating
costs, while in a 'production sharing-contract', the contractor (TNOCs) advances
all funds towards running costs.[153] Joint Venture arrangements impose funding
obligations on all the parties for the joint operations. The level of each party's
participation in the funding and its shares on any oil discovered is directly related
to its interest in the joint venture.[154] The major joint ventures involving foreign
owned oil companies are shown below:

---

[150]   The NNPC subsidiaries are Nigerian Petroleum Development Company (NPDC), Integrated
Data Services Limited (IDSL), Kaduna Refinery and Petrochemicals Company (KRPC), Warri
Refinery and Petrochemical Limited (WRPC), Port Harcourt Refinery and Petrochemical
Company (PHRC), Pipeline and Products Marketing Company (PPMC), National Engineering
and Technical Company Limited (NETCO), National Petroleum Investment Management
Services (NAPIMS). The Eleme Petrochemicals Company Limited, Nigerian Gas Company
(NGC) and Drake Oil Limited, Calson (Bermuda) Limited and Hydrocarbon Services Nigeria
Limited (Hyson) are other partly owned subsidiary companies.
[151]   See Udeme Ekpo, *op. cit.*, p.13.
[152]   Patrick D. Okonmah, Right to a Clean Environment: The Case for the People of Oil-Producing
Communities in the Nigerian Delta, *op. cit.*, p.45; Akpan Wilson, Oil, People and the
Environment: Understanding Land-Related Controversies in Nigeria's Oil Region, *op. cit.*
[153]   Kenneth Omeje, The Rentier State: Oil-Related Legislation and Conflict in the Niger Delta,
Nigeria, 6 (2) *Conflict, Security and Development* 211–230, 218 (2006).
[154]   Godfrey Etikerentse, *op. cit.*, p.498.

Table 1:2. Major oil multinational corporations and joint ventures in the Nigerian upstream oil sector

Consortium	Shareholders	Joint venture operator	Production barrel/day (2003 estimates)	Production percentage (%)
Shell Petroleum Development Company of Nigeria Ltd.	NNPC (55%), Shell (Dutch/British, 30%) ELF (France, 10%), Agip (Italy, 5%)	Shell	950,000	42.2
Mobil Producing Nigeria Ltd.	NNPC (58%), Mobil (US, 42%)	Mobil	500,000	21.2
Chevron Nigeria Limited	NNPC (58%), Chevron (US, 42%)	Chevron	485,000	18.6
Nigeria Agip Oil Company	NNPC (60%), Agip (Italy, 20%), Philips (US, 20%)	Agip	150,000	7.5
Elf Petroleum Limited	NNPC (60%), ELF (France, 40%)	Elf	145,000	6.1
Texaco Overseas (Nigeria) Petroleum Company	NNPC (60%), Texaco (US, 20%), Chevron (US, 20%)	Texaco	55,000	2.7
Other producers	Ashland (US), Deminex (Germany), Pan Ocean (Switzerland), British Gas (GB), Sun Oil (US), Conoco (US), BP (GB), Statoil (Norway) Conoil (Nigeria), Dubri Oil (Nigeria)	Various	35,000	1.7
Total			2,320,000	100

Source: Uwafiokun Idemudia (2009).[155]

The above shows that although the Nigerian State through the NNPC theoretically holds the controlling shares in each of the six major oil companies, operational and hence real control is vested in the international oil corporations.[156] Each joint venture has a Joint Operating Agreement (JOA) with NNPC, which governs the

---

[155]   Uwafiokun Idemudia, Assessing corporate-community involvement strategies in the Nigerian oil industry: An empirical analysis, 34 *Resources Policy*, 133–141 at 134 (2009); U. Idemudia and Ite U., Corporate-community relations in Nigeria's oil industry: challenges and imperatives, *Corporate SocialResponsibility and Environmental Management Journal*, 194–206 (2006).

[156]   See Festus Iyayi , "Oil Companies and the Politics of Community Relations in Nigeria", in Wumi Raji, Ayodele Ale and Eni Akinsola (eds) (2000), *Boiling Point. A CDHR Publication on the Crises in the Oil Producing Communities in Nigeria*, p.156.

administrative arrangements between the partners, along with the Memorandum of Understanding (MOU) which stipulates that "the operating company in a joint venture receives a fixed sum per barrel provided the price of oil per barrel remains within certain margins". About 80 per cent of oil and gas production in Nigeria is currently subject to JOAs.

In the existing joint ventures, the foreign oil companies are the designated 'operators', responsible for the day-to-day business of searching for oil, developing oil fields, laying and maintaining pipelines, managing the export terminals, acting as custodians of the crude oil tanks as well as managing the operating budgets.[157] This "external control" of so many sensitive aspects of Nigeria's oil sector by foreign companies partly explains why ordinary Niger Delta residents sometimes refer to Nigeria as a Shell colony.

One noticeable problem in the JVs relationship is NNPC's inability to timeously release funds to the 'operators' as its part of the funding obligations in a joint venture – an issue known throughout the industry as 'cash call problem'. A key factor in funding problems has been attributed to the inadequate allocation of the Government's contributions to oil funding in the country's federal budgets.[158] Joint venture cash calls sometimes fall into arrears of several hundred million U.S. dollar.[159] A few years ago, NNPC arrears are reportedly approaching US$ 1.0 billion, a very substantial sum.[160] This either delays the implementation of projects, deferring associated tax revenues and more general economic benefits, or results in the build up of significant interest cost liabilities for NNPC, in the event that NNPC's partners go ahead with the project, financing NNPC's shortfall through bank loans as allowed under the Joint Operating Agreement which regulates relations between the joint venture partners.[161] Paradoxically, the oil multinationals do lend money to NNPC to meet its cash call shortfalls. As observed by Akpan, a pattern of financial relationship in which oil companies become lenders to their 'senior partner' could theoretically hinder the 'senior partner's' ability to exercise its full regulatory and monitoring powers over the lenders.[162] It must be pointed out at this juncture that the transnational oil

---

[157] Wilson Akpan, Oil, People and the Environment : Understanding Land-Related Controversies in Nigeria's Oil Region, *op. cit.*

[158] Jedrzej George Frynas, Political instability and business: focus on Shell in Nigeria, *Third World Quarterly*, Vol. 19, No 3, pp.457–478, at 463 (1998).

[159] Wilson Ndarake Akpan, *Between the 'Sectional' and the 'National': Oil, Grassroots Discontent and Civic Discourse in Nigeria*, Unpublished Thesis Submitted in Fulfilment of the Requirements for the Degree of Doctor of Philosophy of Rhodes University, October 2005; Nigeria Exchange News (2000), *Energy sector limps wearily on low funding, faulty equipment*, May 29, at www.ngex.com/news/020600.htm [accessed 13 May 2009]; P. Asiodu, *Improving Investment Flows: New Focus on Financing Projects*, Keynote Address at the 2nd Annual Oil and Gas Investments in Nigeria Conference, London, 27 April 2001.

[160] Joint UNDP/World Bank Energy Sector Management Assistance Programme (ESMAP) Report, *Taxation and State Participation in Nigeria's Oil and Gas Sector*, August 2004, p.54.

[161] *Ibid.*

[162] Wilson Ndarake Akpan, *Between the 'Sectional' and the 'National': Oil, Grassroots Discontent and Civic Discourse in Nigeria*, op. cit.

companies do contribute to the disputes surrounding cash calls as some of them fraudulently incur all manners of expenses that cannot be explained in real terms on projects without approval and turn to the NNPC for reimbursement or for exchange with crude oil. Without investing in tangible resources upstream, they claim they have spent huge sums of money which they ask the NNPC to reimburse. One of the several scandals perpetrated by the oil transnationals in collaboration with some dubious NNPC officials was the recent overshooting by Shell of its JV budget by $1.2 billion, which led to a serious controversy between it and the NNPC. The latter maintained that this was spent by Shell without regulatory approval and in a manner not transparent.[163] The Acting NNPC Group Managing Director, Abubakar Yar'Adua maintained that:

> *"There was a programme and a budget but Shell over-performed by $1.2 billion. They found money somewhere and went ahead with the project without discussing or getting the approval of the bigger partner in the joint venture only to come back and ask for reimbursement. For Shell to claim that Government was not paying its counterpart fund in the JV was deceptive as such statement failed to portray the true picture of the case. The company over-performed, and the National Petroleum Investment Services that was supposed to approve it was not aware, so how can Government pay back."[164]*

Production Sharing Contracts: Following the difficulties of the Nigerian Government in meeting its financial obligations in its joint ventures, government policy started to shift away from joint ventures to production sharing contracts (PSC) in the 1990s. Under PSC, which is the direction in which government policy is currently focused, one party contributes to the acquisition, exploration or development of an oil property, and receives as consideration, an interest in the production to which the contribution is made.[165] PSC became popular in the 1950s and 1960s in countries like Iran and Indonesia because ownership in the underlying resources was clearly retained in the States.[166] This model is also in use in countries like Gabon, Malaysia and India. Nigeria was emulating these countries in adopting this scheme. Under this scheme, the contractor takes full responsibility for all production activities and income from output is shared with NNPC according to agreed terms. The contracting oil company only recovers its costs when there is a commercial discovery. The oil produced is usually shared into Cost oil (a proportion that the producer/contractor takes annually to offset defined costs in accordance with the production sharing contract), Equity oil (a proportion that enables the producer to get guarantee return on investment),

---

[163]   See Ifeanyi Izeze, NNPC: A joint venture of fraud?, Daily Triumph, Friday 27 June 2008.

[164]   Quoted in Ifeanyi Izeze, *Ibid.*

[165]   Kayode Soremekun and Ebenezer Obadare, *op. cit.*, p.41.

[166]   Cynthia L. Quarterman, *Transparency and Change Management White Paper for Nigeria's Extractive Industries Transparency Initiative* ("NEITI"), 12 April 2005, at www.neiti.org.ng/ files-pdf/ChangeManagement.pdf. [accessed 3 March 2010].

Tax oil (a proportion that goes into settling the tax and royalty obligations of the producer) and Profit oil (a proportion shared between the Nigerian Government and the producer based on conditions specified in the contract).[167]

PSCs are most favoured by the Government due to their attribute of freeing Government's finances for other endeavours, while retaining to Government the ownership of the concession and benefiting from the result of operations which it has not funded upfront.[168] There is less risk of political interference to the foreign investor, since a PSC entails no capital expenditure from the State oil company. New prospecting licences and mining leases granted in the deep water fields off the Nigerian coast have been on these terms, and the oil companies have been pushing for the onshore joint ventures to be converted, freeing them from the annual budget struggle.[169] Among those operating under PSCs are Statoil, SNEPCO (Shell), Esso, Nigerian Agip Exploration Limited, Addax, Elf, Conoco, Star Deep Water, Ocean Energy, Petrobas, Chevron, Oranto and Phillips. A typical PSC would include a contract term which is usually 30 years, inclusive of a 10 year exploration period.

In spite of its obvious advantages, the PSC does have certain drawbacks. For instance, there is always the possibility of the contractor concentrating its investment efforts on existing prolific fields while reducing or even stopping altogether investment on the exploration of new and potentially risky fields for economic reasons. There is also the likelihood of 'the contractor incurring unqualified expenditure to the disadvantage of the National Oil Corporation (NNPC) which would have to concede an increased volume of available crude oil for cost-recovery purposes.'[170] As contended by Frynas, their control over

---

[167] Okechukwu Ibeanu (2006), *Civil Society and Conflict Management in the Niger Delta: Scoping Gaps for Policy and Advocacy, op. cit.,* pp.27–28.

[168] Godfrey Etikerentse, *op. cit.,* p.499. In recent years, the PSCs are increasingly becoming the trend in Nigerian oil industry, numbering 25 in early 2006. According to Nwokeji, "PSC is projected to contribute 644,000 or 20% of the expected total daily production of 3.218 mbd by 2010. It accounted for about 110,000 barrels or less than 5% of Nigeria's daily production of 2.485 mbd in 2005, and 17,284,593 barrels or 8.8 per cent of Nigeria's total production of 194,590,903 during the second quarter of 2006." See G. Ugo Nwokeji, *The Nigerian National Petroleum Corporation and the Development of the Nigerian Oil and Gas Industry: History, Strategies and Current Directions,* being a report prepared in Conjunction with an Energy Study sponsored by the James A. Baker III Institute for Public Policy and Japan Petroleum Energy Center, Rice University, March 2007, p. 9, at www.rice.edu/energy/publications/docs/ NOCs/Papers/NOC_NNPC_Ugo.pdf. [accessed 3 March 2010]. The figures are gotten from NNPC (2006) Second Quarter Petroleum Information, at www.nnpcgroup.com/mpi/index. php?order=nom&direction=1&directory=Quarterly&.

[169] Human Rights Watch (1999), The Price of Oil: Corporate Responsibility and Human Rights Violation in Nigeria's Oil Producing Communities, *op. cit.,* p.31. See also United Nations Conference on Trade and Development UNCTAD/CALAG African Oil and Gas Services Sector Survey Volume 1- Nigeria Creating Local Linkages by Empowering Indigenous Entrepreneurs UNCTAD/DITC/COM/2005/6, United Nations Publications, New York and Geneva, 2006.

[170] Sola Adepetun, Production Sharing Contracts – the Nigerian Experience, *J. Energy Nat. Resources L.* 21–28 at 27 (1995).

operating costs by foreign oil companies is probably the key to the understanding of high profits in the Nigerian oil industry.[171] Frynas continued that, 'the rules for the calculation of profits within a company are not publicly known. Shell as a multinational company sets prices and administrative charges between affiliate companies in order to reflect the services performed by its multinational system. The Government with a 55% share is liable to pay 55% of all sorts of expenditure before tax is assessed, while the operational budget is decided by Shell. The company has a financial incentive to inflate costs.'[172] This fact was attested to by a former Managing Director of the Nigerian National Petroleum Corporation when he stated that, 'proper cost monitoring of their operations has eluded us and one could conclude that what actually keeps these companies in operation is not the theoretical margin but the returns which they build into their costs.'[173] Commenting on the production sharing contracts opted for by the Nigerian Government in 1993, Dr. Rilwanu Lukman,[174] the Minister of Petroleum Resources noted with dismay that the PSCs were rather bad deals for Nigeria from an international perspective in that the royalties were 0%, the taxes included a generous tax credit that wiped out much of the tax to be collected and made the profit oil shares to Government abysmally low compared to most other nations.

Risk Service Contracts (RSC): There is a third category termed Risk Service Contracts, wherein the company provides all the funds for exploration, development and production. The primary duration is between two and five years, after which if there is no discovery, the contractor forfeits all rights in the

---

[171] Jedrzej George Frynas, Political instability and business: focus on Shell in Nigeria, *op. cit.*, p. 469. It is estimated as far back as 1995 that Shell makes $170–190 million in profits out of Nigeria every year and this may be an understatement.

[172] *Ibid.* These assertions were denied by Shell PR staff (Detheridge and Pepple) as they alleged that the joint venture's operational budget is not decided by Shell and that Shell does not inflate its costs. According to Shell, the company proposes a budget, but its partners (among whom the Nigerian State oil company holds the majority share) must agree to this budget. Alan Detheridge and Noble Pepple (Shell), A response to Frynas, *Third World Quarterly*, Vol. 19, No 3, 479- 486 at 483–484 (1998).

[173] Cyril Obi and Kayode Soremekun, "Oil and the Nigerian state: an overview", in Kayode Soremekun (ed) (1995), *Perspectives on the Nigerian Oil Industry*, Lagos: Amkra Books, Lagos, p.22, quoted in Jedrzej George Frynas, Political instability and business: focus on Shell in Nigeria, *op. cit.*

[174] Being a Keynote address by the Honourable Minister of Petroleum Resources on the Proposed Petroleum Industry Bill (PIB) in Abuja on 16 July 2009, at http://elendureports.com/index. php? [accessed 3 March 2010]. In the most recent contracts under the PSCs, 'it was evident that the State was in a much weaker bargaining position' as Khan has argued. See Khan, *Nigeria: The Political Economy of Oil, op. cit.*, p.94. It can therefore be seriously contended that the weaker position of the State has given Shell and other oil companies better deals. As pointed out by Frynas: 'The best proof is the NLNG contract that provides for various concessions, waivers and exemptions from the provisions of Nigerian law, including a tax holiday of up to 10 years starting from the first day of production- not expected until 1999'. See Jedrzej George Frynas, *Political instability and business: focus on Shell in Nigeria, op. cit.*, p.468.

contract area.[175] Though the service contract is similar to PSC, it differs in certain
important matters. For instance, the duration of the service contract is only for
five years, and each contract is in respect of one service block. The contractor
pays all funds necessary for exploration appraisal and development operations,
and also any other obligations assumed under the contract.[176] Where commercial
discovery is made within the term of the contract, the funds expended by the
contractor are recoverable in addition to compensation for the risk taken and
remuneration for services rendered. Although the service contractor has no title
to crude oil produced, he has an option to be repaid his investment and to take
his remuneration in crude oil, as well as the first option to purchase the crude
oil produced.[177] Once commercial production has started, the NNPC may take
over production operations. At present, only Agip Energy and Natural Resources
(AENR) operate under a Service Contract in Nigeria. This new partnership
agreement introduced in 2000 seems to be the most progressive of all the
contractual forms currently in operation. Commenting on its advantages, Yinka
Omorogbe stated that:

> "The service contract seems to be regarded as the most progressive.…It is clearly an
> improvement on the production sharing contract which is itself criticised solely for
> not being an efficient revenue earner for the country. A general analysis of the two
> contractual forms however indicates that the service contract is better in all res-
> pects. Its terms are more favourable to the host country and its terms are clearer. Its
> short duration gives incentive to the company to explore and make a discovery early,
> unlike in the joint venture and the production sharing contract. In real terms howe-
> ver the service contract has made little difference to the Nigerian legal framework
> simply because there are so few contracts of this type."[178]

---

[175] See Kayode Soremekun, Nigerian Petroleum Policy and External Relations, Unpublished PhD
Thesis Submitted to the Department of International Relation, University of Ife, 1984.

[176] Yinka Omorogbe, The Legal Framework for Production of Petroleum in Nigeria, 5 (4) *J. Energy
Nat. Resources Law*, 273–292 at 281 (1987). While also contributing to the differences between
service contracts and other joint venture agreements, G. Ugo Nwokeji, *op. cit.,* pp.9–10 stated
that:
"*Unlike JVs where a single company is the operator, this service contract involves NNPC (through
its E&P subsidiary) as a joint operator. The service contract differs from the PSC because investment is distributable according specific (sic) agreements, unlike the PSC where the operator
assumes all of the risk. Although the service contract with Agip involves no direct fund investment on the part of NNPC, NNPC contributes technical and support personnel to the arrangement. The corporation's role as a joint operator also marks this particular arrangement from the
PSC.*"

[177] Yinka Omorogbe, *Ibid,* at pp.281–282. See also Fola Sasegbon, Current Developments in
Oil and Gas Law in Nigeria- with Comparative Analysis with other African Oil Producing
Countries, *International Bar Association Energy Law,* Vol. 1, 371 (1981).

[178] *Ibid,* at p.282. Professor Gao went further to prescribe it as an interesting option for host countries wishing to assure a greater degree of control over the investors and to keep a survey of the
operations: 'Under the risk service formula, Brazil's State oil monopoly remains unharmed as
a result of the use of "hired services". For this reason, the RSC is recommended to those developing countries that are considering moving in the same direction, but fear being deprived of
their sovereignty over petroleum resources'. Balancing the interests of the host country with

What can be inferred from these joint venture programmes is that the State appears to be playing a more active role in the oil industry and maintaining a tight grip on the purse strings. This participation by the State is seen by Ayo Ajomo as a positive phenomenon in the Nigerian oil industry. According to him, there are three main advantages in participation. The first is the transfer of technological and managerial skills from the oil companies to Nigeria; the second is the element of control, which according to him, the participation venture will ensure, while the third benefit is the growth of the Nigerian National Oil Company (NNOC).[179] It appears, however, that these hopes have been largely misplaced as the State-owned corporation has been turned essentially into a 'rent collecting political partner of the foreign operators'.[180] They are also misplaced to the extent that to date, the requisite skills in the oil industry are yet to be transferred, while the element of control, which is another assumed fruit of participation, has proved to be a grand illusion, Finally, the third expectation has also been dashed since the NNPC is yet to come into its own in any meaningful way.[181] The more startling dimension to participation is that what the oil companies appeared to have lost at the upstream level has been compensated for or recouped at the downstream.[182] In other words, the joint venture agreement is lopsided in the sense that the technical operators are still the oil transnationals, the State corporation been left with ownership without control. As stated by Omoweh:

> "The NNPC is what the State wants it to look like. That is to say, in mediating State capitalism, the corporation oversees the State's interest in its various lopsided joint venture agreements with the operating foreign oil companies, and maintains on behalf of the State, ownership of the concessional blocks in both the on- and off-shore locations. It is a lopsided joint venture agreement because the technical operators are still the oil transnationals holding on to the oil technology, leaving the corporation with ownership without control of the critical sector of the industry. Even the entry of some indigenous exploration companies into a hitherto State-owned upstream sector has not changed the situation as both the State and private

---

the international oil companies, some view risk contracts as less favourable to the oil companies: 'The RSC is an arrangement that can finally ensure the host country's full ownership of its oil, direct control of its exploitation, and complete appropriation of the production. On the other hand, this form is the "least attractive" of the options open to oil transnationals, since despite assuming all the exploration and development risks, the remuneration to the company does not include access to crude oil. Thus, the legal nature of the service type of contract is: risk without title of oil'. Zhiguo Gao (1994), *International Petroleum Contracts: Current Trends and New Directions*, Graham & Trotman/M. Nijhoff, London, at 141, 203, quoted in Marilda Rosado De Sa Ribeiro, The New Oil and Gas Industry in Brazil: An Overview of the Main Legal Aspects, *Tex. Int'l L. J.* Vol. 36, 141–166 at 146–147 (2001).

[179]   Cited in Kayode Soremekun, Nigerian Petroleum Policy and External Relations, *op. cit.*

[180]   See Douglas A. Yates, "Changing Patterns of Foreign Direct Investment in the Oil-Economies of the Gulf of Guinea", in Rudolf Traub-Merz/Douglas Yates (eds) (2004), *Oil Policy in the Gulf of Guinea. Security and Conflict, Economic Growth, Social Development, op. cit.*, p.44.

[181]   Kayode Soremekun and Ebenezer Obadare, *op. cit.*, p.42.

[182]   *Ibid* at p.42.

oil capital are dependent on the major oil companies and the foreign oil servicing companies for technology particularly the equipment component. And the country's technological dependence on the oil transnationals will remain so for a long time to come as the country's capital goods-producing industry where some of the basic oil tools are to be manufactured is itself underdeveloped and import-dependent for inputs. The steel sector that ought to have laid the foundation for the effective take-off of that industry is ridden with conflicts right from its onset similar to other public companies that are used to lubricate State capitalism".[183]

Through JV and PSC arrangements, the oil transnationals operate, manage, contribute funds and indeed control the operations of the industry since they provide the technology, capital and more specifically equipment and servicing. As noted by Hutchful, "Nigerian governments had not taken measures to consolidate control over the industry to a degree commensurate with the growth of State participation and investment".[184] Equity interests has not meant real control and participation.[185] Thus, despite State participation in the oil companies, the issue of technology transfer remains a great barrier to the full control over its oil industry. As observed by Olorunfemi:

"The country has not developed the capability to manage its petroleum resources by itself: all the crude oil is still produced by foreign operators. Even though some Nigerians who work in the industry occupy important management positions, the key management roles are performed largely by foreigners."[186]

State participation in the oil sector is not sufficient without technology acquisition. The dream of technology transfer can only be achieved when more Nigerians are able to acquire the needed expertise required for employment in the industry. Even the Government's plans of achieving 45% local content in the industry by 2007, and 70% by 2010 were neither realistic nor impressive when compared with other major world oil producers like Norway, Venezuela, Malaysia, Mexico, Libya, and

---

[183] Daniel A. Omoweh, "Oil Exploration and Production in Nigeria: A Theoretical Overview", in Wumi Raji, Ayodele Ale and Eni Akinsola (eds) (2000), *Boiling Point, A CDHR Publication on the Crises in the Oil Producing Communities in Nigeria, op. cit.*, p.37.

[184] Hutchful Eboe, Building Regulatory Institutions in the Environmental Sector in the Third World: The Petroleum Inspectorate in Nigeria (1997–1987), *Africa Development*, Vol. XXIII No. 2, 121–160 (1998), quoted in Augustine Ikelebe, "Interrogating a Crisis of Corporate Governance and the Interface with Conflict: The Case of Multinational Oil Companies and the Conflicts in the Niger Delta", in *International Conference on The Nigerian State, Oil Industry and the Niger Delta, op. cit.*, p.117.

[185] Augustine Ikelebe, *Ibid*.

[186] Olorunfemi M.S., "Managing Nigeria's Petroleum Resources", OPEC Bulletin (December/January 1986), 24 at 25–26; See also M.M. Olisa (1987), *Nigerian Petroleum Law and Practice*, Fountain Press, Ibadan, p.1, where Olisa expressed a similar view.

Brazil.[187] The last has a local content record of 100%. All these countries practice government ownership of the oil industry in contrast to Nigeria's deregulation and privatization of the industry.[188] Norway is not only a leading oil producer in Europe but also the third largest oil exporter in the world.[189] Statoil of Norway was created in 1972 as a national oil company to begin exploration and production of the North Sea. Initially it had to call on the International Oil Companies (IOCs) such as Mobil and Phillips Petroleum to develop its offshore fields, yet even then Statoil maintained a 50% share of the joint venture and the Government decided the terms and conditions of the partnerships and controlled the revenue of the oil fields. As Statoil gained technical expertise it started operating some fields on its own.[190] In April 2001, the Norwegian Parliament agreed to make Statoil a publicly traded company thereby marking the beginning of change from state to private ownership. Although, the State still retains majority control, it has pulled back from what many considered to be a provincial, meddling approach to the Norwegian oil industry.[191] Today, the State still owns 81.8% of the company. Some believe that Norway will sell even more of its share down to 66% that it must own by law to give Statoil more freedom.[192] Also, the IOCs are 'players on the Norwegian oil field since they own 40% of equity in ventures. This means that Statoil and the newly emerging Norwegian companies have to compete and cooperate with the IOCs.'[193]

Also, in Norway, the requirement to transfer competence and to cooperate in the development of new technology introduced in the early 1970s greatly assisted

---

[187] According to NAPIMS, the level of local content in the Nigerian oil industry increased from 5% in 1999 to 14% in 2003 and close to 20% in 2004. This percentage is said to be much lower for natural gas than it is for crude oil. Local content in Nigeria is defined as the quantum of composite value added to, created in the Nigerian economy through a deliberate utilization of Nigerian human and material resources and services in the petroleum industry in order to stimulate the development of indigenous capabilities without compromising acceptable quality, health, safety and environmental standards- See United Nations Conference on Trade and Development UNCTAD/CALAG African Oil and Gas Services Sector Survey Volume 1- Nigeria Creating Local Linkages by Empowering Indigenous Entrepreneurs UNCTAD/DITC/COM/2005/6, United Nations Publications, New York and Geneva, 2006.
[188] Steve Azaiki, *Oil, Gas and Life in Nigeria, op. cit.*, p.90.
[189] Daphne Eviatar, *Petrol Peril: Why Iraq's Oil Wealth May Do More Harm than Good*, The Boston Globe, April 13, 2003, at www.boston.com/news/packages/Iraq/globe_stories/041303_ideas2.htm [accessed 13 March 2009]. Emeka Duruigbo, Permanent Sovereignty and Peoples' Ownership of Natural Resources in International Law, 38 *Geo. Wash. Int'l L. Rev.* 33–100 at 82 (2006).
[190] Arwa Mohammad Abulhasan, *Future Relations Between Kuwait Petroleum Corporation and the International Oil Companies: Success or Failure?*, being Master of Arts in Law and Diplomacy Thesis Presented to the Fletcher School of Law and Diplomacy May 2004.
[191] Sains Ariane, Statoil Eyes Gas-Powered Growth, Businessweek 28 July, 2003, at www.business-week.com/magazine/content/03_30/b3843712.htm [accessed 13 March 2009].
[192] Arwa Mohammad Abulhasan, *op. cit.*
[193] Arwa Mohammad Abulhasan, *Ibid.*

in the training of Statoil by the international oil corporations. According to
Øystein Noreng:[194]

> *"The transfer of technology and the cooperation in research and development have
> been among the most successful aspects of Norway's petroleum policy. By compel-
> ling oil companies to transfer competence and to cooperate in the development of
> new technology, Norway could assume the role of a leader in international petro-
> leum development. Within a relatively short period of time, Norwegian competence
> and technology for Norwegian conditions were developed. Competence strengthe-
> ned Norway's bargaining position with the international oil industry. Technology
> development led to a significant cost reduction and an ensuing expansion of the
> resource base. During the 1990s, investment costs per barrel of oil equivalent in new
> oil and gas fields on the Norwegian continental shelf were reduced by around 4–5%/
> year. The background was the strong research and development effort during the
> 1990s and the cooperation between oil companies, the supply industry and research
> institutions."*

Brazil, on its part, had a monopoly on the exploration and development of
petroleum, through the State oil corporation Petroleo Brasileiro S.A. (Petrobras)[195]
created in 1953 by Law No. 2.004. The foreign companies participate in oil
exploration through service contracts carried out at their own risks. They are
subject to 25 per cent divided tax, and royalties are paid to Petrobras.[196] Upon the
commencement of commercial operation, Petrobras takes over the operations of
the well, and the foreign company is reimbursed in cash but with an option to
purchase a limited amount of the oil it produces at the market price. It was not
until the Brazilian National Congress enacted Constitutional Amendment No. 9
in 1995 that an end was put to Petrobras' monopoly in exploring for, developing
and producing oil and gas in Brazil. With the passing of the "Petroleum Law" (Law
No. 9.478) in 1997 and the formation in 1998 of the Agencia Nacional do Petroleo
(ANP) to oversee deregulation and restructuring, Petrobras lost its monopoly over
exploration and production rights in Brazil, with the ANP overseeing control of

---

[194] Øystein Noreng, *Norway: Economic Diversification and the Petroleum Industry*, being an
abridged version of a paper delivered at the 10th Annual Energy Conference of the Emirates
Center for Strategic Studies and Research (ECSSR), 26–27 September, 2004 at Abu Dhabi,
UAE, Middle East Economic Survey, Vol. XLVII No. 45, and 8 November 2004, at www.gasan-
doil.com/goc/news/nte44790.htm. [accessed 18 May 2009]. The attitudes that were promoted
in Norway were *'The sky's the limit'* and *'Everything that foreign companies can do, local companies can learn'*. The Norwegian Government signed agreements with foreign oil companies
to secure the transfer of skills and know-how to Norwegian actors and today, it has become a
world leader in exploration, production and services, exporting expertise to many countries,
Nigeria included.

[195] Yinka Omorogbe, The Legal Framework for Production of Petroleum in Nigeria, *op. cit.*, p. 288;
Barrows (Firm), *World Petroleum Arrangements, 1982* (1983), Barrows, pp.121–128; Steven P.
Otillar, Kristina A.McQuaid, *et al*, Recent Developments in Brazil's Oil & Gas Industry: Brazil
Appears to be Stemming the Tide of Resource Nationalism, 30 *Hous. J. Int'l L.* 259–287 at 262
(2007–2008).

[196] Yinka Omorogbe, *Ibid*. p.288.

the country's energy sector. Though Petrobras continues to hold the rights to the most promising fields and prospects, including in the oil-rich Campos Basin and continues to dominate the ANP's bidding rounds, the corporatization of Petrobras has produced an integrated company capable of competing economically with its peers in the turbulent international energy marketplace.[197] Though not without its own challenges, Petrobras has equally become an internationally respected, integrated energy company that operates throughout the world and possesses technical expertise and capabilities that rival any international oil company, especially in deep water exploration and development.[198] Since the enactment of the Petroleum Law, Petrobras has become the fourteenth largest oil company in the World with 2005 net revenues of $47 (U.S.) billion.[199]

Statoil and Petrobras are just two of several examples of national oil companies that are presently competing in the market with the IOCs in developing their natural resources. The Nigerian Government can also achieve this feat by adopting the approaches of Norway and Brazil. It can also enact laws or pass regulations that ensure preferences to local vendors for certain goods and services. In Brazil, regulations were adopted requiring oil companies to allocate a percentage of their investments to local vendors.[200]

When it was realized that technology would not flow from the owner to the acquirer without some help, the National Office of Industrial Property (NOIP) Act was passed in Nigeria to facilitate technology transfer.[201] Among the functions of the NOIP are:

(1) the encouragement of a more efficient process for the identification and selection of foreign technology; and
(2) the development of the negotiating skills of Nigerians so that they may secure optimal contractual terms and conditions in any agreement dealing with the transfer of technology.[202]

In spite of this, the position has not shown marked improvement. Perhaps, by now, it is clear that indigenization is not the same as technology acquisition. The

---

[197] See James A. Baker III Institute for Public Policy, "Critical Issues in Brazil's Energy Sector", Report of the James A. Baker III Institute for Public Policy of Rice University, March 2004, at www.rice.edu/energy/publications/docs/BrazilEnergySector_MainStudy.pdf [accessed 2 October 2011].
[198] Steven P. Otillar, Kristina A.McQuaid, *et al, op. cit.,* p.263; Matt Moffett, How a Sleepy Oil Giant Became a World Player, *Wall St. J.,* August 30, 2007, at A1.
[199] Regina Cunha, U.S. Commercial Serv., U.S Department of Commerce, *Overview: Brazilian Oil and Gas Industry-* August 2007 (August 2007), quoted in Steven P. Otillar, Kristina A.McQuaid, *et al, op. cit.,* p.263.
[200] See Cynthia L. Quarterman, *op. cit.*
[201] Cap. 268 LFN 1990. The Organisation is now known as the National Office for Technology Acquisition and Promotion (NOTAP).
[202] Momodu Kassim-Momodu, Nigeria's Transfer of Technology, *Journal of World Trade* 22, No. 4 (August 1988), pp.58–59.

various attempts to indigenize the industry have not resulted in any appreciable
technology gain.[203] In an interview with Oke-Samuel, an environmentalist on
the issue of technology transfer, he stated that: 'Nigeria is but a true story of a
failed state, that in the face of wanton destruction of its human and economic
resources, it looks elsewhere while its citizens' rights are being violated. Equally,
the refusal of Nigeria to pursue technological development, and its dwelling in
the comfort zone of leadership of the underdeveloped nations in Africa, has
hopelessly and helplessly left the sleeping giant at the mercy of the multinationals,
who because of the overdependence of the host nation do things their own way,
while the slothful leadership that is enmeshed in corruption indolently watches
its citizens being deprived daily in their homeland under the guise of economic
growth brought about by oil development. The absence of will to act on the part
of the Government of Nigeria, which has been demonstrated over the decade, is
itself a criminal breach of trust and the sacred promise of the Nigerian State to its
own people as enshrined in the preambles to the Constitution.'[204]

Happily, on 22 April 2010, Nigerian Oil and Gas Industry Content Development Act 2010 (the Act) was enacted into law. The Act is, *inter alia*, aimed at
correcting the low levels of indigenous participation especially in the oil and gas
industry by ensuring equitable and improved participation of Nigerians. Prior to
the promulgation of the Nigeria Local Content legislation, it is estimated that out
of U.S.$12 billion annual budget spent in the upstream sector of the Nigerian oil
and gas industry, over 80 per cent by value of work was carried out abroad, which
contributed insignificantly to the nation's Gross Domestic Product (GDP).[205] The
most important element of the Act is to promote and enhance the participation
of 'Nigerian content' in the oil and gas industry. Section 106 defines "Nigerian
Content" as 'the quantum of composite value added to or created in the Nigerian
economy by a systematic development of capacity and capabilities through the
deliberate utilization of Nigerian human, material resources and services in the
Nigerian oil and gas industry.' Section 70 of the Act established the Nigerian Content Monitoring Board to, *inter alia*, implement the Act and supervise, coordinate, administer and monitor the implementation and development of Nigerian
content as specified in the Schedule to the Act in the operations of operators,
contractors and all other entities in the Nigerian oil and gas industry.

The Act provides that Nigerian operators must be given first consideration in
the award of oil blocks, oil field licences, and all projects for which contracts are to
be awarded in the oil and gas industry subject to fulfilling the conditions that may

---

[203]   Odiase-Alegimenlen, "Oil and Nigerian Development: An Overview", in Ayua I.A & Guobadia
        D.A (eds.), (2001), *Political Reform and Economic Recovery in Nigeria*, *op. cit.*, pp.579–580.
[204]   Interview with Olugbenga Oke-Samuel, an Environmentalist and Director, Environment and
        Justice Initiative, an NGO based in Akure, Ondo State, Nigeria, in January 2011.
[205]   Momoh, Hadiza Tijjani Sule, Nigerian Local Content Act: The Role of the Petroleum Training
        Institute, Effurun in Human Capital Development, *Petroleum Technology Development
        Journal: An International Journal*, Vol.3 No.1, pp.35–54 at 35 (2013).

be specified by the Minister of Petroleum.[206] An operator submitting a Nigerian Content Plan must ensure that it gives first consideration to services provided from within Nigeria and to goods manufactured in Nigeria; and Nigerians must be given first consideration for training and employment in the work programme for which the plan was submitted.[207] In order to address the challenge of skill shortages in the industry, section 30 of the Act provides that where Nigerians are not employed because of their lack of training, the operator must ensure to the satisfaction of the Board that every reasonable effort is made within a reasonable time to supply such training locally or elsewhere. Such effort and the procedure for its execution must be contained in the operator's Employment and Training Plan. For each of its operations, the operator is required by section 31(1) to submit to the Board a succession plan for any position not held by Nigerians, which shall provide for Nigerians to understudy each incumbent expatriate for a maximum period of four years and at the end of the period the position shall become Nigerianised. Section 32 makes allowance for expatriate positions as it provides that an operator or project promoter may retain, for each of its operations, a maximum of five per cent of management positions as may be approved by the Board as expatriate positions to take care of investor interests.

Again, section 41(2) provides that Nigerian subsidiaries of international/ multinational companies shall own 50 per cent of equipment deployed for use in the execution of work in Nigeria. This requirement may be difficult to achieve. This is because the oil and gas industry is highly capital intensive. Most equipment (such as drilling rigs) are leased from the owners and used for operations around the world; thus, the requirement for Nigerian companies to own such high value equipment might therefore be a herculean task.[208] Section 37 provides that for every project for which a plan is submitted, an operator must carry out a programme and make expenditure, to the satisfaction of the Board, for the promotion of education, attachments, training, research and development in Nigeria in relation to its work programme and activities.

With regards to technology transfer, section 45 provides that: 'The operator shall give full and effective support to technology transfer by encouraging and facilitating the formation of joint ventures, partnering and the development of licensing agreements between Nigerian and foreign contractors and service or supplier companies Agreements for all such joint ventures/alliances must meet the requirements of Nigerian Content development to the satisfaction of the Board.' On the penalty for breach of the provisions of the Act, section 68 provides that any operator, contractor or subcontractor who carries out any project contrary to

---

[206]   Nigerian Oil and Gas Industry Content Development Act, 2010, section 3(1).
[207]   *Ibid*, section 10(1).
[208]   KPMG, Nigerian Oil and Gas Industry Content Development Act, 2010, at www.kpmg. com/NG/en/IssuesAndInsights/ArticlesPublications/Documents/Newsletter%20on%20 Nigerian%20Oil%20and%20Gas%20Industry%20Content%20Development%20Act%20-%20 June%202010.pdf [accessed 30 May 2013].

the provisions of the Act, commits an offence and will be liable upon conviction
to a fine of five per cent of the project sum for each project in which the offence is
committed or cancellation of the project.

It is important to state that with the enactment of the Act, the multinational
oil companies have started to use made-in-Nigeria materials. For example,
'ExxonMobil used locally manufactured pipes at its Edop-Idoho offshore field,
laying of over 100 kilometres of pipeline by SCC [Nigeria Ltd.] in Abuja as well as the
development of Nigerian Oil and Gas Employment and Training Strategy, which
has resulted in the absorption of over 5,000 engineers, geologists and welders into
the industry. Recently, Nigerdock built two platforms for ExxonMobil's satellite
fields at its yard in Snake Island in Lagos.'[209] Also emphasizing the gains of the
Act, Ernest Nwapa, the Executive Secretary of the Nigerian Content Development
and Monitoring Board (NCDMB), states that 'prior to the advent of the Act,
more than 95 per cent of the jobs in the industry were done abroad. Specifically
... U.S.$214 billion worth of procurement and U.S.$9 billion worth of research
and development were done in North America, while U.S.$78 billion worth of
technical services and U.S.$39 billion worth of engineering work were done in
Europe. Asia dominated the fabrication aspect to the tune of U.S.$39 billion...
[W]ith the coming into place of the Act, U.S.$107 billion procurement, U.S.$20
billion fabrication, U.S.$14 billion technical services, U.S.$20 billion engineering
and U.S.$7 billion research and development are domiciled in Nigeria.'[210]

Notwithstanding the above successes recorded, there are some challenges
facing the effective implementation of the Act. Some of these include the fact that
it is unlikely that Nigeria would be ready in three years (as provided by the Act),
for all items required for use in the oil and gas industry to be produced locally as
a result of the poor infrastructural development (such as lack of industrial base,
regular electricity supply) needed for development of the manufacturing and
fabrication industry.[211] The Nigerian Government must take adequate measures
in investing in uninterrupted power supply and other requisite infrastructure to
develop local content. Also, the success or otherwise of the provisions of the Act
in transforming the business and operating structure in the Nigerian oil and gas
industry will largely depends on the political will of the Nigerian Government in
ensuring full implementation of the provisions of the Act by the relevant bodies.
Clauses on the training of manpower and on technology transfer without this, will
not have the same effect, no matter how stringently they are worded.[212] If properly

---

[209]   Oghenekevwe Laba, Appraisal of Reforms in the Oil and Gas Sector, *The Nigerian Voice*, 28
        November 2012, at www.thenigerianvoice.com/nvnews/102145/1/appraisal-of-reforms-in-
        the-oil-and-gas-sector.html [accessed 30 May 2013].
[210]   Quoted in Sebastine Obasi and Michael Eboh, Savouring Gains of Nigerian Content,
        Vanguard, 7 May 2013, at www.vanguardngr.com/2013/05/savouring-gains-of-nigerian-con-
        tent/ [accessed 30 May 2013].
[211]   KPMG, Nigerian Oil and Gas Industry Content Development Act, 2010, *op. cit.*
[212]   Yinka Omorogbe, *The Legal Framework for Production of Petroleum in Nigeria*, *op. cit.*,
        pp.287–288. Suffice it to say that section 404 of the Petroleum Industry Bill 2012 (initially

implemented, the Act has the potential to build the local capacity and competences through mandatory use of local expertise; enhance technology transfer; generate employment opportunities; develop the local skills, knowledge and technology; boost the industry's contributions to the growth of Nigeria's GDP; stem the tide of capital flight and enhance local participation in the activities of the oil and gas industry. It is hoped that Nigeria will join the rank of the several major oil-producing countries of the world such as Norway, Indonesia, Venezuela, Angola, and Brazil with successful local content policy. Emphasis should be shifted to the development of manpower and technical resources rather than simply on maximizing returns from oil. In view of the relevance of indigenous technology in the oil sector, the Nigerian government must as a matter of urgency develop an indigenous technology base in the sector.

Another challenge is that JVs are prone to abuse. The public are not privy to the negotiating process or the ultimate terms of the agreements. NNPC operations are shrouded in secrecy thereby making it difficult for the public to know the arrangements between it and its JV partners. JV contracts determine, among other things, the distribution of the value of every barrel of oil produced, and as confirmed by Michael Watts,[213] the details in Nigeria are never made public, but it is clear that at least two thirds of the value of every barrel of oil flows directly to the Government. Under this situation, corruption, favouritism, politicization, etc cannot be ruled out. The oil transnationals have also been accused of "overcharging for specific services, and imputing unneeded services and personnel into joint venture and production sharing arrangements".[214]

It is clear from the above that State participation, through the NNPC and its subsidiaries/agencies, in oil exploration and production in Nigeria has not been impressive. The monitoring and regulation of the operations and practices of the

---

drafted as, the Petroleum Industry Draft Bill 2008) presently before the Nigerian National Assembly provides that a licensee of a petroleum prospecting licence must within twelve months of the grant of his licence, and the lessee of a petroleum mining lease must on the grant of his lease, submit for the Minister's approval, a detailed programme for the recruitment and training of Nigerians and the programme must provide for the training of Nigerians in all phases of petroleum operations whether the phases are handled directly by the licensee or lessee or through their agents and contractors. Section 8(1) further provides that the Federal Government shall at all times promote the involvement of indigenous companies and manpower and the use of locally produced goods and services in all areas of the petroleum industry in accordance with existing laws and policies. Section 223(1) establishes a Fund to be known as the Petroleum Technology Development Fund which shall be used among others to generally facilitate the attainment of 100 per cent Nigerian content in the petroleum industry. If these provisions are fully implemented after the passing of the bill into law, it will go a long way in solving the problem of technology transfer.

[213] Michael Watts, *Has globalization failed in Nigeria?* (2009 Dialogue), an interview conducted and edited by Ted O'Callahan, at http://qn.som.yale.edu/downloads/Q5Nigeria.pdf [accessed 3 March 2010].

[214] Green (1975), quoted in Augustine Ikelegbe, "Interogating a Crisis of Corporate Governance and the Interface with Conflict: The Case of Multinational Oil Companies and the Conflicts in the Niger Delta", in *International Conference on The Nigerian State, Oil Industry and the Niger Delta, op. cit.*, p.114.

industry, particularly the behaviour and conduct of the industry operators by
the agencies of the State have been very weak. For example, the Directorate of
Petroleum Resources (DPR) has not been effective in its monitoring, oversight
and enforcement functions as can be seen from the reckless and unethical
behavior of the oil industry operators. The reason for this has been attributed to
several factors including lack of adequate technologically competent manpower
to effectively monitor and oversee the industry, overlapping functions among the
agencies of control, distrust between DPR and other agencies of government, etc.
Ikelebe has identified several difficulties faced by the Petroleum Inspectorate in
the regulation of powerful multinationals:

> *"First, the Department found it difficult to regulate a critical resource exploitation,
> in which the Nigerian State was extensively involved. Particularly it was difficult
> to regulate the negative externalities of oil and gas production, which itself consti-
> tuted the revenue base of the government. The inspectorate and indeed the State is
> expected to supervise and regulate an industry in which the State was a major stake
> hold (sic) and beneficiary. As an equity holder in the MNOCs, the State and the
> Inspectorate lacked the "Distance and arms-length relationship required to impose
> costly regulations (Hutchful 1998: 151). More specifically, powerful political elite
> and bureaucrats benefitted from the MNOCs and the negative externalities of their
> operations and production. Second, the multinational oil companies which were
> supposed to be overseen were powerful, large, technologically advanced and very
> influential. Third, the regulatory agencies, in this case the Petroleum Inspectorate
> Department did not have the capacity and ability to effectively supervise and moni-
> tor the oil industry. The inspectorate staff were not adequately trained and equipped
> and they did not have the logistic capability to effectively supervise the petroleum
> industry. Furthermore, the capacity to gather, process, analyze and interpret data
> and materials was poor because of poor logistic, research, scientific and laboratory
> capabilities. Finally, the inspectorate staff did not match the MNOCs in terms of
> competence, incentives, commitment and technical and operational experience and
> equipment and infrastructural support."[215]*

In the same vein, Izeze while commenting on the challenges in the Nigerian oil
industry stated that:

> *"These companies knew very well that the NNPC lacks the in-house capacity-tech-
> nically and even the will-power to monitor the activities of the operators in the pro-
> duction sharing relationships. Neither the DPR nor the NAPIMS has the technical
> capabilities in-house to do even actual fiscalisation of crude quantities at the termi-
> nals. They have to pathetically depend on the foreign multinational operators to col-
> lect the data for the Nigerian government. This is true. The most interesting aspect
> is that the DPR and NAPIMS staff hangs on the facilities and comfort provided by*

---

[215]   Augustine Ikelegbe, *Ibid* pp.112–113. See also, Hutchful Eboe, *op. cit.*, 121–160.

*these foreign operators at the nation's oil and gas export terminals. This pathetic
scenario would make policing of the nation's crude oil business even very difficult
for saints not to talk of the peculiar people in the NAPIMS (NNPC) and DPR."*[216]

If the essence of a State's responsibility is to ensure that its citizens receive adequate
benefits, then something urgent must be done through the general overhaul of the
Nigerian legal and regulatory system. In doing this, Nigeria can borrow a leaf
from the experiences of National Oil Companies in Brazil (Petrobras), Norway
(Statoil), Malaysia (Petronas), Venezuela (PDVSA), Algeria (Sonatraco), Mexico
(PEMEX) and Saudi (Aramco). Unlike NNPC, Petrobras's and Statoil's presence
in the oil and natural gas sectors remains pervasive, competing favourably with
other oil multinationals in a competitive marketplace around the world. As
observed by experts in the oil industry, there are essentially two mechanisms for
a Government to exercise control over its oil and gas regime: "It may be done
directly through a governmental agency, which attempts to develop reserves
itself, or indirectly through the means of [an] authorizing department".[217] It is
suggested that Nigeria adopt the latter and completely disengage the regulation
and administration of its oil and gas fiscal regime from its State-owned company
NNPC.[218] This can be done by discontinuing the NNPC's mandatory involvement
in future oil and gas contractual arrangements, privatise the company by selling
a majority of its equity to the public and make it compete as a commercial entity
with other oil companies in its own right in Nigeria and all around the World just
as do Petrobras and Statoil. The new Indonesian Oil and Gas Law (Law No. 22 of
2001) forced State-owned oil company Pertamina to relinquish its role in granting
new oil development licences and limited the company's monopoly in upstream
activities. Pertamina's regulatory and administrative functions were transferred
to the new regulatory body, Badan Perlaksanaan Minyak Gas, or BP Migas and
Pertamina was formed into the limited liability company PT Pertamina (Persero)
by Presidential Decree in 2003, although it remains a State-owned entity.[219] It
has been a source of unease for the Indonesian Government for many years that
Pertamina was used by Malaysia as a model for its oil and gas company, Petronas.
Petronas has become increasingly successful, producing around 33% of the
country's output in 2000, while Pertamina has not maximised its opportunities,
producing only approximately 7.2% of Indonesia's total output as at 2001.[220]

It is further recommended that Nigeria set in motion a transition and review
process similar to the one in Brazil to decide on the extent to which NNPC

---

[216]   Ifeanyi Izeze, NNPC: A joint venture of fraud?, Daily Triumph, Friday June 27, 2008.
[217]   Typical Arrangements at 9–12, quoted in Cynthia L. Quarterman, *op. cit.*
[218]   Cynthia L. Quarterman, *Ibid.*
[219]   Indonesia Energy Data, Statistics and Analysis – *Oil, Gas, Electricity, Coal, Energy Information
       Administration, Country Analysis Briefs Indonesia,* January 2007, at www.eia.doe.gov/emeu/
       cabs/Indonesia/Oil.html [accessed 5 July 2009].
[220]   Mark Newbery, New Indonesian Oil and Gas Law, *J. Energy Nat. Resources L.* Vol. 20 No. 4,
       355–363 at 355–356 (2002).

should remain involved in its formerly granted concessions; disassemble or
relocate oil and gas oversight functions now within NAPIMS to an independent
organization, evaluate the role of DPR; secure public disclosure of revenue
information like the Sao Tome law, without prejudicing the companies involved
in oil and gas operations; enforce public transparency and accountability to
avoid the practice of 'double invoicing' – that is, contractors devising a system
of invoicing the true production and export figures for their own accounting,
while declaring false figures to the authorities; create an independent oversight
and verification process; set up of a stabilization fund; create an agency to oversee
leasing, exploration, development, production and revenue collection functions
and institute a means by which citizens can become involved in Government's
decision-making processes with respect to oil and gas projects.[221]

As a result of the involvement of the Nigerian Government in the joint
ventures, its paramount interest now lies in the uninterrupted flow of profits
irrespective of negative impacts on the local inhabitants and the ecosystem. This
is why the Government often viewed advocates of environmental crusades with
suspicion and hatred, and used all Governmental powers of the State to silence
such moves. In the words of Ikelegbe, 'given the centrality of oil to Nigeria's
politics and survival ... given the very high stakes of oil, constrict the State to be
sluggish on the dialogue, negotiation and concessions, and expansive in terms of
the repressive responses.'[222] The mono-cultural nature of the Nigerian economy
explains why the Government elected to use the repressive approach as a response
to any form of opposition from the host communities. A host of practices employed
by operators in the oil industry are not monitored or regulated by the DPR and
other agencies under the NNPC because of their status as Government agencies.
They cannot effectively be both equity partners and the regulator of joint venture
companies. According to Owarieta, 'A regulatory body such as DPR has a major
role to play in ensuring that a system of rules is in place'.[223] For these regulatory
agencies to be able to meet their challenges, it is important that they be granted
more autonomy and independence.

1.6   CONCLUSION

This chapter has examined problems associated with the definition of what
constitutes the Niger Delta, the history and development of oil exploration in

---

[221]   See generally Cynthia L. Quarterman, *op. cit.*

[222]   Augustine Ikelegbe, Civil Society, Oil and Conflict in the Niger Delta Region of Nigeria:
Ramifications of Civil Society for Regional Resource Struggle, 39 (3) *J. of Modern African
Studies*, pp.437–469 at 461 (2001).

[223]   G. Owarieta, "Sustaining Industrial Harmony in Nigeria's Petroleum Industry", in Nigerian
Petroleum Business: A Handbook (1997), Advent Communications Limited, Lagos, p. 149;
Olayiwola Owolabi and Iwebunor Okwechime, Oil and Security in Nigeria: The Niger Delta
Crisis, *Africa Development*, Vol. XXXII, No. 1, pp.1–40 at 33 (2007).

Nigeria, the location and history of the oil producing communities of the Niger Delta, the evolution of State participation in oil exploration, and has examined the multinational oil companies operating in the oil producing communities of Niger Delta. It has further dealt with the various contractual arrangements that exists in the Nigerian oil industry – their merits and inadequacies, and suggested ways forward based on the most positive and proven practices of the operations of oil industry in other oil-producing countries of the world, including Norway, Brazil, and Indonesia. It has been shown that the problem of acquisition of manpower and technology, among others, have been major impediments facing the development of the energy sector in the country.

Nigeria has already started the process of amending the legal and regulatory framework regulating the oil industry through the Petroleum Industry Bill (PIB) 2012 presently before the National Assembly.[224] The PIB which is based on the report of the Oil and Gas Reform Implementation Committee, OGIC, set up by the Federal Government in 2000 to carry out a comprehensive reform of the oil industry, combines 16 different Nigerian petroleum laws into a single transparent and coherent document thus making the legal framework more accessible. The Bill is aimed, amongst other things, at streamlining the legal and regulatory framework for the petroleum industry, removing much secrecy to ensure transparency and openness[225] in the oil industry (especially, making payments to the government of Nigeria public information), avoiding overlapping

---

[224] Under the 1999 Constitution of the Federal Republic of Nigeria (as amended), legislation, execution and adjudication of disputes are vested in separate arms of government. These arms of government are independent of one another in terms of their existence and personnel, hence based on the separation of powers. The law making is vested in the National Assembly (the Senate and House of Representatives) at the Federal Level and House of Assembly in the States and they are made up of representatives from local constituencies into which the country is divided. The National Assembly is empowered to make laws for the peace, order and good government of the Federation with respect to any matter included in the Exclusive Legislative list to the exclusion of the States Houses of Assembly, and it also has power to make laws on matters contained in the concurrent list to the extent prescribed.

[225] The Bill makes provision granting the members of the public access to the activities of the proposed institutions. For example, by section 270 of the Bill, the processes of awarding licences are by a competitive and open bidding process, unlike the situation in the past where mining and prospecting licences were given discretionally to people who lack the technical know-how or the means. Section 270(2) specifically prohibits discretional awards. Also germane are Sections 306 and 344 of the Bill. Section 306 makes it clear that registers of technical licences issued under sections 301 and 302 should be open to members of the public who can also receive certified true copies of the documents upon payment of the prescribed fee. Section 259(1) voids confidentiality clauses in respect of royalties, bonus payments of whatever sort, taxes and any other financial matters that directly affect the revenues derived by the State from exploration and production of petroleum including but not limited to production costs of the operating partner. However, section 259(3), which gives the Directorate the power to determine whether a piece of information is proprietary industrial property rights and which also make such decision final and thus outside the openness clause in section 259(1) is likely to detract from the benefits to be derived from the clause. There should be in existence an objective criteria for determining such an important question. See Bamidele Aturu, *Petroleum Industry Bill 2008: Combustible but Curable*, Sahara Reporters Tuesday, 28 July 2009, at www.saharareporters.com/index.php? [accessed 23 November 2009].

and conflicting roles among the institutions/agencies operating in the industry, making the oil companies responsible and ensuring true democratization of the oil wealth of the Niger Delta so that the people in the oil-producing communities can adequately benefit from the resources of their region. These developments taking place would make the Nigerian oil and gas sector one to be watched carefully over the next few years. Notwithstanding the various challenges facing the Nigeria oil and gas sector, the fact that the Government is now taking steps to overhaul the entire sector for the nation is a very hopeful sign for the future of the country. One only hopes that there will be the political will on the part of the Government to implement the Bill when it finally becomes law.

CHAPTER TWO

NIGER DELTA PEOPLE UNDER INTERNATIONAL LAW AND THE PROBLEMS OF RESOURCE CONTROL

2.1 INTRODUCTION

The Niger Delta people often lay claims to indigenous rights under international law, particularly, the right to ownership of land and natural resources. This section critically analyses extant definitions and descriptions of the terms 'indigenous' and 'minority' under international law to determine whether indigenes of the Niger Delta fit into either, or, both connotations. This analysis provides the necessary backdrop to determine whether the claims of the indigenes of the Niger Delta to the land they occupy and the oil resources beneath it are really unassailable under international law. This is because, the claims by the Niger Delta people to land and natural resources can only be validly considered if, and only if, first, they fall within the meaning of minority and/or indigenous people under international law. It also undertakes a detailed analysis of the evolution of resource control agitation in the Nigerian federation as well as determines the viability of resource control as a means of achieving justice, equity and sustainable peace in the oil producing communities of Nigeria. It further examines the genuineness or otherwise of the claims of the Niger Delta people in their various Declarations, like the Kaiama Declaration 1998 that some of the Nigerian laws such as the Land Use Act (LUA), the Constitution, the Petroleum Act deprive them of their rights to ownership of land and natural resources, particularly oil and thus constitute environmental injustice. In doing this, the chapter deals with the issue of ownership of land and oil in Nigeria and examine whether they are in line with the rights of the indigenous peoples (rights to land and natural resources) under international law.

2.2 STATUS OF THE NIGER DELTA PEOPLE IN THE NIGERIAN STATE

In view of the fact that under international law, minority and indigenous rights can only be claimed by those who enjoy the status and considering the different positions maintained between the Nigerian State and the oil producing communities over who has a legitimate claim to land and the minerals under it, determining the status of the Niger Delta people becomes very important. The State is of the believe that it is the owner of the natural resources and, so, must determine how best the exploitation of such resources can bolster national development objectives.[226] On the other hand, the inhabitants of the Niger Delta region often claim that they are minorities/indigenous peoples and so entitled to enjoy the rights belonging to such people under international law. Are the Niger Delta people really entitled to the status being claimed by them? An examination of the various Declarations of Rights of the various groups in the Niger Delta and their claims to rights belonging to minorities/indigenous peoples will help to determine the status of the Niger Delta people.

For proper determination of the status of the Niger Delta people, it is necessary to examine the definition of 'minorities' and 'indigenous people', as the criteria identified will help to determine their status within the Nigerian State. Indeed, international law treats 'indigenous people' and 'minorities' as distinct categories of people with separate legal instruments catering for each of them despite the fact that the difference between these conceptions is not always clear-cut. Different rights accrue to each category which suggests that under international law, indigenous peoples are distinguishable from minorities.[227] While indigenous rights, to a large extent, apply to people collectively rather than individually, minority rights are vested in the individual but are to be exercised in 'community with other members of their group'.[228] Indeed, some measure of collective rights is implicit in this language, but it is the individual, rather than the minority as a group, that holds the right.[229]

2.2.1 DEFINITION OF MINORITIES

Minority is an ambiguous term capable of being defined through an endless combination of interacting variables such as race, culture, language, ethnicity, physical features and many other traits. As a result of these ambiguities inherent in the concept of minority, international law has found it difficult to give any specific guidelines in relation to defining the concept.[230] Several definitions have been proposed by scholars, officials appointed by international agencies, and in

---

[226] Akpan Wilson, Oil, People and the Environment: Understanding Land-Related Controversies in Nigeria's Oil Region, op. cit.

[227] See Marquardt, S., International Law and Indigenous Peoples, International Law on Group Rights 3, p.70 (1995).

[228] Fergus MacKay, The Rights of Indigenous Peoples in International Law, in Lyuba Zarky (ed.) (2002), Human Rights and the Environment: Conflicts and Norms in a Globalizing World, Earthscan Publications Ltd., p.10.

[229] Ibid p.10.

[230] Javaid Rehman (2000), The Weaknesses in the International Protection of Minority Rights, Kluwer Law International, Netherlands, p.14.

international documents emanating from international bodies. The failure on a consensus definition of minorities has been attributed 'mainly to a feeling that the concept is inherently vague and imprecise and that no proposed definition would ever be able to provide for the innumerable minority groups that could possibly exist.'[231] One of the earliest attempts was provided by the Permanent Court in the *Greco-Bulgarian Communities Case*,[232] where the court defined a minority as a group characterized by attributes of race, religion, language, and tradition and which was possessed of 'a sentiment of solidarity', having as its goal the preservation of the enumerated attributes of the group.

The United Nations Sub-Commission on the Prevention of Discrimination and Protection of Minorities also attempted, in 1954, a definition of minority as follows: 'the term minority shall include only those non-dominant groups in the population which possess and wish to preserve ethnic, religious or linguistic traditions or characteristics markedly different from those of the rest of the population'.[233]

In all, the definition that appears to have gained the widest currency is that proposed by Special Rapporteur Francesco Capotorti in 1979 in his Study on the Rights of Persons Belonging to Ethnic, Religious and Linguistic Minorities.[234] He described a minority as follows:

> *"A group numerically inferior to the rest of the population of a State, in a dominant-position, whose members – being nationals of the State – possess ethnic, religious or linguistic characteristics differing from those of the rest of the population and show, if only implicitly, a sense of solidarity, directed towards preserving their culture, traditions, religion or language".*[235]

Good as Capotorti's definition appears to be, it has been challenged and criticised on several grounds. For example, the onerous task of evaluating both the objective (a factual analysis of a group as a distinct entity within the state 'possessing stable ethnic, religious or linguistic characteristics that differ sharply from those of the rest of the population') and subjective criteria (that there exists 'a common will in the group, a sense of solidarity, directed towards preserving the distinctive characteristics of the group'), can make identification of a minority group difficult.[236] Also, to put in place an absolute principle that an entity has to be 'numerically inferior' for it to be recognised as a minority, 'places an unnecessary

---

[231]   Javaid Rehman, *Ibid.*
[232]   (1930) PCIJ Reports, Series B, No. 17, 4 at 21, quoted in Thomas Musgrave (1997), *Self Determination and National Minorities*, Clarendon Press, Oxford, pp.168–169.
[233]   ECOSOC OR. 18th Sess. Supp. No. 7. Commission on Human Rights Report of 10th Sess., 23 February – 16 April 1954, p. 48, para. 420.
[234]   UN Doc. E/CN.4/Sub.2/384/Rev. 1 (1979).
[235]   *Ibid.* This definition was formulated specific to Art. 27 of the ICCPR.
[236]   Javaid Rehman, *op. cit.*, p.15.

heavy burden on the group, and may well be factually incorrect',[237] as facts reveal
that in some cases, minorities are disadvantaged not so much by their weaknesses
in numbers, but by their exclusion from power.[238] More importantly, Capotorti's
definition has been challenged on the basis that it only centred on 'minorities
by will' without taking into consideration the position of 'minorities by force'.[239]
Explaining the distinction between the two kinds of minorities, Laponce has
stated that 'two fundamentally different attitudes are possible for a minority in its
relationship with the majority: it may wish to be assimilated or it may refuse to be
assimilated. The majority that desires assimilation but is barred is a minority by
force. The minority that refuses assimilation is a minority by will'.[240]

Another good definition of a minority was handed down by Jules Deschênes,
a former Canadian member of the United Nations Sub-Commission on the
Prevention of Discrimination and Protection of Minorities. He defines a minority
as:

> "A group of citizens of a State, constituting a numerical minority and in a non-
> dominant position in that State, endowed with ethnic, religious or linguistic cha-
> racteristics which differ from those of the majority of the population, having a sense
> of solidarity with one another, motivated, if only implicitly, by a collective will to
> survive and whose aim is to achieve equality with the majority in fact and in law".[241]

Deschênes' definition refined Capotorti's definition only minimally (replacing
'numerical inferior' with 'numerical minority', and preferring the word 'citizens'
to the 'nationals'), with a view to avoiding the vagueness characterised in
Capotorti's definition. It has, however, been noted that both 'formulae perhaps
carry an incorrect implication through contrasting 'the rest of the population'
(Capotorti) and 'the majority' (Deschênes) with minorities, as if the majority were
a monolithic cultural block in opposition to the minority, which is not the case in
many States'.[242] This definition may not be appropriate in Nigeria where there are
three different blocks of majorities, Hausa, Ibo and Yoruba.

Further, Special Rappoteur Asbjørn Eide in his final report on *Possible Ways
and Means of Facilitating the Peaceful and Constructive Solution of Problems
Involving Minorities*, has defined a minority as 'any group of persons resident
within a sovereign State which constitutes less than half of the population of

---

[237] *Ibid.*
[238] *Ibid*, p.16. A commentator once pointed out that the 'distinction…between nations and minorities is one of power. The element of power or powerlessness is the distinguishing characteristic
of national and minority discourses.' See H. Cullen, Nations and its Shadows: Quebec's Non-
French Speakers and the Courts, 3(2) *Law and Critique*, 219 at 219 (1992).
[239] J.A. Laponce, (1960), *The Protection of Minorities*, University of California Press, Berkeley and
Los Angeles, pp.12–13.
[240] *Ibid*, at p.12. Groups therefore wishing to assimilate are not covered by Capotorti's definition.
[241] UN Doc. E/CN.4/Sub. 2/1999/21, para. 28.
[242] P. Thornberry (1991), *International Law and the Rights of Minorities*, Oxford, pp.7, 9–10.

the national society and whose members share common characteristics of an ethnic, religious or linguistic nature that distinguish them from the rest of the population'.[243] A look at this definition shows a close resemblance to those of Capotorti and Deschênes, as each of them are based on numerical 'inferiority' with the minority having common characteristics in terms of ethnic, linguistic or religious nature, which characteristics distinguish them from the rest of the population. Thus, it has been contended that the criticisms earlier levelled against Capotorti's definition would equally apply to Eide's definition,[244] and this is an indication that the concept of minority in international law poses particular difficulties and the quest for consensus is an ongoing exercise.[245] Thus, in trying to determine what a minority is, it may be more effective, Rehman has suggested, to 'analyse every situation independently', and 'treat the existence and identification issue as a question of fact'.[246]

In spite of these divergences in the definitions of minority and the small likelihood of arriving at a consensus definition, the elements that are common in every attempt to formulate a definition include numerical ratio as compared to the total population, non-dominant position in the State, a cultural, linguistic, ethnic or religious identity different from the rest of the population, and a sense of solidarity, collective will and aspirations.[247] These will provide the basic guidelines for determining below the status of the Niger Delta people in Nigerian State.

2.2.2 DEFINITION OF INDIGENOUS PEOPLES

At present, there is no official or widely accepted definition of indigenous[248] peoples under international Law. In an in-depth study on the question of definition of 'indigenous peoples' conducted by the UN Working Group on Indigenous Populations (WGIP), Chairperson-Rapporteur Erica-Irene Daes noted that a definition was neither necessary nor desirable and thus concluded that 'the concept of "indigenous" is not capable of precise, inclusive definition which can be applied in the same manner to all regions of the world.'[249] However,

---

[243]   Asbjørn Eide, *Possible Ways and Means of Facilitating the Peaceful and Constructive Solution of Problems Involving Minorities*, E/CN.4/Sub.2/1993/34, para. 29.

[244]   See Javaid Rehman, *op. cit.*, p.19.

[245]   *Ibid*, p. 23.

[246]   Javaid Rehman, *op. cit.*, p.24; Asbjørn Eide, *op. cit.*, p.39, para. 195.

[247]   Kaniye Ebeku (2006), *Oil and the Niger Delta in International Law. Resource Rights, Environmental and Equity Issues*, Rudiger Koppe Verlag, Germany, p.50; N. Lerner, The Evolution of Minority Rights in International Law, in Catherine Brolmann, *et al* (eds) (1993), *Peoples and Minorities in International Law*, Martinus Nijhoff Publishers Dordrecht, The Netherlands, p.79.

[248]   The term indigenous is often used interchangeably with others, such as "tribal", "traditional", "native", "original", "first nations", "aboriginal" or other similar concepts.

[249]   E.I. Daes (1996), Working Paper by the Chairperson-Rapporteur, Mrs Erica-Irene A. Daes. On the Concept of 'Indigenous People'. UN Doc. E/CN.4/Sub.2/AC.4/1996/2.

several attempts at a definition have been put forward by different scholars.
A definition that is commonly cited is that given by Jose R. Martinez Cobo that:

> *"Indigenous communities, peoples and nations are those which, having a historical*
> *continuity with pre-invasion and pre-colonial societies that developed on their terri-*
> *tories, consider themselves distinct from other sectors of the societies now prevailing*
> *in those territories, or parts of them. They form at present non-dominant sectors of*
> *society and are determined to preserve, develop and transmit to future generations*
> *their ancestral territories, and their ethnic identity, as the basis of their continued*
> *existence as peoples, in accordance with their own cultural patterns, social institu-*
> *tions and legal systems".*[250]

To some, Cobo's definition is utterly unacceptable, particularly, the African and
Asian States who have in the past argued that indigenous peoples do not exist
in their regions, and that indigenous groups are in fact minority groups.[251] The
deferral sought by the African Group concerning the consideration in 2006 of
the UN Draft Declaration on the Rights of Indigenous Peoples was informed by
the concerns raised regarding lack of a formal definition on 'indigenous people',
collective rights, the concept of self determination, ownership of land resources,
and national and territorial integrity. While the Nigerian observer at the Working
Group indicated the need for a clear-cut definition to assist in identifying the
distinction between indigenous peoples and minorities, the Bangladesh observer
claimed that their entire population of about 120 million was indigenous. The
African Group questioned the right to self determination which they believe
could lead to possible secession of some sections of a national population thereby
threatening the political unity and national integrity of the country.

Self determination is an important right in international law, and it is a right
of all people. It has been classified as *jus cogens*, a peremptory norm of customary
international law. By reason of its normative status, it is 'valid and binding on all,
irrespective of consent, and only a subsequent norm of similar status can abridge
or set it aside'.[252] Articles 1 and 55 of the United Nations Charter provide for equal
rights and self determination of peoples,[253] but fail to define the 'peoples' upon

---

[250]   Jose R. Martinez Cobo, *Study of the Problem of Discrimination Against Indigenous Populations*
        para. 379, UN Doc. E/CN.4/Sub.2/1986/7/Add.4, UN Sales No. E.86.XIV3 (1986).
[251]   See Megan Davis, Indigenous Struggles in Standard-Setting: The United Nations Declarations
        on the Rights of Indigenous Peoples, 9 *Melb. J. Int'l L.* 439 at 443 (2008); Sarah Pritchard,
        "Working Group on Indigenous Populations: Mandate, Standard-Setting Activities and
        Future Perspectives", in Sarah Pritchard (ed) (1998), *Indigenous Peoples, United Nations and
        Human Rights*, Zed Books Ltd, London, p.42.
[252]   Chinedu Reginald Ezetah, International Law of Self Determination and the Ogoni Question:
        Mirroring Africa's Post-Colonial Dilemma, 19 *Loy. L.A. Int'l & Comp. L.J.* 832 (1996–1997);
        Ian Brownlie, *Principles of Public International Law* (1990), 4th ed., Oxford, pp.514–515.
[253]   This right is also incorporated in several other international instruments like Art. 1(1) of the
        International Covenant on Civil and Political Rights (ICCPR) (G.A. RES. 2200A (XXI), 21
        UN GAOR Supp. (No. 16) at 52, U.N Doc. A/6316 (1966), 999 U.N.T.S. 171, entered into force

whom these rights are conferred. In the same vein, the African Charter does not define the "peoples" whom it bestows these rights on. This has created a division between States and indigenous groups over the meaning of the phrase "peoples". Whilst indigenous groups insist on the use of the term "indigenous peoples", the States are adamant on the use of the term "indigenous populations". As some scholars have observed, the reasoning of the States is unsurprising because using indigenous "peoples" would be a tacit acknowledgement of their right to self-determination.[254]

Legal scholars are divided on the definition of the notion of peoples. Notwithstanding the absence of any authoritative international legal definition of the notion of peoples today, scholars agree that 'overriding considerations in the right to be called "people" include territoriality, a common history, culture, language, and a conscious desire to maintain a distinctive identity from other groups'.[255] However, the absence of, or weakness of, one of these elements need not invalidate a claim.[256] In the words of Erica-Irene Daes:

> *"Indigenous peoples are unquestionably "peoples" in every social, cultural, and eth-nological meaning of the term. They have their specific languages, laws, values, and traditions; their own long histories as distinct societies and nations; and a unique economic, religious, and spiritual relationship with the territories in which they have so long lived. It is neither logical nor scientific to treat them as the same "people" as their neighbours, who obviously have different languages, histories, and cultures, and who have often been their oppressors. The United Nations should not pretend, for the sake of a convenient legal fiction, that those differences do not exist"*[257]

---

23 Mar. 1976); Art. 1 of the International Covenant on Economic, Social and Cultural Rights (ICESR), (G.A. Res. 2200A (XXI) of 16 December 1966, entered into force 3 January 1976. Article 1 of these Covenants provides that: 'All peoples have the right to self- determination. By virtue of that right they freely determine their political status and freely pursue their economic, social and cultural development'. See also Part 2 of the Declaration on Granting Independence to Colonial Countries and Peoples (GA Res. 1514 (XV), 14 December 1960, the Declaration on Principles of International Law Concerning the Friendly Relations and Co-operation Among States in Accordance with the Charter of the UN (G.A. Res. 2625 (XXV), 24 October 1970, Art. 20 of the African Charter on Human and Peoples' Rights ILM 21 (1982), 58.

[254] Jeff J. Corntassel and Tomas Hopkins Primeau, Indigenous "Sovereignty" and International Law: Revised Strategies for Pursuing "Self-Determination", 17 *Hum. Rts. Q.* 353 (1995). Anaya S. James, The Capacity of International Law to Advance Ethnic or Nationality Rights Claims, 13 *Hum. Rts. Q.* 34 (1991) noted that the source of the States' resistance is a concern that an acknowledged 'right to self-determination for indigenous groups may imply an effective right of secession'.

[255] See Obiora Okwu-Okafor, Self determination and the Struggle for Ethno-Cultural Autonomy in Nigeria: The Zangon Kataf and Ogoni Problems, 6 *ASICL Proc.* 114 at 94 (1994), quoted in Chinedu Reginald Ezetah, *op. cit.*, p.835.

[256] Erica-Irene A. Daes, Some Considerations on the Right of Indigenous Peoples' to Self Determination, 3 *Transnat'l L. & Contemp. Probs.* 5 (1993).

[257] *Ibid*, p.6.

One of the often-cited definitions of indigenous peoples was laid out by the International Labour Organization (ILO) in its Convention Concerning Indigenous and Tribal Peoples in Independent Countries. The definition given by ILO is in two-parts, and according to Lindsey Wiersma,[258] a group needs to satisfy only one part to be considered an indigenous people. The first part includes those "whose social, cultural and economic conditions distinguish them from other sections of the national community, and whose status is regulated wholly or partially by their own customs or traditions or by special laws or regulations."[259] The second part includes those who are "descen[ded] from the populations which inhabited the country, or a geographical region to which the country belongs, at the time of conquest or colonisation or the establishment of present state boundaries and who, irrespective of their legal status, retain some or all of their own social, economic, cultural and political institutions."[260] Article 1(2) provides that self-identification as indigenous or tribal shall be regarded as a fundamental criterion for determining the groups to which the provisions of the Convention apply.

In 2003, a Working Group under the African Commission on Human and Peoples' Rights (ACHPR) came out with a Report on Indigenous Populations/Communities in Africa where it concluded that a strict definition of indigenous peoples is "neither necessary, nor desirable", as many Governments may use it as an excuse for not recognising indigenous peoples within their territories[261] thus excluding certain groups. Rather than defining indigenous peoples, it recommended an identification approach based on a set of major criteria and stressed the following characteristics of African indigenous peoples: their cultures and ways of life differ considerably from those of the dominant society; their cultures are under threat, in some cases on the verge of extinction; the survival of their particular way of life depends on access and rights to their traditional land and resources; they often live in inaccessible, geographically isolated regions; and they suffer from various forms of marginalization, both politically and socially, and are subject to domination and exploitation within national political and economic structures that are commonly designed to reflect the interests and activities of the national majority. It contended that the focus should be on the more recent approaches focusing on *self-definition*, *special attachment to and use of their traditional land*, and on an experience of

---

[258]   Lindsey L. Wiersma, Indigenous Lands as Cultural Property: A New Approach to Indigenous Land Claims, *Duke Law Journal* Vol. 54, 1063–1064 (2005).

[259]   Convention Concerning Indigenous and Tribal Peoples in Independent Countries, 27 June 1989, 169 I.L.O. 1989, art. 1(1)(a).

[260]   *Ibid* at art. 1(1)(b).

[261]   Report of the African Commission's Working Groups of Experts on Indigenous Populations/Communities, adopted by the ACHPR, at its 28th Session, 2005, published by the ACHPR and IWGIA, p.87; see also Indigenous & Tribal Peoples' Rights in Practice – *A Guide to ILO Convention No. 169 Programme to Promote ILO Convention No. 169 (PRO 169)*, International Labour Standards Department, 2009, at http://pro169.org/res/materials/en/general_resources/IPsRightsCover-english-part2-1lorez.pdf [accessed 3 March 2010].

subjugation, marginalization, dispossession, exclusion or discrimination.[262] This position was again reaffirmed in the 2007 African Commission's Working Group of Experts on Indigenous Populations/Communities Report[263] which stated that in the absence of a universally agreed test that captures the characteristics of indigenous populations, it is more practically useful to indicate the main characteristics which allow for the identification of the indigenous populations and communities in Africa. These include, among others: 'a) self-identification; b) a special attachment to and use of their traditional land whereby their ancestral land and territory have a fundamental importance for their collective physical and cultural survival as peoples; c) a state of subjugation, marginalisation, dispossession, exclusion, or discrimination because these peoples have different cultures, ways of life or modes of production than the national hegemonic and dominant model.'[264]

Recently, the World Bank, while denying that it was defining "indigenous peoples", has implicitly in its Operational Policy (OP 4.10) given a definition of indigenous peoples in a manner similar to the ILO's definition. Paragraph 4 states that:

> For purposes of this policy, the term "Indigenous Peoples" is used in a generic sense to refer to a distinct, vulnerable, social and cultural group possessing the following characteristics in varying degrees:
> (a) self-identification as members of a distinct indigenous cultural group and recognition of this identity by others;
> (b) collective attachment to geographically distinct habitats or ancestral territories in the project area and to the natural resources in these habitats and territories;
> (c) customary cultural, economic, social or political institutions that are separate from those of the dominant society and culture; and
> (d) an indigenous language, often different from the official language of the country or region.[265]

Evident from the ILO's definition and that of the World Bank is the criterion of 'self identification' by the claimants of the rights available to the indigenous

---

[262] *Ibid*, pp.89, 92–93.
[263] Advisory Opinion of the African Commission on Human and Peoples' Rights on the United Nations Declarations on the Rights of Indigenous Peoples, adopted by the African Commission on Human and Peoples' Rights (ACHPR) at its 41st Ordinary Session held in May 2007 in Accra, Ghana, ACHPR and International Work Group for Indigenous Affairs (IWGIA), 2010, pp.30–31.
[264] *Ibid.*
[265] World Bank, Operational Policies: Indigenous Peoples (OP 4.10, July 2005). On the other hand, Benedict Kingsbury, in "Indigenous Peoples" in International Law: A Constructivist Approach to the Asian Controversy, 92 *Am. J. Int'l L.* 453 (1998) offers four criteria for international legal recognition of indigenous peoples: "self-identification as a distinct ethnic group; a historical experience of…severe disruption, dislocation or exploitation; long connection with the region; and the wish to retain a distinct identity".

peoples. However, this criterion has been criticised on the ground that the mere fact that a 'community identifies itself as an indigenous population does not provide a sufficient explanation of why international law should recognise it in these terms',[266] otherwise, numerical minorities, cultural minorities, national minorities, religious minorities, linguistic communities, impoverished majorities, who chose to identify themselves as indigenous peoples will be laying claims to the rights inherent therein.[267] Except for the difficulties of distinguishing between indigenous peoples from minorities as a result of lack of a clearly identifying index,[268] we do not need a formal definition for us to be able to adequately protect the interest of the people under this category. The position taken by Dias appears to be the best in the circumstances. He noted that we may not have a definition of indigenous peoples, 'but we do have a concept. They are the peoples of the world who still face the risk of being displaced from their traditional and ancestral homelands. They are the peoples of the world whose cultural and traditional practices may be eroded because of forced displacement of their population.'[269]

It can be seen from the above that the problem of definition of indigenous peoples still rages on among scholars. Even the UN Declaration on the Rights of Indigenous Peoples[270] does not contain a definition of indigenous peoples. However, Article 9 of the Declaration provides that: "Indigenous peoples and individuals have the right to belong to an indigenous community or nation, in accordance with the traditions and customs of the community or nation concerned." Again, Article 33 maintains: "[I]ndigenous peoples have the right to determine their own identity or membership in accordance with their customs and traditions." Thus, despite the fact that self identification as a criterion did not formally appear in the text of the Declaration, 'the spirit of the Declaration

---

[266]   Patrick Macklem, Indigenous Recognition in International Law: Theoretical Observations, 30 *Michigan J. Int'l L.* 177–210 at 207 (2008–2009). Macklem, at p.209 while calling for an interpretative stand on the nature and purpose of international indigenous rights opined that the 'criteria by which indigenous peoples can be said to exist in international law relate to their historic exclusion from the distribution of sovereignty initiated by colonization that lies at the heart of the international legal order'. He further argued this does not exclude 'additional criteria that condition recognition on distinctive identities, experiences of exclusion, dislocation or exploitation, and self-identification. Nor does it preclude international law from recognizing indigenous peoples in Africa and Asia.'

[267]   *Ibid*, p.207; See Jeff J. Corntassel and Tomas Hopkins Primeau, *op. cit.*, pp.349–350.

[268]   Kaniye Ebeku (2006), *Oil and the Niger Delta in International Law. Resource Rights, Environmental and Equity Issues, op. cit.*, p.56.

[269]   Dias K. Ayesha, *International Standard-Setting on the Rights of Indigenous Peoples: Implications for Mineral Development in Africa*, at www.dundee.ac.uk/cepmlp/journal/html/vol7/article7-3.html [accessed 23 March 2009].

[270]   General Assembly, United Nations Declaration on the Rights of Indigenous Peoples, A/RES/61/295, 13 September 2007, adopted by a landslide affirmative vote of 144 States. While the United States, Canada, Australia and New Zealand voted against it, Nigeria, Azerbaijan, Kenya, Bhutan, Burundi, Bangladesh, Columbia, Georgia, Samoa, Russia and Ukraine abstained. It can be argued that the overwhelming support received during the adoption of this Declaration is a reflection of its global acceptance, hence making it more than a statement of mere aspirational goals.

remains based on a self identification perspective with a right for indigenous individuals to belong to an indigenous community'.[271] The ILO Convention 169[272] remains the only legally binding international instrument that contains a definition of indigenous peoples. It is binding on States parties, but it has been argued that it can be politically binding on non-party States, like Nigeria, especially as it has been incorporated into the official policy of the World Bank, of which Nigeria is a Member State.[273] Likewise, in a quite different context, the American courts have asserted and applied the various principles in Rio Declaration on Environment and Development (though not binding) in decisions relating to alleged environmental violations.[274]

2.2.3 ASSESSMENT OF THE STATUS OF THE NIGER DELTA PEOPLE

This section examines the position of the Niger Delta people *vis-à-vis* the criteria to qualify as 'minorities' and/or 'indigenous peoples.' In doing this, a few of the Declarations of Rights[275] issued by the different ethnic groups in the Niger Delta articulating the demands and positions of the Niger Delta communities will be considered. In the first place, a look at the contents of these Declarations *vis-à-vis* the guidelines for identifying a minority group reveals that the Niger Delta

---

[271] Jérémie Gilbert, The United Nations Declaration on the Rights of Indigenous Peoples: Towards Partnership and Mutual Respect, at www.liv.ac.uk/law/ielu/docs/UN_Declaration_on_the_Rights_of_Indigenous_Peoples-JG.pdf [accessed 3 March 2010].

[272] ILO Convention 169 is a revision of an earlier ILO Convention 107 that had been adopted in 1959. Suffice it to say that Convention 107 which is now closed for ratification remains binding on the 18 countries (Angola, Bangladesh, Belgium, Cuba, Dominican Republic, Egypt, El Salvador, Ghana, Guinea Bissau, Haiti, India, Iraq, Malawi, Pakistan, Panama, Portugal, Syria and Tunisia) that have ratified it and which have not yet denounced it or ratified Convention No. 169. As at October 2009, only 20 countries (Argentina, Bolivia, Brazil, Chile Columbia, Costa Rica, Denmark, Dominica, Ecuador, Fiji, Guatemala, Honduras, Mexico, Nepal, Netherlands, Norway, Paraguay, Peru, Spain and Bolivarian Republic of Venezuela) have ratified Convention No. 169 since 1989. Whereas only five Africans ratified Convention 107, no African country has yet ratified Convention 169.

[273] Kaniye Ebeku (2006), *Oil and the Niger Delta in International Law. Resource Rights, Environmental and Equity Issues, op. cit.* relying on Plant, R., *Land Rights and Minorities*, London, 1994, p.12 where Plant contended that 'an instrument like the ILO's Convention No. 169 can have influence beyond ratifying States, if it is incorporated into the official policy of one of the major international financial Institutions'.

[274] See Dias K. Ayesha, *International Standard-Setting on the Rights of Indigenous Peoples: Implications for Mineral Development in Africa, op. cit.* where he noted that the United States District Court in *Aguinda v. Texaco* applied Principle 2 of the Rio Declaration on Environment, a non-binding international instrument, as evidence of State practice in the United States, even though the Plaintiffs had not alleged a violation of a treaty.

[275] Such Declarations include the Ogoni Bill of Rights 1990 (and its addendum of 1991), at www.nigerianscholars.africanqueen.com/docum/ogoni.htm [accessed 7 June 2009]; the Kaiama Declaration 1998, at www.essentialaction.org/shell/kaiama.html [accessed 7 June 2009]; the Aklaka Declaration of Egi People; Ikwerre Rescue Charter 1999; and the Oron Bill of Rights 1999.

people are a minority in the Nigerian State. For example, the Declarations show
that the Niger Delta people are a non-dominant people within the Nigerian State,
dominated by the major ethnic groups in the country, the Hausa, Yoruba and
Ibo.[276] The Ogoni Bill of Rights states that the Constitution of Nigeria 'does not
protect any of our (Ogoni) rights whatsoever as an ethnic minority of 500,000
in a nation of about 140 million people and that the voting power and military
might of the majority ethnic groups have been used remorselessly against us at
every point in time'.[277] Still on domination, the Declaration further avers that 'the
languages of Gokana and Khana are undeveloped and are about to disappear,
whereas other Nigerian languages are being forced on us'.[278] In a country
with over 250 distinct ethnic groups with several distinct languages, the 1999
Constitution of Nigeria declares in section 55 that 'the business of the National
Assembly shall be conducted in English, and in Hausa, Ibo and Yoruba when
adequate arrangements have been made therefor', ignoring the non-majority
spoken languages, including the languages of the Niger Delta people.

The Declarations also reveal that the Niger Delta people are different from
the rest of the population (Nigeria) in the area of cultural, linguistic, ethnic and
religious identity. Their traditions and culture are peculiar to them. The Ogoni
Bill of Rights demands that they be allowed to enjoy the rights to develop their
'languages and culture' as a separate and distinct ethnic nationality within
Nigeria.[279]

Furthermore, the Declarations claim in several respects that the people of
Niger Delta are a minority. For example, the Kaiama Declaration states that
'the division of the Southern Protectorate into East and West in 1939 marked
the beginning of the "Balkanization" of a hitherto, territorially contiguous and
culturally homogenous Ijaw people into political and administrative units,
much to our disadvantage. This trend is continuing in the "Balkanization"
of the Ijaw into six States – Ondo, Edo, Delta, Bayelsa, Rivers and Akwa Ibom
States, mostly as minorities who suffer socio-political, economic, cultural and
psychological deprivations.' Also, the Ogoni Bill of Rights avers that they cannot
seek any restitution in the courts of law in Nigeria as the Constitution of Nigeria
does 'not, in any way, protect minority rights or bear resemblance to the tacit
agreement made at Nigerian independence.'[280] As observed by Kaniye Ebeku,[281] if

---

[276]   Going by the 2006 census, the total population of all the nine States of the Niger Delta was 31,
        224, 577, in a country of over 140 million people.
[277]   See para. 3 of Addendum to the Ogoni Bill of Rights.
[278]   See para. 12 of Ogoni Bill of Rights. This was articulated by Dr. Leton G.B., an Ogoni leader
        in his preface to the Ogoni Bill of Rights: 'All one sees and feels around is death. Death is eve-
        rywhere in Ogoniland. Ogoni language is dying. Ogoni culture is dying. Ogoni people, Ogoni
        animals, Ogoni fish are dying because of 33 years of hazardous environmental pollution and
        resulting in food scarcity...' See Comment, The News (Nig.), 17 May 1993, at 18–19.
[279]   See paras. d and e of Ogoni Bill of Rights & para. d of Addendum to the Ogoni Bill of Rights.
[280]   See para. 6 of the Addendum to the Ogoni Bill of Rights.
[281]   Kaniye Ebeku (2006), *Oil and the Niger Delta in International Law. Resource Rights,
        Environmental and Equity Issues, op. cit.*, p.59. He further contended that unlike their former

the comparison made here between the population of the Ogonis and the whole of Nigeria is correct (as there is no evidence to the contrary), this implies that Ogonis (as well as other Niger Delta communities) are numerically inferior to the rest of the population, thus satisfying the criteria of minority status (numerical inferiority).

On whether the Niger Delta inhabitants satisfy the requirement of having a 'sense of solidarity, collective will and aspirations', it is pertinent to refer to the coming together of Ogonis under the Movement for the Survival of the Ogoni people (MOSOP) and their sustained campaign for self-determination notwithstanding the State suppression. In view of the above, it can be argued that the Niger Delta inhabitants satisfy the conditions for recognition as a minority group.

To determine the qualification (or otherwise) of the inhabitants of the Niger Delta to be regarded as 'indigenous peoples', reference will be made in the absence of a universally agreed test that capture the characteristics of indigenous populations, to the afore-mentioned criteria suggested by the African Commission's Working Group of Experts on Indigenous Populations/Communities Report. These include, among others: self-identification; a special attachment to and use of their traditional land; and a state of subjugation, marginalisation, dispossession, exclusion, or discrimination because these peoples (indigenous peoples) have different cultures, ways of life or modes of production.[282]

In the first place, the Kaiama Declaration states in its preamble that their meeting in Kaiama is to 'deliberate on the best way to ensure the continuous survival of the indigenous peoples of the Ijaw ethnic nationality of the Niger Delta within the Nigerian State', thus showing that they identify themselves as indigenous peoples. Also, the people's claim to the right to internal self-determination in the Declarations shows that they identify themselves as indigenous peoples in Nigeria, thereby satisfying the requirement of ILO Convention 169. For example, the Ogoni Bill of Rights asserts that the Government of Nigeria 'has ... since independence in 1960 till the present date, denied us our political rights to self determination, economic rights to our resources, cultural rights to the development of our languages and culture, and social rights.'[283] While reaffirming their wish to remain part of Nigeria, the Ogoni Bill of Rights further asserts that 'the Ogoni ... demand political autonomy as a distinct and separate unit within the Nigeria

---

claim to regional minority, the minority status claimed by the Declarations appears to be of 'national minority' and not 'regional minority.'

[282] Advisory Opinion of the African Commission on Human and Peoples' Rights on the United Nations Declarations on the Rights of Indigenous Peoples, adopted by the African Commission on Human and Peoples' Rights (ACHPR) at its 41st Ordinary Session held in May 2007 in Accra, Ghana, *op. cit.*

[283] Addendum to the Ogoni Bill of Rights, para. 1. Summarising the demands contained in the Bill of Rights at the Rally, Garrick Leton said: 'We are not asking for the moon but the basic necessities of life – water, electricity, roads, education, and a right to self determination so that we can be responsible for our resources and our environment'. Quoted in Eghosa Osaghae, The Ogoni Uprising: Oil Politics, Minority Agitation and the Future of the Nigerian State, *African Affairs* 94, at 336–337 (1995).

nation with the full right to (i) control political affairs, [and] (ii) use at least fifty per cent of Ogoni economic resources for Ogoni development…'[284] Indeed, Dias notes that the 'Ogoni peoples claim to have a distinct culture, language, history, political system and religion – a self identification that would allow them to be considered indigenous peoples.'[285] These claims in these Declarations are nothing but a claim to internal self-determination to control their own affairs within the Nigerian State.

On the criteria of special attachment to and use of their traditional land, it suffices to say that land and water are important to the Niger Delta people as they attach spiritual importance to them. For example, in some parts of the Niger Delta, rivers and streams are not just regarded as sources of water for use but also abodes of gods where they take their new born babies for initiation eight days after birth, or use the rivers to carry out their traditional festivals. The traditional economic activity – means of subsistence (fishing and farming) – of the people is defined by land and the natural resources in the region. Hence, access to land for farming and water for fishing activities becomes important for the survival of the people since they depend on the resources of the wetlands for their food. Unfortunately, several laws passed by the Nigerian Government including the Petroleum Act and the Land Use Act which among others, vest the ownership of oil and land respectively in the Federal Government disrupt the traditional economic activities of the local inhabitants of the Niger Delta region upon the commencement of oil-related activities, hindering their access to land and other natural resources.[286] Today, farming in the communities in the region has become an exercise in futility. The land on which their livelihood depends has been deprived of its fertility through the continuous exploitation and irresponsible practices of the oil MNCs, with lakes, rivers and creeks still being polluted through oil spillage and leakage.[287]

The final element to be considered within the criteria set by the African Working Group is to determine whether indigenes of the Niger Delta suffer from subjugation, marginalisation, dispossession, exclusion, or discrimination within national political and economic structures. It is important to note that the violent conflicts in the region are largely driven by the feelings of dispossession, exclusion and marginalization. As noted by the World Bank:

---

[284] *Ibid*, para. 7. The Kaiama Declaration further states in para. 10 that 'we agreed to remain within Nigeria, but to demand and work for self government and resource control for the Ijaw people. Conference approved that the best way forward for Nigeria is a federation of ethnic nationalities. The federation should run on the basis of equality and social justice'.

[285] Dias K. Ayesha, *International Standard-Setting on the Rights of Indigenous Peoples: Implications for Mineral Development in Africa, op. cit.*

[286] Ako, R. and Okonmah, P., 'Minority Rights Issues in Nigeria: A Theoretical Analysis of Historical and Contemporary Conflicts in the Oil-Rich Niger Delta Region', 16 *International Journal on Minority and Group Rights* 57–58 (2009).

[287] Murray B. Rutherford *et al.*, 'Assessing Environmental Losses: Judgements of Importance and Damage Schedules', 22 *Harv. Envtl. L. Rev.* 51–101 at 58 (1998).

"The widespread perception of relative deprivation in the core Niger Delta states is driven by the considerable mismatch between the level of wealth extracted from the region and the benefits accruing to the region and its people. Levels of self-assessed poverty are much higher in the Delta than those revealed by household income and expenditure data. In the South South Zone, over three quarters of the population (77 percent) consider themselves to be living in poverty, compared to the official figure of one third (35 percent)."[288]

This confirms the description given of the Niger Delta region as 'poor, backward and neglected',[289] by the Willink Commission set up in 1958 to enquire into fears of Minorities. This description still remains true as far as the conditions of the region is concern.

In addition to the above criteria, the area known as the Niger Delta today historically "predates Nigeria's emergence as a British Colony by at least a decade. British Niger Delta Protectorate and the Niger Delta Coast Protectorate were already well established by the mid-1880s and the late 1890s".[290] The Kaiama Declaration notes that 'it was through British colonization that the Ijaw nation was forcibly put under the Nigerian State'. It claims further that 'but for the economic interests of the imperialists, the Ijaw ethnic nationality would have evolved as a distinct and sovereign nation, enjoying undiluted political, economic, social and cultural autonomy'.[291] In a similar vein, the Ogoni Bill of Rights asserts that 'the Ogoni people, before the advent of British colonialism, were not conquered or colonized by any other ethnic group in present-day Nigeria',[292] and that it was the British colonialism that forces them into the administrative division of Opobo from 1908 to 1947 and later forcibly included them in the Eastern Region of Nigeria in 1951. This suggests that prior to colonialism, the Niger Delta people already existed as nations, and so were indigenous peoples in the area.[293] Kaniye Ebeku[294] has contended that 'the use of the word "nation" in the Declarations to describe the group implies a claim to the status of people', which is in line with the claim for self-determination, a right associated with indigenous peoples.

---

[288]   World Bank, *Niger Delta Social and Conflict Analysis*, Washington, DC, 2008, pp.8–9.
[289]   Willink Commission, *Report of the Willink Commission Appointed to Enquire into the Fears of Minorities and the Means of Allaying them*, C.O.957/4, Colonial Office, July 1958, 94, London.
[290]   A. Onduku, *Environmental Conflicts: The Case of the Niger Delta*, being a paper presented at the One World Fortnight Programme, University of Bradford, UK, November 2001, at www.waado.org/nigerdelta/essays/resourcecontrol/Onduku.html [accessed 3 March 2010]; See also Victor Ojakorotu, The National Question: Federalism and Oil Violence in the Niger Delta of Nigeria, in Garbutt, R. (ed) (2008), *Activating Human Rights and Peace: Universal Responsibility Conference 2008 Conference Proceedings*, Byron Bay, NSW, 1–4 July, Centre for Peace and Social Justice, Southern Cross University, Lismore, NSW, p. 279 at www.scu.edu.au/research/cpsj/human rights/.p.279 [accessed 3 March 2010].
[291]   Kaiama Declaration 1998, paras. i and ii respectively.
[292]   Paras. 1, 2, 3, and 4 of Ogoni Bill of Rights.
[293]   Kaniye Ebeku (2006), *Oil and the Niger Delta in International Law. Resource Rights, Environmental and Equity Issues, op. cit.*, p.61.
[294]   *Ibid* p.61.

The opportunity to determine the status of the inhabitants of the Niger Delta region arose in the case of *Attorney-General of the Federation v. Attorney-General of Abia State & 35 others (No. 2).*[295] The Supreme Court, on the issue of indigenity of the Niger Delta people noted that:

> *"Until the advent of the British colonial rule in what is now known as the Federal Republic of Nigeria, there existed at various times various sovereign States known as emirates, kingdoms and empires made up of ethnic groups in Nigeria. Each was independent of the other with its mode of government indigenous to it. At one time or another, these sovereign States were either making wars with each other or making alliances, on equal terms. This position existed throughout the land now known as Nigeria. In the Niger Delta area, for instance, there were the Okrika, the Ijaw, the Kalabari, the Efik, the Ibibio, the Urhobo, the Itsekiri, etc. Indeed certain of these communities (e.g., Calabar) asserted exclusive rights over the narrow waters in their area. And because of the terrain of their area, they made use of the rivers and the sea for their economic advancement in fishing and trade – and in making wars too. The rivers and the sea were their only means of transportation. Trade then was not only among themselves but with foreign nations, particularly the European nations who sailed to their shores for palm oil, kernel and slaves."*

From the above discussion, it can arguably be concluded that the Niger Delta people satisfy both the definition of 'minority' and also as 'indigenous peoples' within the Nigerian State and so are entitled to benefit from the two sets of rights. We shall however limit our discussion of these rights to those that are relevant to this study, particularly their rights to land and natural resources, as indigenous peoples.

2.3 OWNERSHIP OF OIL IN NIGERIA

An examination of Nigerian law shows that the subjects of natural or mineral resources in Nigeria are within the legislative competence of the Federal Legislature. This is confirmed by section 44(3) of the 1999 Constitution of the Federal Republic of Nigeria (as amended), which provides as follows:

> *"Notwithstanding the foregoing provisions of this section, the entire property in and control of all minerals, mineral oils and natural gas in, under or upon any land in Nigeria or in, under or upon the Territorial Waters and the Exclusive Economic Zone in Nigeria shall vest in the Government of the Federation and shall be managed in such a manner as may be prescribed by the National Assembly."*

---

[295]   (2002) 6 NWLR (pt. 764) 542.

It can be safely stated that the above provisions had its root in the Minerals Act of 1945,[296] which established the legal foundation for the ownership, and control of petroleum or minerals resources in any part of Nigeria in the Crown (State). This was retained with minor amendments in the 1960 independence Constitution of Nigeria, the 1963 Republican Constitution,[297] was entrenched in the 1979 Constitution of Nigeria,[298] and similarly provided for in section 42(3) of the aborted Constitution of the Federal Republic of Nigeria 1989.

---

[296] Section 3(1) of the Minerals Act 1945 (the Act came into operation on 25 February 1946) states that: "the entire property in and control of all mineral oils, in, under or upon any land in Nigeria, and of all rivers, streams and water courses throughout Nigeria is and shall be vested in the crown, save in so far as such rights may in any case have been limited by any express grant made before the commencement of this Act". Suffice it to say that the first major colonial statute on mineral oil was the Mineral Oils Ordinance No. 7 of 1914 promulgated to regulate the exploitation and exploration of oil in Nigeria and which was amended in 1925, 1950, and 1959. Under section 2 of the 1925 amendment, "mineral oil" was defined as including "bitumen, asphalt and all other bituminous substances" with the exception of coal (covered by the 1945 Minerals Act). A new section was added by the 1950 amendment whereby the submarine areas of Nigeria's territorial waters were brought under the ambit of the ordinance. By the 1959 amendment, the legislative competence of Nigeria's federal legislature (under the 1959 colonial Constitution, Nigeria was a federation with a centre and three regions) was extended to cover the submarine areas of other waters on which the federal legislature may make legislation in future, in matters relating to mines and minerals. This amendment might have been made in the exercise of the right under Article 2 of the Geneva Convention on the Continental Shelf which states that: 1. The coastal State exercises over the continental shelf sovereign rights for the purpose of exploring it and exploiting its natural resources. 2. The rights referred to in paragraph 1 of this article are exclusive in the sense that where the coastal State does not explore or exploit the continental shelf or exploit its natural resources, no one may undertake these activities without the express consent of the coastal State. 3. The rights of the coastal State over the continental shelf do not depend on occupation, effective or notional, or on any express proclamation.
There was, however, no provision in the 1914 Mineral Oils Ordinance dealing with ownership of oil. This lacuna was filled by section 3(1) Minerals Ordinance 1916, and also in the 1945 Minerals Act which replaced it. See Kaniye Ebeku (2006), *Oil and the Niger Delta in International Law. Resource Rights, Environmental and Equity Issues, op. cit.*, pp.75–76; Kekong Bisong (2009), *Restorative Justice for Niger Delta*, Maklu-Publishers Antwerpen, pp.76–77.

[297] Section 158 of the 1963 Republican Constitution of Nigeria vested in the President of the Federation all property hitherto held by the Crown.

[298] Section 40(3) of the 1979 Constitution provides that: "… the entire property in and control of all minerals, minerals oil and natural gas in, under or upon any lands in Nigeria or in, under or upon the territorial waters, and the Exclusive Economic Zone of Nigeria shall vest in the Government of the Federation and shall be managed in such manner as may be prescribed by the National Assembly". See also Section 1(1) of the Minerals and Mining Act No. 20, 2007 (which repealed the Minerals and Mining Act No. 34 of 1999 Cap. M. 12 LFN 2004), which provides that 'the entire property in and control of all Mineral Resources in, under or upon any land in Nigeria, its contiguous continental shelf and all rivers, streams and water courses throughout Nigeria, any area covered by its territorial waters or constituency and the Exclusive Economic Zone is and shall be vested in the Government of the Federation for and on behalf of the people of Nigeria.' The Minerals and Mining Act No. 20, 2007, however, defined 'Minerals or Mineral Resources' to mean 'any substance whether in solid, liquid or gaseous form occurring in or on the earth, formed by or subjected to geological processes including occurrences or deposits of rocks, coal bed gases, bituminous shales, tar sands, any substances that may be extracted from coal, shales, or tar sands, mineral water, and mineral components in tailings, and waste piles, but with the exclusion of Petroleum and waters without mineral content.

The use of the words "the entire property in" and "under or upon" in section 44(3) of the 1999 Constitution shows that the ownership of natural resources (oil) in Nigeria including the seabed and subsoil of the territorial waters and the Exclusive Economic Zone (EEZ) of Nigeria is vested in the Federal Government. The exclusive legislative competence of the Federal Government on this subject is further guaranteed by item 39 in the Exclusive Legislative List[299] of the 1999 Constitution of Nigeria which vest in the Federal Government the exclusive power to legislate on "mines and minerals, including oil fields, oil mining, geological surveys and natural gas".

In the same vein, the Petroleum Act[300] vested in the Federal Government the entire ownership and control of all petroleum in, under or upon any lands in Nigeria, including the territorial waters, the continental shelf and the Exclusive Economic Zone (EEZ) in Nigerian State.[301] The territorial waters have been defined to mean any part of the open sea within 12 nautical miles of the coast of Nigeria (measured from low water mark) or of the seaward limits of inland waters.[302] While the continental shelf is defined in the Petroleum Act as:

> "... the sea bed and subsoil of those submarine areas adjacent to the coast of Nigeria the surface of which lies at a depth not greater than two hundred metres (or, where its natural resources are capable of exploitation, at any depth) below the surface of the sea, excluding so much of those areas as lies below the territorial waters of Nigeria."[303]

Part VI of the 1982 U.N Convention on Law of the Sea (UNCLOS) deals with the continental shelf, and Article 76 of the Convention defines a continental shelf of a coastal State as comprising "the seabed and the subsoil of the submarine areas that extend beyond its territorial sea throughout the natural prolongation of its land territory to the outer edge of the continental margin, or to a distance 200 nautical miles from the baselines from which the breath of the territorial sea is measured where the outer edge of the continental margin does not extend

---

[299]   Section 4(2) of the 1999 Constitution of Nigeria confers powers on the National Assembly to make laws for the order and good government of the Federation with respect to any matter included in the Exclusive Legislative List to the exclusion of the House of Assembly and item 39 in the Exclusive Legislative List (Part 1 of the Second Schedule to the Constitution) is one of such matters.

[300]   Sections 1 and 2, Cap 10 LFN 2004. This Act was promulgated as Petroleum Decree No.51 of 1969. It repealed the Mineral Oils Act Cap 120 1958 Laws of Nigeria and the Petroleum Act Cap 150 1958 Laws of Nigeria.

[301]   The word "State" as used in the Act implies the Federal Republic of Nigeria and not its component units.

[302]   Section 18 of the Interpretation Act, Cap 192, LFN (now Cap I 23 LFN 2004) as amended by Decree No. 1 of 1998. Note that section 318(4) of the 1999 Constitution provides that the Interpretation Act shall apply for the purposes of interpreting the provisions of the Constitution.

[303]   Section 15(1) of the Petroleum Act.

up to that distance". UNCLOS clearly defines the continental shelf of a coastal State with precision and makes no reference to the exploitability test as does the Petroleum Act. UNCLOS however has provisions regarding the exploitation of natural resources in the continental shelf. Article 77 provides in this regard that the coastal State exercises over the continental shelf sovereign rights for the purpose of exploring and exploiting its natural resources, and these rights are exclusive in the sense that where the coastal State does not explore or exploit the natural resources, no one may undertake these activities without the express consent of the coastal State.

The Exclusive Economic Zone (EEZ) is defined in Article 55 of the 1982 Convention as meaning: '... an area beyond and adjacent to the territorial sea, subject to the specific legal regime established in this part, under which the rights and jurisdiction of the coastal State and the rights and freedom of other states are governed by the relevant provisions of this Convention.' And by Article 57,[304] the zone shall not extend beyond 200 nautical miles from the baselines from which the breath of the territorial sea is measured.

In the same vein, the Exclusive Economic Zone (EEZ) Act 1978 which has been integrated into section 44(3) of the 1999 Constitution of Nigeria provides in section 2(1) that:

> "Without prejudice to the Territorial Waters Act, the Petroleum Act or the Sea Fisheries Act, sovereign and exclusive right with respect to the exploration and exploitation of the natural resources of the seabed, subsoil and superadjacent water of the Exclusive Zone shall vest in the Federal Republic of Nigeria and such rights shall be exercisable by the Federal Government or by such Minister or Agency as the Government may from time to time designate in that behalf either generally or in any special case."

The offshore resources of the continental shelf were also legislated upon by the Federal Government in 1971 by the Offshore Oil Revenue Decree.[305] As noted by Ayodele-Akaakar, the Federal Government's assumption of ownership of oil reached its zenith with the promulgation of the Offshore Oil Revenue Decree in 1971 in that the law abrogated the rights of the Regions (States) in the minerals in their continental shelves and vested the title to the territorial waters, continental shelf as well as royalties, rents and other revenues derived from petroleum operations in the Federal Government.[306] Ako, however, argues

---

[304] This is specific in section 1(1) of the Exclusive Economic Zone (EEZ) Act Cap 116 LFN 1990 (Cap E17 LFN 2004).
[305] Cap 428 LFN 1990.
[306] F.O. Ayodele-Akaakar, *Appraising the Oil & Gas Laws: A Search for Enduring Legislation for the Niger Delta Region*, at www.jsd-africa.com/Jsda/Fallwinter2001/articlespdf [accessed 23 November 2009]. See generally the decision of the Supreme Court of Nigeria in *Attorney General of the Federation v. Attorney General of Abia State and 35 others* 10 NSCQR 163.

that it is the Land Use Act which transferred ownership of land to the Federal
Government in 1978 that vested absolute ownership and control of oil resources
in the Federal Government.[307] He contends that before the coming into being of
that Act, even though the ownership of the oil resides in the Federal Government,
the communities owned the land, beneath which the resource was situated and
so had to be consulted before oil operations began on the land.[308] Upon the
commencement of the Act, communities no longer had the right to question the
entry of an oil company for oil operations as same became vested solely on the
federal government.

It can be seen from the above that the deprivation of the oil-producing
communities of Niger Delta of their property rights in crude and other hydrocarbons can be traced back to the period of colonial administration. By virtue of
these laws, the communities and individuals in the oil-producing communities
on or under whose parcels of land minerals are found, are accordingly denied
assertion of any right to such minerals. The result however is the clamour for
resource control by the respective oil-producing States. Thus, while the Niger
Delta people are desirous of owning and controlling the natural resources in their
region, it is beyond doubt from the above statutory and constitutional provisions
that the ownership of oil in Nigeria lies absolutely in the Federal Government.

2.4 LAND OWNERSHIP IN NIGERIA AND THE LAND USE ACT (LUA)

The importance of land for oil operations cannot be overemphasized. It is needed
by the oil multinational companies for most of their oil operations, beginning
from exploration through production to transportation of crude oil by pipeline.
This informs the content of the Land Use Decree of 1978, a decree that 'vested sole
ownership of all lands where oil is explored, transported and stored in the State'.[309]
Prior to the promulgation of the Land Use Act in 1978,[310] Nigeria operated a plural
land tenure system. In the Southern States of Nigeria, there were in existence two
systems of land tenure, namely: customary land tenure system (this varied from
community to community, which variations may not be unconnected with the
'unique historical development of each political grouping and the consequent
variation of legal and institutional structures in different polities',[311] though some

---

[307] Rhuks T. Ako, Nigeria's Land Use Act: An Anti-Thesis to Environmental Justice, 53 (2) *Journal of African Law*, 296–297 (2009).

[308] Rhuks T. Ako, *Ibid*, p.297.

[309] Daniel A. Omoweh (2005), *Shell Petroleum Development Company, the State and Underdevelopment of Nigeria's Niger Delta: A Study in Environmental Degradation*, Africa World Press, Inc., Trenton, NJ and Asmara, Eritrea, p.115.

[310] Cap. 202 LFN 1990, now Cap. L5 LFN 2004.

[311] Kwamena Bentsi-Enchill, "Do African Systems of Land Tenure Require a Special Terminology?", in Gordon R. Woodman and A.O. Obilade (eds) (1995), *African Law and Legal*

common legal principles existed) and land tenure under the received English law, otherwise known as the statutory land tenure system. In the Northern States however, there was in place a system of public ownership of land under a colonial statute (Land and Native Rights Ordinance 1910) and this was retained and reenacted after Independence in 1960.[312] We shall however focus our attention on customary land tenure in the Southern States where the indigenous peoples of the Niger Delta are located.

Land holding under the customary land tenure was based on customary laws and premised on common ownership. What the individuals have is only the right of usufruct.[313] The basic legal principle of customary land tenure was stated by the Privy Council in *Amodu Tijani v. Secretary, Southern Nigeria*[314] in this way:

> *"The next fact which it is important to bear in mind in order to understand the native law is that the notion of individual ownership is quite foreign to native ideas. Land belongs to the community, the village or the family, never to the individual. All the members of the community, the village or family have an equal right to the land, but in every case the Chief or Headman of the community or village, or a head of a family, has charge of the land, and in a loose mode of speech is sometimes called the owner. He is to some extent in the position of a trustee, and as such holds the land for the use of the community or family. He has control of it, and any member who wants a piece of it to cultivate or build upon, goes to him for it. But the land still remains the property of the community or family. He cannot make any important disposition of the land without consulting the elders of the community or family, and their consent must in all cases be given before a grant can be made to a stranger."*[315]

Notwithstanding the various criticisms[316] of this statement, there appears to be agreement that the traditional basis of customary land tenure is "common ownership" (in fee simple/absolute title), whether it is within a family or a

---

Theory, Dartmouth Publishing Co. Ltd., England, p.266. Notwithstanding these variations, there are certain uniformities or common legal principles inherent in these systems.

[312] Land Tenure Law 1962. The Land and Native Rights Proclamation 1910 in the North declared all land in the Northern Nigeria as native land, and all the rights exercisable in respect of native lands were subject to the control and disposition of the Colonial Governor- Section 4. The lands were held and administered for the use and common benefit of the natives only and no valid title could be created without the Governor's consent. According to Olayide Adigun, "An Egalitarian Land Policy for Nigeria", in J.A. Omotola (ed) (1991), *Issues in Nigerian Law*, Faculty of Law, University of Lagos Publication, p.123, the land tenure law can in some sense be described as the precursor of the Land Use Act, because it was the Land Tenure Law that first introduced the concept of the right of occupancy. See Kaniye Ebeku, Oil and the Niger Delta People: The Injustice of the Land Use Act, *Law and Politics in Africa, Asia and Latin America*, Verfassung und Recht in Übersee (VRÜ) 35, pp.208–209 (2002).

[313] This is the legal right to use and derive profit or benefit from a property that belongs to another person, as long as the property is not damaged. The usufructuary is conferred with the full right to use the property but cannot dispose of the property nor can it be destroyed.

[314] (1921) A.C. 339.

[315] *Ibid* at p.404.

[316] For example, A.A. Utuama (1989), in *Nigerian Law of Real Property*, Shaneson, Ibadan, p. 6 contends that in as much as the statement denies the existence of individual ownership of land,

community.[317] Another important feature of customary land tenure is the power
of control and management vested in the Chief or Headman of the community
or village, or the head of a family, to allocate family land to any member in need
of it, and the power to share any money realized from sale, rent or compensation
for the land among all the members of the family or within the community as the
case may be. This was the position before the enactment of the LUA in 1978 and
was well respected by all members of the community including the Government.
The result with respect to oil operations was that 'although oil was vested in
the State and the oil-bearing/landowning communities/villages or families did
not participate in granting concessions to the oil prospecting and production
companies, the companies could only enter the affected land after reaching an
agreement with the land owning communities/villages or families on (i) the
amount of compensation to be paid to them for any damage to the surface rights
and (ii) compensation as an annual rent for the use of the land in its natural state
or other corporeal hereditament'.[318]

Another important issue for consideration is whether the English principle of
quicquid plantatur solo solo cedit is a rule of customary law. Literally, the maxim
connotes that whatever is affixed to the soil belongs to the soil. In other words,
buildings, trees, minerals and other fixtures on the land form part of the land and
so belong to the owner of the land. There is a conflict of both academic and judicial
opinions on this.[319] Even though it appears settled under the customary law that
the owner of land owns anything that is affixed to the land without expenditure of
labour, in accord with the legal maxim, this is only a presumption of law and will
hold good only in the absence of agreements to the contrary. As a presumption,
its application in Nigeria has been limited by law – both statutory and judicial
decisions.[320] This implies that no one is allowed, including the indigenous peoples

---

it is incorrect. T.O. Elias, in *Nigerian Land Law*, 4th ed., Sweet & Maxwell, London, 1971 at p.74
argues that the basis of customary ownership is the family, and not the community.

[317] Kaniye Ebeku, Oil and the Niger Delta People: The Injustice of the Land Use Act, *op. cit.*, p.210.

[318] Kaniye Ebeku (2006), *Oil and the Niger Delta in International Law. Resource Rights,
Environmental and Equity Issues, op. cit.*, p.84.

[319] For example, G. Coker (1966), in *Family Property Among the Yorubas*, Sweet & Maxwell,
London, pp.45–46 is of the view that the principle applies under the Yoruba Native Law and
Custom. According to him: 'Land is by far the simplest object of property in any system of
jurisprudence. In this connection also, land in any application of the term includes buildings
thereon. The maxim *quicquid plantatur solo solo cedit*, which is a maxim of most legal systems,
is also a part of Yoruba native law and custom.' However, B.O. Nwabueze (1982), in *Nigerian
Land Law*, Nwamife Publishers, Enugu, p. 10 opined that '... it must not be supposed, however,
that the maxim *quicquid plantatur solo solo cedit*, applies inflexibly in all situations. Its application in any particular case depends first upon the circumstances of that case, such as the
nature of the object which it is claimed has become part of the soil by attachment thereto, and
secondly upon any statutory enactments modifying the operation of the maxim'.

[320] The Interpretation Act, 1978 provides that though the rule in *quicquid plantatur solo solo cedit*
is applicable in the State, it does not include minerals. The Minerals Act, Cap. 226, LFN 1990
(repealed by Mineral and Mining Act Cap. M12 LFN 2004) provides that the property and
control of all mineral oil, in, under or upon any land in Nigeria, and of all rivers, streams,
and water courses throughout Nigeria is vested as far as the nation is concerned, in the

of Niger Delta to extract, or remove any minerals from any land in Nigeria without the consent and permission of the Federal Government of Nigeria, being the absolute owner of all the minerals found in any soil in Nigeria by virtue of the various laws discussed above.

2.4.1 THE LAND USE ACT AND THE NIGER DELTA PEOPLE

The Land Use Act 1978 is the major statute regulating the administration of land in Nigeria and it was promulgated into law on 29 March 1978. This law was not only revolutionary but equally meant to reassert and preserve the right of all Nigerians to the land of Nigeria. Considering the preamble to the Act, it is obvious that the Land Use Act was aimed at providing a uniform land tenure system in Nigeria, making land easily and cheaply available to the Government and people of Nigeria, and to check 'the scramble and battle over land and the uncertainty surrounding security of and title to land'[321] in Nigeria.

Although, the Federal Military Government inaugurated the Land Use Panel to review Nigeria's land tenure system and make appropriate recommendations for reform, it accepted the recommendation of the minority report which recommended the nationalization of land, and jettisoned the majority report which had advised against nationalization or the extension of the Northern State's land tenure system to the entire country. Based on the recommendation of the minority, the Federal Military Government promulgated the Land Use Decree No. 6 of 1978, which in effect extended the land tenure law as obtained in the Northern part to the whole country. Indeed, section 4 of the LUA provides that the provisions of the Land Tenure Law shall continue to have effect with such modifications as would bring it into conformity with the LUA and its general intendment. Ako[322] notes that the inference that may be drawn from the conduct of the Government in adopting the minority report is that the control of oil resources was to be the absolute and exclusive preserve of the Federal Government (under the control of the major ethnic groups) and so to 'obviate "minority" agitation over any form of ownership or participatory rights'.

State. However, section 5(1) of the Minerals Act provides that: 'Nothing in this Act contained shall be deemed to prevent any citizen of Nigeria from winning, subject to such conditions as may be prescribed, iron ore, salt, soda, potash, or galena from lands (other than lands within the area of mining lease or mining right) from which it has been since before the material date the custom of members of the community to which he belongs to win the same.' See also section 7 (1) of the Minerals and Mining Decree 1999. These accords recognition to the customary rights of the landowners in the community to the minerals found on the land. See Kekong Besong, *op. cit.*, p.75.

[321] I.A. Umezulike, Does the Land Use Act Expropriate?, 5 *J.P.P.L.* pp.61–69 (1986).

[322] Rhuks T. Ako, Nigeria's Land Use Act: An Anti-Thesis to Environmental Justice, *op. cit.*, p.295.

Since the promulgation of the Act, a lot of controversies have been generated in the real property law in Nigeria. President Olusegun Obasanjo (under whose Military Administration, the Act was Promulgated) referred to the Land Use Act 1978 as a controversial law.[323] Similarly, Hon. Justice Augustine Nnamani (of blessed memory) stated that: "No legislation promulgated in this country has elicited so much controversy, so much criticism, so much divergence in the interpretation of its provisions, and so much discourse in academic and business/finance circles as "the Land Use Act".[324] While so many scholarly works have been written on the reformative impacts of the LUA, not so much work has been done on the impact of the LUA on the people in the oil-producing areas of Niger Delta. This study will now investigate and expansively examine the impact of the Nigeria's LUA on the Niger Delta people.

Section 1 of the LUA makes no secret of its intention and purpose. It vests "all land comprised in the territory of each State in the Federation…in the Governor of that State and such land shall be held in trust and administered for the use and common benefit of all Nigerians in accordance with the provisions of the Act". The general effect of this provision is the transferring of ownership of land from the communities to State Governments with the citizens given 'a right of occupancy' in which the interest may not be more than a lease. This is confirmed by the decision of the Supreme Court of Nigeria in *Abioye v. Yakubu*[325] where the court held that the effects of the Act with regards to land ownership included:

> "(1) the removal of the radical title in land from individual Nigerians, families, and communities and vesting the same in the Governor of each State of the Federation in trust for the use and benefit of all Nigerians (leaving individuals, etc, with 'rights of occupancy'); and
>
> (2) removal of the control and management of lands from family and community heads/chiefs and vesting the same in the Governors of each State of the federation (in the case of urban lands) and in the appropriate Local Government (in the case of rural lands)".

As regards its effects on the Niger Delta people, the Act expropriates the land in the region for oil exploitation to take place thus denying the people access to

---

[323] "Vanguard" of September 26, 2001. Ajomo, in "Ownership of Mineral Oils and the Land Use Act," *Nigerian Current Law Review* p. 330 (1982) says: 'From the view point of pure jurisprudence, it is easy to condemn it (i.e., the Act) as a piece of legislation which has not been rooted in the national consciousness of the Nigerian people which as a result would die a natural death'. Ben Epega, in "The Question Mark on the Nigeria's Land Law Reform", *Daily Times*, 17 May 1982, p.17, however, finds nothing amiss with the Act. He contends that the Act represents 'a hallmark of civilization'. In *Nkwocha v. Governor of Anambra State* (1984) 6 SC 362 at 363, Irikefe JSC (as he then was) observed that: 'The Land Use Decree is indisputably the most impactful of all legislations touching upon the land tenure system of this country before and after nationhood'.

[324] Hon. Justice Nnamani, The Land Use Act – 11 years After, May 1989 *GRBPL* 3.

[325] (1991) 5 NWLR (pt. 190) 130 at 223, per Obaseki JSC.

their land. Of note is section 28 of the Act, which provides that the Governor can revoke a right of occupancy for "overriding public interests", which is defined to include the 'requirement of the land for mining purposes or oil pipelines or for any purpose connected therewith'. Udombana notes that the LUA's definition of the phrase 'overriding public interests' is so broad that it renders the constitutional guarantee of proprietary rights useless or, at best, redundant,[326] and this 'gives the Governor unchecked power that could be, and often is abused.'[327] This implies that the Niger Delta people may be deprived of their land at will by the Government for oil exploration or mining purposes by private or public oil companies at little or no cost. Apart from the loss of means of economic sustenance, forced eviction is capable of causing psychological and emotional trauma and the break up of families. Explaining the excruciating effect of the Act, Daniel Omoweh[328] states: 'To the State ..., the inhabitants of the oil-bearing areas are no less than mere squatters in their own ancestral homes and this explains why they are denied or even entirely stripped of rights to protest against environmental pollution', sue the oil TNCs for trespass, claim for damages done to their land and ask for compensation for crops.

As just indicated, the Act deprives the inhabitants of the region the right to be adequately compensated. For example, section 29(2) of the Act provides that where land is revoked by the Governor for oil operations, the Minerals Act or the Petroleum Act or any superseding legislation shall apply. Section 77 of the Minerals Act states that any person prospecting or mining shall pay to the "holder or occupier" of private land such sums as may be a fair and reasonable compensation for any disturbance of the surface rights of that owner or occupier and for any damage done to the surface of the land upon which his prospecting or mining is being or has been carried on; and shall compensate the owner for any crops, economic trees, buildings or works damaged, removed or destroyed by him or by his agent or servant. This means that the *future* economic benefit of trees or property at the time of the revocation and the inherent value of the land itself and its expected economic yield are excluded from the calculation.[329] Also, 29(3) of the

---

[326]   Nsogurua Udombana, "Weighed in the Balances and Found Wanting: Nigeria's Land Use Act and Human Rights", in I.O. Smith (ed) (2003), *The Land Use Act- Twenty Five Years After*, published by Department of Private and Property Law, University of Lagos, p.80.

[327]   *Ibid*. Indeed, the Act has now given a blanket licence to Government officials, the rich, the multinationals and corrupt politicians to acquire a large mass of land in the region under the guise of farming, to the detriment of the original landholders. Lands are revoked by the Governor on the fraudulent ground of 'public purposes' and reallocated to their cronies. The rich now speculate for land in the region, purchase same and then lease or resell to the oil companies thereby depriving the local people from being involved in the management of the land in the region. Apart from the economic deprivation in the form of rent and participation in decision-making process on land use and compensation, this unholy conduct further deepens poverty in the region. See Rhuks T. Ako, Nigeria's Land Use Act: An Anti-Thesis to Environmental Justice, *op. cit.*, p.297.

[328]   Daniel A. Omoweh, *Oil Exploration and Production in Nigeria: A Theoretical Overview, op. cit.*, p.36.

[329]   Rhuks T. Ako, Nigeria's Land Use Act: An Anti-Thesis to Environmental Justice, *op. cit.*, p.298.

LUA,[330] which relates to revocation of a statutory or customary right of occupancy for overriding public interest, implies that the State Governor has the discretion to determine who receives the money and/or its utilization. Worst still, evidence indicates that Governors now cite this provision to receive such compensation for land compulsorily acquired under the Act (presumably, on behalf of the State).[331]

Prior to 1978, the oil companies had to approach the oil-producing communities for access to the land, by either purchasing the plot of land or to paying annual rent for the use of the land. This was in addition to the payment of compensation for any alteration to the land in form of damaged crops or buildings destroyed. Aside from the direct economic benefit, the communities felt a sense of participation in oil operations and were happy that their rights were being respected in matters that affected them. But after 1978, the compensation paid by the oil companies for damage done to land during oil exploration is for improvements to the said land,[332] and the oil companies rarely consult the oil communities for access to their land before the commencement of oil operations. The oil companies often defend their actions by claiming to be acting in compliance with the laws in place, such as the LUA. For instance, Shell claimed that: 'As a responsible Nigerian company SPDC obeys the laws of the country, one of which is the Land Use Decree of 1978 which vests ownership of all land with the Government ... Today we pay compensation for the surface rights of all land acquired for our use and for damage ... from subsequent activity, including oil spills ...'[333] The communities however, who had before the LUA been in control of the land, find it difficult to come to terms with the Act that caused a sudden loss of their land rights. Farmers are displaced from 'the soil they have been using for so many years and all of these losses are not adequately addressed by either the compensation paid or the system of paying compensation'.[334] The result is that the people have become antagonistic to the oil companies and the Government.

Furthermore, the powers of management and control of land which was pre-1978 entrusted in the traditional authorities (elders) to allocate land to members of the family/strangers have been eroded by the Act. Also eroded by

---

[330]   Section 29(3) provides that: 'If the holder entitled to compensation under this section is a community the Governor may direct that any compensation payable to it shall be paid – (1) to the community; or (2) to the chief or leader of the community to be disposed of by him for the benefit of the community in accordance with the applicable customary law; or (3) into some fund specified by the Governor for the purpose of being applied for the benefit of the community.

[331]   Kaniye Ebeku (2006), *Oil and the Niger Delta in International Law. Resource Rights, Environmental and Equity Issues, op. cit.*, p.94. See also Rhuks Ako, Nigeria's Land Use Act: An Anti-Thesis to Environmental Justice, *op. cit.*, p.298.

[332]   Jedrzej George Frynas, Corporate and State Responses to Anti-Oil Protests in the Niger Delta, *African Affairs* 100, p.31 (2001); See also Kenneth Omeje, The Rentier State: Oil-Related Legislation and Conflict in the Niger Delta, Nigeria, *Conflict, Security and Development*, 6(2) 211–230 at 220–224 (2006).

[333]   Quoted in Kaniye Ebeku, Oil and the Niger Delta People: The Injustice of the Land Use Act, *op. cit.*, p.225.

[334]   Constitutional Rights Project (CRP) (1999), *Land, Oil and Human Rights in Nigeria's Delta Region*, CRP, Lagos, p.16.

the Act is the power given to the traditional authorities to give consent to oil companies concerning damages in respect of compensation for damages and for use of the family land. It is worth emphasising that traditional rulers play a major role in the administration of justice in land matters, particularly in the Southern Nigeria, where land is very sensitive. They help to mediate in matters between individuals, families and oil companies. This is also true with the people of the Niger Delta. With the loss of authority of the traditional rulers following the LUA, coupled with the loss of faith in the regular courts due to a number of factors,[335] young people forcibly took over the struggle, and with some element of criminality in the form of kidnapping, pipeline vandalism, shutting down of flow-stations, riots, hostage-taking, killing, maiming and with other violence that now characterizes the region. As pointed out by Ebeku,[336] violent actions and social disharmony have become rife in the Niger Delta as a result of the inability of the traditional authorities to effectively manage complaints owing to loss of their rights and powers (a direct result of the loss of their land rights). Also, in a monstrous demonstration of repressive power, the LUA provides in section 47(2) that "no court shall have jurisdiction to inquire into any question concerning or pertaining to the amount or adequacy of any compensation paid or to be paid under this Act"; moreover, any dispute between the occupier or holder and the Government regarding the amount of compensation payable is to be finally determined by the Land Use and Allocation Committee,[337] whose members are appointed by the State Governors. Happily enough, the courts have consistently held that the ouster clause in section 47 of the LUA, in so far as it conflicts with the provisions of the Constitution is void.[338]

Indeed, the LUA has failed to secure the human security of Nigerians, particularly the oil-producing community and without security – food, shelter, and clothing – there can be no freedom. Men in need are not free men.[339] This idea is well captured by Isaiah Berlin when he said that "[Men] who live in conditions where there is no sufficient food, warmth, shelter, and the minimum degree of scarcity can scarcely be expected to concern themselves with freedom of contract or of the press".[340] This is the situation that the LUA has foisted on the people in the

---

[335] These factors include poverty, slow judicial process, unwholesome attitude of the judiciary in environmental matters, lack of access to justice and the formidable power of the MNCs.

[336] Kaniye Ebeku, Oil and the Niger Delta People: The Injustice of the Land Use Act, *op. cit.*, p.219.

[337] Sections 30 and 47 LUA.

[338] See *Kanada v. Kaduna State & Anor* (1986) 4 NWLR (pt 38) 361; In *Lemboye v. Ogunseyi* (1990) 6 NWLR (pt. 155) 210 at 224–225, the court held that "Sections ... 47 of the Land Use Act 1978 do not ... have the same legislative force as section 236 of the Constitution mainly because the Act is an existing law and therefore to the extent that those sections ... are inconsistent with sections 1, 4(2) and (8) and 6 of the Constitution they are void or incapable of overriding the said section 236".

[339] Nsongurua J. Udombana, "Weighed in the Balances and Found Wanting: Nigeria's Land Use Act, and Human Rights", *op. cit.*, p.66.

[340] Isaiah Berlin, Four Essays on Liberty XIII (1969). Little wonder Kenneth Omeje (2006), in *High Stakes and Stakeholders: Oil Conflict and Security in Nigeria*, Ashgate Publishing Ltd.,

oil-producing areas, as it snatched from individuals in the community, families and the communities their inalienable right to property and source of livelihood and turned them into beggars and squatters in their ancestral homes. The result is that there is discontent against what the people regard as injustice as can be seen from the various protest and demands by ethno-nationalist community groups and social movements in the Niger Delta region for resource control. The Ogoni Bill of Rights (1990) and the Kaiama Declaration of 11 December 1998 are worthy of note here. As part of the measures to put an end to the exploitation of their ancestral lands and resources by extractive industries with deleterious impacts on their human rights and environment, over 5,000 youths drawn from about 40 clans of the Ijaw ethnic nationality in the Niger Delta declared as follows:

> *"All lands and natural resources (including mineral resources) within the Ijaw territory belong to the Ijaw communities and are the basis of our survival ... We cease to recognize all undemocratic decrees that rob our peoples/communities of the right to ownership and control of our lives and resources, which were enacted without our participation and consent. These include the Land Use Decree and the Petroleum Decree ..."*[341]

The conclusion that can be drawn from the above is that these legislations [Petroleum Act of 1969, Offshore Revenue Act of 1971, Petroleum Control Act of 1967, Exclusive Economic Zone Act of 1978, and the Land Use Act of 1978] have not only given absolute control over oil resources to the Federal Government, but have also 'excluded the communities from participation in agreements with multinational oil companies, thereby denying them any share in the royalties paid by the companies or the opportunity to negotiate other terms and conditions of oil exploration and production including employment and other social benefits for members of the communities, environmental impact assessments, and compensation for environmental degradation and other hazards'.[342] In spite of the fact that they bear the direct brunt of the environmental hazards of oil exploration on their ancestral lands, the only benefit they can lay claim to is the meager compensation they receive from the oil companies for surface rents.

England, p.47 described the LUA as the 'most dramatic of the barrage of pro-oil statutes' ... 'which technically facilitates the acquisition/use of land for oil activities'.

[341] The Kaiama Declaration, Communiqué of the All Ijaw Youths Conference held 11 December, 1998, quoted in Patterson Ogon, *Land and Forest Resource Use in the Niger Delta: Issues in Regulation and Sustainable Management*, at www.globetrotter.berkeley.edu/GreenGovernance/papers/ogon2006.pdf. [accessed 18 May 2009].

[342] Eghosa E. Osaghae, Social Movements and Rights Claims: The Case of Action Groups in the Niger Delta of Nigeria, 19 *Voluntas*, 189–210 at 201 (2008).

2.5 REVENUE ALLOCATION AND RESOURCE CONTROL

The concept of revenue allocation and resource control, which has attracted the attention of scholars, politicians and statesmen over the years in Nigeria can be best appreciated and understood in a federal structure where great emphasis is placed on fiscal federalism. Federalism has been described to be an arrangement whereby powers within a multi-national country are shared between a federal or central authority, and a number of regionalized Governments in such a way that each unit, including the central authority, exists as a Government separately and independently from the others, operating directly on persons and property within its territorial area, with a will of its own and its own apparatus for the conduct of affairs and with an authority in some matters exclusive of all others.[343] Each level of government (Federal and State Governments) enjoys autonomy in the sense of being able to exercise its own will regarding the conduct of its own affairs. As opined by K.C Wheare, "… the fundamental and distinguishing characteristic of a federal system is that neither the central nor the regional governments are subordinate to each other, but rather, the two are co-ordinate and independent".[344]

Fiscal federalism is actually the existence in one country of more than one level of government, each with different expenditure, responsibilities and taxing powers. The fiscal structure relates to the disposition of the powers to raise revenue and to incur expenditure between tiers of authorities.[345] It deals with the division of functions and resources among the tiers of government in a Federation. Fiscal federalism has its peculiar problems. One very important problem is the strong probability of a mis-match between the functions assigned to a tier or unit of government and its revenue, and it is this divergence between assigned functions and resources that renders revenue allocation an unsettled and acrimonious exercise.[346] Thus, in any Federal system, the autonomy, authority, financial self-sufficiency, independence and self-determination of these levels of Government must be unequivocally guaranteed in clear terms. No level of government should be subordinate to another. However, there must exist some degree of interdependence amongst the levels of government, most especially in revenue matters.

The practice of Federalism in Nigeria in terms of these fundamental principles has been exceedingly problematic. Ben Nwabueze has criticized the principle

---

[343]   I. E. Sagay, "Anatomy of Federalism with Special Reference to Nigeria", in Olubayo Oluduro *et al.*, (eds) (2007), *Trends in Nigeria Law: Essays in Honour of Oba DVF Olateru-Olagbegi III*, (2007) Constellation (Nig.) Publishers, Ibadan/Abuja, p.190.

[344]   Wheare, K.C. (1963), *Federal Government*, 4th ed., Oxford University Press, London.

[345]   See P.C.N. Okigbo (1965), *The Nigerian Public Finance*, Longman, London, p.3.

[346]   Uka Ezenwe, *Revenue Allocation under the 1995 Draft Constitution: Some Comments*, being a paper presented at the 32nd Annual Conference of the Nigerian Association of Law Teachers held at the Nigerian Institute of Advanced Legal Studies, University of Lagos, Lagos, 10–14 May 1994, p.1.

referred to above, and which are apparent in the 1999 Constitution of the Federal
Republic of Nigeria. In his words:

> *"The Federal system in Nigeria ... contradicts the cardinal principle of true federal-*
> *ism which requires that the arrangement should not place such a predominance*
> *of power and resources in the hands of either the national or regional government*
> *as to make it so powerful that it is able to bend the will of the other to its own. The*
> *power and resources sharing arrangement should be so weighted as to maintain a*
> *fair balance between the national and regional governments. Federalism presup-*
> *poses that the national and regional government should stand towards each other in*
> *a relation of meaningful autonomy and equality, resting upon a balanced division*
> *of powers and resources, sufficient to support the structure of a functioning govern-*
> *ment, able to stand on its own against each other. The sharing arrangement under*
> *Nigeria's federal system assigns to the Federal government powers and resources ...*
> *overwhelmingly greater than those assigned to the States, thereby depriving the lat-*
> *ter of any meaningful autonomy in relation to the Federal government ..."*[347]

This is the heart of the problem because in practice it has not always been easy to
maintain the ideal of complete equilibrium in resources and responsibilities as
between the two levels of government. What we now have in Nigeria is a tendency
towards financial centralization, and a situation where the States are financially
dependent on the Federal Government.

Two divergent motives come to the fore in terms of sharing the revenue
that accrues from resources, *viz:* the amalgamation motive and the separation
motive. These are conflicting claims that are present in fiscal federalism. The oil-
producing States are pressing for amendment of the Constitution with a view
to reviewing the ownership and control of the mineral resources of the country
and the formula for sharing its mineral wealth – this represents the separation
motive. However, those with the amalgamation motive contend that the Federal
Government owns all the minerals, which constitute national resources, and are
as it were, a gift of nature. For which reason, the entire Federation should benefit
directly and fiscally from the petroleum wealth, given its strategic position as the
mainstay of the Nigerian economy.[348] The controversies over revenue allocation
and resource control explain the need now to examine the trends in the sharing
of revenue in Nigeria.

---

[347]   Ben Nwabueze, *Reflections on the 1999 Constitution: A Unitary Constitution for a Federal*
       System of Government, being a paper delivered at a Seminar in Abuja, organized by the
       International Commission of Jurists, 4–16 February, 2000, pp.4–5.
[348]   I.A. Ayua, "Constitutional Scheme on the Sharing of Revenue Resources and its Implementation:
       An Assessment", in I.A. Ayua. *et al* (eds) (2001), *NIGERIA: Issues in the 1999 Constitution*,
       NIALS Publication, Lagos, pp.133–134.

2.5.1 REVENUE-SHARING IN HISTORICAL PERSPECTIVE

Although real fiscal unification started in the 1926/27 fiscal year when the budgetary policy of the country was centralized, this unification itself did not pose any serious problems until the constitutional reforms of Richards Constitution of 1946, which introduced regionalism with its creation of three regions (Western, Northern and Eastern). One can therefore assert that it was in the granting of some measure of administrative autonomy and responsibility to the regions that the issue of finding a suitable fiscal arrangement for the constituent units reared its ugly head.[349] Since then, various ad hoc Commissions/Decrees[350] have been set up/promulgated to work out an acceptable and equitable revenue-sharing formula for the country, and have fashioned a number of different criteria for revenue-sharing, which include derivation, need, national interest, population, equality of States, land mass and terrain, etc.

It is important to note that the criteria or principle of allocation of State revenue in Nigeria has been revised frequently, with the setting up of various Commissions in recognition of the inadequacies of the existing structure and the need to fashion out better criteria that would ensure a more equitable distribution of the country's resources. Nineteen attempts have been made in the Nigeria's history to evolve a formula acceptable to all Nigerians but without success. Since 1970, the Federal Government has always been allocating more resources to itself when compared with the ones allocated to the States and Local Governments, all in the name of maintaining the national unity of the country.[351] The problem emanated from the politicization and the mis-application of the formulae agreed

---

[349]   Peter Terkaa Akper, "Socio-Political Issues in Oil and Gas Exploitation in Political and Economic Reform in Nigeria", in I.A. Ayua *et al* (eds), *Political Reform and Economic Recovery in Nigeria, op. cit.*, pp.526–527.

[350]   These Commissions/Decrees include: Phillipson (1946) (Derivation, Even progress, Population); Hicks- Philipson (1951) (Derivation, Need, National Interest); Chick (1953) (Derivation and Fiscal Autonomy); Raisman (1958) (Need and Derivation); Binns (1964) (Basic Need and Financial Comparability); Dina (1968) (Basic Needs, Balanced Development, Derivation and Minimum National Standard); Aboyade (1977) (Equality of Access to Development opportunities, National Minimum Standards, Independent Revenue and Tax Effort, Absorptive Capacity and Fiscal Efficiency); Okigbo (1979) (Minimum Responsibility of Government, Population, Social Development and Internal Effort); Allocation of Revenue (Federation Account etc) Act Cap 1 (1982) (Equality of States, Population, Social Development represented by Primary School Enrolment and Internal Revenue Effort); National Revenue Mobilisation and Fiscal Commission (1989) (Equality of States, Population, Social Development Factor, Tax Effort and Land Mass/Terrain); Allocation of Revenue (Federation Account etc) Decree No. 106 (1992) (Equality of States, Land Mass and Terrain, Social Development Factors represented by Education, Health, Water and Derivation); Constitution Debate Co-ordinating Committee (1998) (As reflected in the 1999 Constitution – Population, Equality of States, Internal Revenue Generation, Land mass, Terrain and Population density).

[351]   A.A. Adesopo and Asaju A.S., Natural Resource Distribution, Agitation for Resource Control Right and the Practice of Federalism in Nigeria, *J. Hum. Ecol.*, 15(4), 277–289 at 284 (2004).

upon for revenue-sharing.[352] Another problem that arose from the criteria has to
do with the appropriate weight to be assigned to each of the various principles.

The most contentious of the principles is "derivation".[353] The percentage
which has been allocated on the basis of derivation has shifted from 50% to 1%,
and back today to 13% in favour of the States where the resource comes from.
For instance, under the Raisman Commission of 1958, 50% went to the region
where the minerals were extracted, 20% to the Federal Government and 30% to
the Distributive Pool Account (DPA) in which the State of origin also partook
as well as keeping personal income tax and receiving export duty proceeds on
their produce. Oil mineral exploitation was yet to commence significantly at this
period. This was the situation during the first Republic (1960–1966).

When the Military took over power in 1966, it created a twelve State structure
out of the existing four regions. There was an increase in oil revenues and most
of the oil-producing communities were in Biafra, which wanted to secede,
thereby leading to the civil war of 1967–1970. Upon the successful "liberation"
of the oil communities from Biafran control in 1969, the Nigerian Government
promulgated the Petroleum Decree (No. 51) of 1969, which vested all the lands
and resources in, under or upon the land on the Federal Military Government.
Substantial alterations were made to the system of revenue allocation by the
Federal Government between 1970 and 1979, and it greatly reduced the weight
given to derivation as a principle.

In 1970, under the Distributive Pool Account (DPA) Decree No. 13 of that
year, (backdated to 1969), the formula for the sharing of mining rents and royalties
became 50% to the DPA, 45% to the State of derivation and 5% to the Federal
Government.[354] In 1971, through Decree No. 9 of 1971, the Federal Government
made a distinction between revenue from on-shore and off-shore production
by assigning to itself 100% of off-shore revenue, further reducing the financial
strength of the oil-producing States. This was criticized by the Niger Delta people,
and they called for its abolition on the ground that it represented 'yet another
clever political device to deprive the oil-producing States of additional revenue'.[355]
Persuaded by their arguments, the Political Bureau of 1987 recommended that
the dichotomy between onshore and offshore in the allocation of revenue be

---

[352] Pius Okigbo manuscript, "Notes on Revenue Generation and Distribution in a Federation",
(Unpublished Manuscript).

[353] The point or origin from which something comes. Derivation is a long-standing principle
of revenue allocation in Nigeria and it requires that a significant proportion of the revenues
derived from a community or an area should be returned to that community.

[354] I.A. Ayua, "Constitutional Scheme on the Sharing of Revenue Resources and its Implementation:
An Assessment," *op. cit.*, pp.137–138; See also John Boye Ejobowah, Who Owns the Oil? The
Politics of Ethnicity in the Niger Delta of Nigeria, *Africa Today*, Vol. 47, No. 1, pp.28–47 at 35
(2000). In 1975, the Military government promulgated the Constitution Decree No. 6 of 1975
increasing the share of oil revenue going to the DPA to 80% and slashing to 20% the share that
went to the States of derivation.

[355] See Report of the Political Bureau (1987:170), para. 10.012.

abolished. This was accepted by the Federal Government, and it was abolished by the Federation Account (Amendment) Decree 1992[356], which provides that:

> *"For the avoidance of doubt, the distinction hitherto made between the on-shore oil and offshore oil mineral revenue for the purpose of revenue sharing and the administration of the fund for the development of the oil producing areas is hereby abolished."*

In 1980, the Okigbo Commission was set up, and it recommended the abolition of derivation principle. This recommendation caused a lot of ripples, following which the Federal Government was taken to the court.[357] A new revenue allocation arrangement was later passed into law under the Revenue Allocation Act No. 1 of 1982[358], which came into force on 22 January 1982. This gave the Federal Government 55%, States 30.5%, Local Governments 10% whilst 4.5% was given to the oil-producing States and disbursed as follows: 1% for ecological problems, 2% based on derivation principle (paid in direct proportion to the value of minerals extracted from the territory of the States concerned) and 1.5% for the development of mineral producing areas. This in effect means a drastic reduction in the derivation from 50% in 1960 to 2% in 1982. It is this Act that the Military Government amended in 1992 by Decree 106 of 1992. By the amendment, 1% of the revenue accruing to the Federation Account derived from minerals was to be shared among the mineral-producing States in proportion to the amount of mineral produced from each State whether onshore or off shore. Cap 16 (as amended by Decree 106, 1992) thus provided the formula in use for revenue allocation before the coming into force of the 1999 Constitution on 29 May 1999.

It is, however, sad to note that as mineral exploration replaced agricultural exports as the principal source of government revenue and foreign exchange earnings, successive Nigerian Governments deliberately suppressed the principle of derivation in revenue allocation. This has been 'denounced by ethnic minority elements as a politically motivated assault by the majority nationalities on the economic rights of minority communities who are perceived as too small and weak to threaten the stability of the Federation'.[359] Enahoro and two others in 1992 vividly captured the position at Independence as follows:

---

[356]   No. 106 of 1992.

[357]   See *Attorney General of Bendel State v. Attorney General of the Federation & 22 Ors* (1982) 4 NCLR 178 (known as the revenue allocation case). In this case, the Supreme Court declared the Revenue Allocation Act of 1981 (No. 1 of 1981) unconstitutional, and therefore illegal, null and void, and directed all Federal and State Government officials and functionaries to refrain from dividing or otherwise allocating Federal revenue according to the provisions of the said Act.

[358]   Cap. 16, Laws of Federation (LFN) of Nigeria 1990.

[359]   Rotimi T. Suberu (1996), *Ethnic Minority Conflicts and Governance in Nigeria*, Spectrum Books Ltd., Ibadan, p.29. In the words of Saro-Wiwa, 'if the oil had been in any of the majority areas, in Hausa/Fulani country or Yoruba country, the (federal government) would never have seized (sic) the royalties'. Interview in Tell, 8 February 1993, p.31. This claim is supported by

*"At the attainment of independence in 1960, derivation as the basis of revenue allo-
cation gave the State of origin 50% and the Federal Government 50%. This had been
whittled down under successive administrations until the figures are now 3% to the
State of origin and 97% to the Federal Government".*[360]

The Ijaw Youth, in their Kaiama Declaration of 1998, also made a similar statement
on revenue allocation and the principle of derivation when they said:

*"... The principle of derivation in Revenue Allocation has been consciously and
systematically obliterated by successive regimes of the Nigerian State. We note the
drastic reduction of the Derivation Principle from 100 percent in (1953), 50 percent
(1960), 45 percent (1970), 20 percent (1975), 2 percent in (1980), 1.5 percent (1982)
and 3 percent (1992) to date."*[361]

2.5.2 DISTRIBUTION OF REVENUE RESOURCES UNDER THE 1999 CONSTITUTION

The allocation of revenue between the Federal Government, the States and Local
Government Councils under the 1999 Constitution can be found in sections
162–168 as well as in items A and D of paragraph II in the Second Schedule.
Section 162 makes provision for how public revenue will be shared vertically

---

the fact that when the revenues to Nigeria were from commodities such as cocoa, oil palm, cotton, Rubber, groundnuts which were largely from the major ethnic groups, Yoruba in the West
(cocoa), the Hausa-Fulani in the Northern region (groundnut and cotton) and Igbo Eastern
region (oil palm)), derivation was generally accepted as the basis of revenue allocation. But as
revenue from oil mainly derived from the minority ethnic group started to displace revenue
from commodities, emphasis began to shift from derivation as a principle of revenue allocation to other factors such as needs for development, population, etc which are obviously in
favour of the major ethnic groups rather than on the more reasonable superior productive
capacity of States. See Ike Oguine, Nigeria's Oil Revenues and the Oil Producing Areas, 17
J. Energy Nat. Resources L. 112, 114–115 (1999); Edlyne E. Anugwom, Oil Minorities and the
Politics of Resource Control in Nigeria, *Africa Development* Vol. XXX, No. 4, 2005, pp.87–120
at 02, 114; Ejobowah, J.B., Who Owns the Oil? The Politics of Ethnicity in the Niger Delta of
Nigeria, *op. cit.*, p.40.

[360] Enahoro Anthony and Ors (1992), "Position Paper, Movement for National Reformation." A
General Brief, Saros International Publishers, Port Harcourt, p.17. See also Okilo, where he
noted that '... there have been disheartening contradictions and inconsistencies in Nigeria, a
nation that recognized 100 per cent derivation as the basis for revenue allocation in 1950, but
reduced it to 50 per cent at independence in 1960; to 45 per cent in 1970; 20 per cent in 1975;
1.5 per cent in 1982 and 3 per cent in 1992 as crude oil, found in the Ijaw country [Niger Delta],
became the main source of national revenue' – Melford Okilo National Concord, 11 December
1992: B2, quoted in Rotimi T. Suberu, *Ibid* pp.29–30.

[361] Onosode, G., In offi's "Giving Hope a Chance", quoted in Chegwu Emeka, *Legal and
Regulatory Challenges of Resource Control*, Proceedings of the 38th Annual Conference of the
Nigerian Association of Law Teachers held at the Faculty of Law, LASU on 23–26 April 2003,
pp.247–248.

and horizontally.[362] Section 162(1) provides that: "The Federation shall maintain a special account to be called Federation Account into which shall be paid all revenues collected by the Government of the Federation except ..."

By section 162(2), the President must table before the National Assembly proposals for revenue allocation from the Federation Account upon the receipt of advice from the Revenue Mobilization Allocation and Fiscal Commission. In determining the formula for revenue allocation, the National Assembly must take into account certain principles: especially those of population, equality of States, internal revenue generation, land mass and terrain, as well as population density. The principle of derivation shall be constantly reflected, by the National Assembly, in any approved formula as being not less than thirteen per cent of the revenue accruing to the Federation Account directly from any natural resources. The thirteen per cent was arrived at by the 1995 Constitutional Conference to be set aside as derivation revenue to assist the development of oil-producing communities and to financially empower them to tackle the enormous problems of horrendous environmental degradation. This was expected to placate the people from these communities, thereby reducing the tension and agitation coming from them.

However, it must be noted that the derivation formula was inadequate to address the enormous environmental or ecological disaster involving pollution and degradation resulting from the oil and gas activities, mining of the solid minerals etc. The derivation formula is even more flawed with respect to been contrary to the tenets of true fiscal centralism which 'ensures that each unit of Government contributes to the national coffers and receives equitably in return through revenue allocation.'[363] Needless to say that the over-centralisation of fiscal policy is contrary to the tenets of Federalism 'since it emasculates the power of the sub-national governments and makes them over-dependent on the centre'[364] and this has been the lot of the indigenous peoples of the Niger Delta region. The derivation principle first appeared under the 1960 Independence Constitution,[365] and was repeated in the 1963 Republic Constitution[366] wherein 50% was attached

---

[362]   Vertical allocation refers to revenue allocation among the three tiers of government and the appropriate ratio to be used for determining the relative shares of the levels of government, while horizontal allocation deals with allocation to different States at the same (horizontal) level of government and raises the question of the criteria or principles of allocation e.g. derivation, responsibility, population etc. See Bade Onimode, Resources *Derivation, Allocation, and Utilisation*, in M.A. Ajomo *et al* (eds), Constitutions and Federalism: Proceedings of the Conference on Constitutions and Federalism, held at the University of Lagos, Nigeria 23–25 April 1996, Friedrich Ebert Foundation, Lagos, 1997, p.175.

[363]   Rhuks Temitope Ako, Resource Control or Revenue Allocation: A Path to Sustainable Peace in Nigeria's Oil Producing Communities, in Ademola O. Popoola (ed) (2008), *Proceedings of the 35th and 36th Annual Conferences of the Nigerian Society of International Law 2005 & 2006*, Nigerian Society of International Law, p.189.

[364]   Edlyne E. Anugwom, Oil Minorities and the Politics of Resource Control in Nigeria, *op. cit.*, p.100.

[365]   Section 136 of 1960 Constitution.

[366]   Section 140 of 1963 Constitution.

to it in the two Constitutions. The principle suffered set backs during the periods
of military rule, and the country has continued to tinker with both the spirit
and the letter of the derivation formula and the very essence of fiscal federalism.
Fortunately, the 13% derivation principle was enshrined in the 1999 Constitution.

However, instead of paying the 13% in full, the Federal Government interpreted
this provision to mean that revenue derivable from off-shore production of oil
cannot be credited to the States to which that off-shore geographically belongs,
using the Off Shore Revenue (Registration of Grants) Act 1971.[367] On the basis
of this interpretation, the Federal Government split oil revenue into 60%: 40%
as on-shore/off shore revenue and proceeded to base payment of the minimum
13% derivation revenue from only the 60% and thus, merely paid 7.8% revenue as
derivation.[368] The oil-producing communities argued that the Constitution made
no such distinction, and that it was an attempt to subvert the spirit of the minimum
13% derivation provision in the Constitution and to immorally expropriate their
properties. It was this agitation that led to the filing of the suit by the Federal
Government against the 36 States at the Supreme Court[369] for a determination of
the seaward boundary of the littoral States within the Federal Republic of Nigeria
for the purpose of calculating the amount of revenue accruing to the Federation
Account, directly from any natural resources derived from those States pursuant
to section 162(2) of the 1999 Constitution.

The action of the Federal Government immediately escalated the issue of
resource control as it became a major constitutional issue, which resulted in
political confrontation between the Federal Government and the Southern
Governors where the resources were obtained. The littoral defendant States relied
on the revenue allocation provisions in previous Constitutions and Decrees,
particularly the Allocation of Revenue (Federation Account etc) (Amendment)
Decree No. 106 of 1992, which expressly provided that in the application of its
provisions, the dichotomy of on-shore/off-shore oil production and mineral oil/
non-mineral oil revenue was abolished. They relied on this provision to assail
the Federal Government's claim, which they saw as a reintroduction of that
dichotomy. Justice Ogundare JSC in his lead judgment stated that:

> "With the introduction of federalism in Nigeria, our Constitutions made provision
> for revenue allocation among the component units of the federation. For instance,
> in the 1960 Constitution that ushered in independence, elaborate provisions were
> made in sections 130–139 for revenue allocation. Of particular importance is section
> 134. Except for the percentage payable, subsection (1) appeared to be on all fours
> with the proviso to subsection (2) of section162 of the 1999 Constitution for both are
> based on the principle of derivation. There is however, no provision in section 162

---

[367]   Cap 366 LFN 1990.
[368]   David Edevbie, *The Politics of 13 Percent Derivation Principle*, at www.waado.org/Environment/
         FedGovt-NigerDelta/RevenueAllocation/13Percent/Allocation.htm [accessed 3 March 2010].
[369]   *A.G Federation v. A.G Abia State* (2002) FWLR (pt. 102) 1.

or anywhere else in the 1999 Constitution similar to subsection (6) which made it possible for revenue derived from the continental shelf contiguous to a Region to be payable to that Region … It is the absence in the 1999 Constitution of a provision similar to subsection (6) of section 134 of the 1960 Constitution that has given rise to the dispute resulting in this case. I do not, however, see section 134 (6) as stopping the plaintiff from contending that the continental shelf is not part of the territory of a State contiguous to it."[370]

The court held that the seaward boundary of a littoral State within the Federal Republic of Nigeria, for the purpose of calculating the amount of revenue accruing to the Federation Account directly from any natural resources derived from that State pursuant to section 162(2) of the 1999 Constitution of the Federal Republic Nigeria, is the low-water mark of the land surface thereof, and so, the littoral defendants were not entitled to a share in the revenue accruing to the Federation Account from natural resources derivable from the continental shelf of Nigeria. Having regard to the negative impacts of oil exploration on the people of Niger Delta, it is obvious that the 13% derivation coupled with the Supreme Court decision on dichotomy between onshore and offshore will only exacerbate the already existing equality gap between the majority ethnic groups and the indigenous peoples of Niger Delta.

As expected, the oil-producing communities were not happy with the decision of the Supreme Court, particularly on the on-shore/off-shore dichotomy. In order to avert a wave of protests and conflicts that the judgment could have caused, particularly in the Niger Delta region, the Nigerian National Assembly, in what might be called a 'political settlement', passed the Offshore/Onshore Oil Dichotomy Abolition Act, which was signed into law by President Obasanjo on 20 February 2004. This new Act purports to abolish the 'onshore/offshore oil rent dichotomy by extending the payment of the 13% oil derivation revenue to part of offshore oil resources'.[371] The Act has however been subjected to fierce criticisms by commentators on several grounds such as the lack of clarity about the "200 meters depth isobaths", which according to Douglas Oronto and O.C.J. Okocha (SAN)[372] may result in the communities and the people of the Niger Delta been

---

[370] *Ibid*, pp.97–98.

[371] Kenneth Omeje, The Rentier State: Oil-Related Legislation and Conflict in the Niger Delta, Nigeria, *op. cit.*, p.226. Omeje argued that the Federal Government has shrewdly chosen the rather controversial '200 metres water depth isobath' as against the widely recognised international maritime law concepts and practices of the 'contiguous zone' (i.e. 24 nautical miles from the coast) and 'continental shelf and exclusive economic zone' (200 nautical miles from the coast) as the parameter for paying the 13% derivation revenue to littoral States under the new Act.

[372] Quoted in Emmanuel Ojameruaye, *The Offshore/Onshore Oil Dichotomy Abolition Act-Matters Arising*, available at http://nigerdeltacongress.com/oarticles/offshoreonshore_oil_dichotomy_ab.htm [accessed 3 March 2010].

the ultimate losers. Sagay captured the injustice inherent in the new Act in this
way:

> "The implication of this new Act is that ... any part of the Nigerian Continental
> Shelf, deeper than 200m, is outside the derivation zone, and proceeds of resources in
> this area of the sea will go straight to the Federation account. Coastal States derive
> nothing from this vast area ... This is a far cry from the 200 miles of the continental
> shelf of the Niger Delta States as stipulated in the founding Constitutions of Nige-
> ria and Article 7 of the 1982 Convention on the Law of the Sea. By far the most
> disturbing consequence of the coastal States' limitation to a 200m depth belt for
> derivation purposes, is that all the major off-shore oil and gas finds are now in the
> deep off-shore zone between 1,000 and 2,500m as against the 200m limitation for
> coastal States".[373]

Even though the so-called 'political settlement' yields a better result for the Niger
Delta region when compared with the Supreme Court decision, it is doubtful if it
will bring to an end the agitation for resource control and the call for a true fiscal
federalism as the agitation for resource control has assumed a wider mission than
the mere abolition of the dichotomy.

2.6   MEANING AND NATURE OF RESOURCE
CONTROL

The term "resources" is not defined in the 1999 Constitution. It includes natural
resources and money and other man-made resources capable of being acquired
through the exploitation of such natural resources.[374] The term natural resources
is defined elsewhere as:

> "Any material in its native state which when extracted has economic value ... The
> term includes not only timber, gas, oil, coal, minerals, lakes and submerged lands,
> but also, features which supply human need and contribute to the health, welfare,
> and benefit of a community, and are essential to the well-being thereof and proper
> enjoyment of property devoted to park and recreational purposes".[375]

Oil, natural gas, minerals and coal come within this definition. Resource control
therefore means the ability or capacity to authorize or direct the course of

---

[373]   Quoted in Eghosa E. Osaghae, Social Movements and Rights Claims: The Case of Action
Groups in the Niger Delta of Nigeria, *op. cit.,* pp.200–201.

[374]   E.S. Nwauche *et al., Legal and Regulatory Challenges of Resources Control in Nigeria*, being a
paper presented at the Nigerian Association of Law Teachers, Proceedings of the 38th Annual
Conference, Faculty of Law, LASU, Ojo held between 23–26 April 2003, p.215.

[375]   *Black's Law Dictionary,* 6th ed., quoted by Ogundare JSC in *Attorney General, Federation v.
Attorney General, Abia State* (2002) FWLR (pt. 102) 1 at pp.111–112.

exploitation, or the right to manage the revenue accruing from the oil exploitation or other natural resources and to enjoy its benefits. The Third Summit of the 17 Nigerian Southern States Governors in Benin, defined resource control as 'the practice of true federalism and natural law in which the federating units express their rights to primarily control the natural resources within their borders and make agreed contribution towards the maintenance of common services of the Government at the centre'.[376] Resource control in the view of Sagay connotes:

1. the power and right of a community or State to raise funds by way of tax on persons, matters, services and materials within its territory;
2. the exclusive right to the ownership and control of resources, both natural and created, within its territory;
3. the right to customs duties on goods destined for its territory and excise duties on goods manufactured in its territory.[377]

The most vital aspect of resource control, from the text of Delta State's Memorandum to the National Political Conference in 2005, is 'ownership', from which flows actual control and management of the resource.[378] Mere increase in revenue without control and management, according to them, is short-sighted.[379] Leaning on Nwokedi's phrasing of the concept, the States which demand resource control seek to "exercise their freedom to develop their natural resources in the best way they deem fit without undue Federal interference".[380] Ako on his part introduced what he termed the 'local' variant – of resource control in addition to the other broad conceptions of resource control highlighted above. To him, 'Local resource control' refers to giving the inhabitants of the Niger Delta region the opportunities to enjoy access to the environmental resources and benefits of their ancestral land.[381]

---

[376]   Quoted in Steve Azaiki (2006), *Oil, Politics and Blood: The Niger Delta Story*, Y-Books, Ibadan, p.296.

[377]   Itse Sagay, *NIGERIA: Federalism, the Constitution and Resource Control*, being the text of a speech delivered at a sensitization programme organized by the Ibori Vanguard at London Restaurant, Lagos on 19 May 2001. It is about the 'demand by the littoral States and other Southern States of Nigeria (where the nation's resources are derived) to be allowed to be controlling/managing the revenue accruing from the oil and other natural resources in line with the tenets of true federalism' – A.A. Adesopo and Asaju A.S., Natural Resource Distribution, Agitation for Resource Control Right and the Practice of Federalism in Nigeria, *op. cit.*, p.289.

[378]   We Must Breakout of Authoritarian Headmaster-Cum-Father Christmas Complex, being memorandum of Delta State to the National Political Reform Conference, Abuja in the Guardian, Wednesday, 13 April 2005, p.8.

[379]   See *Ibid.*

[380]   Ralph Chiemeka Nwokedi (2003), *Revenue Allocation and Resource Control in Nigerian Federation*, 2nd ed., Snaap Press Ltd., Enugu, 2003, p.142.

[381]   Rhuks Ako, Resource Control in the Niger Delta: Conceptual Issues and Legal Realities, *e-International Relations*, 25 May 2012, at www.e-ir.info/2012/05/25/resource-control-in-the-niger-delta-conceptual-issues-and-legal-realities/ [accessed 23 May 2013].

Resource control is a legal incidence of ownership of natural resources. Nigeria is one of the rare countries in the world that is blessed with the classes of natural resources mentioned above. What is most intriguing has been the fact that communities where some of these resources are found have never had the chance of managing or controlling those natural resources. Accordingly, the distortion of the original Federal structure, which laid emphasis on regional autonomy, power sharing and revenue allocation based on derivation, has been central to the agitation for resource control and conflicts in the Niger Delta.[382]

2.6.1 AGITATION FOR RESOURCE CONTROL IN NIGERIA

The struggle against exploitation, environmental degradation and for control of resources dates back to pre-independence Nigeria. The deportation of King Jaja of Opobo and other coastal kings was the result of the battle for the control of the coastal trade.[383] This continued till 1945 with the enactment of the Minerals Ordinance of 1946. Section 3(1) of that enactment vested in the Crown the entire property in and control of all mineral oils, on, under or upon any lands in Nigeria, and on all rivers, streams and water-courses throughout Nigeria. This provision was attacked by many nationalists as being obnoxious and draconian. Nnamdi Azikwe contended that the British Crown had no right to expropriate land which is the people's mainstay as an agrarian people, nor was it right for it to appropriate minerals in the land to itself.[384]

This hostility continued unabated through the penultimate moments of colonialism, and was inspired by the spirit of self determination, and the fear

---

[382] See Programme on Ethnic and Federal Studies (PEFS) (2004), *The Niger Delta Question: Background to Constitutional Reform*, Monograph New Series No. 8, Department of Political Science, University of Ibadan, Ibadan, pp.13, 44. Eghosa E. Osaghae, Human Rights and Ethnic Conflict Management: The Case of Nigeria, *Journal of Peace Research*, Vol. 33 No. 2, p.181 (1996), argues that 'as a system of opportunities, federalism not only guarantees that the identities and differences of the various groups will be preserved, but also that they will be able to share in the power, resources and benefits of the union', and this informs the incessant quest by the Niger Delta people for the restructuring of the country in a manner that enhances fiscal federalism and the principle of derivation.

[383] E.J. Alagoa, "The Eastern Niger Delta and the Hinterland in the 19th Century", in O. Ikime (ed), *Ground Work of Nigerian History*, Heinemann Educational Books Ltd., Ibadan, p.250; Gertzel C., Relations Between African and European Traders in the Niger Delta 1880–1896, 3 *The Journal of African History* pp.361–366 (1962); Rhuks T. Ako and Patrick Okonmah, Minority Rights Issues in Nigeria: A Theoretical Analysis of Historical and Contemporary Conflicts in the Oil-Rich Niger Delta Region, *International Journal on Minority and Group Rights* 16, pp.55–56 (2009). Victor Ukaogo, "From Injustice to Injustice: The Ethnicity of Resistance and Rebellion in the Niger Delta", in *International Conference on The Nigerian State, Oil Industry and the Niger Delta, op. cit.*, p.837. King Jaja was deposed and deported to the West Indies in 1887 as a result of his fierce opposition to British imperialism and his insistence on African independence. The same fate befell Nana of Itsekiri who resisted British attempts to extend the powers of the newly established Oil Rivers Protectorate in 1887 to cover his territory.

[384] Quoted in E.S. Uwauche, *et al, op. cit.*, p.217.

of inequity amongst the regions especially the Western and Northern regions and the numerous minorities of the South-south regions (then under the Eastern region).[385] This was the period when the minority groups in Nigeria, threatened by their fears of economic domination by the larger groups, caused the setting up of the Willink Commission to look into the fears of minorities. This Commission, which recommended the Constitutional safeguards and protections for minority interests, was the formal outcome of the agitation for resource control in Nigeria.[386] Nevertheless, the visibility and tempo of the agitation for resource control increased with the formation of the Movement for the Survival of Ogoni People (MOSOP) in August, 1990, with the November 1995 hanging of Saro-Wiwa and Eight Ogoni compatriots, the punitive expedition against the inhabitants of Odi in February, 2000, the formation of the Ijaw Youth Council in December 11, 1998 and the famous Kaiama Declaration.[387]

Since the return of Nigeria to democratic rule in 1999, all the Governors and the political leaders of the oil-producing areas, including their people, have embraced the struggle for resource control. Although each of these resource control groups differs considerably in their agendas, strategies and modes of operation, the common objective is that 'a greater percentage of the oil revenue should accrue to and be retained by the oil-producing region as opposed to the Federal Government'.[388] Commenting on the essence of this struggle, Itse Sagay emphasized that:

> "The struggle is not merely one for increased revenue from the proceeds of one's resources, but more importantly, it is a move by the people of the Niger Delta to take their destinies into their hands in order to ensure the environmental protection and restoration of the Niger Delta territory to a productive and living one, and to insist on environmentally friendly and best oil field practice in the oil and gas extraction process. It is a programme to work for the re-investment of proceeds of petroleum sales in infrastructure development, environmentally sensitive industries, and in

---

[385]   *Ibid.*

[386]   Udoma, U. (1994), *The History and the Law of the Constitution of Nigeria*, Spectrum Books Ltd., Ibadan, pp.206–207.

[387]   For example, the "Kaiama Declaration" of the Ijaw people, proclaimed on the 11th of December 1998, represented the most articulate presentation of the inhabitants of Niger Delta conception of 'resource control' and it set the tone for the present debate on the matter. Article 1 of the Declaration declares that ownership of "All land and natural resources (including mineral resources) within the Ijaw territory belong to Ijaw communities" because they are "the basis of our survival". While Article 2 insists on the peoples' and communities' "right to ownership and control of our lives and resources", Article 4 advises all oil companies and staff operating in the Ijaw area to withdraw from Ijaw land "pending the resolution of the issue of resource ownership and control in the Ijaw area of the Niger Delta". See Eghosa Osaghae *et al.*, *Youth Militias, Self Determination and Resource Control Struggles in the Niger-Delta Region of Nigeria*, August 2007, at www.ascleiden.nl/Pdf/cdpnigeriaRevisedOsaghae%5B1%5D2.pdf [accessed 3 March 2010].

[388]   Kenneth Omeje, The Rentier State: Oil-Related Legislation and Conflict in the Niger Delta, Nigeria, *op. cit.*, 224.

*agriculture and, aquaculture. It is a campaign for the re-afforestation, renewal,
detoxification and restoration of the land and water of the Niger Delta and the
introduction and development of renewable resources. Thus, resource control has as
part of its primary objective, how to ensure life and a good livelihood for the people
of the Niger Delta, long after the exhaustion of its petroleum resources, which have
become its enemies".*[389]

It therefore becomes clear that the struggle is for an end to injustice, discrimination,
exclusion, oppression, domination and exploitation, systematic destruction of
the ecosystem, corporate and environmental bad governance, a call for equitable
federation of Nigeria's economic policy, a demand for the practice of true
federation in which the federated units express their rights to primarily control
of the natural resources within their area and ensure the effective management
of resources to achieve good livelihood for the people in the area. This is well
captured by Ken Saro-Wiwa in his presentation on why he championed the Ogoni
cause:

*'I looked at Ogoni [Niger Delta] and found that the entire place was now a waste-
land; and that we are victims of an ecological war, an ecological war that is very
serious and unconventional. It is unconventional because no bones are broken, no
one is maimed. People are not alarmed because they can't see what is happening.
But human beings are at risk, plants and animals are at risk. The air and water are
poisoned. Finally, the land itself dies … Oil has brought nothing but disaster to our
people [Niger Delta]'.*[390]

What can be inferred from this is that the 'failure of the Nigerian State and
its institutions to address the development needs of the minority areas and to
evolve and implement a resources allocation formula built on fairness, ethnic
equity, contribution and needs',[391] has led to the feeling by these groups [Niger
Delta people] that they can do better, hence the struggle for resource control.
The agitation for resource control has therefore been on the increase as a result
of the dissatisfaction of the indigenous peoples of the Niger Delta with the gross
deprivation of their right to enjoy the benefits of the natural resources on their
land, a situation bolstered by the freedom of expression created by the advent of
democracy, and unlike the situation under the Military.

---

[389]   Itse Sagay, *Federalism, the Constitution and Resource control: My Response*, at www.nigerdelta-
congress.com/farticles/federalism_the_constitution_and_html. [accessed 7 September 2009].
[390]   Ken Saro-Wiwa, "Why I championed Ogoni Cause," in Omotoye Olorode, *et al* (eds) (1998),
Ken Saro-Wiwa and the Crises of the Nigerian State, Committee for the Defence of Human
Rights (CDHR) Publication, Lagos, p.379.
[391]   Edlyne E. Anugwom, Oil Minorities and the Politics of Resource Control in Nigeria, *op. cit.*,
p.112.

However equitable, progressive and federatively necessary the quest for resource control in Nigeria may be, its greatest challenges, or support, must lie in the language of the relevant laws that govern the subject in Nigeria.[392] The implication of the Land Use laws when read together with the Petroleum Act, the Constitution and other relevant statutes, is that all resources in Nigeria do not only belong to the Federal Government, but their control, and also the land on or in which they are found, are so owned.[393] Thus, the Supreme Court in *Attorney General of Federation v. Attorney General of Abia State & 35 ors*[394] held that the Federal Government alone, and not the littoral States, can lawfully exercise legislative, executive and judicial powers over the maritime belt or territorial waters and sovereign rights over the exclusive economic zone subject to universally recognized rights. This represents the position of the law in Nigeria today.

2.6.2 A CRITICAL APPRAISAL OF THE LEGAL REGIME OF FULL RESOURCE CONTROL IN NIGERIA

Section 44(3) of the 1999 Constitution and other legislation examined above has shown that true federalism has been jettisoned in favour of an over-centralized control of the nation's resources. Mines, minerals, including oil fields, oil mining, geological survey and gas were put in the Exclusive Legislative List in the 1960 and 1963 Constitutions. This was a carry-over from the provisions of the 1946 Minerals Act, under which the Colonial Government gave itself the exclusive ownership and control of all minerals in Nigeria. This was understandable under a colonial regime whose objective was the exploitation of the colonized peoples, but certainly not acceptable in an independent country constituted by autonomous (Federal) Regions.[395] The direct consequence of concentration of resource-control in the centre been in the Federal Government eclipsing other levels of Government, has led to the denial of the oil-producing areas of any right to the ownership, control and management of their resources, alienation by the oil-producing communities of their oil; all resulting in poverty and gross environmental degradation and giving rise to militancy within the local populations, violent disruption of oil production and pronounced agitation for resource control in the oil-producing areas.

One of the greatest disadvantages of the current over-centralisation of powers and resources in Nigeria is that many States and nearly all the local governments

---

[392] Yinka Omorogbe, *Communities and the Natural Resource Industries: The Route to Survival*, being the text of a paper presented at the World Women Lawyers Conference organized by the International Bar Association, London 1–2 March 2001.

[393] E.S. Nwauche *et al.*, *op. cit.*, p.222.

[394] *Supra* at p.243.

[395] Itse Sagay, *NIGERIA: Federalism, the Constitution and Resource Control*, *op. cit.*

have become indifferent about other sources of revenue in their territories, and
complacent about generating other incomes for themselves. This debilitating
consequence of the abandonment of fiscal federalism in favour of concentration
of resources at the centre was well illustrated by Omokhodion in his article
entitled "Anatomy of the Nigerian Economy":

> "At the end of every month, the 36 honourable Commissioners of Finance of all
> the States of the federation gather in a classroom session in Abuja presided over by
> the Federal Minister of Finance to share money that has accrued to the federation
> account based on a formula no one really understands. This money comes from
> three main sources – the oil money from the Niger Delta, the customs duty collecti-
> ons from the coastal/ports States and the VAT money mainly from Lagos State. After
> the sharing, the commissioners ... head back to their respective governors to report
> what they have received and how to allocate to the areas of defined priority. The
> way the funds [are] used is not the subject of this article but as you know easy come,
> easy goes and because over two-thirds of the States do not suffer any pain in the
> generation of this federation account, they fritter the money away and wait for the
> next month allocation. At the end of the month, they all troop back to Abuja for the
> monthly routine. It is inconceivable for any State to grow with this type of economic
> structure that puts State governments on welfare benefits or what the Americans
> call the "dole".
>
> If the States are not challenged to reap where they sow, the economy of this country
> will go nowhere. As a result of cheap money from the Niger Delta, all the Northern
> States and other Southern States have just allowed their natural and mineral resour-
> ces to go untapped and where they are tapped, the proceeds go to enrich indivi-
> dual foreign bank accounts. The great agricultural potential of the entire Mambilla
> Plateau has continued to lie fallow and seriously under-utilized because the North
> Eastern States that would have benefited directly from its exploitation do not want
> to be bothered with the initial difficulties of establishing a framework for its cultiva-
> tion. As in [the] human form, any child who depends perpetually on the parents to
> spoon-feed him for the rest of his life can never grow. Depending on Abuja to dish out
> handouts called revenue allocation to State governments cannot grow this economy.
> Power and wealth [is] being unduly concentrated at an unwieldy centre."[396]

In other words, the monthly pilgrimage to Abuja encourages laziness, profligacy
and greed in the States. Worst still, it promotes corruption, as the centre has been
turned to a gold mine where 'gold diggers' aspire to go 'milk' the nation.

Suffice it to say that resource-control has within it the potential to unlock the
enormous potential that exists in the Nigerian union and to release the presently
idling energies for its development.[397] Agiobenebo & Azibaolanari have argued

---

[396] Lawson Omokhodion, *Anatomy of the Nigerian Economy*, Vanguard Newspaper, Thursday, 2
       January 2003, p.35.
[397] See Tamunopriye J. Agiobenebo and Nelson Azibaolanari, *Rights, Freedom, Resource Control
       and Politico-Economic Equilibrium of the Market for National Union*, Selected Papers pre-
       sented at the 2001 Annual Conference of the Nigerian Economic Society, 2001, p.433.

that resource-control would enhance and develop the capacity for self reliance for all the levels of government, and for the entire country, because it will promote diversification of the Nigerian economy from oil to other sectors, like agriculture, which Nigeria has long abandoned.[398]

In spite of these arguments, there are fears in some quarters that there may be problems if the States are allowed to control their resources. There is a fear that if the States assume that role, then local government is likely to agitate for further local government control. A worse fear lies in the possibility of endless agitation with communities challenging local government; individual family challenging the community, while the individual within the family having his own claim thereafter against the family.[399] This is confirmed by various inter-communal/ethnic conflicts in the South-South zone, which in most instances is associated with access to, and control/ownership of, mineral resources. For example, there are the Urhobo-Itsekiri conflicts in Warri, Delta State, the Andoni-Ogoni conflicts in Rivers State and several other conflicts in the contiguous oil communities in both Delta and Rivers State. Also discernible since the advent of democracy in 1999 is the subtle use of a distinction between the core Niger Delta States and other Niger Delta States,[400] thus leading to definitional problem of what constitutes 'Niger Delta' and the States to be included in it, as discussed in Chapter one of this work. The worries about resources-control are aptly captured by Christopher Odetunde in this way:

> "First of all, the infrastructures necessary to develop the oil and the steel sectors were derived from revenues from cocoa, groundnuts, hides and skin, steel, palm oil products et cetera from other parts of Nigeria. Secondly, if the Federal Government gives control of resources to the States, it would have mortgaged the trust and confidence of the people of Nigeria who contributed in the first instance to the development of the resources. Third, if the resources are controlled by the States, there is no guarantee that even within such States there will be no splinter groups fighting for control and therefore Nigeria, [which] is struggling to keep the fragile unity together, may end up indirectly splitting her[self] into different warring fragments. Fourth, how would Federal Government guarantee its contractual obligations under the investments of the multinational companies? How would Federal Government assure other States that when States control resources, the benefit would translate to prosperity in other States? ... Finally, what will become of States when resources are no longer available? ... Some resources are highly political on the global stage and highly capital intensive. The States may not have resources to perform or buy the shares from joint venture partners. The long and short of it is that once the foreign

---

[398] *Ibid*; See A.A. Adesopo and Asaju A.S., *op. cit.*, p.283.
[399] E. S. Nwauche, *et al*, pp.223–224.
[400] See Edlyne E. Anugwom, Oil Minorities and the Politics of Resource Control in Nigeria, *op. cit.*, p.108.

*partners pull out, the infrastructure necessary to get resources going may go down
the drain just like all other infrastructures in Nigeria.*[401]

There is also the fear that the States may become more powerful than the centre,
to the extent of challenging the authority of the centre because of their enormous
resources. This, it is believed may lead to secession of the States, and a collapse of
the Federal structure.

While some of these reasons appear quite cogent, there are some that are
more apparent than real, as they are motivated by selfish rather than by genuine
reasons. This has created a dilemma. The dilemma is the problem of determining
the genuineness of those clamouring for the ownership and control of natural
resources, as greed, avarice, and the stealing of public funds occur both at the
Federal and State levels. The basic problem is not which level of government owns
and controls natural resources in Nigeria but the absence of good governance.
Good governance involves transparency, accountability, the rule of law, respect for
human rights etc. It also includes equitable distribution of income, development of
the country with particular attention to the communities where the resources are
obtained, equality in the sharing of public offices, and elimination of corruption
in all facets of the economy. That is, responsible and responsive government. The
current absence of these things, accounts for the incessant agitation by the oil-
producing areas for resource-control. But without good governance guaranteed
to the people, change in ownership and control of natural resources in Nigeria
from Federal Government to State Governments will merely result in the shift of
these evils from the Federal level to the State level.[402]

2.6.3 COMPARATIVE ANALYSIS OF RESOURCE CONTROL

In most developing countries in Africa, the ownership and/or the right of control
of natural resources is vested in the State. Leading examples of these countries are
Algeria,[403] Gabon,[404] Libya[405] and Egypt.[406] For example, Article 12 of the Angolan
Constitution provides that: all natural resources in the soil and subsoil, in internal
and territorial waters, on the continental shelf and in the exclusive economic area
shall be the property of the State.[407] Nigeria falls within this group of countries.

---

[401]   Christopher Odetunde, *Resource Control: Legal Action, Arbitration or Meditation?*, at www.
        nigerdeltacongress.com/articles/resource_control%201.htm. [accessed 3 March 2010].
[402]   Okon, Emmanuel, "The Legal Aspect of Ownership and Control of Natural Resources in
        Nigeria", in *Contemporary Issues in the Administration of Justice, Essays in Honour of Justice
        Atinuke Ige* (2002), Treasure Hall Konsult Rehoboth Publishing, Lagos, p.204.
[403]   Statute No. 58–111 November 22, 1958 Articles 1 and 18.
[404]   Law No. 64 LF-3, 26th April 1964 Article 4(1).
[405]   Law No. 25 of 1995, The Petroleum Article 1(2).
[406]   Law No. 66 of 7953 on Mines and Quarries.
[407]   Angola Constitution adopted by the People's Assembly on 25 August 1992.

The reasons for the public control of resources may not be unconnected with their common colonial experiences and having regard to the mineral laws in these countries before their independence, and the United Nations Resolutions on Permanent Sovereignty over Natural Resources[408] on the need for the newly independent States to own and control their resources.

In developed countries like Canada, Australia, Northern Ireland and the United States of America (USA), there is mixed control of resources. Here, individual, States and Federal ownership is allowed. In the USA, for example, minerals on private land vest in landowners, who are allowed to control their exploitation according to regulatory provisions governing the operation of the industry, especially with regards to health and safety. Where mineral resources occur on public land, they are owned and controlled by the various States, e.g. the State of Alaska in the USA owns all the land in the State currently producing oil and collects royalties on production in respect of its public lands. Local governments in several States such as Texas, Montana and Wyoming also collect property taxes on deposits of natural resources. Thus, what exists in the USA is a dual-ownership system in which the private 'landowner owns mineral rights of onshore areas while the State and the Federal Government owns minerals in/on public lands including offshore areas'.[409] Canada practices regional ownership of oil as each Province owns and administer oil within its borders. Also, while each Province collects and allocates its oil revenues in its chosen manner, the Canadian Federal Government is empowered to levy taxes, and regulate certain aspects of the oil industry of each Province, through its powers over foreign investment.[410] In Australia, States collect royalties but not taxes as only the Federal government can impose taxes.[411] Moreover, where such public land is owned by the Federal Government, it is the government of the Federation that is vested with the right of ownership and control.

With regards to ownership and control of minerals in the continental shelf, that is, in the seabed and subsoil adjacent to the USA's coast, it was established in *United States v. Maine*,[412] *United States v. California*,[413] *United States v. Texas*[414] and *United States v. Louisiana*,[415] that the Federal Government of the USA owns, controls and develops this area. The question as to which tier of Government owns the resources on the seabed and subsoil adjacent to the coast of the USA

---

[408]   Adopted by the United Nations General Assembly, 14 December 1962, Resolution 1803 (XVII).

[409]   F.O. Ayodele-Akaakar, *Appraising the Oil & Gas Laws: A Search for Enduring Legislation for the Niger Delta Region, op. cit.*

[410]   Mercy O. Erhun, "A Comparative Evaluation of Resource Exploitation and Management in Global Deltas: A Case for the Niger Delta Region in Nigeria", in *International Conference on The Nigerian State, Oil Industry and the Niger Delta, op. cit.*, pp.687–688.

[411]   Leaflet produced by the Citizens' Forum for Constitutional Reform (CFCR) on the Review of the 1999 Constitution: What are the Issues? 2001, p.3.

[412]   420 US 515(1974).

[413]   332 US 19 (1947).

[414]   399 US 707 (1950).

[415]   333 US 699 (1950).

was statutorily settled later through the passing of the Submerged Land Acts of 1953, which granted ownership of the mineral rights within the three mile limit to States that comprise the Federation of the USA, with the Federal Government being granted ownership and control outside the three mile limit of the USA's submerged lands.[416]

A few months later, the US Congress implemented its view that the USA has paramount right to the seabed beyond the three-mile limit when it enacted the Outer Continental Shelf Lands Act (OCSLA) 1953.[417] This Act was passed in order to enable the Federal Government to have a fair share of leasing in offshore waters and territory, by reserving some offshore territory exclusively to itself. The OCSLA of 1953 (as amended) delineates the seaward boundary of the Coastal States, vis-à-vis that of the Federal Government, with the Coastal States having an exclusive territorial jurisdiction or competence within the 3 nautical miles offshore (in Texas and Western Florida, the limit is 9 nautical miles) as opposed to the situation in Nigeria where there is no law that delineates the offshore boundary between the Coastal States and Federal Government. The Nigerian Federal Government assumes it has exclusive proprietary right over offshore lands and this was given recognition by the Supreme Court of Nigeria when it held that littoral States cannot claim that revenue accruing from mineral resources offshore belongs to them and that whatever revenue accrues from drilling offshore belongs to the whole Federation of Nigeria based on section 162 of 1999 Constitution.[418]

It is important to note that by the 1958 Convention, the breadth of the territorial sea is a maximum of 3 miles. This has now been extended to 12 nautical miles by Article 3 of the 1982 United Nations Convention on the Law of the Sea, which supercedes the Geneva Convention of 1958. Article 33 extends the breadth of the contiguous zone from 12 miles to 24 nautical miles. In the light of this, it is believed that the rationale in *Maine, Louisiana cases* etc, and the provisions of Submerged Lands Act and Outer Continental Shelf Lands' Act with regards to States sovereign rights over the seabed and subsoil underlying the three miles limit of US Coast will be reviewed to twelve nautical miles along the lines of the 1982 Law of the Sea for Coastal States.[419]

Whilst Justice Ogundare JSC who wrote the lead judgment in *Attorney-General of Federation v. Attorney General of Abia State and 35 Ors*[420] opines that the boundary of the littoral States ends at the "low water mark,"[421] his colleagues' say it ends at the sea.[422] The question is, between the "low watermark" and the

---

[416] 43 US CJ 1310 (1975), and the Submerged Lands Act was declared constitutional in *Alabama v. Texas*, 347 US 272 (1954); See Okon Emmanuel, *op. cit.*, p.198.

[417] 67 State 462, 43 U.S.C.S. 1331.

[418] Per Wali JSC in *Attorney General of Federation v. Attorney General of Abia State and 35 Ors*, *Supra*, at p.197.

[419] Okon Emmanuel, *op. cit.*, p.199.

[420] *Supra.*

[421] *Ibid* at p.91 .

[422] *Ibid* at p.164, per Uwais CJN; p.197, per Wali JSC.

"Sea," where should we place the exact boundary.[423] In the USA, the coastal states have an exclusive territorial jurisdiction within the 3 nautical miles offshore (compared with the low water mark in the case of Nigeria). Even in Texas and Western Florida, the limit is 9 nautical miles.[424]

Also, even though the USA Outer Continental Shelf has been declared to be Federal Lands, by the 106th Congress, the Coastal States receive 50% of revenues from licences, leases, royalties etc; 40% to a Reclamation Fund with only 10% to the Federal Treasury. This is in recognition of their proximity to these fragile ecological zones; infrastructural wear and tear accompanying Outer Continental Shelf, oil and gas activities and for the development of the coastal communities. This kind of equitable sharing formula is absent in Nigeria. Even the 13% derivation recognized by the 1999 Constitution has being whittled down by the Supreme Court's introduction of the 'offshore' and 'onshore' dichotomy, which was abolished by the Allocation of Revenue (Federation Account etc) (Amendment) Decree No.106 of 1992, and, was never contained in the 1979 and 1999 Constitutions.[425] While not advocating that 10% should go to the Federal Government, a leaf can be borrowed from the USA regarding the equitable sharing formula.

2.6.4 IS RESOURCE CONTROL A VIABLE OPTION?

The twin issues of Derivation Formula and Resource Control dominated the discussion at the 2005 National Political Reform Conference which was held to seek an arrangement so that justice would be done to all stakeholders in the Nigerian nation.[426] However, the Conference could not resolve the issues as members from the South/South, where the oil came from, left the venue unceremoniously. Discussions were centered on the need to effecting fiscal federalism among the different tiers of government, while also trying to ensure that Nigerians who are not part of the revenue-producing States are not deprived of the gains of a nation in whose unity they have an equal interest.

Indeed, a lot has been said on the need to allow States to own, develop and control their natural resources located within their areas. D.A. Ijalaye[427] has posited that the owner and producer States should then cede an agreed percentage of their revenue to the Federal Government as tax for the maintenance of the common services of the Federation such as Defence, Foreign Affairs, Currency,

---

[423] David Dafinone, Supreme Court's Verdict on Resource Control: The Political Imperatives, at www.nigerdeltacongress.com/sarticles/supreme_courts_verdict_on_resour.htm [accessed 4 June 2010].
[424] *Ibid.*
[425] *Ibid.*
[426] D.A. Ijalaye (2001), *The Imperatives of Federal/State Relations in a Fledgling Democracy: Implication for Nigeria,* NIALS publication, Lagos, p.22.
[427] *Ibid* p.22.

Immigration, Customs etc. References have been made to some older and mature
federations like USA, Canada, and Australia etc that have this arrangement in
place. While this suggestion appears good and perhaps acceptable, it begs a lot
of questions, which include the following: Is there any assurance that the States'
Governments would perform better than the Federal Government in the matter?
Should it be the local government, community, family or the individual on whose
land oil is discovered that should own it? Have the proponents of this view fully
contemplated the degree of communal clashes, and the individual battles, that
would result in determining the ownership claims to the land with crude oil or
even land through which crude oil pipelines are to traverse? With our level of
sophistication, would an individual owner (particularly at the village level where
oil is generally discovered) be adequately equipped to negotiate a fair contract
(relating to the discovered oil) with a multinational operating oil company?[428]
Again, will the Nigerian government, controlled by the majority ethnic groups,
institutionalize in law the resource-control option as presently been demanded by
the oil-producing communities considering the total reliance by the Governments
(Federal and States) on the huge financial revenue which oil from the Niger Delta
generates?

Any adequate solution must stem, and logically flow from, a rigorous analysis
of the root causes of the communities' restiveness and the persistent agitation
for resource-control in the country. The pauperization of the Nigerian Southern
minorities oil enclave – the goose that literally lays the golden eggs – by the
Federal Government, aided by the operation of multinational oil companies
led to the environmental degradation which devastates the traditional peasant
economy of the oil-producing enclaves and dislodges their basic social life. Worse
still, the Federal presence, massively registered in these areas, has never been
effectively translated into gainful jobs and other economic opportunities for
the predominantly rural communities[429] whose land and environment are daily
destroyed. It is these factors, coupled with the non-provision of commensurate
viable economic alternatives that have led to the increase in the agitation of
the oil-producing areas for resource control. This is graphically painted in the
Memorandum of Delta State to the 2005 National Political Reform Conference
in this way:

> "Unfortunately, this great deposit of oil and gas has become a mixed blessing for
> the people of the State. They are denied the benefit of this wealth and exposed to
> devastating environmental pollution and degradation....Oil spillages have become

---

[428] See Godfrey Etikerentse, "Oil and Gas Exploration in Nigeria: Challenges for the 21st Century",
in I.A Ayua and D.A. Guobadia (eds.) (2001), *Political Reform and Economic Recovery in
Nigeria*, NIALS Publication, Lagos, pp.511–512.

[429] Inya A. Eteng, *Minority Rights Under Nigeria's Federal Structure*, in Constitutions and
Federalism, Proceedings of the Conference on Constitutions and Federalism, held at the
University of Lagos, Nigeria 23–25 1996, Friedrich Ebert Foundation, Lagos, 1997, pp.134, 141.

recurrent and routine in the Niger Delta. It is now well known that these spillages in combination with other toxic wastes and effluents dumped into the waters and lands at virtually every stage of oil exploration and exploitation destroy farm lands, economic crops, waters, including groundwater resources, biodiversity, etc. There is now a growing concern that some of these toxins may have already entered the food chain, thereby placing the health of the human population of these areas at more direct risk.

Furthermore, the people are impoverished and marginalized due to the inequit-able and defective federal system of government practised by the Nigerian State. The existing structure is characterized by over-concentration of power, imbalance among the constituent units, and consequently inequitable distribution of resources. The structural inequity is further re-institutionalised by a host of obnoxious, sup-pressive and offensive laws.

The pain, anguish and the deep-seated resentment of institutionalized injustice, amongst the grossly neglected communities of Delta State, are heightened by the gen-uine concern that these wasting assets will be completely depleted in a few decades. This scenario of simultaneous presence of a modern global oil and gas industry, bac-ked by Federal might, harvesting stupendous wealth from communities in a manner that dislocates the ecological foundations of their traditional modes of livelihood, yet excludes them from participation in the new wealth, has created desperate levels of poverty and anger. It is this new social ecology that has created conditions for agitation and restiveness, hence the unrelenting demand for resource control."[430]

This extract has been set out at length to emphasize that strangulated or subverted federalism gave rise to the present agitation for resource control. The clamour for resource-control is a clamour for adequate compensation, a cry for redistribution of the revenue allocation formula, a cry against degradation of the environment and dislocation of the economy, for a more defined and humane form of decentralised federalism that guarantees regional autonomy, for control of resources and development, and for fair, just and equitable treatment of all people. With the right leadership, and good government committed to improving the life of the people in these areas, ensuring good oil practices, payment of adequate compensation to those from whose lands wealth is derived, ensuring that poorer units (Niger Delta) partake in the enjoyment of the benefits belonging to the Federation, it will be possible to contain the agitation for resource-control arising from neglect, injustice, and environmental degradation.

---

[430]   We Must Break Out of Authoritarian Headmaster-Cum-Father Christmas Complex, The Guardian, Wednesday, 13 April 2005, p.8. Again, capturing the reasons for the Niger Delta struggle, Eghosa Osaghae *et al.*, *op. cit.* state that: 'The struggle is perceived as one for devel-opment attention, resource benefits, inclusion and representation and fight against economic deprivation, neglect and negative oil externalities. The region is seeking adequate attention, recognition and participation in the management or control of the benefits of its oil resources and fair, just and equitable treatment as minority groups. The ethnic groups in the region want massive development, resource control or at least adequate derivation based share, and a better federal framework that guarantees equitable, fair and just treatment and regional autonomy.'

2.7 OWNERSHIP OF INDIGENOUS LAND AND NATURAL RESOURCES WITHIN THE CONTEXT OF INTERNATIONAL LAW

Having considered the position of Nigerian domestic laws on the issue of ownership of land and natural resources, we shall now investigate what the position is under international law and find out whether the laws of Nigeria as discussed above are in conformity with the current position under international law. Suffice it to say that the rights to land and natural resources are among the most important rights of indigenous peoples all over the world, and have been receiving considerable attention since the early 1980s in international law. This is because of the importance attached to land and natural resources by indigenous peoples as their source of livelihood and sustenance and the reason for their existence as identifiable territorial communities. Several international and regional instruments on the subject include the African Charter on Human and Peoples' Rights, the International Labour Organization (ILO) Conventions (Nos. 107 and 169), the UN Declaration on the Rights of the Indigenous Peoples, the Declaration of the World Conference to Combat Racism and Racial Discrimination 1983, the Convention on Biological Diversity (CBD) 1992, and International Standards on Indigenous Rights and State Practices. We shall focus on the major instruments: the African Charter on Human and Peoples' Rights, the ILO Conventions (Nos. 107 and 169), the Convention on Biological Diversity, the UN Declaration on the Rights of the Indigenous Peoples, and the State practices on indigenous rights relating to the ownership and control of indigenous lands and natural resources.

2.7.1 INTERNATIONAL LABOUR ORGANISATION (ILO) CONVENTIONS (NOS. 107 AND 169)

The ILO, which is the main body within the UN concerned with the welfare of workers, has since its inception been concerned with the promotion of the rights of the indigenous peoples through its national and regional projects. The ILO Conventions (Nos. 107 and 169)[431] are a clear manifestation of the growing concern of the body concerning indigenous peoples all over the world, and they represent the only binding international instruments solely concerned with indigenous peoples. The first of the two Conventions, Convention No. 107 adopted in 1957, had as its aim the integration and assimilation of indigenous peoples. It enshrined, amongst other things, a right of indigenous ownership of

---

[431] International Labour Organization (ILO), Convention Concerning Indigenous and Tribal Persons in Independent Countries (ILO No. 169), 27 June 1989, 1650 U.N.T.S. 383; ILO Convention Concerning the Protection and Integration of Indigenous and Other Tribal and Semi-Tribal Populations in Independent Countries (ILO No. 107), 26 June 1957, 328 U.N.T.S. 247.

communal land and makes provision for compensation where the land is taken by the Government for the purpose of development.[432] Commenting on these provisions, Kaniye Ebeku has stated that:

> "Article 11 [which recognizes the land rights of indigenous peoples] provides a right in this Convention which is delineated in a 'strong' manner; Article 12 [which forbids removal of indigenous peoples from their habitual territories without their consent, except in exceptional cases, provides (inter alia) for the payment of compensation where removal was inevitable] is not quite as categorical, but it none-the-less contains important constraints on the State Parties' freedom of action...; Article 13 relates back to the general question of indigenous laws and customs in the context of land rights...; [And] Article 14... is equality provision..."[433]

As a result of its lack of respect for indigenous peoples' culture and identity, due to its integrationist and assimilationist orientation, ILO 107 became an 'embarrassment' to the ILO, and this led to a decision taken in 1986 to revise it in line with the principle that indigenous peoples should 'enjoy as much control as possible over their own economic, social and cultural development'.[434] Following a two year thorough revision process to remove the weaknesses identified in it, the International Labour Conference finally adopted ILO 169 in 1989. However, ILO 107 still remains in force for the States that have ratified it, but have not yet ratified ILO 169.

ILO 169 represents a clear departure from the philosophy of integration and assimilation which characterized ILO 107. This can be inferred from its preamble, which contains as its basic theme of the right of indigenous peoples to live and develop their own identities, languages and religions as distinct communities. While it did not declare a right to environment, it is 'the first international instrument to relate environmental concerns explicitly to indigenous peoples'.[435] The Convention provides additional new rights on the international legal register, most importantly that which relates to indigenous peoples' management of natural

---

[432] See sections 11, 12, 13 and 14 of the Convention. See Kaniye Ebeku, *op. cit.*, p.100.

[433] Kaniye Ebeku (2006), *Oil and the Niger Delta in International Law. Resource Rights, Environmental and Equity Issues op. cit.*, at pp. 100–101, quoting from Thornberry P. (1991), *International Law and the Rights of Minorities*, Clarendon Press, Oxford, p.356.

[434] See Fergus MacKay, "The Rights of Indigenous Peoples in International Law", in Lyuba Zarky (ed) (2002), *Human Rights and the Environment: Conflicts and Norms in a Globalizing World*, Earthscan Publications Ltd. London, p.16; ILO (1988) Partial Revision of the Indigenous and Tribal Populations Convention, 1957 (No. 107), Report VI (1), International Labour Conference, 75th Session, Geneva. Geneva: International Labour Organization. The Group of Experts convened by the ILO Office to revise the ILO 107 agreed that "the Convention's integrationists approach is inadequate and no longer reflects current thinking". See Russel Lawrence Barsh, Revision of ILO No. 107, 81 *Am. J. Int'l L.* 761 (1987).

[435] Fergus MacKay, *Ibid*, p. 16. For instance, Article 4(1) requires States to take 'special measures to protect the environment of indigenous peoples, and these measures include environmental impact studies of proposed development activities (art. 7(3)), the recognition of subsistence rights (art. 23), and protection of natural resources (art. 15(1)).

resources. Article 15(1) states that "the rights of the peoples concerned to the natural resources pertaining to their lands shall be safeguarded", in addition to the "right of these peoples to participate in the use, management and conservation of these resources." Where the State retains the ownership of mineral or sub-surface resources or rights to other resources pertaining to lands, as in Nigeria, Article 15(2) provides that governments shall establish or maintain procedures through which they shall consult these peoples, with a view to ascertaining whether and to what degree their interests would be prejudiced, before undertaking or permitting any programmes for the exploration or exploitation of such resources pertaining to their lands and the peoples concerned shall wherever possible participate in the benefits of such activities, and shall receive fair compensation for any damage which they may sustain as a result of such activities. Articles 14 (recognized rights of ownership and possession of the peoples concerned over the lands which they traditionally occupy), 16 (preventing unjust removal of indigenous peoples from the lands which they occupy and requiring their free and informed consent before removal in case it becomes necessary, with full compensation) and 17 (provides for recognition of indigenous law tenure systems) in ILO 169 afford better protection to the land and natural resources of the indigenous peoples than does ILO 107.

Despite the above provisions which appear to safeguard the rights of indigenous peoples, the Convention has been criticized for various reasons. These include the fact that indigenous peoples did not participate in the drafting stages; that it has been ratified only by a small number of States, the absence of the language of self determination; and numerous qualifications in the Convention's main provisions that hamper its practical effectiveness.[436] Whatever its shortcomings, the spirit of consultation and participation that constitute the core of the Convention makes it mandatory that the indigenous peoples must be allowed to have a say in any resource exploration activities on their lands and to partake in the benefit of such operations.

2.7.2 AFRICAN CHARTER ON HUMAN AND PEOPLES' RIGHTS AND INDIGENOUS RIGHTS

The African Charter on Human and Peoples' Rights (ACHPR) was adopted in 1981 but came into force only on 21 October 1986. Unlike its European and

---

[436] See generally, Fergus MacKay, *Ibid*, p.17; James Anaya, Indigenous Peoples' Participatory Rights in Relation to Decisions about Natural Resource Extraction: The More Fundamental Issue of What Rights Indigenous Peoples Have in Lands and Resources, 22 *Ariz. J. Int'l & Comp. L.* 10 (2005). ILO 169 has been further criticised for containing no mechanism for redress of alleged violations or even a regular reporting requirement with a monitoring system. See Bradford Morse, "Indigenous Rights as a Mechanism to Promote Environmental Sustainability", in Laura Westra *et al.* (eds) (2008), *Reconciling Human Existence with Ecological Integrity: Science, Ethics, Economics and the Law*, Earthscan U.K. 2008, pp.167–168.

American counterparts, which are basically concerned with individual rights, the African Charter guarantees both individual and collective rights and does not place a hierarchy on these rights. Regarding the provisions dealing with the right to land and natural resources, Article 21(1) provides that 'all peoples shall freely dispose of their wealth and natural resources. This right shall be exercised in the exclusive interest of the people. In no case shall a people be deprived of it'. Article 21(2) further states that 'in case of spoliation the dispossessed people shall have the right to the lawful recovery of its property as well as to an adequate compensation'. In the landmark case of the *Social and Economic Rights Action Center and the Center for Economic and Social Rights v. Nigeria,*[437] the African Commission on Human and Peoples' Rights recognized that the Ogoni people, one of the constituent peoples of Nigeria, are entitled to this right in relation to the natural resources within its territory

The African Commission's Working Group on Indigenous Populations/ Communities (formed on 6 November 2000) has dealt with African indigenous rights in detail. Its Report confirms that 'the protection of rights to land and natural resources is fundamental for the survival of indigenous communities in Africa and such protection relates both to Articles 20, 21, 22 and 24 of the African Charter'.[438] It further noted in its Report that the alienation and the dispossession of the 'indigenous peoples of their customary rights to land and other natural resources has led to an undermining of the knowledge systems through which indigenous peoples have sustained life for centuries and it has led to a negation of their livelihood systems and deprivation of their means.'[439] It concluded that this is a serious violation of the African Charter (*Articles 20, 21 and 22),* which states clearly that all peoples have the right to existence, the right to their natural resources and property, and the right to their economic, social and cultural development.[440] The Working Group recognized the concerns over the use of the term *indigenous peoples* in the African context, the availability of collective rights, formulated as rights of 'peoples', to indigenous peoples, the right to self determination as a right of indigenous peoples and posited that the 'principle of self-identification as expressed in ILO Convention 169 and by the Working Group on Indigenous Populations is a key principle that should also guide the further deliberations of the African Commission'[441] in identifying indigenous peoples.

---

[437]   Communication 155/96.

[438]   *Report of the African Commission's Working Group of Experts on Indigenous Populations/ Communities,* adopted by the African Commission on Human and Peoples' Rights at its 28th ordinary session (May 2003), 2005, p.21 at www.pro169.org/res/materials/en/identification/ ACHPR%20Report%20on%20indigenous%20populations-communities.pdf [accessed at 6 June 2011].

[439]   *Ibid,* p.108. For more on the work of the African Commission Working Group, see Kealeboga N.Bojosi and George Mukundi Wachira, Protecting Indigenous Peoples in Africa: An Analysis of the Approach of the African Commission on Human and Peoples' Rights, 6 *Afr. Hum. Rts. L.J.* 382–406 (2006).

[440]   *Ibid.*

[441]   *Ibid,* p.101.

2.7.3 THE CONVENTION ON BIOLOGICAL DIVERSITY (CBD)

This is the main international legal framework for biodiversity conservation and
it is legally binding on party members. It was one of the agreements adopted at
the Rio Earth Summit of 1992,[442] which came into force on 29 December 1993
and was ratified by the Nigerian Government on 8 August 1994. As at February
2013, the party members to the Convention are 193. This Convention is unique in
the sense that it affords some protection to the indigenous peoples who had often
been marginalised in earlier efforts to conserve biodiversity, despite the fact that
their territories encompass vast areas of the remaining biological biodiversity.
It establishes three main goals *viz*: conservation of biodiversity, sustainable use
of biodiversity, and the fair and equitable sharing of benefits arising from the
commercial and other utilization of genetic resources. Amongst other things, it
also provides indirect protection to the indigenous peoples. For example, Article
8(j) establishes that '[E]ach Contracting Party shall, as far as possible and as
appropriate: ... Subject to its national legislation, respect, preserve and maintain
knowledge, innovations and practices of indigenous and local communities
embodying traditional lifestyles relevant for the conservation and sustainable use
of biological diversity and promote their wider application with the approval and
involvement of the holders of such knowledge ... and encourage the equitable
sharing of the benefits arising from [their] utilisation'. However, these rights are
weakened by the use of the phrases "as far as possible" and a qualifier "subject to
its national legislation", as these give States the discretion to limit their obligations
under the provision.[443]

Article 10(c) may be relevant with regards to land and resource rights of
indigenous peoples. It provides that States shall 'protect and encourage customary
use of biological resources in accordance with traditional cultural practices that
are compatible with conservation or sustainable use requirements'. Although, the
meaning and scope of this article is yet to be articulated, it is likely to 'include
indigenous agriculture, agro-forestry, hunting, fishing, gathering and the use of
medicinal plants and other subsistence activities'.[444] Relying on the analysis of the
secretariat of the CBD in its background on Traditional Knowledge and Biological
Diversity, which interpreted article 10(c) to require respect for indigenous tenure
over terrestrial and marine estates, control over and use of natural resources and

---

[442] Convention on Biological Diversity, UN Conference on Environment and Development,
EP.Bio.Div./CONF. L2.1992 (1992). As at February 2013, the party members to the Convention
are 193.
[443] See Cherie Metcalf, Indigenous Rights and the Environment: Evolving International Law, 35
Ottawa L. Rev. 101–140 at 113 (2003–2004).
[444] Fergus MacKay, *op. cit.*, p.25.

respect for indigenous self-determination and self government,[445] MacKay[446] declared that this article, by implication, should be read to include protection for the land base, ecosystem and environment in which those resources are found.

Even though the Convention was drafted without the involvement of indigenous peoples, and so is deficient in some respects concerning the rights of the indigenous peoples to natural resources, it nonetheless provides 'support for the participation, consultation and compensation rights of indigenous peoples in connection with their traditional knowledge'.[447]

2.7.4 THE UNITED NATIONS DECLARATION ON THE RIGHTS OF INDIGENOUS PEOPLES

The adoption of the UN Declaration on the Rights of Indigenous Peoples on 13 September 2007 marked the greatest development on indigenous rights in the last decade, and it is indeed a triumph for indigenous peoples in their age-long struggle for an international instrument that will recognise their distinct cultural rights and provide remedies for the injustices of dispossession, marginalisation and neglect. The Declaration does not have legally binding effect, but may, however, serve as a framework that States can adopt to strengthen their relationship with indigenous peoples and in the development of their municipal law. UN Secretary-General, Ban Ki-moon has noted:

> *"The Declaration is a visionary step towards addressing the human rights of indigenous peoples. It sets out a framework on which States can build or rebuild their relationships with indigenous peoples. The result of more than two decades of negotiations, it provides a momentous opportunity for States and indigenous peoples to strengthen their relationships, promote reconciliation and ensure that the past is not repeated."*[448]

---

[445] Traditional Knowledge and Biological Diversity, UNEP/CBD/TKBD/1/2, 18 October 1997.
[446] *Op. cit.*, pp.25–26. See also, Indigenous Peoples' Rights, Extractive Industries and Transnational and Other Business Enterprises. A Submission to the Special Representative of the Secretary-General on human rights and transnational corporations and other business enterprises, Jointly produced by Forest Peoples Programme and Tebtebba Foundation, 29 December 2006, pp.35–36.
[447] Cherie Metcalf, *op. cit.*, p.113. For example, para. 22 of the Decision VII/28 on Protected Areas adopted by the 7th Conference of Parties to the CBD provides that "the establishment, management and monitoring of protected areas should take place with the full and effective participation of, and full respect for the rights of, indigenous and local communities consistent with national law and applicable international obligations". Decisions Adopted by the Conference of Parties to the Convention on Biological Diversity at its Seventh Meeting. UNEP/BDP/COP/7/21, pp.343–364.
[448] Ban Ki-moon, "Protect, Promote, Endangered Languages, Secretary-General Urges in Message for International Day of World's Indigenous People", SG/SM/11715, HR/4957, OBV/711 (23 July 2008).

In many of its provisions, it addresses issues that border on economic rights and
the right of indigenous peoples to their lands, territories and resources. Most
importantly, in contrast with ILO 107 and 169, it declares that 'indigenous peoples
have the right to self-determination' and provides that 'by virtue of that right they
freely determine their political status and freely pursue their economic, social
and cultural development'.[449] By so doing, it 'comprehends indigenous peoples as
international actors. But indigenous peoples as international legal actors do not
occupy the same international legal plane as sovereign States'.[450] It also provides
for the right to maintain their own political, legal, economic, social and cultural
institutions and 'to participate fully, if they so choose, in the political, economic,
social and cultural life of the State'.[451]

As in ILO 107 and 169, indigenous rights, as contained in the UN Declaration,
presuppose complex relations between the State and the indigenous peoples within
the State. They neither entitle indigenous peoples to acquire sovereign power as of
right nor vest sovereignty in them, as sovereignty is understood in international
law.[452] This can be implied from the provisions of Article 4 of the Declaration which
restrict the right to self determination to an internal aspect of self determination,
thereby not meeting the desires of the indigenous peoples to self determination.
In support of Article 4, Article 46 of the Declaration, known as the 'saving clause',
specifically guarantees the territorial integrity of States, thereby, foreclosing the
possibility of such a broad misrepresentation of the conferred self-determination
right.[453] Article 46(1) states: 'Nothing in this Declaration may be interpreted as
implying for any State, people, group or person any right to engage in any activity
or to perform any act contrary to the Charter of the United Nations or construed as
authorizing or encouraging any action which would dismember or impair, totally
or in part, the territorial integrity or political unity of sovereign and independent
States'. In the same vein, the Declaration provides in Article 46(2) that: "In the
exercise of the rights enunciated in the present Declaration, human rights and
fundamental freedoms of all shall be respected. The exercise of the rights set forth
in this Declaration shall be subject only to such limitations as are determined
by law, in accordance with international human rights obligations." Article 46,
which renders its provisions subject to existing domestic and international law,
'has become a catch-all provision to arrest State fears about the implications of

---

[449] Art. 3.
[450] Patrick Macklem, Indigenous Recognition in International Law: Theoretical Observations, 30
Mich. J. of Int'l L. 202 (2008).
[451] Art. 5. Art. 20(1) & (2) also declares that indigenous peoples have the right to maintain and
develop their political, economic and social systems or institutions and should they be deprived
of their means of subsistence and development, they are entitled to just and fair redress.
[452] Patrick Macklem, *op. cit.*, p.203. See also Benedict Kingsbury, Reconciling Five Competing
Conceptual Structures of Indigenous Peoples' Claims in International and Comparative Law,
34 *N.Y.U. J. Int'l. & Pol.* 189, 225 (2001).
[453] Christopher J. Fromherz, Indigenous Peoples' Courts: Egalitarian Juridicalpluralism, Self-
Determination, and the United Nations Declaration on the Rights of Indigenous Peoples, 156
University of Pennsylvania Law Review, 1341–1381 at 1346 (2008).

the recognition of cultural rights for municipal legal systems and concerns about the impact of the United Nations Declaration on the Rights of Indigenous Peoples upon the rule of law'.[454]

The provisions concerning land and resources are particularly reflected in Articles 24–30 of the Declaration. But importantly, Articles 26 and 28[455] provide novel and far-reaching rights. They enshrines the right of indigenous people to own, develop, control, and use the lands and territories that they have traditionally owned or otherwise occupied and used, including the right to restitution of lands confiscated, occupied, or otherwise taken without their free and informed consent, with the option of just, fair and equitable compensation whenever such return is not possible. Also recognised by the Declaration is the collective nature of the land rights of the indigenous peoples, and this goes to show that the recognition of collective rights does not necessarily amount to the denial of the rights of individuals.[456] For example, the bearers of the rights under Article 26 of the Declaration undoubtedly are indigenous peoples, and so, 'despite the political debates surrounding the issue of collective rights, the UN Declaration reflects the emerging legal acknowledgment of the collective nature of property rights for indigenous peoples'.[457]

---

[454]   Megan Davis, Indigenous Struggles in Standard Setting: The United Nations Declaration on the Rights of Indigenous Peoples, 9 *Melb. J. Int'l L.* 439, 461 (2008). Article 4 of the UN Declaration provides that: 'Indigenous peoples, in exercising their right to self-determination, have the right to autonomy or self-government in matters relating to their internal and local affairs, as well as ways and means for financing their autonomous functions'.

[455]   Article 26(2): Indigenous peoples have the right to own, use, develop and control the lands, territories and resources that they possess by reason of traditional ownership or other traditional occupation or use, as well as those which they have otherwise acquired.
(3) States shall give legal recognition and protection to these lands, territories and resources. Such recognition shall be conducted with due respect to the customs, traditions and land tenure systems of the indigenous peoples concerned.
Article 28(1) Indigenous peoples have the right to redress, by means that can include restitution or, when this is not possible, just, fair and equitable compensation, for the lands, territories and resources which they have traditionally owned or otherwise occupied or used, and which have been confiscated, taken, occupied, used or damaged without their free, prior and informed consent.
(2) Unless otherwise freely agreed upon by the peoples concerned, compensation shall take the form of lands, territories and resources equal in quality, size and legal status or of monetary compensation or other appropriate redress.

[456]   Jérémie Gilbert, The United Nations Declaration on the Rights of Indigenous Peoples: Towards Partnership and Mutual Respect, at www.liv.ac.uk/law/ielu/docs/UN_Declaration_on_the_Rights_of_Indigenous_Peoples-JG.pdf [accessed 3 March 2010].

[457]   Jérémie Gilbert, *Ibid*, Gilbert stressed that the IACHR in the *The Mayagna (Sumo) Awas Tingni Community v. Nicaragua*, (Ser. C) No. 79 (31 August 2001) Inter-Am. Ct. H.R. at 148 clearly affirmed the right to property in lands for "members of indigenous communities within the framework of commonality of possession (..)". He further posits that the ILO Convention No. 169 also recognises the collective nature of property in lands for indigenous peoples, and the jurisprudence of the HRC and CERD also emphasise the collective nature of this connection. CERD, General Recommendation XXIII (51) on the Rights of Indigenous Peoples (adopted at the Committee's 1235th meeting, on 18 August 1997), see para. 5.

However, none of the articles in the Declaration expressly provides for indigenous peoples' exclusive rights over the natural resources on the lands they occupy. What they vest in the indigenous peoples is essentially 'a right to effective participation in consultation and decision-making regarding the management of natural resources as well as for benefit-sharing'.[458] This is established by Article 32 of the Declaration.[459] In the absence of any international legal instrument vesting indigenous peoples directly with the right to permanent sovereignty over natural resources, it implies that laws such as the LUA and other statutes that expropriated the land of the indigenous peoples of the Niger Delta are legitimate (subject to duty to compensate) even when these expropriatory statutes have been condemned by international human rights bodies.[460]

Be that as it may, it seems plausible to argue that given the recognition that has been accorded international standards on indigenous rights; particularly by international financial institutions (IFIs), whose activities most often affect the interests of the indigenous peoples, these rights may have developed to become customary international law.[461] We shall now examine this argument.

2.7.5 INTERNATIONAL FINANCIAL INSTITUTIONS AND INDIGENOUS PEOPLES

The operations of the international financial institutions that give development assistance to developing countries affect the indigenous peoples living within the territory where the project concerned is to be carried out, in the form of the

---

[458] Nico Schrijver, 'Unravelling State Sovereignty? The Controversy on the Right of Indigenous Peoples to Permanent Sovereignty over their Natural Wealth and Resources', in Ineke Boerefijn and Jenny Goldschmidt (eds) (2008), Changing Perceptions of Sovereignty and Human Rights: Essays in Honour of Cees Flinterman, Intersentia Antwerp-Oxford-Portland, p.98.

[459] Article 32(1) Indigenous peoples have the right to determine and develop priorities and strategies for the development or use of their lands or territories and other resources.
(2) States shall consult and cooperate in good faith with the indigenous peoples concerned through their own representative institutions in order to obtain their free and informed consent prior to the approval of any project affecting their lands or territories and other resources, particularly in connection with the development, utilization or exploitation of mineral, water or other resources.
(3) States shall provide effective mechanisms for just and fair redress for any such activities, and appropriate measures shall be taken to mitigate adverse environmental, economic, social, cultural or spiritual impact.

[460] Concluding Observations of the Human Rights Committee: Canada. 7/4/99. UN Doc. CCPR/C/79/Add.105, at para. 8; Concluding Observations of the Human Rights Committee: Australia. 28/7/2000. UN Doc. CCPR/CO/69/AUS,para.8; Concluding observations of the Committee on Economic, Social and Cultural Rights: Canada. 10/12/98. UN Doc. E/C.12/1/Add.31, at para. 18. See also Special Rapporteur Mrs. Daes, in her final report to the Sub-Commission on the Promotion and Protection of Human Rights, Indigenous Peoples' Permanent Sovereignty over Natural Resources. Final Report of the Special Rapporteur, Erica-Irene A. Daes, E/CN.4/Sub.2/2004/30, 13 July 2004, para. 55.

[461] See Kaniye Ebeku (2006), *Oil and the Niger Delta in International Law. Resource Rights, Environmental and Equity Issues, op. cit.*, p.108.

adverse consequences of such operations on their culture, language, environment and most importantly, their land and natural resources. This is common in projects like mining and petroleum extraction, and agricultural programmes, all of which have serious implications for the resource rights of the indigenous peoples. In most cases, their lands are 'invaded' with little or no regard for their human rights and general well-being, as it is evident in the case of the Niger Delta people of Nigeria. As a result, 'many indigenous groups [have] felt themselves to be essentially "victims of progress", because the majority of development projects appeared to be in the interests of Governments, international agencies, and non-local people. It was for this reason that indigenous leaders began to press for greater recognition of their social, economic, and cultural rights and particularly for the right of self-determination'.[462] As stated by Victoria Tauli-Corpuz, an indigenous leader from the Philippines, "for many indigenous peoples throughout the world, oil, gas and coal industries conjure images of displaced peoples, despoiled lands, and depleted resources. This explains the unwavering resistance of most indigenous communities with any project related to extractive industries."[463]

However, the growing international concern for the protection of the indigenous peoples and their land and natural resource rights all over the world has had tremendous impact on the policies of these international financial institutions, particularly in their various projects in these communities. Worthy of note is the 2004 revision of the World Bank' Operational Policy 4.10 of 10 May 2005.[464] Paragraph 1 declares that OP 4.10 "contributes to the Bank's mission of poverty reduction and sustainable development by ensuring that the

---

[462]   Hitchcock, R.K., International Human Rights, the Environment, and Indigenous Peoples', 5 *Colo. J. Int'l Env. L. & Pol'y* 10 (1994).

[463]   Extracting Promises: Indigenous Peoples, Extractive Industries and the World Bank, in E. Caruso *et al.*, (eds) (2003), Tebtebba Foundation & Forest Peoples Programme: Capitol Publishing House, Manilla), at 9, quoted in Indigenous Peoples and the Human Rights-Based Approach to Development: Engaging in Dialogue Cordillera Indigenous Peoples' Legal Centre (DINTEG) and UNDP Regional Initiative on Indigenous Peoples' Rights and Development (RIPP) United Nations Development Programme Regional Centre in Bangkok, Serving Asia and the Pacific (2007), p.63.

[464]   Since early 1982, the World Bank Group has adopted a number of policies aimed at mitigating harm to indigenous peoples in WBG-financed projects. It adopted in 1982 a policy called *Operational Manual Statement 2.34 Tribal People in Bank-Financed Projects* – OMS 2.34. Following criticisms by NGOs, Indigenous peoples and several other people, coupled with problem of its implementation, OMS 2.34 had to be revised leading to the adoption in 1991 of another Policy called *Operational Directive 4.20 on Indigenous Peoples* ("OD 4.20"). OD 4.20 was an improvement over OMS 2.34 as it, amongst other things, 'strengthened Bank policy on indigenous peoples by requiring indigenous peoples' informed participation; accounting for indigenous preferences in project design; strengthening domestic legislation on indigenous peoples' rights; paying special attention to securing indigenous land and resource rights; and developing specialized Indigenous Peoples' Development Plans to provide for culturally appropriate benefits and mitigation plans in all projects affecting indigenous peoples'. See Indigenous Peoples and the Human Rights-Based Approach to Development: Engaging in Dialogue Cordillera Indigenous Peoples' Legal Centre (DINTEG) and UNDP Regional Initiative on Indigenous Peoples' Rights and Development (RIPP), *Ibid* p.46. In spite of its laudable provisions, critics called for its revision on the ground that it did not afford much

development process fully respects the dignity, human rights, economies and cultures of indigenous peoples." Paragraph 1 further provides that the Bank will only finance projects that comply with its operational policy, whose measures include the avoidance of potential adverse effects of the project on the people or where avoidance is "not feasible" to "minimize, mitigate, or compensate for such effects." Paragraph 16 provides that as a result of the indigenous peoples' close ties to lands and natural resources, when a project affects indigenous peoples, special considerations apply which require that the borrower "pays particular attention" to customary rights, both individual and collective, pertaining to traditionally owned lands or territories, to lands and territories customarily used or occupied, where access to natural resources is "vital to the sustainability of their cultures and livelihoods." Footnote 16 defines 'customary rights' to lands and resources as "patterns of long-standing community land and resource usage in accordance with indigenous peoples' customary laws, values, customs and traditions, including seasonal or cyclical use rather than formal legal title to land and resources."[465] The operational policies of other financial institutions like the Asian Development Bank (ADB) and the Inter-American Development Bank (IDB) are similar to those of World Bank.

The main point of interest though is that most countries of the world belong to at least one IFI (especially the World Bank) which are subjects of international law because they have rights and obligations that are determined by international law.[466] Therefore, as Member-States of these IFIs, countries are bound to respect and adhere to the institutions' Operational Policies which recognize indigenous peoples' rights. This is all the more so because these OPs, as in the case of the World Bank's OP 4.10, are developed in consultation with borrower Governments (Nigeria inclusive).[467] Such is the allure of the official policies of IFIs that Plant suggested that 'an instrument like the ILO's Convention No. 169 can have influence beyond ratifying States alone, if it is incorporated within the official policy of one of the major international financial institutions.'[468] However, in practice, the Bank's have not always adhered strictly to these principles. This is confirmed by a study undertaken by the Bank itself in 1992, which made it clear that more than a third of the Bank's projects affecting indigenous communities had not taken into account Operational Directive 4.10 on indigenous peoples, including that

---

protection to the indigenous peoples and their land rights. This was replaced in May 2005 by *Operational Policy 4.10 on Indigenous Peoples* ("OP 4.10" or "the OP").

[465] Indigenous Peoples and the Human Rights-Based Approach to Development: Engaging in Dialogue Cordillera Indigenous Peoples' Legal Centre (DINTEG) and UNDP Regional Initiative on Indigenous Peoples' Rights and Development (RIPP), *Ibid*, p.61.

[466] Anaya S. James, International Human Rights and Indigenous Peoples: The Move Toward the Multicultural State, 21 *Ariz. J Int'l & Comp. L.* 13, 47 (2004); Daniel Bradlow, The World Bank, the IMF and Human Rights, 6 *Transnat'l L. & Contemp. Probs.* 63 (1996).

[467] Kaniye Ebeku, (2006), *Oil and the Niger Delta in International Law. Resource Rights, Environmental and Equity Issues, op. cit.*, p.111.

[468] R. Plant, *Land Rights and Minorities*, Minority Rights Group, London, 1994, p.12, quoted in Kaniye Ebeku *Ibid*.

part of the directive mandating consultation with affected communities.[469] In spite of these shortcomings, IFI Operational Policy documents have contributed immensely to the jurisprudence on the recognition of Indigenous Peoples' rights; especially to land and natural resources.

2.7.6 INDIGENOUS PEOPLES' RIGHTS IN INTER-NATIONAL LAW AND PRACTICES OF STATES

A number of indigenous peoples' rights, including the rights to 'demarcation, ownership, development, control and the use of lands they have traditionally owned or otherwise occupied and used',[470] reflected in the various international instruments discussed above have been considered by a number of scholars to have become a part of customary international law. It is the aim of this subsection to examine the various laws, policies and national Constitutions of countries (especially those with large numbers of indigenous peoples) in order to determine to what extent these documents may have crystallised into norms of customary international law binding on States.

The question, however, is: What constitutes customary international law? Article 38 (b) of the Statute of the International Court of Justice provides that the Court shall apply, *inter alia*, 'international custom, as evidence of a general practice accepted as law', while adjudicating on an international disputes brought before it. The actual elements that must be present to establish a rule of customary international law are not provided in Article 38 and neither is there any unanimity among scholars on this. One scholar has given a four-part test for creation of a customary norm in international law by combining usage and psychological element (*opinio juris*[471]). These are State practice (the 'quantitative' element), *opinio juris* ('psychological' element), adherence to the norm by a majority of "specially affected States" ('qualitative' element) and continuation of the practice

---

[469] See Anaya S. James, *op cit*, p.58; John Swartz and Jorge Uquillas: *Aplicación de la Política del Banco sobre Poblaciones Indígenas (OD 4.20) en América Latina (1992–1997)*, World Bank, Regional Office for Latin America and the Caribbean, at 2 (1999).

[470] S.J. Anaya and Wiessner, S., *The UN Declaration on the Rights of Indigenous Peoples: Towards Re-empowerment*, Jurist Forum, School of Law, University of Pittsburgh, 3 October 2007, at http://jurist.law.pitt.edu/forumy/2007/10/un-declaration-on-rights-of-indigenous.php [accessed 23 November 2009]. See also Siegfried Wiessner, The Rights and Status of Indigenous Peoples: A Global Comparative and International Legal Analysis, 12 *Harv. Hum. Rts. J.* 57 (1999) for comparative research on State practice on indigenous matters where he concluded based on what he sees as positive changes in State statutes and practices, that indigenous land rights and rights to natural resources have acquired the status of customary international law.

[471] *Opinio juris*, according to Arthur M. Weisburd, Customary International Law: The Problem of Treaties, 21 *Vand. J. Transnat'l L.* 1, 7 (1988), exists "when a State believes that it is legally obliged to obey a certain rule". In a similar vein, M.E. Villiger (1985), *Customary International Law and Treaties*, Martinus Nijhoff Publishers, Dordrecht, p.26 contends that *opinio juris* is the "conviction of a State that it is following a certain practice as a matter of law and that, were it to depart from the practice, some form of sanction would, or ought to, fall on it".

over some period of time ('temporal' element).[472] To Cheng, *opinio juris* of States is the only true element of custom, and that 'usage instead of being a constitutive and indispensable element, merely provides evidence of the underlying rule and of the requisite *opinio juris*';[473] and that *opinio juris* operates "prospectively" and can attach to any given rule "instantaneously".[474] The court in *North Sea Continental Shelf Cases*[475] stated that two conditions must be met in order to create a binding customary norm:

> *"Not only must the acts concerned amount to a settled practice, but they must also be such, or be carried out in such a way, as to be evidence of a belief that this practice is rendered obligatory by the existence of a rule of law requiring it. The need for such a belief, i.e., the existence of subjective element, is implicit in the very notion of the opinio juris sive necessitatis. The States concerned must therefore feel that they are conforming to what amounts to a legal obligation. The frequency, or even habitual character of the act is not in itself enough. There are many international acts, e.g., in the field of ceremonial and protocol, which are performed almost invariably, but which are motivated only by considerations of courtesy, convenience or tradition, and not by any sense of legal duty."*[476]

The court further recognised that rules embodied in a treaty may play a role in the formation of customary international law. From the subsequent cases and opinions of ICJ in the *Western Sahara* and the *Nicaragua cases*, the Court is of the opinion that *opinio juris* may be manifested also in UN Resolutions, in that, 'the cumulative impact of many Resolutions, when similar in content, voted for by overwhelming majorities and frequently repeated over a period of time may give rise to a general *opinio juris* and thus constitute a norm of customary international law'.[477] Discussing how an emergent rule can crystallise into a binding norm of

---

[472] Dennis Arrow, The Proposed Regime for the Unilateral Exploitation of Deep Sea-bed Mineral Resources by the United States, 21(2) *Harv. Int'l L.J* 337–417 (1980), referred to by Jo Lynn Slama, *Opinio Juris* in Customary International Law, 15 *Okla. City U. L. Rev.* 603, 617–618 (1990).

[473] Cheng, Bin, United Nations Resolutions on Outer Space: "Instant" International Customary Law? 5 *Indian J. Int'l L.* 23 at 46 (1965).

[474] Cheng, *Ibid*, at 46–47, quoted in Jo Lynn Slama, *op. cit.*, pp.639–640.

[475] (W. Ger. v. Den.) (W. Ger. v. Neth.), 1969 I.C.J. 4.

[476] *Ibid* at 44.

[477] *Western Sahara* (Advisory Opinion), 1975 I.C.J. 12, 121; *Case Concerning The Military And Paramilitary Activities In And Against Nicaragua (Nicaragua v. United States of America)* (Merits) Judgment of 27 June 1986, at www.icj-cij.org/docket/index.php? [accessed 8 August 2009]. In *Sedco, Inc. v. National Iranian Oil Co.*, 10 Iran-U.S.C.T.R. 180 at 186, the Tribunal indicated that "United Nations General Assembly Resolutions are not directly binding upon States and generally are not evidence of customary law. Nevertheless, it is generally accepted that such resolutions in certain specified circumstances may be regarded as evidence of customary international law or can contribute- among other factors- to the creation of such law". This is possible where the legal effects of specific political standards contained within a resolution is recognised by States and they subsequently support their position through State practice. Quoted in Jo Lynn Slama, *op. cit.*, p.647; Stephen Allen, *The UN Declaration on the Rights of Indigenous Peoples: Towards a Global Legal Order on Indigenous Rights?*, at http://ilreports.

customary law, Anaya argues that 'actual state conduct is not the only or necessarily determinative indicia of customary norms'.[478] According to him:

> "With the advent of modern international intergovernmental institutions and enhanced communications media, states and other relevant actors increasingly engage in prescriptive dialogue. Especially in multilateral settings, explicit communication of this sort may itself bring about a convergence of understanding and expectation about rules, establishing in those rules a pull towards compliance even in advance of a widespread corresponding pattern of physical conduct. It is thus increasingly understood that explicit communication among authoritative actors whether or not in association with concrete events, is a form of practice that builds customary rules".[479]

Despite these divergent views on the actual elements for the formation of customary international law, certain distinct elements can be discerned. Also, *opinio* and usage operate interdependently to qualify each other and so, *opinio* is a constitutive element of custom which combines with usage to create rules of customary international law.[480]

Applying the above guidelines, evidence abounds to show that the provisions of the ILO Conventions and UN Declaration on the Rights of Indigenous Peoples have been accepted and incorporated not only into the national laws of State parties, and some non-State parties, but its principles have continuously been applied by the courts in these countries in the determination of indigenous rights.

Several international treaty monitoring bodies have started referring to the UN Declaration (although not legally binding) and making use of it in the interpretation of the rights of indigenous peoples and individuals and related State obligations. This practice, it has been contended, shows its significance and its implementation at all levels – international, regional and national.[481] For example, the Committee on the Rights of the Child in its General Comment No. 11 (2009) 'urges States parties to adopt a rights-based approach to indigenous children based on the Convention and other relevant international standards,

---

blogspot.com/2009/05/allen-un-declaration-on-rights-of.html [accessed 23 November 2010]; Cassese A. (1998), *Self-Determination of Peoples: A Legal Reappraisal,* Cambridge University Press, Cambridge, pp.69–70.

[478]   Anaya S. James and Robert A. Williams, The Protection of Indigenous Peoples' Rights over Lands and Natural Resources Under the Inter-American Human Rights Systems, 14 *Harv. Hum. Rts. J.* 33, 54 (2001).

[479]   *Ibid,* 54–55. See also Anaya S. James, The Emergence of Customary International Law Concerning the Rights of Indigenous Peoples, *Law & Anthropology,* Vol. 12, pp.127–139 at 128 (2005).

[480]   See Jo Lynn Slama, *op. cit.,* p.656.

[481]   Paul Joffe, Global Implementation of the *UN Declaration on the Rights of Indigenous Peoples-* and Canada's Increasing Isolation, September 2009, at http://thestar.blogs.com/files/joffe-2. doc [accessed 3 April 2010].

such as ILO Convention No. 169 and the United Nations Declaration on the
Rights of Indigenous Peoples'.[482]

Also important are Government statements and reports in the ILO and
Working Group processes about relevant domestic policies and initiatives been
taken concerning indigenous rights. For instance, a number of States, including
New Zealand, Mexico, Guatemala, Canada and Australia submitted information
to the Special Rapporteur, Ambassador Jose R. Martinez-Cobo during the
course of the 'Study of Discrimination against Indigenous Populations'.[483]
Mexico reported that since 1977, its indigenous policy 'is based on the tenet
that the strengthening of national consciousness will be achieved by respecting
ethnic pluralism'.[484] New Zealand reported that 'in recent years, the policy of
the Government has recognized the fact that New Zealand society embraces
more than one culture in one citizenship. This means first of all, that all citizens
regardless of race have the same rights and liabilities and that every citizen is
entitled to the same opportunity as others; but at the same time full recognition
is given to the fact that New Zealand is a multiracial and multicultural country.
This combined policy provides that, while being in every sense a full citizen of the
State, the Maori is entitled to retain his social and cultural institutions and that all
other citizens should be taught to know and respect those institutions'.[485] These
statements and reports lend credence to the fact that the distinctive character of
indigenous peoples is being daily recognized at the international level in line with
the ILO Conventions and UN Declaration.

Furthermore, the Inter-American Commission on Human Rights and
the Inter-American Court on Human Rights have greatly contributed to
the development of indigenous rights at the international level, particularly,

---

[482] Committee on the Rights of the Child, *Indigenous children and their rights under the
Convention*, General Comment No. 11, UN Doc. CRC/C/GC/11 (30 January 2009), para. 82.
See also Committee on Economic, Social and Cultural Rights, *Concluding observations of the
Committee on Economic, Social and Cultural Rights: Nicaragua*, UN Doc. E/C.12/NIC/CO/4
(28 November 2008), para. 35, culled at Paul Joffe, *op. cit.* The Committee on the Elimination of
All Racial Discrimination, in May 2008, referred to the UN Declaration on Indigenous Peoples
Rights in its comments on US obligations under CERD, when it stated that: 'While noting
the position of the State party with regard to the United Nations Declaration on the Rights of
Indigenous Peoples (A/RES/61/295), the Committee finally recommends that the Declaration
be used as a guide to interpret the State Party's obligations under the Convention relating to
indigenous peoples'- Despite the fact that US objected to the Declaration, the Committee still
regarded it as relevant to the implementation of the CERD. UN Committee on the Elimination
of Racial Discrimination, Concluding Observations of the Committee on the Elimination of
Racial Discrimination: United States of America, 72nd sess, UN Doc CERD/C/USA/CO/6 (8
May 2008) 10, See Megan Davis, Indigenous Struggles in Standard Setting: The United Nations
Declaration on the Rights of Indigenous Peoples, 9 *Melb. J. Int'l L.* 439, 466 (2008).
[483] This was commissioned in 1971. See UN Doc. E/CN.4/Sub.2/1983/21/Add.1, 10 June 1983.
[484] *Ibid*, para. 114.
[485] *Ibid*, para. 115. Australia, Canada, Norway, Denmark, Colombia and other countries similarly
gave positive reports concerning their fundamental policies in relation to indigenous populations in their countries.

land rights and natural resources. *Awas Tingni v. Nicaragua*,[486] was the first international decision to interpret the American Convention in such a way as to accord recognition to the collective rights of the indigenous peoples. The court upheld the rights of the indigenous peoples of Nicaragua to their land and natural resources, and found that they are entitled, under the Convention, to have the State demarcate and grant title to the land as property of the Awas Tingni community in accordance with their customary law. This is in line with Article 14(2) of ILO 169, which provides that 'Governments shall take steps as necessary to identify the lands which the peoples concerned traditionally occupy, and to guarantee effective protection of their rights of ownership and possession'. The court arrived at this decision by applying what it called the "evolutionary" method of interpretation taking into consideration modern developments in the international realm regarding the rights of indigenous peoples. Even though Nicaragua is not a party to the ILO Convention, Judge Garcia Ramirez expounded upon this interpretative methodology by making specific references to the relevant provisions of ILO 169, and parts of the UN Draft and the OAS Declarations on the Rights of Indigenous Peoples.[487]

Further, the court concluded in *Saramaka People v. Suriname*[488] that 'the natural resources found on and within indigenous and tribal people's territories, that are protected under Article 21, are those natural resources traditionally used and necessary for the very survival, development and continuation of such

---

[486]   *Mayagna (Sumo) Awas Tingni Community v. Nicaragua* (2001) Inter-Am Court HR (ser C) No. 79; See also *Mary and Carrie Dann v. United States*, 11.140 (U.S.), Inter-Am. Comm. H.R., Report No. 75/02 (merits decision of 27 December 2002), where the court summarised what it felt are the "general international legal principles" that are applicable in the context of indigenous human rights both within and outside the Inter-American system:

(1)   the right of indigenous peoples to legal recognition of their varied and specific forms and modalities of their control, ownership, use and enjoyment of territories and property;

(2)   the recognition of their property and ownership rights with respect to lands, territories and resources they have historically occupied; and

(3)   where property and user rights of indigenous peoples arise from rights existing prior to the creation of a state, recognition by that state of the permanent and inalienable title of indigenous peoples relative thereto and to have such title changed only by mutual consent between the state and respective indigenous peoples when they have full knowledge and appreciation of the nature or attributes of such property. This also implies the right to fair compensation in the event that such property and user rights are irrevocably lost.

It is evident from the above that 'certain minimum standards concerning indigenous land rights, rooted in accepted precepts of cultural integrity, property, non-discrimination, and self-determination, have made their way not just into conventional law but also into general or customary international law'. Anaya S. James, International Human Rights and Indigenous Peoples: The Move Toward the Multicultural State, 21 *Ariz. J Int'l & Comp. L.* 13, 47 (2004).

[487]   Anaya S. James, *Ibid*, p. 44 (2004). See also Anaya S. James, Divergent Discourses About International Law, Indigenous Peoples, and Rights Over Lands and Natural Resources: Towards a Realist Trend, 16 *Colo. J. Int'l Envtl. L. & Pol'y* 237–258 at 253 (2005).

[488]   *Saramaka People v. Suriname* (2007) Inter-Am Court HR (ser C) No. 172 (122). See also *Yakye Axa Indigenous Community v. Paraguay*, 2005 Inter-Am. Ct. H.R. (ser. C) No. 125 (June 17, 2005); *Sawhoyamaxa Indigenous Community v. Paraguay*, 2006 Inter-Am. Ct. H.R. (ser. C) No. 146 (March 29, 2006).

people's way of life'. The Supreme Court of Belize[489] applied the Declaration, just barely one month after its adoption regarding the Mayan rights to land and resources. The judge held *inter alia*, that: 'both customary international law and general international law would require that Belize respect the rights of its indigenous people to their lands and resources'. As noted by Megan Davis, the 'transmission of this decision throughout indigenous networks globally arguably gives weight to Anaya's version of Franck's "pull toward compliance", the idea that explicit communication among authoritative actors is a form of practice that may bring about a convergence of understanding and expectation that builds customary rules.'[490]

Also, the Australian High Court in *Mabo* v. *Queensland (No. 2)*[491] recognised the traditional ownership of the Meriam (indigenous) people of Australia to their land and held that the British annexation of the Murray Islands in 1879 did not extinguish Native title. Justice Brennan who made copious references to international and comparative law maintained that '… whatever the justification advanced in earlier days for refusing to recognise the rights and interests in land of the indigenous inhabitants of settled colonies, an unjust and discriminatory doctrine of that kind can no longer be accepted'.[492] Also relying on the principles of the UN Declaration, the High Court of Botswana has recognised recently land rights to San hunter-gatherers.[493]

Furthermore, State parties to ILO Conventions and even some non State parties have incorporated its provisions into their municipal laws. For example, the Brazilian Constitution of 1988, for the first time in the history of that country, includes a chapter (Article 231) on Indian rights into its Constitution. This chapter recognises the Indians' rights to their culture and languages, access to the judicial system as well as their original rights to the lands they traditionally occupied. Article 231(2) provides that Indians are entitled to the permanent ownership of the lands traditionally occupied by them including the exclusive usufruct or enjoyment of existing resources, rivers and lakes. This is a great development because under the pre-1988 Constitution, under which the country

---

[489] *Cal v. Attorney General of Belize*, Claim No. 171 of 2007, Judgment, Oct. 18, 2007, 127, at www.law.arizona.edu/depts/iplp/advocacy/maya-belize/documents/ClaimsNos17land172of2007.pdf.

[490] Megan Davis, *op. cit.*, p.467. See also Thomas Franck, Legitimacy in the International System, 82 *Am. J. Int'l L.* 705 (1988).

[491] (1992) 175 CLR 1. See also *The Wiks Peoples v. The State of Queensland* 134 ALR 637 (1996) where the Federal Court of Australia held that pastoral leases did not extinguish native title. This view was also maintained in the US in *Montana v. US* (1981) 450 US 544. In New Zealand, the Court of Appeal has recognised Maori rights over the foreshore and seabed in *Ngati Apa v Attorney General* [2003] NZLR 643. This led to the enactment of the Foreshore and Seabed Act 2004 which provided that while the Maori could become the guardians of these areas, they belonged to the State. See Stephen Allen, *op. cit.*

[492] *Ibid*, 42.

[493] *Sesana & Ors v. Attorney General* (52/2002) [2006] BWHC 1 (13 December 2006). See also the South African case of *Alexkor Ltd. v. Richtersveld Community* (2004) 5 SA 460 (CC) ('Richtersveld').

was pursuing the assimilationist goal of integration, lands occupied by forest-dwelling aborigenes were part of the patrimony of the Union.

In 1997, "The Law Concerning Promotion of Ainu Culture and Dissemination and Enlightenment of Knowledge about Ainu Traditions" was enacted by the Japanese government. The Japanese legislature passed a law[494] aimed at protecting and preserving the culture and traditions of Ainu, an indigenous minority group in the country. The new law replaced the "Former Aboriginal Protection Law" that had been in effect for over 100 years, and had served as the legal basis for assimilating the Ainu into mainstream society.[495] This, again, represents a significant change in the lives of Ainu who before then were banned from fishing and hunting, which had been the traditional way of supporting themselves. The restoration of their cultural rights is seen 'as a way of atoning for the shameful decimation of Ainu society, disintegration of Ainu culture, and wounding of Ainu pride over the course of Japanese history'.[496] Notwithstanding the fact that only very few States have ratified ILO 169, suffice it to say that most of those that have ratified it belong to the indigenous world. Besides, the failure of other States to ratify it can likely be 'attributed more to political inertia than to a rejection of the Convention's essential terms',[497] as they have manifested their agreement with the Convention's core precepts while pointing out certain limited problem areas inherent in it.

Again, the UN Declaration was adopted in Bolivia at the national level as Law No. 3760 of 7 November 2007 and it was incorporated into their new Constitution (promulgated on 7 February 2009). Bolivia stresses that it "has elevated the obligation to respect the rights of indigenous peoples to Constitutional status, thereby becoming the first country in the world to implement this international instrument".[498] The Government of the Democratic Republic of the Congo has endorsed the Declaration, and further, the "Constitution has reaffirmed in that

---

[494] Japan Brief, Law enacted to protect Ainu Culture, Tradition, [Society] June 19, 1997, at www.fpcj.jp/old/e/mres/japanbrief/jb_464.htmloted [accessed 8 June 2009]. Also, Columbia's Constitution of 1991, among other developments, abandons the integrationist approach, expands indigenous peoples' social, economic and political rights and recognises their rights to exploit the natural resources within their territories- Articles 159, 246, 286, 321, 329, 246, 330. Ecuador's 1998 Constitution contains several provisions relating to indigenous rights. For example, article 84 recognises and guarantees to the indigenous peoples collective rights to retain ownership of community lands, participate in the use, enjoyment, management and conservation of renewable natural resources on their lands and further commits the State to promote indigenous peoples' practices of biodiversity management, traditional forms of social life and collective intellectual property.

[495] Masamii Wasaki-Goodman et al., Traditional food systems of Indigenous Peoples: the Ainu in the Saru River Region, Japan, at ftp://ftp.fao.org/docrep/fao/012/i0370e/i0370e08.pdf [accessed 8 July 2011].

[496] Ibid; See also Siegfried Wiessner, Rights and Status of Indigenous Peoples: A Global Comparative and International Legal Analysis, 12 Harv. Hum. Rts. J. 57, 89 (1999).

[497] Anaya S.J., The Emergence of Customary International Law Concerning the Rights of Indigenous Peoples, Law & Anthropology, Vol. 12, pp.127–139 at 131 (2005).

[498] Permanent Forum on Indigenous Issues, Information received from Governments: Bolivia, E/CN.19/2009/4/Add.2 (24 February 2009), para. 57; Columbia, which had previously abstained

regard the attachment of the Democratic Republic of the Congo to human rights
and fundamental freedoms such as those proclaimed by the international legal
instruments to which it has acceded.'"[499]

Even, in its draft form, the Declaration formed the basis for legislation in some
countries. For instance, the Indigenous People's Rights Act in the Philippines.[500]
The domestic practice of the four opposing States to the Declaration (Australia
(whose courts had revitalized the international indigenous peoples rights with their
decisions in *Mabo* and *Wik*), Canada (whose Government 'had proceeded with land
settlement claims and treaties'), the U.S. (whose observations on the Declaration
show that it only objected to what it felt 'to be the "overly broad and inconsistent"
language of the provisions on land and resources'), and New Zealand (whose
government recognizes the Maori's right to own, use and manage their lands and
resources according to Maori ways)), makes those States also according to Anaya
and Wiessner, 'part of the world consensus on customary international law'.[501]

From the above discussion on State practice,[502] as evidenced in the decisions
of their courts, national legislation, reports, claims of their Governments, and
declarations *in abstracto*, coupled with the second element – *opinio juris* – the
States, particularly the non-party States, are convinced that the recognition of
indigenous rights is a practice allowed by customary international law.[503] It can be

---

during the General Assembly vote on the Declaration, announced its endorsement of the
Declaration in April 2009. See Paul Joffe, *op. cit.*

[499] Permanent Forum on Indigenous Issues, Information received from Governments: Democratic
Republic of the Congo, UN Doc. E/C.19/2009/4/Add.3 (27 February 2009), para. 10.

[500] An Act to Recognize, Protect and Promote the Rights of Indigenous Cultural Communities/
Indigenous Peoples, Creating a National Commission on Indigenous Peoples, Establishing
Implementing Mechanisms, Appropriating Funds Thereof, and for Other Purposes, Rep. Act
No. 8371, § 2(a)-(f), (1997) (Phil.), at www.grain.org/brl_files/philippines-ipra-1999-en.pdf.
[accessed 8 June 2009].

[501] Anaya and Wiessner, *op. cit.* It has been further contended that the fact that 'the four States
contributed to the formation of the Declaration for many years before deciding to vote against
it points to a sense of *opinio juris*: if the final draft had reflected their desired changes and preferences, the States, including New Zealand, would likely have voted for the Declaration'- See
Sarah M. Stevenson, Indigenous Land Rights and the Declaration on the Rights of Indigenous
Peoples: Implications for Maori Land Claims in New Zealand, 32 *Fordham Int'l L.J.* 298–343
at 325, 326–327 (2008–2009).

[502] The practice does not need to involve a large number of States and neither does it need to have
lasted for a long time. Ebeku, relying on Malancczuk, contended that in the absence of any practice that 'goes against an alleged rule of customary international law, it seems that a very small
amount of practice is sufficient to create a customary rule, even though the practice involves
only a small number of States and has lasted for only a short time'. Kaniye Ebeku (2006), *Oil
and the Niger Delta in International Law. Resource Rights, Environmental and Equity Issues,op.
cit.*, p.118; P. Malancczuk (1997), *Akehurst's Modern Introduction to International Law*, 7th ed.,
Routledge, London, p.42.

[503] Kaniye Ebeku, *Ibid* p.119. F. Maes, "Environmental Law Principles, their Nature and the
Law of the Sea: A Challenge for Legislators", in M. Sheridan and Lavrysen L. (eds) (2002),
Environmental Law Principles in Practice, Bruylant Brussels, p.62. However, one is not unmind-
ful of the positions taken by few scholars that States are inclined to comply with indigenous
norms not on legal but rather on the basis of moral obligation. As argued by Oguamanam,
this position has been significantly weakened as a result of State practice upholding indigenous claims, coupled with the fact that 'international legal theory is inclined to undermine

arguably concluded that indigenous rights to land and natural resources are now established in customary international law. Indeed, John Alan Cohan, argues, based essentially on the content of international human rights Conventions and custom apart from domestic laws, that "there appears to be little doubt that the international community now regards indigenous peoples as having environmental rights that rise to the status of international norms" and that "because indigenous peoples' ways of life and very existence depend on their relationship with the land, their human rights are inextricable from [their] environmental rights".[504] He continued that these environmental rights can include "the right of indigenous peoples to control their land and other natural resources as a necessary means to maintain their traditional way of life".[505]

On whether Nigeria is bound by this rule of general customary law, it has been suggested that 'the principle of the "persistent objector" constitutes the single exception to the generally accepted premise that a rule of customary international law is "universally binding", even though participation in the formation of the custom is not universal'.[506] Even though it was not shown that Nigeria contributed to the State practice of indigenous peoples as discussed above, it is bound by the emerging customary international law to recognize, respect, promote, and enforce those rights, particularly the indigenous rights to land and natural resources.[507] Its failure to oppose or even protest against such rights supports a finding of the necessary *opinio* in customary norm creation,[508] and so, an inference of consent to the rights could be drawn from Nigeria's inaction. As noted by Maes, 'a non-reaction in a certain situation applicable to a state may be interpreted as an

---

the supposed divide between moral and legal subjectivities upon which the normative theory is premised'. See Chidi Oguamanam, Indigenous Peoples and International Law: The Making of a Regime, 30 *Queen's L.J* 348, 388 (2004).

[504] John Alan Cohan, Environmental Rights of Indigenous Peoples Under the Alien Tort Claims Act, the Public Trust Doctrine and Corporate Ethics, and Environmental Dispute Resolution, 20 *UCLA. J. Envtl. L. & Pol'y* 133, 154 (2001–2002), cited in David H. Getches, Indigenous Peoples' Rights to Water Under International Norms, 16 *Colo. J. Int'l Envtl. L. & Pol'y* 259–294 at 264–265 (2005).

[505] *Ibid.*

[506] Jo Lynn Slama, *op. cit.*, p.627; F. Maes, "Environmental Law Principles, their Nature and the Law of the Sea: A Challenge for Legislators", *op. cit.*, pp.62–63. Stein Ted L., The Approach of the Different Drummer: The Principle of the Persistent Objector in International Law, 26 *Harv. Int'l L.J* 457 (1985). It is important to stress that all States are bound by customary and general principles of international law, and so, a claim by a State that it is not a party to such and therefore not bound by it may not avail the State.

[507] See Kaniye Ebeku (2006), *Oil and the Niger Delta in International Law. Resource Rights, Environmental and Equity Issues op. cit.*, p.120.

[508] See Jo Lynn Slama, *op. cit.*, p. 628. Even for countries like New Zealand that voted against the Declaration, it has been contended that it is doubtful whether they can prevent the formation of a binding customary international law right, more so, when the Declaration received an overwhelming votes of States in favour of it, when several countries have acted to implement it into municipal law and their courts have used it as proof of international law. See Sarah M. Stevenson, *op. cit.*, p.341.

implicit consent to be bound.'[509] These international instruments evinced the direction of global thought and vision of what the indigenous peoples of the World are individually and collectively entitled to. Government policies must therefore move in this direction, so that policies that can enhance participation of indigenous peoples in the control of their land and natural resources in line with the trends and aspirations of the international instruments and the State practice of other progressive countries, as described above, are pursued.

In view of this, it is submitted that Nigeria's laws, particularly the LUA and the Petroleum Act, which exclusively vest ownership of land and natural resources in the State are inconsistent with the relevant international laws and regional instruments discussed above.

2.8   CONCLUSION

Indigenous peoples are closely tied to the land and natural resources of their traditional territories for their survival and cultural integrity. This chapter has examined the status of the Niger Delta people in Nigerian State and discussed the question of ownership of land and natural resources, both under the customary law and the relevant statutes including the Constitution of Nigeria. It has established a connection between the rise in oil-related conflicts and the recent agitation for resource-control by the Niger Delta people under the strangulated form of Federalism that is presently being practiced in Nigeria. On the whole, it contends that the laws relating to ownership of land and natural resources in Nigeria are incompatible with the various international standards concerning indigenous peoples' rights to land and natural resources, and so confirms the claim of the Niger Delta people that some of the Nigerian statutes negate their rights to land and natural resources and thus interfere with their ability to protect their territories from massive environmental degradation. Therefore, repealing and/or amending some of these laws in line with the emerging international standards can be a major vehicle in the movement for the transformative change that the oil producing communities of Nigeria so desperately need. This will be considered, further, in Chapter Three.

---

[509]   F. Maes, "Environmental Law Principles, their Nature and the Law of the Sea: A Challenge for Legislators", *op. cit.*, p.60.

CHAPTER THREE

LEGAL AND INSTITUTIONAL FRAMEWORK FOR OIL OPERATIONS IN NIGERIA AND THE STATE RESPONSES TO ENVIRONMENTAL INSECURITY IN THE NIGER DELTA

3.1 INTRODUCTION

Oil is the mainstay of the Nigerian economy, being the major source of revenue that the nation depends on. However, 'one of the worst features of the Nigerian oil industry is the increased social cost to the oil-producing areas by way of pollution,'[510]caused by oil spills, pipeline leakages, oil-well blowouts and gas flaring. The role of the law in ensuring a balance between the goals of economic development and the right of the people to a healthy and clean environment becomes imperative. This chapter examines the various laws aimed at regulating the oil industry and ensuring the protection of the environment in Nigeria. Although these laws do not employ the conventional language of rights, they are nevertheless designed to ensure that the environment is conducive for the present generation and is adequately preserved for future generations. These laws are also intended to provide effective remedies for people whose rights may be violated as a result of the damage to the environment.[511] The chapter addresses the adequacy or otherwise of these laws and the effectiveness of its enforcement machinery in protecting the environment and the people in the oil-producing areas of Nigeria.

The chapter also examines some of the developmental initiatives and committees set up by the Government to address the economic, social and environmental problems that have become the lot of the people in the oil-producing areas of Nigeria. It determines to what extent these initiatives have helped in ameliorating the plight of the people in this region, particularly as they relate to the promotion of respect for their human rights and in ensuring sustainable development of the Niger Delta region.

---

[510] Augustine Ikein (1991), *The Impact of Oil on a Developing Country: The Case of Nigeria*, Evans Brothers Nigeria Ltd., Ibadan, p.180.
[511] Akeem Bello, Environmental Rights in Nigeria: Issues, Problems and Prospects, *Igbinedion University Law Journal* Vol. 4, pp.60–95 at 75 (2006).

3.2 LEGAL FRAMEWORK OF NIGERIAN LAWS ON OIL AND THE ENVIRONMENT

3.2.1 CRIMINAL CODE

There are some sections of the Nigerian Criminal Code[512] that, although not targeted against the activities of the oil companies, may be applied in instances of oil pollution of rivers and streams (including gas flaring). For example, section 245 of the Nigerian Criminal Code provides that: 'Any person who corrupts or fouls water of any spring, stream, well, tank, reservoir, or place so as to render it less fit for the purpose for which it is ordinarily used, is guilty of a misdemeanour and is liable to imprisonment for six months'. This section may be used as a protective measure against water pollution. Equally relevant is section 247 of the Act, which may be used against gas flaring. It provides that any person who: '(a) vitiates the atmosphere in any place so as to make it noxious to the health of persons in general dwelling or carrying on business in the neighbourhood, or passing along the public highway; or (b) does any act which is, and which he knows or has reason to believe to be, likely to spread the infection of any disease dangerous to life, whether human or animal, is guilty of a misdemeanour, and is liable to imprisonment for six months.'

The use of these provisions in the protection of environment may, however, be difficult. For instance, the phrases "corrupts or fouls" and "render it less fit for the purpose for which it is ordinarily used" are too general for precise judicial interpretation.[513] Besides, it may pose great difficulties for the prosecution who may be required under the criminal justice system to produce scientific evidence to prove the charge beyond reasonable doubt. Also, one wonders why the offences under these sections are classified as misdemeanours, and so treated lightly, when recent information about pollution has revealed its seriousness.[514] Thus, in spite of the importance of these sections, there is no proof that any of the multinational oil companies that are daily polluting the water and the air in the Niger Delta have ever been charged with violating these provisions of the law.

---

[512]   Cap. C38, LFN, 2004.

[513]   M.T. Okorodudu-Fubara, Statutory Scheme for Environmental Protection in the Nigerian Context: Some Reflections of Legal Significance for the Energy Sector, *Nigerian Current Law Review*, pp.1–39 at 12 (1996).

[514]   See A.A. Adedeji and Ako R.T., Hindrances to Effective Legal Response to the Problem of Environmental Pollution in Nigeria, *Ibadan Bar Journal* Vol. 4, pp.12–23 at 18 (2005). Akin Ibidapo-Obe, "Criminal Liability for Damages Caused by Oil Pollution", in Omotola J.A. (ed) (1990), *Environmental Laws in Nigeria Including Compensation,* Faculty of Law, University of Lagos, pp.231–252.

3.2.2 HARMFUL WASTE (SPECIAL CRIMINAL PROVISIONS ETC) ACT 1988[515]

This Act was enacted after the 1988 Koko Toxic Waste Incident in Delta State, Nigeria.[516] It prohibits the carrying, depositing, dumping, transporting, importing, selling and buying etc of harmful wastes within the territorial jurisdiction of Nigeria.[517] Section 15 defines "harmful waste" to include "injurious, poisonous, toxic or noxious substances, if the waste is in such quantity as to subject any person to the risk of death, fatal injury or incurable impairment of physical or mental health". Oil pollutants, no doubt, come within the purview of the Act, as they are harmful, noxious and toxic.[518] The Act provides for both criminal and civil liability. Violators are liable to life imprisonment upon conviction.[519] Any carrier used in the transportation or importation of the harmful waste, and any land on which the harmful waste was deposited or dumped will be forfeited and vested in the Federal Government.[520] Section 12 provides that any person responsible for dumping or depositing shall be liable for any damage caused by the harmful waste. The Act also makes provision for the exclusion of diplomatic immunity which some foreigners may want to use to shield themselves away from prosecution,[521] while its provision also extends to corporate bodies and their erring officers.[522] These are quite laudable provisions, most especially when viewed against the background that most African countries have become dumping grounds for harmful wastes from developed countries in recent times.

The definition of "harmful waste" under the Act is, however, restrictive as it does not cover serious injury or impairment that may not be fatal or incurable. As rightly argued by one scholar,[523] the use of the word 'include' in the definition does not appear to cure the deficiency as injuries to be included can only be in the class (fatal or incurable) of those enumerated. Again, just like several other environmental laws in Nigeria, the prosecutorial powers are not conferred on the regulatory bodies to institute legal proceedings against the violators of the provisions of the Act and neither does it provide for citizens suit. The duty of prosecuting is vested in the Attorney-General of the Federation or in some

---

[515] Cap. H1 LFN 2004.
[516] In 1988, an Italian firm dumped toxic waste in the Port town of Koko. Before this incident, Nigeria was ill-equipped to manage such an environmental crisis, as there was no institutional capacity or laws to address such matters. See Sylvia F. Liu, The Koko Incident: Developing International Norms for the Transboundary Movement of Hazardous Waste, 8 *J. Nat. Resources & Env't. L.* 121 (1993).
[517] *Supra,* Section 1.
[518] Nwosu E.O., Petroleum Legislation and Enforcement of Environmental Standards in Nigeria, *The Nigerian Juridical Review* Vol. 7, pp.80–108 at 95 (1998–1999).
[519] *Supra,* Section 6.
[520] *Ibid.*
[521] *Ibid,* Section 9.
[522] *Ibid,* Section 7.
[523] Nwosu E.O, *supra* p.95.

situations the Police, who are not adequately equipped to deal with environmental problems. Hence, violators are rarely prosecuted.

3.2.3 OIL IN NAVIGABLE WATERS ACT[524]

This Act was enacted in 1968 to implement the 1954 International Convention for the Prevention of Pollution of the Sea by Oil (to which Nigeria is a signatory) so as to protect navigable waters from oil pollution. Generally, the Act prohibits the discharge of certain oils, such as crude oil, fuel oil, lubricating oil, and heavy diesel into the sea area. Section 1 makes it an offence for any ship to discharge 'any mixture containing not less than 100 parts of oil' into a prohibited sea area.[525] What constitutes '100 parts of oil' is not defined by the Act, though, the prohibited sea areas are stated in the Schedule to the Act. The Act further makes it an offence for any person to discharge oil or oily mixture into waters from any vessel or from any place on land or from any apparatus used in transferring oil from or to any vessel (whether to or from a place on land or to or from another vessel).[526] Section 3 is important for this work in that it covers cases of oil pollution, most especially, the ones from oil pipelines and also effluent discharges from oil refineries.

By virtue of section 6, any person who violates the provisions of sections 1, 3 or 5 of the Act shall on conviction by the High Court or a Superior Court, or on summary conviction by any court of inferior jurisdiction, be liable to a fine, provided that a summary conviction by an inferior court shall carry a fine not exceeding two thousand naira. Considering the grave and devastating consequences of discharging oil into waters on the health, the ecosystem and the socio-economic life of the people, one is of the view that the fine of N2,000 naira (24 USD) is no more than a slap on the wrist for multinational oil companies who are noted for causing environmental degradation in the region. This ridiculous amount cannot in any way deter the multinational oil companies and obviously is a far cry from the amount paid by the oil companies in developed countries for similar breach.[527]

Also, apart from failing to prescribe the minimum amount of the fine, the Act also fails to prescribe any term of imprisonment for offenders. It is suggested that these inadequacies should be reviewed to prevent arbitrariness on the part of the court. The amount payable as fine should be increased.[528]

---

[524] Cap. O6, LFN 2004.

[525] *Ibid*, Section 20.

[526] *Ibid*, Section 3 (1).

[527] Abimbola Salu, Can Laws Protect the Environment in Nigeria?, *Modern Practice Journal of Finance and Investment Law*, Vol. 2 No. 2, 140–154 at 147 (1998). In *N.R.A v. Shell (UK)* 1990 Water Law 40, the court imposed a fine of £1 million pounds on Shell (UK) Ltd. for polluting the River Mersey.

[528] Abimbola Salu, Securing Environmental Protection in the Nigeria Oil Industry, *Modern Practice Journal of Finance and Investment Law*, Vol. 3 No. 2, pp. 337–356 at 346 (1999).

Another problem with the Act is that it contains too many sweeping defences, thereby putting its efficacy into question. Section 4 of the Act creates several defences to the offences created under sections 1 and 3. For instance, an erring party may be exculpated if he is able to establish that the oil was discharged for the purpose of securing the safety of a vessel, for the purpose of preventing damage to any vessel or cargo, for the purpose of saving life, or that the discharge was accidental due to damage to the vessel or leakage and all reasonable care was taken to contain and put an end to the pollution. Other defences include sabotage, absence of negligence, and proving that the oil discharged was contained in an effluent produced by operations for the refining of oil which it was not reasonably practicable to dispose of otherwise than by discharging it into water. As rightly stated by a learned writer, 'by the time all these defences are pleaded, it is hardly feasible to convict anybody under the provision of these enactments'.[529] Taking into consideration the grave consequences that always followed pollution incidents it is suggested that, as in most jurisdictions, liability should be strict so that a culprit cannot escape liability merely by presenting one of these ready-made defences.

Another major limitation on the effectiveness of the Act in affording environmental protection to the Niger Delta people against pollution is contained in section 12. This section stipulates that no action can be brought under the Act without the consent of the Attorney-General of the Federation in a matter of oil spillage. The implication of this is that where a spillage occurs in a remote village, the local authority has to first be notified, then the latter will inform the State Government and then the State will finally inform the Federal Attorney-General. This obviously leads to waste of time, energy and resources. The law needs to be reviewed to grant the State Attorneys-General power to commence such actions.[530] However, it should be noted that the State itself will be a major shareholder in the oil operation business in Nigeria and so may not be willing to prosecute or commence any proceeding against the erring multinational oil companies. This may partly explain the outright reluctance on the part of the Attorney-General of the Federation, and other authorities concerned, in prosecuting offenders or enforcing compliance under these laws.

3.2.4 OIL PIPELINES ACT[531]

This Act was enacted in 1956 as one of the earliest laws on oil pollution and contains some important provisions that could be used effectively to protect the Niger Delta people and their environment from the negative impacts of

---

[529]   See Oluwole Akanle (1991), *Pollution Control Regulation in the Nigerian Oil Industry*, Nigerian Institute of Advanced Legal Studies (NIALS) Publication Series, p.9.
[530]   Abimbola Salu, Securing Environmental Protection in the Nigeria Oil Industry, *op. cit.*, p.347.
[531]   Cap. O7, LFN 2004.

oil operations. It was to 'make provision for licences to be granted for the
establishment and maintenance of pipelines incidental and supplementary to
oilfields and oil mining and for purposes ancillary to such pipelines.'[532] It provides
for the issuance of permits to survey, and for oil pipeline licences. As a way of
regulating environmental degradation, section 17(4) of the Act provides that:

> *"Every licence shall be subject to the provisions contained in this Act as in force at
> the date of its grant and to such regulations concerning public safety, the avoidance
> of interference with works of public safety in, over and under the land included in
> the licence and the **prevention of pollution of such lands or any waters** as may
> from time to time be in force."* (bold mine)

The Act also makes provision for the duration of an oil pipeline licence, which is
for a term not exceeding twenty years.[533] This may be in recognition of the fact
that 'the nature of pipelines may make them less fit due to corrosion and other
wear and tear arising from pressure and long usage.'[534] This provision will go a
long way in preventing the recurring incidence of oil spillages caused by ruptured
old pipelines. The Act confers a right of action on victims of pollution arising
from any breakage of, or leakage from, an oil pipeline or ancillary installation.
Section 11(5) provides that:

> *"The holder of a licence shall pay compensation ...; (c) to any person suffering
> damage (other than on account of his own default or on account of the malicious act
> of a third person) as a consequence of any breakage of or leakage from the pipeline or
> an ancillary installation. If the amount of such compensation is not agreed between
> any such person and the holder, it shall be fixed by a court in accordance with Part
> IV of this Act."*

This section is highly commendable in that it create strict liability for the licence
holder. The claimant is not required to establish negligence on the part of the
pipeline licence holder. However, this provision has been under-utilised probably
as a result of ignorance on the part of the claimants and their counsel,[535] and also
because of the defence of sabotage mostly raised by oil multinational companies.
In order to discourage sabotage-induced oil spillages, this section prohibits the
payment of compensation for damages arising from sabotage. In spite of the
good intention of this provision, it has its own shortcoming. Sabotage is an act
of individual or groups of individuals but is not a community action, usually

---

[532]   Preamble to the Act.
[533]   Section 17 (1) of the Act.
[534]   E.O. Nwosu, *op. cit.*, p.87.
[535]   A.O. Ekpu, Environmental Impact of Oil on Water: A Comparative Overview of the Law and
        Policy in the United States and Nigeria, *Denver Journal of International Law and Policy*, Vol.
        24 No. 1, p.89 (1995).

caused for economic gains. 'In many cases, it appears that sabotage is carried out by contractors likely to be paid to clean up the damage, sometimes with the connivance of the oil company staff.'[536] The Act fails to take into consideration the innocent individuals in the community who may not be involved in the sabotage and yet suffer considerable loss as a result of the act of sabotage. This is coupled with the fact that arrests of the perpetrators are rarely made. It is submitted that in the absence of proof of complicity, it is wrong to deny innocent claimants their right to be compensated for their damaged properties caused by an unknown third party. Such a refusal to pay them compensation amounts to violation of their human rights.[537]

3.2.5 ASSOCIATED GAS RE-INJECTION ACT[538] AND THE REGULATIONS

This Act was primarily made to compel every company producing oil and gas in Nigeria to submit to the Minister charged with responsibilities for oil (not later than 1 April 1980) preliminary programmes for (a) schemes for the viable utilization of all associated gas produced from a field or groups of fields and (b) projects to re-inject all gas produced in association with oil but not utilized in an industrial project. The Act also made it a duty for oil companies to submit detailed plans for implementation of gas re-injection, not later than 1 October 1980.[539] The Act also provides that no company engaged in the production of oil and gas shall after 1 January 1984 flare gas produced in association with oil without the permission in writing of the Minister.[540] Section 3 provides that:

> "Where the Minister is satisfied after 1st January, 1984 that utilisation or re-injection of the produced gas is not appropriate or feasible in a particular field or fields, he may issue a certificate in that respect to a company engaged in the production of oil or gas-(a) Specifying such terms and conditions, as he may at his discretion choose to impose, for the continued flaring of gas in the particular field or fields; or

---

[536]   Human Rights Watch (HRW), *The Price of Oil: Corporate Responsibility and Human Rights Violations in Nigeria's Oil Producing Communities*, New York, 1999, p.83.

[537]   Ibaba Samuel Ibaba and John C. Olumati, Sabotage Induced Oil Spillages and Human Rights Violation in Nigeria's Niger Delta, *Journal of Sustainable Development in Africa*, Vol. 11 No. 4, 51–65 at 61–62 (2009); O. Adewale, *Sabotage in the Nigerian Petroleum Industry: Some Socio-Legal Perspective*, Nigerian Institute of Advanced Legal Studies Occasional Paper, 1990, p. 17; Kaniye Ebeku (2006), *Oil and the Niger Delta People in International Law: Resource Rights, Environmental and Equity Issues, op. cit.*, p.274.

[538]   Cap. A25, LFN 2004.

[539]   *Ibid*, Section 2 (1).

[540]   *Ibid*, Section 3 (1).

(b) Permitting the company to continue to flare gas in the particular field or fields if the company pays such sum as the Minister may from time to time prescribe for every 28.317 Standard cubic metre (SCM) of gas flared ..."

The penalty for non-compliance with section 3 is forfeiture of the concessions which have been granted to the violator in the particular field(s) in relation to which the offence is committed. In addition, 'the Minister may order the withholding of all or part of any entitlements of any offending person towards the cost of completion or implementation of a desirable re-injection scheme, or the repair or restoration of any reservoir in the field in accordance with good oil field practice.'[541]

Close to the end of 1984, evidence revealed that no oil company had complied with the provisions of the Act and there was no evidence that the Minister had insisted that the oil companies comply with it. The reason which was related to the 'adverse effects it could have on the nation's economy if its enforcement results in a halt to oil production operations.'[542] Rather than ensuring the enforcement of the law, the Minister made the Associated Gas Re-Injection (Continued Flaring of Gas) Regulations 1984, which provide for exemptions to the earlier general ban on flaring. The Regulations, which became effective from 1 January 1985 stipulated conditions for the issuance of certificates for the continued flaring of gas. These were:

(a) where more than seventy-five per cent of the produced gas is effectively utilized or conserved;
(b) where the produced gas contains more than fifteen per cent impurities, rendering it unsuitable for industrial purposes;
(c) where an on-going utilization programme is interrupted by equipment failure;
(d) where the ratio of the volume of gas produced per day to the distance of the field from the nearest gas line or possible utilization point is less than 50,000 scf/km provided that the gas to oil ratio of the field is less than 3,500 scf/bbl, and that it is not technically advisable to re-inject the gas in that field;
(e) where the Minister, in appropriate cases as he may deem fit, orders the production of oil from a field that does not satisfy any of the conditions specified in these regulations.[543]

---

[541]   *Ibid*, Section 4 (2).
[542]   M. Kassim-Momodu, Gas Re-Injection and the Nigerian Oil Industry, *Journal of Private & Property Law* 6 & 7, 1986/1987, p. 83, quoted in Kaniye Ebeku (2006), *Oil and the Niger Delta People in International Law: Resource Rights, Environmental and Equity Issues, op. cit.*, p.206.
[543]   Regulation 1. It was contended that one of the underlying reasons for this gradual easing of the provisions on re-injection was probably the realisation that the NNPC, as majority share-holder in all the ventures, would be bound to pay up its own percentage of costs of re-injection, which amounts to a substantial sum. See Omorogbe Yinka, Pollution and the Nigerian Oil Industry, in Wole Owaboye and Osuntogun Abiodun (eds) (1992), *Thoughts on Petroleum*

To date, despite requests from environmental organisations, neither the oil companies nor the NNPC has disclosed whether any such Ministerial certificates have been issued, nor have they disclosed such certificates for their lawfulness to be assessed. The current position, as far as the public is concerned, is therefore that the lawfulness of the continued flaring has not been demonstrated.[544]

In reality, this Regulation defeated the aim of the Associated Gas Re-Injection Act, which was aimed at putting an end to gas flaring in Nigeria. As observed by one scholar, 'a total of 86 out of 155 fields thereby remained exempted from the anti-flaring provisions. The remaining fields were subject to a fairly insignificant penalty which made it far more economical for the companies to flare than to utilise or re-inject gas.'[545] This position was confirmed by the provisions of the Associated Gas Re-Injection (Amendment) Decree 1985,[546] which permits a company engaged in the production of oil or gas to continue to flare gas in a particular field(s) on the payment of a fee prescribed by the Minister. This Decree fixed a fine of 2 kobo (equivalent to USD0.0009 in 1985 when Nigerian currency was still strong) against any erring oil companies for each 1000 standard cubit feet (scf) of gas flared. Unsurprisingly, this paltry sum did not deter the oil companies from the continued flaring of gas to the detriment of the health and environment of the Niger Delta as it is far more economical and effective to flare than to re-inject or utilized the associated gas. The fines were raised in January 1998 to USD11 for every 1000 scf of gas flared[547] but the companies still continued with the flaring. The Government responded with the Associated Gas Re-Injection Act 2004 and the Associated Gas Re-Injection (Amendment) Act 2004, which made it compulsory for all oil-producing companies in the country to submit detailed plans for utilisation of their gases. Flaring of associated gas without the written permission of the Minister was also prohibited, but all these seem to have been inadequate to deter the oil companies, as the gas flaring still continues unabated.

Suffice it to say that 1985 was initially promoted by the Government and the oil operators as the year to which to end gas flaring. This was then shifted to 2003, 2004, 2006, 2008, 2010 and then to 2012 with the draft version of the Petroleum Industry Bill (PIB) mandating the oil firms to end gas flaring in

---

Law, being a Report of National Workshop on Petroleum and Industrial Law, The Law Society, Faculty of Law, University of Lagos (Special Publication), p.25.

[544] Environmental Rights Action/Friends of the Earth Nigeria/Climate Justice Programme Report (2005), *Gas Flaring in Nigeria: A Human Rights, Environmental and Economic Monstrosity,* at www.climatelaw.org/cases/case-documents/nigeria/report/section9 [accessed at 26 February 2010].

[545] Omorogbe Yinka, Law and Investor Protection in the Nigerian Natural Gas Industry, 14 *J. Energy Nat. Resources L.* 179–192 at 181 (1996).

[546] Decree No. 7 of 1985.

[547] Garba I. Malumfashi, Phase-Out of Gas Flaring in Nigeria by 2008: The Prospects of a Multi-Win Project (Review of the Regulatory, Environmental and Socio-Economic Issues), *Petroleum Training Journal* Vol. 4 No. 2, p.116 (2007).

December 2012.[548] This apparently shows the little regard felt by the Government
for the impact of gas flares on the environment and human life in the Niger Delta
and neighbouring communities. And whether the December 2012 or the 2013
recently suggested by the oil MNCs will become realistic will depend much on
the Government's commitment and political will, the oil companies and most
especially the prospects and success of the various Liquefied Natural Gas (LNG)
projects in the country.

3.2.6 PETROLEUM ACT 1969[549] AND THE PETROLEUM (DRILLING AND PRODUCTION) REGULATIONS

This Act empowers the Minister in section 9(1)(b)(iii) to make Regulations for
the prevention of the pollution of water-courses and the atmosphere during
petroleum operations. Pursuant to this Act, the Minister issued the Petroleum
(Drilling and Production) Regulations 1969, which contains some important
provisions on environmental protection. Regulation 25 thereof provides that:

> "The licensee or lessee shall adopt all practicable precautions including the provision
> of up-to-date equipment approved by the Director of Petroleum Resources to prevent
> pollution of inland waters, rivers, water courses, the territorial waters of Nigeria or
> the high seas by oil, mud or other fluid or substances which might contaminate the
> water, bank or shore line which might cause harm or destruction to fresh water or
> marine life and where any such pollution occurs or has occurred, shall take prompt
> steps to control and, if possible, end it."

This Regulation has been criticised for the vague legal duty it imposes, as all the
'operator is enjoined to do is to take prompt steps "to control and, if possible,
end" the pollution in question.'[550] Also, the provision for the adoption of "all
practicable precautions" may be difficult to apply in reality because present day
economic pressures may be adduced to defeat the ecological and environmental
concerns. The use of the term "up-to-date equipment" appears to be relative
and vague as it does not assert certainty in terms of period or time in which a

---

[548]   Tim Cocks, 'Nigeria Oil Bill to Outlaw Gas Flaring by end-2012,' *Reuters Africa*, 28 May 2012,
        at http://af.reuters.com/article/investingNews/idAFJOE84R0A820120528 [accessed at 6 June
        2010].

[549]   Cap. P10, LFN 2004.

[550]   Omorogbe Yinka (2001), *Oil and Gas Law in Nigeria*, Malthouse Press Ltd., Lagos, p.136.
        Similar provision is contained in paragraph 43(3) of the Petroleum Refining Regulations, 1974,
        which provides: "The Manager [of a Refinery] shall adopt all practicable precautions includ-
        ing the provision of up-to-date equipment as may be specified by the Director [of Petroleum
        Resources] from time to time, to prevent the pollution of the environment by petroleum or
        petroleum products; and where such pollution occurs the Manager shall take prompt steps to
        control and, if possible, end it."

particular equipment must be replaced. This Regulation may partly explain why most oil companies in Nigeria use substandard and outmoded equipment in their operations, thus leading to the high frequency of oil spillages experienced in the oil-producing communities of Nigeria. As rightly noted, 'the use of poorly defined terms permits maximisation of production rather than protection of the environment'.[551]

Regulation 36 provides that 'the licensee or lessee shall maintain all apparatus and appliances in use in his operations, and all boreholes and wells capable of producing petroleum, in good repair and condition, and shall carry out all his operations in a proper and workmanlike manner in accordance with these and other relevant Regulations and methods and practices accepted by the Director of Petroleum Resources as good oil field practices'. The Regulation further provides that the licensee or lessee must take reasonable steps to control the flow and prevent the escape of waste out from relevant areas; prevent the escape of petroleum into any water, well, spring, river, lake, reservoir, estuary, or harbour; and cause as little damage as possible to the surface of the relevant area and to the trees, crops, buildings, structures and other property. This provision is highly relevant in view of environmental impacts of seismic operations most especially on buildings and vegetations, and the impact of oil spills on mangrove trees.[552] However, the terms 'businesslike manner', 'workmanlike manner,' and 'good oilfield practices' whose interpretation is important for the enforceability of the provisions of this law are not defined by the Regulations.

Also important for environmental protection is Regulation 40, which obliges the licensee or lessee to drain all waste oil, brine and sludge or refuse from all storage vessels, boreholes and wells into proper receptacles, constructed in compliance with safety Regulations made under the Act or any other applicable Regulations; and for these to be disposed of in a manner approved by the Director of Petroleum Resources or as provided by any other applicable Regulations.

Furthermore, the Regulations require a licensee or a lessee to pay "adequate compensation" to any person whose fishing rights are interfered with by the unreasonable exercise of the licensee's or lessee's rights. This provision which seeks to assist victims of oil pollution has some inherent weaknesses. Aside from the fact that it contains vague terms, such as 'adequate compensation', the scope is limited to fishing rights while other interests that may be affected by the unreasonable exercise of the licensee's rights are not covered. Also, the victim is only entitled to compensation if he is able to prove that the licensee or lessee exercised its right 'unreasonably'. It has been observed that this will be a herculean, if not an impossible, task for the victim, who often is a poor and illiterate fisherman.[553] It

---

[551]   Ekpu A.O., *op. cit.*, p.79.
[552]   Kaniye Ebeku (2006), *Oil and the Niger Delta People in International Law: Resource Rights, Environmental and Equity Issues, op. cit.*, p.197.
[553]   See A.O. Ekpu A, *op. cit.*, p.80.

is unthinkable for a poor and illiterate fisherman to procure expert evidence that
will be able to match that of the oil multinationals.

Another shortcoming is that there is no specific sanction or penalty
imposed upon the licensee or lessee for contravening any of the provisions of
the Regulations aside from the general power given to the Minister of Petroleum
Resources to revoke the licence or lease of the licensee or lessee[554] or to order the
suspension of their operations[555] for non-compliance with the enabling Act or any
regulations issued thereunder. The economic consequences for the nation may
make the imposition of penalties unrealistic unless the offence is a particularly
grave one. Equally important to note is that while the penalty of a fine of N100[556]
(less than US1) can have no deterrent effect on the oil companies, the prison term
is inapplicable to corporate offenders.

3.2.7 NATIONAL ENVIRONMENTAL STANDARDS AND REGULATIONS ENFORCEMENT AGENCY (NESREA) ACT

In 1988, the Federal Government promulgated the Federal Environmental
Protection Agency Act (Decree No. 58 of 1988),[557] and established an agency
called Federal Environmental Protection Agency (FEPA), charged with the
responsibility of protecting and developing the environment. FEPA and other
relevant departments in other Ministries were merged to form the Federal
Ministry of Environment in 1999, but without an appropriate enabling law on
enforcement issues. This situation created a vacuum in the effective enforcement
of environmental laws, standards and regulations in the country.[558] To address
this situation, the National Environmental Standards and Regulations
Enforcement Agency (NESREA) was established as an agency of the Federal
Ministry of Environment, Housing and Urban Development. The NESREA Act
was assented to by the President of Nigeria on 30 July 2007[559] and this repealed
the FEPA Act. NESREA, the new environment regulator of Nigeria is tasked with
the fundamental responsibility of protecting and maintaining environmental
quality in Nigeria. However all regulations, authorisations and directions made
pursuant to the FEPA Act, and which were in force at the commencement of the
NESREA Act, continued to be in force and have effect as if made by the NESREA

---

[554] Paragraph 24 of Schedule 1 to the Petroleum Act.

[555] Section 8(1)(f).

[556] Regulation 45(1) provides for a fine of N100 or imprisonment for a term of six months against violation of any of the Regulations.

[557] Cap. F10, LFN, 2004.

[558] Stan Okenwa, Nigeria: Odey wants Reversal of CITES Ban as NESREA Raises Stake in Wildlife Protection, *Daily Champion*, 4 February 2010.

[559] See the Federal Republic of Nigeria Official Gazette, Government Notice No. 61, Act No. 25. Section 36 of the Act repealed the FEPA Act.

Act.[560] Until it was repealed, the FEPA Act was the most important environmental protection law in Nigeria.

NESREA has as its objectives the responsibility for the protection and development of the environment, biodiversity conservation and sustainable development of Nigeria's natural resources in general and environmental technology. The objectives of the agency include coordination and liaison with relevant stakeholders within and outside Nigeria on matters of enforcement of environmental standards, regulations, rules, laws, policies and guidelines.[561] Its functions are stated in section 7 of the Act, and these include to:

(a) 'enforce compliance with laws, guidelines, policies and standards on environmental matters;

(b) coordinate and liaise with stakeholders, within and outside Nigeria, on matters of environmental standards, regulations and enforcement;

(c) enforce compliance with the provisions of international agreements, protocols, conventions and treaties on the environment, including climate change, biodiversity, conservation, desertification, forestry, oil and gas, chemicals, hazardous wastes, ozone depletion, marine and wildlife, pollution, sanitation and such other environmental agreements as may from time to time come into force …

(h) enforce through compliance monitoring, the environmental regulations and standards on noise, air, land, seas, oceans and other water bodies other than in the oil and gas sector …

(k) conduct environmental audit and establish data bank on regulatory and enforcement mechanisms of environmental standards other than in the oil and gas sector …'

The Agency is given wide enforcement powers. These include the ability to prohibit processes and the use of equipment or technology that undermines environmental quality,[562] the establishment of mobile courts to expeditiously decide cases of violation of environmental regulations,[563] to conduct public investigations of pollution and the degradation of natural resources, except the investigation on oil spillages.[564] It can be seen from the above that the Agency is empowered to enforce compliance, control and monitor environmental regulations generally

---

[560] *The International Comparative Legal Guide to: Environment Law 2008*, Published by Global Legal Group Ltd., London, p.299, at www.iclg.co.uk/khadmin/Publications/pdf/2032.pdf [accessed 2 March 2010]. The following Regulations aimed at controlling and protecting the environment were made by FEPA pursuant to the NESREA Act: Guidelines and Standards for Environmental Pollution Control in Nigeria 1991; National Environmental Protection (Effluent Limitation) Regulations 1991; National Environmental Protection (Pollution Abatement in Industries and Facilities Generating Wastes) Regulations 1991; National Environmental Protection (Management of Solid and Hazardous Wastes) Regulations 1991.

[561] Section 2 of the Act.

[562] Section 8(d).

[563] Section 8(f).

[564] Section 8(g).

other than in the oil and gas sector. In my visit to the NESREA's office in Abuja
during the course of my fieldwork in January 2011, one of the officers of the
Agency who pleaded for anonymity confirmed that the Agency does not have the
legal capacity to deal with issues relating to oil and gas. However, while section
7(h)[565] of the NESREA Act empowers NESREA to enforce compliance with any
environmental legislation on, among others, disposal of hazardous chemicals and
wastes, and any environmental regulations and standards on noise, air, etc *other
than in the oil and gas sector*, section 7(c) of the same Act includes 'oil and gas' in
the list of international treaties on the environment to be enforced by NESREA.
For effective enforcement of the standards, rules, policies and regulations by
NESREA; and to avoid conflict between it and the National Oil Spill Detection
and Response Agency (NOSDRA) – the body charged to deal specifically with
matters of oil spill management/pollution, there is therefore a need to review
this section to clarify the mandate of NESREA in order to avoid overlapping of
responsibilities and functions between the two agencies.

In spite of the laudable provisions of the Act, one of its shortcomings is in
the area of environmental health protection. Notwithstanding the provision of
section 7(d) of the Act which empowers NESREA to 'enforce compliance with
policies, standards, legislation and guidelines ... [on] environmental health and
sanitation', membership of its Governing Council is limited to representatives
from the environment, minerals, agricultural and natural resources, water,
science and technology, standards organizations, manufacturers association, oil
companies and civil society. The exclusion of the health sector in this important
implementation board has the potential to undermine efforts aimed not only at
addressing the health implications of environmental pollution, but also efforts at
promoting environmental health generally.[566]

Another major challenge facing this agency is the lack of awareness of
the people about the Agency and its functions. Not much is known about this
Agency – the major Nigerian environmental agency – by the Nigerian people and
the industries it is meant to regulate. A lot needs to be done about this as the
educational awareness is the greatest means towards empowerment of citizens
and the beginning of a sound, healthy and sustainable green environment.

The Agency's former Director-General, Ngeri Benebo, has noted that the
Agency is confronted with the challenges of inadequate human and institutional
capacity, inadequate baseline information data; inadequate budgetary
provision, inadequate public awareness and education on enforcement, and
poor information exchange and feedback mechanisms between the relevant

---

[565]   See also section 7(g), (j) & (k).
[566]   William Onzivu, Tackling the Public Health Impact of Climate Change: The Role of Domestic
Environmental Health Governance in Developing Countries, *International Lawyer*, Vol. 43
No. 3. pp.1311–1335 at 1325 (2009).

stakeholders and the Agency.[567] Whether the Agency will be able to meet its mandate of addressing the vacuum in effective enforcement of environmental laws, standards and regulations in Nigeria will depend, *inter alia*, on adequate funding, partnership with public sector including the State governments and civil society, cooperation with industries, an aggressive advocacy programme, competent and well-trained personnel, political will on the part of the Government, and collaboration with other countries and some international organizations.

3.2.8 NATIONAL OIL SPILL DETECTION AND RESPONSE AGENCY (ESTABLISHMENT) ACT 2006[568]

The National Oil Spill Detection and Response Agency (NOSDRA), a Federal Government body established under the Federal Ministry of Environment, Housing and Urban Development, was established under the National Oil Spill Detection and Response Agency (Establishment) Act 15, 2006 as the institutional framework for the coordination and implementation of the National Oil Spill Contingency Plan for Nigeria (itself devised in accordance with the International Convention on Oil Pollution Preparedness, Response and Co-operation (OPRC) 1990,[569] to which Nigeria is a signatory). Prior to the enactment of NOSDRA, it can be said that there were no adequate legal and institutional frameworks in place to directly address oil spills, and clearly defining oil spill preparedness and response principles. NOSDRA was therefore created specifically for the oil industry, and to serve as a policing body of oil spills.

NOSDRA is also mandated to establish, *inter alia*, a viable national operational organization to ensure safe, timely, effective and appropriate responses to major oil spills and to identify high risk/priority areas in the oil-producing environment for protection and clean-up, as well as ensuring clean-up and remediation of all impacted sites to the best practical extent.[570] Sections 6 and 7 of the Act set out the functions of the Agency, which includes that it shall:

(i) be responsible for surveillance and ensure compliance with all existing environmental legislation and the detection of oil spills in the petroleum sector;

---

[567] Mustapha Suleiman, NESREA highlights achievements, challenges, *Daily Trust*, Thursday, 19 November 2009 at http://news.dailytrust.com/index.php?option=com_content&view=artic le&id=9823:nesrea-highlights-achievements-challenges&catid=34:environment&Itemid=30 [accessed 2 March 2010].

[568] Act No. 15 of 2006 A.407 Acts and Subsidiary Legislation 2006 Vol. 1.

[569] Its objectives are to advance the adoption of adequate response measures in the event that an oil-pollution incident occurs; and to provide for mutual assistance and co-operation between States.

[570] See section 5 of the NOSDRA Act for the objectives of the Agency.

(ii) receive reports of oil spillages and coordinate oil-spill response activities throughout Nigeria;

(iii) co-ordinate the implementation of the National Oil Spill Contingency Plan (NOSCP) as may be formulated, from time to time, by the Federal Government;

(iv) co-ordinate the implementation of the NOSCP for the removal of hazardous substances as may be issued by the Federal Government;

(v) undertake surveillance, reporting, alerting and other response activities as they relate to oil spillages.

In carrying out these functions, the Agency is empowered to co-opt all the Government Ministries and Agencies mentioned in the Second Schedule to the Act, in the management of a Tier 3 or a major Tier 2 oil spill.[571]

This Act is commendable as it tries to address the issue of environmental degradation emanating mostly from oil pollution which is one of the root causes of the crisis in the Niger Delta. Pollution from oil exploration and exploitation activities in the Niger Delta impacts heavily on the health of humans and resources such as agricultural land, fresh water, mangroves, fish and shellfish and results in high costs for the remediation of contaminated sites. Oil spills from leaking underground pipelines and storage tanks are a regular occurrence, rendering vast tracts of land and water bodies unproductive.[572] Indeed, the conclusion reached after a Natural Resource Damage Assessment and Restoration Scoping Team visited the Niger Delta from 21–29 May 2006[573] was that an estimated 9–13 million barrels (1.5 million tons) of oil has spilled in the Niger Delta ecosystem

---

[571] *Ibid*, Section 7(g)(ii). According to Bamidele Ajakaiye, 'Tier 1 handles spills less than or equal to 7 tonnes (50 bbls), that may occur at or near a company's own facility. Tier 2 handles spills greater that 7 tonnes, but less or equal to 700 tonnes (5,000 bbls), in the vicinity of a company's facility where resources from another company or industry are possible. Government Response Agencies in the area can be called in, on a mutual aid basis. Tier 3 handles spills greater than 700 tonnes (5,000 bbls), where substantial further resources would be required and support from a national or international cooperative stockpile, such as the Oil Spill Response Limited (OSRL), may be necessary. Such an operation is subject to government control and direction.' See Bamidele Ajakaiye, *Role of NOSDRA in Environmental Management Protection and Enforcement in the Oil and Gas Industry*, being a paper delivered at the 2008 Manufacturers Association of Nigeria (M.A.N.), Environmental Management Seminar Theme: Preparing Businesses in Nigeria for Environmental Challenges and Opportunities, held on 4 November 2008 at the Conference Hall, M.A.N. House 77, Ikeja, Lagos, at www.man-greencourses.com/sr.pdf [accessed 2 March 2010].

[572] Nigeria Vision 2020 Program, *Report of the Vision 2020 National Technical Working Group on Environment and Sustainable Development*, July 2009, p.41 at www.npc.gov.ng/downloads/Environment%20&%20%20Sustainable%20Devt%20NTWG%20Report.pdf [accessed 2 March 2010].

[573] A group of independent environmental and oil experts, with participation by Nigeria's Ministry of Environment, WWF UK and the IUCN Commission on Environmental, Economic and Social Policy visited Niger Delta communities and spill-damaged sites in Rivers, Bayelsa and Delta states. Despite this alarming figure, the Nigerian Government and the oil companies are yet to take drastic measures aimed at preventing oil spills from recurring, or addressing the impact of oil spills on the ecosystem and the people of the region.

over the past 50 years, representing about 50 times the estimated volume spilled in the Exxon Valdez Oil Spill in Alaska in 1989; an amount equivalent to about one "Exxon Valdez" spill in the Niger Delta each year. This, according to the team, makes the Delta one of the five most oil polluted environments in the world.[574] Pollution from oil spills continues unabated.

An oil spiller is required by the Act to report an oil spill to the Agency in writing not later than 24 hours after the occurrence of the oil spill, in default of which the failure to report shall attract a penalty in the sum of Five Hundred Thousand Naira (N500,000.00) (approximately US$3,500) for each day of failure to report the occurrence. The failure to clean up the impacted site, to all practical extent including remediation, shall attract a further fine of One Million Naira (N1,000,000.00) (approximately US$7,000) per day.[575] Suffice it to say that these penalties imposed on defaulting companies are quite inadequate to ensure compliance with the law when viewed against the background that failure, for example to clean up and remediate oil impacted sites, exacerbates human rights violations.

Another important provision of the Act is section 19, which empowers the Agency, in the event of a major oil spill, to assess the extent of damage to the ecology by matching conditions following the spill against those which existed before; to undertake a post-spill impact assessment to determine the extent and intensity of damage and long term effects; advise the Governments (Federal and State) on possible effects on the health of the people, and ensure that remedial action is taken for the restoration and compensation of the environment. The section further provides that the Agency shall assist in mediating between affected communities and the oil spiller; monitor the response effort during emergencies so as to ensure full compliance with legislation and the protection of highly sensitive areas, habitats, and the salvation of endangered wildlife; assess any damage caused by an oil spillage and monitor the clean-up operations to ensure full rehabilitation of the affected areas.

It can be seen from the Act that the Agency does not pay compensation to oil spill impacted communities. The Agency may only assess or assist in the assessment of damages caused by the spill and assist mediation between the oil spiller and the affected communities. It is the defaulting oil company or party that is responsible for payment of compensation on the basis of polluter-pays-principle.[576] It is noteworthy that the NOSDRA adopted the polluter pay principle in line with international best practice in the oil industry. The Act emphasizes the responsibility of polluters for cleaning up the environment, paying compensation and restoring the environment to its natural state. If sections 6(2) & (3) and

---

[574]   *Ibid.*
[575]   Section 6(2) & (3).
[576]   *Ibid*, Section 19.

section 19 of the Act are properly implemented, they may help in bringing to an end the hardship faced by victims of oil pollution.

However, while this system of compensation has its advantages, it presents a lot of problems. There is a problem of imbalance of power and knowledge between the oil companies and the communities in that the former has a considerable control over how the cause of an oil spill is determined. Also, the rates of compensation set by the Oil Producers' Trade Section of the Lagos Chamber of Commerce and Industry in 1997 (OPTS – the association of oil producing companies operating in Nigeria), based on the Government compensation rates, are set in Lagos without the involvement of the affected communities. This implies that the polluter plays a significant role in setting the terms of compensation.[577] Besides, the compensation paid, based on the OPTS rate, usually undervalues the injuries suffered by the victims in that it only covers a limited subset of resources. Further, the rate has not been revised to take into account inflation or increases in the value of trees over time; the rates do not cover non-consumptive uses, like sacred groves of trees and finally, the rates are basically much lower than the real value of the resource, in particular for fruit trees.[578]

Where a spill affects the community, the community leaders often represent the community. Apart from the fact that this type of negotiation is open to abuse, and may be discriminatory against women and the vulnerable in the community, damages suffered by individual members may be lost in the process of negotiation. Again, many kinds of damage are either inadequately covered or not covered at all. For instance, compensation is not paid for damage to the health of the people, long term damage to livelihood, to moving water bodies, such as rivers and streams, or to those unable to prove they are a landlord but whose crops and other property is damaged by an oil spill. This is because these situations are not usually factored into standard compensation calculations.[579] Some of these injustices were raised by the World Bank in 1995: '[T]he compensation rates do not include long term, non-market goods, or off-site effects. For example, only crops from a single year are considered for compensation. Similarly, long term ecological changes including vegetation changes from dredging and mangrove destruction are not covered. The program also neglects to include indirect economic impacts, like the disruption of breeding grounds for marine fish.'[580]

---

[577] Amnesty International Report (2009), *Nigeria: Petroleum, Pollution and Poverty in the Niger Delta*, p.71 at www.amnesty.org/en/library/asset/AFR44/017/2009/en/e2415061-da5c-44f8-a73c-a7a4766ee21d/afr440172009en.pdf [accessed 5 March 2010].
[578] Environmental Law Institute (ELI), *Natural Resource Valuation and Damage Assessment in Nigeria: A Comparative Analysis*, Environmental Law Institute, August, 2003, p.23 at www.elistore.org/Data/products/d13-18.pdf [accessed 18 April 2010].
[579] *Ibid.*
[580] World Bank (1995), *Defining an Environmental Development Strategy for the Niger Delta*, World Bank, Washington DC., Vol. II, Industry and Energy Operations Division West Central Africa Department, p.76.

This is coupled with the fact that there are some forms of damage which require expertise as regards quantification of damage, which the communities or even the oil companies may not be able to handle, e.g. calculation of the damage from multiple pollution events affecting water. As a result of the above, it is suggested that a new compensation regime that will engage the use of an independent consultants be put in place to avoid the current oppressive regime where the oil communities are left at the mercy of the all-powerful oil companies.

Another major challenge is the poor adherence to the provisions of the Act by the oil companies, particularly as regards the early reporting of oil spills and prompt clean-up and remediation of impacted sites. NOSDRA recently called on Chevron Nigeria Limited to step-up remediation efforts at oil impacted sites in Abiteye-Escravos in Delta State and at Ilaje in Ondo State whose pipeline oil spillages occurred in October 2006 and June 2007 respectively to ensure certification of the sites by the Agency. The Agency warned it will no longer condone delay in effecting clean-up of oil impacted sites by Chevron, as witnessed in Ilaje, where it was more than a year before any reasonable action was taken.[581] Again, in an oil spill that occurred at Ogbodo on 25 June 2001, where a massive oil spill occurred, clean-up of the site was delayed for months. It was reported by the Amnesty International that, when it visited the site on 4 October 2003, oil residues clearly remained on the water and the land, and many people claimed that they could no longer fish or hunt.[582] This incident affected some 42 communities as the oil which moved through the water system contaminated the communities' water supply, destroying fishing and the crops of the people. Also, a SPDC pipe that burst on 28 August 2008 resulted in a significant oil spill into Bodo Creek in Ogoniland. According to an Amnesty International Report, the leak was not stopped until 7 November.[583] The Report continued that as of May 2009, the site of the spill had still not been cleaned up, while a second spill was reported at the site on 2 February 2009.[584] Although Shell has pledged to clean-up spills as fast as possible, no matter what their cause, it has cited security concerns, and the desire of some communities to win clean up-contracts or extract greater compensation, as reasons for delays.[585] These reasons are rather spurious and weak considering the fact that delays can increase the impact of oil spills on the people and the environment. One begins to wonder whether there 'are there no ground rules as to the cost range and the source of contractors for the clean-up of oil spills in the

---

[581]   Emmanuel Onwubiko, *Environmental Friendly Oil Industry: How Feasible?*, at www.point-blanknews.com/artopn1147.htm [accessed 3 March 2010].

[582]   Amnesty International Report (2009), *Nigeria: Petroleum, Pollution and Poverty in the Niger Delta, op. cit.*, p.19; See also Christian Aid, *Behind the mask, Sustained Misery: Shell in the Niger Delta*, pp.28–30 at www.evb.ch/cm_data/public/Shell%20Award%20Nominierung_Behind%20the%20mask_0.pdf [accessed 7 March 2010].

[583]   *Ibid*, p.7.

[584]   *Ibid*, pp.7, 27.

[585]   See Shell Sustainability Report 2009, at http://sustainabilityreport.shell.com/2009/ouroperationsinfocus/nigeria/cleaningupspills.html?cat=b [accessed 23 May 2010].

joint venture operations production programme.'[586] The joint venture agreement
between the multinational oil companies and the Government should have made
provisions for contractors to be engaged for the clean-up in case of oil spills and
the range of cost to be expended.

The procedures for detecting oil spills, and to determine the extent of damage,
and for clean up are rather cumbersome, inadequate, time-wasting, semi-crude
and environmentally unfriendly with a resultant high impact on the ecosystem.[587] When an oil spill occurs, the community is expected to report the oil
spill incident to the local government which will then report to the oil company
that owns the facilities or the NNPC. The oil company should notify the regulators
including the NOSDRA, the Department of Petroleum Resources (DPR) and
the responsible State Ministry of Environment (STMENV). Within twenty-four
hours, it is expected that a Joint Inspection Team (JIT) will be constituted, which
will include the Operators (oil company) representatives, the regulators (DPR,
NOSDRA, STMENV) and the communities and other stakeholders, to ascertain
the extent of spill, the volume of oil spilled into the environment, the causes of
spill and the clean-up strategies to be adopted and whether it is necessary to pay
compensation.[588] According to Oluseyi Fabiyi, the problems associated with the
current procedures include:

i.   *"If the oil spill is within the operator's right of way, the oil company is not
     mandated to pay compensation to the community. Therefore, the community
     may wait until the spill gets out of the right of way before they alert the
     responsible oil company.*

ii. *When it is ascertained by the Joint Inspection Team (JIT), that the spill is as a
     result of [third party] human interference with the oil facilities, the company
     is absolved of paying any form of compensation to the community irrespective
     of the damage caused. Therefore the tendency is for the operators to drag
     foot [their feet] in addressing oil spills if it is as a result of the activities of the
     vandals. In most cases the people responsible for the pipeline blow up don't
     usually reside within the communities. Most of the times the affected members
     of the community are not ... involved in the oil facilities vandalisation but they
     directly bear the brunt of [the] oil spill on their environment ...*

iii. *The methods of clean up and reaction time are not only ineffective but often
     inefficient. Usually [the] oil company assigns contractors to clean up oil spills ...*

iv. *There is no real-time detection of oil spill in the entire Niger delta, therefore
     oil spills spread into the ecosystem before they are detected and reported.
     Usually there is [a] time lapse before the Joint Inspection Team is constituted to*

---

[586]   *Shell's 2009 Sustainability Report*, Editorial Opinion, The Guardian, 20 May 2010, at www.
       nigeriamasterweb.com/paperfrmes.html [accessed 23 May 2010].
[587]   See Oluseyi Fabiyi, *Mapping Environmental sensitivity index of the Niger delta to oil spill: The
       policy, procedures and politics of oil spill response in Nigeria*, at http://gisdevelopment.net/pro-
       ceedings/mapafrica/2008/maf08_44.pdf [accessed 5 March 2010].
[588]   *Ibid.*

inspect the spill [and to] determine the cause and the extent of damage before [the] clean-up exercise can commence. The procedure is time-wasting to the detriment of the ecosystem ..."[589]

As a result, the local inhabitants are left to cope alone with the ongoing impacts of the pollution on their livelihoods and health, so human rights violations persist. Bradford Houppe, Vice-President of Shell's newly established Ethical Affairs Committee, recently openly apologised to all the inhabitants of Nigeria's Niger Delta for the several years of human rights violations, for which Shell has taken full responsibility. In his words, 'our failure to deal with these spills swiftly and the lack of effective clean-up greatly exacerbate their human rights and [the] environmental impact'.[590] There is therefore a need for NOSDRA to establish proper oversight measures over the multinational oil companies to ensure the prompt and effective response to oil spill incidents and cleanup.

The involvement of several bodies and agencies in spill detection and clean up is not only cumbersome and time-wasting but also results in a clash of functions among the agencies, particularly NOSDRA and the DPR.[591] This conflict situation, leading to unhealthy competition, calls for the Nigerian Government to clarify and define the roles of the various bodies/agencies responsible for the protection of environment. It also leads to the additional problem of bureaucracy, which continues to hinder the effective performance of the Agency.[592] In order to ensure a quick, adequate, transparent and credible oil spill assessment process, it is suggested that matters relating to oil spill contingency programme for preventing and responding to spills should be handled by a single agency independent of the

---

[589]   *Ibid.*

[590]   Bradford Houppe, *Shell Apologises for Human Rights Violations in Niger Delta*, being a Public Statement by Shell made at The Hague on 27 March 2010, at http://shellapologises.com/statement.html [accessed 17 April 2010].

[591]   DPR is given the responsibility of supervising all petroleum industry operations, including enforcing safety and environmental regulations. While NOSDRA is responsible for oil spill management, DPR is also involved, and lines of reporting and authority in this regard are not clear.

[592]   Amnesty International Report (2009), *Nigeria: Petroleum, Pollution and Poverty in the Niger Delta, op. cit.,* p.19. Analysing the dangers involved in the process, Amnesty International at p.46 of the Report noted that the companies appear to exert significant influence over the investigation into oil spills. In some instances, it was alleged that following the joint inspection with the regulator and the community, the oil companies would not specify the cause of the spill in the field, insisting that they complete that part in their offices. A clear example was an oil spill that occurred in Batan, Delta State in 2002, where 'SPDC rejected the findings of a joint investigation its staff signed, stating the spill was due to sabotage, claiming its staff were intimidated although video footage of the investigation contradicts SPDC's [Shell Petroleum Development Company of Nigeria] account.' Similarly, the World Bank, in *Nigeria Rapid Country Environmental Assessment, Final Report*, 30 November 2006, p.39 pointed to the limitations and conflicts that may occur in the process, stating that: "The multi-national oil companies pay public sector supervising officers high *per diem* or feeding allowances for their participation in the JITs. This makes participation in such teams sought after and potentially compromises the neutrality of the monitoring process."

oil companies. The agency would be responsible for oil spill detection, spill cleanup and remediation and should have operational offices in all the oil-producing local government areas. The cost of doing the cleanup would be passed on to the responsible oil company.[593] This agency should work in conjunction with all the communities affected by oil. On the other hand, these communities need to be educated and empowered to detect, report and monitor oil spills and participate in clean-up, monitoring, and restoration. The environmental education of the oil-producing communities should extend to making them to realize that the oil spills they create through sabotage of pipelines/installations, illegal oil bunkering/oil theft, artisanal refineries, *inter alia*, are causing long term damage to their future and their children's rather than looking at oil spills as a commercial asset.[594] An independent agency with a strong coordinating centre, whose event response operations would not be hindered by red-tape bureaucracy, will not only help in the timely response to oil spill incidents, and compensation and restoration of impacted areas but will further ensure adequate protection of the environment and the rights of the people in the oil-producing areas of Nigeria.

Another challenge is that the agency still lacks necessary equipment to function, such as boats or helicopters, which are vital for monitoring oil spills in a region with both onshore and offshore oil operations.[595] More often, they have to rely on oil companies for analysis of soil and water samples and for other data, all of which makes them unable to effectively enforce compliance on the oil companies. There is also a need for constant capacity training programmes and the procurement of high-tech equipment to enable NOSDRA to fulfill its mandate of preventing oil spills and clean-up and securing the restoration of affected areas.

3.2.9 ENVIRONMENTAL IMPACT ASSESSMENT DECREE 1992

Prior to the promulgation of the Environmental Impact Assessment (EIA) Decree,[596] the EIA culture regarding the physical, biological and socio-economic impacts of major developmental projects was to a large extent flimsy, ad hoc, fragmented, and in some situations non-existent.[597] The recognition of EIA as

---

[593] Oluseyi Fabiyi, *op. cit.*

[594] *Niger Delta Natural Resource Damage Assessment and Restoration* Project Phase 1 – Scoping Report Federal Ministry of Environment, Abuja, Nigeria Conservation Foundation, Lagos WWF UK CEESP- IUCN Commission on Environmental, Economic, and Social Policy, 31 May, 2006, at www.ngps.nt.ca/Upload/Interveners/World%20Wildlife%20Fund%20%20 Canada/Niger_Delta_scoping_report_2006.pdf [accessed 5 March 2010].

[595] Amnesty International Report (2009), *Nigeria: Petroleum, Pollution and Poverty in the Niger Delta, op. cit.*, p.44.

[596] Decree No. 86 of 1992, now Cap. E12, LFN 2004.

[597] See Femi Olokesusi, Legal and Institutional Framework of Environmental Impact Assessment in Nigeria: An Initial Assessment, 18 *Environ Impact Asses. Rev.* 159–174 at 160 (1998).

a planning tool for evaluating the environmental consequences of a proposed project started in Nigeria in the early 1980s with the 1981–1986 National Development Plan. The Plan stated that 'feasibility studies for all projects both private and public should be accompanied by environmental impact assessment'. This was also reflected in the National Environmental Policy of 1989 (revised in 1999) and other various national documents on environment, construction and agricultural policy. In the oil and gas sector, 'the Department of Petroleum Resources, required operators in the oil and gas sector to carry out EIA under the guidelines prepared by its Environment and Safety section. These guidelines were, however, not binding but mere administrative codes of procedures'.[598] It was the EIA Decree that actually established a legislative framework for EIA in Nigeria.

The Decree states 'albeit in very ungrammatical language',[599] that there is a duty to incorporate environmental considerations in any proposed activity by person, authority or governmental body that may likely or to a significant extent affect the environment or have environmental effects' and to encourage the dissemination of information relating to the environmental impacts of any proposed activities to relevant interested parties generally.[600] It requires that before the commencement of any new project, its environmental impacts must be evaluated in order to mitigate its effects on the environment.[601] Section 4 prescribes the minimum content of an EIA as follows:

(a) a description of the proposed activities;
(b) a description of the potential affected environment including specific information necessary to identify and assess the environmental effects of the proposed activities;
(c) a description of the practical activities, as appropriate;
(d) an assessment of the likely or potential environmental impacts of the proposed activity and the alternatives, including the direct or indirect cumulative, short-term and long-term effects;

---

[598] Olawale Ajai, Environmental Impact Assessment and Sustainable Development: A Review of the Nigerian Legal Framework, *Nigerian Current Legal Problems* (Vols. 2 & 3), p.16 (1998).
[599] *Ibid.*
[600] Section 1.
[601] Section 2(1) provides that the 'public or private sector of the economy shall not undertake or embark on public [sic] or authorise projects or activities without prior consideration, at an early stages, or [sic] their environmental effects'. See also section 2(2), which provides that: 'Where the extent, nature or location of a proposed project or activity is such that is likely to *significantly affect the environment*, its environmental impact assessment shall be undertaken in accordance with the provisions of this Decree.' (emphasis added). The phrase 'significantly affect the environment' used here and in some other sections of the Decree (for example, sections 1(a), 2(3)) is nebulous. However, the relevant criterion, as revealed in sections 26 and 40, is the adversity of the effect. See Olawale Ajai, *op. cit.*, p.27.

(e) an identification and description of measures available to mitigate adverse
environmental impacts of the proposed activity and an assessment of those
measures;

(f) an indication of gaps in knowledge and uncertainties which may be
encountered in computing the required information;

(g) an indication of whether the environment of any other state or local government area or areas outside Nigeria is likely to be affected by the proposed
activity or its alternatives;

(h) a brief and non-technical summary of the information provided under
paragraphs (a) to (g) of this section.

It is the duty of the Agency (FEPA now enlarged into the Federal Ministry of
Environment)[602] to hold wide consultations with all the stakeholders and then
come to a decision after evaluating all submissions. In doing this, it is expected to
be impartial, meticulously transparent and state clear reasons for its decisions.[603]
Section 14 of the Decree provides for when EIA is required. This includes *inter
alia*, where a Federal, State or Local Government body is itself the proponent of the
project and does any act or thing which commits the Government to carry out the
project in whole or in part.[604] Also, EIA must be carried out in respect of projects
listed in the Mandatory Study List (specified in the Schedule to the Decree),[605] or
the project is likely to cause significant adverse environmental effects that may
not be mitigable; or where public concern respecting the environmental effects
of the project warrants it.[606] However, section 15 dispenses with the need for EIA
for some projects. The section provides that EIA shall not be required where in
the opinion of the Agency (Federal Ministry of Environment) the President of
Nigeria is of the opinion that the environmental effects of the project are likely
to be minimal; the project is to be carried out during a national emergency for
which temporary measures have been taken by the Government; the project is to
be carried out in response to circumstances where, in the opinion of the Agency,
the project is in the interest of public health or safety.

It is important to note that petroleum projects,[607] and waste treatment and
disposal are placed under the mandatory study list and the implication is that

---

[602] This was done in 1999 by President Olusegun Obasanjo's regime. There is therefore the need to
review the EIA Decree to tally with the developments.

[603] See sections 6, 7, 8 and 9.

[604] See also section 2(4).

[605] These are agriculture, airport, drainage and irrigation, land reclamation, fisheries, forestry,
housing, industry, infrastructures, ports, mining, petroleum, power generation and transmission, quarries, railways, transportation, waste treatment and disposal and water supply. See
also section 2(4).

[606] Section 26(a).

[607] Listed under the petroleum projects are: Oil and gas fields development; Construction of offshore pipelines in exceed of 50 km in length; Construction of oil and gas separation, processing, handling, and storage facilities; Construction of oil refineries; Construction of product
depots for the storage of petrol, gas or diesel (excluding service stations) which are located

most of the activities or projects of oil operations, given their locations (mangrove forests in the Niger Delta)[608] are legally required to be preceded by an EIA.[609] The Department of Petroleum Resources (DPR) is the principal regulator in the oil and gas sector and it has published its EIA procedure in its own Environmental Guidelines and Standards (EGASPIN) 1991, reviewed in 2002. It is specifically provided in the EGASPIN that 'issuance of this guideline in no way absolves the operator or licensee from complying with other legislations'.[610] This implies that the oil industry must comply with both the EGASPIN of the DPR as well as the provisions of the EIA Act.[611]

However, this Decree suffers from a lot of defects. In the first place, apart from the poor grammar, it is a badly drafted legislation with a lot of ambiguous and meaningless provisions. For example, the goals and objectives of the Decree provided in section 1 are incoherent.

> "*The objectives of any Environmental Impact Assessment…shall be*
> (a) *to establish before a decision taken by any person, authority corporate body or unincorporated body including the Government of the Federation, State or Local Government intending to undertake or authorise the undertaking of any activity that may likely or to a significant extent affect the environment or have environmental effects on those activities shall first be taken into account.*"

The word "is" is omitted between the word 'decision' and 'taken' thereby rendering the entire objectives meaningless. Again, the concluding portion which requires an assessment of the effect of the environment on an activity appears illogical. It is the effect of the activity on the environment that seems appropriate.[612] Also, section 13 provides that 'when a project is described on the Mandatory Study List … until the Agency has taken a *cause* of action conducive to its power' (italics mine). The word 'cause' as used in the section is inappropriate. The more appropriate word capable of giving meaning to the section is 'course'. Section 14(i) provides that 'where a Federal, State or *Local Government Agency Authority* established by the Federal, State or Local Government Council …' (italics mine). There is no such body or agency as a 'Local Government Agency Authority'.

---

608 within 3 km of any commercial, industrial or residential areas and which have a combined storage capacity of 60,000 barrels or more.
  Section 2(2).
609 Kaniye Ebeku (2006), *Oil and the Niger Delta People in International Law: Resource Rights, Environmental and Equity Issues, op. cit.*, pp.213–214.
610 Part VIII, Article 1.5 EGASPIN.
611 See Rhuks T. Ako, Ensuring Public Participation in Environmental Impact Assessment of Development Projects in the Niger Delta Region of Nigeria: A Veritable Tool for Sustainable Development, *Environtropica, An International Journal of the Tropical Environment*, Vol. 3 Nos. 1 & 2, 1–5 at 10 (2006).
612 Olawale Ajai, *op. cit.*, pp.24–25.

In addition, the entire section 12 is completely omitted as it jumps from section 11 to 13. The Decree is also full of wrong internal cross-referencing. Among these are sections 17(1)(b)(d) & (2)(d), 26(a), 27, 28, 29, 47(a), 49(1), 53(1) & (2), 54(1)(b), 55(1) and 56(1) & (2). For example, cross referencing in section 47(a) to section 11 is wrong. While the latter deals with notification of environmental effect to… affected states, section 47 is on the conditions for screening. And the reference in section 56(1) and (2) to section 15(b) and (c) is wrong for the reason that while the former deals with international agreement, the latter is on 'excluded projects'. Commenting on the drafting of this Decree, Olawale Ajai has noted that:

> *"Badly drafted legislation may be worse than no legislation at all, either because it encourages undue litigation or because it unduly compels the courts to embark on judicial legislation in order to ensure that effect is given to otherwise otiose and redundant provisions. The EIA decree appears to have been drafted by lay-men because of the unlawyerly style of language [and the] vague, ambiguous and meaningless provisions... it contains. What is unpardonable is the very poor grammar used in many provisions..."*[613]

These monumental inadequacies will no doubt weaken the protection it affords the people in the Niger Delta region concerning their environment and their right to a healthy and sound environment.

Also, the Decree uses a narrow definition of the word "environment" and so confines its meaning to the biophysical environment. Section 63(1) defines 'environment' as 'the components of the Earth, and includes –

(a) land, water and air, including all layers of the atmosphere;
(b) all organic and inorganic matter and living organisms, and
(c) the interacting natural systems that include components referred to in paragraphs (a) and (b).

It further defines "environmental assessment" to mean, 'in respect of a project, an assessment of the environmental effects of the project' and defines "environmental effect" of a project as any change that the project may cause to the environment, whether within or outside Nigeria, and includes any effect of any such change on health and socio-economic conditions. It appears from the above that the relevant effects to guard against are significantly adverse environmental effects. It follows therefore that 'the direct socio-economic and cultural impacts of a project on local communities and human beings are not relevant and need not be assessed'.[614] This runs contrary to the belief that environment exists for man. Again, the yardsticks – health and the socio-economic – adopted in the definition appears to be too

---

[613]   *Ibid*, p.24.
[614]   *Ibid*, p.26.

narrow. A more elaborate or expansive definition of 'environmental effect' is suggested, and the definition of 'environmental effect' given by the Canadian Environmental Assessment Act 1992, c. 37[615] is suggested.

Another defect in the Decree is section 15(1), which empowers the President to exclude some projects from EIA on the grounds of 'minimal environmental impact of the project'. Apart from the fact that this criteria may be susceptible to political considerations and abuse, the cumulative effects of what seems a minimal impact over a long period of time may, if care is not taken, become significant and calamitous to the people and environment. Furthermore, section 62 of the Decree makes it a criminal offence to fail to comply with the provisions of EIA. For individuals, on conviction the offender shall be liable to N100,000 fine or to five years imprisonment and in the case of a firm or corporation to a fine of not less than N50,000 and not more than N1,000,000. This, as with most of the earlier statutes considered, is rather too small to serve as a deterrent, particularly to corporate bodies (the oil companies and Governments), most especially, when the adverse effect of the projects are high and the environment cannot be restored back to its natural state. The section is inelegantly drafted in that while a corporate offender may be liable to a fine as low as N50,000, the measure of punishment for an individual offender is unqualified, that is, 'N100,000 fine or to five years imprisonment'.

Another major pitfall of the Decree is in the area of public participation. While it explicitly provides that the public be given a chance to participate in EIA process,[616] the extent of participation given to interested parties appears to fall far short of what is required under the international law on the rights of indigenous peoples. Part of the discussion below in chapter seven will be on the issue of Niger Delta Peoples' participation in the EIA procedures.

Also important is the fact that the EIA requirements under the decree only touch on future projects. It fails to provide for 'environmental audit' of projects

---

[615] As amended by the Canadian Environmental Assessment Act 2003, C.9. It provides that: "environmental effect" means, in respect of a project,
  (a) any change that the project may cause in the environment, including any change it may cause to a listed wildlife species, its critical habitat or the residences of individuals of that species, as those terms are defined in subsection 2(1) of the *Species at Risk Act*;
  (b) any effect of any change referred to in paragraph (a) on
    (i) health and socio-economic conditions;
    (ii) physical and cultural heritage;
    (iii) **the current use of lands and resources for traditional purposes by aboriginal [indigenous] persons**, or
    (iv) any structure, site or thing that is of historical, archaeological, paleontological or architectural significance, or
  (c) any change to the project that may be caused by the environment, whether any such change or effect occurs within or outside Canada." (emphasis added).
  This definition is more encompassing as it will afford better protection to the Niger Delta people and the ecosystem.
[616] While section 25 provides for guidelines for notification of the public, sections 7, 8 and 9 enjoin the Agency to disseminate information about an EIA in respect of proposed activities.

in place prior to coming into being of the Decree in 1992. This is appalling as evidence abounds that most of the environmental impacts of oil operations in the oil-producing communities of Niger Delta are caused by facilities which had been constructed over three decades before the enactment of the Decree and which are rarely maintained or replaced.[617] This is a serious shortcoming which creates suspicion as to the protection the Decree affords the Niger Delta people.

For the Decree to be able to fulfill its mandate of regulating and controlling environmental degradation arising from oil operations for the betterment of the present generation and engender sustainable development, these shortcomings need to be promptly addressed.

3.2.10 PETROLEUM INDUSTRY BILL

The Petroleum Industry Bill (PIB) 2012, which is currently before the National Assembly, is aimed at setting out a new legal and regulatory framework for the organisation and operation of the entire oil industry in Nigeria. The PIB combines 16 different Nigerian petroleum laws into a single transparent and coherent document. It is therefore 'a reform legislation which aims to put in place of the existing myriad of legislative and administrative instruments governing the petroleum industry one omnibus [piece of] legislation that establishes clear rules, procedures and institutions for the administration of the petroleum industry in Nigeria.'[618] It makes provision for three separate and clearly defined principal entities,[619] plus several other bodies, to deal with petroleum industry, and all these agencies and bodies are put under the Ministry of Petroleum Resources. It proposes the replacement of the current NNPC-dominated system with a new oversight structure in which a National Petroleum Directorate would set policy and the three new agencies would regulate implementation. The Bill also aims at filling the lacunae that exist in the existing laws regulating the oil industry.

However, with regard to the protection of the environment and the human rights of the people in the oil-producing areas, the Bill offers less protection. For example, the provisions on compensation in the Bill are more or less the same as in the existing laws. Section 280(1) provides: 'In the course of exploration and production activities in respect of petroleum, no person shall injure or destroy any tree or object which is: (a) of commercial value; (b) the object of veneration, to the

---

617 Kaniye Ebeku (2006), *Oil and the Niger Delta People in International Law: Resource Rights, Environmental and Equity Issues, op. cit.*, pp.214, 139–141.

618 Rilwanu Lukman, being Keynote Address by the Honorable Minister of Petroleum Resources on the Proposed Petroleum Industry Bill (PIB) delivered at Abuja on the 16 July 2009, at www.nnpcgroup.com/pib/petIndsBillDocs/SpeechByHonorableMinisterToIndustry.pdf [accessed 13 March 2010].

619 The Nigerian Petroleum Inspectorate, which shall be responsible for all matters "upstream", which includes oil and gas petroleum exploration and production; the National Midstream Regulatory Agency; and the Petroleum Products Regulatory Authority.

people resident within the petroleum prospecting licence or petroleum mining lease area, as the case may be.' It provides further that an offender shall pay 'fair and adequate compensation' to the persons or communities directly affected by the said damage or injury.[620] The protection that the section seeks to afford the people in the oil-producing areas seems to be more limited than that provided under the existing laws because things like water resources, farmland and fishing rights[621] are not covered in the Bill. Also, as with the existing legislations, the term 'fair and adequate compensation' is not defined by the Bill.

Another major change in the Bill is in the area of restoration and remediation following environmental degradation. Section 409(1) provides that a licensee or lessee shall 'as far as it is reasonably practicable, rehabilitate the environment affected by exploration and production operations, whenever environmental impacts occur as a result of licensees and lessees operations.' However, subsection 2 thereof states that the 'licensee or lessee shall not be liable for, or under an obligation, to rehabilitate where the act adversely affecting the environment has occurred as a result of sabotage of petroleum facilities, which also includes tampering with the integrity of any petroleum pipeline and storage systems.' The costs of restoration and remediation of pollution found to have occurred as a result of sabotage, shall be borne by the Local and State Governments in whose jurisdiction the said act occurred, using the Remediation Fund.[622] As demonstrated by the Amnesty International Report, 'the designation of the cause of oil pollution as sabotage is heavily dependent on the oil companies' own assessment.'[623] On this issue of dispute as to whether the cause of an act that has resulted in harm was as a result of sabotage, section 409(3) provides that such shall be referred to the Petroleum Inspectorate for adjudication. There is, however, doubt as to whether the Petroleum Inspectorate will operate differently from the

---

[620] Section 280(2). Again, section 412(1) provides that a licence or a lease holder shall be liable to pay 'fair and adequate compensation for the disturbance of surface or any other rights to any person who owns or is in lawful occupation of the licensed or leased lands...' Apart from the fact that the term 'any other rights' is also not defined, the Bill does focus on surface goods.

[621] Amnesty International Report (2009), *Nigeria: Petroleum, Pollution and Poverty in the Niger Delta, op. cit.*, p.53.

[622] Section 286 requires every State and Local Government within which any licence or lease is located to pay a sum equal to 1% of the state's annual derivation allocation, and 0.5% of the Local Government's annual derivation allocation into a Remediation Fund which would be utilised exclusively for the restoration and remediation of the environment where the damage has been caused by sabotage. However, the Bill neither stipulates any procedure for its collection, nor makes any provision for the management of the Fund. The Federal Government should also be made to contribute to this fund, as it basically controls the security apparatus of the State that is supposed to be preventing sabotage. For more discussion of the PIB, see Social Development Integrated Centre (Social Action) (2009), *Communities and the Petroleum Industry Bill* (PIB), being Report of Communities and Civil Society Consultation Forum on the Petroleum Industry Bill 2009, organized by Social Action, Stakeholder Democracy Network (SDN) in collaboration with the Bayelsa State NGO Forum (BANGOF), Yenagoa, Bayelsa State, 27–28 November 2009.

[623] Amnesty International Report (2009), *Nigeria: Petroleum, Pollution and Poverty in the Niger Delta, op. cit.*, p.54.

way the DPR is presently operating, most especially having regard to its lack of independence and its lack of capacity and resources.[624]

By virtue of section 283 of the bill, oil companies are required to submit an environmental program or environmental quality management plan to the Inspectorate for approval, and prior to the approval, the companies are further required, by section 285, to pay a sum to the Inspectorate for site rehabilitation or management of any negative environmental impacts. These are laudable provisions aimed at protecting the environment from harm and ensuring that communities enjoy a safe environment. However, the Bill fails to 'delineate clear guidelines by which the Inspectorate can assess the plans, set or update the cost estimates, or determine the appropriate time to intervene for damage remediation.'[625] There is no clear mandate given to the Inspectorate on how to make these vital decisions, the absence of which exposes Nigeria to the risk of having the oil companies dictating and setting environmental procedures, thereby defeating the goals[626] of the Bill. A situation where important environmental safety decisions are put in the hands of corporations predominantly driven by profit is certainly dangerous.

Again, in spite of the fact that the bill commits the Federal Government to promoting development of the petroleum producing areas, ensuring regular consultation with all stakeholders including oil community areas,[627] and ensuring that damage to the communities is minimal, there are no concrete measures in the Bill that would give force to these commitments, such as 'mandating community consultations or government oversight of community development plans or social impact assessments.'[628] Besides, the oil-producing communities of Niger Delta have complained of lack of adequate consultation on the Bill.

It is expected that these omissions will be addressed before the final passing of the Bill into law so that the Bill will be able to accomplish the goals set out by it.

3.2.11 BIODIVERSITY LAWS

Nigeria has signed and ratified a number of international treaties and agreements on biodiversity conservation, and these include the Convention on Biological

---

[624]   *Ibid.*

[625]   Patrick Heller, *The Nigerian Petroleum Industry Bill: Key Upstream Questions for the National Assembly*, Revenue Watch Institute, at www.revenuewatch.org/images/RWI_Nigeria_PIB_Analysis.pdf [accessed 13 March 2010].

[626]   The goals of the PIB include among others – to ensure peace and development of petroleum development areas, transform the oil industry into an engine of sustainable development, enhance transparency and governance, better fiscal benefits for Nigeria and eliminate harmful social and environmental impacts on oil producing communities.

[627]   For example, see sections 7 and 13.

[628]   Patrick Heller, *op. cit.*

162

Diversity (CBD) 1992,[629] the Ramsar Convention,[630] the Convention on International Trade in Endangered Species of Wild Fauna and Flora (CITES 1973),[631] the African Convention on the Conservation of Nature and Natural Resources 1968,[632] and several others, all of which impose varying duties on Nigeria to pursue conservation programmes. Article 6(a) of the CBD, for example, provides that: 'Each Contracting Party shall, in accordance with its particular condition and capabilities develop national strategies, plans or programmes for the conservation and sustainable use of biological diversity, or adapt for this purpose existing strategies, plans or programmes which shall reflect, *inter alia*, the measures set out in this Convention relevant to the Contracting Party concerned.' Article 8 (a) provides that each contracting party shall as far as possible and appropriate establish a system of protected areas or areas where special measures need to be taken to conserve biological diversity.

In recognition of the need to protect her biological resources, Nigeria has put in place some laws. These include the National Parks Decree 1991,[633] the Sea Fisheries Decree 1992,[634] the Endangered Species (Control of International Trade and Traffic) Act 1985,[635] Forestry Laws,[636] and Wild Animals Preservation Laws.[637]

The **Endangered Species (Control of International Trade and Traffic) Act 1985**[638] was made pursuant to the Convention on International Trade in Endangered Species of Wild Fauna and Flora (CITES 1973). The Endangered Species Act contains a list of endangered species for protection. However, in spite of the fact that the Niger Delta region have some of the species listed under the Act for protection, it does not cover the problem of habitat destruction by

---

[629] Nigeria signed the Convention in June 1992 and ratified it on 29 August 1994.
[630] Nigeria became a party to the Convention in 2000 and the Convention entered into force on 2 February 2001.
[631] This was signed by Nigeria in February 1974 and ratified in May 1974 but came into force for her on 1 August 1975.
[632] This Convention was revised on 11 July 2003 at the Second Ordinary Session of the Assembly of the African Union in Maputo, Mozambique. This revised version was signed by Nigeria on 16 December 2003 but it is yet to ratify it as at 30 March 2013. This Convention, which contains important developments concerning environmental protection, needs 15 ratifications before it can enter into force but has only been ratified by 8 (Burundi, Comoros, Ghana, Lesotho, Libya, Mali, Niger and Rwanda) out of 53 countries as at 30 March 2013.
[633] Decree No. 36 of 1991 (repealed by the National Park Service Decree No. 46 1999, now Cap. N.65 LFN 2004). The Decree established five National parks: the Chad Basin National Park, the Cross River National Park, the Gashaka-Gumti National Park, the Kainji Lake National Park, the Old Oyo National Park. Then, the Yankari National Park was added. In 1999, Kamuku and Okomu National Parks were added through the promulgation of Decree No. 46 of 1999, making the number on National Parks to be eight. It also has 445 forest reserves, 12 strict nature reserves and 28 game reserves. See *Nigeria First National Biodiversity Report,* July 2001, at www.cbd.int/doc/world/ng/ng-nr-01-en.pdf [accessed 20 April 2010].
[634] Decree No. 17 of 1992.
[635] Cap. E9, LFN 2004.
[636] For example Forestry Law (Western Region) 1958 as applicable to Delta State.
[637] For example, Wild Animals Preservation Law (Western Region) 1959 as applicable to Delta State.
[638] *Op. cit.*

---

human activities such as forest clearing, oil operations etc. contrary to Article
8(d) of the CBD.[639] Human-related activities pose serious threats to biological
resources as forests and many other important habitats throughout the country
are being lost through forestry operations, industrialization and pollution,
urbanization and solid wastes, wild fires, flooding and erosion, invasive species,
and poor environmental policy.[640] It has been argued that the major reason for
the loss of aquatic genetic diversity is water pollution.[641] Saro-Wiwa wrote in 1992
concerning the effects of oil exploration on the biodiversity of Ogoni land:

> *"I hear the plaintive cry of the Ogoni plains mourning the birds that no longer sing at
> dawn; I hear the dirge for trees whose branches wither in the blaze of gas flares. The
> brimming streams gurgle no more, their harvest floats on waters poisoned by oil spil-
> lages. Where are the antelopes, the squirrels, the sacred tortoises, the snails, the lions
> and tigers which roamed this land? Where are the crabs, periwinkles, mudskippers,
> cockles, shrimps and all which found sanctuary in mudbanks, under the protective
> roots of mangrove trees?"*[642]

It is now widely recognized that global warming over the past 50 years is
principally as a result of human activities that have released green-house gasses
such as carbon dioxide, nitrous oxides and methane into the atmosphere.[643] The
impact of oil operations activities – gas flaring, pollution and horrendous habitat
destruction in the construction of oil pipelines and other infrastructures – on the
Nigerian biodiversity is quite enormous.

Also, unlike CITES which aims at protecting both plants and animals, the
Endangered Species Act only makes provisions for animals. In addition, the
Minister has not altered the list of animals since the enactment of the Act even
when some species of animals have been recently pronounced endangered by
international organizations or scientists.[644]

The **National Park Service Decree**[645] provides, *inter alia*, that a person shall
be guilty, unless authorized to do so under the Decree or Regulations made

---

[639] Kaniye Ebeku, Biodiversity Conservation in Nigeria: An Appraisal of the Legal Regime in
Relation to the Niger Delta Area of the Country, 16 *J. Envtl. L.* 361–375 at 370–371 (2004).
Article 8(d) of CBD enjoins the contracting parties to the Convention to promote the protection of ecosystems, natural habitats and the maintenance of viable populations of species in
natural surroundings.
[640] *NIGERIA: National Biodiversity Strategy and Action Plan*, at www.cbd.int/doc/world/ng/ng-
nbsap-01-en.pdf [accessed 20 April 2010].
[641] Emma-Okafor, Lilian Chinenye *et al.*, Biodiversity Conservation for Sustainable Agriculture
in Tropical Rainforest of Nigeria, 3(1) *New York Science Journal* 81–88 at 83 (2010).
[642] Ken Saro-Wiwa (1992), *Genocide in Nigeria: The Ogoni Tragedy*, Saros International Publishers,
London, Lagos & Port Harcourt, p.83.
[643] Emma-Okafor Lilian Chinenye *et al.*, *op. cit.*, p.83.
[644] Bola Adewale, "An Overview of Biological Biodiversity Laws in Nigeria", in I.A Ayua (ed)
(1995), *Law, Justice and the Nigerian Society: Essays in Honour of Hon. Justice Mohammed
Bello*, NIALS, Lagos, p.334.
[645] National Park Service Decree No. 46 1999, now Cap. N.65 LFN 2004.

thereunder, if he introduces a chemical or otherwise causes any form of pollution; carries out an undertaking connected with forestry, agriculture, grazing, or excavation; or does any leveling of the ground or construction or any act tending to alter the configuration of the soil or the character of the vegetation; or does any act likely to harm or disturb the fauna or flora, in the National Park.[646] For these offences, section 37(2)(b) provides for a penalty of imprisonment for a term of not less than six months but not exceeding five years without the option of a fine. In the case of other offences under the section, 30 of the Decree, to a fine of not less than N10,000 but not exceeding N50,000 or imprisonment for a term of not less than one year but not exceeding five years or to both such fine and imprisonment. But where the offence is committed by a body corporate, to a fine of not less than N100,000 but not exceeding N1,000,000. These penalties will assist the government in enforcing the provisions of the statute.

The **Sea Fisheries Decree 1992** provides for the control and protection of sea fisheries within the territorial waters of Nigeria. Its relevance to the Niger Delta people is that this Decree prohibits the killing of fish by explosive substances or any noxious or poisonous matter, thus satisfying the concept of sustainability.

The **National Policy on Environment** launched in 1989, and which was revised in 1999, contains among other things some strategies for biological diversity and conservation of natural resources, including the promotion of *in situ* and *ex situ* biodiversity conservation and the implementation of a National Strategy and Action plan for biodiversity conservation. Importantly, the Policy notes that 'in Nigeria economic development has not been sustainable partly because biological resources are improperly managed.' The implementation strategies also cover mining and mineral resources, wildlife, marine and coastal area resources, industry, energy, oil and gas, etc.

In spite of the above, the provisions of Nigerian laws as well as international laws on biodiversity conservation are largely defective or inadequate thereby rendering them ineffective as instruments for the conservation of the rich biodiversity in the Niger Delta region.[647] One of the major defects is the non-inclusion of any part of the country's coastal area, and by extension, the Niger Delta, into the protected area system notwithstanding that the Niger Delta contains 'abundant species of national and international importance, some of which are listed as endangered under domestic law and international treaty.'[648] This point was also made by a scholar who notes that 'there is no legislation that directly protects species outside national parks and forests reserves.'[649] This no doubt runs contrary to Article

---

[646] *Ibid*, section 30(g), (m), (n) & (o).

[647] Kaniye Ebeku (2006), *Oil and the Niger Delta People in International Law: Resource Rights, Environmental and Equity Issues*, *op. cit.*, p.223.

[648] Kaniye Ebeku, Biodiversity Conservation in Nigeria: An Appraisal of the Legal Regime in Relation to the Niger Delta Area of the Country, *op. cit.*, p.372; See also NIGERIA: National Biodiversity Strategy and Action Plan, *op. cit.*

[649] O. Ajai, Implementing the Biodiversity Convention in Nigeria: Some Problems and Prospects, *Nigerian Current Law Problems*, p.167 (1995), quoted in Kaniye Ebeku (2006), *Oil and the*

8(e) of the CBD[650] and Article 4(1) of the Ramsar Convention on Wetlands 1971
(as amended in 1982 and 1987)[651] and other international instruments to which
Nigeria is a signatory. There is therefore an urgent need to address this matter. The
non-applicability of the national laws on biodiversity conservation to the Niger
Delta areas may not be unconnected with the fear that they would adversely affect
oil exploration activities, and damage the economic interests of the country. This
fear is obviously borne out of ignorance of Nigerian authorities, not appreciating
that biodiversity conservation is germane to the country's development. The
Nigerian Government should ensure conservation of the biodiversity of the Niger
Delta areas in the interest of the present and future generations.[652] At present,
there is no agency, State or Federal that is exclusively established to look into
biodiversity issues. There is therefore an urgent need to establish a Biodiversity
Agency to take care of biodiversity conservation.

It is also important to stress that Nigeria was suspended in 2005 from
membership of CITES for alleged breaches of its provisions on illegal trade in
endangered species. The suspension was however lifted on August 2011 at the
61st CITES Standing Committee held in Geneva, Switzerland,[653] following
the assurance by the Nigerian Government that it would put in place relevant
legislation on illegal trade in wildlife as well as establish inter-agency committee
to monitor and enforce the law.

3.3   COMMON LAW

Aside from the statutory provisions discussed above, common law remedies in
negligence, nuisance and the rule in *Rylands v. Fletcher*[654] are available to victims
of oil pollution. Common law forms part of the Nigeria's legal system and its
importance lies in the fact that such an action can be brought where there is a
lacunae in the provisions of the statutes. It provides an avenue for an individual to

---

*Niger Delta People in International Law: Resource Rights, Environmental and Equity Issues, op.
cit.*, p.223.

[650]   This section requires contracting parties to promote environmentally sound and sustainable
development in areas adjacent to protected areas with a view to furthering the protection of
these areas.

[651]   It provides that 'each contracting party shall promote the conservation of wetlands and water-
fowl by establishing nature reserves on wetlands, whether they are included in the List or not.'
Nigeria became a party to the Convention in 2000 and the Convention entered into force on 2
February 2001.

[652]   Kaniye Ebeku, Biodiversity Conservation in Nigeria: An Appraisal of the Legal Regime in
Relation to the Niger Delta Area of the Country, *op. cit.*, 374.

[653]   Paul Obi, Nigeria's Suspension from CITES Trades Lifted, *This Day*, 23 August 2011, at www.
thisdaylive.com/articles/nigeria-s-suspension-from-cites-trades-lifted/96928/.   In   fulfillment of its promise, the Nigerian Government has published the National Environmental
(Protection of Endangered Species in International Trade) Regulations, 2011 in its Official
Gazette.

[654]   (1866) L.R. [Ex. 265; (1866) L.R.] H.L. 330.

seek redress against perpetrators of acts cause 'in the context of injury suffered in respect of the individual's right to enjoy his property and immediate environment free from interference or disturbance.'[655] This could serve as an effective instrument in the hands of the Niger Delta people to enforce some of their rights.

However, the ingredients which the claimants have to prove to succeed, and the several defences of which the defendant may avail himself have made these torts unappealing for seeking redress against a polluter. As rightly observed by Emole, "the remedies offered by common law under the law of tort are ill-suited for the purpose of contending with oil pollution."[656] For instance, in the case of negligence, which is often used against oil companies, the plaintiff has the burden of proving that the defendant was careless in the exercise of his duty of care. In addition to showing that damage occurred, he must also show that the damage occurred as a result of the negligence of the defendant, that is, through his fault. In oil pollution cases this is usually a difficult task for a poor victim, given the technical nature of oil operations and the fact that the poor litigant may not be able to match the oil companies who have what it takes to provide expert evidence and technical knowledge to justify their actions.[657]

In diverse cases of oil-related infringements of the rights of the oil communities, such as in cases of nuisance attributable to seismic surveys and gas flaring, the courts have encountered enormous difficulties in attributing causality.[658] However, in some situations, the plaintiff may shift the burden of proof to the defendant by pleading *res ipsa loquitur,* meaning, the thing speaks for itself.

The *Rylands v. Fletcher* rule states that "the person who for his own purpose brings on his land and collects and keeps there anything likely to do mischief if it escapes, must keep it in at his peril, and if he does not do so, is prima facie answerable for all the damage which is the natural consequence of its escape." Here, the principle of strict liability applies so that the polluter may be held liable for the damage that occurs from his activities, irrespective of whether he was at fault or not. However, one of the exceptions that may affect the plaintiff's claim under the rule is that he must prove that the escape was as a result of a 'non-natural user' of the land by the defendant polluter – a requirement to which no

---

[655]   Kent Nnadozie, "Environmental Regulation of the Oil and Gas Industry in Nigeria", in Beatrice Chaytor and Kevin R. Gray (eds) (2003), *International Environmental Law and Policy in Africa,* Environment and Policy Vol. 36, Kluwer Academic Publishers, Dordrecht Netherlands, p.115.

[656]   Emole C.E., Regulation of Oil and Gas Pollution, *Journal of Environmental Policy and Law,* Vol. 28 No. 2 p.108 (1998).

[657]   See *Chinda & Ors v. Shell BP* (1974) 2 RSLR 1; *Anthony Atunbi v. Shell BP Petroleum Company of Nigeria* Suit No. UCH/48/73 Ughelli High Court delivered on 12 November 1974.

[658]   Kenneth Omeje, The Rentier State: Oil-related Legislation and Conflict in the Niger Delta, Nigeria, *op. cit.,* p.223. For instance, in cases relating to seismic survey, the claims of the victims of oil pollution could not succeed in court as a result of the difficulty in establishing causality and consequential damage. See *Seismograph Service Ltd. v. Onokpasa* [1972] 1 All NLR 343; *Seismograph Service Ltd. v. Akporuovo* [1974] 1 All NLR 104; *Seismograph Service v. Ogbeni* (1976) 4 S.C. 85; *Seismograph Service v. Saturday Mark* (1993) 7 NWLR (pt. 304) 203.

objective or universal test can be applied.[659] A further exception to the rule is where the defendant is empowered by statute to perform certain acts, such as where the polluter has a licence to carry out the activity that resulted in the harm complained of.[660]

In situations where a claimant succeeds in an action in tort, the damages awarded by the court are usually ridiculously low[661] to the point that the award may just be the amount of compensation that was earlier offered by the defendant.[662] However, the court has sometimes been liberal and progressive, as can be seen in *F.B. Farah & Ors v. Shell BP Petroleum Company of Nigeria*[663] where the court awarded a total sum of N4,621,307.00 as damages to the plaintiffs who were victims of oil pollution. We only hope that Nigerian courts will be able to sustain this progressive trend so as to provide adequate compensation for victims of oil pollution.

3.4 TRANSNATIONAL CORPORATIONS AND INTERNATIONAL ENVIRONMENTAL STANDARDS IN THE OIL INDUSTRY

The frequent and extensive pollution of the Niger Delta area as a result of the activities of the oil companies has given rise to questions whether these companies are actually employing internationally recognized standards to prevent and control pollution in the form of oil spillage, gas flaring, etc. As discussed earlier in this chapter, there are several provisions of Nigerian laws that require the oil companies to ensure 'good oil practice.'[664] Even though some of these laws do not define that term, recourse may be had to the Mineral Oils (Safety) Regulations 1962 which expressly provide that good oil field practice compliance 'shall be considered to be adequately covered by the appropriate current Institute of Petroleum Safety Codes, the American Petroleum Institute's [API] Codes or the American Society of Mechanical Engineer [ASME] Codes.' This effectively makes

---

[659] Kent Nnadozie, *op. cit.*, p.116.

[660] See *Sam Ikpede v. Shell-BP Petroleum Development Company Nigeria* (1973) M.W.S.L. 61 (Selected judgements of High Court of Mid-Western State) where the rule was held not applicable because the defendant's fell under the exception of statutory authority as they had a licence to lay pipes.

[661] In *R. Mon & Anor v. Shell BP.* (1970–1972) 1R.S.L.R. 71, the court awarded the sum of N200 as damages to the plaintiffs.

[662] This was the situation in *Godspower Nweke v. Nigerian Agip Oil Company Ltd.* (1976) 10 S.C. 101. See Yinka Omorogbe, *Oil and Gas in Nigeria, op. cit.*, p.156.

[663] (1995) 3 NWLR. (pt. 382) 148; *Shell BP Petroleum Dev. Co. Ltd. v. Tiebo VII* (1996) 4 NWLR (pt. 445) 657 (the court awarded N400,000.00 as special damages and N5,600,000.00 as general damages).

[664] See Regulations 25 and 36 of the Petroleum (Drilling and Production) Regulations 1969 discussed above.

it binding on oil companies to respect international standards in their operations in Nigeria.[665]

The standards of the American Petroleum Institute (API), American Society of Mechanical Engineer (ASME), the U.S. Integrity Management (IM) for High Consequence Areas (HCAs), and the Alaska Best Available Technology (BAT) Industry represent a widely accepted 'good oil field practise' standard for petroleum pipeline management.[666] These standards are aimed, *inter alia*, at ensuring the use of safe and interchangeable equipment, effective detection of internal leaks in pipelines, the development of pipeline codes for pressure piping, the incorporation of Best Alternative Technology into all the stages of oil field operations and the making of provision for Third Party Damage (TPD) such as accidental damage to buried pipelines during construction, or cases of sabotage and illegal bunkering as occurs in the Niger Delta areas. Members of the API, to which Shell and some other oil companies operating in the Niger Delta belong, are responsible for "obeying all laws and best practice" as part of their pledge to a program of continuous health, safety and environmental improvements,[667] in all areas of their operations.

The oil companies are required by Nigerian laws to comply with the API standards for High Consequence Areas. This is because most of the Niger Delta region meets the criteria defined in the U.S. as High Consequence Areas for oil spills (populated areas, drinking water areas, or productive ecosystems) in addition to the fact that the areas are susceptible to damage from third parties.[668] It is important to stress that all the major oil companies operating in Nigeria (including Shell, Eni, Total) are members of the International Petroleum Industry Environmental Conservation Association (IPIECA), established in 1974 with the aim of developing and promoting 'scientifically-sound, cost-effective, practical, socially and economically acceptable solutions to global environmental and social issues pertaining to the oil and gas industry.'[669] IPIECA has developed a wide range of documents on issues like the impact of oil spills on aquatic life, oil spill response, social impact assessment, and human rights training package to assist the industry in their operations.

---

[665]   Human Rights Watch (1999), *The Price of Oil: Corporate Responsibility and Human Rights Violations in Nigeria's Oil Producing Communities, op. cit.*, p.55.

[666]   Richard Steiner, *Double Standards? International Standards to Prevent and Control Pipeline Oil Spills, Compared with Shell Practices in Nigeria*, Friends of the Earth Netherlands November 2008.

[667]   American Petroleum Institute (API), *API Environmental Stewardship Pledge for CAREFUL Operations*, at www.api.org [accessed 23 November 2010], quoted in Alexandra S. Wawryk, Adoption of International Environmental Standards by Transnational Oil Companies: Reducing the Impact of Oil Operations in Emerging Economies, 20 *J. Energy Nat. Resources L.* 402–434 at 403 (2002).

[668]   Richard Steiner, *op. cit.*

[669]   IPIECA, *Bringing together the oil and gas industry on global, environmental and social issues*, at www.ipieca.org/ipieca_info/about.php [accessed 21 April 2010].

In recognition of the above, and the need to fulfill their obligations under the relevant national laws, most of these companies now published their environmental principles and policies, indicating that they abide by the relevant laws concerning their operations or are taking necessary steps to comply. The publication of these principles, sometimes called 'codes of conduct', by the TNCs and their various promises to behave ethically and to abide by 'international standards' or 'best practices' for environmental protection have considerably raised the hopes of the affected communities and the Government that the oil companies will improve their environmental performance. For example, Shell declares that one of its several responsibilities to society is, 'to conduct business as responsible corporate members of society, to comply with applicable laws and regulations, to support fundamental human rights in line with the legitimate role of business, and to give proper regard to health, safety, security and the environment.'[670]

However, events in the Niger Delta region have shown that these cosmetic statements are not enough to guarantee environmental protection. The oil companies have not only failed to comply but also are not willing to provide information required to verifying their claims to environmental excellence or of effective compliance with applicable international standards and best practices. For instance, a lack of willingness on the part of Shell Nigeria, in spite of their professed transparency principle to 'provide full relevant information about their activities to legitimate interested parties'[671] has been separately revealed by both Steiner[672] and Christian Aid.[673] They disclosed their unsuccessful attempts at getting Shell Nigeria to provide information on the situation of their pipelines, the efficacy of their pipeline management, their Oil Spill Contingency Plan (OSCP), amongst other. Christian Aid observed that there is 'no publicly available information from SPDC [Shell Petroleum Development Company] on the lifespan of its pipelines in Nigeria, nor on the application of the lifespan criteria commonly used by the international oil industry, such as those applied by the American National Standards Institute (ANSI) and the US Environmental Protection Agency.'[674] In fact, Shell's Alan Detheridge admitted that Shell Nigeria's 'overall picture' of the age and condition of its pipelines with respect to industry standards was incomplete.[675] This not only violates the company's code of conduct but also all environmental international standards in the oil industry.

---

[670] See generally, Revised Shell General Business Principles 2005, at www.static.shell.com/static/public/downloads/corporate_pkg/sgbp_english.pdf [accessed 22 April 2010]; See also Shell Code of Conduct 2006, *How to live by the Shell General Business Principles*, at www.static.shell.com/static/public/downloads/corporate_pkg/code_of_conduct_english.pdf [accessed 22 April 2010].

[671] Shell, 1997, Shell General Business Principles.

[672] Richard Steiner, *op. cit.*

[673] Christian Aid, *Behind the mask, Sustained Misery: Shell in the Niger Delta*, pp.28–39 at www.evb.ch/cm_data/public/Shell%20Award%20Nominierung_Behind%20the%20mask_0.pdf [accessed 7 March 2010].

[674] Christian Aid, *Ibid*, p.30.

[675] *Ibid.*

Information on the incidence of oil spills, gas flaring and the oil pipelines that criss-cross the entire Niger Delta region further confirms the non-compliance by the oil companies with international environmental standards.

Shell does not, and can never, deny the fact that its operations result in damage to the environment. What it has continued to dispute is the extent of the damage and amount of the damage that is attributable to it. For example, Shell reports incidence of oil spills every year – 262 in 2002, 221 in 2003, 236 in 2004, 224 in 2005 and 241 in 2006,[676] and attributes more than half of these to sabotage. According to Shell, of the 241 incidents that occurred in 2006, sabotage accounted for 165 (69%), while 50 (20%) were controllable incidents (resulting from equipment failure, corrosion or human error).[677] Shell again recorded that in 2008, 53 spills involving 8,325 barrels (about 15% of the total volume spilled) were the result of the failure of equipment, corrosion or human error, and this they claimed is a significantly lower volume than the previous year (11,723 barrels).[678]

Similarly, Tuodolo notes that, 'between 1995 and 2006, Shell alone recorded 3,213 oil spill incidents (annual average of 300 incidents) resulting in the spillage of over four hundred and fifty thousand barrels of oil (450,000 bbls) into the Niger Delta environment, along with the daily flaring of huge volumes of gas (about 604 million scf per day).'[679] Further, oil companies are noted for under-reporting incidents of oil spillage. Comparing the rate of oil spillage in the U.S. (that has over 165,000 miles of oil transmission lines) with the Niger Delta (that has 10,000 miles of high pressure oil pipelines and flow lines), it was revealed that more oil is being spilled from the pipeline system in the Niger Delta whose pipeline is 16 times shorter than that of U.S. and the spill rate (spills/km of pipeline) is immensely greater in Nigeria than in U.S.[680] Debunking the long-standing claim of Shell that sabotage[681] is the single most important cause of oil pollution in the

---

[676] Shell Petroleum Development Company (SPDC) (2007). *Shell Nigeria Annual Report 2006: People and the Environment,* at http://narcosphere.narconews.com/userfiles/70/2006_shell_nigeria_report.pdf [accessed 21 April 2010].

[677] Shell Petroleum Development Company (SPDC), *Ibid.* There is no year in which Shell Nigeria records no spills caused by corroding pipelines. For example, it reported in 2005 that 'the number of spills caused by corrosion decreased slightly from 38 in 2004 to 33 in 2005'; there were 2.500 barrels of oil spilled at the Nembe-IV pipeline in 2006; in 2007, a spill occurred 'along a 28-inch pipeline in the Cawthorne Channels due to corrosion', and in 2008 'Trans Niger Pipeline (TNP) near the Bodo community in Ogoni land leaked spilling 4,140 barrels'- all caused by corrosion as compared to Trans Alaska Pipeline in the U.S. that has operated for over 30 years with no record of oil spills caused by corrosion- Cited in Richard Steiner, *op. cit.*; See also Shell in Nigeria, *Environmental Performance: Managing Oil Spills,* Shell in Nigeria, May 2009, at http://www-static.shell.com/static/nga/downloads/pdfs/briefing_notes/environ-mental_performance.pdf [accessed 21 April 2010].

[678] Shell in Nigeria, *Environmental Performance: Managing Oil Spills, op. cit.*

[679] Felix Tuodolo, Corporate Social Responsibility: Between Civil Society and the Oil Industry in the Developing World, 8 (3) *ACME: An International E-Journal for Critical Geographies* 530–541 at 537 (2009).

[680] Richard Steiner, *op. cit.*

[681] Shell in its Sustainability Report 2009 alleged that most oil spills onshore in Niger Delta – 98% in 2009 – were as a result of sabotage and oil theft, with the remaining 2% due to operational

Niger Delta, Terisa E. Turner, a Canadian Professor and UN-based International
Oil Working Group Expert, in her post-visit interview after a fact finding visit to
the Niger Delta communities in 2001, stated that:

> *"The claim of sabotage is patently false … There has been almost no arrest for sabo-
> tage of petroleum pipelines. Much less prosecution of any accused. The oil companies
> have been claiming that the oil spills, the pipeline explosions were all caused by sab-
> otage. But there is no evidence to this so far. These are just lies, distraction, shirking
> of responsibility on the part of the oil companies – and Shell here is the most serious
> culprit. Shell has not replaced its pipelines, [and] has not carried out proper mainte-
> nance. It is well known … that should the pipelines not be replaced within 20 years
> or even sooner, then inevitably, they will leak, [or] they may explode any day … It
> so happened in the case of Yorla [in Ogoni] that Shell jumped to the false accusation
> and the cowardly denial of responsibility by citing villagers guilty of sabotage. This
> false allegation was then proved false by the very contractor – Boots and Coots – that
> Shell brought in from Texas to install a new X'mas tree which regulates that flow of
> crude oil in the pipelines. So then we have the petroleum experts showing the claim
> of sabotage to be false."*[682]

This position has been confirmed by several other scholars and researchers.[683]

With regards to the flaring of gas, while 99 per cent of associated gas is used
or re-injected into the ground in the U.S. and Western Europe, more than half
the associated gas is flared in Nigeria in spite of Regulations introduced over
two decades ago to limit this practice.[684] Furthermore, most of the gas flare sites
are located within residential areas.[685] As revealed by the Nigerian Extractive

---

failures. See Shell Sustainability Report 2009, at www.shell.com/home/content/environment_
society/society/nigeria/environment/ [accessed 21 April 2010].

[682] Terisa E. Turner, being her Assessment of the Aftermath of Shell's Oil Spill Disaster at Ogbudu,
Niger Delta: *Oil Companies Lie, Deceive, Play Ethnic Card to Divide Host Communities*, published by National Interest (Lagos), Vol. 221, 31 July 2001, pp.29–30, at www.waado.org/
Environment/OilCompanies/States/Rivers/OgbuduSpill/TerisaTurner_Interview.html
[accessed 22 April 2010]. Nigerian courts have had course to refute the claims of sabotage by
oil companies. In *Shell v. Isaiah* (1997) 6 NWLR (pt. 508) 236, Shell's defence of sabotage in
an action for negligently failing to contain the oil spills caused by an old tree which fell on the
pipeline causing extensive pollution on the plaintiffs land, failed as the Court of Appeal considered the defence to have been an afterthought.

[683] See Kaniye Ebeku (2006), *Oil and the Niger Delta People in International Law: Resource
Rights, Environmental and Equity Issues,op. cit.*, pp.139–141; Frynas J.G., Corporate and State
Responses to Anti-Oil Protests in the Niger Delta, *African Affairs* 100, 27–54 at 47 (2001).

[684] Shell Guilty Campaign: Oil Change International, Friends of the Earth (International, Europe,
U.S. and The Netherlands), PLATFORM, and Greenpeace UK (2009), *Shell's Big Dirty Secret:
Insight into the world's most carbon intensive oil company and the legacy of CEO Jeroen van der
Veer*, at www.foeeurope.org/corporates/Extractives/shellbigdirtysecret_June09.pdf [accessed
13 March 2011].

[685] In the small village of Orugbiri, which is 'a small settlement not larger than 100 metres in
length, two gas flaring sites exist,' in contravention of the rule that flare sites must be located far
away from communities to avoid the hazardous effect of gas flaring on the health of the people.
See Amos Adeoye Idowu, Human Rights, Environmental Degradation and Oil Multinational

Industries Transparency Initiative (NEITI) audit, between 1999 and 2004 Shell was the highest flarer in Nigeria, 'burning off an average of 52 per cent of gas it produced in Nigeria.'[686] And this is notwithstanding Government Regulations, the decisions of the courts and even the several promises by the oil companies to put an end to gas flaring, something aptly described by a critic as "constant night and day pollution."[687] Angered by the situation, Saro-Wiwa wrote in 1992 that:

> *"As a final remark of their genocidal intent and insensitivity to human suffering, Shell and Chevron refuse to obey a Nigerian law which requires all oil companies to re-inject gas into the earth rather than flare it. Shell and Chevron think it cheaper to poison the atmosphere and the Ogoni and pay the paltry penalty imposed by the Government of Nigeria than re-inject the gas as stipulated by the Regulations...Shell has won prizes for environmental protection in Europe where it also prospects for oil. So it cannot be that it does not know what to do. Now, why has it visited the Ogoni people with such horror ... The answer must lie in racism."[688]*

Another practice of the oil companies that is quite worrisome relates to the high-pressure pipelines that pass above ground through the communities and criss-cross over their homes and land, inhibiting them from making use of that land for agricultural purposes, thus rendering it economically useless.[689] This is unlike the practice in developed countries where the pipelines are buried below the ground to prevent environmental pollution. As pointed out by one scholar, international safety and standards regulations prescribe a minimum distance of one kilometre between oil installations and residential houses.[690] This is often ignored by the

---

Companies in Nigeria: The Ogoniland Episode, *Netherlands Quarterly of Human Rights*, Vol. 17 No. 2, 161–184 at 171 (1999).

[686] Shell Guilty Campaign: Oil Change International, Friends of the Earth (International, Europe, U.S. and The Netherlands), PLATFORM, and Greenpeace UK (2009), *op. cit.*, relying on the Nigeria Extractive Industries Transparency Initiative Report on the Physical Audit 1999–2004 Appendix C: Gas System (2006), prepared by Hart Resources Ltd., at www.neiti.org.ng/FinalAuditReports-Sept07/PhysicalReports/Appendicies/AppCGasSystemBinder.pdf [accessed 22 April 2010].

[687] Claude Ake, *Interview with Andy Rowell*, December 1, 1995. Suffice it to say that Shell publicly stated in its Sustainability Report 2003 that it had "set a corporate objective to end all flaring of gas by 2008," but as usual, it shifted the goal-posts a year later to 2009, which also passed with the situation remaining almost the same. See Shell Guilty Campaign: Oil Change International, Friends of the Earth (International, Europe, U.S. and The Netherlands), PLATFORM, and Greenpeace UK (2009), *Ibid*. See Shell Petroleum Development Company of Nigeria, *Environment 1996*, February 1997.

[688] Ken Saro-Wiwa, *Genocide in Nigeria: The Ogoni Tragedy, op. cit.*, p.82.

[689] Gabriel Eweje, Environmental Costs and Responsibilities Resulting from Oil Exploitation in Developing Countries: The Case of the Niger Delta of Nigeria, 69 *Journal of Business Ethics* 27–56 at 40 (2006).

[690] Isuwa B. Dogo, *Transnational Corporations and Environmental Pollution and Degradation*, being the text of a paper presented at the 1997 Annual Conference of the Nigerian Society of International Law in Lagos on 15 August 1997, p.6, quoted in Amos Adeoye Idowu, *op. cit.*, p. 171.

oil companies who lay their pipelines in front of residential buildings. The oil
companies have however argued that '[M]uch of the area in which oil companies
are operating is swamp, so burying pipelines could, in fact, exacerbate the
risk of fractures and spillages. From time to time the positioning of pipelines
is reviewed, especially when it is known that communities have expanded onto
land neighbouring a pipeline, and if considered a hazard then the pipelines are
re-routed.'[691] In response to this argument, the Ogonis contend that their land
is neither swampy nor has a pipe ever been re-routed in their communities.[692]
They allege double standards by the oil companies as they carry out proper
environmental surveys in laying their pipelines, and also bury their pipelines,
in the UK and the EU.[693] Burying of pipelines will not only reduce the various
incidences of sabotage, but will further help to prevent pollution of waters and
farmlands.

Shell's clean up of oil spills and the repair of its pipelines in Nigeria has been
found by Christian Aid to be scandalously inadequate, and such as would never
be tolerated in Europe or North America.[694] It continued that the "oil spills, made
inevitable by a network of ageing pipes, many of which are still routed above
ground, are left for weeks, sometimes months, without being cleaned up. Oil is
carried downstream, visiting a deadly black plague on communities miles away
from the original spillage. This makes a nonsense of Shell's claims of 'integrity
and respect for people,' and its 'commitment to support human rights and to
contribute to sustainable development' in Nigeria."[695] Note, in contrast, the swift
and immediate response of BP to the 20 April 2010 explosion of its Deepwater
Horizon oil rig that resulted in the death of eleven workers and caused a horrendous
ecological disaster around the Gulf of Mexico. This incident, according to Keating,
'may have been the worst oil spill in U.S. history, but it pales in comparison to the
ongoing catastrophe that has afflicted Nigeria's Niger River Delta over the last five
decades. As many as 546 million gallons of oil are believed to have spilled since oil
exploration began in this region – the equivalent of an Exxon Valdez spill every
year.'[696] The environmental disaster that occurred in the Gulf of Mexico has been
going on in the Niger Delta for years, resulting in deaths, diseases, displacement

---

[691] Tookey R.W.: 9 December 1992, 'Letter to Shelley Braithwaite, London Rainforest Action Group,' Shell International Petroleum Company Limited, quoted in Gabriel Eweje, *op. cit.* 41.
[692] Gabriel Eweje, *Ibid.*
[693] See Tetsuya Morimoto, Growing industrialization and our damaged planet: The extraterritorial application of developed countries' domestic environmental laws to transnational corporations abroad, *Utrecht Law Review*, Vol. 1, Issue 2, pp.134–159 at 137 (2005) where he stated that 'in the case of Shell's pipeline running from Stanlow in Cheshire to Mossmoran in Scotland, some seventeen environmental surveys had been commissioned before a single turf was cut.'
[694] Christian Aid, *Behind the mask, op. cit.*, p.23.
[695] *Ibid.*
[696] Joshua E. Keating, *The World's Ongoing Ecological Disasters*, Foreign Policy, 16 July 2010, at www.foreignpolicy.com/articles/2010/07/16/the_world_s_worst_ongoing_disasters?page=0,0 [accessed 8 June 2011].

and destruction of the means of livelihood of the people, without any apology, regrets, compensation or necessary remedial actions by the multinational oil companies responsible. When these occur in developed countries, like recently in America's Gulf coast in the Gulf of Mexico, BP, Halliburton and Transocean Limited, according to Adujie, engaged in purely voluntary actions to remediate and clean up, in offering compensation to individuals and companies, and as well as offering U.S.$170 million dollars, within one month, to the US Gulf Coast States of Alabama, Florida, Louisiana, and Mississippi; and did this even well before the effects and consequences of the pollution become apparent.[697] In clear cases of the devastating effects of their actions on the people and the environment, the oil companies in the Niger Delta are, in contrast, not willing to respond, even under compulsion by court judgments, protests and demonstrations as they constantly deny liabilities. The swift and voluntary response of BP has clearly revealed a sharp contrast in the protection and rights afforded in different parts of the world to the local inhabitants of the oil producing communities and their environment. While BP immediately responded to the disaster in America, the minorities in the Niger Delta 'continue to suffer environmental degradation, a complete lack of benefit from oil extraction and outright repression in an environment devoid of effective protective mechanisms.'[698] The application of different standards by the oil multinationals, between the developed and developing countries, in oil exploration, prospecting, drilling and disaster-management control amounts to double standards. This discriminatory practice against victims of similar harmful oil pollution is an injustice which further worsens the human rights of the local inhabitants.

Confirming the double standards, Shell Nigeria for example did not initiate its Asset Integrity Review (covering wells, pipelines, flow lines and other production facilities) and Pipeline Integrity Management System (PIMS) until 2003/2004 when these important management plans date back internationally several years – the Leak System standard in 1995, the ASME standard in 1998 (updated in 2002), the Alaska BAT requirement in 1997, and the U.S. Integrity Management Requirement in 2001.[699] These could have averted most of the large pipeline spills occurring in the region. Commenting on the poor environmental practices of Shell in Nigeria, Bopp van Dessel, the former head of environmental studies for Shell Nigeria between 1992 and 1994, and who had to quit Shell in 1994 as a result of 'professional frustration' stated that Shell's operations in Nigeria breached international standards and caused extensive pollution.[700] He continued

697 Paul I. Adujie, *American Oil Spills in Gulf of Mexico: Lessons for Nigerians, Ecuadorians and Others*, New Liberian, at http://newliberian.com/?p=1228 [accessed 23 May 2010].
698 Alex Free, *Africa: Multinational Oil, the U.S and Nigeria – a Crude Contrast*, Pambazuka News 14 May 2010, at http://allafrica.com/stories/201005140634.html [accessed 23 May 2010].
699 Richard Steiner, *op. cit.*
700 Quoted in Richard Steiner, *op. cit.* In 2007, Shell in its advertisements in various European Newspapers and Magazines claimed: "We used our waste [carbon dioxide] to grow flowers," thus suggesting that its operations have little or minimal impact on the environment. Both the

that: 'Wherever I went, I could see that Shell were not operating their facilities properly. They were not meeting their own standards, they were not meeting international standards. Any Shell site that I saw was polluted, any terminal that I saw was polluted. It is clear to me that Shell was devastating the area.'[701]

In an interview, Basil Omiyi, Country Chair for Shell Nigeria and Managing Director of SPDC, stated that, '[W]e do, however, have a substantial backlog of asset integrity work to reduce spills and flaring. That backlog is caused by under-funding by partners over many years, operational problems and, more recently, the lack of safe access to facilities.'[702] These statements are admissions that Shell Nigeria is operating below the international best practice standards, Shell corporate standards worldwide and the Nigerian laws regulating the oil and gas industry, and call into question its claim of environmental leadership.

Despite abysmal track record of Shell in Nigeria, it falsely continues to portray itself as "green" in its advertisements, which claims the U.K's Advertisement Standards Authority (ASA) has described not only as "a ridiculous claim" but also found violated advertisement rules.[703] It is important to note that Shell's attitude to Nigeria's environment is not an isolated case as all other oil multinationals operating in Nigeria have acted similarly in their operations regarding adherence to international standards.[704] They have variously demonstrated a lukewarm

---

Dutch and U.K. Advertising Standard Authorities declared that Shell had misled the public on its environmental performance. See Shell Guilty Campaign: Oil Change International, Friends of the Earth (International, Europe, U.S. and The Netherlands), PLATFORM, and Greenpeace UK (2009), *op. cit.*

[701] *Ibid.*

[702] Basil Omiyi, being a statement made in an interview by Roger Hammond, Development Director, Living Earth, on *Meeting the Energy Challenge*, The Shell Sustainability Report 2006, www.shell.com/static/envirosoc-en/downloads/sustainability_reports/shell_sustain_report_2006.pdf [accessed 21 April 2010].

[703] Center for Constitutional Rights and EarthRights International, *Shell's Environmental Devastation in Nigeria*, at http://wiwavshell.org/shell%E2%80%99s-environmental-devasta-tion-in-nigeria/ [accessed 21 April 2010]; See also J.G. Frynas, Corporate and State Responses to Anti-Oil Protests in the Niger Delta, *op. cit.*, p.47.

[704] For example, at the fire incident that struck at the Chevron Escravos Tank farm on 20 July 2002, it took the company no less than five days to end the disaster. At the end of the five days, 'there was estimated 180,000 barrels of oil in the affected tank, from which the company suc-cessfully pumped out about 80,000 barrels,' with the 100,000 barrels unaccounted for. This incident affected the five communities- Madagho, Ajidagbo, Ajala, Ogidighen and Ogorodo which make up the Escravos. Apart from the fact that Chevron only attempted a botched clean up of the oil spill, it is reported that the communities are still appealing to Chevron for com-pensation. This is unlike the fire and explosion incident at Chevron's Richmond California refinery in America in April 1989, where it was reported that "the State Labour Department fined Chevron U.S.$877,000 for 114 safety violations in connection with the fire, 5 of them classified as 'serious' legal violations. The company eventually settled for U.S.$275,000 in pen-alties and as part of the settlement agreed to reinforce its fire protection efforts at the U.S. refineries." Cited in Kenneth Omeje (2006), *High Stakes and Stakeholders: Oil Conflict and Security in Nigeria*, Ashgate Publishing Ltd. England, pp.127–128; Manuel A., *The Dirty Four: The Case Against Letting BP Amoco, ExxonMobil, Chevron, and Philips Petroleum Drill in the Artic Refuge*, US Public Interest Research Group Washington DC. March 2001, cited in Kenneth Omeje, *Ibid* p.128.

attitude to responding to incidents of oil spillages, halting gas flaring and other activities deleterious to the health of the communities and the ecosystem where they operate.[705] It is certain that the environmental regimes in Europe and America would not permit these unwholesome and lax attitudes, as companies so operating there could be sued out of business.[706]

Shell's excuse of underfunding by the Nigerian Government or security[707] (militancy) problem as reasons for not been able to conform to 'good oil field practice' in Nigeria is no longer tenable since it has the technical know-how, the financial wherewithal and the corporate mandate to achieve a significant improvement in its oil field operations in the Niger Delta.[708] Shell has the option of renegotiating the Joint Operating Agreements (JOA) and the Memorandum of Understanding (MOU) if they are making it violate international best practices in the industry.

Sadly, for a co-owner in the industry and as equally liable to claims for environmental damage, the Government hardly performs its oversight and regulatory function in the industry and this has contributed immensely to the non-compliance of the oil companies with the Nigerian relevant laws, their own environmental and business standards and with internationally recognised best practice. As a shareholder in the oil industry, the Nigerian State faces a substantial conflict of interest regarding its regulatory responsibilities.[709] Under the joint venture partnership agreements, Government and the multinational oil companies share the operational cost of crude oil production in proportion to their equity shares. This implies that governmental attempts to regulate the oil industry will amount to Government regulating itself, since it would bear any additional costs arising from such regulation.[710] And because the oil MNCs retain

---

[705] For example, the Qua Iboe oil spillage exposed the inadequacy of Mobil's safety measures. A major oil spillage occurred on 12 January 1998 in one of the Mobil's oil wells in its Qua Iboe onshore terminal in Akwa Ibom State which covered a distance of two hundred kilometres affecting about twenty communities in the area. Mobil could not engage in the shoreline clean up until 28 January 1998, and some sites were still visibly contaminated as late as March 1998. This can be contrasted with a similar incident involving Exxon Corporation in 1989 in Alaska, where Exxon Corporation responded swiftly by bringing in experts and five plane loads of modern equipment to contain the spill. See Aghalino S.O. and Eyinla B., Oil Exploitation and Marine Pollution: Evidence from the Niger Delta, Nigeria, 28(3) *J. Hum Eco.* 177–182 (2009); Human Rights Watch (HRW) (1999), *The Price of Oil: Corporate Responsibility and Human Rights Violations in Nigeria's Oil Producing Communities*, New York, p.35.

[706] S.O. Aghalino and Eyinla B., *Ibid.* at 181.

[707] For example, Shell stated that it has not been able to put an end to gas flaring in Nigeria 'mainly due to security issues and funding difficulties with its main partners.' See Shell Sustainability Report 2009, at http://sustainabilityreport.shell.com/2009/servicepages/downloads/files/all_shell_sr09.pdf [accessed 23 May 2010].

[708] Richard Steiner, *op. cit.*

[709] See Stuart Kirsch, "Mining and Environmental Human Rights in Papua New Guinea", in Jedrzej George Frynas and Scott Pegg (eds) (2003), *Transnational Corporations and Human Rights*, Palgrave Macmillan, New York, pp.115–136 at 117.

[710] Uwafiokun Idemudia, "Corporate Social Responsibility and the Rentier Nigerian State: Rethinking the Role of Government and the Possibility of Corporate Social Development in

direct operational control of the day-to-day operations, they take important decisions, regarding how oil installations are constructed, or how to handle a protest by the local people, all of which can influence the human rights impact of their operations.[711] From the continuous environmental devastation of the Niger Delta area, and the worsening human rights situations of the people in the region, it can be concluded that Shell and other oil companies operating in the Niger Delta are not employing internationally recognized standards used in developed countries to prevent pollution and environmental damage. In order to make the oil companies take the protection of environment seriously, Government must free itself from the joint venture agreements with the oil companies so that it will be able effectively to enforce the environmental standards.[712] Adherence to international environmental standards will help to prevent environmental damage and the attendant violations of the rights of the people.

3.5 CHALLENGES TO EFFECTIVE REGULATION OF THE ENVIRONMENTAL PRACTICES OF TRANSNATIONAL OIL CORPORATIONS IN NIGERIA

The pertinent question at this juncture is: In spite of the litany of environmental laws in place, why are the MNCs not brought to book for their activities which bring about environmental injustice to the marginalized and the economically dispossessed people of the Niger Delta?

The unwholesome attitude of the judiciary in prioritizing the economic interests of the State over the environment is a major challenge. The judges' reason for not granting an injunction in favour of a plaintiff whose land, fish pond and creek had been polluted by the defendant's mining operations in *Allar Irou v. Shell. BP*[713] was because "[T]o grant the order … would amount to asking the defendants (Shell-BP) to stop operating in the area … It is needless to say that mineral oil is the main source of the country's revenue." Commenting on this case, Ajomo

---

the Niger Delta", Rethinking Extractive Industry: Regulation, Dispossession, and Emerging Claims, *Canadian Journal of Development Studies* (Special Issue) XXX (1–2) pp.131–151 at 141 (2010).

[711] Jedrzej George Frynas, "The Oil Industry in Nigeria: Conflict Between Oil Companies and Local People", in Jedrzej George Frynas and Scott Pegg (eds), *Transnational Corporations and Human Rights, op. cit.*, p.103.

[712] S.O. Aghalino, Corporate Response to Environmental Deterioration in the Oil Bearing Area of the Niger Delta, Nigeria, 1984–2002, *Journal of Sustainable Development in Africa*, Vol. 11, No. 2, pp.281–294 at 290 (2009).

[713] Unreported Suit No. W/89/71. In *Onyor v. Shell BP* (1982) 12 C.A 144 at 159–160 the Judge, while finding that the amount claimed by the plaintiff against the oil company was justified, nonetheless, reduced the amount of compensation in order not to "sour the good relationship which already exists between the parties".

has observed that 'in the oil sector where environmental degradation is most prevalent, the all-pervading influence of the oil companies and the paternalistic attitude of the judges towards them in matters relating to environmental hazards created by the companies have made the enforcement of environmental laws ineffective…What the judges fail to realize is that economic development can be compatible with environmental conservation.'[714] The attitudes of Nigerian judges place the people at a disadvantaged position.

That aside, the slow judicial process, in which cases take several years before being disposed of is another factor. For instance, *SPDC v. HRH Chief Tiebo VII & 4 others*[715] was filed in the High Court in 1992 and only got to the Court of Appeal in 1996. Also, *Elf Nigeria Ltd. v. Opeme Sillo & Daniel Etseni*,[716] which relates to damages suffered since 1967, was heard at the High Court in 1987, the Court of Appeal in 1990 and the Supreme Court in 1994. This delay makes people lose hope in the judiciary, thus forcing them to embark on self-help.

Another major challenge is the formidable positions of the MNCs (in terms of human, financial and technological strength). As a result of their enormous power and resources the MNCs pose a great threat to their opponents in any litigation. They have the resources to engage the best lawyers and experts. In terms of technical operations, they have the resources to access the best information and are able to assess and interpret scientific information in whatever form they desire.[717] As a result of this, many litigants prefer to settle matters amicably out of court at a very low level of compensation, often dictated by the MNCs. This formidable position puts them in a position to be able to manipulate the Nigerian Government to do what is in their interest, not minding the impact of such activities on the lives of the people in the local communities where they operate. The result is that they often get away with non-compliance with laws and regulations made by the Nigerian Government to check the problem of environmental pollution in the oil industry.[718] This is well exemplified in the unending broken promises to end gas flaring, as previously discussed.

Furthermore, the laws do not pay much regard to preventive measures as they appear to be more concerned with the outcome of pollution.[719] Provision is not made in the law to ensure that pollution does not occur or to minimize its

---

[714]   M.A. Ajomo, "An Examination of Federal Environmental Laws in Nigeria", in Ajomo, M.A. and Adewale, O. (eds) (1994), *Environmental Law and Sustainable Development in Nigeria*, NIALS, Lagos, pp.22–23.

[715]   (1996) 4 NWLR (pt. 445) 657.

[716]   (1994) 6 NWLR (pt. 350) 258.

[717]   See Engobo Emeseh, *The Limitations of Law in Promoting Synergy between Environmental and Development Policies in Developing Countries: A Case Study of the Petroleum Industry in Nigeria*, at http://web.fu-berlin.de/ffu/akumwelt/bc2004/download.htm [accessed 6 March 2010].

[718]   Adedeji A.A. and Ako R.T, Hindrances to Effective Legal Response to the Problem of Environmental Pollution in Nigeria, *op. cit.*, p.21.

[719]   E.O. Nwosu, Petroleum Legislation and Enforcement of Environmental Laws and Standards in Nigeria, *op. cit.*, p.104.

occurrence, considering its devastating effect on the people and the ecosystem. Once there is an oil spill, it is difficult if not impossible to restore the environment back to its *status quo* no matter how prompt and meticulous the clean-up operation is. Therefore, there is a need for provisions concerning precautionary measures to be inserted in Nigerian laws in line with the precautionary principle, which provides for the taking of action that anticipate, prevent or minimize environmental hazards.[720] Also, most of these enactments do not expressly provide for the "polluter pays" principle to address the issue of liability for removal of pollution. This principle which required the polluter to bear the financial cost of cleaning up the pollution needs to be entrenched within the oil-related laws as it encourage companies to avoid polluting the environment as much as possible so as to avoid the ensuing cost. This will result in the reduction of pollution and ensure a pollution free environment. In addition, this principle will help to relieve the victim of oil pollution from the burden of having to prove the cause of pollution, negligence and fault of the polluter: matters which the victim has little or no knowledge of.[721]

Another challenge is the inadequacy of legislative protection of rights. The Niger Delta requires rights-respecting regimes to ensure the protection of the rights of the people. Laws are rights-respecting when the communities are able to easily access the legal process and use it to compel public officers to carry out duties that promote and protect their rights.[722] Unfortunately, the laws regulating the business of oil exploration and exploitation in Nigeria today do not guarantee either a clear and coherent process or the accessibility of such process.[723] The problems with these Acts, as already discussed, include the unenforceability of some parts of the Acts, inelegant provisions, and more.

Our review of the law has also revealed that Nigeria places undue emphasis on command and control instruments for its environmental management and pollution control. No doubt, this may be efficient in deterring polluters where the fines and punishments are stringent and effectively implemented.[724] However, as discussed above, this is not the situation in Nigeria. It is suggested that the use of various economic measures like pollution charges, marketable permits, subsidies, deposit and return systems, and enforcement incentives would introduce more flexibility, efficiency and cost-effectiveness into pollution control efforts.[725] It will

---

[720] E.O. Nwosu *Ibid.*
[721] Rose Ohiama Ugbe, The "Polluter Pays Principle": An Analysis, *The Calabar Law Journal,* Vols. VI-VII, 127–157 at 154 (2002–2003).
[722] Social and Economic Rights Action Center (SERAC) (2005), *Perpetuating Poverty, Consolidating Powerlessness: Oil and the Niger Delta,* SERAC, Lagos, p.48.
[723] *Ibid,* pp.48–49.
[724] Adedeji A.A. and Ako R.T., Towards achieving the United Nations' Millennium Development Goals: The Imperative of Reforming Water Pollution Control and Waste Management Laws in Nigeria, *Desalination* 248 642–649 at 647 (2009).
[725] Anthony Nzodinma Egbu, Constraints to Effective Pollution Control and Management in Nigeria, *The Environmentalist,* Vol. 20, pp.13–17 at 16 (2000). For more on the advantages of market-based instruments for pollution control in Nigeria, see Joseph Adelegan, *Environmental*

complement the command and control approach in the fight against oil-induced environmental pollution in the oil producing communities.

In addition, as earlier observed, some of the provisions in much of the legislation are grossly inadequate to deter an intending environmental delinquent. For instance, under the Oil in the Navigable Waters Act, the penalty for discharging oil into waters with devastating effect on aquatic and socio-economic life is a sum not exceeding N2,000.00, which cannot in any way deter the MNCs who are the major culprits of environmental degradation. In view of the extensively damaging effects of environmental pollution on the pristine ecosystems and on the people in the community, penalties should be high enough to be a real deterrent. For example, in the United Kingdom, the maximum penalty for oil spillage under the Oil Pollution Act 1971 was increased from £1,000.00 to £50,000.00.[726] Also, the Petroleum Act contains nebulous terms such as "practicable precautions"; "up-to-date equipment" and "prompt steps", none of which is defined in the Act or Regulations.[727] The enforceability of the provisions of this law in terms of environmental protection is much dependent on the interpretation of these terms.[728]

Furthermore, there is also lack of an authoritative statute governing all areas of oil-related human rights violations and environmental pollution.[729] The various laws regulating the oil and gas industry are scattered all over the statute book, thus serving as an obstacle to accessibility to justice. The local inhabitants often find it difficult to access these laws in the preparation of their cases, and in the assessment of their rights, since they may not have the wherewithal to access and review all the available statutes and regulations that may be relevant to their cases.[730] They are therefore put at a disadvantaged position when compared to the oil companies, which have the resources to get good counsel who can access all the laws and put better arguments in their defence. There is therefore a need for these laws to be put together into a single and comprehensive statute for easy accessibility. It is hoped that the Petroleum Industry Bill (PIB) 2008, presently before the National Assembly, which is aimed, *inter alia*, at streamlining the legal and regulatory framework for the Petroleum Industry, will help overcome this challenge.

Compliance, Policy Reform and Industrial Pollution in sub-Saharan Africa: Lessons from Nigeria, being excerpt from the Proceedings of the International Network for Environmental Compliance and Enforcement's (INECE) Eighth International Conference, Linking Concepts to Actions: Successful Strategies for Environmental Compliance and Enforcement, held 5–11 April 2008, in Cape Town, South Africa, pp.109–118.

[726] S.O. Aghalino and Eyinla B., *op. cit.*, p.180.

[727] Yinka Omorogbe, "Regulation of Oil Industry Pollution in Nigeria", in E. Azinge (ed), *New Frontiers in Law* (1993), p.147, quoted in A.A. Adedeji and Ako R.T., *op. cit.*, p.19.

[728] *Ibid.*

[729] Social and Economic Rights Action Center (SERAC) (2005), *Perpetuating Poverty, Consolidating Powerlessness: Oil and the Niger Delta*, *op. cit.*, p.49.

[730] *Ibid.*

Another major challenge is the poor enforcement mechanisms of the existing laws. As earlier discussed, most Government institutions involved in environment resources management lack trained staff, technical expertise, adequate information, analytical capability and other prerequisites for policies and programmes.[731] For example, in 1995 the World Bank found that the Regional Office of FEPA in Rivers State had only 25 staff, which included 10 environmental professionals, out of which only 3 were concerned with pollution.[732] Also worrisome is the poor funding which has resulted in the regulatory bodies not having the equipment required to monitor effectively environmental standards. In this regard, they rely on the MNCs that they are supposed to regulate for this equipment. The regulated, that is MNCs, are in effect the regulators. Egbu,[733] asserts that neither the Federal Environmental Protection Agency's Zonal Office in Port Harcourt nor the Rivers State Ministry of Environment has a well-equipped laboratory. The result is that where there is an oil contamination incident in Rivers State, the authorities often request that the oil companies responsible should provide soil and water sample analysis.[734] The effect of unskilled personnel in the detection and enforcement of rules was most evident in the failure of the customs officials to detect the harmful substances in the "koko" incident, when they were deceived into believing that 3,800 tons of toxic wastes were chemicals for manufacturing fertilisers.[735] Little wonder that oil companies operating in the Niger Delta are rarely found wanting by the regulating authorities for environmental pollution. All this is to the detriment of the local communities in the area.

Also important is the fact that most of these statutes do not offer much hope to victims of oil pollution as regards their right to be compensated. This is coupled with the inadequacy of compensation usually awarded to the oil communities by the courts. Compensation is rarely awarded by the courts, and where it is, the damages are so paltry and contemptible that they hardly cover litigation expenses. It is a double-tragedy of unimaginable proportion for people to lose their means of livelihood and at the same time not to be adequately compensated.[736] By entrenching a regime of low compensation, the law is used to facilitate the

---

[731]   Environmental Resource Manager Limited (1998), *Niger Delta Environmental Survey Final Report*, Phase 1, Vol. 1, Niger Delta Environmental Survey, Lagos, p.763.

[732]   Kaniye Ebeku, (2006), *Oil and the Niger Delta People in International Law: Resource Rights, Environmental and Equity Issues,op. cit.*, p.238.

[733]   Anthony Nzodinma Egbu, *op. cit.*, p.15.

[734]   *Ibid.* See Kenneth Omeje, *High Stakes and Stakeholders: Oil Conflict and Security in Nigeria, op. cit.*, pp.52–53.

[735]   Newswatch 1988, 4 July, p.16, quoted in Ali Ahmad, "Policing industrial Pollution in Nigeria", in Beatrice Chaytor and Kevin R. Gray (eds) (2003), *International Environmental Law and Policy in Africa*, Environmental and Policy Vol. 36, Kluwer Academic Publishers, Dordrecht Netherlands, p.138.

[736]   Aturu, Bamidele, *Justice for Oil Communities in Oil and the Nigerian Environment*, Benin City, Environmental Rights Action (ERACTION), Nigeria 1998, quoted in Aluko M.A.O. (2008) 'Sustainable Development, Environmental Degradation and the Entrenchment of Poverty in the Niger Delta of Nigeria, 15(1) *J. Hum. Ecol.* 63–68, p.65 (2008).

exploitation of the people of the Niger Delta which further worsens their poor economic situation.

The over-dependence on oil revenue by the Government means that most of the policies of Government are directed towards minimizing any loss of the revenue from oil at the expense of environmental protection or the protection of citizen's rights. As contended by Ikporukpo C.O.,[737] given the importance of petroleum to the Nigerian economy, the laxity in enforcing existing legislation may actually be a deliberate policy to encourage foreign direct investment in the oil industry. Since the State is more concerned with national wealth accumulation and how to maximize oil rents, it bothers little about issues of environmental protection and how to put in place the necessary institutional framework for enforcing the relevant laws.[738] In this sense, Government does not perceive harm to the environment as a problem except where it inhibits the free flow of profit. The result is that there are several oil-related environment protection laws which are not enforced to regulate the activities of the oil companies due to the economic interests of the nation. Considering the huge cost of pollution control and clean up, it is the belief of the Nigerian Government that the enforcement of these laws would not only decrease the revenue base of the Government but might lead to the flight of oil companies from the country, hence further diminishing the revenues accruing.[739] The Nigerian Government have misinterpreted the 'right to development', as declared by the United Nations General Assembly,[740] to mean the pursuit of economic development to the detriment of environmental protection. This sordid situation is put pungently by Orford:

> *"It has become accepted by many States and some commentators that the right to development is a right of States to pursue a narrow economic model of development over the human rights of the people of the State invoking the right. The right to development is presented as allowing States where necessary to put the interests of investors over the interests of other human beings."*[741]

---

[737]   Ikporukpo, C.O., The Management of Oil Pollution of Natural Resources in Nigeria, *Journal of Environmental Management*, Vol. 20, No. 3, pp.199–206 (1985), quoted in Uwafiokun Idemudia, *op. cit.*, p.21. Amos Adeoye Idowu, *op. cit.*, p.176.

[738]   Kenneth Omeje, *High Stakes and Stakeholders: Oil Conflict and Security in Nigeria*, *op. cit.*, p. 93.

[739]   Joshua P. Eaton, The Nigerian Tragedy, Environmental Regulation of Transnational Corporations, and the Human Right to a Healthy Environment, 15 *B.U. Int'l. L.J.* 261–307 at 291 (1997).

[740]   Declaration on the Right to Development was adopted by General Assembly resolution 41/128 of 4 December 1986, at http://www2.ohchr.org/english/law/pdf/rtd.pdf [accessed 25 April 2010].

[741]   A. Orford, *Globalization and the Right to Development*, in Alston P. (ed) (2001), *Peoples' Rights*, Oxford University Press, Oxford, p.135, quoted in Kaniye Ebeku, Kaniye Ebeku (2006), *Oil and the Niger Delta People in International Law: Resource Rights, Environmental and Equity Issues, op. cit.*, p.241.

Failure to halt continued degradation of the environment by the oil companies on the specious excuse that trade should not be jeopradized will not only worsen the human rights situation of the people whose lives depend on the sustainability of the environment but will affect the capacity of future generations in meeting their needs for sustainable national development.[742] The pursuit of economic development and of human rights is never antithetical. One should therefore not be traded off for the other. In order to ensure adequate protection to the people of the oil-producing communities of Nigeria, and the ecosystem of the region, there is a need for a change of attitude by the Government and the judiciary in the form of effective balancing of economic interests with the needs of environmental protection.

Other challenges like corruption, lack of accountability in Government, problems of access to justice and environmental information, and lack of public participation in environmental matters will form part of the discussion in Chapters Five and Six below.

3.6 INSTITUTIONAL FRAMEWORKS FOR NIGER DELTA DEVELOPMENT

The need for the development of the Niger Delta region has long been recognized and several initiatives have been made in this regard. The response of the Government to the claims of the oil-producing areas has been classified by Suberu[743] into three forms: redistributive, reorganizational and regulatory state responses. These have included the creation of separate Federal States in the Niger Delta, *viz* Akwa Ibom, Delta, and Bayelsa States in 1987, 1991 and 1996, respectively (reorganizational policies),[744] the increase in the percentage of revenue allocation based on derivation from 1.5% to 3% in 1992 and 13% in 1999,[745] the installation of His Excellency, Dr. Goodluck Jonathan, the former Governor of Bayelsa State, an Ijaw man, as Vice-President of Nigeria in 2007 under the People's Democratic Party (PDP) (now President of the Federal Republic of Nigeria since

---

[742]   Amos Adeoye Idowu, *op. cit.*, p.181.

[743]   R.T. Suberu (1996), *Ethnic Minority Conflicts and Governance in Nigeria*, Spectrum Books Ltd., Ibadan, pp.35–47. According to Suberu, 'redistributive policies are state decisions that consciously dispense valued resources to one group at the expense of other claimants to state resources. Reorganizational policies refer to state efforts to restructure or reconfigure political or administrative institutions and relationships in order to accommodate group demands or strengthen the efficacy of centralized state power. Regulatory policies entail the mandatory imposition of sanctions or restrictions on individuals or groups that are perceived to pose a threat to state cohesion and order'- p.35.

[744]   Shola Omotola, From the OMPADEC to the NDDC: An Assessment of State Responses to Environmental Insecurity in the Niger Delta, Nigeria, *Africa Today*, Vol. 54 No. 1, pp.73–89 at 74 (2007).

[745]   Eghosa E. Osaghae, Social Movements and Rights Claims: The Case of Action Groups in the Niger Delta of Nigeria, 19 *Voluntas* 189–210 at 203 (2008).

May 2010 following the death of President Umaru Yar'Adua on the 5th May 2010) and the establishment of development agencies, such as the Niger Delta Development Board (NDDB), the Oil Mineral Producing Areas Development Commission (OMPADEC), the Niger Delta Development Commission (NDDC), etc (redistributive policies). The repressive response of the State has included the statutory proscription of parties or associations perceived to be working against the Government,[746] the execution of Ken Saro-Wiwa and eight other Ogoni leaders in 1995,[747] the Umuechem massacre of 1990,[748] the Ogoni genocide,[749] the Odi Massacre of 1999,[750] the Odioma killings in 2005[751] and the Gbaramatu Massacre

---

[746]   For example, the promulgation of Decree No. 21 of 1992, which empowered the President of the Federal Republic of Nigeria to "dissolve and proscribe any association of individuals of three or more persons ... which in his opinion is formed for purposes of furthering the political, religious, ethnic, tribal, cultural or social interest of a group of individuals contrary to the peace, order and good governance of the Federation." Several associations fighting for the environmental justice in the oil producing areas of Niger Delta were dissolved by the government under this Decree. These include Association of Minority Oil Producing States (AMOS), Commonwealth of Oil Producing Areas, etc. In the wake of increasing restiveness in Ogoniland, another draconian Decree was promulgated known as the Treason and Treasonable Offences Decree of 1993 which imposed death penalty on "advocates of ethnic autonomy who conspire with groups within or outside the country and profess ideas that minimise the sovereignty of Nigeria." It was this Decree that was used against Saro-Wiwa and other eight Ogoni activists.

[747]   The execution or what the British Prime Minister, John Major then called a 'judicial murder' of Ken Saro-Wiwa and other eight Ogoni leaders by the Military government of late Gen. Sani Abacha were premised on the belief that they instigated the killings of the four "moderate" Ogoni leaders (Edward Kobani, Albert Badey, Samuel Orage and Theophilus Orage) by the youth wing of Movement for the Survival of the Ogoni People (MOSOP) which Saro-Wiwa was the leader, the National Youth Council of Ogoni People (NYCOP) in May 1994. See *The Daily Telegraph*, Outrage at Nigeria executions, 11 November 1995, quoted in Boris Holzer, Framing the Corporation: Royal Dutch/Shell and Human Rights Woes in Nigeria, 30 *J. Consum. Policy* 281–301 at 287 (2007).

[748]   This occurred in November 1990, the law enforcement agencies sacked Umuechem community killing about twenty persons, including a law enforcement officer, the community's traditional leader and two of his sons. See African Concord, 3 December 1990, pp.23–27, quoted in R.T. Suberu (1996), *Ethnic Minority Conflicts and Governance in Nigeria, op. cit.*, p.35.

[749]   For example, the police opened fire on a peaceful protest against Shell contractors in the Ogoni village of Biara in April, 1993, leaving at least eleven people seriously injured and one person dead. See The News, 17 May 1993, pp.18–20, quoted in R.T. Suberu, *Ibid.*

[750]   This occurred in 1999 under President Olusegun Obasanjo when the State carried out a scorched earth action against Odi- a town in Bayelsa State in the Niger Delta in retaliation for the killing of law enforcement agents, who had been drafted to the area to quell riots. More than 2000 people were allegedly killed, many injured, several women raped, unquantifiable resources destroyed with several people displaced. Describing the situation, Senator Chuba Okadigbo, the then Senate President of Nigeria who visited the community a week after the gory incident stated that: 'the facts speak for themselves...there is no need for speech because there is nobody to speak to.' See S.O. Aghalino, The Olusegun Obasanjo Administration and the Niger Delta Question, 1999–2007, 7(1) *Stud Tribes Tribals* 57–66 at 64 (2009); Emily Lenning and Sara Brightman, Oil, Rape and State Crime in Nigeria, 17 *Crit. Crim.* 35–48 (2009).

[751]   The soldiers bombarded the town of Odioma, in Bayelsa State on 19 February 2005 allegedly pursuing militants. Not less than 17 people were killed, including an elderly woman and a two year old child, both burnt to death and several women were raped. See S.O. Aghalino, *Ibid*; Emily Lenning and Sara Brightman, *Ibid.*

of 2009.[752] A scholar has noted that, 'the people of the Niger Delta, as well as the human rights movements around the world, [have] described the experience of the Odi people as genocide'.[753] He continued that, 'they are right because even the soldiers that came to Odi left behind statements (in graffiti) to that effect.'[754] The weapons usually used by the police or soldiers such as FN rifles, AK47s, heavy artillery, general purpose machine guns, bazookas, aircraft, bombs, etc as if they are going to war front, shows that the operations against the environmental crusaders within these communities were nothing but operational genocide.[755] The protesters not only have had their properties destroyed but have also been killed, maimed, raped, displaced and forced into exile. The local inhabitants see this as a form of repression to keep them (as minorities) from voicing even the most moderate claims. Indeed, this is nothing but a grave violation of the rights of the people, whose resources bring fortunes to the Nigerian State and multinational oil companies but, paradoxically, pain, agony and death to the inhabitants of the region. The execution of these dastardly acts, even during the civilian regime, is a clear indication that the brutality and egregious human rights violations under the previous military regimes is also very much a feature of democratic governance.

We shall now examine some of the developmental agencies that have been put in place by the Government to address the Niger Delta issues and examine the adequacy or otherwise of their efforts in meeting the various socio-economic and human rights challenges of the region.

---

[752] In May 2009, President Umaru Yar'Adua ordered a military operation in the Gbaramatu Kingdom (which covered Oporoza, Okerenkoko, Kunukunuma, Kurutie, Kokodiaghene, Ibafa among others, all in the Niger Delta region) to apprehend some militants suspected to have murdered 12 members of a Joint Task Force, including a Lt. Colonel, on 13 April 2009. This military operation which was more a colossal massacre and genocide claimed more than 2,000 persons, mostly aged men and women as well as children. This is aside from the lootings, raping, maiming and burning of these communities by the soldiers. All these bombardments, including that of Zaki Biam and its environs in 2001 by the Federal government, have been largely among the minority groups when similar situations occur among the majority ethnic groups, but without similar response. There is a need for Government to 're-examine the system of rewards and sanctions to ensure more equity and even-handedness in both regions of majority and minority ethnic groups.' See O. Alubo, Citizenship and Nation Making in Nigeria: New Challenges and Contestations Identity, *Culture and Politics*, Vol. 5, Nos. 1 & 2, pp.135–161 at 148 (2004).

[753] Isaac Olawale Albert, The Odi Massacre of 1999 in the Context of the Graffiti Left by the Invading Nigerian Army, University of Ibadan, Ibadan, PEFS Monograph, New Series No. 1, 2003, quoted in Programme on Ethnic and Federal Studies (PEFS) (2004), *The Niger Delta Question: Background to Constitutional Reform, op. cit.*, p.28.

[754] *Ibid.*

[755] *Ibid.*

3.6.1   THE NIGER DELTA DEVELOPMENT BOARD (NDDB)

The peculiar development challenges of the Niger Delta were recognized long before the political independence of Nigeria, with the setting-up of the Henry Willink's Commission of Inquiry in 1958 to look into fears of the people of the Niger Delta, as well as other minorities in the country. Although the Willink Commission rejected the demands of the minorities for a separate State, it observed that a case was 'made out for special treatment of this area [the Niger Delta].'[756]

In the defence of its rejection for separate State to be created for the minorities, the commission recommended, *inter alia*, the creation of a board at the Federal level to address the issues raised in the agitations. Consequently, the Niger Delta Development Board (NDDB) was created. The Board came into existence in 1960 to manage the developmental needs and challenges of the Niger Delta region. In its seven years of existence, the NDDB had achieved nothing significant to show, before it faded away following the military coup of 1966 and the outbreak of civil war in 1967.

3.6.2   NIGER DELTA BASIN DEVELOPMENT AUTHORITY (NDBDA)

Following the massive failure of the NDDB, the Federal Government established the Niger Delta Basin Development Authority[757] in 1980, to provide irrigation, drainage systems, to check flooding and erosion, to gather hydro-meteorological data, to provide potable water, to ensure quality water management, widen waterways, dredge silted canals and carry out soil analysis in the area. Decree 35 of 1987 readjusted the boundaries and expanded the Authority's area of jurisdiction to include eighteen Local Government areas of Delta State.[758]

The Federal Government also established River Basin Development Authorities (RBDA) throughout the country. The members of the Boards of these authorities often comprise politicians who have regarded their tenures as opportunities to reap the "dividends of democracy". They have often been viewed as drains on the nation's finances.[759] Equally important to note is that none of the Board members of the NDBDA, appointed by the Federal Government to run the Authority, came from the Niger Delta. Also, while attention was focused on the establishment and funding of RBDAs, not much attention was paid to the

---

[756]   Willink Commission, 1958: 41–42, para. 18, quoted in Kaniye Ebeku, Niger Delta Oil, Development of the Niger Delta and the New Development: Some Reflections from a Socio-Legal Perspective, *Journal of Asian and African Studies* pp.389–425 at 401 (2008).
[757]   Vide Decree 37 of 1976.
[758]   See Steve Azaiki, *Inequities in Nigerian Politics, op. cit.*, p.116.
[759]   UNDP Report (2006), *Niger Delta Human Development Report*, p.12.

developmental needs of the Niger Delta region. This increased the frustration of
the people in this region and further exacerbated in them their feeling of neglect
by the Federal Government. All these contributed to the failure of the Board.

Following growing agitation for a special focus on the development of the
region, the Shehu Shagari administration set up a Presidential task force in 1980,
known as the 1.5 Percent Committee to examine the developmental peculiarities
of the region. 1.5 per cent of the Federation Account was allocated to the committee
to carry out its mandate.[760] But curiously, perhaps as an oversight, the law did
not create an effective administrative organ to administer the fund.[761] Upon the
assumption of the leadership of General Ibrahim Babangida, as the Head of State
and Commander-in-Chief of Armed Forces in Nigeria in 1985, he established a
Presidential Implementation Committee (PIC) in 1987 to administer the 1.5 per
cent derivation fund. In spite of the Committee's determination to transform the
area, it could not achieve much due to inadequate funding and logistics. More
important was the fact that the Committee operated from Lagos, far way from
its area of assignment. This, as would be expected, made it lose touch with the
realities in the Niger Delta – the travails of the oil-producing communities, their
woes, agitations and aspirations.[762] The failure of the PIC to meet the yearnings
and aspirations of the people of the Niger Delta naturally increased those people's
anger, frustration and restiveness. As a result, a Judicial Commission of Inquiry
headed by Hon. Justice Alfa Belgore, then Justice of the Supreme Court, was set
up in 1992 to, amongst other things, identify the root causes of the restiveness,
and suggest the way forward. The Commission recommended the setting up of
a development agency for the region to ameliorate the problems arising from oil
production. This led to the establishment of the Oil Mineral Producing Areas
Development Commission (OMPADEC) in 1992.

3.6.3 OIL MINERAL PRODUCING AREAS DEVELOPMENT COMMISSION (OMPADEC)

The Oil Minerals Producing Areas Development Commission (OMPADEC) was
established in 1992 by President Ibrahim Babangida to replace the PIC, which
had by then become almost moribund. The Commission was established by a
Decree,[763] to address the special developmental needs of the oil producing areas.
Its responsibilities included (i) 'tackling ecological problems that have arisen from
the exploitation of oil minerals,' (ii) consulting 'with the relevant Federal and
State Government authorities on the control and effective methods of tackling
the problem of oil pollution and spillages,' (iii) ensuring 'fair and equitable

---

[760]   *TELL* Nigeria's Independent Weekly News magazine, No. 23, 4 June 2007, p.29.
[761]   U. Ekpo (2004) *The Niger Delta and Oil Politics, op. cit.*, p.68.
[762]   *Ibid*, at p.69.
[763]   See the Oil Minerals Producing Areas Development Commission Decree No. 23 of 1992.

distribution of projects, services and employment of personnel in accordance with recognized percentage production', that is, based on the percentage of oil derivable from each of the oil-producing areas and (iv) liaising 'with the various oil companies on matters of pollution control.'[764]

Section 2(1)(c) of the Decree provided that the sum received by the Commission was to be used for the rehabilitation and development of the oil-producing areas on the basis of the proportion of the oil produced in a particular State, local government area or community. This formula has been criticized for not taking into account the level of devastation to the ecology of the place where oil is exploited. This is because it was possible to produce many barrels of oil with minimal ecological damage but, on the other hand, produce a few barrels of oil with much greater ecological damage.[765] This approach also has the potential of marginalizing those communities, like Oloibiri, which were major oil producers in the past, but which no longer produce oil in appreciable quantities.[766]

Again, Section 3(5) of the Decree provided that the Commission was not subject to the direction, control or supervision of any other authority or person in the performance of its functions other than the President and Commander-in-Chief of the Armed forces. In the view of Akper P.T.,[767] this provision appeared to have watered down whatever influence the oil-producing communities would have had over the activities of the Commission and which may have accounted for its lack of success.

The Commission did not make any noticeable impact on the lives and environment of the Niger Delta people. It was characterized by official profligacy, corruption, excessive political interference, mismanagement, inadequate and irregular funding, lack of transparency and accountability, and sometimes insensitivity to the needs of the communities in whose interests it was set up. There were also allegations of arbitrary distribution of benefits and projects.[768] Contracts were awarded in anticipation of funds, with the result that contracts worth billions of naira were awarded which were not eventually backed with cash. At the time it folded the Commission owed its contractors billions of naira and left the Niger Delta with several abandoned projects.[769] According to the Niger Delta Human Development Report 2006, the Chief Executive of OMPADEC had identified three pressing problems in respect of the Commission. There were no

---

[764] Section 2(1).
[765] P.T. Akper, "Socio-Political Issues in Oil and Gas Exploitation in Political and Economic Reform in Nigeria", in I.A. Ayua and Guobadia D.A. (eds) (2001), *Political Reform and Economic Recovery in Nigeria, op. cit.*, p.536.
[766] *The Guardian*, 14 May 1993, p.24.
[767] *Ibid.*
[768] See P. Fregence, "Oil Exploration and Production Activities: The Socio-Economic and Environmental Problems in Warri-Itsekiri Homeland", in Funmi Adewunmi (ed.) (1997), *Oil Exploitation, The State and Crises in Nigeria's Oil Bearing Enclave*, Friedrich Ebert foundation, Lagos, p.59.
[769] UNDP Report (2006), *Niger Delta Human Development Report*, p.12.

available data for planning purposes, such as crude oil production quotas by State; the Commission had no means to cope with the volume of demands upon it given decades of physical neglect and deprivation; and funding was inadequate. While the decree setting up OMPADEC stipulated that it should receive three per cent of the Federation Account, the Commission claimed that what it actually got was three per cent of net revenues from the Federation Account.[770] Besides, much of the funds released ended up in the accounts of private individuals, as the number of projects completed cannot justify the amount received.[771] Its first two leaders – Albert K. Horsfall and Professor Eric Opia were unceremoniously dismissed in quick succession as a result of corrupt deals.[772] Although, reorganizations and changes of leadership were effected several times to reposition the Commission in such a way that it could serve the needs of the people in the oil-producing region, the problems still persisted. There was an amendment to the principal statute in 1996, through the promulgation of the Oil Minerals Producing Areas Development Commission (Amendment) Decree No. 7 of 1996, in terms of the composition of the board,[773] *inter alia*, but this did not bring about any meaningful impact to the people for the region.

Another reason alleged for its inefficiency was that OMPADEC was not given the power to craft regulations, enforce laws, or even impose sanctions for violation of environmental laws,[774] thus preventing it from achieving the environmental objectives stated in the Decree. The establishment of the Commission was viewed as a diversionary attempt to pre-empt the claims of the oil-bearing communities to exclusive control of oil rents and royalties.[775] Thus, in the words of Ken Saro-Wiwa: "OMPADEC is illogical, an insult and an injury. If you have your own

---

[770] *Ibid.*

[771] E. Ojameruaye, *Lessons from the Chadian Model for Distribution of Oil Wealth in Nigeria's Niger Delta*, at htpp://www.waado.org/Environment/Remediation/Chadian_model_niger_delta.htm [accessed 5 May 2010].

[772] Shola Omotola, *The Next Gulf? Oil Politics, Environmental Apocalypse and Rising Tension in the Niger Delta*, Occasional Paper Series: Vol. 1 No. 3, published by the African Centre for the Constructive Resolution of Disputes (ACCORD), p.18. The removal of Eric Opia in September 1998 was as a result of his inability to account for N6.7 billion (then almost U.S.$80 million). See J.G. Frynas, Corporate and State Responses to Anti-Oil Protests in the Niger Delta, *op. cit.*, p.38; S.O. Aghalino, The Olusegun Obasanjo Administration and the Niger Delta Question, 1922–2007, *op. cit.*, p.59.

[773] The Amendment Decree of 1996 amended sections 3 and 4 of the principal statute. The amendment provided that all members of the Board except the Managing Director and Executive Directors were to be part-time members. Unlike under the Principal Decree, the Managing Director was to be the Chief Executive of the Commission and not the Chairman. Again, by section 3 of the Amendment Decree, which amended section 4 of the Principal Decree, all the members of the Commission were to enjoy a 4-year tenure, subject to renewal for another term, except the Managing Director and the Executive Directors who were to enjoy a 5-year tenure also subject to renewal for another term. See P.T. Akper, *op. cit.*, pp.532–538.

[774] Emeka Duruigbo, Managing Oil Revenues for Socio-Economic Development in Nigeria: The Case for Community-Based Trust Funds, 30 *N.C.J. Int'l. & Com. Reg.* 122–196 at 137 (2004–2005); Joshua P. Eaton, The Nigerian Tragedy, Environmental Regulation of Transnational Corporations, and the Human Right to a Healthy Environment, *op. cit.*, p.289.

[775] R.T. Suberu (1996), *Ethnic Minority Conflicts and Governance in Nigeria, op. cit.*, p.38.

money, why should Government set up a Commission to run your money? They are treating us like babies here … OMPADEC is (designed) to bait us and destroy our will to resist injustice".[776]

As a result of these inadequacies levied against OMPADEC, the people of the region got disappointed. The bulk of its projects had little to do with poverty reduction, and so the vast majority of the poor people in the region were not helped in any significant way. Rather than abating the restiveness in the region, the Commission further accentuated it, and at an alarming rate. The Commission was finally scrapped in 1999.

3.6.4 NIGER DELTA DEVELOPMENT COMMISSION (NDDC)

In order to address the renewed and heightened wave of youth restiveness in the region, following years of neglect and underdevelopment in the midst of oil wealth, and in an attempt to defuse the demands for "resource control," President Obasanjo introduced to the National Assembly, soon after his inauguration in May 1999, a Bill to establish the Niger Delta Development Commission (NDDC). This law which had a stormy passage through the National Assembly, was eventually passed in July 2000 in accordance with section 56(5) of the 1999 Constitution.[777]

The NDDC Act establishes a governing board for the Commission, appointed by the President, and compromising: the Chairman; one person who shall be an indigene of an oil-producing area to represent each of the following member States, that is, Abia, Akwa Ibom, Bayelsa, Cross River, Delta, Edo, Imo, Ondo and Rivers; three persons to represent non-oil mineral producing States drawn from the remaining geo-political zones which are not represented in the Commission; one representative of oil-producing companies in the Niger Delta nominated by the oil-producing companies; one person to represent the Federal Ministry of Finance; one person to represent the Federal Ministry of Environment; the

---

[776] The News 17 May 1993, p.25, quoted in Suberu R.T., *Ibid*, p.38.
[777] Signed by Speaker of the House of Representatives on 11 July 2000 and the Senate President on 12 July 2000. Section 55(5) in combination with section 58(4) of the 1999 Constitution of the Federal Republic of Nigeria provides that where a Bill is presented to the President for assent, he shall within thirty days signify his assent or withhold same. Where the latter is the case, and the Bill is again passed by a two-thirds majority of each House, the Bill shall become law and the assent of the President shall be dispensed with. 'The National Assembly amended the draft Bill to reflect some concerns, including reducing the percentage of funds to come from the Federation Account to 15% and increasing a proposed levy on the oil companies from 0.5 to 3% of their budget. President Obasanjo vetoed these amendments in March 2000, but in May both Houses of the National Assembly passed the Bill again by a two thirds majority, overriding the President's veto. After further argument and requests to agree on the amendments, the President finally accepted this version of the Bill.' See Human Rights Watch (2002), *The Niger Delta: No Democratic Dividend*, Vol. 14 No. 6(A), p. 25, at www.hrw.org/reports/2002/nigeria3/nigerdelta.pdf.

Managing Director of the Commission; and two executive directors. The Act
provides for the rotation of the office of Chairman of the Commission amongst
the member States of the Commission in alphabetical order as listed above.
The Chairman and other members of the Board are appointed by the President
subject to the confirmation of the Senate in consultation with the House of
Representatives.

The NDDC specific functions and powers as provided for in section 7 of the
NDDC Act, include to: (i) formulate policies and guidelines for the development
of the Niger Delta area (ii) conceive, plan and implement, in accordance with
set rules and regulations, projects and programmes for sustainable development
of the area in the fields of transportation, health, education, employment,
industrialization, agriculture and fisheries, housing and urban development,
water supply, and electricity and telecommunications (iii) prepare master plans
and schemes to promote the physical development of the Niger Delta area and
estimate the cost of implementing such master plans and schemes (iv) tackle
ecological and environmental problems that arise from the exploration of
mineral oil in the Niger Delta area and advise the Federal Government and
the member States on the prevention and control of oil spillage, gas flaring and
environmental pollution and (v) liaise with the oil companies on all matters of
pollution prevention and control.

In order to avoid ugly repetition of the past, when activities and programmes
of previous Commissions were negatively affected by inadequate funds, the
NDDC Act requires the Federal Government to contribute from the Federation
Account 15% of the monthly statutory allocations due to member States of the
Commission, and the oil companies are expected to contribute three per cent of
their annual budgets to the Commission. Also, member states are expected to
contribute fifty per cent of the ecological fund allocated to them by the Federal
Government.[778] Other sources of funds include proceeds from other NDDC assets
and other miscellaneous sources. Although, the recent Supreme Court decision
in the Resource Control case has upset the arrangement for the funding of the
Commission, section 14 of the Act, which lists the sources of the funds of the
Commission,[779] is an improvement on the equivalent provision in the OMPADEC

---

[778] See Idemudia Uwafiokun, Host Nation- Oil Transnational Corporation Partnership for
Poverty Reduction in the Niger Delta, Nigeria – Diagnosis and Recommendations, *Exploration
and Production Vol. 7 Issue 1, Touch Briefings*, pp.128–130 at 128 (2009).

[779] Member States are supposed to contribute 50% of the sum due to them from the Ecological
Fund. However, the decision in the case of *A.G of the Federation v. Abia State and 35 others
(Supra)*, may have affected this arrangement. In this case, the Supreme Court held *inter alia*,
that the first line charges on the Federation Account such as the 1% direct allocation to the
Federal Capital Territory, service of external debts, payments to NNPC and funding of the
Judiciary are unconstitutional. Although, no direct reference was made by the decision to the
Ecological Funds, which is equally a first charge on the Federation Account, it may also by
inference be subject to the decision as it applies to similar charges. The result is that the contribution of the States to the NDDC, through their allocations from the Ecological Fund may
be unenforceable. The President has sent an amendment to the National Assembly to make all

Decree.[780] Section 28 repealed the former OMPADEC Decree and dissolved the Commission established under it; and the NDDC inherited all its assets, funds, resources, personnel and liabilities.

In a bid to fulfill its mandate, NDDC has continued to take on projects that cut across every strata of life in the Niger Delta, such as roads and rehabilitation, education, youth empowerment, health, water supply, electricity supply and skills acquisition. Some of these road projects include the construction of the Ogbia Nembe Road in partnership with Shell Petroleum Development Company. This cuts across the Local Government Areas (LGAs) where oil production started in Nigeria (Oloibiri is in Ogbia LGA, the old Brass Division) and will help to connect 13 major communities in Bayelsa State to the capital in Yenegoa.[781] Indeed, between 2002 and 2003, NDDC claimed it had executed 810 projects in different sectors of the region.[782]

As a development agency, the NDDC quickly identified the need for a master plan as part of its overall strategy, and in 2006, it launched the Niger Delta Regional Development Master Plan (NDRDMP). This will be discussed later.

As a result of the above achievements of NDDC, some members of the civil society and other Nigerians have accorded it some credit. Notwithstanding the above, youth discontent, ethnic militias, restiveness, and environmental and developmental crises continue to suggest that all is not well with the Commission. The Commission is faced with a lot of challenges inhibiting it from fulfilling its mandate. One of these is inadequate funding, which is exacerbated by the fact that it has become difficult to earn revenue from some expected sources. Evidence abounds that the Federal Government has consistently refused to meet its obligations to the Commission, as it is contributing 10%, instead of the 15% provided for in the Act.[783] Even some of the oil companies are not contributing the full 3% of their budget as stipulated in the Act.[784] While the Federal Government

---

the member States contribute 10% of their monthly statutory allocation to the Commission. See Y. Akinseye-George, "Niger Delta Development Commission (NDDC) Act: Human Rights Dimension", in Ogungbe, M.O. (ed) (2003), *Nigerian Law: Contemporary Issues. Essays in Honour of Sir, Chief (Dr.) Gabriel Osawaru Igbinedion*, College of Law, Igbinedion University, Okada Publication, p.207.

[780]   Y. Akinseye-George, *Ibid*.

[781]   See Idemudia Uwafiokun, Host Nation – Oil Transnational Corporation Partnership for Poverty Reduction in the Niger Delta, Nigeria – Diagnosis and Recommendations, *op. cit.*, p.128; *TELL* Nigeria's Independent Weekly News Magazine No. 23 June 4, 2007 p.50.

[782]   Shola Omotola, From the OMPADEC to the NDDC: An Assessment of State Responses to Environmental Insecurity in the Niger Delta, Nigeria, *op. cit.*, p.81.

[783]   E. Ojameruaye, *Lessons from the Chadian Model for Distribution of Oil Wealth in Nigeria's Niger Delta, op. cit.*; See also Reuben Adeolu Alabi, Comparative Analysis of Socio-Economic Constraints in Niger Delta, *European Journal of Economics, Finance and Administrative Sciences*, Issue 10, pp.63–74 at 66 (2008).

[784]   Shola Omotola, From the OMPADEC to the NDDC: An Assessment of State Responses to Environmental Insecurity in the Niger Delta, Nigeria, *op. cit.*, pp.73–89 at 84; Emeka Duruigbo, Managing Oil Revenues for Socio-Economic Development in Nigeria: The Case for Community-Based Trust Funds, *op. cit.*, p.142. For example, in 2001, the approved budget for Shell was U.S.$2.004 billion but it remitted U.S.$380.074 million (1.30%) as against three per

by law was expected to allocate N318 billion to the NDDC between 2001 and 2006, it remitted only N93 billion, and while the oil MNCs were expected to contribute N182 billion during the same period, they allocated only N142 billion.[785] The failure of Government to meet its responsibilities makes it morally untenable for it to accuse the oil companies of moral bankruptcy when they fail to meet their responsibilities for the development of the region.[786]

An amendment has been proposed by the Federal Government to the NDDC Act which will reduce its contribution from 15% to 10% and that of oil companies from 3% to 2%. It also wants the oil-producing States to contribute 10% of their statutory allocations to the Commission, but the States are opposed to this because they are also to contribute 50% of their Ecological Fund Allocation to the Commission.[787] The States claim there is no legal basis for their continued contribution to a Commission that is an appendage of the Presidency and outside their sphere of influence.[788] This situation is worrisome when coupled with the attendant delays in the release of approved allocations, due in part to prolonged face-offs between the legislature and the executive which delays the passage of Appropriation Bills. The controversy over the funding of NDDC since its establishment rages on and has continued to cripple the effectiveness of the Commission. There is a need for the NDDC to be properly funded to be able to deliver its mandate.

Another major challenge, which affects the Commission is that it is entangled in the same corruption crises that plagued the previous initiatives. This frequently leads to misapplication of funds that should have been utilized for developmental purposes. In spite of the efforts of the Government to combat corruption in Nigeria, through the setting up of different agencies,[789] corruption still remains entrenched in our entire system. In less than six years the leadership of the NDDC has been changed thrice, and 'a recent allegation of corruption that led to the indefinite suspension of Mr. Godwin Omene, the Managing Director of NDDC is very much a reenactment of history'.[790] Appointments to

---

cent of its annual budget stipulated by the NDDC Act; Mobil's approved budget was U.S.$1.029 billion, but it remitted $26.631 million (2.55%); Chevron's approved budget was U.S.$1.100 billion but it remitted U.S.$29 million (2.69%); Agip's approved budget was U.S.$461.551 million but it remitted U.S.$11.173 million (2.41%). See Reuben Adeolu Alabi, *Ibid* p.66.

[785] Uwafiokun Idemudia, Corporate Social Responsibility and the Rentier Nigerian State: Rethinking the Role of Government and the Possibility of Corporate Social Development in the Niger Delta, *op. cit.*, p.145.

[786] Uwafiokun Idemudia and Uwem E. Ite, Corporate-Community Relations in Nigeria's Oil Industry: Challenges and Imperatives, 13 *Corp. Soc. Responsib. Environ. Mgmt.* 194–206 at 203 (2006).

[787] E. Ojameruaye, *Lessons from the Chadian Model for Distribution of Oil Wealth in Nigeria's Niger Delta*, *op. cit.*

[788] *Ibid.*

[789] Independent Corrupt Practices & Other Related Offences Commission (ICPC) 2000, Economic and Financial Crimes Commission (EFCC) 2002, Money Laundering Act 1995, etc.

[790] Shola Omotola, From the OMPADEC to the NDDC: An Assessment of State Responses to Environmental Insecurity in the Niger Delta, Nigeria, *op. cit.*, p.84; V. Jike, "The Political

the NDDC have also become a matter of political cronyism and a process of capturing political votes. Because of the delicate political configuration of power in Nigeria, and how this configuration has been bureaucratized, appointments and the disciplining of errant officials are usually politicized.[791] This lack of transparency and accountability undermines the Commission's legitimacy amongst its stakeholders[792] and affects the Commission's capacity to deliver its mandate. Since only a very small proportion of its budgeted funds trickle down to the intended beneficiaries as a result of corruption, developmental objectives are inhibited and this denies local inhabitants the right to a good quality of living.[793]

Another challenge is the excessive level of political control over the Commission. The NDDC Act provides that the Commission shall be subject to the direction, control and supervision in the performance of its functions of the President, Commander-in-Chief of the Armed Forces. Also, for reasons which are not very clear, the NDDC Act not only made in section 7, the NDDC virtually an agent of the Presidency, but also made the organization one of the most bureaucratic, through an endless maze of monitoring Committees. The Commission has a Board comprising appointees of the President, who are nominated by their Governors, a Management Committee, a Governor's Committee, a Presidential Monitoring team, a Ministerial team, a Senate Monitoring Team, and a House Committee.[794] It is doubtful whether these bureaucratic bottlenecks will permit the Commission to effectively tackle the numerous problems of human rights violations caused by the operations of the multinational oil companies. To be able to achieve the objectives for which it is set up, the NDDC should be given some measure of independence to carry out its functions, avoiding unnecessary interference with its operations.

Again, as an agency of the Federal Government, the Commission is perceived by local communities as existing to facilitate the self-serving political goals of the ruling party by means of non-transparent overpriced contracts and payments.[795] It is therefore seen as lacking what it takes to develop the region.

Sociology of Resource Control in the Niger Delta", in Hassan A. Saliu (ed) (2005), *Nigeria Under Democratic Rule, 1999–2003*, Vol. 2, University Press, Ibadan, p.159.

[791] Social and Economic Rights Action Center (SERAC) (2005), *Perpetuating Poverty, Consolidating Powerlessness: Oil and the Niger Delta, op. cit.,* p.34.

[792] Idemudia Uwafiokun, Host Nation- Oil Transnational Corporation Partnership for Poverty Reduction in the Niger Delta, Nigeria- Diagnosis and Recommendations, *op. cit.,* p.130.

[793] Ibaba Samuel Ibaba, "State Intervention in the Niger Delta: A Critical Appraisal of the Ideology of Developmental Commission", in *International Conference on The Nigerian State, Oil Industry and the Niger Delta, op. cit.,* p.534.

[794] Mittee L., *Civil Society and Implementation of the Master Plan,* being Notes of the Presentation at the Niger Delta Stakeholders Networks Workshop on the Implementation of the Niger Delta Regional Development Master Plan, held at the Marina Resort, Calabar, 11–13 November 2007.

[795] A.I. Osuoka, *Oil and Gas Revenues and Development Challenges for the Niger Delta and Nigeria,* being a paper presented at the Expert Group Meeting on the Use of Non-Renewable Resource Revenues for Sustainable Local Development, organised by the UN Department of Economic and Social Affairs, Friday 21 September 2007, UN Headquarters, New York, at www.

The concept of popular participation in the process of development is almost absent from the scheme of the NDDC Act, hence the top-down approach to the implementation of projects. There is an absence of true representation of the Niger Delta communities in the NDDC. While it may be true that community members are represented in the Commission, one representative from each community is grossly insufficient to represent the interests of the varying communities.[796] These criticisms were well captured by a scholar in this way:

> "The greatest problem relates to the Commission's composition. Moreover, the Act lacks other appropriate and necessary participatory provisions. Specifically, the NDDC Act does not make provision for the representation of the indigenous people (for whose benefit the Act was made) in the executing body nor is there provision for their participation in the planning and execution of projects. The provision for the representation of state members in the Commission cannot be properly regarded as affording representation to the local people, since they have no input in the process of appointment. The problem with this situation lies in the fact that such appointees are likely to see themselves as representing the state authorities that appointed them, and not the people. Moreover, they may be persons who are unfamiliar with the problems and needs of the local people."[797]

The Commission has been accused of not engaging the communities, civil society, and sometimes, the State, in planning development projects in the Niger Delta. Even in the preparation of the Master Plan for the development of the region, there were complaints that it was crafted by expatriates (GTZ of Germany) in collaboration with a few of the Nigerian political elite with no substantial input from the inhabitants of the region.[798] The NDDC Act should encourage popular participation in all spheres of the development process in line with the provisions of Article 8(2) of the UN Declaration on the Right to Development. It is only through a participatory and interactive process, built on genuine and transparent stakeholder consultations, that sustainable solutions will emerge.[799] The success recorded in the Akassa development project, which is a Statoil-BP participatory community development initiative in the Niger Delta, provides perfect example. This programme initiated in Akassa, a coastal community in Bayelsa State in 1997, and executed directly by the locals partnering with two leading NGOs,

---

un.org/esa/sustdev/sdissues/institutional_arrangements/egm2007/presentations/isaacosuok. pdf [accessed 5 May 2010].

[796] Emeka Duruigbo, Managing Oil Revenues for Socio-Economic Development in Nigeria: The Case for Community-Based Trust Funds, *op. cit.*, p.148.

[797] Kaniye Ebeku, Critical Appraisal of Nigeria's Niger Delta Development Act 2000, *Int'l. Energy L. & Tax'n Rev.* 203, 204 (2003), quoted in Emeka Duruigbo, *Ibid* pp.147–148.

[798] See Akeem Ayofe Akinwale, Re-Engineering the NDDC's Master Plan: An Analytical Approach, *Journal of Sustainable Development in Africa*, Vol. 11, No. 2, pp.142–159 at 151 (2009); Kenneth Omeje, Development Securitisation in Nigeria's Niger Delta: An Appraisal of the Niger Delta Development Commission (NDDC), *African Renaissance*, Vol. 1 No. 1, pp.124–133 at 130 (2004).

[799] Y. Akinseye-George, *op. cit.*, p.208.

ProNatura International and Niger Delta Wetland Centre, has components like poverty alleviation, human resource management, and natural resource management,[800] and should serve as a model for NDDC in its effort towards achieving its set objectives.

Consultation with NGOs/civil society and the communities is important. NGOs and Community based organizations (CBOs) could assist in consulting with the local people, producing action plans to address local problems and encouraging communities to establish control over local decisions in the process of development.[801] Consultation with the communities will go a long way in correcting the impression of ordinary people that the loyalty of the NDDC is to the Federal Government and the oil companies that provide the bulk of its budget, and not to the Niger Delta. A situation where decisions about the projects which the Commission intends to carry out are taken without the input of the affected communities is not only unpalatable but violates their right to participation. Identifying and appreciating the needs of the community may be a problem for the Commission. For example, the NDDC built a landing jetty for the Isua-Joinkrama community in Ahoada West Local Government Council of Rivers State. The facility was meant to aid motorised boat transportation. But it was not needed at Isua-Joinkrama, which is accessible by tarred road and so does not use motorised boats for mass transportation.[802] This is one of several wasteful expenditures by the Commission on projects not of priority to communities, in the face of the community's pressing need for pipe borne water, medical facilities, educational facilities, etc. Also, the NDDC's top-down decision making process, according to Anyankwe Nsirimovu, impairs the quality of decisions that the commission makes by restricting the information that groups and affected communities can offer.[803] A bottom-up strategy should be adopted as that constitutes an important, well-tested strategy for developing a consensus-building mechanism for facilitating regional harmony, cohesion, stability, and the efficient/effective management of development.[804]

---

[800]   Kenneth Omeje, Development Securitisation in Nigeria's Niger Delta: An Appraisal of the Niger Delta Development Commission (NDDC), *op. cit.*, pp.131–132.

[801]   Y. Akinseye-George, *op. cit.*, p.208.

[802]   A.I. Osuoka, *op. cit.*

[803]   Social and Economic Rights Action Center (SERAC) (2005), *Perpetuating Poverty, Consolidating Powerlessness: Oil and the Niger Delta, op. cit.*, p.36.

[804]   G. Onosode, Environmental Management and Sustainable Development in the Niger Delta, in Osuntokun A. (ed) (2000), *Environmental Problems of the Niger Delta*, Friedrich Ebert Foundation, Lagos, p.16.

3.6.5 THE DEVELOPMENT OF NIGER DELTA REGIONAL DEVELOPMENT MASTER PLAN

When the NDDC was inaugurated in January 2001, part of the brief given to the Commission by President Olusegun Obasanjo was to produce a master plan for the development of the Niger Delta region. The Master Plan was provided for in the enabling Act for the establishment of the NDDC.[805] It took the Commission five years to produce the document but finally in 2006, the NDDC launched the Niger Delta Regional Development Master Plan (NDRDMP). During the launch, President Obasanjo said that the inauguration of the master plan was based on his commitment to reverse the trend of abject poverty, gross neglect, underdevelopment and lack of infrastructure in the region.[806]

The master plan is unique in every sense. Importantly, it is the first regional development plan of any sort in the history of the Nigerian Nation, and it is a product of rigorous region-wide consultations and stakeholder participation. The master plan is a 15-year development roadmap for the region from 2006 to 2020 to be implemented in three phases of five years each, *viz.* the Foundation Phase, 2006–2010; the Expansion Phase, 2011–2015; and the Consolidation Phase, 2016–2020. The Foundation Phase provides the framework for the empowerment of the Niger Delta, and it targets the infrastructural backbone for development by creating favourable conditions for greater productivity and economic enterprise in rural and urban areas for all segments of the population.[807] The Expansion phase will build on the foundation laid by the first phase by harnessing the improved climate and infrastructural backbone. The Consolidation phase will build on the gains of the preceding two phases to entrench peace and prosperity.[808] The major goals for the developmental themes in the Master Plan include interventions in many sectors of activity, grouped under five general themes: Economic Growth, Human and Community Needs, the Natural Environment, Physical Infrastructure, and Institutional Development. Under the economic growth goal, wealth is expected to be generated to reduce poverty and support better living standards for the growing population. Human and Community Needs which targets the welfare of individuals is intended to improve the quality of life of the individual, family and community at large and to enhance the sense of identity and pride of each community.[809] The National Environment goal is to protect and conserve the rich biodiversity resources of the region, remediate and restore environmentally impacted sites and degraded resources, and set appropriate standards for the

---

[805] This was provided for in Part II, section 7(1) of the enabling Act for the establishment of the NDDC, and reflects President Olusegun Obasanjo's vision of a clearly defined, people-oriented and multi-stakeholder development strategy for the region.

[806] *Punch Newspaper*, Saturday, 31 March 2007, p.43.

[807] *TELL*, Nigeria's Independent Weekly News Magazine, No. 23, 4 June 2007, pp.34–35.

[808] *Ibid.*

[809] Niger Delta Regional Development Master Plan – Popular Version, NDDC Publication 2006, p.21.

environmental regulation and control in the region. Under Infrastructure, the Plan sets to provide adequate infrastructure to support industrialization and economic growth as well as human and community welfare. Institutional Development is targeted at building adequate human capacity at all levels of society to drive the development process.[810]

Realizing that the resources needed to implement the NDRDMP are not at the disposal of any one development stakeholder, the Plan stresses the need for stakeholders to partner, collaborate and pool their resources towards the common goal – the development of the Niger Delta region. It is the primary responsibility of the NDDC, the nine State Governments and the Local Governments in the Niger Delta region to champion this process of building partnerships (Public-Private Partnership).[811] Specific steps towards achieving collaboration among the various development stakeholders include the establishment of the Niger Delta Partners for Sustainable Development Forum (PSD) at Regional, State and Local Government levels. The Master Plan targets a funding mix of a public-private partnership, PPP, to cover the $50 billion estimated expenditure in the 15-year development plan. About 24% of this will come from the private sector and private individuals, while 76% will be borne by the public sector, NGOs, donor agencies, and local and international development finance institutions.[812]

As laudable as this document is, it faces some challenges. Firstly, it fails to address some of the oil-related activities that negatively impact on the human rights of the inhabitants of the oil-producing communities, like the issue of how to end gas flaring.

There is also the funding challenge, which has been previously discussed. NDDC requires better funding to meet the set objectives and implement the strategic programmes and initiatives contained in the Master Plan. All the stakeholders must be prepared to make their contributions – the Federal Government, States, Local Government, oil companies, even the donor agencies and the NDDC. Some measures must be taken to ensure that the budgets of the various levels of Government, the NDDC and other stakeholders are prepared to cover issues in the Master Plan.

Another major challenge must be in getting all stakeholders, State and Local Governments, the oil companies, and so on to "buy into" the Master Plan so that the vision can be achieved.[813] This can be better achieved if the Commission can get legislative support for the plan, that is, get the State Houses of Assembly to pass appropriate laws to give legislative teeth to the plan. This will institutionalize the plan and commit subsequent Governments to the implementation.[814]

---

[810]   *Ibid.*
[811]   *Ibid*, p.40.
[812]   *Ibid.*
[813]   T. Alaibe, *TELL* Nigeria's Independent Weekly News Magazine, No. 23, 4 June 2007, p.41.
[814]   *Ibid.*

The peace and order of the region is another factor. Frequent crises, occasioned by political, social, economic and other reasons has affected the developmental programmes in the region. Sustainable development can only take place in a peaceful environment. For example, most of the engineers handling the Commission's projects are expatriates, and are increasingly wary of carrying out any project in the region for fear of being kidnapped or murdered. The spate of insecurity that has enveloped the region has affected the region negatively. Besides, the Commission needs a peaceful atmosphere to plan and execute programmes and projects. It is therefore imperative for all the stakeholders to swing into action to find a permanent solution to the atmosphere of insecurity that pervades the entire region.

3.6.6 CONSOLIDATED COUNCIL ON SOCIAL AND ECONOMIC DEVELOPMENT OF COASTAL STATES OF THE NIGER DELTA (COSEND)

This development body was established by the Federal Government on 18 April 2006 and is charged with responsibility for the development of the Niger Delta region. It was established because of the perceived failure of NDDC. This point was well noted by the former President Obasanjo when he declared that NDDC was 'not doing 100 per cent what we want it to do.'[815] While inaugurating COSEND, the President announced a nine-point Plan for the socio-economic development of the Niger Delta area, covering: employment generation; transportation; education; health; telecommunications; environment, agriculture; power; and water resources.[816] However, unlike the earlier development agencies, like OMPADEC and NDDC that were created by statutes, COSEND was not established by any statute, thus making its future doubtful. In fact, not much has been heard about its operations and activities since it was set up till date. Even though it still exists, the administration of President Umaru Yar'Adua, who assumed the leadership of the country in 2007, did not specifically state whether it would continue with the agency.[817]

---

[815] *Guardian*, New Development Plan for Niger Delta, 19 April, 2006, at http://odili.net/news/source/2006/apr/19/6.html, quoted in Kaniye Ebeku, Niger Delta Oil, Development of the Niger Delta and the New Development: Some Reflections from a Socio-Legal Perspective, *Journal of Asian and African Studies*, p.408 (2008).

[816] Kaniye Ebeku, *Ibid* p.408.

[817] *Ibid* p.417.

3.6.7 NIGER DELTA PEACE AND CONFLICT RESOLUTION COMMITTEE

This Committee was set by President Umaru Yar'Adua's administration in July 2007. This body is charged with the task of studying the causes of conflicts in the region and making appropriate recommendations.[818] In carrying out its task, the Committee is required *inter alia*, to 'liaise with the groups in the region'. Its membership is made up of a Chairman, Secretary, two persons representing each State of the Niger Delta, four from the oil companies and one each from the NDDC and NNPC.[819] The Committee aims at bringing about genuine and peaceful negotiations with the people.

3.6.8 TECHNICAL COMMITTEE ON THE NIGER DELTA

This 45-member Committee was inaugurated by President Umaru Yar'Adua's administration on 8th of September 2008 to collate and review all past reports, starting from the 1958 Willinks' Report, appraise their recommendations and make other proposals that will help the Federal Government to achieve sustainable development, peace, and human and environmental security in the Niger Delta Region. One good thing about this Committee is that it builds on reports of all the previous committees that have been set up by Governments over the past 50 years to address the Niger Delta environmental crisis. The Committee under the Chairmanship of Mr. Ledum Mitee, the Movement for the Survival of the Ogoni People (MOSOP) President, submitted its Report[820] to the Federal Government on 1st of December 2008.[821] In spite of calls by Nigerians, and even the members of the Committee, for the Government to review the report and prepare a White Paper on it, Government has remained silent and has failed to respond on the report.[822]

One can only hope that the Government will implement the recommendations made and not throw the Report into dustbin as has been the case with previous Reports. The Committee's recommendations include appointing a mediator to facilitate discussions between Government and the militants; granting an

---

[818]   Government sets up Niger Delta Peace and Conflict Resolution Committee, at www.nigeriafirst.org/printer_7476.shtml [accessed 6 May 2010].
[819]   *Ibid.*
[820]   See the Report of the Technical Committee on the Niger Delta, November 2008, at www.mosop.org/Nigeria_Niger_Delta_Technical_Committee_Report_2008.pdf [accessed 6 May 2010].
[821]   L. Mitee, *The Niger Delta: A Vision to Nigeria's Development*, being the text of a paper presented at the 5th All Nigerian Editors Conference, Kaduna, on 3 April 2009, at www.nigerianguildofeditors.com/index.php? [accessed 6 May 2010].
[822]   See David Smock, *Crisis in the Niger Delta*, USI Peace Briefing, September 2009, p.1, at www.usip.org/files/resources/niger_delta_crisis.pdf [accessed 6 May 2010].

amnesty to some militant leaders; launching a disarmament, demobilisation and rehabilitation campaign; increasing the percentage of oil revenue to the Delta to 25% from the current 13%; establishing regulations to compel oil companies to have insurance bonds; making the enforcement of critical environmental laws a national priority; exposing fraudulent environmental cleanups of oil spills and prosecuting operators; and ending gas flaring by 31 December 2008 as previously ordered by the Federal Government.[823] It is the general consensus of Nigerians, particularly the Niger Delta people, that the Committee's Report provides the best road towards bringing peace to the crisis-ridden region. The Federal Government should without delay put in place machinery to implement the recommendations of the Report of the Technical Committee on the Niger Delta.

3.6.9   MINISTRY OF NIGER DELTA

In fulfilment of President Umaru Yar'Adua's promise to address the neglect of the Niger Delta region, he made the development of the Niger Delta region one of his seven point Agenda. In furtherance of the determination of the Government to promote the cause of the region, the Ministry of Niger Delta Affairs was set up on 10 September 2008 with the aim of addressing the region's developmental challenges, just like the Ministry of Lagos Affairs and the Ministry of Federal Capital Territory created before it. The NDDC is placed under the new Ministry as an agency. It is hoped that the new ministry, being part of the civil service, will not be bogged down by the bureaucratic rules characteristic of the Nigerian civil service. Government needs to fund the Ministry adequately so that the fate that befell the previous development agencies will not render it ineffective.

3.6.10 PRESIDENTIAL PANEL ON AMNESTY AND DISARMAMENT OF MILITANTS IN THE NIGER DELTA

In line with the determination of the Government to address the Niger Delta problem, a Presidential Panel on Amnesty and Disarmament of Militants in the Niger Delta was set up on 5 May 2009. In its recommendations submitted to the President, this Panel set out the terms, procedures and processes for the grant of an amnesty to the Niger Delta militants.

---

[823]   *IRIN News,* NIGERIA: Timeline of recent events in Niger Delta, at www.irinnews.org/Report. aspx?ReportId=84606 [accessed 6 May 2010]; For more on the recommendations, see the Report of the Technical Committee on the Niger Delta, November 2008.

Accepting the recommendations, President Umaru Yar'Adua, pursuant to section 175 of the Constitution of Nigeria,[824] granted 'amnesty and unconditional pardon to all persons who have directly or indirectly participated in the commission of offences associated with militant activities in the Niger Delta.'[825] The amnesty which was unveiled on 25 June 2009 was scheduled to run between 6 August to 4 October 2009, that is, a 60 day period; and was 'predicated on the willingness and readiness of the militants to give up all illegal arms in their possession, completely renounce militancy in all its ramifications unconditionally, and depose to an undertaking to this effect.'[826] In the declaration, the President acknowledged the fact that the challenges in the Niger Delta arose as a result of the inadequacies of previous attempts at meeting the yearnings of the people of the region, which thus led to the restiveness witnessed in the Niger Delta. The high incidence of violence in the Niger Delta led to the amnesty initiatives.

Disarmament, Demobilization and Reintegration (DDR) adopted by the Nigerian Government under the amnesty programme is one of the most important ways of resolving conflicts and managing post-conflict situations in the world. It has been used by the United Nations and other similar bodies as an instrument for achieving sustainable peace.[827] It was adopted by the Nigerian Government in its amnesty programme in the Niger Delta. There are three phases to the amnesty programme, *viz.*, the disarmament and demobilisation of militants; the rehabilitation and integration of ex-militants, and the post-amnesty package of huge infrastructural development. The disarmed militants were taken to designated collection points and camps in six Niger Delta states, with a promise of a payment of N65,000 [approximately $407 USD] monthly, payment of their rent and an offer of vocational training.[828] During the first phase which has already been implemented, a lot of militants turned in arms and ammunitions.[829]

---

[824]   Under Section 175, the President may, after consultation with the Council of State (a) grant any person concerned with or convicted of any offence created by an Act of the National Assembly a pardon, either free or subject to lawful conditions; (b) grant to any person a respite, either for an indefinite or for a specified period, of the execution of any punishment imposed on that person for such an offence; (c) substitute a less severe form of punishment for any punishment imposed on that person for such an offence; or (d) remit the whole or any part of any punishment imposed on that person for such an offence or of any penalty or forfeiture otherwise due to the State on account of such an offence.

[825]   President Umaru Musa Yar'Adua, Yar'Adua "Niger Delta" Amnesty Proclamation, *Sahara Reporters*, Thursday, 25 June 2009 at www.saharareporters.com/index.php?option=com_con tent&view=article&id=3088:yaradua-qniger-deltaq-amnesty-proclamation&catid=42:exclusi ve&Itemid=160 [accessed 6 May 2010].

[826]   *Ibid.*

[827]   I.S. Ibaba, Amnesty and Peace-Building in the Niger Delta: Addressing the Frustration-Aggression Trap, *Africana: The Niger Delta* (Special Issue), Vol. 5(1), 238–271 at 244 (2011).

[828]   O.O. Oluwaniyi, Post-Amnesty Programme in the Niger Delta: Challenges and Prospects, *Conflict Trends*, Issue 4, 46–54 at 50 (2011).

[829]   K. Kuku, being a Communiqué stating the stand of the Amnesty Office on the Issue of those Niger Delta Youths Clamouring for inclusion in the Amnesty Programme, 8 December 2011, at www.nigerdeltaamnesty.org/index.php?option=com_content&view=article&id=251:press-statement&catid=36:news&Itemid=18 [accessed 2 February 2012].

Indeed, it was recorded that about 26,358 ex-militants accepted the amnesty offer (first phase – 20,192 militants representing those that accepted the offer on or before 4 October 2009, while the second phase of the amnesty programme that occurred in November 2010 comprised 6,166 militants representing those that accepted the offer post 4 October 2009). This appeared to have reduced both the incidence of conflict and the accumulation of arms by militants in the region. Rehabilitation centres were provided for the second stage, which was tailored to meet the training needs of the ex-militants. The training was to be done in batches as the centres could only accommodate a few of the registered ex-militants. It was expected that each batch would spend four weeks in the rehabilitation programme, which involved reorientation, counseling and moral/spiritual regeneration.[830] A survey of the career aspirations of the ex-militants reveals a great preference for about ten (10) sectors ranging from Oil/Gas, Maritime Services, Fabrication and Welding Technology, Exploration and Production and Processing Engineering. The duration of training ranges between 3 and 18 months.[831] Those desirous of going back to school for further education were also given that opportunity under this programme.

Reports from the Nigerian Government indicate that following the relative peace ushered in by the cease-fire, as a result of the amnesty declaration, the country's oil output rose to 2.3 million barrels a day from 800,000 barrels per day (in the 2006–2008 period) as a result of the improvement in security in the region.[832] This increment of 1.5 million barrels per day adds 120.45 million dollars of revenue to national coffers every day.[833] Some companies also took the opportunity to repair some of their damaged oil facilities.

This programme can be seen as one of the concrete steps taken by the Federal Government to bring peace to the Niger Delta. However, the Federal Government on 2 December 2009 scrapped the Presidential Committee on Disarmament and Amnesty for Militants in the Niger Delta, and in its place are five new committees

---

[830]   A.A. Akinwale, Amnesty and human capital development agenda for the Niger Delta, *Journal of African Studies and Development*, Vol. 2 (8), 201–207 at 205 (2010).

[831]   *Ibid.*

[832]   U. Igwe, 'Is the Niger Delta Amnesty Working?', *The African Executive*, November 2010, at www.africanexecutive.com/modules/magazine/articles.php?article=5517 [accessed 3 March 2012].

The economic loss incurred by Nigeria while the Niger Delta crisis lasted has recently been put by the Federal Government at over N308.7 billion with N3billion lost in 2008. This according to the Government translates to the production loss of one million barrels of oil per day. See Timi Alaibe, Presidential Adviser on Niger Delta and former Managing Director, NDDC, speaking during an interactive session with Journalists on 12 May 2010 at Abuja, quoted in Ike Abonyi, Nigeria: Government Loses N308 Billion to Niger Delta Crisis, *ThisDay* 13 May 2010, at http://allafrica.com/stories/201005130218.html [accessed 6 May 2010].

[833]   *Ibid.*

which will handle the post-amnesty programmes and fast-track development challenges in the region.[834]

There are several challenges facing the post-amnesty programme. The total number of ammunitions/weapons handed in by the militants, totaling 1,798 rifles, 1,981 guns of various types, 70 RPGs, 159 pistols, one spear and six cannons,[835] is certainly low when compared with the 26,358 militants that registered for the amnesty programme. The region is still ridden with arms, and this is evident in the various attacks that have been carried out by militants even after the disarmament exercise. The disarmament programme needs to be firmed up because as long as many arms are still at large, the region remains very unsafe and at risk of relapsing into violence.[836]

The recent spate of bombings across the region shows that all is not well with the amnesty programme. For instance, the Movement for the Emancipation of the Niger Delta (MEND) set off two car bombs on 15 March 2010 in Warri, the Delta State capital, where a post-amnesty dialogue was being held, and this left one person dead and several others injured.[837] Also important is the 1 October 2010 car bombing that killed about 12 people and disrupted Nigeria's 50th anniversary celebrations. This led to the trial of MEND leader, Henry Okah, at his base in Johannesburg, South Africa, for terrorism on the suspicion of having masterminded the operation; and the trial of his brother, Charles Okah, and three others before the Federal High Court in Abuja, Nigeria on suspicion of involvement.[838] The South Guateng High Court in South Africa had found Okah guilty of the 13-count charge of acts of terrorism and sentenced him on 26 March 2013 to 24 years imprisonment. The Judge, Neels Claaseen, in his judgment stated that: "The group's agitation for improved environmental situation and provision of infrastructure in the area is aimed at attracting the Federal Government attention to the plight of the people in the area. Though a good cause, but it does not justify any act of violence and terrorism."[839] Also, on 4 February 2012, the militant group also bombed a trunk pipeline at Brass in Bayelsa State belonging

---

[834] Sola Adebayo, N'Delta: FG Scraps amnesty committee, raises five new panels, *The Punch*, Friday 11 December 2009, at www.punchng.com/Articl.aspx?theartic=Art20091211285762 [accessed 6 May 2010].

[835] D. Agbo, Arms recovered from ex-Niger Delta militants destroyed. *Legal Oil*, 29 May 2011, at www.legaloil.com/NewsItem.asp?DocumentIDX=1307016053&Category=news [accessed 2 February 2012].

[836] O. Joseph, Analysis: Nigeria's Delta amnesty at risk of unraveling. *Spero News*, 23 April 2010, at www.speroforum.com/a/31526/Analysis--Nigerias-Delta-amnesty-at-risk-of-unravelling [accessed 2 February 2012].

[837] S. Ofehe, Features on Niger Delta Amnesty. *Ex Ponto Magazine*, 11 May 2011, at www.expon-tomagazine.com/nl/reportages/2279-features-on-niger-delta-amnesty [accessed 2 February 2012].

[838] K. Nwajiaku-Dahou, *The Politics of Amnesty in the Niger Delta. Challenges Ahead*, Paris and Brussels: The Institut français des relations internationales (Ifri), 2010, pp. 9–10.

[839] Sola Adebayo *et al.*, 2010 Independence Day Bombing: Henry Okar Jailed 24 Years, *National Mirror*, 27 March 2013, at http://nationalmirroronline.net/new/2010-independence-day-bombing-henry-okah-jailed-24-yrs/.

to Italy's Eni SpA, ENI, from which it lost 'around 4,000' barrels per day of 'equity production' from the incident.[840] The group further claimed responsibility for the bombing of the Ogbogbabene country home of the Minister of Niger Delta Affairs, Elder Godsday Orubebe in the Burtutu Local Government Area of Delta State on 28 January 2012.[841]

Importantly, 'the amnesty is exclusive; it targets only militants without consideration for the victims of militancy and hostage-taking in the region.'[842] The interests of mothers and children who had lost fathers and sons and homes and have been displaced by the conflict were not taken into consideration in the amnesty package,[843] presumably as a result of their lack of means of violence. The exclusion of grassroots organizations, and the exclusion of local knowledge from the construction of the peace-building process in the Niger Delta raises questions on the sustainability of the current peace in the region.[844]

In addition, it was revealed that some of the rehabilitation centres and demobilising camps lack even the basic facilities for proper impartation of knowledge and skills. Shortages of bed spaces, beds and other basic facilities in some of the centres allow only a few militants to be accommodated.[845] Also in compliance with the UN code on Disarmament, Demobilization and Reintegration (DDR), it is expected that in the implementation of DDR programmes, the ex-militants should be taken away from their natural habitats for transformation and reintegration.[846] For better coordination of the programme, it is suggested that the Government agencies involved need to draw on the experience and professionalism of similar exercises in other countries, including those administered by the United Nations[847] in countries like Liberia and Sierra Leone. They can learn from some Nigerians that have helped in formulating and administering similar programmes in other countries. There is an urgent need

---

[840] E. Mamah & E. Amaize, Nigeria: MEND Resumes Hostilities- Blows Up Agip Trunk Line in Bayelsa, *Vanguard*, 6 February 2012, at http://allafrica.com/stories/201202060224.html [accessed 2 February 2012].

[841] *Ibid.*

[842] A.A. Akinwale, Amnesty and human capital development agenda for the Niger Delta, *Journal of African Studies and Development*, Vol. 2 (8), 201–207 at 204 (2010).

[843] K. Nwajiaku-Dahou, *op. cit.*, p.15.

[844] C. Obi & S.A. Rustad, "Conclusion: amnesty and post-amnesty peace, is the window of opportunity closing for the Niger Delta?.", in C. Obi & S.A. Rustad (eds.) (2011), *Oil and Insurgency in the Niger Delta: Managing the complex politics of petro-violence*. London/New York: Zed Books, p.208.

[845] A. Ikelegbe, *Oil, Resource Conflicts and the Post Conflict Transition in the Niger Delta Region: Beyond the Amnesty*, Centre for Population and Environmental Development (CPED) Monograph Series No. 3. Benin City: Ambik Press, 2010 p.69.

[846] E. Amaize, 'Amnesty: Nigeria, EU to partner on Niger Delta,' *Vanguard*, 13 August 2011, at www.vanguardngr.com/2011/08/amnesty-nigeria-eu-to-partner-on-niger-delta/ [accessed 2 February 2012].

[847] N. Obasi, Yar'Adua Should Draw Up Roadmap to Delta Peace, *International Crisis Group*, 30 November 2009, at www.crisisgroup.org/en/regions/africa/west-africa/nigeria/op-eds/obasi-yar-adua-should-draw-up-roadmap-to-delta-peace.aspx bid [accessed 2 February 2012].

for assistance and cooperation from international communities in the areas of technical assistance, capacity building, vocational training and skill acquisition.

Government also needs to work out long-term strategies for human capacity development and the re-integration of ex-militants, which should include resettlement, training and skills acquisition, capacity building, provision of alternative employment, and make provisions for funds to address effectively the DDR programme. Beyond amnesty, the underlying economic, social and environmental problems that triggered militancy in the Niger Delta need to be addressed holistically, as without this, it is doubtful whether the amnesty, without more can bring any durable peace to the volatile region.

Amnesty alone will only bring a temporary peace to the region. Sooner or later, new and more dangerous groups may emerge in the region if nothing is done adequately to address the root causes of the Niger Delta crisis. Interestingly, following the amnesty proclamation, the President also announced the relinquishment of ten per cent of the Federal Government's holdings and interests in the oil and gas resources directly to the oil producing communities of the Niger Delta.[848] This could give the Niger Delta communities direct financial stake in the revenues derived from oil production, rather than having the money flow primarily to the Federal and State Governments, and often, to the pockets of the individuals. If properly utilized, it will go a long way in enhancing the development of the region in terms of the development of infrastructure, human capital and the protection of its environment, which could help to curtail the propensity of militants to destroy oil MNCs' facilities and disrupt oil production. However, there is a need for machinery to be put in place to ensure transparency and accountability regarding the use of the money at the local level. There is a challenge concerning the method to be used in managing the funds, as the communities where oil is presently being explored may want to claim a monopoly over the monies to the detriment of the communities where oil is presently not being exploited.[849] This may lead to another round of hostilities and conflicts in the region if not properly handled. The amnesty should not be seen as a ploy on the part of the Government to ensure continued and uninterrupted extraction of oil in the Niger Delta, but one that should help to promote and consolidate peace, jump-start development, raise standards of living, and promote environmental justice and other important peace-related needs.

---

[848] Y.Y.D. Dadem, Current Challenges for Environmental and Economic Justice in the Niger Delta of Nigeria, *Kogi State University Bi-Annual Journal of Public Law*, Vol. 1 Part 1, pp.219–231 at 231 (2009).
[849] Y.Y.D. Dadem, *Ibid*, p.231.

3.7 HOW EFFECTIVE ARE THE NIGER DELTA DEVELOPMENT INITIATIVES IN ADDRESSING THE ENVIRONMENTAL AND HUMAN RIGHTS CHALLENGES?

From the above discussion, it can be seen that none of the above institutions established by the Government to address the developmental problems of the Niger Delta articulated explicitly any view on the nexus between oil exploration and human rights concerns of the people in the region, despite the massive environmental degradation and human rights violations that the people in this region are face daily. The enabling statutes of these agencies are silent on important issues of social and economic rights, poverty alleviation, an active role for women, population displacement and human security.[850] Though, it is possible to assume that these should ultimately be the end result of the projects to be implemented by these agencies, events in the past have shown in Nigeria that this is often not the case. Projects were often seen not as a means of improving the conditions of the populace but rather as a means for enriching a few contractors, political supporters, and sycophants,[851] at the expense of the intended beneficiaries of the projects. Hence, there is still poverty, squalor, inequitable allocation of resources, underdevelopment, neglect, alienation and pollution of the environment in the entire region. Certainly, the projects carried out by these agencies/commissions 'do not include [the] political and many economic rights still denied the people of Niger Delta.'[852] By filling institutional gaps and providing for infrastructural facilities and skill-acquisition, without addressing issues of environmental degradation that negatively impact on the human rights of the people in the oil producing areas, the human rights violations will continue unabated. The narrow and limited focus of these agencies makes them inadequate to protect the rights of the Niger Delta inhabitants.

Again, the NDDC and other developmental agencies have little or no influence over how multinational oil companies conduct their core business operations,[853] and so do not facilitate plans capable of controlling the activities of the oil companies that will reduce the negative impact of oil operations which undermine the human rights of the local inhabitants. Oil spills and gas flaring with their negative consequences on fishing and farming, still continue as a result of the acts and omissions of the multinational oil companies, thus worsening the human rights situation in the region. There is no amount of infrastructural

---

[850]   Y. Akinseye-George, *op. cit.*, p.208.
[851]   *Ibid.*
[852]   Programme on Ethnic and Federal Studies (PEFS) (2004), *The Niger Delta Question: Background to Constitutional Reform, op. cit.*, p.39.
[853]   Idemudia Uwafiokun, Host Nation – Oil Transnational Corporation Partnership for Poverty Reduction in the Niger Delta, Nigeria – Diagnosis and Recommendations, *op. cit.*, p.130.

development that 'can compensate for 24 hours of daylight resulting from gas flaring by the oil companies.'[854] A large reduction in the negative impact of the oil operations, coupled with meaningful development programmes, will go a long way in bringing desired peace to the region. According to Okechukwu Ibeanu, the development efforts of the Government in the Niger Delta have failed because, '[F]irst, there is no accountability, transparency and public participation in development programmes and spending. Secondly, development projects have been patently exclusionary of vulnerable groups like women, children and the disabled. Thirdly, development projects have been unsustainable, particularly in creating alternatives to the petroleum industry and in environmental protection and remediation.'[855]

It is suggested that in the formulation of policies, in setting up developmental agencies and in the prioritization of projects to address the objective needs of the "ecologically endangered and economically dispossessed communities"[856] of the Niger Delta, 'human rights' standards and 'sustainable development' should serve as a bedrock. These should reflect contemporary thinking around the world regarding the human rights dimensions of environmental management. Unsustainable exploitation of oil in the Niger Delta, with its negative impacts threatens the rights of the local inhabitants and the ecosystem, and undermines the future prospects of the inhabitants. A balance must be struck between demands for economic development and the pursuance of sustainable development 'on the basis and principles of social, economic and environmental sustainability.'[857] The discussion of the relevant international instruments will form part of the discussion in Chapter Four below. Sustainable peace in the Niger Delta can only be guaranteed when there is a political will on the part of the Government and a strong commitment on the part of the oil companies and other stakeholders, towards the establishment of a decentralized, integrated, bottom-up participatory development process that can adequately ensure quality of life of the inhabitants, including their social and economic rights,[858] while also guaranteeing a safe, clean and healthy environment.

---

[854] Uwafiokun Idemudia and Uwem E. Ite, Corporate-Community Relations in Nigeria's Oil Industry: Challenges and Imperatives, *op. cit.*, p.202.

[855] Okechukwu Ibeanu, *Affluence and Affliction: The Niger Delta as a Critique of Political Science in Nigeria*, being 27th Inaugural Lecture of the University of Nigeria delivered on 20 February, University of Nigeria Press Ltd., 2008, pp.32–33.

[856] R.T. Suberu (1996), *Ethnic Minority Conflicts and Governance in Nigeria*, *op. cit.*, p.37.

[857] Uwafiokun Idemudia and Uwem E. Ite, Demystifying the Niger Delta Conflict: Towards an Integrated Explanation, 33 *Review of African Political Economy*, 109–406 at 404 (2006).

[858] Y. Akinseye-George, *op. cit.*, p.211.

3.8 CONCLUSION

This Chapter has revealed that the various interventionist agencies set up to tackle the problems of the Niger Delta have not really changed the situation of things in the region. Rather they have all been bedeviled by similar shortcomings: corruption, abuse of human rights, bureaucratic inefficiency, underfunding, adoption of a top-down approach to developmental issues, lack of public participation, and undue political interference. As observed by one scholar, most of the legal and other interventions in the Niger Delta region exhibit 'characteristics which do not enhance environmental justice, human rights and sustainable development. Firstly, these laws often centralize the management of the environment in core institutions that are far removed from the host communities. Secondly, the existing laws are largely rule-oriented in that they either prohibit or declare certain forms of activities unlawful and then subjecting them to prior authorization by the regulatory agencies, which often lack the expertise to monitor compliance with regulations. Thirdly, since they are largely informed by the assumption that all mineral resources are Federally owned, the existing laws often do not recognize the rights of the host communities to participate in the management of natural resources.'[859] Despite these institutional and developmental initiatives, no significant success has been recorded in the reduction of environmental degradation and the consequent violations of the rights of the local inhabitants. Rather, there has been tremendous increase in violations of environmental laws to the detriment of the people and environment.

The chapter has further noted that Nigeria has laws and regulations in place capable of regulating the activities of the multinational oil companies operating in the region but fails to ensure enforcement and compliance. It then went on to confirm that the possession of well-developed and extensive environmental laws does not guarantee adequate remedies.[860] As explained by Adewale 'a thread that runs through these [Nigerian] statutes is the inability to effectively ensure an enforcement process to enable the workability of these laws. Enforcement requires adequate monitoring equipment, staff, and funding. It is doubtful if presently these facilities exist for the monitoring of the environment.'[861] Besides, some of these laws are defective and/or inadequate, and so are not able to prevent abuses by the oil MNCs or be effective against a state's own violations. The unenforceability of these laws, coupled with some of their inadequacies, tends to diminish the faith of the oil-producing communities in the ability of laws to protect their rights to enjoy clean and healthy environment, and weakens their hope of getting

---

[859]   *Ibid* p.203.
[860]   John Lee, The Underlying Legal Theory to Support a Well-Defined Human Right to a Healthy Environment as a Principle of Customary International Law, 25 *Colum. J. Envtl. L.* 283–346 at 289 (2000).
[861]   Omobolaji Adewale, The Right of the Individual to Environmental Protection: A Case Study of Nigeria, 12(4) *Rivista Giuridica Dell' Ambiente* 649 at 650 (1991).

justice. The non-enforcement of the laws perpetuates the deprivation, alienation, exclusion and insecurity of the local inhabitants and this breeds their contempt and hatred for the multinational oil companies and Government. This predisposes them to exhibit the culture of violence characterised by disruptive and anti-oil protests, attacks on and forcible closures of oil installations, kidnappings of local and foreign oil expatriates, pipeline vandalisation, oil bunkering and other forms of criminality, and in rare cases murder. In fact, the inadequacies and non-enforcement of these laws underpins the quest of the local inhabitants for environmental rights and justice as can be seen in their demands for resource control and self determination as a way of protecting themselves from further domination and oppression.[862] There is a need for the Nigerian Government to address these inadequacies and ensure that the laws are effectively applied and enforced by all those charged with the responsibility of enforcing the laws.

---

[862] Victor Ukaogo, "From Injustice to Injustice: The Ethnicity of Resistance and Rebellion in the Niger Delta", in *International Conference on The Nigerian State, Oil Industry and the Niger Delta, organized by the Department of Political Science, op. cit.*, p.837.

CHAPTER FOUR

NIGER DELTA, ENVIRONMENTAL DEGRADATION AND HUMAN RIGHTS

4.1   INTRODUCTION

> *"[C]urrent global human rights systems offer little protection against human rights abuses by companies, except very indirectly via the duty of the state to protect against abuse by third parties. The same situation applies at the level of the regional institutions. That leaves only two possible tracks: the application of domestic law, either of the home country of the company or of the host country, or not applying law at all but striving towards compliance by using non-legal means such as self regulation by the companies (introducing human rights as a corporate standard of excellence, particularly for global companies), or public opinion campaigns focusing on naming and shaming."*[863]

With the wind of economic globalization blowing across the globe, human rights are currently exposed to significant violation by powers other than the State, including MNCs. Unfortunately, for several reasons, a lot of states, most especially developing countries, hardly regulate the activities of the MNCs thus creating a regulatory vacuum. In this situation, the catalogue of civil, political, social, cultural and economic rights of people, as expressed under both domestic and international human rights laws, are adversely affected by the MNCs. Mostly affected are the already marginalized groups in society, who are made to trade their health, safety and human rights for the growth and prosperity promised by such economic ventures. A classic example has been the indigenous people of the Niger Delta region of Nigeria who live in the country's most vulnerable ecosystem and where the oil MNCs carry out their oil exploration activities.

This chapter looks at the human rights provisions in the 1999 Constitution of the Federal Republic of Nigeria (CFRN) as an instrument for environmental justice, and will examine some of the rights that are vulnerable to the activities of the MNCs and the extent to which the Constitution has served as a valuable tool for the protection of the environment and the Niger Delta people. The chapter also

---

[863]   Koen De Feyter (2005), *Human Rights: Social Justice in the Age of the Market*, Zed Books Ltd., London & New York, p.166.

examines the legal regimes that regulate corporations, and their effectiveness or
otherwise in affording protection to victims of environmental and human rights
violations, in particular, the Niger Delta people.

4.2 THE RELATIONSHIP BETWEEN ENVIRON-
MENTAL DEGRADATION AND HUMAN RIGHTS

Environmental degradation has direct effects on the enjoyment of a lot of
human rights, and conversely, the violation of several human rights may impair
the environment. The two concepts are inextricably intertwined and as such
environmental injustice represents an aspect of human rights abuse.[864]

Rich and poor alike are affected by the collapse of ecosystems. Still,
vulnerable groups, such as the indigenous communities in the Niger Delta, are
the ones that are more likely to be affected the greatest since they are the ones
that are least able to mobilize against abuses.[865] Environmental degradation
generates further poverty by the exhaustion of natural resources, and prejudices
the exercise of basic rights, eventually raising new humanitarian issues, such as
the plight of environmental refugees.[866] In addition, resource constraints related
to environmental degradation, like lack of water, food shortages, and disrupted
access to means of livelihood, can lead to skirmishes, violence and even wars. In
view of this, environmental degradation is a threat to human survival since it
inhibits the quality of life and the development of human personality. It can be
seen that the need to protect and improve 'man's environment arise[s] directly out
of a vital need to protect human life, to assure its quality and condition, and to
ensure the prerequisites indispensable to safeguarding human dignity and human
worth and the development of the human personality.'[867] Therefore, respect for
human rights is related to environmental protection, for human beings depend
upon it to survive.[868]

---

[864] Francis O. Adeola, Environmental Injustice and Human Rights Abuse: The States, MNCs and
Repression of Minority Groups in the World System, *Human Ecology Review*, Vol. 8, No. 1,
39–59 at p.40 (2001); Klaus Bosselmann (2008), *The Principle of Sustainability: Transforming
Law and Governance*, Ashgate, Aldershot, Hampshire, p.131.

[865] Center for International Environmental Law (CIEL), *Human Rights and Environment:
Overlapping Issues*, at www.ciel.org. [accessed 3 March 2010].

[866] Jorge Daniel Taillant, *Environmental Discrimination*, Center for Human Rights and
Development (CEDHA) November 2000, at www.cedha.org.ar/en/documents. [accessed 3
March 2010].

[867] R.S. Pathak, "The Human Rights System as a Conceptual Framework for Environmental
Law", in E.B. Weiss (ed) (1992), *Environmental Change and International Law*, United Nations
University Press, p.209.

[868] Sueli Giorgetta, The Right to a Healthy Environment, Human Rights and Sustainable
Development, 2 *International Environmental Agreements: Politics, Law and Economics* 173–
194 at 175 (2002).

Human rights cannot be secured in a degraded or polluted environment and many national Constitutions recognise this fact by acknowledging a human right to a safe/clean environment. Acknowledging the link between environmental protection and human rights, Justice C.G. Weeramantry, former Vice President of the International Court of Justice (ICJ), in his separate opinion in the Case Concerning the Gabcikovo-Nagymaros Project noted that:

> *"The protection of the environment is likewise a vital part of contemporary human rights doctrine, for it is a sine qua non for numerous human rights such as the right to health and the right to life itself. It is scarcely necessary to elaborate on this, as damage to the environment can impair and undermine all the human rights spoken of in the Universal Declaration and other human rights instruments."*[869]

The link between human rights and the environment in international law was first made in 1972, in the Stockholm Declaration,[870] and was aimed at inspiring Governments to preserve and enhance the human environment.[871] The Declaration proclaimed that man's natural and man-made environment 'are essential to his well-being and to the enjoyment of basic human rights – even the right to life itself.' Principle 1 states that: 'Man has a fundamental right to freedom, equality and adequate conditions of life, in an environment of a quality that permits a life of dignity and well-being, and he bears a solemn responsibility to protect and improve the environment for present and future generations.' It further declared more pungently in Principle 6 that 'the just struggle of the peoples of all countries against pollution should be supported.' Though this Declaration is non-binding and does not proclaim a fundamental human right to a healthy environment, it recognises that basic environmental health is imperative for the free enjoyment and exercise of human rights.[872] Thus, environmental degradation may interfere with fundamental human rights to such an extent as to violate those rights.[873]

A number of non-binding, but widely accepted, Declarations supporting the individual's right to a clean environment were subsequently adopted.[874] One of these is the 1982 World Charter for Nature.[875] The Charter does not expressly provide for the individual's right to a clean environment, but it was one of the first instruments to recognize rights of nature, distinct from the rights of

---

[869]   See Gabcikovo-Nagymaros Project, 37 I.L.M. at 206.

[870]   UN G.A. Res. 2398 (XXII) (1968).

[871]   F. Maes, "Environmental Law Principles, their Nature and the Law of the Sea: A Challenge for Legislators", in M. Sheridan & L. Lavrysen (eds) (2002), *Environmental Law Principles in Practice*, Bruylant Brussels, p.67.

[872]   Dinah Shelton, Human Rights, Environmental Rights, and the Right to Environment, 28 *Stan. J. Int'l L.* 1103 at 112 (1991); Sueli Giorgetta, The Right to a Healthy Environment, Human Rights and Sustainable Development, *op. cit.*, p.176.

[873]   Dinah Shelton, *Ibid.*

[874]   J. Thornton and Beckwith S. (2004), *Environmental Law*, 2nd edition, Sweet & Maxwell's Textbook Series, Sweet & Maxwell, London, p.388.

[875]   World Charter for Nature, UN General Assembly Res. No. 37/7, adopted on 28 October 1982.

human beings,[876] that is, adopting environmental protection in an eco-centric manner. Its uniqueness also lies in the fact that it is one of the first instruments to recognize the right to participate in decision-making, and to have access to means of redress, when one's environment has suffered damage or degradation.[877] The Charter also provides that assessments of the effects on nature of proposed policies and activities 'shall be disclosed to the public by appropriate means in time to permit effective consultation and participation.'[878] It thus makes provision for environmental impact assessment (EIA) process.

There is also the 1989 Declaration of the Hague on the Environment[879] which recognized not only 'the fundamental duty to preserve the ecosystem' but also the 'right to live in dignity in a viable global environment, and the consequent duty of the community of nations *vis-à-vis* present and future generations to do all that can be done to preserve the quality of the atmosphere.'

In 1990, the United Nations General Assembly passed a resolution '[r]ecogniz[ing] that all individuals are entitled to live in an environment adequate for their health and well-being; and call[ing] upon Member States and Intergovernmental and non-governmental organizations to enhance their efforts towards ensuring a better and healthier environment.'[880]

Also worthy of consideration is the 1994 Draft Declaration of Principles on Human Rights and the Environment, appended to the Report of the UN Special Rapporteur on Human Rights and the Environment, Mrs. Fatma Zohra Ksentini.[881] The Report regarded the 'right to a healthy and flourishing environment' as 'evolving', while also acknowledging a 'universal acceptance of environmental rights recognized at the national, regional and international levels.'[882] The Draft Declaration provides that '[a]ll persons have the right to a secure, healthy and ecologically sound environment' and that this right and other human rights, including civil, cultural, economic, political and social rights, are universal, interdependent and indivisible.[883] It further provides that '[a]ll persons have the right to an environment adequate to meet equitably the needs of present generations and that does not impair the rights of future generations to meet

---

[876] Sumudu Ataputtu, The Right to a Healthy Life or the Right to Die Polluted?: The Emergence of a Human Right to a Healthy Environment under International Law, 16 *Tul. Envtl. L.J.* 65 at 75 (2002).

[877] See Udombana N.J., "The Right to a Healthy Environment: Foreground and Forecasts", *Political Reform and Economic Recovery in Nigeria, op. cit.*, p.111.

[878] Paras 16 & 11, World Charter for Nature, UN General Assembly Res. No. 37/7, adopted on 28 October 1982.

[879] Declaration of the Hague on the Environment, 11 March 1989, 28 I. L. M (1989), 1308.

[880] *Need to Ensure a Healthy Environment for the Well-Being of Individuals*, UN G.A.O.R, 45th Sess., 68th Ple. Mtg., UN Doc. A/RES. 45/94 (1990).

[881] The Report was presented to the Sub-Commission on Prevention of Discrimination and Protection of Minorities, at its 46th Session, U.N DOC, E/CN.4/Sub. 2/1994/9.

[882] *Ibid*, paras 5, 240.

[883] *Ibid*, principle 2.

equitably their needs.'[884] Even though the report is right in recognizing that the right to environment is evolving, it has been criticized for being politically motivated, and for being, at best, vague.[885] It is further contended that it deals more with *lex ferenda* (what the law should be) than with *lex lata* (what the law is).[886] Despite these criticisms and its non-legal binding nature, this Draft Declaration has been used by various national courts when making decisions on environmental matters. In the Columbian case of *Fundepublico v. Mayor of Bugalagrande and Others*,[887] the court relied on the Draft Declaration and on the rights contained in the Columbian Constitution in deciding in favour of the protection of the fundamental right to a healthy environment.

Although, more recently drafted international human rights instruments do not embody a distinct right to a healthy environment, they do specifically mention the value of the environment in their systems of protection.[888] These include the Convention on the Rights of the Child (1989) and the 1989 International Labour Organization (ILO) Convention No. 169. The Convention on the Rights of the Child (1989),[889] in Article 24, recognizes the 'right of the child to the enjoyment of the highest attainable standard of health' and mandates that State Parties consider the 'dangers and risks of environmental pollution.' Article 29 includes respect for the environment as one of the goals of educational programmes. This Convention also emphasizes the role of the environment in the fulfillment of other human rights such as the right to health.[890] It is the only international human rights

---

[884]   *Ibid*, principle 4.

[885]   Ole W. Pedersen, European Environmental Human Rights and Environmental Rights: A Long Time Coming? 21 *Georgetown Int'l Envtl. Law Review* 73–111 at 78 (2008); Dinah Shelton, Human Rights, Environmental Rights and the Right to Environment, *op. cit.*, p.131; Alan E. Boyle, "The Role of International Human Rights Law in the Protection of the Environment", in Alan E. Boyle and Michael R. Anderson (eds) (1996), *Human Rights Approaches to Environmental Protection*, Clarendon Press, Oxford, p.50, where he notes that the report 'cannot make up its mind, referring variously to the right to a "healthy and flourishing environment" and to a 'satisfactory environment.'

[886]   Ole W. Pedersen, *Ibid*, pp.78–79. Sumudu Ataputtu, The Right to a Healthy Life or the Right to Die Polluted?: The Emergence of a Human Right to a Healthy Environment under International Law, *op. cit.*, at 79.

[887]   Decision of the Constitutional Court of Columbia, Juzgado Primero superior, Interlocutorio # 032, Tulua, 19 Dec. 1991 where the court stated: 'It should be recognized that a healthy environment is a *sine qua non* condition for life itself and that no right could be exercised in a deeply altered environment;' See also Emilie Filmer-Wilson and Michael Anderson, *Integrating Human Rights into Energy and Environment Programming: A Reference Paper*, May 2005, at http://hurilink.org/tools/Integrating_HRs_into_Energy_and_Environment_Programming. pdf. [accessed 13 March 2009].

[888]   See Emilie Filmer-Wilson and Michael Anderson, *Ibid*.

[889]   Adopted and opened for signature, ratification and accession by General Assembly Resolution 44/25 of 20 November 1989. It entered into force on 2 September 1990, in accordance with art. 49. www2.ohchr.org/english/law/crc.htm [accessed 3 July 2009].

[890]   Ole W. Pedersen, *op. cit.*, at p.78.

---

convention of universal application which comes close to addressing issues of environmental pollution.[891]

The 1989 International Labour Organization (ILO) Convention No. 169 concerning Indigenous and Tribal Peoples requires state parties to adopt special measures, as appropriate, to safeguard the environment for indigenous peoples,[892] and ensure that studies are carried out, in co-operation with the indigenous peoples, to assess the environmental impact on them of planned development activities.[893]

Also important is the 2007 UN Declaration on the Rights of the Indigenous Peoples[894] which provides a link between indigenous communities and the protection of the environment. Article 29 of the Declaration provides that:

> *"1. Indigenous peoples have the right to the conservation and protection of the environment and the productive capacity of their lands or territories and resources. States shall establish and implement assistance programmes for indigenous peoples for such conservation and protection, without discrimination.*
> *2. States shall take effective measures to ensure that no storage or disposal of hazardous materials shall take place in the lands or territories of indigenous peoples without their free, prior and informed consent."*

Rights to environmental protection have also increasingly come to be accorded a pride of place by the various committees charged with interpreting international human rights standards.[895] The links between the environment and some of the substantive rights enshrined in the Covenant on Economic, Social and Cultural Rights have been clarified by the Committee on Economic, Social and Cultural Rights (CESR).[896] For instance, the CESR, commenting on Article 12(2)(b) of the ICESR has stated: 'The improvement of all aspects of environmental and industrial hygiene (art. 12.2(b)) comprises, *inter alia*, preventive measures in respect of occupational accidents and diseases; the requirement to ensure an adequate supply of safe and potable water and basic sanitation; the prevention and reduction of the population's exposure to harmful substances such as radiation and harmful chemicals or other detrimental environmental conditions that directly or indirectly impact upon human health.'[897] In its comment on the Right to Adequate Food, the Committee interpreted the phrase 'free from

---

[891] Sumudu Ataputtu, The Right to a Healthy Life or the Right to Die Polluted?: The Emergence of a Human Right to a Healthy Environment under International Law, *op. cit.*, at 98.

[892] Convention concerning Indigenous and Tribal Peoples in Independent Countries, 1989 C169, Article 4.

[893] *Ibid.*, art. 7.

[894] Adopted by General Assembly Resolution 61/295 on 13 September 2007.

[895] Emilie Filmer-Wilson and Michael Anderson, *op. cit.*

[896] *Ibid.*

[897] United Nations Committee on Economic, Social and Cultural Rights Twenty-second session Geneva, 25 April-12 May 2000 Distr. GENERAL E/C.12/2000/4, adopted on 11 May 2000.

adverse substances' in Article 11 of the Covenant to mean that the State must set requirements for food safety and adopt other protective measures to prevent contamination of foodstuffs through 'bad environmental hygiene.'[898]

Also relevant is the final text of the Conference on Security and Co-operation in Europe (CSCE) Meeting on the Environment in Sofia in 1989. It reaffirmed respect for the right of individuals, groups, and organizations concerned with the environment, to express freely their views, to associate with others and to assemble peacefully, to obtain and distribute relevant information and to participate in public debates on environmental issues.[899]

The Rio Declaration on Environment and Development, adopted at the United Nations Conference on Environment and Development in 1992, endorsed the link between human beings and the environment. However, rather than repeating the direct approach that had been taken in the Stockholm Declaration, it shifted the vocabulary away from human rights towards the theme of sustainable development,[900] stating that: 'Human beings are at the centre of concerns for sustainable development. They are entitled to a healthy and productive life in harmony with nature.'[901] Comparing the Stockholm Declaration with the Rio Declaration, Pallemaerts notes: 'By contrast, the first principle of the Rio Declaration, where it states that "human beings are at the centre of concerns for sustainable development," sounds like the triumph of a delirious anthropocentricism.'[902] In spite of the sparse references to human rights in the 1992 Rio Declaration and its anthropocentric nature, Principle 10 of the Rio Declaration has proved to be of particular importance in enabling concerned individuals and groups to take action for environmental protection. It provides, stating that:

> "Environmental issues are best handled with participation of all concerned citizens, at the relevant level. At the national level, each individual shall have appropriate access to information concerning the environment that is held by public authorities, including information on hazardous materials and activities in their communities, and the opportunity to participate in decision-making processes. States shall facilitate and encourage public awareness and participation by making information

---

[898] Para 10, CESCR Committee on Economic, Social and Cultural Rights Twentieth session Geneva, 26 April-14 May 1999, General Comment 12, E/C. 12/1999/5.

[899] See CSCE/SEM. 36. See also EC Directive 90/313, 1990.

[900] See J. Thornton and S. Beckwith, *op. cit.*, p.388.

[901] Principle 1. Even though the Rio Declaration did not explicitly mention a right to a healthy environment, Principle 1, which was accepted without reservation by almost all nations, captures the ideal of the right to a healthy environment, if not the right itself. See John Lee, The Underlying Legal Theory to Support a Well-Defined Human Right to a Healthy Environment as a Principle of Customary International Law, 25 *Colum. J. Envtl. L.* 283–346 at 308 (2000).

[902] Marc Pallemaerts, International Environmental Law in the Age of Sustainable Development: A Critical Assessment of the UNCED Process, 15 *Journal of Law & Commerce* 623–676 at 642 (1996).

*widely available. Effective access to judicial and administrative proceedings, inclu-
ding redress and remedy, shall be provided."*

This principle has provided the impetus for establishing detailed mechanisms, in
the domestic law of States, for the exercise of procedural rights relating to access
to environmental information and participation in decision-making.[903]

The shift of emphasis apparent in the Rio Declaration continued at the 2002
UN World Summit on Sustainable Development in Johannesburg, convened
to assess progress made since the 1992 Rio Conference. The Johannesburg
Declaration on Sustainable Development makes some oblique references to
'human dignity' but otherwise focuses on sustainable development.[904]

4.2.1 REGIONAL INSTRUMENTS

The right to a healthy environment has been given recognition in some of the
regional multilateral instruments. The African Charter on Human and Peoples'
Rights and the Additional Protocol to the American Convention on Human
Rights explicitly mention the right to a healthy environment.

The African Charter on Human and People's Rights (ACHPR) 1981[905]
expressly provides for the right to a healthy environment. Article 24 of the Charter
states that 'all peoples shall have the right to a general satisfactory environment
favourable to their development.' Although failure of the Charter to provide for
the meaning of 'satisfactory environment' in Article 24 makes it rather vague, it
is nevertheless the first broadly ratified international human rights instrument
specifically recognizing a right to the environment.[906]

The Additional Protocol to the American Convention on Human Rights
1988,[907] which was adopted in San Salvador, stipulates that 'everyone shall have
the right to live in a healthy environment and to have access to basic public
services' and 'the States Parties shall promote the protection, preservation and
improvement of the environment.'[908] Unlike the African Charter, which does not
actually recognize the right to environment as an individual human right, but

---

[903]   *Ibid*, pp.388–389.
[904]   See J. Thornton and Beckwith S., *op. cit.*, p.388.
[905]   Adopted June 27, 1981 and entered into force 21 October 1986, OAU Doc. OAU/CAB/
        LEG/67/3/Rev. 5 (hereinafter called the African Charter).
[906]   Ole W. Pedersen, *op. cit.*, p.79; Sueli Giorgetta, *op. cit.*, p.177.
[907]   Organization of American States: Additional Protocol to the American Convention on Human
        Rights in the Area of Economic, Social and Cultural Rights 'Protocol of San Salvador,' O.A.S.
        Treaty Series No. 69 (1988), reprinted in Basic Documents Pertaining to Human Rights in
        the Inter-American System, OEA/Ser. L.V/II.82 doc.6 rev.1 at 67 (1992). It was adopted on 17
        November 1988, and entered into force on 16 November, 1999.
[908]   Article 11(1) & (2). The San Salvador Protocol distinguishes between the right of individuals
        to "live in a healthy environment" and the positive obligation of States to protect, preserve
        and improve the environment. The failure of a State to carry out that obligation can, there-

rather as a collective right vested in peoples, the San Salvador Protocol explicitly recognize the right to an environment as an individual right.[909]

The Aarhus Convention makes a further important contribution. It was the first occasion on which the right to a healthy environment *per se* was explicitly accorded recognition in the operative provisions of an international legal instrument at the European level.[910] The 1998 Aarhus Convention, developed under the auspices of the United Nations Economic Commission for Europe, codifies various environmental dimensions of the right to information, the right to participation and the right of equal access to judicial and administrative remedies because 'adequate protection of the environment is essential to human well-being and the enjoyment of basic human rights, including the right to life itself.'[911] Aimed at ensuring 'the protection of the right of every person of present and future generations *to live in an environment adequate to his or her health and well-being*,' the Aarhus Convention provides that each Party shall guarantee rights of access to information, public participation in decision-making, and access to justice in environmental matters. It recognizes the link between human rights and environmental protection including the procedural environmental rights. This will be considered in detail later. Although the Aarhus Convention is a regional instrument, its global relevance is widely recognized, and it is open to accession by non-ECE countries, subject to the approval of the Meeting of the Parties.

Despite the above, environmental degradation and pollution still persist. In May 1998, the UN Committee on Economic, Social and Cultural Rights 'note[d] with alarm the extent of the devastation that oil exploration has done to the environment and quality of life in areas such as Ogoniland [Niger Delta] where oil has been discovered and extracted without due regard to the health and well-being of the people and their environment,' and recommended that '[t]he rights of minority and ethnic communities – including the Ogoni people – should be respected and full redress should be provided for the violations of the rights set forth in the Covenant that they may have suffered.'[912] As a party to the ICCPR and

---

fore, give rise to an enforceable right of action. See Udombana N.J., "The Right to a Healthy Environment: Foreground and Forecasts," *op. cit.*, p.112.

[909] Marc Pallemaerts, "Proceduralizing Environmental Rights: The Aarhus Convention on Access to Information, Public Participation in Decision-Making and Access to Justice in Environmental Matters in a Human Rights Context", in *Human Rights and the Environment*, Proceedings of a Geneva Environment Network Roundtable, UNEP Publication, Geneva, 2004, p.17.

[910] Marc Pallemaerts, A Human Rights Perspective on Current Environmental Issues and their Management: Evolving International Legal and Political Discourse on the Human Environment, the Individual and the State, *Human Rights and International Legal Discourse*, Vol. 2 No. 2, pp.149–178 at 157 (2008).

[911] UN Economic Commission for Europe, Convention on Access to Information, Public Participation in Decision-Making and Access to Justice in Environmental Matters (25 June 1998) (Aarhus Convention), at www.unece.org/env/pp/documents/cep 43e.pdf.

[912] UN Committee on Economic, Social and Cultural Rights (CESCR), *UN Committee on Economic, Social and Cultural Rights: Concluding observations: Nigeria*, 16 June 1998, E/C.12/1/

the ICESCR, the Nigerian Government has failed to meet its obligations under
these Covenants, particularly to the Niger Delta people. This has led to a renewed
effort by human rights crusaders, environmentalists, international organizations
and UN's agencies to look for ways to abate these negative effects by presenting
in clear terms the link between environmental issues and human rights violation.

It is because of the above that the conflict in the Niger Delta region should be
seen in the context of the close relationship between human rights in general and
environmental protection in international and Nigerian law.

4.3 CONSTITUTIONAL RECOGNITION OF
ENVIRONMENTAL RIGHTS IN NIGERIA

The right to a decent or healthy environment is not enshrined in the Constitution
of the Federal Republic of Nigeria (CFRN) 1999 (as amended). Section 20 of the
Constitution provides that 'the State shall protect and improve the environment
and safeguard the water, air, and land, forest and wildlife of Nigeria.' Furthermore,
section 17(2)(d) of the Constitution provides that 'exploitation of human or
natural resources in any form whatever for any reasons, other than the good
of the community, shall be prevented.' This implies that the Government of
Nigeria must always take into consideration the rights of the people in decisions
concerning the exploitation of human or natural resources. These include taking
precautions against environmental harms capable of destroying life and property
as well as the provision of relief and compensation for victims of environmental
degradation caused by the exploitation of natural resources by the Government.[913]

Unfortunately, these provisions are contained in Chapter II of the Constitution
entitled 'The Fundamental Objectives and Directive Principles of State Policy';
and these provisions are not justiciable. They are not enforceable against the State
in view of section 6(6)(c) of the Constitution, which provides that:

> *"The Judicial powers vested in accordance with the foregoing provisions of this sec-
> tion –*
>
> *(c) shall not, except as otherwise provided by this Constitution, extend to any
> issue or question as to whether any act or omission by any authority or person
> or as to whether any law or any judicial decision is in conformity with the
> Fundamental Objectives and Directive Principles of State Policy set out in
> Chapter II of this Constitution."*

Add.23, paras. 29 and 38, at www.unhcr.org/refworld/docid/3ae6ae690.html [accessed 6 May
2009].

[913] Amos Adeoye Idowu, *op. cit.*, p.162.

These provisions on the peoples' right to a protected environment are non-justiciable in the sense that they are capable of vindication by legal remedies.[914] If they were a provision under the fundamental rights contained in Chapter IV of the CFRN 1999, they would have been justiciable. The non-justiciability of the provisions of section 6(6)(c) of the Constitution is quite startling, especially when viewed against the background of the first specific goal of Nigerian National Policy on the Environment.[915] This identified the need to 'secure for all Nigerians a quality of environment adequate for their health and well-being.' Paragraph 6 of the Policy provides that action shall be taken to '(c) make it a Constitutional duty of Governments – Federal, States and Local – to safeguard the environment and aspire to have a safe and healthy nation.' Worthy of note is that the provisions of paragraph 6(c) were deleted in the updated version of the National Policy on the Environment, presumably because of the inclusion of section 20 in the 1999 Constitution.[916] It is submitted that this glowing but judicially unenforceable provision on the right to clean environment is consistent with the Government apathy towards this right.[917] Okorodudu-Fubara, while commenting on this Constitutional apathy observed that: 'While there are a fair number of constitutional or other legal provisions which impose a basic duty on the State to protect (certain parts of) the environment, there are only very few provisions which provide for a specific right of individual human beings to an adequate environment.'[918]

The Nigerian Government's reluctance to make environmental rights justiciable intriguingly started during the era of environmental policy revolution in Nigeria in the mid 90s.[919] While the Federal Military Government established by Decree, the Federal Environmental Protection Agency (FEPA) in December 1988, and launched the National Policy on the Environment in November 1989, the Constitution of the Federal Republic of Nigeria (Promulgation) Decree, 1989

---

[914] This position was confirmed in *Okogie v. Lagos State Government* (1981) 2 NCLR 337, where the Court of Appeal held that the directive principles of state policy in chapter II of the 1979 Constitution of the Federal Republic of Nigeria is non-justiciable and must conform to and run subsidiary to the fundamental rights. The Supreme Court of Nigeria again in *Attorney-General of Ondo State v. Attorney-General Federation* (2002) 9 N.W.L.R. (pt. 772) 222 maintained that the fundamental objectives and directive principles of state policy in chapter II of the Nigerian constitution remain non-justiciable. They are mere declarations that lack the force of law and cannot be enforced by legal process except when translated or elevated to the status of law by legislation.

[915] See The National Policy on the Environment (1989).

[916] Akeem Bello, Environmental Rights in Nigeria: Issues, Problems and Prospects, *Igbinedion University Law Journal*, Vol. 4, pp.60–95 at 70 (2006).

[917] Olubayo Oluduro, 'Environmental Rights: A Case Study of the 1999 Constitution of the Federal Republic of Nigeria,' *Malawi Law Journal*, Vol. 4, Issue 2, pp.255–270 at 257 (2010).

[918] M.T. Okorodudu-Fubara (1998), *Law of Environmental Protection: Materials and Text,* Caltop Publications Ltd., Lagos, p.87.

[919] S.M. Adam, "Human Rights and Environmental Protection in Nigeria", in J.M. Nasir *et al* (eds) (2008), *Contemporary Readings in Governance, Law and Security: Essays in Honour of (Sir) Mike Mbama Okiro, Inspector-General of Police,* Constellation (Nig.) Publishers, Ibadan/Abuja, p.321.

which was enacted on 3 May 1989 (which was eventually abandoned following the military coup of General Sani Abacha in November 1993) failed to incorporate the right to environment.

For environmental rights to have any practical importance, they must be supported by enforceable obligations on the part of the State to act for the benefit of the people.[920] It is submitted that this hypocrisy of making elaborate and hallowed policy statements without providing accompanying enforcement mechanisms is a deliberate elitist strategy of sustaining environmental degradation which is beneficial to the State and its elites, while the poor and the defenceless bear the mortal consequences.[921]

No less than 130 countries have Constitutions that make some specific reference to the environment, and about sixty include the right to a healthy environment as a fundamental right.[922] For example, in Africa, at least 35 countries

---

[920] Neil A.F. Popovic, Pursuing Environmental Justice with International Human Rights and State Constitutions, 15 *Stan. Env'l L.J.* 338–374 at 362 (1996).

[921] *Ibid*. This is exemplified in the Niger Delta struggle in Nigeria where the State, the elites and the MNCs benefit from the resource exploitation by the latter to the detriment of the vulnerable groups in the oil-producing communities where the oil is being exploited.

[922] These include Angola, Argentina, Azerbaijan, Belarus, Belgium, Benin, Brazil, Bulgaria, Burkina Faso, Cameroon, Cape Verde, Chad, Chechnya, Chile, Columbia, Congo, Costa Rica, Croatia, Cuba, Czech Republic, Democratic Republic of Congo, Ecuador, El Salvador, Ethiopia, Finland, France, Georgia, Honduras, Hungary, Kyrgyzstan, Latvia, Macedonia, Mali, Moldova, Mongolia, Mozambique, Nicaragua, Niger, Norway, Paraguay, Philippines, Portugal, Russia, Sao Tome and Principe, Seychelles, Slovakia, Slovenia, South Africa, South Korea, Spain, Tajikistan, Togo, Turkey, Ukraine, Yugoslavia. See Lynda Collins, Are We There Yet? The Right to Environment in International and European Law, 3 *McGill Int'l J. Sust. Dev. L. & Pol'y* 119–153 at 136 (2007); James R. May, Constituting Fundamental Environmental Rights Worldwide, 23 *Pace Envtl. L. R.* 113–182 at 114–115 (2005–2006); Luc Lavrysen and Jan Theunis, "The right to the protection of a healthy environment in the Belgian Constitution: retrospect and international perspective", in Isabelle Larmuseau (ed) (2007), *Constitutional rights to an ecologically balanced environment*, V.V.O.R. Report 2007/2, being the Report of the International conference organised by the Flemish Environmental Law Association, in collaboration with the European Environmental Law Association on 28 September 2007, p. 9; Kaniye S.A. Ebeku, Constitutional Right to a Healthy Environment and Human Rights Approaches to Environmental Protection in Nigeria: *Gbemre v. Shell* Revisited, *RECIEL* 16(3) 312–320 at 312–314 (2007). Dinah Shelton, Human Rights and the Environment: What Specific Environmental Rights Have Been Recognized?, 35 *Denv. J. Int'l L. & Pol'y* 129–171 at 164–165 (2006); Shubha Harris, *Establishing a Constitutional Right to Environmental Quality*, 5 May, 2008, at http://apps.americanbar.org/environ/committees/lawstudents/writingcompetition/2008/WillMitSoL/ShubhaHarris.pdf [accessed 6 July 2009]. Interestingly, Ecuador which shares with Nigeria the same history of pollution from state-run and private oil companies on 28 September 2008 approved a new Constitution that includes a Chapter on Nature's Rights (Chapter Seven). Article 71 of the Chapter grants nature or *Pacha Mama*, the right to 'integral respect for its existence and for the maintenance and regeneration of its life cycles, structure, functions and evolutionary processes),' and further grants legal standing to any person to ventilate those rights in court. See Republic of Ecuador Constitution of 2008. It is important to stress that while a considerable number of countries have included some type of provision guaranteeing the right to healthy environment in their Constitutions, there is paucity of case law interpreting these provisions.

have Constitutional provisions ensuring the right to a healthy environment.[923] This is a significant improvement from the position in mid 1980s where it was just two countries, Equatorial Guinea and Ethiopia, which had environmental provisions in their Constitutions.[924] Now, for example, in South Africa, Section 24 of the 1996 Constitution provides that:

> *"Everyone has the right –*
> *(a) to an environment that is not harmful to their health or well-being; and*
> *(b) to have the environment protected, for the benefit of present and future generations, through reasonable legislative and other measures that –*
> > *(i)   prevent pollution and ecological degradation;*
> > *(ii) promote conservation; and*
> > *(iii) secure ecologically sustainable development and use of natural resources while promoting justifiable economic and social development."*

Sadly enough, the right to a healthy environment is not enshrined in the CFRN 1999. The non-justiciable character of the provisions relating to the right to a healthy environment under the Nigerian Constitution has reduced this right to sheer rhetoric. As a result of this, the environmental degradation in the oil-producing communities in the Niger Delta region continues to increase in leaps and bounds with deleterious effects on human beings, vegetations and animals. It is submitted that there is a need for the inclusion of the right to a clean and decent environment in the enforceable part of the Constitution, as is the case in many States in the U.S.[925] It should be elevated from its present insignificant level as part of the fundamental objective principles of State policy to a substantive right as in Chapter IV of the Constitution. As noted by Hayward, 'a human right to an environment adequate for one's health and well-being is not a luxury.'[926]

However, several arguments have been canvassed against the recognition of a right to environment. One of these is the difficulty in definition. The various

---

[923] Carl Bruch and Wole Coker, Breathing life into Fundamental Law in Africa, at www.eli.org/pdf/breathinglife.pdf. [accessed 3 March 2010].

[924] See Charles Okidi, *Environmental Rights and Duties in the Context of Management of National Resources*, Constitution of Kenya Review Commission, available at www.Kenyaconstitution.org/index.shtml. [accessed 3 March 2010]. See Rhuks T. Ako, Entrenching the Right to Environment into Nigeria's Constitution, *Ikeja Bar Journal*, Vol. 1 Part 1, p. 121 (2005).

[925] See Ala. Constitution Art. VIII; Fla. Constitution Art. II section 7; Cal. Constitution Art. X, section 2; Tex. Constitution, Art. XVI, section 59; Ohio Constitution, Art. II, section 36; Mont. Constitution, Art. IX, section 1; Mich. Constitution, Art. IV, section 52; Mass Constitution, section 179; N.Y. Constitution Art. XIV; Va. Constitution Art. XI, section 1; La. Constitution Art. IX. For general discussions on these provisions, see Robert A. McLaren, Comment, Environmental Protection Based on State Constitutional Law: A Call for Reinterpretation, 12 *U. Haw. L. Rev.* 123, 126–127 (1990); Dinah Shelton, "Environmental rights in the State Constitutions of the United States", in Isabelle Larmuseau (ed) (2007), *Constitutional rights to an ecologically balanced environment, op. cit.*, pp.106–133.

[926] T. Hayward (2005), *Constitutional Environmental Rights*, Oxford University Press, Oxford, p.210.

---

definitions of an environmental human right demonstrate that the right is
often formulated in vague and abstract terms. For instance, the right does not
usually elaborate on what a State must do to protect the environment, and
adjectives such as 'sound', 'decent' or 'clean' are not defined.[927] Some argue that
environmental rights are imprecise and that such imprecision makes it difficult
to enforce environmental rights. Further, since the scope of the right cannot be
clearly defined, the determination of its scope and judicial enforcement of the
right, depends on the court's chosen interpretation of 'environment' and this may
pitch the court against the legislature in a never-ending battle.[928] On this, it is
submitted that vagueness or lack of specificity is not uncommon to human rights;
they are indeed common features in the articulation of most human rights,
especially economic, social and cultural rights, and this should not be a basis of
rejecting the need for environmental human rights. Alan Boyle argues that this
definitional problem arose also in relation to "sustainable development", but this
did not prevent the UN's efforts at promoting sustainability: 'Indeterminacy is
thus a problem, but not necessarily an insurmountable one.'[929] Boyle notes that
the definitional problem can be addressed by 'adopting a more specific focus,
for example on health, rather than on the vaguer and more subjective criteria of
decency, satisfaction, or viability.'[930] An alternative is to let supervisory institutions
and courts develop their own interpretations, as they have done with respect to
many other human rights.[931] This will give the courts an opportunity to define

---

[927] Prudence E. Taylor (1998), *An Ecological Approach to International Law. Responding to
Challenges of Climate Change*, Routledge, London and New York, p.230; Luis E. Rodriguez-
Rivera, Is the Human Right to Environment Recognized Under International Law? It Depends
on the Source, 12 *Colo. J. Int'l Envtl. L & Pol.'y* 1–46 at 10–11 (2001); Schwartz, Michelle
Leighton, International Legal Protection for Victims of Environmental Abuse, 18 *Yale J. Int'l
L.* 355–387 at 374 (1993); Prudence E. Taylor, From Environmental to Ecological Human
Rights: A New Dynamic in International Law?' 10 *Georgetown International Environmental
Law Review* 309–397 at 351 (1998); Paula M. Pevato, A Right to Environment in International
Law: Current Status and Future Outlook, 8(3) *Rev. Eur. Cmty. &Int'l Envt'l L. (RECIEL)* 309–
321at 312 (1999); Karen E. MacDonald, Sustaining the Environmental Rights of Children: An
Exploratory Critique, 18 *Fordham Envtl. L. Rev.* 1–65 at 14–15 (2006–2007).

[928] Oludayo G. Amokaye, Human Rights and Environmental Protection: The Necessary
Connection, *UNILAG Journal of Human Rights Law*, Vol. 1 No. 1, pp.104–105 (2007); Noralee
Gibson, The Right to a Clean Environment, 54 *Sask. L. Rev.* 5–18 at 9 (1990), where Gibson
asserts that the scope and form of the right to a clean environment is yet to be determined,
too vague to be justiciable and is no more than a slogan. To ensure the enforcement of this
proposed right, he posited that rigorous standards such as a clearly defined object and an identifiable subject should be applied to the definition of this right.

[929] Alan Boyle, "The Role of International Human Rights Law in the Protection of the
Environment", in Alan Boyle and Michael Anderson (eds) (1996), *Human Rights Approaches to
Environmental Protection, op. cit.*, p.51; See also T. Hayward, "Constitutional Environmental
Rights: A Case for Political Analysis", in Andrew Light and Avner de-Shalit (eds) (2003), *Moral
and Political Reasoning in Environmental Practice*, The MIT Press, Cambridge, England,
pp.117–120.

[930] Alan Boyle, *Ibid* p.50.

[931] Alexandre Kiss and Dinah Shelton (1995), International Environmental Law, Transnational
Publishers, p.10; Dinah Shelton, Human Rights, Environmental Rights and the Right to
Environment, *op. cit.*, pp.103–138; Sumudu Atapattu, The Right to a Healthy Life or the

and adapt the provisions on environmental rights to meet modern needs and challenges in the field of environmental law. This is evident in the interpretation given to the right to a general satisfactory environment, as contained in Article 24 of the African Charter, by the African Commission in the case of *Social and Economic Rights Action Center (SERAC) and another v. Federal Republic of Nigeria*.[932]

Another problem is the fundamentally anthropocentric character[933] of viewing environmental standards through a human rights focus, without giving any thought to the non-human beings that coexist with man within the environment. A number of negative consequences arising from the anthropocentrism of environmental human rights have been identified by Taylor.[934] These include the fact that anthropocentrism deprives the environment of direct and comprehensive protection, that is, the environment is only protected as a consequence of, and to the extent needed to protect, human well-being, thus subjugating all other needs, interests and values of nature (such as the flora, fauna and micro-organisms that shape and condition the environment) to those of humanity. Also, that humans are the beneficiaries of any form of relief from infringement of the right, that is, there is no guarantee of its utilization for the benefit of the environment, nor is there any recognition of nature as the victim of the degradation.[935] These arguments have, however, been dismissed by Boyle, making reference to several international treaties[936] which are not exclusively for human benefit.[937]

Right to Die Polluted?: The Emergence of a Human Right to a Healthy Environment Under International Law, *op. cit.*, p.112.

[932] Communication 155/96. This will be discussed below.

[933] Principle 1 of the Rio Declaration of 1992 provides that 'human beings are at the centre of concerns for sustainable development. They are entitled to a healthy and productive life in harmony with nature.' This has been heavily criticized for its manifestly anthropocentric nature. Comparing this Declaration with the Stockholm Declaration, Marc Pallemaerts, opined that: 'By contrast, the first principle of the Rio Declaration, where it clamours that "human beings are at the centre of the concerns for sustainable development," sounds like the triumph of a delirious anthropocentricism.' See Marc Pallemaerts, The Future of Environmental Regulation: International Environmental Law in the Age of Sustainable Development: A Critical Assessment of the UNCED Process, 15 *J.L. & COM.* 623 p.642 (1996). On the other hand, the World Charter for Nature adopted in 1982 was the first, and so far the only instrument of its kind, to recognize the rights of nature, distinct from the rights of human beings. In other words, it adopted an ecocentric approach unlike most international instruments that approach environmental protection in an anthropocentric manner. It does not embody the rights of man in human rights parlance, rather, it endorses the right of every form of life, 'warranting respect regardless of its worth to man.' See Sumudu Atapattu, *op. cit.*, pp.75–78.

[934] Prudence E. Taylor, *An Ecological Approach to International Law. Responding to Challenges of Climate Change, op. cit.*, p.234.

[935] *Ibid.*

[936] These include the World Heritage Convention 11 ILM (1972), 1358; the Berne Convention on the Conservation of European Wildlife and Natural Habitats UKTS 56 (1982), Cmnd. 8738; the Convention on International Trade in Endangered Species 993 UNTS 243; the Biological Diversity Convention 31 ILM (1992), 822; the World Charter for Nature UNGA Res. 37/7 (1982), reprinted in 22 ILM (1983), 455.

[937] Alan Boyle, *op. cit.*, p.52.

In addition, Handl believes that a right to environment would be difficult
to conceptualize as an inalienable right in the sense of not being subject to
derogation. He argues that environmental entitlements will continue to be
susceptible to restrictions for the sake of other socio-economic objectives.[938] It is,
however, important to note that apart from a few human rights like the right to
life, the prohibition of slavery or the right against torture, all other human rights
can be derogated from in times of emergency or in the interests of a democratic
society.

In spite of the above, it is submitted that these arguments do not justify
outright rejection of the concept of a right to a healthy environment. The absence
of a positive codification of the right in the enforceable part of the Constitution
means that MNCs and Government have a great latitude to pursue profitability
without constraints. The failure of the Nigerian Government to make section 20
on environment justiciable is not only evidence of its insensitivity to the plight of
the sick, homeless, poor, illiterate and marginalized citizens of the Niger Delta
but also evidence of its deliberate ignorance of the internationally recognised
interdependence and indivisibility principle of all human rights. It depicts a
deliberate ignorance of developments in other African countries like South Africa.
The advantages of following the approach elsewhere are that it would require the
State to take protective action, and secondly, it would establish the personal rights
of all inhabitants of the Nigerian Nation to a non-deteriorated environment.[939]

The Constitutional recognition of a distinct right to a healthy environment
would elevate it to the status of other fundamental rights, according it with the same
importance, and allowing victims to resort to the same machinery.[940] If enacted,
the right to environment would grant the public a right to a healthy environment
and introduce a series of reforms to increase the powers of the private citizens
to protect themselves and their environment from the effects of pollution.[941] As
suggested by one scholar, one of the most effective ways of ensuring the protection
and preservation of the environment is to leave it in the hands of the ordinary
citizen by granting the citizen a right to a clean environment.[942] In relation to the

---

[938]   See Gunther Handl, "Human Rights and Protection of the Environment: A Mildly "Revisionist"
    View", in Antonio Trindade (ed) (1992), *Human Rights, Sustainable Development and the
    Environment*, Instituto Interamericano de Derechos Humanos, San Jose, Costa Rica, pp.119–
    120, quoted in Sumudu Atapattu, *op. cit.*, p.116. According to Atapattu, it is not intended that
    the right to environment should be framed in absolute terms or be a non-derogable right,
    but rather, like the right to privacy or an adequate standard of living, a balancing of compet-
    ing interests test will have to be applied in relation to the right to environment, in line with
    standard practice in relation to human rights; For further objections to Handl, see Luis E.
    Rodriguez-Rivera, *op. cit.*, pp.33–37.

[939]   Olarenwaju Fagbohun, Reappraising the Nigerian Constitution for Environmental
    Management, *Ambrose Alli University Law Journal*, Vol. 1 No1. p.46 (2002).

[940]   Sumudu Atapattu, *op. cit.* at 91.

[941]   Emmanuel Kasimbazi, *The Environment as Human Rights: Lessons from Uganda, African
    Society of International and Comparative Law*, p.148 (1998).

[942]   O. Adewale, The Right of the Individual to Environmental Protection: A Case Study of
    Nigeria, *Environment and Urbanization*, Vol. 4, No. 2, 176–183 at 176 (1992); See also

people of Niger Delta, it would provide a standard to which claims could be made in cases of environmental damage by the oil companies, thus helping them to combat environmental degradation. Since this right is addressed not only to the State, but also to third persons, who are also bound to refrain from actions that can degrade the environment,[943] this will go a long way to instill fear in the oil companies operating in the Niger Delta, thus curtailing their non chalant attitude regarding the adoption of international best practices in their oil exploration activities. Such a right would increase the power to sue in civil courts for damages caused by pollution and to initiate private suits or claims where Government has refused to act.[944] It would grant increased access to information and rights to participate on standard settings and other processes.[945]

Also, the recognition of the right to environment could help in removing some of the obstacles encountered by litigants in environmental suits under the common law actions of public nuisance, negligence, and the rule in *Ryland v. Fletcher;* and also the problems of *locus standi.*[946] It may help to liberalize the rules of standing in relation to the right to seek legal redress in environmental matters, including 'rights to object to ministerial and agency environmental decisions; and rights to bring actions against departments, agencies, firms and individuals that fail to carry out their duties according to law.'[947] For example, in Illinois, it was noted that the Constitutional right to a clean and healthy environment creates no new cause of action,[948] but it does give 'standing to an individual to bring an environmental action for a grievance common to members of the public,'[949] even in cases where a resident may not be able to demonstrate the 'particularized' harm that is normally required.[950] Hence, the recognition of the right to environment

---

Richard L. Ottinger, Legislation and the Environment: Individual Rights and Government Accountability, 55 *Cornell L. Rev.* 666–673 at 673 (1970).

[943] Tonia Pediaditaki, "The right to the protection of the environment in the Greek Constitution", in Isabelle Larmuseau (ed), *Constitutional rights to an ecologically balanced environment, op. cit.*, p.63.

[944] Lawrence Atsegbua, A Critical Appraisal of Environmental Rights Under the Nigerian Courts, *Benin Journal of Public Law* Vol. 2. No. 1. p.46 (2004). According to Shedrack C. Agbakwa, Reclaiming Humanity: Economic, Social and Cultural Rights as the Cornerstone of African Human Rights, 5 *Yale Human Rights and Development Law Journal* 177, 181 (2002), 'the greatest benefit of guaranteeing enforceable [justiciable] rights is the assurance it gives people that effective mechanisms for adjudicating violations or threatened violations of their rights are available.'

[945] Lawrence Atsegbua, *Ibid* p.46.

[946] Akeem Bello, *op. cit.*, p.92.

[947] Robyn Eckersley, "Greening Liberal Democracy: The Rights Discourse revisited", in Brian Doherty and Marius de Geus (eds) (1996), *Democracy and Green Political Thought: Sustainability, Rights and Citizenship*, Routledge, London, p.230, quoted in T. Hayward, Constitutional Environmental Rights: A Case for Political Analysis, *op. cit.*, p.116.

[948] *City of Elgin v. County of Cook*, 660 N.E. 2d 875 (Ill. 1995).

[949] *Glisson v. City of Marrion*, 720 N.E 2d 1034, 1041 (Ill. 1999), quoted in Dinah Shelton, "Environmental rights in the State Constitutions of the United States", in Isabelle Larmuseau (ed), *Constitutional rights to an ecologically balanced environment, op. cit.*, p.123.

[950] Dinah Shelton, *Ibid.*

as fundamental under the Nigerian Constitution could assist in liberalizing the standing rules for environmental organizations who might want to challenge environmental harms caused to a community or private individual by the Government or non-state actors, as daily witnessed in the Niger Delta.

The right to environment implies that there is a duty to protect and preserve the environment as well as defend it when violated by others. This right is linked to the duty of both the State and individuals to protect the environment for the present and future generations.[951] The establishment of a right to a healthy environment both in national and international law will not only work to protect the environment and victims of environmental harm, but will help to safeguard those human rights contained in the Constitution and those already accepted and revered by the international community.[952] So imperative is the Constitutional right to environment that 'the nations that haven't it yet in their fundamental laws live with a crippled Environmental Law System.'[953] More responsibilities are therefore placed on the Government not only to ensure a better and healthy environment through initiation of sound policies but also to provide adequate remedies to victims of environmental pollution. Constitutional guarantee of the right to environment could assist in clarifying and establishing values that without such a provision would not be recognized by the Judges in their interpretation of the law.[954]

Although, there is as yet no international treaty which guarantees a fundamental right to a healthy environment, there is hope that this may sometime occur.[955] This is because the right is presently gaining ground as a norm of international law, receiving explicit recognition in authoritative international documents, and is explicitly provided for in many national constitutions.[956] For the purposes of customary international law, the verbatim reproduction and acceptance of the language of Principle 1 of the Rio Declaration without reservation by 179 nations

---

[951]   Akeem Bello, *op. cit.*, p.93.

[952]   Joshua P. Eaton, The Nigerian Tragedy, Environmental Regulation of Transnational Corporations, and the Human Right to a Healthy Environment, *op. cit.*, p.300.

[953]   Branca Martins da Cruz, "The constitutional right to an ecologically balanced environment in Portugal", in Isabelle Larmuseau (ed), *Constitutional rights to an ecologically balanced environment, op. cit.*, p.56.

[954]   Tim Hayward, Constitutional Environmental Rights: A Case for Political Analysis, *op. cit.*, p.125.

[955]   Okorodudu-Fubara M.T., *Dynamics of a New World Environmental Legal Order*, An Inaugural Lecture delivered at Oduduwa Hall, Obafemi Awolowo University, Ile-Ife, Nigeria on Tuesday, 13 April 1999, Inaugural Lecture Series 133, Obafemi Awolowo University Press Limited, Ile-Ife, p.15.

[956]   T. Hayward, Constitutional Environmental Rights: A Case for Political Analysis, *op. cit.*, p.123; Thomas T. Ankersen, Shared Knowledge, Shared Jurisprudence: Learning to Speak Environmental Law Creole (Criollo), 16 *Tul. Envtl. L.J.* 807–830 at 820 (2003); Carl Bruch, Wole Coker and Chris VanArsdale, Constitutional Environmental Law: Giving Force to Fundamental Principles in Africa, 26 *Colum. J. Envtl. L.* 131–211 at 163 (2001); Dinah Shelton, Developing Substantive Environmental Rights, *Journal of Human Rights and the Environment*, Vol. 1 No. 1, 89–120 at 89–90 (2010).

at the 1994 UN Conference on Population and Development;[957] by 186 nations at the 1995 World Summit for Social Development;[958] by 175 nations at the 1996 Second Conference on Human Settlements (Habitat II);[959] and by 17 nations at the OAS-sponsored 1997 Hemispheric Summit on Sustainable Development,[960] is evidence of a widespread and consistent State practice.[961] As argued by one scholar, the 'repetition of the same principle [Principle 21 of Stockholm Declaration] in various international texts, even if none of them is legally binding, can be considered as equivalent [to] a constant practice... Thus, it may be concluded that Principle 21 of the Stockholm Declaration formulates customary international law rule.'[962] Also, the recognition of a substantive right to the environment under Article 24 of the African Charter and Article 11 of the San Salvador Protocol represents regional customary law and adds to the notion of an emerging right.[963] This practice can contribute to the creation of a right to a healthy environment as a principle of customary international law.[964] This right is almost certain to become enforceable 'hard law,' that is, becoming legally binding obligations.[965] As observed by Victor Hugo: 'An invasion of armies can be resisted, but not an idea whose time has come.'[966]

4.4 CATEGORIES OF HUMAN RIGHTS VULNERABLE TO THE ACTIVITIES OF OIL MULTINATIONAL COMPANIES

Human rights violations are no longer associated solely with Governments, but also with MNCs. The Business and Human Rights Resources Center – widely acknowledged as providing the broadest array of 'balanced information on business and human rights' – has documented abuses ranging from health and safety violations in the workplace, to murder, torture, and forced displacement

---

[957] Programme of Action, UN Doc. A/CONF.171/13 (1994), principle 2. It was held in Cairo, Egypt, though it is legally non-binding.

[958] Copenhagen Declaration, UN Doc A/CONF.166/7/Annex (1995), principle 6. This Declaration is also legally non-binding.

[959] The 1996 UN Conference on Human Settlements, UN Doc/Conf.165/PC.3/L.3 (1996), chapter 1, preamble 2. This is legally non-binding.

[960] Declaration of Santa Cruz, O.A.S. G.T/CCDS-51/96, rev. (26 November, 1996), at www.summit-americas.org/boliviadec.htm [accessed 7 June 2009]

[961] John Lee, *op. cit.*, pp.308–309.

[962] Prue Taylor (1998), *An Ecological Approach to International Law. Responding to Challenges of Climate Change*, Routledge, London and New York, p.77, quoted in Joanna E. Arlow, The Utility of ATCA and the "Law of Nations" in Environmental Torts Litigation: *Jota v. Texaco, Inc.* and Large Scale Environmental Destruction, 7 *Wis. Envtl. L.J.* 93–138 at 128 (2000).

[963] Ole W. Pedersen, *op. cit.*, p.82.

[964] John Lee, *op. cit.*, p.309.

[965] Barry E. Hill, *et al*, Human Rights and the Environment: A Synopsis and Some Predictions, 16 *Geo. Int'l Envt'l. L. Rev.* 359–402 at 400 (2004).

[966] Victor Hugo, *Histoire D' Un Crime* (1877).

at the hands of military and security forces protecting company facilities.[967] One
reason for focusing on alleged abuses in the extractive sectors is that this sector
has been the subject of intense public scrutiny and criticism for its human rights
performance. Also, this sector illustrates corporate human rights responsibilities,
and their implications for corporate policies that are applicable to most other
sectors.[968] Human rights provisions are intended to protect individuals and
groups against abuses such as violence and killing, torture, inhuman and
degrading treatment, state-induced starvation, and deprivation of means of
livelihood. Nevertheless, ecological imperialism, which connotes wanton natural
resource exploitation, degradation, and inequitable bearing of the associated
environmental hazards (or external costs of production) by MNCs or other
powerful foreign or local vested interests, remains a serious threat to the nations
of the world.[969]

Since human rights involve the assurance of people's means of livelihood and
well-being, any significant threats to the environmental bases of that livelihood
risks violation of fundamental human rights.[970] The enjoyment of most of the
internationally recognized human rights are severely affected by environmental
degradation. We shall now examine some of the major human rights affected
by environmental harms and see how the Government and multinational
corporations have contributed to the continuous violation of human rights of the
people in the oil-producing communities of Nigeria.

4.4.1 RIGHT TO LIFE

The right to life is guaranteed, in almost all human rights instruments – by the UN
at the global level, the African Union (AU) at the regional level and the Constitution
at the national level in Nigeria. For example, the International Covenant on Civil
and Political Rights (ICCPR),[971] which was ratified by the Nigerian Government
alongside the International Covenant on Economic, Social and Cultural Rights

---

[967] C. Kaeb, Energy Issues of Human Rights Responsibility in the Extractive and Manufacturing
Industries: Patterns and Liability Risks, 6(2) *Northwestern Journal of International Human
Rights,* p.328 (2008).

[968] *Ibid.*

[969] F.O. Adeola, *op. cit.* at p.41.

[970] Articles 3, 17 and 25 of the Universal Declaration of Human Rights are particularly important to global environmental justice. In Article 3, everyone has the right to life, liberty, and
security; Article 17 stipulates that everyone has the right to own property and no one shall be
arbitrarily deprived of his/her property, and in Article 25, everyone has the right to a standard
of living adequate for the health and well-being of him/herself and his/her family, including
food, clothing, housing, and medical care and necessary social services, and the right to security. See F.O. Adeola, *Ibid,* p.55.

[971] Adopted Dec. 16, 1966, and entered into force March 23, 1976, G.A Res. 2200 A (XXI).

(ICESCR)[972] provides that, 'every human being has the inherent right to life. This right shall be protected by law. No one shall be arbitrarily deprived of his life.'[973] In the same vein, the African Charter on Human and Peoples' Rights (African Charter)[974] which Nigeria ratified[975] and enacted as part of her law,[976] provides that 'human beings are inviolable' and therefore, 'every human being shall be entitled to respect for his life and the integrity of his person.' At the national level, the 1999 CFRN provides in Section 33(1) that 'every person has a right to life, and no one shall be deprived intentionally of his life, save in execution of the sentence of a court in respect of a criminal offence of which he has been found guilty in Nigeria.'

A lot of innocent people, including women and children, have been massacred by the Nigerian military and security agents in the guise of protecting oil infrastructures. These include the following instances.

1. **The MOSOP and Ogoni Incident**: The Movement for the Survival of Ogoni People (MOSOP) was formed in 1990 by Ken Saro-Wiwa, and other Ogoni elites, *inter alia*, to agitate for Ogoni self determination, resource control and political autonomy in order to bring an end to the devastation of their environment, their political marginalization and their economic strangulation.[977] Ken Saro-Wiwa was a writer and an environmental activist. He was a member of the Ogoni community in the Niger Delta region, whose community has suffered extreme and unremediated environmental destruction since the 1950s when the MNCs started the crude oil exploitation. He was actively involved in mobilizing the Ogoni in their non-violent struggle to stop the ecological destruction that Shell and the Nigerian Government were permitting

---

[972] Adopted 16 December 1966 and entered into force 3 January 1976, G.A Res. 2200 A (XXI). ICCPR and ICESCR were both ratified by Nigeria on 29 July 1993, 'Status of Ratifications of the Principal International Human Rights Treaties,' at www.193.194.138.190/pdf/report.pdf [accessed 3 June 2009]. However, as at March 2011, Nigeria is yet to sign the first Optional Protocol (1966) to the ICCPR, under which an individual, who asserts that his rights as contained in the ICCPR have been violated and who has exhausted all domestic remedies, can submit written communications to the United Nations Human Rights Committee.

[973] Art. 6(1) of ICCPR.

[974] *Op. cit.*

[975] The African Charter was ratified by Nigeria on 22 June 1983.

[976] The African Charter was domesticated by Nigeria as part of her law through the African Charter on Human and Peoples' Rights (Ratification and Enforcement) Act, Cap. A9, Laws of the Federation 2004 so as to enable it to have effect at municipal level. The Supreme Court, while commenting on the status of the Charter *vis-à-vis* municipal enactments in *Abacha v. Fawehinmi* (2000) 6 NWLR (pt. 660) 228, held *inter alia* that the Charter has some international flavour and in that sense, it cannot be amended or watered down or sidetracked by any Nigerian law.

[977] Ken Saro-Wiwa (1995), *A Month and a Day: A Detention Diary,* Penguin Books, New York, p.80; R. Boele *et al.*, Shell, Nigeria and the Ogoni. A Study in Unsustainable Development: The Story of Shell, Nigeria and the Ogoni People – Environment, Economy, Relationships: Conflict and Prospects for Resolution, 9 *Sustainable Development* 79 (2001).

in Ogoniland.[978] On 4 January 1993, MOSOP staged a peaceful mass rally
of around 300,000 Ogoni people – more than half of the Ogoni population
– through four Ogoni centres, so drawing international attention to the environmental degradation of Ogoniland by Shell.[979] This protest was followed by
a violent riot on 21 May 1994 in which four Ogoni Chiefs were murdered in
gruesome fashion by the National Youth Council of Ogoni People (NYCOP),
militants who apparently were irritated by the non-militant approach toward
Shell and the Government that the victims had promoted.[980] Saro-Wiwa, who
had on the day of the murders been denied entry to Ogoniland, was later
arrested for inciting the murder. He was incarcerated and found guilty on 31
October 1995 by a special tribunal in a trial considered unfair and fraudulent
across the world, and was sentenced to death by hanging along with 8 other
MOSOP leaders on 10 November 1995.[981] This provoked international outrage
and eventually led to the suspension of Nigeria from the Commonwealth of
Nations, including the recall of many foreign diplomats by their home countries. These and other sanctions were eventually lifted with the coming to
power of the civilian government in 1999. Although Saro-Wiwa and the other
8 MOSOP leaders were unjustly executed, they were able to create awareness
among the local people which has sustained the struggle till today.

2. **The Odi Massacre of 1999**: This involved the Federal Government's sacking
of Odi – a town in Bayelsa State in the Niger Delta. In mid-November 1999
some restive youths, protesting the neglect of the community, murdered
twelve policemen sent to the community to restore order.[982] Rather than
looking for the perpetrators, President Olusegun Obasanjo, on 20 November
1999, ordered a military invasion of Odi, in retaliation for the killing of

---

[978] A Rowell *et al., The Next Gulf: London, Washington and Oil Conflict in Nigeria, op. cit.*, pp.2–3.

[979] International Crisis Group Policy Briefing, *Nigeria: Ogoni Land after Shell, op. cit.*

[980] Roland Ogbonnaya, Ogoni and quest for autonomy, *ThisDay*, Friday 14 November, 2008, at
https://lists.mayfirst.org/pipermail/friends/2008-November/004300.html [accessed 3 July
2009].

[981] See B Holzer, Framing the Corporation: Royal Dutch/Shell and Human Rights Woes in
Nigeria, 30 *J Consum Policy* 287 (2007); Amnesty International Report, *Nigeria: The Ogoni
Trial and Detentions*, 14 September 1995, AI Index: AFR 44/020/95, at www.amnesty.org/en/
library/asset/AFR44/020/1995/en/ [accessed 20 July 2010]; Amnesty International Report,
Nigeria: A Travesty of Justice: The Secret Treason Trial and Other Concerns, 26 October 1995,
AFR 44/023/1995, at www.unhcr.org/refworld/docid/3ae6a98fc.html [accessed 20 July 2010];
Amos Adeoye Idowu, *op. cit.*, pp.179–180; Sigrun I Skogly, Complexities in Human Rights
Protection: Actors and Rights Involved in the Ogoni Conflict in Nigeria, 15(1) *Netherlands
Quarterly of Human Rights*, 47–60 at 57–58 (1997), lists some of the features of the trial as
including "insufficient evidence that any of the defendants either killed or incited anyone else
to kill; redefining the law of murder, to the extent that 'a death was caused in the course of a
civil disturbance and anyone who in any way contributed to or encouraged the *disturbance*
could be convicted of murder; and a reversal of the burden of proof both in terms of unchal-
lenged evidence must be true; and construction of the evidence."

[982] I. Okonta, *The lingering crisis in Nigeria's Niger Delta and suggestions for a peaceful resolution*, at http://nigerdeltacrises.blogspot.com/2008/09/lingering-crisis-in-nigerias-niger.html
[accessed 3 March 2010].

the policemen. The military mob leveled the entire village of Odi, killed over 2000 defenceless villagers and raped several women.[983] Major General T.Y. Danjuma, then Minister of Defence, explained to the public, five days later, that the action was taken to protect oil installations in the territory.[984] According to the Minister, 'Operation Hakuri II [that is, the invasion of Odi] was initiated with the mandate of protecting lives and property – particularly oil platforms, flow stations operating rig terminals, and pipelines, refineries and power installations, in the Niger Delta.'[985] Describing the situation, Senator Chuba Okadigbo, the then Senate President of Nigeria who visited the community a week after the gory incident stated that: 'the facts speak for themselves…there is no need for speech because there is nobody to speak with.'[986] Government's reaction generated worldwide condemnation, most especially, given that this dastardly act was committed in the 20th century under a democratic government.

3. **The Gbaramatu Massacre of 2009**: Gbaramatu is an Izon Clan in the south-west of Warri, Delta State. It has a population of over 65,000 people and is made up of more than fifty communities, with Oporoza acknowledged as the headquarters and ancestral home of the clan/kingdom.[987] On 13 May 2009, the late President Umaru Yar'Adua ordered a military operation in the Gbaramatu Kingdom, which covered Oporoza, Okerenkoko, Kunukunuma, Kurutie, Benikurukuru, Goba, Abiteye (Kiangbene), Kokodiaghene, Ibafa among others, all in the Niger Delta region, to apprehend some militants suspected of killing eighteen military officers guarding oil facilities.[988] This military operation, which was more a genocidal massacre, claimed, according to Chief Bello Oboko, a community leader in the kingdom, more than 2,000 persons, mostly elderly men and women as well as children and women.[989] This is aside from the lootings, maiming and burning of these communities by the soldiers.

---

[983]   See S.M. Adam, *op. cit.*, 329; SO Aghalino, The Olusegun Obasanjo Administration and the Niger Delta Question, 1999–2007, *op. cit.*, p.64; E Lenning and S Brightman, Oil, Rape and State Crime in Nigeria, *op. cit.*, pp.35–48.

[984]   E. Courson, *Movement for the Emancipation of the Niger Delta (MEND): Political Marginalization, Repression and Petro-Insurgency in the Niger Delta*, Nordiska AfrikaInstitutet, Discussion paper 47, Uppsala 2009, p.15.

[985]   Civil Liberty Organisation of Nigeria (1999), 'Genocide in Odi,' Press Conference by Leaders of Human Rights and Civil Society Groups who Visited Odi, Bayelsa State on Wednesday December 8th 1999, quoted in Chijioke J. Evoh, Green Crimes, Petro-violence and the Tragedy of Oil: The Case of the Niger-Delta in Nigeria, *In-Spire Journal of Law, Politics and Societies*, Vol. 4, No. 1, pp.40–60 at 54 (2009).

[986]   A Rowell *et al.*, *op. cit.*, p.24.

[987]   E. Courson, *The Burden of Oil: Social Deprivation and Political Militancy in Gbaramatu Clan, Warri South West LGA, Delta State, Nigeria*, Niger Delta Economies of Violence Working Paper No. 15, 2007, 2–3.

[988]   *Ibid*, 23.

[989]   Quoted in S Adebayo, Niger Delta: We have lost over 2000 persons – Gbaramatu Kingdom, *Saturday Punch*, May 23, 2009, p.10.

4. **The Umuechem Massacre of 1990**: This is one of the several incidents in
   which the oil MNCs invited the state security forces to deal with peaceful
   demonstrations by the local people. In October 1990, youths from the
   Umuechem community, in Rivers State, demanded provision of electricity,
   water and roads; and compensation for oil pollution of crops and water
   supplies, by mounting a peaceful protest at a road junction 3 km from
   Shell's flow station.[990] In anticipation of an impending attack, the manager of
   SPDC's eastern division, J.R Udofia, wrote to the Rivers State Commissioner
   of Police to request security protection, with preference for the mobile police,
   notoriously known for their abuses.[991] On 30 October, the protest moved
   to the Shell premises. SPDC again made a written report to the Governor
   of Rivers State, a copy of which was sent to the Commissioner of Police.[992]
   On 31 October, the Police attacked the peaceful demonstrators leaving
   about 80 people dead, and burned Umuechem to the ground, destroying
   495 houses.[993] No evidence of a threat by the villagers was found by the
   Judicial Commission of Inquiry set up by the Government. The Commission
   concluded that the Mobile Police had displayed 'a reckless disregard for lives
   and property.'[994] No compensation has been paid to the families of those
   killed or whose homes were destroyed and neither has any of the perpetrators
   been brought to book for these heinous crimes.[995]

Similar massacres took place against the Odioma people in 2005.[996] In most cases,
oil companies actively supported the suppression of anti-oil protests by providing
both financial and logistic support to the state security forces. For instance, it
was reported that Chevron helicopters and boats were used in attacks on anti-
oil protesters in 1998 and 1999 and a secret memo from May 1994 revealed that
oil MNCs provided the infamous Rivers State Internal Security Task Force with
financial assistance which they used to suppress the anti-oil protesters in Ogoni
area.[997] The then Chairman of the Rivers State Internal Security Task Force, Major

---

[990]   Human Rights Watch, *The Price of Oil: Corporate Responsibility and Human Rights Violations
        in Nigeria's Oil Producing Communities, op. cit.*, p.112.
[991]   *Ibid.*
[992]   *Ibid.*
[993]   Christian Aid, Christian Aid, *Behind the mask, Sustained Misery: Shell in the Niger Delta*, at
        www.evb.ch/cm_data/public/Shell%20Award%20Nominierung_Behind%20the%20mask_0.
        pdf [accessed 7 March 2010].
[994]   Rivers State Government, Report of the Judicial Commission of Inquiry into the Umuechem
        Disturbances, quoted in Human Rights Watch, *The Price of Oil: Corporate Responsibility and
        Human Rights Violations in Nigeria's Oil Producing Communities, op. cit.*, p.112.
[995]   *Ibid.*, pp.112–113.
[996]   E. Courson, *Odi Revisited?: Odi and State Violence in Odioma, Brass LGA, Bayelsa State*,
        Niger Delta Economies of Violence Working Paper No. 7-r, at http://geography.berkeley.edu/
        ProjectsResources/ND%20Website/NigerDelta/WP/7-Courson.pdf [accessed 3 March 2010].
[997]   Jedrzej George Frynas, "The Oil Industry in Nigeria: Conflict Between Oil Companies
        and Local People", in Jedrzej George Frynas and Scott Pegg (eds) (2003), *Transnational
        Corporations and Human Rights*, Palgrave Macmillan, New York, pp.99–114 at 105.

Paul Okuntimo, wrote in the same memo that 'Shell operations are impossible unless ruthless military operations are undertaken for smooth economic activities to commence.'[998] The above revealed the reign of violence visited on the Niger Delta people by the State (in connivance with the oil companies) through the use of the Police and the Army to suppress protests of the people against the destruction of their environment and to seek improved livelihoods. A situation in which people defending their land, and God-given natural resources, were treated to bullets. It is likely that the level of death and destruction in the Niger Delta in the last decade is comparable to that witnessed during the recent invasion of Iraqi with thousands dead, tens of thousands injured and hundreds of thousands (perhaps millions) displaced.[999]

Although Ken Saro-Wiwa and the other eight Ogonis were ostensibly charged and tried for murder, it is obvious to the world that they were actually arrested and executed for expressing their discontent with the environmental harm caused by Shell and the Government in their native Ogoniland. These extrajudicial killings were committed, ostensibly, to rid of from the Niger Delta region criminals that engages in illegal oil bunkering, pipeline vandalization and kidnapping of oil workers. Unfortunately, the security forces unleash their reign of terror on those who have not committed any crime but have simply protested at oil operations by the MNCs and the use made by the Government of the oil revenues, in the exercise of their rights to freedom of expression, assembly, and association.[1000] Even today, many communities in the Niger Delta live under heavy military surveillance – the Joint Military Task Force established in 2003 – all in the bid to ensure the protection of oil installations and the continued flow of crude oil.[1001] While there may be legitimate concerns on security issues, relating to the kidnappings of oil workers, inter-communal conflicts in the region, among others, these do not justify the ongoing human rights abuse being perpetrated by the security agents in the Niger Delta region.

More than 50 years of oil MNCs activity in the Niger Delta has led to a very high level of water and air pollution, thousands of oil spills,[1002] and more flared

---

[998]   Memo written by Major Paul Okuntimo, to the then Military Governor of Rivers State, Lt. Col. Dauda Komo, 12 May 1994, quoted in International Crisis Group Policy Briefing, *Nigeria: Ogoni Land after Shell, op. cit.,* p.4.

[999]   Silvia Federici, *Struggles on the Nigerian Oil Rivers*, at www.radicalpolytics.org/caffentzis/10-struggles_nigerian_oil_rivers.pdf [accessed 3 March 2010].

[1000]   Arvind Ganesan, "Human Rights, the Energy Industry, and the Relationship with Home Governments", in Asbjørn Eide *et al.* (eds) (2000), *Human Rights and the Oil Industry*, Intersentia, Groningen-Oxford, p.57.

[1001]   In the course of this research, I carried out a field trip to some of the communities in the Niger Delta region, including Ubeji and Iwherekan in Delta State. These communities were highly militarised. They were surrounded by a sizeable number of military personnel, thus giving the impression that the war in the region is not over.

[1002]   It has been estimated that more than 300 oil spills occur in the region per year. See, Emmanuel O. Emmanuel of the Port Harcourt-based Centre for Social and Corporate Responsibility (CSCR), in "Oil and Conflict in Nigeria", *The Corporate Examiner*, Vol. 33, No. 5, 15 (2005). However, the U.S. Energy Information Administration quotes more than 4,000 spills in

gas than all other countries, except Russia. During the course of my fieldwork to some Niger Delta communities, such as Ubeji and Iwherekan, in Delta State in January 2011, in order to understand the impact of the oil exploratory activities on the people and the environment, the most persistent complaint was about the effects of the oil pollution and gas flaring. For example, in the Ubeji community in Delta State, with a population of about 10,000 inhabitants, as reported by the 2006 Nigeria's National Population Census,[1003] and which is host to the Warri Refining and Petrochemical Company and the Nigeria Gas Company, the community receives almost all the refinery wastes containing oil residues, solid waste disposal and atmospheric emissions, as there is no pit dug by the Government through which the waste could be properly channeled into. The water in the community is all polluted and the gas flares from the refinery enveloped the community. The community leaders interviewed said that the pollution had not only 'spoiled' their land but their health had equally been adversely affected. When asked why they think these impacts are caused by oil exploitation, Paul Eneuntowose Keku, one of the community leaders retorted: 'In the past, everything was okay with us in that we never experienced all these. But since the commencement of oil exploitation in the community, we have never had it as good… And it seems reasonable to assume that these negative developments are signs of the impacts of oil exploitation in the community.' Each day several local inhabitants of the Niger Delta lose their lives from gas flare-induced cancer, pollution of the water and air, or destruction of their means of livelihoods. Gas flaring has also been said to lead to local and global warming, loss of fertility in soils and the strange growth of fauna and plants, resulting in hunger, starvation and ultimately the slow death of people in the Niger Delta region. During the field work carried out by the researcher to Awoye, in Ilaje community of Ondo State, in January 2011, the elders and youths of the community interviewed complained, *inter alia*, that the land is becoming uninhabitable, and the community may likely disappear. Being close to the ocean, they stressed that the seismic activities of Chevron Nigeria Ltd., have exposed the community to the incursions, thus making the community live in perpetual fear. Several inhabitants have been displaced with most of their means of livelihood destroyed. The dangers are that community, faced with the threat of being submerged, may be forced to relocate and this could lead to the problem of environmental refugees with its attendant socio-economic problems.

The right to life is not limited to protection against the termination of life; it also involves any activities whose effects may cause danger to life. As a normative principle in the contemporary framework of human rights, it includes a very wide variety of rights loosely connected together around the four issues of the

---

Nigeria between 1960 and 2003. See 'Nigeria: Environmental Issues,' July 2003, at www.eia. doe.gov/emeu/cabs/Nigenv.htm, quoted in International Crisis Group Africa Report, *Fuelling the Niger Delta Crisis*, Africa Report No. 118, 28 September 2006, p.19.

[1003] Marcus O. Edino *et al.*, Perceptions and attitudes towards gas flaring in the Niger Delta, Nigeria, 30 *Environmentalist* 67–75 at 69 (2010).

termination, prevention, preservation and fulfillment of human life.[1004] The right to life is perhaps the most basic human right from which all other human rights derive their roots, and once the right to life is infringed, all other rights of the individual are automatically affected. As stated by the African Commission, 'the right to life is the fulcrum of all other rights. It is the fountain through which other rights flow, and any violation of this right without the due process amounts to arbitrary deprivation.'[1005] The relationship between the right to life and the environment is such that serious environmental harm will have a far reaching effect on the lives of the people exposed to such harm. And where a claimant can show that he will suffer some risk of death from the impact of environmental degradation arising from oil exploitation, he may be able to claim a violation of his right to life. The Supreme Court of Nepal has categorically stated, in *Surya Dhungel* v. *Godavary Marble Industry*,[1006] that a clean and healthy environment is a part of the entirety of life. Therefore, a polluted environment is a threat to life and it is one of the most important obligations of the State to protect the environment. Again, in *Advocate Prakashmani Sharma* v. *His Majesty's Government (HMG), Cabinet Secretariat and others*,[1007] the Supreme Court emphasized the adverse effects of the polluted River Ragmati, situated at the heart of Kathmandu city, on the health of the population living in the city, and issued directions to His Majesty's Government to take necessary action in this regard.

In *Shantistar Builders* v. *Narayan Khimalal Totame*,[1008] the Supreme Court of India found a right to shelter in the right to life; and in *Tellis and ors v. Bombay Municipal Corporation and Ors*,[1009] the Supreme Court in India derived a right to livelihood from the right to life.

The case of *Awas Tingni Mayagna (Sumo) Indigenous Community* v. *Nicaragua*,[1010] decided by the Inter-American Court of Human Rights, is equally important. This involved the protection of Nicaraguan forests in lands traditionally owned by the Awas Tingni. The case commenced as an action against the Government-sponsored logging of timber on native lands by Sol del Caribe, S.A. (SOLCARSA), a subsidiary of the Korean company Kumkyung Co.

[1004]   N.J. Udombana, "Weighed in the Balances and found Wanting: Nigeria's Land Use Act and Human Rights", in I.O. Smith (ed) (2003), *The Land Use Act – Twenty Five Years After, op. cit.*, p.68.

[1005]   African Commission in Communication 223/98 – *Forum of Conscience* v. *Sierra Leone*, at Para. 19.

[1006]   Nepal Kanoon Patrika, Special Issue 2052, p.169. The Indian Court also held in *Subhash Kumar v. State of Bihar* (1991) AIR 420 that the right to life guaranteed in the Indian Constitution of 1949 includes the right to a healthy environment. See also the Supreme Court of Pakistan decision in *Zia v. WAPDA* (1994) PLD 693; Bangladesh Supreme Court decision in *Mohiuddin Farooque v. Bangladesh and Others* (1997) 17 BLD (AD) 1.

[1007]   Supreme Court Judgment on Constitutional Issues, Narendra Pathak, p.198.

[1008]   AIR (1990) S.C 630 (India).

[1009]   (1987) L.R. C'Wealth 351, 368–369 (India).

[1010]   Quoted in D. Shelton, *Human Rights and the Environment*, Background Paper No. 2, Joint UNEP-OHCHR Expert Seminar on Human Rights and the Environment 14–16 January 2002, Geneva.

Ltd. The Government had granted SOLCARSA a logging concession without consultation with the Awas Tingni community, although the Government had agreed to consult them consequent to the granting of an earlier logging concession. The Awas Tingni filed a case at the Inter-American Commission, alleging that the Government had violated their rights to cultural integrity, religion, equal protection and participation in Government. The Commission found, in 1998, that the Government had indeed violated the human rights of the Awas Tingni.

In *Yanomami* v. *Brazil*,[1011] the Inter-American Commission established a link between environmental quality and the right to life in response to a petition brought on behalf of the Yanomami Indians of Brazil. The petition alleged that the Government had violated the American Declaration of the Rights and Duties of Man[1012] by constructing a highway through Yanomami territory and authorizing the exploitation of the territory's resources. The Government action had serious effects on the well-being of the community, including, the alteration of their traditional organization, forced displacement to lands unsuitable to their ways of life, emergence of female prostitution, diseases and epidemics, and death of hundreds of Yanomamis. The Commission found that the Government had violated Yanomami rights to life, liberty, and personal security guaranteed by Article I of the Declaration, as well as the rights of residence and movement (Article VIII) and the right to the preservation of their health and well-being contained in Article XI.

It is hoped that Nigerian courts will embrace these liberal, and people-oriented, interpretations of constitutionally protected rights.

4.4.2 THE RIGHT TO HEALTH

The right to health in Nigeria falls within the category of what are called the "second generation" rights, that is, economic, social and cultural rights. In acknowledgment of the importance of this right, various international human rights instruments contain the right to health. Article 25(1) of the UN Universal Declaration of Human Rights 1948 provides that: 'Everyone has the right to a standard of living adequate for the health and well-being of himself and of his family, including ... medical care ... and the right to security in the event of ... sickness, disability ...'

Both the ICCPR and ICESCR provide for the right to health. For instance, Article 12 of the ICESCR provides that the right to health includes 'the rights of everyone to the highest attainable standard of physical and mental health.'

[1011] Case 7615 (Brazil), INTER-AM. CH. R., 1984–1985 Annual Report 24, OEA/Ser. L/V/II.66, doc.10, rev. 1 (1985).

[1012] Pan American Union, Final Act of the Ninth Conference of American States, Res. XXX, at 38 (1948), reprinted in OAS, Basic Documents Pertaining to Human Rights in the Inter-American System (1996).

State parties to the Covenant are required to take steps to achieve the realization of this right. Paragraph 2 of Article 12 provides some steps to be taken, which include the improvement of all aspects of environmental and industrial hygiene; the prevention, treatment and control of epidemic, endemic, occupational and other diseases; and the creation of conditions which will assure to all medical service and medical attention in the event of sickness. A recent resolution adopted by the United Nations General Assembly expresses the link between health and environment, stating that 'all individuals are entitled to live in an environment adequate for their health and well-being.'[1013]

The African Charter is not left out. Article 16 thereof provides that 'every individual shall have the right to enjoy the best attainable standard of physical and mental health.' Paragraph 2 of Article 16 goes on to say that parties to the Charter 'shall take the necessary measures to protect the health of their people and to ensure that they receive medical attention when they are sick.' Article 24 of the African Charter, which entitles all people to a general satisfactory environment favourable to their development, is relevant.

At the national level, section 17(3)(c) of the Constitution of the Federal Republic of Nigeria (CFRN) 1999 (as amended) provides that: 'The State shall direct its policy towards ensuring that ... the health, safety and welfare of all persons in employment are safeguarded and not endangered or abused.'

Section 20 of the Constitution further provides that the State shall protect and improve the environment and safeguard the water, air and land, forest and wildlife of the country. Thus, every human being has the right to environmental protection because the quality of life and health care that an individual enjoys and the survival of man depend entirely on the survival of the natural environment from which man derives his livelihood.[1014]

Since the provisions relating to the right to health under the Nigerian Constitution of 1999 fall within the chapter II provisions on Fundamental Objectives and Directive Principles of State Policy, by virtue of section 6(6)(c) of the Constitution, they are non-justiciable. However, since this right is provided for by international and regional instruments, highlighted above, to which Nigeria is a party, including the African Charter, it therefore implies that the Nigerian courts can have recourse to these international instruments in matters that come before them. Therefore, it does not really matter that the Nigerian Constitution does not expressly provide for an enforceable right to health, so long as it provides for the right to life, which will be endangered if a person's health is threatened by activities sanctioned by the State.[1015] The Nigerian courts can enforce the right to health by reading it into other rights, such as the right to

---

[1013] United Nations General Assembly Resolution 45/94.

[1014] M.T. Ladan, "Human Rights and Environmental Protection", in Obilade, A.O (ed) (1999), *Text for Human Rights Teaching in Schools*, CRP, Lagos, pp.99–100.

[1015] L. Atsegbua, A Critical Appraisal of Environmental Rights Under The Nigerian Constitution, *Benin Journal of Public Law* Vol. 2. No. 1, June, p.50 (2004).

life. The failure of Nigerian Government to take adequate step in preventing the MNCs from polluting the environment (land, water and air), including enacting or enforcing laws, constitute a violation of the rights contained in these domestic and international instruments.

The right to health, which has been closely linked to the right to life, is infringed when environmental degradation pollutes land, air or water as witnessed in the Niger Delta. Researchers have reported that there is a correlation between exposure to oil pollution and the development of health problems. A recent study by Rodriguez-Trigo, *et al* on the health effects of oil spill on workers, volunteers, and local residents associated with five previous oil spills (Exxon Valdez (1989), the Braer oil spill (1993), the Sea Empress oil spill (1996), the Erika oil spill (1999) and the Prestige oil spill (2002)), revealed that workers and local residents do suffer from health effects after oil spills.[1016] The main symptoms found were acute headaches, dizziness, skin rashes, irritation of the eyes and throat, and breathing problems. While the Government and the oil companies take the benefits (oil), the toxins are left permanently in the region. It is also common in the Niger Delta to see women at the flare sites using the toxic flames to dry their *kpokpo garri* and fish. The oil companies have paradoxically counted this as an economic benefit to the local inhabitants.[1017] The result is that the products of these processes, the *kpokpo garri* and the dried fish, are poisoned and harmful to human health.[1018] All those who rely on these locally produced foods – whether from their own production or bought at the market – risk contamination.[1019] These unwholesome practices have continued in this region for ages without the Government or the oil companies educating the people on the adverse impacts of these practices to their health, or providing safe dryers for this purpose.

The Environmental Rights Action and the Climate Justice Programme, in a study carried out in 2005, attempted to assess the harm done by the toxic cocktail of pollutants, including benzene and dioxins, produced by gas flaring. It estimates that in Bayelsa State alone, flaring is likely to cause 49 premature deaths, 4,960

[1016] Rodriguez-Trigo *et al.*, Arch Bronconeumology Vol. 43(11), 628–635 (2007), quoted in the daily green, *The Health Effects of Oil Spills,* at http://dailygreen.com/environmental-news/latest/oil-spill-health-effects-0510 [accessed 3 March 2010]. *See* O.S. Olusi (1981), *Nigerian Oil Industry and the Environment,* Proceedings of the 1981 International Seminar, NNPC, Lagos, quoted in Augustine A. Ikein (1990), *The Impact of Oil on a Developing Country: The Case of Nigeria,* Evans Brothers (Nigeria Publishers) Ltd., Ibadan, p.134.

[1017] L. Oxburgh, a Non-Executive Chairman of Shell, while responding to an interview on the gas flaring in the region insisted that 'the locals appreciate the flares as a heat source to dry their fish.' See Restricted document (1995), Subject My Tel. No: Trial of Ken Saro-Wiwa, February, quoted in Andy Rowell *et al.* (2005), *The Next Gulf: London, Washington and Oil Conflict in Nigeria,* Constable and Robinson, London, p.68.

[1018] Nnimmo Bassey, *Gas Flaring: Assaulting Communities, Jeopardizing the World,* being a paper presented at the National Environmental Consultation hosted by the Environmental Rights Action in conjunction with the Federal Ministry of Environment at Reiz Hotel, Abuja 10–11 December 2008.

[1019] P. Bond and Rehana D. (2005), *Trouble in the Air, Global Warming in the Privatised Atmosphere,* Civil Society Reader, Durban, p.194.

child respiratory illnesses among children, 120,000 asthma attacks, and 8 additional cases of cancer each year.[1020] The resultant adverse effects of gas flaring include premature deaths, respiratory illnesses like coughing and difficulty in breathing, decreased lung function, aggravated asthma, blood disorders, and cancer.[1021] However, in spite of the above study, Shell has continued to maintain that it 'has seen no evidence, not even from sources such as the World Health Organisation, to suggest that flaring has an impact on health.'[1022] Gas flaring is reportedly responsible for fall in life expectancy in the Niger Delta. The Economist reported in 2008 that 'Life expectancy, once just below 70 years in the Niger Delta, is now around 45.'[1023] The above data is more worrisome when it is realized that the oil MNCs and the Nigerian government give priority to how much profits can be maximized rather than the preservation and protection of the environment for safety of the lives and property of the people in the region.[1024]

One important case that illustrates the right to health is the Brazilian case of *Commission v. Brazil*.[1025] Here, as a result of the Brazilian Government's sanctioning of the exploitation of the Amazonians by means of a road-building program, the Yanomami Indians were displaced from their ancestral land and were exposed to epidemics including influenza, TB and measles. They contended that the Government had not adequately taken action to address these health issues. The Commission decided that the failure of the Brazilian Government to fulfill their positive obligations to provide the Yanomami Indians with a park for the protection of their cultural heritage, or to protect them from disease and ill-health, amounted to, *inter alia*, a violation of their right to residence and movement and their right to preservation of health and well-being as recognized in Articles VIII and XI of the American Declaration of the Right and Duties of Man.

Efforts should be made by all stakeholders in the oil sector to guard against the destructive and unsustainable way in which the natural resources in the Niger Delta are exploited. The environment must be adequately protected to ensure the health of the people.

[1020] Environmental Rights Action/Friends of the Earth Nigeria/Climate Justice Programme Report, *Gas Flaring in Nigeria: A Human Rights, Environmental and Economic Monstrosity*, *op. cit.*, p.25.

[1021] *Ibid*; A. Rowell *et al.*, *op. cit.*, p.68.

[1022] B. Briggs, *Strategic Relations Manager at Shell, talked to Shell World UK magazine about one of his hot topics: Shell in Nigeria*, at www.shell.co.uk/home/content/gbr/aboutshell/media_centre/annual_reports_and_publications/swuk/summer_2010/nigeria.html [accessed 23 November 2010].

[1023] Economist, *Nigeria: Another deadline goes up in flames*, 3 April 2008, www.economist.co.uk, quoted in Ecumenical Council for Corporate Responsibility (ECCR) Report, *Shell in the Niger Delta: A Framework for Change*, sponsored by Cordaid, February 2010, p.10, at http://allafrica.com/download/resource/main/main/idatcs/00020052:f1951c2ce1554d231761a0196fbc9b5b.pdf [accessed 10 March 2009].

[1024] L. Atsegbua, A Critical Appraisal of Environmental Rights Under The Nigerian Constitution, *op. cit.*, p.51.

[1025] (1984) Inter-American Commission on Human Rights, Case 7615 (Brazilian).

4.4.3 THE RIGHT TO FOOD

The right to food and the right to life are intertwined and interdependent. Without the right to food, all other rights will be meaningless. Thus, '[w]hether one speaks of human rights or basic human needs, the right to food is the most basic of all. Unless that right is first fulfilled, the protection of other human rights becomes a mockery for those who must spend all their energy merely to maintain life itself.'[1026]

This right is firmly entrenched in international and regional instruments. The UDHR provides that everyone has the right to a standard of living adequate for his/her health and well-being and his/her family, including food.[1027] Also, the ICESCR recognizes that every person has a right to be free from hunger.[1028] Similarly, the Universal Declaration on the Eradication of Hunger and Malnutrition is another important step taken by the international community for the protection of the right to food.[1029] The African Commission has further stated that the right to food is implicit in the African Charter, in such provisions as the right to life,[1030] the right to health,[1031] and the right to economic, social and cultural development.[1032] The CESCR, in its General Comment 12, has explained the meaning of the right to food as stated in the ICESCR.[1033] The right to adequate food is realized when every man, woman and child alone or in community with others, has physical and economic access at all times to adequate food, or the means for its procurement.[1034] According to the Committee, the core content of the right to food implies availability and accessibility. Availability in this sense means that there should be food in a quantity and quality sufficient to satisfy the dietary needs of individuals, free from adverse substances and acceptable within a given culture. Accessibility means that food should be accessible in ways that are sustainable and that do not interfere with the enjoyment of other

---

[1026] Presidential Commission on World Hunger 1980, cited in Philip Alston, "International Law and the Right to Food", in Asbjon Eide *et al.* (eds) (1984), *Food as a Human Right*, United Nations University, Tokyo, p.162.

[1027] UNDHR Article 25.

[1028] ICESCR Article 11.

[1029] Adopted on 16 November 1974 by the World Food Conference convened under General Assembly resolution 3180 (XXVIII) of 17 December 1973; and endorsed by General Assembly resolution 3348 (XXIX) of 17 December 1974; See K.P. Poudyal, *The Protection of Socio-Economic Rights with Special Reference to the Right to Food, Right to Education and the Right to Health*, at www.interights.org/doc/WS2_Poudyal_final.doc. [accessed 3 March 2010].

[1030] Article 4 of the African Charter, *Supra*.

[1031] *Ibid*, Article 16.

[1032] *Ibid*, Article 22. See African Commission, in Communication 155/96- *The Social and Economic Rights Action Center and the Center for Economic and Social Rights v. Nigeria*, at para. 64, quoted in N.J. Udombana, "Weighed in the Balances and Found Wanting: Nigeria's Land Use Act and Human Rights", *op. cit.*, pp.71–72.

[1033] CESR, General Comment No. 12 (1999), Article 11 of the International Covenant on Economic, Social and Cultural Rights, E/C.12/1999/5.

[1034] *Ibid*, para 6.

human rights.[1035] States have a core obligation to respect and protect this right and to fulfill and facilitate its enjoyment by ensuring adequate conditions for that purpose. As part of their obligations to protect people's resource base for food, the UN Committee on CESR has stated that States parties 'should take appropriate steps to ensure that activities of the private business sector and civil society are in conformity with the right to food.'[1036] However, the fulfillment of this right in relation to the Niger Delta people has been jeopardized by the activities of the oil companies and the Government due to the negative impacts of oil exploitation in the region.

The Niger Delta people are predominantly farmers and fishermen, and land is seen as an important commodity. The picture of the Ogoni [Niger Delta] pre 1958 was captured thus:

> "*The Ogonis grow mostly yam, cassava and plantain from which bumper harvest[s] are recorded at the end of each farming season. Ogoni fishermen needed not [to] foray into the deep seas, the banks were rich enough with fishes to make business 'boom.' The soil of Ogoni was rich and loamy. Its natural position on coastal plains, nourished by creeks, rivers running slowly into the Atlantic coast guaranteed successful farming. But all these were before 1958. Right after the discovery of oil in Ogoni land the story turned sour.*"[1037]

Today, farming in Ogoni and other communities in the Niger Delta has become an exercise in futility. The land on which their livelihood depends has been deprived of its fertility through the continuous and irresponsible exploitation practices of the oil MNCs, with lakes, rivers and creeks being polluted through oil spillage and leakage.[1038] When oil spills occur on agricultural farmlands, the crops in the ground do not survive as any crop that comes into contact with the oil are destroyed. The oil on the soil results in water-logging, which decreases soil aeration, and decimates soil organisms such as the worms that are necessary for soil fertility and nutrient rich topsoil formation.[1039] The long term effects of these spills include the delayed germination of crops, stunted growth in trees and low yields. In some cases, the land is rendered unusable for years or even decades.[1040] These long term effects are not usually taken into account in compensation deals,

---

[1035]   *Ibid*, para 8.
[1036]   *Ibid*, para. 27.
[1037]   Rekiya Agnes Sha' aba, "MOSOP and the Ogoni Struggle", in Omotoye Olorode *et al* (eds) (1998), *Ken Saro-Wiwa and the Crises of the Nigerian State*, Committee for the Defence of Human Rights (CDHR) Publications, Lagos, p.73.
[1038]   *Ibid*.
[1039]   Jonas E. Okeagu *et al.*, The Environmental and Social Impact of Petroleum and Natural Gas Exploitation in Nigeria, *Journal of Third World Studies*, Vol. XXIII, No. 1, 199–218 at 206 (2006).
[1040]   Amnesty International, *Nigeria: Petroleum, Pollution and Poverty in the Niger Delta*, *op. cit.*, pp.30–31.

as the people are simply compensated for the loss of the crops on the ground without regard to the long term effects on farm yields. For example, in the Shell Petroleum Development Company of Nigeria (SPDC) Bomu Well II blowout in Ogoniland where an oil spill reportedly rendered over 607 hectares of agricultural land in the community unusable for decades, the compensation allegedly paid was only for the loss of the crops and economic trees on the land at the time of the incident but paid no compensation for the damages to their land. This was later corrected in court in *Shell Pet. Dev. Co. v. Farah*[1041] as the Court awarded a total sum of N4,621,307.00 for the damage to the land.

Even a small leak is capable of wiping out a year's food supply for a family, and its income from products expected to be sold for cash.[1042] Given the overwhelming dependency of the Niger Delta people on mangrove and other protein-based sea food, fish, *inter alia*, the oil spillage may lead to food insecurity in the region.[1043] The consequences for many of the local inhabitants are grave as it not only results in famine but violates their right to gain a living through work. And unlike the Gulf of Mexico explosion on the Deepwater Horizon Oil rig, there is not a massive fund to ensure that the local farmers/fishermen can maintain their life.[1044] It may also lead to forced migration.

Oil spills from high pressure pipelines also may destroy artificial fish ponds used for fish farming. Fish are driven away from in-shore or shallow waters into the deep-sea as a result of flaring and become out of the reach of the local inhabitants who do not have the fishing gadgets to go into deep-sea fishing.[1045] The fish that ingest oil become unpalatable, or even poisonous, to consume.[1046] According to a Food and Agricultural Organization of the United Nations Report on Nigeria in 2007, the Niger Delta is the second largest producer of shrimps in the world, but 'the extensive brackish waters have been depleted of their stocks due to pollution

---

[1041] (1995) 3 NWLR (pt. 382) 148.

[1042] Human Rights Watch Report (1999), *The Price of Oil: Corporate Responsibility and Human Rights Violations in Nigeria's Oil Producing Communities, op. cit.*, p.60.

[1043] The Environment and Conservation Program, Centre for Environment, Human Rights and Development (CEHRD) Report, *Persistent oil spillage at Bodo Creek: unprecedented impacts on ecosystem stability, biodiversity and food security of Ogoni communities*, October 2008, at www.cehrd.org/files/Press_Release_on_Persistent_Oil_Spillage_at_Bodo_Creek.pdf [accessed 3 March 2010]; I. Aigbedion and Iyayi S.E., Environmental Effect of Mineral Exploitation in Nigeria, 2(2) *International Journal of Physical Sciences*, 33–38 at 35–36 (2007).

[1044] Scott McKenzie, *Oil Spills in Nigeria Highlight Lack of Accountability*, 4 September 2010, at www.globalpolicyjournal.com/blog/04/09/2010/oil-spills-nigeria-highlight-lack-legal-accountability [accessed 15 June 2011].

[1045] Legborsi Saro Pyagbara, *The Adverse Impacts of Oil Pollution on the Environment and Wellbeing of a Local Indigenous Community: The Experience of the Ogoni People of Nigeria*, being a paper presented at the International Expert Group Meeting on Indigenous Peoples and Protection of the Environment, at Khabarovsk, Russian Federation, on 27–29 August 2007.

[1046] Kaniye Ebeku, *Oil and the Niger Delta People in International Law: Resource Rights, Environmental and Equity Issues, op. cit.*, p.142.

from the petroleum industry. Mangroves are fast disappearing and with them the important shellfish fishery, with which women had been occupied for ages.'[1047]

The right to food requires that the Nigerian Government should not destroy or contaminate food sources, nor allow private parties to destroy or contaminate food sources, thereby preventing peoples' efforts to feed themselves.[1048] Unfortunately, the Constitution of the FRN 1999, does not expressly mention the right to food under the heading of fundamental rights in Chapter IV. Aspects of this right, however, can be discerned in the Chapter II, dealing with the 'Fundamental Objectives and Directive Principles of State Policy.' For example, Section 16(2)(d) of the Constitution provides that the State shall direct its policy to ensure 'that suitable and adequate shelter, suitable and adequate food ... are provided for all citizens.' As earlier mentioned, the provisions of Chapter II under the Nigerian Constitution are non-justiciable. However, considering the fact that the right to food is an integral part of the right to life, there is ample scope to identify this right through interpretation of the Constitution.[1049]

4.4.4 THE RIGHT TO WATER

Water is important to the continuance of life, and the right to water is closely linked to other fundamental rights. Water is essential for securing livelihoods (right to gain a living by work), for enjoying certain cultural practices (right to take part in cultural life), ensuring environmental hygiene (right to health), to sustain life (right to life), to produce food (right to adequate food), etc. The protection of this right is clearly an essential prerequisite to the enjoyment of many other human rights. Without the fulfillment of the right to water, in terms of ensuring that there is access to a sufficient quantity of safe and clean water, other human rights may be jeopardized.

It is sad to note that among the elements of the newly debated environmental human rights such as the right to life, to housing, to food and water, it is only the full recognition of a right to water that has not taken place in a global human rights instrument.[1050] When conceptualizing water as a human right, three facets must be clearly noted:

a.   accessibility – which entails three elements:

[1047]   Food and Agricultural Organization of the United Nations report on the Federal Republic of Nigeria, FID/CP/NIR, March 2007, at ftp://ftp.fao.org/fi/document/fcp/en/FI_CP_NG.pdf [accessed 13 May 2009].
[1048]   See *SERAC et al. v. Nigeria, Supra* at 65.
[1049]   P.K. Poudyal, *op. cit.*
[1050]   John Scanlon, Angela Cassar and Noemi Nemes, *Water as a Human Rights?*, being a paper delivered at the 7th International Conference on Environmental Law, organized by the Law for a Green Planet Institute, Co-sponsored by IUCN Environmental Law Programme, *Water and the Web of Life*, held at Sao Paulo Brazil 2–5 June 2003, p.20.

–   within safe physical reach for all,
–   affordable for all, and
–   accessible to all in law and in fact;

b.   adequate quality – water for personal or domestic use must be safe;

c.   quantity – water supply must be sufficient and continuous for personal and
domestic uses.[1051]

Few international conventions or human rights instruments focus on all these three aspects of a human right to water. However, the Action Plan from the United Nations Water Conference held in Mar del Plata in 1977 recognized for the first time water as a 'right' declaring that all people have the right to drinking water in quantities and of a quality equal to their basic needs.[1052] The Preamble to the 1977 Declaration inspired Chapter 18 of Agenda 21, which repeated the 'commonly agreed premise' that 'all peoples, whatever their stage of development and their social and economic conditions, have the right to have access to drinking water in quantities and of a quality equal to their basic needs.'[1053] Also, the UN Committee on Economic, Social and Cultural Rights raised these concepts when it stated that 'the human right to water entitles everyone to sufficient, affordable, physically accessible, safe and acceptable water for personal and domestic uses …'[1054] Nigeria is a party to the ICESCR, and so is under an obligation to ensure the availability of sufficient, safe, acceptable water for personal and domestic use by its citizens.[1055]

Further, the Millennium Declaration recognizes that supply of drinking water is not simply a matter of quality but also regards both quantity and access as important; it acknowledges the need 'to stop the unsustainable exploitation of water resources by developing water management strategies at the regional, national and local levels, which promote both equitable access and adequate supplies.'[1056]

Environmentally abusive practices on the part of some oil MNCs in the Niger Delta region of Nigeria have caused devastation of the natural resources of the

---

[1051]   John Scanlon, Angela Cassar and Noemi Nemes, *Ibid*, p.28; Committee on Economic, Social and Cultural Rights, General Comments No. 15 on the Right to Water, UN Doc. E/C. 12/2002/11, 20 January 2003, para. 12.

[1052]   Preamble, United Nations. (1977). Report of the United Nations Water Conference, Mar Del Plaza. March 14–25, 1977. No E 77 II A 12, United Nations Publication, New York.

[1053]   Agenda 21, Chapter 18: Protection of the Quality and Supply of Freshwater Resources, at www.gdrc.org/uem/water/agenda21chapter18.html [accessed 13 May 2009]; See John Scanlon, Angela Cassar and Noemi Nemes, *op. cit.*, p.28.

[1054]   United Nations Economic and Social Council, Committee on Economic, Social and Cultural Rights, General Comment No. 15 (2002). The right to water (Arts. 11 and 12 of the International Covenant on Economic, Social and Cultural Rights) Twenty-ninth Session, Geneva, 11–29 November 2002. E/C. 12/2002/11.

[1055]   Amnesty International, *Nigeria: Petroleum, Pollution and Poverty in the Niger Delta*, op. cit., p.25.

[1056]   Para 23 of the Millennium Declaration (2000) Resolution referred by the General Assembly at its Fifty-fourth session (A/55/2). Adoption by Fifty-fifth Session, quoted in See John Scanlon, Angela Cassar and Noemi Nemes, *op. cit.*

people in the region, particularly the pollution of their water in the last decades. The impact of oil related pollution on underground water is also very grave. When oil spills, or when there is an effluent discharge, it seeps into the ground and becomes mixed in the underground water system.[1057] Once this occurred polluted underground water – leading also to a rise in water borne diseases – takes many years to remedy.[1058] Crude oil contains thousands of different chemicals, many of them toxic, and some known to be carcinogenic, with no determined safe threshold for human exposure.[1059] Three-quarters of all rural communities in the Niger Delta do not have access to safe water supplies, and depend on untreated surface water and unsafe wells for drinking water, which results in serious health problems from waterborne diseases.[1060] Most communities in this region draw their water straight from streams and creeks, with no alternatives being available. A spill can cause severe harm for the population dependent on these streams and creeks as source of their water. Even though the oil MNCs provide water to affected communities when oil spillages occur, the water supplied hardly meets the need of the communities and is for a temporary period only. It was reported that following the major Texaco spill of 1980, 180 people died in one community as a result of the pollution.[1061] In January 1998, Nigerian opposition radio reported that about one hundred villagers from communities affected by a major Mobil spill of 12 January had been hospitalized as a result of drinking contaminated water.[1062] Following the Ogbodo oil spill of June 2001, thousands of the local inhabitants of the 42 communities affected lost access to their main source of drinking water with no alternative sources of clean water being provided by the Government.[1063]

Residents in the Niger Delta region interviewed by Human Rights Watch on several occasions not only complained that spills in their area had made people sick who drank the water, especially children, but also complained that often fish taste of paraffin (kerosene), indicating hydrocarbon contamination. In many communities near oil installations, even when there has been no recent spill, an oily sheen can be seen on the water, which in fresh water areas is usually the

---

[1057] Legborsi Saro Pyagbara, *op. cit.*

[1058] *Ibid.*

[1059] Greenpeace U.K., 'Greenpeace Oil Briefing No. 7: Human Health Impacts of Oil,' (London, January 1993), quoted in Human Rights Watch (1999), *The Price of Oil: Corporate Responsibility and Human Rights Violation in Nigeria's Oil Producing Communities, op. cit.*, pp.66–67.

[1060] Amnesty International Report, *Nigeria: Petroleum, Pollution and Poverty in the Niger Delta, op. cit.*, p.25.

[1061] Finine Fekumo, Civil Liability for Damage Caused by Oil Pollution, p.268, quoted in Human Rights Watch (1999), *The Price of Oil: Corporate Responsibility and Human Rights Violation in Nigeria's Oil Producing Communities, op. cit.*, p.61.

[1062] Radio Kudirat Nigeria, 30 January 1998, as reported by BBC, SWB, 4 February 1998, quoted in Human Rights Watch (1999), *Ibid.*

[1063] Amnesty International, *Nigeria: Petroleum, Pollution and Poverty in the Niger Delta, op. cit.*, pp.25–26.

water the people living there use for drinking and washing.[1064] In April 1997, samples taken from water used for drinking and washing by local villagers were analyzed in the U.S. A sample from Luawii, in Ogoni, where there had been no oil production for four years, had 18 ppm of hydrocarbons in the water, 360 times the level allowed in drinking water in the European Union (EU). A sample from Ukpeleide, Ikwerre, contained 34 ppm, 680 times the EU standard.[1065] Even, litigations against the oil companies for compensation in the event of spills include claims for deaths of children caused by drinking polluted water.[1066] Thus, there may just be a 'little difference between a State that arbitrarily executes persons and a State that knowingly allows water to be poisoned by contaminants.'[1067] In both situations, the State can be held liable for depriving the individuals of the right to life.

Unfortunately, the Nigerian Constitution of 1999, like many other Constitutions in the world does not make any explicit provision for the right to water. The South African Bill of Rights 1996 enshrines an explicit right of access to sufficient water. Section 27(1)(b) of the South African Constitution provides, inter alia, that everyone has the right to have access to sufficient water. Section 27(2) requires the State to take reasonable legislative and other measures, within its available resources, to achieve the progressive realization of the right.

However, with the growing trend of constitutionalism globally, courts increasingly view the constitution as an independent source of substantive law and rights, enforceable even in the absence of implementing legislation.[1068] Courts now recognize that Constitutions can serve as an avenue for developing, implementing, and enforcing environmental protections implicitly or indirectly.[1069] Thus, courts do often rely on the environmental provisions in their Constitutions when protecting water from pollution. Where Constitutions lack environmental provisions, reliance has been placed on the right to life, a provision contained in most Constitutions world-wide.[1070] In the *Port Hope case*,[1071] the complainant alleged before the UN Human Rights Committee that dumping of nuclear wastes within Port Hope, Ontario, was causing large scale pollution of residences, thus

---

[1064] Human Rights Watch (1999), *op. cit.*, p.61.

[1065] S. Kretzmann and Wright S., *Human Rights and Environmental Information on the Royal Dutch/Shell Group of Companies, 1996–1997: An Independent Annual Report,* Rainforest Action Network and Project Underground, San Francisco and Berkeley, CA., May 1997, p.6. The EU standard is 0.05 ppm, quoted in Human Rights Watch (1999), *Ibid.*

[1066] For example, *SPDC v. Chief Caiphas Enoch & two others* (1992) 8 NWLR (pt. 259) 335, in which five children were alleged to have died as a result of drinking oil-contaminated water. See Human Rights Watch (1999), *Ibid.*

[1067] Dinah Shelton, Human Rights and the Environment: What Specific Environmental Rights Have Been Recognized?, *op. cit.,* pp.170–171.

[1068] Environmental Law Institute Research Report (2007), *Constitutional Environmental Law: Giving Force to Fundamental Principles in Africa,* 2nd ed., pp.1–3, 7.

[1069] *Ibid,* p.7.

[1070] See John Scanlon, Angela Cassar and Noemi Nemes, *op. cit.*

[1071] *E.H.P. v. Canada,* Communication No. 67/1980 (27 October 1982), UN. Doc. CCPR/C/OP/1 at 20 (1984), quoted in John Scanlon, Angela Cassar and Noemi Nemes, *Ibid.*

threatening the lives of the people. Though the complaint was declared inadmissible as a result of failure to have exhausted local remedies, the Committee noted that the case 'raises serious issues under Art. 6(1)' of the ICCPR, with regards to a State's obligation to protect human life.

In *Vellore Citizens Welfare Forum* v. *Union of Indian*, the Supreme Court of India held that tanneries had violated a citizen's right to life by discharging untreated effluents into agricultural areas and local drinking water supplies, thereby severely polluting the drinking water.[1072] In Pakistan, the Supreme Court, citing *Shala zia v. WAPDA*,[1073] found in the *General Secretary, West Pakistan Salt Miners Labour Union, Khwra, Khelum* v. *The Director, Industries and Mineral Development, Punjab Lahora*, that mining companies had violated the right of citizens by polluting local drinking water supplies.[1074]

Thus, while there might not be a constitutional right to water, Nigerian courts should be prepared to be creative and to interpret liberally existing constitutional provisions to meet the needs of the communities in the Niger Delta region in terms of accessibility, adequate quality and quantity of clean and safe water.

4.4.5 RIGHT TO CULTURE

Environmental degradation has implications for the right to culture. To the Niger Delta people, land is the abode of the gods. The oil exploration activities have broken their spiritual link to the land. Since they have been prevented from performing their annual fishing (religious) festival, during which they appeased their gods, they have noticed strange and unusual phenomena, such as children suddenly dying while out in the bush without any apparent cause whatsoever.[1075] The point being made here is not to argue for belief in metaphysical afflictions, but rather to demonstrate the unhappiness of the people in the region with the degradation of their environment, the desecration or seizure of any of their land and its impact on their culture and tradition. The Shell oil spill that occurred in

---

[1072]   *Vellore Citizens Welfare Reform* v. *Union of India*, 1996 A.I.R (SC) 2715 (1996); *Advocate Prakashmani Sharma* v. *HMG, Cabinet Secretariat and others*, Supreme Court Judgment on Constitutional Issues, Narendra Pathak, p.198.

[1073]   PDL 1994 Supreme Court 693 where the Supreme Court interpreted the constitutionally protected rights to life and dignity to include the right to a healthy environment.

[1074]   *General Secretary, West Pakistan Salt Miners Labour Union Khwra, Khelom* v. *The Director, Industries and Mineral Development, Punjab Lahora*, Human Rights Case No. 120 of 1993, 1994 S.C.M.R 2061 (1994). Also, the Supreme Court in Nepal held in *LEADERS, Inc.* v. *Godawi Marble Industries* (Supreme Court Nepal, 31 October 1995), that a marble mining operation contaminating water supplies and the soil violated the constitutional right to life of the nearby residents. See generally See John Scanlon, Angela Cassar and Noemi Nemes, *op. cit.*, pp.47–50.

[1075]   Constitutional Rights Project (CRP) (1999), *Land, Oil and Human Rights in Nigeria's Delta Region, op. cit.*, p.18.

Yorla Well Head in Ogoniland on 29 April 2001 occured beside a sacred forest.[1076]
The oil companies blatantly disregarded the Nigerian laws (Petroleum Act) which
forbade them from extracting oil in sacred shrines and forests.

Another serious impact of oil pollution on the Niger Delta communities is
that it has led to the death and possible extinction of medicinal plants and herbs
that are rooted in these communities' traditional medicine, and which have deep
spiritual significance to the community.[1077] This is because most of these herbs
and plants are located in sacred groves, shrines and forests, which have been
destroyed in the course of oil exploitation and *via* the toxicity of oil pollution.[1078]
The erosion of the cultural rights of the Niger Delta people can also be seen in
the gradual extinction of their languages, which is attributed to the imposition of
the culture of the dominant ethnic groups. The Ogoni Bill of Rights, for example,
states that the 'the languages of Gokana and Khana are undeveloped and are
about to disappear, whereas other Nigerian languages are being forced on us'.[1079]
The language of most of the Niger Delta communities is fast disappearing due
to the oil exploitation activities, thereby making the region a 'melting pot', in
which all nationalities are assimilated. The indigenous language of the people,
which is a means of communication has reached almost a stage of extinction
('pidgin English' has become the lingua franca (unofficial)), thereby eroding the
people's identity and solidarity.[1080] The right of the people in this region to enjoy
their cultural rights is hindered by the loss of their languages, positive and tested
traditional practices and social values to environmental degradation.

Unfortunately, the right to culture is not recognized under the Nigerian
Constitution. The only portion in the 1999 Constitution that talks about the
protection of Nigerian culture is section 21. It provides that the State shall:

(a) protect, preserve and promote the Nigerian cultures which enhance human
    dignity and are consistent with the fundamental objectives as provided in
    Chapter II; and
(b) encourage development of technological and scientific studies which enhance
    cultural values.

However, section 21, which falls under chapter II of the Constitution is non-
justiciable. The UN Human Rights Committee has interpreted Articles 27(2) of
the Covenant on Civil and Political Rights in a broad manner, observing that
culture manifests itself in many forms, including a particular way of life associated

---

[1076] Fr. Kevin O'Hara, Niger Delta: Peace and Co-operation Through Sustainable Development,
Environmental Policy and Law, 31 (6), pp.302–308 at 305 (2001).
[1077] Legborsi Saro Pyagbara, *op. cit.*
[1078] *Ibid.*
[1079] See para. 12 of Ogoni Bill of Rights.
[1080] Nsirim-Worlu Heoma, 'Oil Production and Changing Cultural Pattern in Ikwerre Ethnic
Nation: A Case of Obio-Akpor,' *Academic Research International,* Vol. 2 No. 1, 102–110 at 106,
108 (2012).

with the use of land resources, especially in the case of indigenous peoples.[1081] That right may include such traditional activities as fishing or hunting, and the right to live in reserves protected by law. The protection of these rights is directed towards ensuring the survival and development of the cultural, religious and social identity of the minorities concerned, thus enriching the fabric of society as a whole.[1082] The UN Human Rights Committee issued a decision, in *Lubikon Lake Band* v. *Canada*,[1083] that oil and gas exploration deprived the Band, a self-identified, relatively autonomous, socio-cultural and economic group, of its right to live its traditional way of life and culture and thus constituted a violation of Article 27 of the ICCPR.

In the Columbian case of *Organización Indígena de Antioquia* v. *Codechoco & Madarien*,[1084] the indigenous peoples claimed that the logging of the forests in their territory violated their human rights. The court held that the devastation of the indigenous forests affected their cultural and ethnic integrity and that the communities were likely to suffer future damage due to their cultural dependency on the tropical forest in which they dwelt.

In addition to relying on section 21 of the Constitution of the Federal Republic of Nigeria, 1999 (as amended), which requires the State to protect, preserve and promote Nigerian cultures, Nigerian courts can borrow a leaf from the decisions from other jurisdictions discussed above to identify the threats to people's cultural survival as a result of harmful effects on the environment through degradation.

4.4.6 RIGHT TO PROPERTY AND TO HOUSING

The right to property implies a right of ownership. It includes a right to have access to one's property and the right not to have one's property invaded or encroached upon.[1085] This right is recognized by international law[1086] and by municipal laws.

[1081]   Shelton D., *Human Rights and the Environment: Jurisprudence of Human Rights Bodies*, Background Paper No. 2, being a paper presented at the Joint UNEP-OHCHR Expert Seminar on Human Rights and the Environment, 14–16 January 2002.

[1082]   General Comment 23 paras. 7, 9, issued by the United Nations Human Rights Committee, in Compilation of General Comments and General Recommendations adopted by Human Rights Treaty Bodies, UN Doc. HRI/GEN/1/Rev. 3 (1997) at 41, quoted in D. Shelton, *Ibid.*

[1083]   Communication No. 167/1984 (26 March 1990), UN Doc. Supp. No. 40 (A/45/40) at 1 (1990).

[1084]   Juzgado Tercero Agrario del circulo Judicial de Antioquia, Medellin. 24 February 1993.

[1085]   See African Commission, in Communication 140/94, 141/94, and 145/95- Constitutional Rights Projects, *Civil Liberties Organisation and Media Rights Agenda* v. *Nigeria*, Thirteenth Annual Activity Report 1999–2000, Annex V. (hereinafter called *CRP et al.* v. *Nigeria*), at para. 54.

[1086]   See UDHR (art. 25), the ICESCR (art. 11), the ICERD (art. 5(e) (iii), and the Convention on the Rights of Child (CRC) (art. 27(3)). The following also supports Housing rights- Vancouver Declaration on Human Settlements (Sec. III(8)); the Declaration on the Right to Development (art. 8(1)); The Draft Declaration on the Rights of Indigenous Peoples (arts. 10, 11(c), 22, 23, 25, 26, 27 and 31; and the UN Sub-Commission on the Prevention of Discrimination and Protection of Minorities Resolution 1994/8.

For example, the UDHR provides that '[e]veryone has the right to own property alone as well as in association with others. No one shall be arbitrarily deprived of his property.'[1087] In the same vein, the African Charter provides that '[t]he right to property shall be guaranteed. It may only be encroached upon in the interest of public need or in the general interest of the community and in accordance with the provisions of appropriate laws.'[1088]

The right to housing which is regarded as a component of the right to property connotes 'the right to live somewhere in security, peace and dignity.'[1089] Its enjoyment, like every other right, must not be subject to any form of discrimination and should be ensured to all persons irrespective of income or access to economic resources.[1090]

The rights to property and housing are recognized by the 1999 Constitution of Nigeria. Aside from the non-justiciable provision of section 16(2)(d) of the Constitution, which refers to the obligation of the State among others to direct its policy towards ensuring 'that suitable and adequate shelter' is provided for all citizens, the Constitution in its justiciable part provides in section 43 the right of every Nigerian 'to acquire and own immovable property anywhere in Nigeria.' This includes, by implication, land and housing.[1091]

The Constitution not only forbids the compulsory acquisition of interests in movable and immovable property without prompt and adequate compensation,[1092] but gives the claimant to compensation 'a right of access for the determination of his interest in the property and the amount of compensation to a court of law or tribunal or body having jurisdiction in that part of Nigeria.'[1093]

This right to housing means that the Government must provide socio-economic and political conditions adequate for the realization of that right and must adopt legislative and other measures to prevent any violation of the individual's right to adequate housing.[1094] With the promulgation of the Land Use Act (LUA) 1978, Nigerians were divested of their land, which became vested in the Governor to hold for the benefit of Nigerians.[1095] This form of expropriation of land, or *de facto* confiscation of land, has impaired the issue of land ownership.

[1087] See Universal Declaration of Human Rights, adopted 10 December 1984, Article 17.

[1088] *Supra*, Article 14.

[1089] Committee on Economic, Social and Cultural Rights, 'The Right to Adequate Housing (Art. 11(1) of the Covenant),' General Comment No. 4 in Committee on Economic, Social and Cultural Rights: Report on the Sixth Session, ECOSOC Official Records, 1992, Suppl. No. 3, UN Doc. E/1992/23, at para. 7.

[1090] See N.J. Udombana, "Weighed in the Balances and Found Wanting: Nigeria's Land Use Act and Human Rights", *op. cit.*, p.76.

[1091] *Ibid*, pp.76–77.

[1092] Section 44(1)(a) of the CFRN, 1999.

[1093] Section 44(1)(b) of the CFRN, 1999.

[1094] E. Onyekpere, The Right to Adequate Housing – The Concept of Legal Security of Tenure, 5(2) *J. Hum. Rts. L. & Prac.* 44, 45 (1997), quoted in N.J. Udombama, "Weighed in the Balances and Found Wanting: Nigeria's Land Use Act and Human Rights," *op. cit.*, pp.77–78.

[1095] Section 1 of the LUA, Cap L5, Laws of the Federation of Nigeria 2004.

Nigerians can no longer alienate any right of occupancy without the consent of the Governor.[1096] The Federal Government relying on the LUA, and other draconian legislation like the Petroleum Act 1969,[1097] and the Lands (Title Vesting, etc.) Decree No. 52 of 1993[1098] has seized mineral resources of the people of the Niger Delta, without adequate compensation to the people whose land were so seized. The LUA in section 47(2) sadly provides that '[n]o court shall have jurisdiction to inquire into any compensation paid or to be paid under this Act.' The courts have, however, declared this provision to be void to the extent of its inconsistency with Constitutional provisions.[1099]

Various examples of violations of the right to housing of the people of the Niger Delta can be cited. The most serious case in which an oil company was directly implicated in abuses by the security forces was the incident at Umuechem in October 1990 where the Mobile Police, summoned by Shell, attacked peaceful demonstrators with tear gas and gunfire, killing eighty unarmed demonstrators and destroying or badly damaging 495 houses.[1100] Events in Ogoniland and other communities in the Niger Delta are not different. In 1987, following a protest against Shell by the Iko community in Akwa Ibom State, the Mobile Police burnt forty houses to the ground. Again, in 1995, the village of Iko was badly affected by a malfunctioning flare which was flooded by salt water at high tide, allowing salt from sea water subsequently to be vaporized and shot out all over the village, killing vegetation and corroding sheet metal roofing.[1101]

The forceful taking over of people's property, forced evictions, flares corroding metal roofs, and the burning and destruction of homes, etc, are extremely traumatic events, causing physical, psychological and emotional distress; and entailing loss of means of economic sustenance, increased impoverishment, the break up families, an increase in levels of homelessness and in some cases even deaths.[1102] It is submitted that the right to shelter obliges the Nigerian Government not to destroy the housing of its citizens and to prevent the violation of any

---

[1096]   See Section 22 of the LUA, *Savannah Bank* v. *Ajilo* (1989) 1 NWLR (pt. 97) 305; *Igbum* v. *Nyarinya* (2001) 9 WRN 15 (CA).

[1097]   See Petroleum Act, Cap. P10 LFN 2004.

[1098]   See Lands (Title Vesting etc.) Decree No. 52 of 1993 which vests in the Federal Government the title to all lands within 100 metres limit of the 1967 shoreline of Nigeria as well as all lands reclaimed from any lagoon, sea or ocean in or bordering Nigeria. The Decree which was promulgated by General Babangida after he had left office, was backdated to 1977, in clear violation of constitutional and international human rights instruments, including the African Charter. See Udombana N.J., *op. cit.*, p.81.

[1099]   See *Nkwocha* v. *Governor of Anambra State* (1984) 6 SC 362; *Lemboye* v. *Ogunseyi* (1990) 6 NWLR (pt. 155) 210.

[1100]   Human Rights Watch (1999), *The Price of Oil: Corporate Responsibility and Human Rights Violations in Nigeria's Oil Producing Communities, op. cit.*, p.112.

[1101]   Environmental Rights Action, *Shell in Iko*; Human Right Watch Interview with Powell B., June 20, 1998, quoted in Human Rights Watch (1999), *Ibid* p.128.

[1102]   See N.J. Udombana, "Weighed in the Balances and Found Wanting: Nigeria's Land Use Act and Human Rights", *op. cit.*, p.85.

individual's right to housing by any other individual or non-State actor. Where
such infringements occur, it should act to preclude occurences.

4.4.7   RIGHT TO RESPECT FOR ONE'S PRIVATE LIFE AND HOME

The right to the respect for private life and the interrelated right to peaceful
enjoyment of one's possessions primarily entail the protection of the individual
against arbitrary interference by public authorities with his private and family
sphere.[1103] This is provided for in section 37 of the 1999 Constitution of Nigeria
as one of the fundamental rights available to all citizens, and is justiciable. The
section provides that 'the privacy of citizens, their homes, correspondence,
telephone conversations and telegraphic communications is hereby guaranteed
and protected.' These rights, which aim to secure to the individual a sphere within
which he can freely pursue the fulfillment and development of his personality,
encompass a person's intimate life and physical well-being, including , his house,
and, to some extent, his workplace.[1104] The enjoyment of this right can be severely
impaired by environmental conditions, such as noise pollution or other acts of
nuisance. Environmental degradation caused by the impact of oil exploitation
has seriously undermined the Niger Delta people's rights to home, privacy and
family life. They are badly affected by pollution – noise, air, water, land – of all
kinds, as a result of the exploration activities of the MNCs with little or no regard
for the lives of the people living in these areas. Noises from outdated machinery
and equipment; and the roaring noise, intense heat and other discomforts from
the gas flares are common occurrences. Nuisance is created everywhere without
any efforts to abate it. Communities in this area are exposed to various health
problems, including, hearing problems. If oil workers fall sick, they are airlifted to
company hospitals in Port Harcourt or Lagos; the local people, meanwhile, have
little or no health care available to them other than traditional remedies.

The European Court of Human Rights decision in *López Ostra* v. *Spain*,[1105]
exemplifies environmental harm as a breach of the right to private life and the

---

[1103] Article 17 ICCPR; Article 8 ECHR; Article 11 ACHR; Article 14 ACHPR, quoted in the World Conservation Union Paper on *Human Rights and Environment: Overlapping Issues*, at www.ciel.org. [accessed 3 March 2010].

[1104] World Conversation Union Paper, *Ibid*. Note that the ECHR interpreted the term 'home' in *Niemietz* v. *Germany* (1992) 16 EHRR 97, Par. 30 as applicable also to professional-business premises, under article 8 ECHR.

[1105] (1994) Series A No. 303-C; (1995) 20 EHHR 277, ECtHR, quoted in World Conservation Union Paper, *Ibid*. See also *Guerra & others* v. *Italy*, 26 EHHR 357 (1998) ECtHR; *Hatton and Others* v. *United Kingdom*, Eur. Ct. H.R. 17 (2001) where the ECHR accepted that excessive noise could constitute a violation of art.8. *Moreno Gomez* v. *Spain*, Application no. 4143/02, Chamber Judgment of 16 November 2004, Unpublished. A similar approach was taken by the IACHR in *Maya Indigenous Communities of the Toledo District* v. *Belize*, Case 12.053, IACHR. Report 40/04 (2004) at 153, 194.

home. The case is about the State's failure to protect the home, private and family life of one of its citizens from the pollution caused by a waste treatment facility. In this case, the Spanish State failed to regulate a privately-owned waste treatment facility that was causing air pollution, which made local residents' living conditions unbearable and caused them serious health problems. The applicant alleged that there had been a violation of her right to respect for her home that made her private and family life impossible (Article 8 ECHR) as a result of the waste treatment facility located a few metres away from her home and also violated her rights to physical integrity (Article 3 ECHR). It was not proven incontrovertibly that there was a causal link between her health damage suffered and the pollutants released from the plant. The European Court of Human Rights found the State responsible for the right to respect for her home and private life, since serious pollution can impact an individual's well-being and prevent her from enjoying her home in such a way that her private and family life is adversely affected. The Court held that the State had failed to succeed in striking a fair balance between the interest of the city's economic development in having a waste-treatment plant, and the applicant's effective enjoyment of her individual right to respect for her home and her private and family life. Therefore, it held that there had been a violation of Article 8 of the Convention and awarded compensation. The Court held, however, that the conditions suffered by the applicant and her family did not amount to degrading treatment within the meaning of Article 3.

In *Selçuk and Asker* v. *Turkey*,[1106] the applicants argued that the deliberate burning of their homes by Turkish security forces was, *inter alia*, a violation of their rights to freedom from inhuman treatment, respect for their homes and peaceful enjoyment of their property. They also claimed that the particular circumstances of the destruction of their homes and their eviction from their village, constituted a breach of Article 3 of the European Convention, which states that no one shall be subject to torture or to inhuman or degrading treatment or punishment. The European Court of Human Rights held that there had been a violation of the applicants' rights to peaceful enjoyment of their property and their right to respect for their homes. Furthermore, the court held that, bearing in mind the manner in which the applicants' homes were destroyed, and their personal circumstances, they had been subject to inhuman treatment in violation of Article 3. Due to the absolute nature of Article 3, any such violation is unjustifiable, even in times of national emergency.

In *Fadeyeva* v. *Russia*,[1107] the applicant alleged that there had been a violation of Article 8 of the Convention on account of the State's failure to protect her

---

[1106]   European Court of Human Rights, App. No. 00023185/94, Judgment 24 April 1998, quoted in Centre on Housing Rights and Evictions, *50 Leading Cases on Economic, Social and Cultural Rights: Summaries*, Working Paper No. 1, June 2003, at www.cohre.org. [accessed 5 March 2010].

[1107]   *Fadeyeva* v. *Russia*, 2005-IV Eur. Ct. H.R. 255, 293 (2005), Application no. 55723/00, Judgment 9 June 2005.

private life and home from severe environmental nuisance arising from the
industrial activities of the Severstal steel-plant. The court observed that the actual
detriment to the applicant's health and well-being reached a level sufficient to
bring it within the scope of Article 8. It therefore found the Russian Government
to be in violation of Article 8 because of its lack of attention to existing domestic
rules to protect citizens from pollution.

These cases may be highly significant in similar Nigerian litigation.

4.4.8 RIGHT TO DIGNITY OF THE HUMAN PERSON

The Constitution of the FRN, 1999, under section 34(1) provides that: 'Every
individual is entitled to respect for the dignity of his person, and accordingly, (a)
no person shall be subjected to torture, or to inhuman or degrading treatment.'
In addition, section 17(2)(b) states that '... human dignity shall be maintained
and enhanced.' Although these provisions of the Constitution do not explicitly
prohibit rape and other sexual violence they clearly extend to offences of this
nature. Besides, the Criminal Code[1108] (as applicable in the Southern part) and
the Penal Code[1109] (as applicable in the Northern part) makes rape a criminal
offence punishable by imprisonment. The Protocol to the African Charter
on Human and Peoples' Rights on the Rights of Women in Africa,[1110] ratified
by Nigeria on 18 February 2005, provides in Article 3 for the right to dignity.
Article 4 dealing with the rights to life, integrity and security of the person states
that 'Every woman shall be entitled to respect for her life and the integrity and
security of her person. All forms of exploitation, cruel, inhuman or degrading
punishment and treatment shall be prohibited.' It requires States to enact and
enforce laws to prohibit, prevent and punish 'all forms of violence against women
including unwanted or forced sex whether the violence takes place in private or
public.'[1111] It further obliges States to 'prohibit and condemn all forms of harmful
practices which negatively affect the human rights of women and which are
contrary to recognised international standards.'[1112] Rape constitutes torture, as
defined by Article 1 of the International Convention Against Torture and Other
Cruel, Inhuman, or Degrading Treatment or Punishment.[1113] Rape also violates

---

[1108]   Cap C38 LFN 2004, sections 357–358, 218, 222.

[1109]   Cap P3, LFN 2004, sections 282, 285.

[1110]   Adopted by the Second Ordinary Session of the Assembly of the Union, Maputo, 11 July 2003,
        at www.achpr.org/english/women/protocolwomen.pdf [accessed 5 July 2009].

[1111]   *Ibid*, Article 4(2).

[1112]   *Ibid*, Article 5.

[1113]   [T]he term 'torture' means any act by which severe pain or suffering, whether physical or men-
        tal, is intentionally inflicted on a person for such purposes as ... punishing him for an act he or
        a third person has committed or is suspected of having committed ... or for any reason based
        on discrimination of any kind, when such pain or suffering is inflicted by or at the instigation
        of or with the consent or acquiescence of a public official or other person acting in an official
        capacity. See also Human Rights Watch/Africa (1995), *Nigeria: The Ogoni Crisis: A Case Study*

the prohibitions against torture in Article 7 of the ICCPR.[1114] It can therefore be seen from the above constitutional and statutory provisions and international instruments that States have obligations to ensure the protection of the dignity of individual citizens, and to prevent and remedy any forms of torture.

Women and girls in the Niger Delta have been subjected to various forms of inhuman and degrading treatment, particularly rape and all forms of sexual slavery, in the hands of Nigerian security personnel sent on peace missions to the region, including those deployed to guard oil flow stations. For example, following a demonstration by youths in Choba against a pipeline construction company called Wilbros Nigeria Ltd. (a subsidiary of Wilbros Group, a US company) on 28 October 1999, the military personnel that were sent to Choba unleashed a reign of terror on the community. The rapes of women by the military personnel were captured on film by a journalist and published in the Nigerian daily press.[1115] The same calamity also befell Ogoniland in November 1993 where the Nigerian military, in a three year campaign, looted, murdered, burnt, raped and perpetrated other inhuman and degrading treatments on the community. During these periods, Ogoni women were sexually harassed, assaulted and battered by the military personnel. The women described in detail, in interviews with members of the Federation of Ogoni Women's Organisations (FOWA), the sexual violence they went through in the hands of the Nigerian Military personnel, purportedly on a peace mission to their community. One woman reported:

"One day we were demonstrating. We sang as we moved from our town to Ken Khana. Singing near the main road we met face to face with the army ... they asked us to lie down on the road. After using the koboko (whip) on us they started kicking us with their foot (sic). They dragged some of the women into the bush. We were naked, our dresses were torn, our wrappers [a loose flowing outer garment] were being loosed by a man who is not your husband. They tore our pants and began raping us in the bush. The raping wasn't secret because about two people are raping you there. They are raping you in front of your sister. They are raping your sister in front of your mother. It was like a market."[1116]

---

of *Military Repression in Southeastern Nigeria*, at www.unhcr.org/refworld/docid/3ae6a7d8c.html [accessed 26 September 2010].

[1114] International Covenant on Civil and Political Rights, adopted and opened for signature, ratification and accession by General Assembly Resolution 2200A (XXI) of 16 December 1966, entry into force 23 March 1976, in accordance with Article 49. Art. 7 thereof provides that: 'No one shall be subjected to torture or to cruel, inhuman or degrading treatment or punishment ...'

[1115] Sokari Ekine, Women's Responses to State Violence in the Niger Delta, 10 *Feminist Africa* 67–83 at 75 (2008).

[1116] Mrs Kawayorko, quoted in Sokari Ekine, *Ibid*, p.77.

More than 50 allegations of rape by the security forces in Odi in 1999 were recorded
by the Women's Aid Collective (WACOL).[1117] In Ugborodo, Delta State, women
were also allegedly raped by the security personnel during a demonstration in
February 2002, in protest against the perceived failure of Chevron Nigeria Ltd.
to implement a Memorandum of Understanding between it and the community
of Ugborodo. The women reported that soldiers used guns to rape them: 'The
women were stripped naked while guns were pointed into their private parts.'[1118]

From the above, it can be seen that the military personnel sent on peace
missions to the Niger Delta have reportedly used rape as an instrument to
intimidate, humiliate, terrorise, and destroy the pride of the local inhabitants,
and get revenge for attacks on oil installations by the militants. The various acts
of the military personnel in the rapes violate Article 5 of the UN Code of Conduct
for Law Enforcement Officials.[1119] The consequences of sexual violence range from
physical injuries to potential sexually transmitted diseases (including HIV/AIDS),
miscarriages, forced and unwanted pregnancies, single parenting, and traumatic
fistulas – debilitating tears in the tissue of the vagina, bladder, and rectum.[1120]
Besides, it results in stigmas as they are avoided by their spouses, relatives and
communities. It is sad to note that the response of the Nigerian Government to
all these violations of the sexual rights and fundamental freedoms of the Niger
Delta women, by State actors in collaboration with the oil companies, has been
inadequate as it has failed to investigate these heinous crimes and bring the culprits
to justice. The Government cannot claim ignorance, as most of these crimes are
not only reported in the media but some of the victim's interviews have been
shown on national television. Such insensitivity on the part of the Government
to the plight of the women further confirms its little regard to the human rights

---

[1117] Women's Aid Collective (*WACOL*), *A cry for justice: the truth about sexual violence against women in Nigeria*, Enugu, 2003, p.3, quoted in Amnesty International, *Nigeria: Rape – the Silent Weapon*, 28 November 2006, p.14.

[1118] Women Advocates Research and Documentation Centre (WARDC), *The 11-day siege: gains and challenges of women's non-violent struggles in Niger Delta*, Lagos, December 2005, p.47, quoted in Amnesty International, *Ibid*, pp.17–18.

[1119] Code of Conduct for Law Enforcement Officials, adopted by General Assembly Resolution 34/169 of 17 December 1979. Art. 5 provides that: 'No law enforcement official may inflict, instigate or tolerate any act of torture or other cruel, inhuman or degrading treatment or punishment, nor may any law enforcement official invoke superior orders or exceptional circumstances such as a state of war or a threat of war, a threat to national security, internal political instability or any other public emergency as a justification of torture or other cruel, inhuman or degrading treatment or punishment.' Even though the UN Code of Conduct is a non-legally binding instrument, 'the prohibitions on torture and other cruel, inhuman, or degrading treatment have acquired the status of customary international law. As such, the Nigerian Government is legally obligated to uphold them, as well as its treaty commitments.' See Human Rights Watch/Africa, *Nigeria: The Ogoni Crisis: A Case Study of Military Repression in Southeastern Nigeria, op. cit.*

[1120] Alexis Arieff, *Sexual Violence in African Conflicts*, Congressional Research Service, 25 November 2009, at www.fas.org/sgp/crs/row/R40956.pdf [accessed 23 November 2010].

of the local inhabitants of the Niger Delta. The Oputa Panel[1121] was set up by the Government to investigate into human rights violation by the security forces (between 15 January 1966 and 29 May 1999). During the Panel's public hearings, the panel listened to the experiences of victims, including women who had been raped by members of the Nigerian security personnel, and their families. The report of the Panel, which has since been submitted, is yet to be made fully public and none of the victims have been compensated, even more than 10 years later.[1122] Having failed to exercise due diligence to prevent, stop, investigate, or prosecute those soldiers who committed rapes or provide reparation to the victims,[1123] it is submitted that the Nigerian Government has violated the Nigerian Constitution, Articles 2 and 4 of the International Convention Against Torture and the other intersanional human rights instruments discussed above.

4.4.9 THE RIGHT TO INFORMATION

The right to information in the context of environmental protection has at least two components: the right to obtain Government-held information on request and the Government's affirmative duty to apprise the people of environmental dangers and emergencies.[1124] The right to information implies that 'States have to distribute data and information relating to facts, activities, practices or projects with a considerable impact or potential impact on the environment and to provide access to data and information concerning or potentially concerning the environment. This information should cover not just cases of pollution but all the factors likely to cause environmental damage, such as over-exploitation of resources, erosion, floods, earthquakes, etc'.[1125] The right to seek, receive

---

[1121] Oputa Report, Vol. 3, at www.nigerianmuse.com/nigeriawatch/oputa/OputaVolumeThree.pdf [accessed 22 April 2010]. The Human Rights Violations Investigation Commission (HRVIC) or the Oputa Panel was established by the then President Olusegun Obasanjo in 1999. It concluded and presented its findings and recommendations in May 2002 to the President, but the Report has never been officially released. Following the submission of the final Report, several individuals challenged Obasanjo's authority to establish the Commission. The Federal High Court, in February 2003 ruled in favour of the petitioners on the grounds that the 1999 Constitution did not make provision for tribunals of inquiry and the HRVIC did not have authority to summon witnesses from outside the Federal Capital Territory of Abuja. See Centre for the Study of Violence and Reconciliation (CSVR), *Human Rights Violations Investigation Commission, Nigeria*, at www.justiceinperspective.org.za/index.php?option=com_content& task=view&id=23&Itemid=57[accessed 23 November 2010].

[1122] Amnesty International, *Nigeria: Rape – the Silent Weapon, op. cit.*, p.12.

[1123] See Amnesty International, *Ibid*, p.19.

[1124] Environmental Rights Report, *Human Rights and the Environment*, Materials for the 61st Session of the United Nations Commission on Human Rights, Geneva, 14 March – 22 April 2005, Prepared by Marcello Mollo, *et al* & Environmental Justice Course Participants, Whittier Law School, Earth Justice, USA, at www.earthjustice.org [accessed 3 March 2010].

[1125] M. Dejeant-Pons, "The Right to Environment in Regional Human Rights Systems", in K.E. Mahoney and Mahoney P. (eds) (1993), *Human Rights in the Twenty-First Century*, quoted in Ayesha Dias, *Human Rights, Environment and Development: With Special Emphasis on*

and impart information without interference has been guaranteed by a series
of international environmental law instruments, as well as by the domestic
legislation in many States.[1126]

It is a common occurrence in the Niger Delta that in carrying out projects
there is either a lack of consultation with regard to the proposed project or that
such consultation is not performed adequately. This will be considered further in
Chapter Six below.

4.4.10 THE RIGHT TO PARTICIPATION

As a means of pursuing environmental protection, participation is based on
the right of those who may be affected by an activity or developmental project
to have a say with regard to that activity. The right to participate in public
affairs is provided for by Article 25 of the ICCPR.[1127] Worthy of mention also
is the UN (ECE) Convention on Access to Information, Public Participation in
Decision Making and Access to Justice in Environmental Matters (the Aarhus
Convention). This Convention elaborates on Principle 10 of the Rio Declaration,
and aims at providing effective means for the exercise of procedural rights in an
environmental context. It was signed at Aarhus, Denmark in June 1998, and came
into force in October 2001. It is regional in scope, it being a Convention of the
UN (ECE) – The Economic Commission for Europe of the United Nations. While
emphasizing the significance of the convention, Kofi Annan, and the former
Secretary-General to the UN, had this to say:

> *"Although regional in scope, the significance of the Aarhus Convention is global.
> It is by far the most impressive elaboration of principle 10 of the Rio Declaration,
> which stresses the need for citizens' participation in environmental issues and for
> access to information on the environment held by public authorities. As such it is the
> most ambitious venture in the area of 'environmental democracy' so far undertaken
> under the auspices of the United Nations."*[1128]

Corporate Accountability, Human Development Report 2000, Background Paper, at http://hdr.
undp.org/en/reports/global/hdr2000/papers/ayesha%20dias%20.pdf [accessed 3 March 2010].

[1126] ICCPR (Article 19), Convention for the Protection of World Cultural and Natural Heritage,
23 November 1972, 27 U.S.T. 37, 1037 UNT. S 151, Article 27(2); UN Framework Convention
on Climate Change, 9 May 1992, UN Doc. A/CONF. 151726, 31I.L.M. 849 (1992), Article 6(a)
(ii); Convention on Civil Liability for Damage Resulting from Activities Dangerous to the
Environment, June 21, 1993, 32 I.L.M. 1228 (1993), Article 14(1); The African Charter (Article
19); The Nigerian Constitution of 1999 (Section 39(1)).

[1127] *Op. cit.* The World Charter for Nature, in its resolution recommends: 'All persons, in accordance with their national legislation, shall have the opportunity to participate, individually or
with others, in the formulation of decisions of direct concern to their environment, and shall
have access to means of redress when their environment has suffered damage or degradation.'
UN General Assembly, A/RES/37/7, 28 October 1982, art. 23. See also Article 13 of the African
Charter on Human and Peoples' Rights, *op. cit.*

[1128] See Aarhus website, at www.unece.org/env/pp [accessed 3 March 2010].

The Aarhus Convention consists of three 'pillars.' While the first pillar gives the public the right of access to environmental information; the second provides the public with a right to participate in environmental decision-making processes; and the third pillar guarantees access to justice for the public in environmental matters. As stated by Thornton J. and Beckwith S.:

> "*The first pillar establishes rules and requirements for Governments to disclose information about the state of the environment, and the factors, policies and activities that affect it. Citizens are entitled to obtain this information within one month of requesting it, and without having to say why they require it. In addition, the Convention places public authorities under an obligation to actively disseminate environmental information. The second pillar requires arrangements to be made by public authorities to enable citizens and environmental organizations to comment on, for example, proposals for projects affecting the environment and for these comments to be taken into account in decision making. The third pillar deals with the right of the public and public interest groups to seek a judicial remedy for non-compliance by Governments and corporations with the legal obligations established by the first two pillars.*"[1129]

Article 19(3) of the Convention provides that 'Any other State, not referred to in paragraph 2 above, that is a Member of the United Nations may accede to the Convention upon approval by the Meeting of the Parties'. In view of the laudable and comprehensive provisions of the Convention, Nigeria will do well in improving its environmental procedural rights regime by acceding to the Aarhus Convention like other UN member Countries.

The human rights violations described above reveal that there exists a close relationship between human rights, environmental degradation and economic development. Abuses of human rights and damage to the environment go *pari passu*. It shows how environmental degradation in the Niger Delta region has led to human rights abuses, including the right of other species to survive (eco-centric approach); economic development through oil exploitation has given rise to environmental problems; and human rights violations have occurred because of environmental issues.[1130] It goes to confirm the view expressed by Kofi Annan, that 'millions are experiencing globalization not as an opportunity, but as a force of disruption or destruction: as an assault on their material standards of living, or on their traditional way of life.'[1131] Despite the human rights consequences of

---

[1129] *Ibid*, pp.407–408.
[1130] See Sumudu Atapattu, The Right to a Healthy Life or the Right to Die Polluted?: The Emergence of a Human Right to a Healthy Environmental Under International Law, *op. cit.*, pp.70–71.
[1131] United Nations Centre for Human Settlements (Habitat), Cities in a Globalizing World – Global Report on Human Settlements 2001, Earthscan Publications, London, 2001, quoted in UNEP/UNICEF/WHO, *Children in the New Millennium: Environmental Impact on Health*, Nairobi/New York/Geneva, 2002, p.23.

the activities of the MNCs around the world, this has received little international attention, with the result that the devastating effects of their activities continue unabated. Unfortunately, Movement for the Emancipation of the Niger Delta (MEND) and a large number militant groups erupted out of the 1990s environmental and human rights abuses committed by the dictatorship of Late Gen. Sani Abacha.[1132]

In a practical sense, the return to civilian Government in 1999 has made little difference to the people in the Niger Delta region in terms of their human rights violations. This was pointed out by the UN Special Rapporteur on Human Rights Defenders[1133] on her visit to Nigeria when investigating human rights in the Niger Delta in April 2005. Also Nick Aston Jones, a British environmentalist, who has spent years monitoring the impact of oil exploratory activities on the Niger Delta environment, had this to say when he visited the region in 2001:

> *"The level of civil discontent and government armed repression is no less than it was in 1993. The difference is that the (mobile) police rather than the army now intimidate civilians. However, my evidence suggests that oil pollution from poorly maintained well heads and pipelines is significantly worse. Shell remains characterised by a negative attitude towards its host communities; a lack of cultural and ecological awareness and sensitivity; a willingness to encourage armed attacks on defenceless communities and to resort to the repression of civil rights in preference to negotiation; poor maintenance of its extraction infrastructure and low engineering standards; ignorance of environmental and social impacts; a tendency to tolerate the inefficient management of its compensation and social programme processes; and to lie repeatedly when challenged until the evidence is irrefutable. Thus, in terms of its respect for human rights, the environment and natural justice, Shell's activities in Ogoni (and elsewhere in the Niger Delta) continue to be cynical and contemptible: Especially, given an advertising campaign that stresses its sensitivity to the environment. In the end, I cannot avoid the conclusion that Shell is badly managed and that its shareholders should be asking why its public statements do not match the facts of its field activities."*[1134]

Human rights defenders have continued to be arbitrarily detained, beaten, their access to information restricted, their protests obstructed, often with

---

[1132]   Roger Bate, Nigeria at 50,' *The Wall Street Journal*, 7 October 2010, at http://online.wsj.com/article/SB10001424052748704483004575524031010682478.html [accessed 3 December 2010].

[1133]   The United Nations Special Representative of the Secretary General for Human Rights Defenders stated '… There is a need for government and the oil companies to review their practices and transparency to genuinely engage with defenders in order to hear and respond to the needs of the affected population,' at www.unhchr.ch/huricane,huricane.nsf/0/ABAA1A82 98C41EBBC1257012006A4701? [accessed 3 March 2010].

[1134]   Quoted in Fr. Kevin O' Hara, Niger Delta: Peace and Co-operation Through Sustainable Development, *Environmental Policy and Law*, 31(6), 302–308 at 305 (2001). Nick Aston Jones visited Ogoniland in 1993 and 1994 as part of the ERA Baseline Participatory Ecological Survey of the Niger Delta region.

the use of force, their houses searched, and in some instances threatened with death,[1135] simply for investigating oil spills and environmental degradation. The continuation of the environmentally abusive practices in the Niger Delta region depicts the failure of the existing legal regimes aimed at regulating the conduct of the multinational oil companies as regards the effects of their activities on the people and environment. It further shows the need to hold MNCs accountable for their impact on environmental human rights.

4.5 STATE RESPONSIBILITIES FOR ACTS OF NON-STATE ACTORS

It is beyond dispute that non-state actors have come to occupy central positions in the provision of the key services and goods which are essential for an individual's day-to-day life. These non-State actors include MNCs, civil society groups, and international organizations, to mention just the most prominent among a wide range of potentially important actors. These actors have all assumed major roles in relation to the enjoyment of human rights, especially in recent years.[1136] This research will, however, limit itself to MNCs operating in the Niger Delta.

Orthodox human rights norms protect the individual against the State, which in certain situations may be a 'little devil' but leave him unprotected against abuse from the 'big devil' – big business, because 'big devil' is private, and not the State.[1137] This shows the crucial need to deconstruct the private-public divide which has inhibited human rights enforcement.[1138]

We shall here examine the responsibilities of States for non-State actors. 'State responsibility' is the phrase used to describe the position of a State which has breached its own obligations or those imposed on it by international law, including the prevention of environmentally destructive conduct by non-state actors. Such obligations include due diligence and cooperation, which will be discussed below. It may also refers to the duty of a State, upon notice of such a breach, to prevent further harm, to obtain compensation for damage to its people, and to ensure proper clean-up and restoration of the environment.[1139] As noted

---

[1135]   Mirror, *RIVPA Frowns at Threats to Harm Local Publishers,* statement by Rivers State Indigenous Publishers Association, 21–27 September 2004, quoted in Amnesty International Report, *Nigeria Ten Years on: Injustice and Violence Haunt the Oil Delta, op. cit.*

[1136]   H.J. Steiner *et al.* (2008), *International Human Rights in Context. Law, Politics, Moral. Text and Materials,* Third Edition, Oxford University Press, Oxford, p.1385.

[1137]   J.K. Minkah-Premo, The Role of Judicial Enforcement of ECOSOC Rights in National Development: The Case of Ghana, *African Society of International & Comparative Law, ASICL Proc.* 11, p.71 (1999).

[1138]   *Ibid.*

[1139]   Patricia Birnie, *et al* (2009), *International Law and the Environment,* Third Edition, Oxford University Press, Oxford New York, pp.214–215, 226.

by Weiler: 'Under conventional international human rights law, states are obliged to ensure that each of their citizens enjoy basic rights and freedoms – not only in so far as states must not breach such rights or freedoms acting in their own capacity, but also by ensuring that the necessary legal and political conditions exist which will promote and protect the enjoyment of such rights and freedoms. This general obligation also includes the need to safeguard the rights of citizens as against the conduct of non-state actors.'[1140] The responsibility of the State in relation to injuries resulting from violation of obligations under international law can be either direct (for acts of the State itself) or indirect and imputed (for acts of its citizens or those under its control). As a general rule, the State is not liable for the action of private parties unless such fault can be attributed to the State.[1141]

The ICCPR, ratified by Nigeria, includes binding obligations on Nigeria to undertake to respect and to ensure to all individuals within its territory and subject to its jurisdiction the rights recognized in that Covenant, without distinction of any kind, such as race, colour, sex, language, religion, political or other opinion, national or social origin, property, birth or other status.[1142] Article 2(3)(a) & (b) of ICCPR also includes the obligation to ensure that any person whose rights or freedoms included in the ICCPR have been violated shall have an effective remedy and that anybody claiming such a remedy shall have this right determined by a competent judicial, administrative or legislative authority or by any competent authority provided for by the legal system of the state.

The ICESCR, also ratified by Nigeria, includes binding obligations upon Nigeria to respect, promote and fulfill economic, social and cultural rights and this includes both obligations of immediate effect and of progressive realization.[1143] The obligation to "respect" requires that States refrain from interfering directly or indirectly with the enjoyment of a human right, the obligation to "protect" obliges States to prevent third parties (that is, individuals, groups, corporations, or other entities) from interfering in any way with the enjoyment of a human right; and the obligation to "fulfill" contains obligations to facilitate, provide and promote as well as to adopt appropriate legislative, administrative, budgetary, judicial, promotional and other measures towards the full realization of the right in question.[1144] It has been suggested that the obligation of the State to "protect" under the ICESR 'includes an obligation for the State to ensure that all other

---

[1140] Todd Weiler, *Balancing Human Rights and Investor Protection: A New Approach for a Different Legal Order*, Oil, Gas and Energy Law Intelligence, Vol. 1, Issue No. 2, March 2003, at www.dundee.ac.uk/cepmlp/journal/html/vol11/article11-5.pdf [accessed 3 March 2010].

[1141] A. Dias, *op. cit.*

[1142] See Article 2(1) of ICCPR.

[1143] See Amnesty International Report, *Nigeria: Are Human Rights in the Pipeline?* AI Index: AFR 44/020/2004, Amnesty International 9 November 2004, p.19.

[1144] *Ibid.*

bodies subject to its control (such as transnational corporations based in that State) respect the enjoyment of rights in other countries.'[1145]

Under international law there are a number of different ways in which the State can be held accountable for human rights abuses committed by non-State actors. The State can be deemed responsible for carrying out the human rights violation because of a specific kind of connection with the non-State actors, or it can be responsible for failing to take reasonable steps to prevent, or respond to, an abuse.[1146] In other words, the State can be responsible when it relies on some other person to carry out an action that falls within its own role, when it has 'participated' in some way, or supported abuses by others, as well as when it has failed in its duty to take adequate measures to prevent the abuse of human rights and where it fails to provide effective remedies.[1147]

The concept of due diligence is used when evaluating the accountability of States for the acts of non-State actors. 'Due diligence' has been defined as the conduct 'to be expected from a good government,' that is, from a government 'mindful of its international obligations'.[1148] It describes the degree of effort which a State should undertake to ensure that human rights are respected by all. The State has an obligation to 'take all appropriate measures', to 'make appropriate efforts', or to 'use best practicable means' to prevent violations (by its official) and abuses (by non-State actors) of human rights. In order to effectively discharge its due diligence obligations towards the environment, a State must take positive steps to create an environmental authority, enact proper laws and regulations, instruct the environmental authority to lay down emission standards and threshold levels and oversee the implementation of these standards.[1149] It must ensure that it discloses information on activities that affect the environment, ensure public participation of citizens in decision-making processes and make provision for the assessment of the environmental impact of development activities.[1150] Where a right has been violated or abused, the State has a duty to redress it as far as possible, and to provide an appropriate remedy, which may include compensation.[1151]

[1145] F. Coomans, "Some Remarks on the Extraterritorial Application of the International Covenant on Economic, Social and Cultural Rights", in F. Coomans and M.T. Kamminga (eds) (2004), *Extraterritorial Application of Human Rights Treaties,* Intersentia, Antwerp and Oxford, p.192, quoted in Robert McCorquodale, Corporate Social Responsibility and International Human Rights Law, 87 *Journal of Business Ethics*, 385–400 at 389 (2009).
[1146] Amnesty International Report, *Nigeria: Are Human Rights in the Pipeline? op. cit.*, p.20.
[1147] *Ibid.*
[1148] Pierre Dupuy, "Due Diligence in the International Law of Liability", in *OECD* (ed) (1977), *Legal Aspects of Transfrontier Pollution,* OECD, Paris, p.369.
[1149] Sumudu Atapattu, The Right to a Healthy Life or the Right to Die Polluted?: The Emergence of a Human Right to a Healthy Environment Under International Law, *op. cit.*, p.113.
[1150] *Ibid.*
[1151] Amnesty International Report, *Nigeria: Are Human Rights in the Pipeline? op. cit.*; Dinah Shelton, Human Rights and the Environment: What Specific Environmental Rights Have Been Recognized?, 35 *Denv. J. Int'l. L. & Pol'y* 129–171 at 130 (2006).

A wide range of international and regional Covenants expressly require
States to regulate the conduct of non-State actors so that they do not violate
economic, social and cultural rights. For example, the Committee on Economic,
Social and Cultural Rights has emphasized the indirect obligations arising out
of the activities of non-State actors with regards to the enjoyment of economic,
social and cultural rights. For instance, it has underlined that State parties 'should
take appropriate steps to ensure that activities of the private business sector and
civil society are in conformity with the right to food.'[1152] Thus, 'failure to regulate
activities of individuals or groups so as to prevent them from violating the right
to food of others' amounts to a dereliction of duty by the State.[1153]

The international experts who drew up the Maastricht Guidelines on
Violations of Economic, Social and Cultural Rights, adopted in 1997, noted that
the State obligation to "protect" 'includes the State's responsibility to ensure that
private entities or individuals, including transnational corporations over which
they exercise jurisdiction, do not deprive individuals of their economic, social
and cultural rights.'[1154]

The Human Rights Committee has noted that 'the positive obligations
on States Parties to ensure Covenant rights will only be fully discharged if
individuals are protected by the State, not just against violations of covenant
rights by its agents, but also against acts committed by private persons or entities
that would impair the enjoyment of Covenant rights in so far as they are amenable
to application between private persons or entities. There may be circumstances
in which a failure to ensure Covenant rights as required by article 2 would give
rise to violations by State parties of those rights, as a result of States Parties
permitting or failing to take appropriate measures or to exercise due diligence
to prevent, punish, investigate or redress the harm caused by such acts by private
persons or entities.'[1155] Again, the CESCR has explained, in its General Comments
concerning certain rights, that the obligation to protect 'requires States Parties
to take measures that prevent third parties from interfering with the enjoyment
of the right.'[1156] In its General Comment on the Right to Water, '"third parties"
include individuals, groups, corporations and other entities as well as agents
acting under State authority. The obligation includes, *inter alia,* adopting the
necessary and effective legislative and other measures to restrain, for example,
third parties from denying equal access to adequate water; or from polluting and

---

[1152] General Comment No. 12 para. 27.
[1153] *Ibid*, para 19, quoted in Chirwa D.M. (2002), *Obligations of Non-State Actors in Relation to Economic, Social and Cultural Rights under The South African Constitution*, Social-Economic Rights Project Community Law Centre, University of the Western Cape, at www.community. lawcentre.org.za [accessed 10 March 2010].
[1154] See Para. 18. A similar Declaration was also made by the African Commission in the *Social and Economic Rights Action Centre and the Centre for Economic and Social Rights & the Centre for Economic and Social Rights v. Nigeria*, Communication 155/96.
[1155] Human Rights Committee, General Comment 31, para. 8.
[1156] See Amnesty International Report, *Nigeria: Are Human Rights in the Pipeline? op. cit.*, p.20.

inequitably extracting from water resources, including natural sources, wells and other water distribution systems.'[1157] The Nigerian Government has frequently failed to meet its obligations to respect, protect and fulfill human rights. In May 1998, the UN Committee on Economic, Social and Cultural Rights considered Nigeria's initial report under the CESCR. The Committee 'note[d] with alarm the extent of the devastation that oil exploration has done to the environment and [the] quality of life in those areas, including Ogoniland, where oil has been discovered and extracted without due regard for the health and well-being of the people and their environment,' and recommended that '[t]he rights of minority and ethnic communities – including the Ogoni people – should be respected and full redress should be provided for the violations of the rights set forth in the Covenant that they have suffered.'[1158]

International law has some mechanism for monitoring the implementation of indirect obligations in respect of non-State actors. One of these mechanisms is the State reporting procedure. However, the judicial enforcement mechanism has also proved to be an important supervisory mechanism.[1159] Thus, the Human Rights Committee, although charged with the monitoring of civil and political rights under the ICCPR, has imposed liability on States for failure to protect citizens from acts of private actors resulting in infringements of the (negative) obligations generated by economic, social and cultural rights, using the family protection and privacy clause.[1160] Further, in *Social and Economic Rights Action Center and the Center for Economic and Social Rights v. Nigeria*,[1161] the African Commission on Human and Peoples' Rights held, *inter alia*, that 'Governments have a duty to protect their citizens, not only through appropriate legislation but also by protecting them from damaging acts that may be perpetrated by private parties. This duty calls for positive action on the part of Governments in fulfilling their obligations under human rights instruments.'[1162] The Commission therefore held that Nigeria was responsible for violations by the oil companies, in addition to those that had been committed by the government itself.

[1157] Committee on Economic, Social and Cultural Rights, General Comments No. 15 on the Right to Water, UN Doc. E/C. 12/2002/11, 20 January 2003, para. 23.

[1158] Concluding Observations of the Committee on Economic, Social and Cultural Rights: Nigeria, UN Document E/C. 12/1/Add. 23, 13 May 1998, para 38.

[1159] D.M. Chirwa, *op. cit.*

[1160] *Ibid.* "Negative obligations", are those that require a limitation of the State's activities so as not to impinge upon the liberty of its citizens. Civil and political rights suggests negative obligations, that is, where the State merely adopts 'do not approach', but it is important to stress that violations of economic, social and cultural rights (positive obligations, one that obliges the State 'to do') often result from the non-fulfillment of negative obligations by the State. See Víctor Abramovich, Courses of action in economic, social and cultural rights: Instruments and allies, transl. by Barney Whiteoak, at www.surjournal.org/eng/conteudos/artigos2/ing/artigo_abramovich.htm [accessed 23 May 2013].

[1161] Communication 155/96.

[1162] *Ibid,* para. 57. See also *Yanomami v. Brazil* Resolution No. 12/ 85 Case 7615 reported in Annual Report of the Inter-American Commission on Human Rights 1985.

The "due diligence" concept developed by the Inter-American Court was
followed by all the human rights systems referred to above. Under this test, the
court considers whether the State took reasonable steps to prevent or respond to a
violation by a private actor, including investigations and the provision of remedies
such as compensation. In *Velasquez Rodriguez* v. *Honduras*,[1163] Rodriguez was
kidnapped, and probably killed by the Honduran Army. The Inter-American
Court of Human Rights stated that: 'An illegal act which violates human rights
and which is initially not directly imputable to a State (for example, because
it is the act of a private person or because the person responsible has not been
identified) can lead to international responsibility of the State, not because of the
act itself, but because of the lack of due diligence to prevent the violation or to
respond to it as required by the Convention.'[1164] It was held that even though the
attackers were private actors, the State was liable because of its failure to take steps
to find the victim or the perpetrators, or to provide any remedy to the victim's
family.

Regarding the oil exploration and production in the Niger Delta, all MNCs
operating in Nigeria are required to enter into a joint venture with the Nigerian
Government, through NNPC, the State oil company, which owns the majority
of the shares in the joint ventures. Thus, as the majority shareholder, the
Nigerian Government is under the obligation to respect, and ensure respect for
international human rights law as well as national law, by its agents and by the
MNCs.[1165] The Nigerian Government must establish, and reinforce, the necessary
legal and administrative framework for ensuring that the relevant national and
international laws are implemented by the transnational corporations and other
business enterprises.

4.5.1 HOST STATE CONTROL

The placing of primary responsibility on the State for ensuring the protection of the
human rights by the MNCs is designed to accord respect to national sovereignty.
However, in countries with serious human rights abuses, as in Nigeria under its
former military dictatorship (Late Gen. Sanni Abacha), and South Africa under
the apartheid regime, leaving regulation of the MNCs activities affecting human
rights in the hands of such Governments would effectively preclude adequate
protection of those rights.[1166] This is coupled with the fact that MNCs are likely

---

[1163] Judgment of 29 July 1988, Inter-American Court on Human Rights Series C. No. 4 (1998);
(1989) 28 ILM 294, para. 172.
[1164] *Ibid*, para. 172.
[1165] Amnesty International Report, *Nigeria: Are Human Rights in the Pipeline?, op. cit.,* p.21.
[1166] Diane F. Orentlicher and Timothy A. Gelatt, *op. cit.,* p.103.

to show a preference to operate in countries with lax regulatory frameworks.[1167] One of the major reasons for the lax regulations in the developing countries is the belief that the development of their natural resources will undoubtedly lead to the growth in the nation's economy and an improvement in the lives of the local communities in the region where the resources are located. Hence, developing countries find it difficult to regulate or control MNCs and they easily agree to any terms dictated by the MNCs. And because domestic legislation has focused on trying to compete successfully to attract foreign investment, it is not surprising that legislators have been more inclined to enact laws that are much less favourable to the individual national interest.[1168]

However, events in countries like Nigeria, Sudan and Columbia, where there has been failure to ensure fair and equitable distribution of the oil wealth, have proved that oil exploration does not inevitably lead to national economic growth and benefits for the people. As reported by the UK Inter-Agency Group in Columbia in early 1999, the development of oil in Casanare had brought no appreciable improvement to the lives of the poor who have suffered unduly from an increase in the political violence and from environmental harms.[1169] The situation in Nigeria is even worse. While production and export of oil has reached about 2.4 million bpd, translating into huge financial resources, it has failed to translate into the good life for the majority of Nigerians, especially the people of the Niger Delta region where the "goose" resides. Most of the 30 million people living in that region have become the living dead, as a result of environmental pollution, whilst the Nigerian Government has left the oil companies to their own devices – laissez faire.

In addition, the absence of the technical and legal expertise that is necessary for monitoring complex activities, involving environmental pollution, also hinders efforts at regulating MNCs in developing countries.[1170] These challenges, coupled with the attendant human rights violations, exemplify the need for the international community to devise measures to hold MNCs accountable for their actions abroad and to protect the rights of the indigenous peoples that are in jeopardy around the world as a result of their activities.

[1167] Emeka Duruigbo, Corporate Accountability and Liability for International Human Rights Abuses: Recent Changes and Recurring Challenges, 6(2) *Northwestern Journal of Human Rights* 222–261 at 249 (2008); Mathew Lippman, Transnational Corporations and Repressive Regimes: The Ethical Dilemma, 15 *Cal. W. Int'l L.J.* 542, 545 (1985).

[1168] M. Curtis (2001), *Trade for Life: Making Trade Work for the Poor*, Christian Aid, London, p.122; John Alan Cohan, Environmental Rights of Indigenous Peoples Under the Alien Tort Claims Act, the Public Trust Doctrine and Corporate Ethics, and Environmental Dispute Resolution, 20 *UCLA J. Envtl. L. & Pol'y* 133–185 at 145 (2002).

[1169] Balance Sheet of Conclusions and Recommendations of the Inter-Agency Group to BP Amoco, April 1999, quoted in Sir Geoffrey Chandler, "The Responsibilities of Oil Companies", in Asbjorn Eide *et al.* (eds) (2000), *Human Rights and the Oil Industry*, Intersentia, Groningen-Oxford, p.14.

[1170] Emeka Duruigbo, Corporate Accountability and Liability for International Human Rights Abuses: Recent Changes and Recurring Challenges, *op. cit.* at 249.

Rather than allowing MNCs to operate entirely under the laws of the host
countries which are often deliberately lax in order to attract foreign investors,
developing host countries could enact laws that require MNCs to comply with
whatever are their home countries' standards.[1171] This approach was recommended,
in a Report from the United Nations Economic and Social Commission for Asia
and the Pacific (ESCAP) which noted that:

> *"Governments should look into the possibility of revising policies and regulations*
> *so that TNCs [Transnational Corporations] are bound to adopt the environmental*
> *standards of their home countries, while at the same time allowing local firms to*
> *be regulated on the basis of local standards ... Local standards should be gradually*
> *upgraded on the basis of a schedule to give local firms time to adjust their operations*
> *according to the new standards required and for them to have time to plan out such*
> *changes."*[1172]

However, this approach has been criticized on the ground that it would require
environmental authorities of developing host countries to identify, understand
and administer differing standards for different MNCs, according to their
country of origin.[1173] Besides, such an approach is discriminatory, and contrary to
the principle of national treatment (that is, giving foreigners the same treatment
as one's own nationals) insofar as TNCs are subjected to stricter rules than those
applicable to local or state-owned industries.[1174] This is quite true as there is no
sufficient evidence that the State owned or local industries are better than the
MNCs in their environmental practices. As argued by Fowler, whether such
measures could be justified as bonafide environmental regulation rather than a
protectionist measure is quite doubtful.[1175]

4.5.2 HOME STATE CONTROL

The above reveals the difficulties that are likely to be faced by host countries in
effectively regulating the activities of MNCs in their domain. A situation in which
the host Government is unable to 'hold multinationals to account for their human

---

[1171] Tetsuya Morimoto, Growing industrialization and our damaged planet: The Extraterritorial
application of developed countries' domestic environmental laws to transnational corporations abroad, 1 (2) *Utrecht Law Review*, pp.134–159 at 144 (2005); Robert J. Fowler, International
Environmental Standards for Transnational Corporations, 25 *Environmental Law* 1–30 at 26
(1995).

[1172] See UN Centre on Transnational Corporations and Economic and Social Commission for Asia
and the Pacific, *Environmental Aspects of Transnational Corporations Activities in Pollution-
Intensive Industries in Selected Asian and Pacific Developing Countries*, ESCAP/UNCTC
Publications Series B, no. 15 (1990), pp.75–76.

[1173] Tetsuya Morimoto, *op. cit.*, p.144; Robert J. Fowler, *op. cit.*, p.26.

[1174] *Ibid.*

[1175] *Ibid.*

rights and environmental transgressions and in which home Governments lack the political will to regulate or provide the conditions for legal redress at home for transgressions perpetrated by their companies overseas, perpetuates an operating environment characterized by effective impunity.'[1176] Consequently, calls have been made for the extraterritorial application of developed home countries' environmental laws to national MNCs operating abroad in developing countries. The advantages of this are quite enormous. Firstly, this will make the MNCs comply with the stringent environmental regulations of their home countries, in addition to complying with the host countries' environmental rules. Secondly, extraterritorial regulation may help to stimulate developing countries to improve their own environmental regulations without jeopardizing the development of domestic industries, since the host countries would no longer need to maintain weak regulations in order to attract foreign investments. In addition to facilitating the transfer of advanced environmental technologies to host developing countries, and boosting the development of environmental training programmes for their personnel, the brunt of the enforcement costs would be borne by the Governments of developed countries.[1177]

Under international law, a State is allowed to exercise prescriptive jurisdiction, that is, jurisdiction to make law, over extraterritorial acts based on four principles, *viz.*: the nationality principle, the passive personality principle, the protective principle, and the universality principle. The nationality principle grants a State an undisputed right to extend the application of its laws to its citizens (those who have their nationality), wherever they may be; (ii) the protective principle allows the State to exercise its legislative jurisdiction, when vital interests of the State are threatened, even if by non-nationals acting outside the territory of the State.[1178] The reason for this principle is linked to the preservation of the interests of the State. A typical example relates to the counterfeiting of a State's currency outside the territory of the State by non-nationals. The passive personality principle allows the national state of the victim of an offence to assert prescriptive jurisdiction over extraterritorial conduct directed against the victim, no matter the nationality of the perpetrator.[1179] Under the universal principle, a State is allowed to define and punish certain criminal offences recognized by the international community to be of universal concern, such as genocide, crimes against humanity, piracy, the slave trade, terrorism and other serious crimes, even where none of the above bases of

---

[1176] Catherine Coumans, "Alternative Accountability Mechanisms and Mining: The Problems of Effective Impunity, Human Rights, and Agency", in *Rethinking Extractive Industry: Regulation, Dispossession, and Emerging Claims, Canadian Journal of Development Studies, op. cit.*, p.32 (2010).

[1177] Tetsuya Morimoto, *op. cit.*, p.146.

[1178] Vaughan Lowe and Christopher Staker, "Jurisdiction", in Malcolm D. Evans (ed) (2010) *International Law*, 3rd Edition, Oxford: Oxford University Press, Oxford, pp.323, 325–326.

[1179] *Ibid*, 330.

jurisdiction is present.[1180] Of these principles, the nationality principle is widely accepted as a basis for prescriptive jurisdiction over extraterritorial conduct, and so could be used by a State to prescribe the application of domestic environmental regulations to the foreign operations of their MNCs.[1181] The practice of State as regards the determination of the nationality of companies differs.[1182] While there is tendency for States under the common law to accord nationality to companies on the basis of their incorporation in the territory of the State, regardless of where their actual business or management is carried out, some civil law States confer nationality rather on the basis of the place where the company has the seat of its management.[1183]

Even though corporations may usually possess the nationality of where they are incorporated, there are complications regarding MNCs. This is because MNCs, being a group of corporations, may have each group formally established in a different State under different laws but with all connected together by common management and financial control. 'If the nationality of an affiliate corporation belonging to a TNC is determined only on the basis of its place of incorporation, this means that a foreign affiliate corporation cannot be regarded as a national of the TNC's home country.'[1184] In this regard, the home country may not be able to exercise extraterritorial jurisdiction over those foreign affiliates on the basis of nationality principle. In order to avoid this situation, Para 414(2) of the Restatement (Third) of Foreign Relations Law of the U.S. provides that for limited purposes, a State may regulate the activities of corporations organized under the law of a foreign state 'on the basis that they are owned or controlled by nationals of the regulating state.' Relying on this, the U.S. has exercised extraterritorial jurisdiction over foreign subsidiaries, and other affiliate corporations, to enforce economic sanctions against hostile countries, although this has been seriously challenged by European Union.[1185]

Suffice to say, the adoption of extraterritorial jurisdiction of developed home countries' domestic environmental laws has been criticized, as it may intrude too far into the internal affairs of sovereign states, indicating a new form of 'cultural imperialism' particularly in its operations in developing countries.[1186] Without doubt, every sovereign State, subject to its treaty commitment, has the right to decide what constitutes a safe and risk-free activity, what the health of its citizens should be, what the standard of the health of its citizens will be, and what level

---

[1180]   Tetsuya Morimoto, *op. cit.*, p.147; Restatement (Third) of Foreign Relations Law of the United States, the American Law Institute, Philadelphia, 1987, para. 404.
[1181]   Tetsuya Morimoto, *Ibid*, p.147.
[1182]   See Barcelona Traction, Light and Power Company, Limited, Second Phase, Judgment, ICJ Reports 1970, p.3.
[1183]   Vaughan Lowe and Christopher Staker, *op. cit.*, pp.323–324.
[1184]   Tetsuya Morimoto, *op. cit.*, p.148.
[1185]   *Ibid.*
[1186]   Robert J. Fowler, *op. cit.*, p.27.

of pollution it will accept as legal within its boundaries.[1187] However, when such activities begin to affect the well-being of those in other jurisdictions, such a State should no longer be allowed to justify its actions by claiming sovereignty. The resistance of the developing countries to higher standards of health, safety and environmental protection has been aptly described by critics as the 'bureaucratization of issues of global concern,' which in the long run, is likely to affect the international community and even future generations.[1188] This fact is particularly important when viewed against the background that human rights and the environment can easily be victimized under a repressive regime which places primacy on economic development, notwithstanding the environmental and human impact of such activities. Therefore, the sovereign rights of a nation should be moderated where the effect of its activity or operation is clearly global or has long-term effects on a nation's population.[1189] Home States are also reluctant to establish jurisdiction over their MNCs because it is felt that in as much as it is not all States that adopt this kind of approach, it produces a competitive disadvantage for those that do.[1190]

4.6 THE RESPONSIBILITY OF NON-STATE ACTORS

Globalization has contributed to, and in part been driven by, the increasingly central role of MNCs in the international and domestic economic orders. Over the last two decades, there has been much growth in the number of transnational corporations and in their global wealth. One often cited way of illustrating their magnitude explains that, 'of the world's 100 largest economies, only 49 of them are countries, the remaining 51 are transnational corporations.'[1191] Moreover, the combined revenue of the top 200 corporations which now exceeds US$7.1 trillion dwarfs the combined economic activity of the poorest four-fifths of humanity,

---

[1187] Sudhir K. Chopra, Multinational Corporations in the Aftermath of Bhopal: The Need for a New Comprehensive Global Regime for Transnational Corporate Activity, 29 *Valparaiso University Law Journal* 235–284 at 256 (1994).

[1188] *Ibid* p.257.

[1189] *Ibid.*

[1190] Marion Weschka, Human Rights and Multinational Enterprises: How Can Multinational Enterprises Be Held Responsible for Human Rights Violations Committed Abroad?, 66 *ZaöRV* 625–661 at 660 (2006).

[1191] World Bank World Development Report 1996 and Fortune's Global 500 of 1994, Fortune, 7 August 1995; See Sarah Anderson and John Cavanagh, *Top 200: The Rise of Corporate Global Power*, Institute for Policy Studies, Washington DC, December 2000, which concluded at p.3 that 'General Motors is now bigger than Denmark; DaimlerChrysler is bigger than Poland; Royal Dutch/Shell is bigger than Venezuela; IBM is bigger than Singapore; and Sony is bigger than Pakistan,' and that combined sales of the top 200 corporations 'are bigger than the combined economies of all countries minus the biggest 10.' See also Joseph E. Stiglitz (2006), *Making Globalization Work*, Allen Lane, an imprint of Penguin Books Ltd., London, p.187.

US$3.9 trillion for over 4.5 billion people.[1192] Thus, in a world where transnational corporations often have revenue and capital that dwarfs that of the world's smaller States, the concept that companies have responsibilities to the community at large other than just to make money has gained increasing currency.[1193]

Along with such greater power and wealth comes an enhanced potential to abuse the environment where they operate since many of them have the capacity to circumvent national and global policies. The tremendous power of MNCs gives them capacity to inflict great damage, while their economic and political strength renders them difficult to regulate.[1194] With technological advancement, coupled with new investment opportunities, corporate powers increases and they are able to get their goods and services produced in several different locations. As a result, the MNCs become 'de-nationalized' and that they view the world, rather than their home or host states, as their base of operations.[1195]

The growing power of MNCs raises some fundamental problems for traditional international law. In the first place, being able to operate in different locations all over the world, States, whose regulatory schemes are largely domestic, find it difficult to regulate the activities of the MNCs, whose operations transcend borders. MNCs can insulate themselves and their officials from liability in any one country by moving their assets and operations elsewhere;[1196] also thereby making it difficult to enforce judgment debt if there is a monetary judgment against it. This brings into question the narrow view of international law, that the main focus of international law should be relations between states.

In some cases, the national security agenda of developing countries is determined by the security concerns of MNCs that operate there. As a result, the need to provide security for the continued exploration of oil takes precedent over national security.[1197] It is extraordinarily difficult to hold the MNCs to account for their human rights abuses in the developing countries because 'of their global presence, their socio-political influence, the impotence of the state, and the

---

[1192] Owens Wiwa, *The Paradox of Poverty and Corporate Globalization*, being Speech at Ghent on 30 October 2001 at the First EU International Conference on Globalization, at www.waado.org/environment/oilcompanies/Globalization_OwensWiwa.htm [accessed 6 September 2009].

[1193] Bronwen Manby, *Shell in Nigeria: Corporate Social Responsibility and the Ogoni Crisis*, A case study published by the Carnegie Council on Ethics and International Affairs, at www.cceia.org/resources/publications/case_studies/20/index.html/:pf_printable [accessed 3 March 2010].

[1194] Beth Stephens, The Amorality of Profit: Transnational Corporations and Human Rights, 20 *Berkeley Journal of International Law* 45–90 at 46 (2002).

[1195] Claudio Grossman and Daniel D. Bradlow, Are We Being Propelled Towards a People-Centered Transnational Legal Order?, 9 *Am. U. J. Int'l L. & Pol'y* 1–25, p.8 (1993).

[1196] Beth Stephens, *op. cit.*, p.83; Joseph E. Stiglitz, *Making Globalization Work*, *op. cit.*, p.196; Steven R. Ratner, Corporations and Human Rights: A Theory of Legal Responsibility,111 *Yale L.J.* 443–545 at 463 (2001); Claudio Grossman and Daniel D. Bradlow, *Ibid* at p.8.

[1197] Akosua K. Darkwah, *The Impact of Oil and Gas Discovery and Exploration on Communities with Emphasis on Women*, at www.g-rap.org/docs/oil_and_gas/netright-akosua_darkwah-2010.pdf [accessed 4 March 2011].

unenforceability of international law.'[1198] In the absence of a clear international standard capable of regulating MNCs, they can get away with their unwholesome activities in their host countries. In such a situation, the local population 'will be left to fall between the twin pillars of hapless Governments and careless corporations.'[1199] Allowing this state of affairs to continue is clearly dangerous globally.

With globalization, human rights are currently greatly exposed to violation by powers other than the State. The list of companies that have inflicted agonizing pains on the lives of the people, particularly in the developing countries, for which they are yet to pay compensation, or for which they have paid just a fraction of what they should pay, is long. Environmental harm caused by the activities of MNCs in the developing countries have been illustrated by several lawsuits, such as against Texaco in Ecuador, Union Carbide in India, Freeport-McMaron in Indonesia and Shell in Nigeria, showing the 'capacity of corporations to affect communities and individuals in ways that would ... be recognized as breaches of international human rights if committed by States.'[1200] For example, Texaco oil operations have reportedly spilled a million gallons of oil and dumped billions of gallons of untreated toxic brine into water and soil in Ecuador. Investigators have accused Freeport-McMaron of dumping hundreds of thousands of tons of toxic mine tailings into local waterways, destroying the environment and polluting the ground water.[1201] The explosion at the Union Carbide Plant in Bhopal, where over 20,000 people were killed and some 100,000 bear lifelong health damage, including respiratory illnesses, eye problem, neurological and neuromuscular damage, and immune system impairment[1202] is still fresh in the memory. The total number of affected people was, in fact, more than this figure (probably close to 600,000 people), and the difference between the harm done and what the company was forced to pay, an estimated US$500 per person (for a death or a life maimed), is huge, by any reckoning.[1203] While Dow Chemicals has acquired the Bhopal plant, taking over all its assets, it has not taken over any of its liability. Also in Papua New Guinea, OK Tedi, dumped 80,000 tons of contaminated material daily into the OK Tedi and Fly rivers over the course of the dozen or so years it operated in the country, while it extracted about $6 billion worth of ore. Following the exhaustion of the mine, the Australian-majority owned company, 'after admitting

---

[1198] Khulumani Support Group, *The Significance of the Successful Appeal Ruling*, at www.khulumani.net/reparations/corporate/223-the-significance-of-the-successful-appeal-ruling.html [accessed 3 August 2011].

[1199] Douglass Cassel, Corporate Initiatives: A Second Human Rights Revolution?, 19 (5) *Fordham International Law Journal* 1963–1984 at 1980 (1996).

[1200] Justine Nolan and Luke Taylor, Corporate Responsibility for Economic, Social and Cultural Rights: Rights in Search of a Remedy? 87 *Journal of Business Ethics* 433–451 at 438 (2009).

[1201] Beth Stephens, *op. cit.*, p.53; Richard L. Herz, Litigating Environmental Abuses Under the Alien Tort Claims Act: A Practical Assessment, 40 *Va. J. Int'l L.* 545, 547–548 (2000).

[1202] Joseph E. Stiglitz, *Making Globalization Work, op. cit.*, p.194.

[1203] *Ibid*, 194–195.

that it had vastly underestimated the environmental impact, just walked away,
turning over its shares to the Government – leaving the Government, already
strapped for funds, with the cleanup costs.'[1204] In Nigeria, Oloibiri, where crude
oil was first struck in June 1956 by Shell D'Arcy shared a similar experience. After
20 years (1958–1978) of oil drilling in this community, Shell decided that the oil
had dried up. Shell dismantled its equipment and left the community in 1978 for
other communities in the region, leaving the community to contend with the
devastating effects of pollution and gas flaring.[1205] While Shell and the Nigerian
Government count their gains in dollars from the oil revenue, the community
bemoans the loss of their means of livelihood. Moreover, the revenue derived
from oil is not put back into the community, even to restore the environment to
what it was before the harm was done to it. Indeed, Oloibiri serves as a warning
of the tragic fate that awaits many more oil producing communities in the Niger
Delta region.[1206]

As shown above, Shell and other oil MNCs move to seek their wealth
elsewhere when the reason for their continued stay in one place is no longer there,
but where will the people of the degraded communities go?[1207] Must the economic
prosperity of a nation always be sacrificed to environmental, health and human
rights concerns? This jobs/environment tradeoff, if judged by recent history, both
in the Niger Delta communities and elsewhere, is however a false one. The reality
is that economic activities of these MNCs, such as those in the Niger Delta, yields
few, if any, jobs for the residents in the host community.[1208] These communities
are faced with pollution of various sorts, and persistent lack of economic
development, thus making the communities to appreciate the hollowness of the
promises of both the Government and the MNCs.[1209] As observed in a report
by a Nigerian Government official investigation headed by Justice Oputa (also
known as the Human Rights Violations Investigation Commission), '[W]hile
their environment and means of livelihood are undermined, little effort is made
to recompense the Niger Delta people with basic infrastructure of electricity,
roads, schools, potable water, cottage industry and employment. As such, wanton
neglect and deepening poverty characterize the Niger Delta communities.'[1210]
Summarising the situation in the region, the report concluded that 'life in the
Niger Delta is nasty, short and brutish.'[1211]

[1204]   *Ibid*, 195.
[1205]   See Anayochukwu Agbo, Oloibiri: Face of the Coming Holocaust, *Tell (Special Edition), 50
         Years of Oil in Nigeria*, 18 February 2008, pp.48–51.
[1206]   Adekunbi Ero, Echoes from the Wasteland, *Tell (Special Edition), Ibid* p.55.
[1207]   *Ibid*, p.56.
[1208]   Sheila Foster, The Challenge of Environmental Justice, *Rutgers University Journal of Law and
         Urban Policy*, Vol. 1, Issue 1, at www.rutgerspolicyjournal.org/1-1.html [accessed 3 March
         2010].
[1209]   *Ibid*.
[1210]   Oputa Report, *op. cit.*
[1211]   *Ibid*.

The fact that the activities of these MNCs seriously pose a threat to several of the rights contained in the Universal Declaration of Human Rights and other international human rights instruments, coupled with the fact that the States are too weak and/or corrupt to be effective, and the MNCs are so powerful that they influence state decision making, provides an argument for the imposition of human rights duties on the MNCs. Thus, any contemporary notion of human rights must contemplate non-state actors as new duty holders.[1212] This is in a context where States have competed for investment and industry by progressively lowering their environmental standards – an international 'race to the bottom.'[1213] For example, it was reported that at one point, the Government of Papua New Guinea passed a law (understood to have been drafted by BHP, an Australian-based corporation operating in the country) making it illegal for any person to sue international mining companies outside the country even for the enforcement of health, environmental, or legal rights. The reason for the law was that such suits might discourage foreign investment in the country.[1214] Such is the imbalance of power between MNCs and the developing countries.

Sadly enough, any negative effects of the activities of the MNCs on the human rights of the local inhabitants are often ignored – relying on the traditional view that human rights is the responsibility of the State, and any mention of human rights on the part of MNCs would be making the latter involved in the domestic political process.[1215] Sometimes, refraining from political intervention creates even more problems for corporations, as witnessed by Shell in Nigeria in the 1990s, when there was serious pressure from NGOs such as Amnesty International on Shell to use its weight to win clemency for Ken Saro-Wiwa and eight other Ogoni activists who were later executed.[1216] Maintaining its policy position not to become involved in domestic politics, Shell stated that '… despite our appeal and those of others, the executions [of Ken Saro-Wiwa and others] went ahead … Like all Shell companies worldwide, SPDC cannot interfere in domestic politics. But the company can, and does, make its views known publicly on human rights matters.'[1217] The position of Shell arose from its belief that to intervene would mean going against its principle of non-involvement in domestic politics. But this failed

---

[1212] Steven R. Ratner, Corporations and Human Rights: A Legal Responsibility, *op. cit.*, p.469.

[1213] Jeffrey L. Dunoff and Joel P. Trachtman, Economic Analysis of International Law, 24 *Yale J. Int'l L.* 1–59 at 54 (1999); Eyal Benvenisti, Exit and Voice in the Age of Globalization, 98 *Michigan Law Review* 167–213 at 167 (1999).

[1214] Joseph E. Stiglitz, *Making Globalization Work*, *op. cit.*, p. 195; Robert McCorquodale, Corporate Social Responsibility and International Human Rights Law, 87 *Journal of Business Ethics*, 385–400 at 387 (2009).

[1215] Sigrun I. Skogly, Complexities in Human Rights Protection: Actors and Rights Involved in the Ogoni Conflict in Nigeria, *Netherlands Quarterly of Human Rights*, Vol. 15 No. 1, 47–60 at 51 (1997).

[1216] See Daniel Malan, Corporate Citizens, Colonialists, Tourists or Activists? Ethical Challenges Facing South African Corporations in Africa, *Journal of Corporate Citizenship*, 18 *Summer*, p.55 (2005).

[1217] See Daniel Malan, *Ibid*, 55.

to recognize the difference between ordinary politics, which rightly should be immune from corporate influence, and human rights which transcend national boundaries. Failures of corporations to raise concerns, for example, against State security forces abuses of rights at MNC sites, or about worker disappearances, and maintaining the posture of political neutrality or cultural relativism, is to fail to fulfill their responsibilities to uphold international human rights standards.[1218]

The MNCs are quick to claim that it is the responsibility of Governments to enact laws against environmental degradation, and not that of the MNCs. This they do to exculpate themselves from liability, ignoring the fact that they routinely lobby strongly against environmental standards that costs them profits, and use their wealth to get laws and regulations passed that free them to pollute at will – thus ensuring that social and private interests are not aligned.[1219] In Nigeria, the Petroleum Industry Bill,[1220] aimed at putting the oil industry on a strong footing in Nigeria, has been stuck in the National Assembly for years partly due to the powerful and strident lobby by the oil MNCs against some sections of the Bill. So strong is this lobby that it is capable of influencing or corrupting any Minister who is not well grounded in oil industry politics or driven by the national interest.[1221]

While the MNCs often take some moral responsibility for their actions at home – doing the right thing even if they are not compelled by laws or regulations or threat of lawsuits, and even if there might be some short-term loss in profits – such moral responsibility seems weaker when they operate in developing countries.[1222] The accountability gap that presently exists has made the oil MNCs operating in the Niger Delta region continue to justify their harmful conduct (such as ecological destruction, protection of their facilities using military security personnel or taking advantage of the forced removal of people for the purpose of oil exploitation) as acceptable so long as it does not run contrary to the Nigerian laws. They exploit the lax regulations and the poverty of developing countries, to despoil the environment and violate the rights of the people.

[1218] Prince of Wales Bus. Leaders Forum & Amnesty Int'l, *Human Rights: Is It Any of Your Business?* 29 (2000), quoted in Steven L. Ratner, *op. cit.*, p.517. As the *New York Times* editorialized, 'Shell, surely, has never hesitated to use its influence on matters of Nigerian tax policy, environmental rules, labor laws and trade policies.' See, Shell Game in Nigeria, *N.Y. Times*, Dec. 3, 1995, at 14. The question then is: why the reluctance on human rights concerns?

[1219] Joseph E. Stiglitz, *Making Globalization Work, op. cit.*, p.196.

[1220] See the discussion in Chapter One. The MNCs have expressed concern over the Bill which they consider a threat to their billions of dollars investment in Nigeria. The Nigerian Government had, in the Bill pushed for a tremendous upward revision of taxes and royalties on deepwater projects, from the unusually generous packages granted in the early 1990s, but this is being met with stiff opposition by the oil MNCs. See Hamisu Muhammad, Petroleum Bill- Federal Government Lobbies U.S., EU on IOCs, *Daily Trust*, 24 July, 2009, at http://allafrica.com/stories/200907240404.html [accessed 5 June 2010]; Tom Burgis, Oil Industry: Controversial Bill Still Hangs in the Balance, *FT.com Financial Times*, 29 September 2010, at www.ft.com/ [accessed 17 November 2010].

[1221] Editorial, Lobbying for the Petroleum Ministry, *ThisDay* 5 April, 2010, at http://allafrica.com/stories/201004050592.html [accessed 17 November 2010].

[1222] Joseph E. Stiglitz, *op. cit.*, 196–197.

It is important to note that the UDHR explicitly imposes direct human rights obligations on private actors. According to the Preamble: '... every individual and every organ of society, keeping this Declaration constantly in mind, shall strive by teaching and education to promote respect for these rights and freedoms and by progressive measures, national and international, to secure their universal and effective recognition and observance ...' The obligations that the Declaration imposes on 'every individual and every organ of society' are not restricted to a particular category of rights but covers both civil and political rights as well as economic, social and cultural rights. Neither 'organ of State' or 'individual' can be said to exclude corporations.[1223] As emphasized by Henkin, '*Every individual* includes juridical persons. *Every individual and every organ of society* excludes no one, no company, no market, no cyberspace. The Universal Declaration applies to them all.'[1224] In addition, the UN Commission on Human Rights has emphasized that:

> *"While the extant international legal framework imposes legal obligations to respect human rights mainly on states and intergovernmental organisations, it cannot be forgotten that the Universal Declaration of Human Rights calls on every individual and every organ of society to take action in order to secure the universal and effective recognition of the rights recognised by it. The Universal Declaration clearly envisions the promotion and protection of human rights as a collective effort of both society and the state; it does not restrict the task only to state action. In fact, article 29(1) declares that 'everyone has duties to the community in which alone the free and full development of his personality is possible.'* **It is not possible for private actors whose actions have a strong impact on the enjoyment of human rights by the larger society ... to absolve themselves from the duty to uphold international human rights standards.***"*[1225]

In its recent general comments, the CESCR has explicitly stated that non-State actors have obligations for the realization of economic, social and cultural rights entrenched in the ICESCR. For example, with respect to the right to food, it stated that: '[A]ll members of society – individuals, families, local communities, non-governmental organizations, civil society organizations, as well as the private business sector – have responsibilities in the realization of the right to adequate food ... The private business sector – national and transnational – should pursue its activities within the framework of a code of conduct conducive to respect for the right to adequate food.'[1226] This statement has found tremendous support in

---

[1223] It has been argued that, 'while companies may not be in the habit of referring to themselves as 'organs of society,' they are a fundamental part of society,' See Amnesty International and Prince of Wales Business Leaders Forum 2000, p.23, quoted in D.M. Chirwa, *op. cit.*

[1224] Louis Henkin, The Universal Declaration at 50 and the Challenge of Global Markets, 25 *Brooklyn J. Int'l L.* 17–25 at 25 (1999) (emphasis in original).

[1225] UN Commission on Human Rights, Sub-Commission on the Promotion and Protection of Human Rights, 2nd session, 1 August 2000, E/CN.4/Sub.2/2000/1/Rev.1, p.17 (bold mine).

[1226] See para. 20 of General Comment No. 12, The Right to adequate food (Article 11) 12 May 1999.

several international Declarations,[1227] and they speak with one voice that private actors have both negative and positive duties concerning socio-economic rights.

As shown above, even though international law norms are often viewed as addressed only to States, many do in fact apply to private individuals as well as corporate persons as well as to States and their officials.[1228]

Many corporations already admit that they have human rights obligations. Shell states in its Code of Conduct that 'Conducting our activities in a manner that respects human rights as set out in the UN Universal Declaration of Human Rights and the core conventions of the International Labour Organization supports our licence to operate ... All employees must understand the human rights issues where they work and follow Shell's commitments, standards and policies.'[1229] Shell reported that in 2009, 165 violations of the Code of Conduct were reported (204 in 2008) as a result of which it ended its relationships with 126 staff and contractors (138 in 2008).[1230] Chevron declares that 'We condemn human rights abuses... Chevron recognizes that companies have a responsibility to respect human rights, and can also play a positive role in the communities where we operate. We conduct our global operations consistently with the spirit and intent of the United Nations Universal Declaration of Human Rights, the International Labor Organization (ILO) Declaration on Fundamental Principles and Rights at Work that are applicable to business, and other applicable international principles, including the Voluntary Principles on Security and Human Rights. All employees are required to comply with Chevron's Human Rights Policy.'[1231] It is therefore a common belief today that MNCs do have human rights responsibilities.

However, several arguments have been canvassed against extending responsibility for human rights to MNCs. These include:

[1227] The United Nations Declaration on the Elimination of All Forms of Racial Discrimination, Adopted on 20 November 1963, by UN General Assembly Resolution 1904 (XVIII). Art. 2; The Rio Declaration on the Environment and Development, Adopted by the UN Conference on Environment and Development, Rio de Janeiro on 13 June 1992, UN Doc. A /CONF. 151/26 (Vol. 1) (1992); the Copenhagen Declaration on Social Development and Programme of Action, Adopted by the World Summit for Social Development in Copenhagen on 12 March 1995, UN Doc. A /CONF. 166/9 (1995). Para. 12(e) of this Declaration states that economic growth and market forces conducive to social development require the encouragement of 'national and transnational corporations to operate in a framework of respect for the environment ... with proper consideration for the social and cultural impact of their activities.'

[1228] Beth Stephens, The Amorality of Profit: Transnational Corporations and Human Rights, *op. cit.*, p.78.

[1229] Shell Code of Conduct, at http://www-static.shell.com/static/aboutshell/downloads/who_we_are/code_of_conduct/shell_code_of_conduct_english_september10.pdf [accessed 13 March 2011].

[1230] Shell Sustainability Report 2009, p.6, at http://sustainabilityreport.shell.com/2009/servicepages/downloads/files/all_shell_sr09.pdf [accessed 13 March 2011].

[1231] Chevron Business Conduct and Ethics Code, at www.chevron.com/documents/pdf/chevron-businessconductethicscode.pdf [accessed 10 March 2010]. Chevron adopted a new corporate Human Rights Policy in 2009 that replaces its existing Human Rights Statement.

i   MNCs are in business. Their only social responsibility is to benefit their shareholders, and not to be moral arbiters concerning human rights issues;

ii   As private non-state actors, they are only obliged to obey the law of the land where they operate and have no obligation to observe human rights. As such, they can only be beneficiaries of human rights protections, not human rights protectors themselves;

iii. There exist questions regarding which of the several human rights corporations must observe. As corporations, they can only ensure that they do nothing to infringe their employees' economic and social rights, but can do nothing to protect civil or political rights more widely which they see as the job of the Government; and

iv. There is also the 'free-rider' problem. That the more conscientious companies disadvantage themselves competitively by spending time, money and energy observing human rights, while less scrupulous competitors make no investment in compliance with human rights.[1232]

Corporate responsibility for the sanctity of fundamental human rights is good for business and good for people.[1233] This fact was well noted in 1998 by the UN Human Rights Commissioner, Mary Robinson. When asked: 'Why should business care about human rights?' she replied that, 'business needs human rights and human rights needs business.'[1234] The reason behind this assertion, in her opinion, was twofold: 'first, business cannot flourish in an environment where fundamental human rights are not respected – what firm would be happy with the disappearance or imprisonment without trial of employees for their political opinions? – and, second, corporations that do not themselves observe the fundamental human rights of their employees, or of the individuals or communities among which they operate, will be monitored and their reputations will suffer.'[1235] This view has also been expressed in the UN Global Compact.[1236] It was exemplified by the furore that greeted the execution of Ken Saro-Wiwa in Nigeria amid accusations that Shell had a hand in the events that led to the arrests

---

[1232] Peter T. Muchlinski, Human Rights and Multinationals: Is there a Problem?, 77 *International Affairs* 31–48 at 35–36 (2001); Peter T. Muchlinski, Corporate Social Responsibility and International Law: The Case of Human Rights and Multinational Enterprises, in Doreen McBarnet *et al.*, (eds) (2007), *The New Corporate Accountability: Corporate Social Responsibility and the Law*, Cambridge University Press, pp.436–437; Nancy L. Mensah, Codes, Lawsuits or International Law: How Should the Multinational Corporation Be Regulated with Respect to Human Rights?, 14 (2) *U. Miami Int'l & Comp. L. Rev.* 243–269 at 248 (2006).

[1233] Michael D. Hausfeld, *The Importance of Corporate Accountability for Human Rights, A Commentary*, September 2008, at www.reports-and-materials.org/Michael-Hausfeld-commentary.pdf [accessed 3 March 2010].

[1234] Mary Robinson, The business case for human rights, *Financial Times Management, Visions of ethical business*, Financial Times Professional, London 1998, p.14, quoted in Peter T. Muchlinski, *op. cit.*, p.38.

[1235] Quoted in Peter T. Muchlinski, *Ibid.*

[1236] The UN Global compact calls on the major MNCs, like the oil MNCs in Nigeria, to observe the fundamental rights of workers, human rights and environmental standards.

and his execution. This was further accentuated by accusations of environmental degradation from oil pollution and gas flares in the Niger Delta, and the growing evidence that the security arrangements of the Shell employees and its installations had, through the calling in of Government security personnel, led to the deaths of innocent local inhabitants of the region at an earlier date.[1237] Apart from the harm this caused to Shell's image, it also subjected it to expensive lawsuits which the company is still engaged in till today.[1238]

MNCs can maintain the trust of local communities where they operate if the fundamental rights of the people are respected. It is not enough for the corporations simply to get the national Government's 'licence to operate'; they also need community support and broad acceptance in order to continue in business, that is a "social licence." Failure of a company to meet its social and community expectations in terms of environmental performance will not only damage its reputation but may lead to a frosty relationship between the company and the community, and ultimately an end to the company's activities in the community, which will have a direct impact on its profitability. The situation in the Niger Delta, particularly in Ogoniland, provides an example. Shell discovered oil in Ogoni in 1957 but mistook the initial social acceptance of the community for social approval to operate.[1239] Several factors contributed to Shell's loss of its social licence in Ogoniland. These include environmental degradation caused by the impacts of seismic surveys, gas flaring and oil spills, lack of benefits from oil and denial of rights, including adequate compensation, lack of respect for the community's culture and tradition, the arrest, trial and hanging of Ken Saro-Wiwa and other eight Ogoni environmental activists, and depletion of the Ogoni's original trust in Shell.[1240] All these led to the company's loss of its social licence to operate in Ogoni leading to the eventual pull out of Shell from the area in mid-1993 following community protests. The possibility of Shell also losing its legal licence to operate in Ogoni was made known by the President of Nigeria, the late President Umaru Yar'Adua, sometime in June 2008. In his words, 'there is a total loss of confidence between Shell and the Ogoni people' and for that reason 'another operator acceptable to the Ogonis' will take over from Shell.[1241] Acceptability is particularly important in the extractive and mining industry because of the environmental impact of their activities. It is only by demonstrating unwavering

---

[1237] Sir Geoffrey Chandler, "The Responsibilities of Oil Companies", in Asbjørn Eide *et al.* (eds), *Human Rights and the Oil Industry, op. cit.,* p.10.

[1238] *Oguru et al* v. *Royal Dutch Shell Plc. & Anor,* Court of the Hague, Civil law section, Case No./ Docket No.: 330891 / HA ZA 09–579 (to be discussed later).

[1239] Legborsi Saro Pyagbara, Shell's Social Licence to Operate: A Case Study of Ogoni, The Ecumenical Council for Corporate Responsibility (ECCR) Report, *Shell in the Niger Delta: A Framework for Change,* February 2010, p.19.

[1240] *Ibid,* 15–27.

[1241] President Umaru Yar'Adua, New operator to replace Shell in Nigeria's Ogoniland, (AFP) 4 June, 2008, at http://afp.google.com/article/ALeqM5ilZcJKFiFVnQf_NOEa1XJUzrjgBQ [accessed 3 March 2010].

commitment towards sustainable development and human rights that MNCs can keep their social licence to operate in these communities. Companies also risk the tightening of their regulatory licences, owing to the fact that the frustrated community may decide to turn to the Government and the regulators of the industry for help.[1242]

It is event like these that led to the emergence of voluntary initiatives by companies to improve the lot of their workers and those of the communities where they carry on business. Efforts to establish binding codes of conduct for multinationals have been, to date, unsuccessful. The next sub-section will examine some of the voluntary codes and initiatives proposed by corporations, non-governmental and inter-governmental organizations, and by individual Governments.

4.7   SOME VOLUNTARY CODES OF CONDUCT

Companies have adopted voluntary codes of conduct that express commitment to respecting human rights. Several organizations relating to the petrochemical industry have drafted specifically designed voluntary guidelines and codes of conduct. Corporate codes of conduct are policy statements that define ethical standards for companies. In the MNC context, they can be considered as 'public welfare' codes, to 'promote socially responsible MNC conduct, largely in the developing world, so as to prevent harm or mistreatment of persons by MNC operations.'[1243] Codes of conduct are voluntary behavioral principles, standards or guidelines that MNCs pledge to abide by because they see it as in their interests to do so.[1244] There are about four types of MNC Codes *viz*: public international codes of conduct, private company codes of conduct, industry association codes of conduct and non-governmental organization (NGO) codes of conduct. Private company codes appear to be the most common because they are created by the MNCs themselves. Industry association codes are similar to the private company codes except that they belong to an entire industry or group of companies within the same industry.[1245] The NGO codes are created by organizations with interests in labour, environmental, human rights, etc, usually in response to a major incident of MNC conduct, e.g.[1246] the Global Sullivan Principles, crafted in 1977

[1242]   Neil Gunningham, "Corporate Environmental Responsibility: Law and Limits of Voluntarism", in Doreen McBarnet *et al.* (eds) (2007), *The New Corporate Accountability: Corporate Social Responsibility and the Law, op. cit.*, p.499.

[1243]   Sean D. Murphy, Taking Multinational Corporate Codes of Conduct to the Next Level, 43 *Colum. J. Transnat'l L.* 389–433 at 392–393 (2005).

[1244]   *Ibid*, 400; Nancy L. Mensch, Codes, Lawsuits or International Law: How Should the Multinational Corporation Be Regarded with Respect to Human Rights?, 14 *U. Miami Int'l & Comp. L. Rev.* 243–269 at 250 (2006).

[1245]   Nancy L. Mensch, *Ibid*, 251–252.

[1246]   *Ibid*, 253–254.

by the Reverend Leon H. Sullivan, with respect to the activities of MNCs in South
Africa in the apartheid era. The original Sullivan Principles were relaunched in
1999 as a more general code, known as the Global Sullivan Principles of Social
Responsibility.[1247] The Global Sullivan Principles refer to support for universal
human rights, equal opportunities, respect for freedom of association, levels of
employee compensation, training, health and safety, sustainable development,
fair competition and working in partnership to improve quality of life.[1248]

4.7.1   ILO TRIPARTITE DECLARATION OF PRINCIPLES

The International Labour Organization (ILO) Tripartite Declaration of Principles
Concerning Multinational Enterprises and Social Policy,[1249] adopted in 1977,
appears to be the most significant of these codes, perhaps because the business
sector itself played a role in drafting it. It provides in paragraph 8 that: 'All the
parties concerned by this Declaration … should respect the Universal Declaration
of Human Rights and the corresponding International Covenants adopted by
the General Assembly of the United Nations as well as the Constitution of the
International Labour Organisation.'

Amongst other things, the Tripartite Declaration calls upon MNCs to take
positive measures like creating employment opportunities, ensuring security
of employment, promoting equality, providing favourable work conditions and
workplace safety, protecting freedom of association and the right to organise
in host countries. Albeit non-binding and lacking in means of enforcement, 'it
provides more detailed guidance on labour issues and a more complete picture of
how companies can maximize their positive contribution to society, and minimize
any negative impacts.'[1250] While the ILO lacks the power to bring the policies of
other international organizations – such as the Bretton Wood Institutions – into
comformity with its standards, it does play a critical role in advising Governments
on steps that can be taken to comply with core labour standards.[1251]

[1247]   The Global Sullivan Principles, at www.mallenbaker.net/csr/CSRfiles/gsprinciples.html
[accessed 3 March 2010].

[1248]   The Global Sullivan Principles of Corporate Social Responsibility, at www.mallenbaker.net/
csr/CSRfiles/Sullivan.html [accessed 3 March 2010].

[1249]   Tripartite Declaration of Principles Concerning Multinational Enterprises and Social Policy
(adopted by the Governing Body of the International Labour Office at its 204th Session
(Geneva, November 1977) as amended at its 279th (November 2000) and 295th Session (March
2006)), at www.ilo.org/wcmsp5/groups/public/---ed_emp/---emp_ent/---multi/documents/
publication/wcms_094386.pdf [accessed 3 March 2010].

[1250]   International Labour Organization, *The Labour Principles of the United Nations Global
Compact: A Guide for Business*, International Labour Office, Geneva: ILO, 2008, p.11.

[1251]   See K.A. Hagen, Policy Dialogue between the International Labour Organization and
the International Financial Institutions: The Search for Convergence, *FES Dialogue on
Globalization* No. 9, October 2003, p.19f.

4.7.2 ORGANIZATION FOR ECONOMIC CO-OPERATION AND DEVELOPMENT (OECD) GUIDELINES FOR MULTINATIONAL ENTERPRISES

The OECD, an institution of thirty-four Governments from only developed countries, has adopted a declaration on international investment and multinational enterprises, which contains sets of guidelines for multinational enterprises.[1252] The first of these guidelines, developed in 1976, contained rather anodyne statements on the corporation's duties to follow the policies of the host country.[1253] Importantly, the Guidelines, as revised in June 2000, expressly call on corporations to '[r]espect the human rights of those affected by their activities consistent with the host Government's international obligations and commitments.'[1254] It fails to provide guidance on how companies can prevent themselves from becoming complicit in human rights abuses by third parties and the specific wording of paragraph 2 above implies that companies are able to operate differently depending on what international human rights instruments the host state is signatory to.[1255] Nigeria is a signatory to the ICESR, thus implying that, under the OECD Guidelines, Shell Nigeria must respect the right to food, the rights to work and to an adequate standard of living, the right to health and the right to a healthy environment.[1256]

Chapter V of the Guidelines states that 'Enterprises should, within the framework of laws, regulations and administrative practices in the countries in which they operate, ... take due account of the need to protect the environment, public health and safety, and generally conduct their activities in a manner contributing to sustainable development,' and in particular prevent 'serious environmental and health damage from their operations, including accidents and emergencies.' Also, Chapter V(6) of the Guidelines requires that enterprises 'adopt technologies and operating procedures in all parts of the enterprise that reflect standards concerning environmental performance in the best performing part of the enterprise.' It is sad to note that the oil companies operating in the Niger Delta are not complying with these provisions.

The complex issue of corporate structure was also dealt with by the Guidelines, as they calls upon MNCs to '[e]ncourage, where practicable, business partners, including suppliers and sub-contractors, to apply principles of corporate conduct

---

[1252] See OECD, Guidelines for Multinational Enterprises, 15 I.L.M. 969 (1976).

[1253] *Ibid*, paras. 1–2. See Steven L. Ratner, *op. cit.*, p.487.

[1254] Section II para. 2 of the OECD Guidelines as revised in 2000, at www.oecd.org/dataoecd/56/36/1922428.pdf. [accessed 3 March 2010].

[1255] Council of Europe Parliamentary Assembly Report, *Human Rights and Business*, Doc. 12361, 27 September 2010, p.12 at http://assembly.coe.int/Documents/WorkingDocs/Doc10/EDOC12361.pdf [accessed 6 June 2011].

[1256] Stichting Onderzoek Multinationale Ondernemingen (SOMO), *Royal Dutch Shell Overview of controversial business practices in 2009*, SOMO Amsterdam, May 2010, p.7.

compatible with the Guidelines.'[1257] Unfortunately, the Guidelines do not provide for how these are to be implemented and do not give corporations any sense of what rights are included and how broadly the group of 'those affected by their activities extend.'[1258] The non inclusion of developing countries (which serves as the home of a sizeable number of businesses and potential victims) as members of OECD, further cast some doubts on the authority of OECD.[1259]

The OECD Guidelines are not legally binding on OECD Governments or OECD-based corporations, but companies are enjoined to respect them wherever they operate. In order to ensure a measure of enforceability, each OECD member has a 'national contact point,' (NCP) usually part of a government agency, vested with responsibility to promote the guidelines within the member State and to gather information regarding compliance.[1260] However, not all adhering States have established NCPs. The Guidelines therefore serves as a link between the Member State and the MNCs. Any dispute concerning the Guidelines can be referred to the OECD's Committee on Investment and Multinational Enterprises (CIME), a political body with no means of enforcing its decisions.[1261] Besides, a situation where NCPs are housed within Government departments tasked with promoting business, trade and investment, can lead to significant conflict of interest.[1262] This is because, it may sometime, has to review complaints against the same investments, hence poor performance.

NCPs are faced with a lack of resources to carry out a proper investigation of complaints or to provide effective mediation.[1263] Since the establishment of the Guidelines, there have been only few cases against corporations, suggesting the ineffectiveness inherent in its current procedures.[1264] Apart from the fact that most businesses are unaware of their existence, the Guidelines are also full of loopholes in relation to implementation, one of the most significant being an exemption 'on grounds of business confidentiality.'[1265] NCPs often find it difficult to take action where they find a company to have been involved in human rights violations as they lack effective mechanisms to implement their decisions. For example, the United Kingdom NCP recently upheld the majority of the allegations brought by Global Witness, one of which was that Afrimex, a UK based company, had been involved in human rights abuse by failing to take adequate steps to

---

[1257]   OECD Guidelines as revised in 2000, *op. cit.*, section II, para. 10.
[1258]   Steven L. Ratner, *op. cit.*, 487.
[1259]   Steven L. Ratner, *Ibid*, 536.
[1260]   Sean D. Murphy, *op. cit.*, 410.
[1261]   *Ibid.*
[1262]   Council of Europe Parliamentary Assembly Report, *Human Rights and Business, op. cit.*, p.12; John Ruggie, *Protect, Respect and Remedy: a Framework for Business and Human Rights*, Report of the Special Representative of the Secretary General on the issue of human rights and transnational corporations and other business enterprises (7 April 2008) UN Doc A/HRC/8/5, para. 98.
[1263]   John Ruggie, *Protect, Respect and Remedy: a Framework for Business and Human Rights, Ibid.*
[1264]   M. Curtis, *Trade for Life: Making Trade Work for the Poor, op. cit.*, p.128.
[1265]   M. Curtis, *Ibid.*

contribute to the abolition of child and forced labour in mines in Democratic Republic of the Congo.[1266] Yet, the NCP was not able to do anything other than issue recommendations, which reportedly have not been acted upon by other government departments.[1267]

The Guidelines have failed to allay public mistrust, to ensure accountability for human rights in corporate activities, and most importantly, to reduce significantly the negative impact of some companies' activities on human rights.[1268] In spite of the existence of the OECD for over 30 years, MNCs from its state parties still constitute the worst violators of the human rights in the host communities.[1269] In recognition of these shortcomings, adhering Governments to the Guidelines have agreed on the terms of reference for carrying out an update of the Guidelines, and launched an update of the Guidelines in June 2010, during a Roundtable on corporate responsibility, where discussions centred on supply chains, human rights and environment/climate change.[1270] On 25 January 2011, Friends of the Earth International and Amnesty International submitted a complaint to the UK and Dutch NCPs under the Specific Instance Procedure of the OECD Guidelines for Multinational Enterprises.[1271] This complaint sets out breaches of the OECD Guidelines (specifically Sections III (Disclosure) and VII (Consumer Interests) as well as Section V (Environment)) by Royal Dutch Shell ('Shell') in relation to statements made concerning incidents, and implications of sabotage to its operations, in pollution and the environment relating to the Niger Delta. The complaint alleges that Shell has (1) provided misleading information and omitted to mention relevant facts about causes of oil spills; (2) based its communications on biased and unverified information, thus failing to provide reliable and relevant information to external stakeholders; (3) gave out incorrect and conflicting messages about causes of oil spills thereby contributing to low quality non-financial information. The complainant alleges that Shell repeated

---

[1266] *Final Statement by the UK National Contact Point for OECD Guidelines for Multinational Enterprises: Afrimex (UK) Ltd*, 28 August 2008, at www.oecd.org/dataoecd/40/29/43750590. pdf [accessed 3 March 2010]. See also Council of Europe Parliamentary Assembly Report, *Human Rights and Business*, op. cit., p.12.

[1267] Council of Europe Parliamentary Assembly Report, *Ibid.*

[1268] Amnesty International USA, Nigeria- Companies fail to live up to human rights principles, at www.amnestyusa.org/business-and-human-rights/chevron-corp/nigeria/page. do?id=1101655 [accessed 23 November 2010].

[1269] Hakeem O. Yusuf, Oil in Troubled Waters: Multinational Corporations and Realising Human Rights in the Developing World, with Specific Reference to Nigeria, 8 *African Human Rights Law Journal* 79–107 at 104 (2008); OECD Watch 1 April 2003, at www.germanwatch.org/tw/ kw-inl01.pdf [accessed 23 November 2009].

[1270] 2010 Update of the OECD Guidelines for Multinational Enterprises, at www.oecd.org/docu ment/33/0,3343,en_2649_34893_44086753_1_1_1_34529562,00.html [accessed 3 November 2011].

[1271] Friends of the Earth International and Amnesty International, *Complaint to the UK and Dutch National Contact Points under the Specific Instance Procedure of the OECD Guidelines for Multinational Enterprises*, submitted on 25 January 2011, at www.business-humanrights. org/media/documents/oecd-complaint-against-shell-re-oil-pollution-in-nigeria-25-jan-2011. pdf [accessed 2 November 2011].

claims that between 70% and 85% and, most recently, 98% of oil spills are due
to sabotage will make Shell to hide under the misleading and incorrect figures
to avoid its responsibility to pay compensation for damage done to the people or
their livelihoods; and also deflect attention away from legitimate criticism of Shell
environmental and human rights impact in the Niger Delta.[1272] The complaint
asks that Shell be called upon to disclose the source of information that it relies
on in continuing to make its public allegations relating to sabotage, and to take
appropriate steps to comply with the OECD Guidelines when it makes statements
on oil spills in the Niger Delta. The response of the UK and Dutch National Contact
Points ("NCPs") to this complaint and its final outcome will indicate the value
or otherwise of the OECD Guidelines for the resolution of environmental and
human rights issues in the Niger Delta region. It is hoped that the Government of
these countries will be able to follow up, and satisfactorily resolve, the complaints
alleged to have been breached in the Guidelines by Shell.

4.7.3 UN GLOBAL COMPACT

In 1999, then UN Secretary-General Kofi Annan launched the Global Compact
(GC) designed to encourage corporations to commit to following a list of
principles in their activities. The GC Principles provide that businesses should:
(1) support and respect the protection of international human rights within
their sphere of influence; (2) make sure that their own corporations are not
complicit in human rights abuses; (3) uphold freedom of association and
the effective recognition of the right to collective bargaining; (4) eliminate all
forms of forced and compulsory labour; (5) effectively abolish child labour; (6)
eliminate discrimination in respect of employment and occupation; (7) support
a precautionary approach to environmental challenges; (8) undertake initiatives
to promote greater environmental responsibility; (9) encourage the development
and diffusion of environmentally friendly technologies and (10) work against
all forms of corruption, including extortion and bribery.[1273] These ten GC
Principles are based on a set of core values in the areas of human rights, labour
standards, the environment and anti-corruption. These core values are derived
from the UDHR,[1274] the ILO Declaration on Fundamental Principles and Rights
at Work,[1275] the Rio Declaration on Environment and Development[1276] and the
United Nations Convention Against Corruption.[1277]

[1272] *Ibid.*
[1273] Initially, the GC contained nine principles, but the tenth principle (corruption) was added
at the GC Leaders Summit in New York, in 2004. See generally, www.unglobalcompact.org
[accessed 23 November 2009].
[1274] UN Doc. A/811, 10 December 1948.
[1275] 37 I.L.M. 1233 (1998).
[1276] 31 I.L.M. 874 (1992).
[1277] UN Doc. A/58/422 (2003)/ (2004) 43 ILM 37.

UNGC is a voluntary and not a regulatory instrument. It therefore does not police, enforce or measure the actions of companies.[1278] Its objective is to activate change and empower businesses with the opportunity to imbibe and entrench the UNGC's 10 Principles as part of their business strategy.[1279] The launching of the UNGC is regarded as 'a key entry point for engaging business and improving the United Nations' ability to work with the private sector.'[1280]

To participate in the GC, the company's chief executive officer is expected to send a letter (endorsed by the company's board of directors) to the UN Secretary General expressing support for the GC and its principles, and then publicly advocate the GC and its principles.[1281] Companies subscribing to the GC are required to submit annually examples of measures taken by them to comply with the principles. This is a condition for participation, and the examples have to be posted on the GC website to ensure that there is an element of transparency in the process.[1282] Failure to comply may lead to the company being listed as a 'non-communicating company.'

Although, the GC has been successful in attracting a large number of participants, estimated in 2008 to be over 4,000 companies from around the world,[1283] it has not been an effective vehicle in pushing the companies to meeting up their human rights responsibilities. The GC contains deficiencies which inhibit it from achieving its objectives. One of these is the lack of clarity of the GC principles in terms of their content and scope. From the outset, the GC adopts an exhortatory rather than a prescriptive approach. It asks companies to 'embrace, support and enact, within their sphere of influence' a set of core values in the area of human rights, the environment, etc.[1284] This makes it promotional rather than fully protectionist in character.[1285]

The GC has also been faulted on its vagueness concerning the scope of its principles. For example, it uses the phrase 'sphere of influence' to delimit business responsibility for rights but fails to define this important term.[1286] In addition, the voluntary nature of GC and 'its emphasis on dialogue and learning makes it primarily an educational tool – rather than a viable means of enforcing corporate

---

[1278] See 'About the GC' at www.unglobalcompact.org [accessed 23 November 2009].

[1279] See D. Asada, *op. cit.*, p.352.

[1280] See S. Williams, The Global Compact: Special Report on Corporate Social Responsibility, *African Business*, February 2007, p.40.

[1281] Justine Nolan, The United Nations' Compact with Business: Hindering or Helping the Protection of Human Rights, 24 *The University of Queensland Law Journal* 445–466 at 462 (2005).

[1282] Sorcha MacLeod, "The United Nations, human rights and transnational corporations: challenging the international legal order", in Nina Boeger *et al.* (2008), *Perspectives on Corporate Social Responsibility*, Edward Elgar Publishing Ltd., Cheltenham UK, p.70.

[1283] Scott Jerbi, Business and Human Rights at the UN: What Might Happen Next?, 31 *Human Rights Quarterly* 299–320 at 304 (2009). These companies include Shell, BP, Rio Tinto, etc.

[1284] Justine Nolan, *op. cit.*, p.460.

[1285] *Ibid.*

[1286] *Ibid.* There is also lack of clarity as regards the exact human rights that business should support and respect.

accountability commitments.'[1287] This factor has hampered ongoing efforts at developing stronger measures both at the international and domestic level to make MNCs accountable for their actions, including human rights.

Also, in cases of violation of any of the principles, the GC does not have an enforcement mechanism. It provides no indication on how compliance will be monitored or how performance data will be verified. Rather, it serves as a platform for free publicity for many MNCs such as Nike and Shell, many of which have bad reputations for violating international human rights, labour and environmental standards.[1288]

The current system of reporting has been criticised on the ground that it makes it possible for companies to report on the issues of their own choice even where they are performing badly in another area of the compact.[1289] Hence, in their comprehensive review of the compact's history, Prakash Sethi and Schepers conclude that the GC has 'failed to meet its mission and goals, and deliberately so.' 'It is long on promises, short on performance, and mostly silent in terms of transparency and objective reporting.'[1290]

4.7.4 NORMS ON RESPONSIBILITIES OF TRANSNATIONAL CORPORATIONS AND OTHER BUSINESS ENTERPRISES WITH REGARD TO HUMAN RIGHTS

Not content with the incrementalism reflected in the approaches discussed above, and the inadequacy of a purely state-centric focus in the sphere of human rights,[1291] some observers, such as the International Commission of Jurists, have insisted upon the need for binding legal rules. A first step in this direction was the adoption of a set of Norms on the Responsibilities of Transnational Corporations and Other Business Enterprises with Regard to Human Rights (the so-called 'UN Norms').[1292] The UN Norms[1293] drafted by a working group of the UN

[1287] *Ibid*, p.464; Nina Seppala, Business and the International Human Rights Regime: A Comparison of UN Initiatives, 87 *Journal of Business Ethics*, 401–417 at 412 (2009).

[1288] M. Curtis, *Trade for Life: Making Trade Work for the Poor, op. cit.*, p. 130; Sean D. Murphy, *op. cit.* at 413; Scott Jerbi, Business and Human Rights at the UN: What Might Happen Next?, *op. cit.* at 304.

[1289] Nina Seppala, *op. cit.*, p.412.

[1290] Quoted in Jon Entine, UN Global Compact: Ten Years of Greenwashing?, *Ethical Corporation*, 1 November 2010, at www.ethicalcorp.com/resources/pdfs/content/201011154314_Last%20word_Page%2050%20ECM.pdf [accessed 3 March 2011].

[1291] Justine Nolan and Luke Taylor, Corporate Responsibility for Economic, Social and Cultural Rights: Rights in Search of a Remedy?, 87 *Journal of Business Ethics* 433–451 at 434 (2009).

[1292] See H.J. Steiner *et al*, *op. cit.*, p.1398.

[1293] Norms on the Responsibilities of Transnational Corporations and other Business Enterprises with Regard to Human Rights, UN Doc. E/CN.4/Sub.2/2003/12/Rev.26 August 2003, adopted at its 22nd meeting, on 13 August 2003.

Sub-Commission on the Promotion and Protection of Human Rights, Chaired by David Weissbrodt, provide the most appropriate basis for developing global standards on the human rights responsibilities of companies. The Norms apply not only to TNCs but also to national companies and local businesses by making each responsible according to 'their respective spheres of activity and influence.' In this way, it 'balances the need to address the power and responsibilities of TNCs' with levelling 'the playing field of competition for all businesses, while not being too burdensome on very small companies.'[1294] The Norms are the most comprehensive statement of standards and rules for companies in relation to human rights, as against the ILO Guidelines that focus only on labour standards, the OECD Guidelines that mention human rights only once, and the Global Compact that contains just ten short sentences.[1295] They establish the right balance between Governments' obligations and companies' responsibilities on human rights.[1296]

The Commentary to the Norms, while elaborating on its general obligations,[1297] states that:

> "Transnational corporations and other business enterprises shall have responsibility to use due diligence in ensuring that their activities do not contribute directly or indirectly to human abuses, and that they do not directly or indirectly benefit from abuses of which they were aware or ought to have been aware. Transnational corporations and other business enterprises shall further refrain from activities that would undermine the rule of law as well as governmental and other efforts to promote and ensure respect for human rights, and shall use their influence in order to help promote and ensure respect for human rights. Transnational corporations and other business enterprises shall inform themselves of the human rights impact of their principal activities and major proposed activities so that they can further avoid complicity in human rights abuses. The Norms may not be used by States as

---

[1294] David Weissbrodt, Business and Human Rights, 74 *University of Cincinnati Law Review* 55–73 at 66 (2005).
[1295] *Ibid.*
[1296] Amnesty International Report (2005), *Nigeria: Claiming Rights and Resources Injustice, Oil and Violence in Nigeria*, at www.amnesty.org. [accessed 5 March 2010].
[1297] Para. 1 of the Norms contains the general obligations. It provides that 'States have the primary responsibility to promote, secure the fulfillment of, respect, ensure respect of and protect human rights recognized in international as well as national law, including ensuring that transnational corporations and other business enterprises respect human rights. Within their respective spheres of activity and influence, transnational corporations and other business enterprises have the obligation to promote, secure the fulfillment of, respect, ensure respect of and protect human rights recognized in international as well as national law, including the rights and interest of indigenous peoples and other vulnerable groups.' This appears to be the most controversial aspect of the norm as it has been criticized for taking a contrary view from the traditional international law.

*an excuse for failing to take action to protect human rights, for example, through the
enforcement of existing laws.*"[1298]

The UN Norms, aside from setting a standard that business can measure itself
against, is also a useful benchmark against which national legislation can be
judged – to determine whether Governments are living up to their obligations to
protect rights by ensuring that appropriate regulatory frameworks are in place.[1299]

The usefulness of the UN Norms in addressing environmental injustices like
that found in the Niger Delta region is further shown in its Article 14, wherein it
is provided that TNCs and other business enterprises shall be responsible for the
environmental and human health impact of their activities. The Commentary to
Article 14 provides that:

(a) Transnational corporations and other business enterprises shall respect the
rights to a clean and healthy environment …
(b) Transnational corporations and other business enterprises shall be responsible
for the environmental and human health impact of all of their activities …
(c) … on a periodic basis (preferably annually or biannually), transnational
corporations and other business enterprises shall assess the impact of their
activities on the environment and human health including impacts from
siting decisions, natural resource extraction activities, the production and sale
of products or services, and the generation, storage, transport and disposal
of hazardous and toxic substances. Transnational corporations and other
business enterprises shall ensure that the burden of negative environmental
consequences shall not fall on vulnerable racial, ethnic and socio-economic
groups.
(e) Transnational corporations and other business enterprises shall respect the
prevention principle … and the precautionary principle …
(g) Transnational corporations and other business enterprises shall take appropriate measures in their activities to reduce the risk of accidents and damage
to the environment by adopting best management practices and technologies … and reporting of anticipated or actual releases of hazardous and toxic
substances.[1300]

The Norms move beyond pure voluntarism to include mechanisms for
implementation. It provides that TNCs 'shall adopt … internal rules of operation

---

[1298] Commentary on the Norms on the Responsibilities of Transnational Corporations and Other
Business Enterprises with Regard to Human Rights, UN Doc. E/CN.4/Sub.2/2003/38/Rev.2
(2003).
[1299] See Amnesty International Report, *Nigeria: Are Human Rights in the Pipeline?, op. cit.*
[1300] Commentary on the Norms on the Responsibilities of Transnational Corporations and Other
Business Enterprises with Regard to Human Rights, UN Doc. E/CN.4/Sub.2/2003/38/Rev.2
(2003).

in compliance with the Norms. Further, they shall periodically report on and take other measures fully to implement the Norms [and] shall apply and incorporate these Norms in their contracts or other arrangements and dealings with contractors, subcontractors, suppliers, licensees, distributors,' and others.[1301] The Norms further provide that TNCs 'shall be subject to periodic monitoring and verification by the United Nations, and other international and national mechanisms already in existence or yet to be created, regarding application of the Norms.'[1302] It provides that this monitoring shall be done in a transparent and independent manner taking into account input from stakeholders, including non-governmental organizations.[1303] It added that States 'should' establish and reinforce the necessary legal and administrative framework for implementing the Norms and other relevant national and international laws.[1304] Suffice it to say that the proposed enforcement procedures were part of the major reasons why many companies opposed the Norms.[1305]

Article 18 enjoins TNCs and other business enterprises to make reparations for any damage done as a result of failure to meet the standards set out in UN Norms. It provides that:

> *"Transnational corporations and other business enterprises shall provide prompt, effective and adequate reparation to those persons, entities and communities that have been adversely affected by failures to comply with these Norms through, inter alia, reparations, restitution, compensation and rehabilitation for any damage done or property taken. In connection with determining damages, in regard to criminal sanctions, and in all other respects, these Norms shall be applied by national courts and/or international tribunals, pursuant to national and international law."*

While the norms were welcomed by human rights groups, others like States and business leaders, reacted negatively against it. Some of the criticisms include the fact that it separated a limited number of rights from the overall universe of human rights, it would make the responsibilities of companies with regards to human rights similar to those of the States, etc.[1306] Unfortunately, as a result of vehement opposition, the Norms were never adopted by the United Nations General Assembly. The Norms were opposed by the International Chamber of Commerce (ICC) and the International Organization of Employers (IOE), because

---

[1301] *Ibid*, para. 15.
[1302] *Ibid*, para. 16.
[1303] *Ibid*.
[1304] *Ibid*, para. 17
[1305] Nina Seppala, *op. cit.* at 411; D. Kinley and R. Chambers, The UN Human Rights Norms for Corporations: The Private Implications for Public International Law, 6(3) *Human Rights Law Review*, 447–497 at 476–478 (2006).
[1306] See Nina Seppala, *Ibid* at 403; D. Kinley and Chambers R., *Ibid* at 462–478.

of their binding and legalistic approach.[1307] Words like 'sphere of influence' and 'complicity', as used in the Norms, have been attacked for lack of precision and clarity. The Norms have been described as an extreme case of the 'privatization of human rights.'[1308] According to the ICC and the IOE: 'The essential problem with the draft Norms is that they privatize human rights by making private persons (natural and legal) the duty bearers. Privatisation leaves the real duty-bearer – the state – out of the picture.'[1309] They were accused of shifting human rights duties from States to civil society actors who are neither democratically elected nor qualified to make decisions concerning human rights that are protected by international law.[1310] Most developing countries were not keen on intrusive regulation and most developed countries were of the view that the Norms were either unnecessary or over-reaching.[1311] The UN Commission on Human Rights, in 2004, noted that the Norms contained 'useful elements and ideas,' but that the draft had no legal standing and that the Sub-Commission should not perform any monitoring function concerning it.[1312] Despite their adoption by the UN Sub-Commission on the Promotion and Protection of Human Rights, and strong support from the civil society and human rights groups, the Norms are not to date recognized by most governments.

4.7.4.1   Ruggie's Position

The debate over the content, form and aims of the Norms led to a call by the Office of the High Commissioner of Human Rights (OHCHR), at its sixty-first session, that the UN Secretary-General should appoint a Special Representative on the issue of human rights and business (SRSG) to continue the extensive consultation process started by the OHCHR.[1313] And in July 2005, Professor John Ruggie was appointed, *inter alia*, to 'identify and clarify standards of corporate responsibility and accountability with regard to human rights' and to 'research and clarify the implications for transnational corporations and other business enterprises of

---

[1307]   International Chamber of Commerce, *Joint views of the IOE and ICC on the draft norms on the responsibilities of transnational corporations and other business enterprises with regard to human rights* UN ESCOR, 55th Sess. UN Doc E/CN.4/Sub.2/2003/NGO/44 (2003).

[1308]   *Ibid.*

[1309]   *Ibid.* This criticism has been held to be misplaced since the preamble to the Norms maintains that the primary obligation for human rights lies in the states. See Nina Seppala, *op. cit.* at 404; Andrew Clapham (2006), Human Rights Obligations of Non-State Actors, Oxford University Press, Oxford, p.228.

[1310]   See David Kinley *et al.*, "'The Norms are Dead! Long Live the Norms!' The Politics behind the UN Human Rights Norms for Corporations", in Doreen McBarnet *et al.* (eds) (2007), *The New Corporate Accountability: Corporate Social Responsibility and the Law, op. cit.*, p.468.

[1311]   H.J. Steiner, *op. cit.*, p.1405.

[1312]   Responsibilities of transnational corporations and related business enterprises with regard to human right, Office of the High Commissioner for Human Rights, 60th Sess., 56th mtg., UN Doc. E/CN.4/DEC/2004/116 (2004).

[1313]   David Kinley *et al.*, "'The Norms are Dead! Long Live the Norms!' The Politics behind the UN Human Rights Norms for Corporations", *op. cit.*, p.461.

concepts such as 'complicity' and 'sphere of influence.' In his report in 2009 to the UN Human Rights Council, Ruggie states:

> "*Company claims that they respect human rights are all well and good. But the Special Representative has asked whether companies have systems in place enabling them to demonstrate the claim with any degree of confidence. He has found that relatively few do. What is required is an ongoing process of human rights due diligence, whereby companies become aware of, prevent, and mitigate adverse human rights impacts ...' [T]he responsibility to respect requires companies to ... become aware of, prevent and address adverse human rights impacts. Moreover, for companies to know they are not infringing on others' rights requires mechanisms at the operational level, to which affected individuals and communities can bring grievances concerning company related impacts and which companies may need to establish where none exist.*"[1314]

Due diligence, according to Ruggie, is 'a process whereby companies not only ensure compliance with national laws but also manage the risk of human rights harm with a view to avoiding it'.[1315] He states that the 'scope of human rights-related due diligence is determined by the context in which a company is operating, its activities, and the relationships associated with those activities.'[1316] He further states that companies do not control some of these factors, but that is no reason to ignore them.[1317] He continues that companies can avoid complicity in human rights abuses when they employ this due diligence process. Even though businesses may not have the full responsibilities of State actors to protect human rights, their duty to 'do no harm' is unambiguous.[1318]

Ruggie notes that business can affect virtually all internationally recognized rights and that any attempt to limit the list will almost certainly miss one or more rights that may turn out to be significant in particular instances.[1319] He therefore discards the approach taken by the UN Norms.[1320] Ruggie refers to an examination of 320 cases of human rights violations that companies were involved in from

---

[1314] John Ruggie, *Business and human rights: Towards operationalizing the 'protect, respect and remedy' framework*, report of the Special Representative of the Secretary-General, UN Human Rights Council, A/HRC/11/13, April 2009, paras. 49, 59.

[1315] John Ruggie, *Protect, Respect and Remedy: A Framework for Business and Human Rights*, op. cit., para. 25.

[1316] *Ibid*, para. 25.

[1317] *Ibid.*

[1318] 'The corporate responsibility to respect human rights [means], in essence, to do no harm'- *Presentation of Report to United Nations Human Rights Council*, Special Representative of the Secretary-General, Geneva, 3 June 2008, quoted in The Ecumenical Council for Corporate Responsibility (ECCR) Report, *Shell in the Niger Delta: A Framework for Change: A Framework for Change*, op. cit., p.11.

[1319] John Ruggie, *Protect, Respect and Remedy: A Framework for Business and Human Rights*, op. cit., para. 6.

[1320] European Parliament, *Business and Human Rights in EU External Relations: Making the EU a leader at home and abroad internationally*, EXPO/B/DROI/2009/2, April 2009, pp.8–9.

2005 to 2007[1321] and maintains that this examination revealed that 'there are few if any internationally recognized rights business cannot impact.'[1322]

In one of his articles, Ruggie states three main reservations he has against legally binding instruments to regulate companies at global level. First, that 'treaty-making can be painfully slow, while the challenges of business and human rights are immediate and urgent;' second, 'a treaty-making process now risks undermining effective shorter-term measures to raise business standards on human rights;' and third, that even if treaty obligations exists, 'serious questions remain about how they would be enforced.'[1323] These points appear unpersuasive as they all apply to most instruments of international law. There would be neither an ICCPR nor an ICESCR if Governments had acted in accordance with Ruggie's logic, since their negotiation and ratification processes also made 'painfully slow' progress.[1324] Also, the negotiations on climate protection provide an example that 'short-term measures of like-minded governments are perfectly conceivable in spite of obstacles during negotiations at global level,' and that 'problems occur in enforcing Conventions would also be an argument against many of the ILO conventions – without their rationale being seriously disputed for this reason.'[1325] However, in response, Ruggie states that he is not opposed to a legal approach, but that his Report reflects the step-by-step process he has been following since the beginning of his mandate. He posits that there are bodies of law and regulation in the form of soft laws applicable to business that have greater leverage over business practices, and secure benefits in a shorter span of time, than harder laws.[1326] Ruggie's Report has been hailed as a significant contribution to closing the gaps that exist 'between the scope and impact of economic forces and actors, and the capacity of societies to manage their adverse consequences.'[1327]

However, the Report has also come under severe criticism. One of these is as regards the way and manner the Special Representative of the UN Secretary-General on Business and Human Rights ("SRSG") treated the obligations of business with regard to human rights. Apart from the fact that its clear distinction between the 'State duty to protect' and the 'corporate responsibility

---

[1321] John Ruggie, *Corporations and Human Rights: A Survey of Scope and Patterns of Alleged Corporate-Related Human Rights Abuse*, published as an Addendum to the third Ruggie Report, A/HRC/8/5/Add.2.

[1322] A/HRC/8/5, para. 52.

[1323] John Ruggie, Business and Human Rights – Treaty Road not Travelled, *Ethical Corporation*, 6 May 2008, at www.ethicalcorp.com/content.asp?ContentID=5887 [accessed 3 March 2010].

[1324] Misereor & Global Policy Forum Europe, *Problematic Pragmatism- The Ruggie Report 2008: Background, Analysis and Perspectives*, June 2008, at www.wdev.eu/downloads/martens-strohscheidt.pdf [accessed 3 March 2010], p.9.

[1325] *Ibid.*

[1326] John G. Ruggie, *Response by John Ruggie to Misereor / Global Policy Forum*, 2 June 2008, at www.reports-and-materials.org/Ruggie-response-to-Misereor-GPF-2-Jun-2008.pdf [accessed 3 March 2010].

[1327] Quoted in Christiana Ochoa, *The 2008 Ruggie Report: A Framework for Business and Human Rights*, ASIL Insights, Vol. 12 Issue 12, June 2008, at www.asil.org/insights080618.cfm [accessed 3 March 2010].

to respect' restricts the extent of corporate duties, it also limits the degree of their commitments.[1328] Legally speaking, 'responsibility' (referred to as 'social expectation' in Ruggie's 2008 report and as a 'social norm' in his 2009 report) is far less strong than 'duty,' thus making the Report a mere description of the current status quo,[1329] and hence unsatisfactory for the regulation of MNCs. Ruggie, in this regard, aimed at further weakening the obligation of MNCs to respect human rights, and this is supported by his 2008 Report: 'Failure to meet this responsibility can subject companies to the courts of public opinion – comprising employees, communities, consumers, civil society, as well as investors – and occasionally to charges in actual courts.'[1330] By implication, Ruggie is clearly steering the UN away from canvassing for binding legislation.[1331] Limiting the responsibility of corporations to merely respecting human rights may encourage them to contract out human rights abuses to their business partners, over whom they often exercise effective control but also usually maintain some distance.[1332]

In his more recent 2010 report, Ruggie has maintained his earlier position that States have the primary role in preventing and addressing corporate-related human rights abuses. He has identified five priority areas through which States could achieve greater policy coherence and effectiveness as part of their duty to protect human rights: (a) safeguarding their own ability to meet their human rights obligations; (b) considering human rights when they do business with business; (c) fostering corporate cultures respectful of rights at home and abroad; (d) devising innovative policies to guide companies operating in conflict-affected areas; and (e) examining the cross-cutting issue of extraterritorial jurisdiction.[1333] Extraterritorial jurisdiction is the ability of a state, through various legal, regulatory and judicial institutions, to exercise its authority over actors and activities outside its own territory.[1334] This often brings about the problem of

---

[1328]   Misereor & Global Policy Forum Europe, *Problematic Pragmatism- The Ruggie Report 2008: Background, Analysis and Perspectives, op. cit.*, p.13.

[1329]   *Ibid.*

[1330]   John Ruggie, *Protect, Respect and Remedy: A Framework for Business and Human Rights, op. cit.*, para. 54.

[1331]   Center for Human Rights and Environment, *UN Special Representative Releases Report on Human Rights and Business Calling for New UN Policy Framework to Address Corporate Abuse of Human Rights*, 18 April 2008, at www.cedha.org.ar/en/more_information/un_special.php [accessed 3 March 2010].

[1332]   Surya Deva, "'Protect, Respect and Remedy': A Critique of the SRSG's Framework for Business and Human Rights", in Karin Buhmann *et al.* (2011), *Corporate Social and Human Rights Responsibilities: Global Legal and Management Perspectives*, Palgrave Macmillan, New York, p.124.

[1333]   John Ruggie, *Business and Human Rights: Further steps toward the operationalization of the 'protect, respect and remedy' framework*, report of the Special Representative of the Secretary-General, UN Human Rights Council, A/HRC/14/27, April 2010, para. 19.

[1334]   See Jennifer A. Zerk, "Extraterritorial Jurisdiction: Lessons for the Business and Human Rights Sphere from Six Regulatory Areas," Corporate Social Responsibility Initiative Working Paper No. 59. 2010, at www.hks.harvard.edu/m-rcbg/CSRI/publications/workingpaper_59_zerk.pdf [acccesed 24 April 2013].

determining where the domestic State's jurisdiction ends, and where the foreign
State's jurisdiction starts.

Even though Ruggie has come up with a variety of ideas on business and
human rights, he is yet to come up with concrete measures that will address what
he calls governance gaps – between the scope and impact of economic forces and
actors, and the capacity of the societies to manage their adverse consequences –
created by globalization[1335] which he sees as the root cause of the business and
human rights predicament today. This is because his framework is based on the
fundamental responsibility of States to maintain and enforce the system.

Notwithstanding the shortcomings regarding their legal status, the UN
Norms have potential[1336] to be developed into a treaty that can be used to hold
MNCs and other business enterprises responsible under international law for
their human rights abuses. It is submitted that if the Norms are turned into a
binding international treaty, the MNCs, such as exists in the Niger Delta region,
could be held accountable under international law for the human rights and
environmental harm they commit.[1337] It will be in this way that the untoward
activities of the MNCs, and the Governments responsible for regulating them,
can be properly put in check. As a common standard, the Norms could serve as
the main tool for monitoring and judging corporate conduct in respect of human
rights. This will be valuable not only for States in fulfilling their obligations to
protect human rights but also for corporations in facilitating competition on an
equal footing, and to eliminate the possibility of companies using a bad human
rights record to competitive advantage.[1338]

Interestingly, the Norms have already started to form the basis upon which
corporate action is based. For example, several leading companies have begun
to road-test the Norms in their own businesses, such as Hewlett-Packard,
Novartis, and other companies that compose the Business Leaders Initiative on
Human Rights; and some NGOs, such as Amnesty International, Christian Aid,
Human Rights Watch, have been using it as a basis for advocacy of Corporate
Social Responsibility (CSR).[1339] If the shortcomings inherent in the Norms are
acknowledged and addressed, the Norms which can be regraded as 'soft law,'
could provide the basis for drafting a human rights treaty on corporate social
responsibility.[1340]

[1335] John Ruggie, *Respect and Remedy: A Framework for Business and Human Rights, op. cit.*
[1336] Unlike other initiatives, UN Norms cover a wide range of human rights and provide for
enforcement mechanisms which include compensation for victims of human rights violations.
[1337] See Marion Weschka, *op. cit.* at 656.
[1338] N. Rosemann, The UN Norms on Corporate Human Rights Responsibilities. An Innovating
Instrument to Strengthen Business, *Human Rights Performance,* Dialogue on Globalization
Occasional papers, Geneva No. 20 August, Published by Geneva office of the Friedrich-Ebert-
Stiftung, 2005, p.37.
[1339] David Weissbrodt, Business and Human Rights, *op. cit.,* 72–73.
[1340] David Weissbrodt, *Ibid* p. 67; David Kinley *et al.,* "'The Norms are Dead! Long Live the Norms!'
The Politics behind the UN Human Rights Norms for Corporations," *op. cit.,* p. 471.

4.7.5 THE VOLUNTARY PRINCIPLES ON SECURITY AND HUMAN RIGHTS (VPs)

This is an international, multi-stakeholder initiative,[1341] launched in 2001, with the aim of assisting energy and mining corporations in both maintaining the security of their operations and ensuring respect for human rights. The need for creating the VPs arose following a series of incidents in the late 1990s concerning the way security forces operated while protecting oil and mining installations in many parts of the world.[1342] Featuring mostly in these allegations of human rights violations were U.S. and UK multinationals, thus prompting those two countries to set machinery in motion to try to address the issues of human rights and security in the extractives sector. Accusations of corporate involvement in the harassment of Government critics, and loans of corporate equipment to military units suspected of human rights[1343] abuses, would come under the company's responsibility to avoid complicity in human rights abuse. More important was the alleged involvement of the Royal Dutch/Shell group of companies in a highly-publicised crackdown by the Nigerian Military Government against Nigerian activists who were very critical of Shell's oil operations in Nigeria, which, led *inter alia*, to a lawsuit against Shell in the U.S.[1344] This event significantly focused the

---

[1341] This was initiated by U.S. and U.K. Governments, in collaboration with certain companies in the extractive and energy sectors, as well as certain NGOs.

[1342] Voluntary Principles on Security and Human Rights, *The Voluntary Principles: Columbia Case Study*, at http://voluntaryprinciples.org/files/vp_columbia_case_study.pdf [accessed 3 March 2011].

[1343] Steven L. Ratner, *op. cit.*, p. 502; There are three main categories of complicity: (a) direct complicity, (b) indirect complicity, and (c) mere presence in a country, coupled with complicity through silence or inaction. Direct complicity involves a 'MNC knowingly assisting a state in violating customary international law.' Indirect complicity concerns a situation where the 'MNC is not itself the direct perpetrator of the crimes but it benefits from human rights abuses committed by the host government... An oft-cited example is a situation in which security forces use repressive measures while guarding MNC facilities or to suppress peaceful protests.' Lastly, mere presence in a country with a repressive host government is seen as perpetuating and aggravating human rights. See Anita Ramasastry, Corporate Complicity: From Nuremberg to Rangoon- An Explanation of Forced Labour Cases and their Impact on the Liability of Multinational Corporations, 20 *Berkeley Journal of International Law* 91–159 at 102–104 (2002).

[1344] Sean D. Murphy, *op. cit.*, p.417. Corporations must not be complicit in human rights violations of the local population where they operate. Complicity under the international legal standards would require a corporation not to lend its equipment to Government with the knowledge that it is going to be used to violate human rights. The oil companies operating in the Niger Delta recruit local security firms to protect their sites. As documented by several NGOs, including Human Rights Watch, Amnesty International, and Christian Aid, these firms often associate themselves with Government or paramilitary security personnel that use force against local communities. A lot of cases have been brought under the U.S. Alien Tort Claims Act (ATCA) against oil companies for their complicity in human rights violations in Colombia, Indonesia and the Niger Delta. See *Wiwa* v. *Royal Dutch Petroleum Co.*, 226 F. 3d 88, 91, 94, 106 (2d Cir. 2000) and later *Wiwa* v. *Royal Dutch Petroleum Co.*, 2002 WL 319887 (S.D.N.Y. Feb. 28, 2002); see generally, Peter Utting and Kate Ives, The Politics of Corporate Responsibility and the Oil Industry, *Stair* 2, No. 1, 11–34 at 20 (2006).

attention of human rights activists on the role and responsibility of oil companies in their uncomfortable coexistence with indigenous peoples.[1345]

The Preamble to the VPs states that their goal is to promote respect for human rights, particularly those set forth in the Universal Declaration of Human Rights and international humanitarian law. The Principles include provisions on: regular consultations between companies and host Governments and local communities; proportionality and use of force; improved company engagement for protection of human rights by their security contractors; monitoring of the progress of investigations into alleged abuses; inclusion of appropriate provisions in contracts; and review of the background of private security firms that companies intend to employ.[1346] The VPs are divided into three categories, *viz*, risk assessments, relations between companies and public security agencies (police, military, etc) and relations with private security contractors hired by the companies. The first provides that where companies provide equipment (including lethal and non-lethal equipment) to public or private security agencies, they should consider the risks of such transfers, and implement appropriate measures to mitigate foreseeable negative consequences. The company must ensure that the equipment is necessary, is appropriate and its use is controlled such that it will not be misused to cause human rights abuses.[1347] The second category enjoins companies to 'use their influence' with public security services so as not to use the services of individuals credibly implicated in human rights abuses; nor use force unless strictly necessary and to an extent proportional to the threat; nor violate the rights of freedom of association and peaceful assembly, or other related rights.[1348] The third category enjoins companies to follow similar principles with regards to private security providers, and also urges them to include such principles, including the International Code of Conduct for Private Security Providers (ICoC) (a multi-stakeholder initiative convened by the Swiss Government), in all contractual agreements with private security contractors, so that they are able to terminate such contracts in cases of breach.[1349] The VPs encourage companies to consult regularly with relevant stakeholders, including civil society knowledgeable about local conditions, to discuss security and human rights. National support is vital to the success of VPs. Indonesia, Turkey, Georgia

---

[1345] Bennett Freeman *et al.*, A New Approach to Corporate Responsibility: The Voluntary Principles on Security and Human Rights, 24 *Hastings Int'l & Comp. L. Rev.* 432–449 at 426 (2001).

[1346] *Ibid.*

[1347] Multilateral Investment Guarantee Agency (MIGA) Working Paper, *The Voluntary Principles on Security and Human Rights: An Implementation Toolkit for Major Project Sites*, July 2008, pp.17, 19.

[1348] Sean D. Murphy, *op. cit.* 418; Bennett Freeman *et al.*, *op. cit.* at 437 (2001).

[1349] *Ibid.*

and Azerbaijan, have included the VPs as part of their contracts with international companies.[1350]

It is important to state that one effect of the executions of Ken Saro-Wiwa and eight others in Nigeria was the recognition by MNCs of the need to have human rights policies. This they have done by adopting voluntary standards on human rights and security. Some oil companies operating in the Niger Delta, including Shell and Chevron, have taken on board the VPs.[1351] Shell stated in its 2009 Report that '[t]he staff and contractors who provide security to Shell operations are expected to perform their duties in line with the Voluntary Principles on Security and Human Rights (VP SHR) ... All new security contracts globally now contain a clause on the VP SHR. We also include the VP SHR clause as contracts come up for renewal and we expect all security contracts to contain it by 2012.'[1352]

However, there are some challenges facing the VPs. Apart from their non-binding nature and limited membership, they have been frequently criticized for using vague language and for a general lack of clarity; a situation that results in some confusion among operational-level staff.[1353] It has been further observed that the VPs are difficult to monitor and audit, thereby making it difficult to evaluate companies' compliance with the Principles,[1354] particularly in Nigeria. For example, the Nigerian Government has not lived up to its obligations to respect, protect and fulfill human rights. While it actually provides security for the oil MNCs (oil being the mainstay of Nigeria's economy), it has failed woefully in ensuring the protection of the local inhabitants of the Niger Delta from the hands of the military posted there to guard the oil installations and the industry. The author during his fieldwork to some of the communities in the region saw the maintenance of a heavy military presence in the Niger Delta communities, with the local inhabitants daily faced with repression at the hands of those security forces. There is a need for some form of independent verification to ensure that companies and institutions actually put the VPs into practice, and to foster greater transparency. The progress of MNCs should then be publicly reported.[1355]

[1350]   Multilateral Investment Guarantee Agency (MIGA) Working Paper, *The Voluntary Principles on Security and Human Rights: An Implementation Toolkit for Major Project Sites, op. cit.*, p. v-6.

[1351]   Amnesty International USA, Nigeria- Companies fail to live up to human rights principles, *op. cit.*

[1352]   Shell Sustainability Report 2009, p.21, at http://sustainabilityreport.shell.com/2009/servicep-ages/downloads/files/all_shell_sr09.pdf [accessed 21 April 2010].

[1353]   Voluntary Principles on Security and Human Rights, *Overview of Company Efforts to Implement the Voluntary Principles*, at http://voluntaryprinciples.org/files/vp_company_efforts.pdf. [accessed 21 April 2010]. For example, as noted in this Report, there is an air of uncertainty as to 'how best to involve host nations in security arrangements, particularly in countries lacking capacity and where companies perceive that they have limited opportunities to have influence.'

[1354]   ERA Report, *When Oil Companies Volunteer*, at www.eraction.org/media/publications/oil-politics/244-when-oil-companies-volunteer [accessed 3 March 2010].

[1355]   *Ibid.*

Significantly, the VPs can be used by the home countries of oil MNCs operating in Nigeria as a framework for working with the Nigerian Government and security personnel to enhance respect for human rights and accountability for abuses, and helping to protect their companies' foreign investments. Thus, the U.S., UK and Dutch Governments should contribute to the implementation of the VP process in Nigeria in the light of the incessant community protests and unrest that often characterizes the Niger Delta region, and forcing the closure of oil production activities.[1356] The Voluntary Principles should also serve as an opportunity for the Nigerian legislatures at the State and Federal levels to take those provisions, review them, and enact them into law. It is possible that the oil companies may have endorsed the Principles primarily as a way of boosting their public image and showing to the world that they really care about human rights. Enacting the Principles into law will force the companies to implement them by making them mandatory principles. This may also help the companies to bridge part of the huge deficits they have accumulated in terms of the transparency in their activities.[1357]

4.8 THE PLACE OF VOLUNTARY CODES OF CONDUCT IN REGULATING THE ACTIVITIES OF MNCs

As shown above, voluntary codes of conduct, while a welcome signal of corporate commitment, are nonetheless voluntary, and as such unenforceable, and so easily violated by unscrupulous MNCs. In addition, voluntary codes are often limited to a few companies. They are limited, in particular, to those sectors where brand names play a decisive role, such as in garments, footwear, sports goods and consumer goods.[1358] The extractive and mining industries, like the oil industry, which perhaps threaten the environment most, are not likely to remain committed to voluntary ethical codes, as a result of the fact that brand names do not play any significant role in those sectors.[1359] Also, since they are often crafted by the companies themselves, these codes regularly involve careful picking and

---

[1356]   Bennett Freeman, Managing Risk and Building Trust: The Challenge of Implementing the Voluntary Principles on Security and Human Rights, *Traditional Dispute Management*, Vol. Issue 1, February 2004, at www.transnational-dispute-management.com/samples/freearticles/tv1-1-article_30.htm [accessed 3 March 2009].

[1357]   Anna Zalik and Michael Watts, Imperial Oil: Petroleum Politics in the Nigerian Delta and the New Scramble for Africa, *Socialist Review*, at www.socialistreview.org.uk/article.php?articlenumber=9712 [accessed 3 March 2010].

[1358]   Abdulai Abdul-Gafaru, *Are Multinational Corporations Compatible with Sustainable Development in Developing Countries?*, being a paper prepared for a conference on Multinational Corporations and Sustainable Development: Strategic Tool for Competitiveness, Atlanta, Georgia, 19–20 October 2006.

[1359]   *Ibid.*

choosing of the rights included.[1360] 'Internal codes only bind those corporations which adopt and implement them, which are by no means all TNCs, thus leaving an un-level playing field in which companies that stick out their necks and do the right thing are penalized.'[1361]

Many codes are vague in regard to human rights commitments which make monitoring difficult. In their Business Principles, the companies often refer to human rights in general, without being specific. Even where the companies refer to some rights, as contained in the 1999 Shell report,[1362] they are referred to only in vague terms – without references to concrete articles in concrete human rights instruments – thus making it easier for them to be adhered to.[1363] For MNCs to be taken seriously as regards their purported commitment to human rights standards, those standards have to be understood in the way they have been formulated in treaties or have become customary international law; and also in the manner in which they have been interpreted by specially created bodies like the European Court of Human Rights or the UN Human Rights Committee.[1364] Lack of clarity and specificity in a code gives room for interpretational problems and allows the rules easily to be evaded.[1365]

Whether unique to a company, or adopted sector-wide, voluntary codes too often lack international legitimacy, and this has resulted in calls for a more detailed, comprehensive, and effective instrument.[1366] As can be seen from the activities of MNCs in the Niger Delta, the fact that the interests of corporations to make profits and to enhance value for shareholders predominates over their concerns for the community where they operate implies that voluntary regulation may only have a positive effect when it coincides with the profit motives of the MNCs. It is difficult to expect MNCs, whose aim is to make profits to make laws that may likely affect their profits and also expect them to sanction themselves in cases of breach. In this way, MNCs should be seen as 'egoistic utility maximizers

---

[1360] David Kinley and Rachel Chambers, The UN Human Rights Norms for Corporations: The Private Implications of Public International Law, op. cit., p.491.

[1361] Ibid, 491–494.

[1362] The Report specifically mentioned among others: employee rights, like health and safety, freedom of association, equal opportunity, pay and conditions, the ILO Declaration 1998; Security policy, like standards and training; and Community rights, such as indigenous people, local people, social equity, right to development, etc. See Shell Report 1999, p.29, at http://sustainabilityreport.shell.com/2008/servicepages/downloads/files/shell_report_1999.pdf [accessed 13 March 2011].

[1363] Willem J.M. van Genugten, "The Status of Transnational Corporations in International Public Law with Special Reference to the Case of Shell", in Asbjørn Eide et al. (eds), Human Rights and the Oil Industry, op. cit., pp.84–85.

[1364] Ibid, 85.

[1365] Helen Keller, "Codes of Conduct and their Implementation: the Question of Legitimacy", in Rüdiger Wolfrum and Volker Röben (eds) (2008), Legitimacy in International Law, Vol. 194, 219–298 at 290.

[1366] Amnesty International Report, Nigeria: Are Human Rights in the Pipeline? op. cit.

who conform to norms because compliance is perceived to be in their own
interest.'[1367]

Another major weakness of voluntary codes is that most of them are adopted
following abuses. For example, in Sudan, the Canadian oil company Talisman
endorsed the Canadian Code of Conduct for Business Abroad after it had been
targeted for its complicity in human rights abuses carried out in the name of
oil exploration.[1368] The adoption of codes in these cases appears to be intended
to cover up negative publicity, avoid risks associated with binding national
regulation, ward off criticism, and advertise a 'caring' public image, thus serving
as a way of deflecting attention away from the abuses already committed and
helping a company evade its responsibilities.[1369] Dealing with this issue, the 2003
OECD Report, which examined a large number of national and international
environmental voluntary initiatives and the extent to which they have been
able to provide sufficient 'regulatory clout' to address the present and future
environmental challenges, found that the majority of the companies had failed
to bring about the needed change in their behaviour beyond that of 'Business-
as-Usual.'[1370] It noted that: 'While the environmental targets of most – but not all
– voluntary approaches seem to have been met, there are only a few cases where
such approaches have been found to contribute to environmental improvements
significantly different from what would have happened anyway. Hence, the
environmental effectiveness of voluntary approaches is still questionable.'[1371]

Another major problem of codes relates to the absence of, or poor, compliance
mechanisms. The MNCs prefer that they themselves should control whether or
not they are complying with their own standards. For example, managers of Shell
companies world-wide are required to write and sign three different letters every
year, covering performance in the areas of: Business Integrity; Health, Safety and
Environment (HSE); and the Statement of General Business Principles.[1372] To show
its importance, it is mandatory for the managers to write and sign these letters
and they are held personally responsible for the accuracy of the contents.[1373] This
is seen as a form of self-regulation and self-control, and a Verification Statement
is made by KPMG Accountants and PricewaterhouseCoopers every year.[1374] In

---

[1367]   Helen Keller, *op. cit.*, p.272.
[1368]   M. Curtis, *Trade for Life: Making Trade Work for the Poor, op. cit.*, p.127.
[1369]   *Ibid*, p.127.
[1370]   OECD (2003), *Voluntary Approaches for Environmental policy: Effectiveness, Efficiency and
Usage in Policy Mixes,* OECD, Paris, p.62; Michael Kerr and Marie-Claire Cordonier Segger,
*Legal Strategies to Promote Corporate Social Responsibility and Accountability: A Pre-requisite
for Sustainable Development*, Centre for International Sustainable Development Law (CISDL)
Legal Brief, April 2004, p.4.
[1371]   OECD, *Ibid* at 14 (italics from the source).
[1372]   The Shell Report 1999, *op. cit.*, p.4.
[1373]   *Ibid*.
[1374]   Willem J.M. van Genugten, "The Status of Transnational Corporations in International Public
Law with Special Reference to the Case of Shell", in Asborne Eide *et al.* (eds), *Human Rights
and the Oil Industry, op. cit.*, p.86.

2005, Shell piloted an External Review Committee of five experts to assess its annual Sustainability Report (according to the AA1000 Assurance Standard) and the committee provides an unedited public statement, which is published in the Report.[1375] This step is quite commendable, but so long as the assessment is being done by experts contracted by Shell, their reports will remain questionable as they may not be free from the biases of interested parties. In a survey of 132 codes carried out by Kolk *et al.*, they found that in 41% of the cases, there was no specific mention of monitoring, and in a further 44% the monitoring systems provided for were internal.[1376] Independent monitoring is essential to ensuring that codes do not simply remain rhetoric, but translate into practice in relation to a company's operations, and also those of its subcontractors.[1377] Oil MNCs should be able to take full responsibility for their human rights conduct by allowing external verification by a committee, preferably consisting of representatives of employers' and workers' organizations, a staff member of a well-respected NGO, and an independent human rights expert.[1378] The formulation of standards around a non-enforceable and sanction-less framework gives room for suspicion that they may be used more for public relations purposes, and does little to advance the rights of the poor and hapless host communities, like those in the Niger Delta.[1379]

However, this is not to suggest that self-regulation through voluntary initiatives is not important. It can undoubtedly be relevant in improving company behaviour where previously there may have been few standards at all, or where the existing laws were grossly inadequate to address the problems. Secondly, it can be used to hold a company to account publicly (though not legally) if its activities do not match the rhetoric.[1380] Private claims may sometimes be brought against any MNC that holds itself out as adopting a voluntary code but fails to comply with same. Such a failure to follow the standards set in a code could, perhaps, be evidence of a breach of contract (where it is stated, or can be implied from, the agreement), or, in certain contexts, of an actionable misrepresentation.[1381] Thus, voluntary initiatives can serve as a powerful weapon to plaintiffs in court cases in which MNCs are accused of human rights violations, to prove that MNCs are not working in accordance with generally accepted standards of behaviour which

---

[1375] Shell Sustainability Report 2005- *Meeting the Energy Challenge*, presented by Ethical Insight Team at Maplecroft, at www.maplecroft.com/pdf/shell2005.pdf [accessed 21 April 2010].
[1376] Ans Kolk *et al.*, International Codes of Conduct and Corporate Social Responsibility: Can Transnational Corporations Regulate Themselves?, *Transnational Corporations* 8 (1) 68 (1999), quoted in *Helen Keller, op. cit.*, 291.
[1377] Helen Keller, *Ibid*, p.290.
[1378] Willem J.M. van Genugten, "The Status of Transnational Corporations in International Public Law with Special Reference to the Case of Shell", in Asborne Eide *et al.* (eds), *Human Rights and the Oil Industry, op. cit.*, p.86.
[1379] Hakeem O. Yusuf, *op. cit.* at 103; Helen Keller, *op. cit.* at 291.
[1380] Helen Keller, *Ibid* at 295.
[1381] Peter Muchlinski, "Corporate Social Responsibility and International Law: The Case of Human Rights and Multinational Enterprises", in Doreen McBarnet *et al.* (eds), *The New Corporate Accountability: Corporate Social Responsibility and the Law, op. cit.*, pp.456–457.

they have agreed to. For example, in France, the *Dassault* case[1382] led to a great legal debate concerning the degree of obligation resulting from a 'code of conduct' adhered to by the company and which it had undertaken to comply with. The ruling of the Cour de Cassation,[1383] delivered on 8 December 2009, established that 'such undertakings could provide grounds for invoking corporate liability, either if the company disregarded the obligations entered into, or if, under cover of a so-called code of '*ethics*,' it violated the fundamental rights and liberties of its employees'.[1384] In addition, such codes of conduct have been used by plaintiffs to demonstrate the extent of control parent companies have over subsidiaries or commercial partners. For instance, Shell's environmental policy and compliance verification system, General Business Principles, and its declarations to abide by the OECD Guidelines, were some of the elements used to determine the influence of the multinational over its Nigerian subsidiaries, in the Shell Nigerian case before Dutch Courts.[1385]

Thirdly, voluntary codes can be used to develop 'best practice' if used transparently, and can form a template for what can later become binding regulation. It has made corporate executives come to a realization that ignoring human rights and environmental concerns can adversely affect their company's profit. The potential power of codes of conduct may be enhanced by references to them in domestic and international courts. And with time, codes may transform from soft law into hard law, on both the national and international level, thus serving as stepping stones in the crystallization of law.[1386] Also, for

---

[1382] Quoted in International Federation for Human Rights (FIDH), *Corporate Accountability for Human Rights Abuses: A Guide for Victims and NGOs on Recourse Mechanisms*, July 2010, at www.fidh.org/Corporate-Accountability-for-Human-Rights-Abuses [accessed 3 June 2011], p.526. This is a case in which a trade union questioned the legal status of the internal code; see also *Kasky v. Nike*, Inc. 27 Cal. 4th 939 (2002), which is a suit arising from alleged Nike's public statements concerning its goods. The Nike case was finally settled out of court in September 2003, with Nike agreeing to pay U.S.$1.5 million to the Fair Labour Association. Even though Kasky's allegations was never tested in court because of the settlement, 'the point was made that specific claims as to one's human rights practices can be just as strictly regulated as are those made in respect of the quality of one's stitching, or the curative effects of one's drugs, or the longevity of one's battery life... the prospect of such litigation appears to have had the salutary effect of making corporations think more carefully about the justifications for their public pronouncements about their respects for or non-compliance with human rights standards.' See David Kinley (2009), *Civilising Globalisation. Human Rights and the Global Economy*, Cambridge University Press, United Kingdom, p.194.

[1383] Cass. Soc. December 8, 2009, no. 08–17.091, quoted in International Federation for Human Rights (FIDH), *Ibid.*

[1384] *Ibid*, July 2010, p.526.

[1385] *Oguru et al* v. *Royal Dutch Shell Plc. & Anor*, Court of the Hague, Civil law section, Case no./ docket no.: 330891 / HA ZA 09–579. See Milieudefensie Factsheet, *The people of Nigeria versus Shell: The first session in the legal proceedings*, Milieudefensie December 2009, at www1.milieu-defensie.nl/english-/publications/Factsheet%20Courtcase%20Nigeria%20first%20session%20 in%20the%20legal%20proceedings.pdf [accessed 3 June 2011]; International Federation for Human Rights (FIDH), *Ibid*, p.527.

[1386] Heller Keller, *op. cit.*, 295; Justine Nolan and Luke Taylor, Corporate Responsibility for Economic, Social and Cultural Rights: Rights in Search of a Remedy?, *op. cit.*, p.434; See

civil society groups, it can be a pragmatic way of working with business to secure improvements in their activities.[1387]

Even though the limitations of codes are real, with effective independent monitoring and compliance mechanisms in place, codes will help in filling some gaps that presently exist at the international level concerning the regulation of MNCs operations.

4.9 NEED FOR A LEGALLY BINDING INSTRUMENT FOR CORPORATE ENVIRONMENTAL ACCOUNTABILITY

Codes are necessary, but not sufficient in addressing the regulatory vacuum that has accompanied globalization, and the exploitation of that vacuum by MNCs for profit maximisation.[1388] As useful as the voluntary initiatives are in the protection of the environment and the promotion of human rights, events in the Niger Delta have clearly shown that they have not been able to stem the flow of human rights abuses by MNCs.[1389] 'Rusted pipelines are still spilling crude oil. Cleanup rarely happens. Most fish and wildlife are long gone and even subsistence agriculture is impossible in many areas. Enormous flares of natural gas still light up villages and fields day and night. The army, still known as the "kill-and-gos," randomly arrests dissidents and ruthlessly destroys whole villages when unrest emerges.'[1390] The human rights violation by the oil MNCs, in conjunction with the Nigerian Government, shows the inadequacy inherent in international law for failing to hold private actors responsible for their activities.[1391] As described by Sacharoff:

> "Shell oil participated in the violation of human rights in Nigeria by conspiring with the Nigerian Government when it economically and politically supported the attacks on the Ogoni villages and, when it bribed witnesses for the prosecution in the trial of Saro-Wiwa. By actively being involved in the internal politics of Nigeria, by paying for the military operations in Ogoni and by providing the weapons and

---

also Peter Muchlinski, "Corporate Social Responsibility and International Law: The Case of Human Rights and Multinational Enterprises", in Doreen McBarnet *et al.* (eds), *op. cit.*, p.457.

[1387] M. Curtis, *Trade for Life: Making Trade Work for the Poor*, *op. cit.*, p.126.

[1388] Wesley Cragg, "Multinational Corporations, Globalisation, and the Challenge of Self Regulation", in John J. Kirton and Michael J. Trebilcock (eds) (2004), *Hard Choices, Soft Law: Voluntary Standards in Global Trade, Environment and Social Governance*, Ashgate Publishing Co. Ltd, England, p.225.

[1389] David Kinley and Rachel Chambers, The UN Human Rights Norms for Corporations: The Private Implications of Public International Law, *op. cit.*, p.491.

[1390] Bill Kovarik, Remembering Ken Saro-Wiwa, *SE Journal* (2005), at www.radford.edu/wko-varik/misc/blog/17.wiwa.html [accessed 3 April 2010].

[1391] Ariadne K. Sacharoff, Multinationals in Host Countries: Can they be Held Liable Under the Alien Tort Claims Act for Human Rights Violations?, 23 *Brook. J. Int'l L.* 927–964 at 963–964 (1998).

vehicles used in the violation of human rights, Shell Oil accepted a state function. By accepting this role, Shell Oil functioned as a state actor... The two actors [Shell Oil and Nigerian Government] conspired as equals to deny the rights of Ogoni people. However, only one of these actors [Nigerian government] can be held liable for these acts. Shell Oil does not face any repercussions for its activities in Nigeria, even though these activities violate international law... Shell Oil was acting in the capacity of the state and it, therefore, should be treated as such."[1392]

Shell Oil can be seen as a *de facto* state actor as it was by its active involvement as shown above, acting under colour of State law. Thus, by 'holding an MNC liable for its activities based on international law, the international community can adjust to this necessary form of regulation and possibly recognize the importance of maintaining control over a potentially lawless entity.'[1393] The failure of the existing mechanisms, at both the national and international level, to address effectively the human rights violations of MNCs shows that there is a need for a mandatory international legal regime, based on at least minimum human rights requirements, to regulate their activities. This would give room for equal treatment among all the MNCs regarding human rights obligations and further ensure predictability and stability concerning compliance with well-defined human rights norms.[1394] Indeed, 'if every nation is forced to abide by the same laws, investors will not be able to pick and choose a country to invest in based on whether or not that country prosecutes companies who destroy the environment. TNCs would not be able to evaluate which country would allow for the largest profit based on its weak environmental standards, lack of prosecution for polluting the environment, or harm to the health of its people. Countries would no longer be forced into trading health for economic development ... A uniform set of binding principles is necessary to level the playing field.'[1395] It will help to bring to an end the current "immunity" enjoyed by MNCs for their human rights violations. Stating the need for legal regulation, McCorquodale[1396] has emphasised that business activity is assisted by the operation of the rule of law. Where the rule of law is in place, corporations are able to reduce their risks, as they can conduct their businesses aware that there is a great degree of certainty, stability and recourse to redress.[1397] The adoption of stricter universal standards of corporate

---

[1392]   *Ibid*, at 963–964.

[1393]   *Ibid*, at 964.

[1394]   Abdullah Al Faruque and M.D. Zakir Hossain, Regulation Vs Self Regulation in Extractive Industries: A Level Playing Field, *MqJICEL* Vol. 3, 45–64 at 59 (2006).

[1395]   Sabaha Khan, *Transnational Corporations Liability on Environmental Harms*, Articlesbase, 27 September 2009, at www.articlesbase.com/health-and-safety-articles/transnational-corporations-liability-for-environmental-harms-1275283.html [accessed 13 April 2010]; Beth Stephens, *op. cit.*, p.82.

[1396]   Robert McCorquodale, Corporate Social Responsibility and International Human Rights Law, 87 *Journal of Business Ethics*, 385–400 at 396 (2009).

[1397]   *Ibid*, 396; Kaufmann *et al.*, *Governance Matters*, at www.worldbank.org/wbi/governance [accessed 3 April 2010].

liability will encourage corporations to behave responsibly in the course of their operations, thereby protecting human rights. Such an international arrangement can help universalize the remedies under the Alien Torts Claim Act (ATCA) (to be discussed later in this chapter); make them available and accessible in many parts of the world; reduce the pressure on the U.S. courts; reduce resentment against the U.S. for serving as the world's judge; remove the competitive disadvantage faced by U.S. companies; and help promote international human rights protection by expanding the pool of people with reasonable prospects of seeking remedies for their environmental and human rights abuse at the relevant forums across the world.[1398] Due to their non-penal nature, voluntary initiatives cannot be made to replace hard sanctions. Since voluntary initiatives help in addressing most of the problems that have proved difficult using hard sanctions, they will be useful in complementing hard sanctions.[1399] Greater reliance should therefore be placed on both voluntary initiatives and hard sanctions; that is, adopting a hybrid forms of regulation that articulate voluntary initiatives and legal frameworks.[1400]

4.10 U.S. TRANSNATIONAL HUMAN RIGHTS LITIGATION

4.10.1 ATCA AND THE PROTECTION OF ENVIRONMENT

The Alien Torts Claim Act (ATCA), a U.S. law enacted in 1789,[1401] provides that '[t] he district courts shall have original jurisdiction of any civil action by an alien for a tort only, committed in violation of the law of nations or by a treaty of the United States.'[1402] Its original purpose was to empower American courts to pass judgment on piracy committed on the high seas. ATCA 'rested unnoticed' for many years,[1403]

[1398]   Emeka Duruigbo, Exhaustion of Local Remedies in Alien Tort Litigation: Implications for International Human Rights Protection, 29 *Fordham Int'l L.J.* 1245–1311 at 1307–1308 (2006).
[1399]   Bede Nwete, *Soft Law and Hard Sanctions in Upstream Oil and Gas in Developing Regions – How International Codes, Principles and Protocols Influence National Projects and Developments*, International Energy Law and Policy Research Paper Series, Working Research Paper Series No: 2010/05, Centre for Energy, Petroleum and Mineral Law and Policy, University of Dundee, p.19.
[1400]   Peter Utting and Kate Ives, The Politics of Corporate Responsibility and the Oil Industry, *Stair* 2, No. 1, 11–34 at 28 (2006).
[1401]   The Judiciary Act of 1789, ch. 20, § 9, 1 Stat. 73, 77 (Sept. 24, 1789).
[1402]   28 U.S.C. § 1350 (2000). ATCA is complemented by the 1991 Torture Victim Protection Act (TVPA) which applies to "individual who, under actual or apparent authority, or color of law, of any foreign nation and: 1) subjects an individual to torture shall, in a civil action, be liable for damages to that individual; or 2) subjects an individual to extrajudicial killing shall, in a civil action, be liable for damages to the individual's legal representative, or to any person who may be a claimant in an action for wrongful death".
[1403]   James Boeving, Half Full ... or Completely Empty?: Environmental Alien Tort Claims Post Sosa v. Alvarez-Machain, 18 *Geo. Int'l Envtl. Law Review* 109–147 at 110 (2005). Judge Friendly called ATCA a 'legal Lohengrin' – 'no one seems to know whence it came.' *IIT v. Vencap, Ltd.*,

until 1980, when it came into limelight in *Filartiga* v. *Pena-Irala*.[1404] In this case, the family of a Paraguayan man, who had been tortured and killed in Paraguay, initiated an action under ATCA against the alleged torturer, a Paraguayan Police official who was then living in New York. The Second Circuit Court of Appeal reversing the decision of the District Court held that 'an act of torture committed by a State official against one held in detention violates established norms of the international law of human rights, hence the law of nations.'[1405] The implication of this decision was considered so great that Professor Harold Koh noted that through the decision, 'transnational public law litigants finally found their *Brown* v. *Board of Education*.'[1406]

For a long period of time, ATCA was only used in matters involving Government officials who had used their powers to abuse people. It was not until the mid-1990s that human rights activists began to make use of the law to bring cases against companies accused of complicity in human rights abuses committed outside the United States.[1407] The law applies only to companies that are connected to the U.S. either because they are registered there or because they are listed on U.S. stock exchanges.[1408]

As noted by Boeving, there are three primary and interconnected reasons why ATCA is been chosen for the protection of the environment: the environment as an international good; lack of local remedies resulting from unequal bargaining power between MNCs and the host economy; and human rights as a proxy for environmental harm.[1409] For Boeving, the first is that the use of ATCA by foreign plaintiffs will remove the unequal bargaining power in which MNCs exert greater influence on the environmental policies of developing nations.[1410] The second rationale, though similar to the first, focuses not on the environment *per se*, but the lack of adequate local remedies to confront MNCs generally. The third rationale focuses on the consequences of environmental degradation on human populations and how MNCs can be held legally accountable for their environmental and human rights abuses, either caused by their direct action or through their complicity in the actions of the State.[1411]

---

519 F.2d 1001, 1015 (2d Cir. 1975) (Friendly, J.), abrogated on other grounds by *Morrison* v. *Nat'l Austl. Bank Ltd.*, 130 S. Ct. 2869 (2010).

[1404] 630 F 2d 876 (2nd Cir, 1980).

[1405] *Ibid.*

[1406] Harold Hongju Koh, Transnational Public Law Litigation, 100 *Yale L.J.* 2347–2402 at 2366 (1991).

[1407] J. Bray, *op. cit.*, p.306.

[1408] *Ibid*, pp. 306–307.

[1409] James Boeving, *op. cit.* at 112.

[1410] *Ibid*, p.114.

[1411] *Ibid*, p.115.

4.10.2 ELEMENTS REQUIRED FOR AN ENVIRONMENTAL CLAIM UNDER ATCA

A claimant bringing an action for environmental harm under ATCA is required to satisfy the requirements of the statute. These are – bringing the action as an alien; suing in tort only; and showing that the tort violated the law of nations or a treaty of the United States.[1412] The third element is the most difficult element for plaintiffs to argue, and for judges to recognize. The law of nations, as it was defined in 1789, is believed to have encompassed what is now known as international law – both treaty based and customary international law.[1413] In determining whether a claim violates the laws of nations, courts claim to do this by consulting the works of the jurists, writing on international law; or the general usage and practice of nations; or judicial decisions recognizing and enforcing that law.[1414] However in practice, the definition that the courts apply is much narrower than what international legal scholars consider as customary international law. For the purpose of ATCA, some conducts that international legal scholars may view as violating customary international law may not yet be recognized as a violation of the law of nations because ATCA further defines the law of nations as 'specific, universal, and obligatory.'[1415] For example, while some international environmental principles, like that of sustainable development … are norms recognized in the international community, they are not so under ATCA as the law of nations. In 2004, the Supreme Court in *Sosa* v. *Alvarez-Machain*,[1416] observed that courts may allow 'any claim based on the present-day law of nations to rest on a norm of international character accepted by the civilized world and defined with a specificity comparable to the features of the 18th-century paradigms we have recognized.'[1417] The 18th-century paradigms referred to were the 'violation of safe conducts, infringement of the rights of ambassadors, and piracy.'[1418] It also permitted ATS claims in relation to a handful of serious human rights violations, such as genocide, crimes against humanity and slavery. Regarding the recognition of new ATCA claims, the court counseled that 'judicial power should be exercised on the understanding that the door is still ajar subject to vigilant door keeping, and thus open to a narrow class of international norms today.'[1419] The court thereby created serious barriers to what could be brought as an ATCA claim. In

---

[1412] Richard M. Buxbaum and David D. Caron, The Alien Tort Statute: An Overview of the Current Issues, 28 *Berkeley J. Int'l L.* 511–518 at 513 (2010); Kathleen Jaeger, Environmental Claims Under the Alien Tort Statute, 28 *Berkeley J. Int'l L.* 519–536 at 520 (2010).

[1413] Natalie L. Bridgeman, Human Rights Litigation Under the ATCA as a Proxy for Environmental Claims, 6 *Yale Hum. Rts. & Dev. L.J.* 1–43 at 5 (2003).

[1414] *Filartiga*, 630 F.2d at 880.

[1415] Natalie L. Bridgeman, *op. cit.* at 5–6.

[1416] 542 U.S. 692 (2004).

[1417] *Ibid* at 749.

[1418] *Sosa* v. *Alvarez-Machain*, *Supra*, p.723 (quoting William Blackstone, 4 Commentaries); Natalie L. Bridgeman, *op. cit.* at 755.

[1419] Natalie L. Bridgeman, *Ibid* at 729.

view of the lack of clarification of the scope of ATCA in *Sosa*, it can be stated that
the current standard for bringing environmental claims under ATCA is similar to
that utilized more than 200 years ago when the statute was drafted, requiring the
demonstration of a universal, definable, and obligatory international law norm[1420]

An alternative avenue employed by environmental plaintiffs is to allege a tort
that violates 'a treaty of the United States.' For a claim to be brought successfully
under this heading, it must be shown that the U.S. is a party to the relevant treaty,
and that the treaty is to be in force in the U.S. The treaty has to self-executing,
that is, one that creates a private cause of action; or the treaty must have been
implemented in the United States pursuant to legislation by the Congress.[1421]
This, no doubt, accounts for why this approach is far less frequently used by
environmental plaintiffs.

4.10.3 ATCA ENVIRONMENTAL JURISPRUDENCE[1422]

The courts in the U.S. have addressed a number of environmental claims brought
under the ATCA by a foreigner who has suffered an environmental harm outside
the U.S. at the hands of an American corporation or a MNC with business
operations in the U.S. This section examines some of these cases.

4.10.3.1 Amlon Metals Inc. v. FMC Corp.[1423]

The plaintiffs brought this action under the Resource Recovery and Conservation
Act (RCRA)[1424] 1976 and the Alien Tort Statute (ATS), alleging the failure of the
defendant to have ensured that the copper residue which Amlon had shipped
to England was free from harmful impurities and not hazardous. The plaintiffs
contended that defendant's conduct violated the 'law of nations,' in particular
Principle 21 of the Stockholm Principles formulated at the United Nations
Conference on the Human Environment. Principle 21 grants the State the
sovereign right to exploit its natural resources pursuant to its own environmental
policies, and prohibits activity that causes damage to the environment of other
States or of areas beyond the limits of national jurisdiction. The plaintiff also

---

[1420] James Boeving, *op. cit.* at 133.

[1421] *Ibid*, at 117.

[1422] See generally, James Boeving, *Ibid.* at 118–128; Kathleen Jaeger, *op. cit.* at 526–534; Natalie L.
Bridgeman, *op. cit.* at 17–26; Simon Baughen (2007), *International Trade and the Protection of
the Environment*, Routledge-Cavendish, London & New York, pp.262–266.

[1423] 755 F. Supp. 668 (S.D.N.Y. 1991).

[1424] 44 U.S.C. §§ 6901–6992 (1985). The Resource Conservation and Recovery Act (RCRA)
addresses solid and hazardous waste management activities in order to ensure proper treatment, storage, and disposal in a manner protective of human health and the environment.

relied on the Restatement (Third) of Foreign Relations Law.[1425] The plaintiff's case was dismissed for lack of subject matter jurisdiction, finding that the plaintiff's reliance on the Stockholm Principles was misplaced because the Principles do not 'set forth any specific proscriptions, but rather refer only in a general sense to the responsibility of nations to insure that activities within their jurisdiction do not cause damage to the environment beyond their borders.' It found that the Restatement was too specific to the U.S., and, did not constitute a statement of universally recognized principles.

This case shows how the courts consider claims based on general principles of international environmental law but it failed to provide direction as to what is sufficient for such claims.[1426] Lack of international consensus on environmental norms, which the court identified in *Amlon* when dealing with Principle 21, has been identified as one reason why courts have been reluctant to recognize environmental abuses brought by affected victims.[1427] It is only when plaintiffs start to appeal to sources of environmental norms that evidence true international consensus that more success will be recorded in establishing causes of action under the ATCA.[1428]

4.10.3.2 Jota v. Texaco, Inc. and Aguinda v. Texaco, Inc.[1429]

In *Aguinda*, the plaintiffs were residents of the Oriente region of Ecuador, and an adjoining area in Peru. They brought an action under the Alien Tort Statute (ATS), alleging that Texaco had polluted their rain forests and rivers by large scale disposal of toxic by-products of their drilling processes resulting in environmental harm and personal injuries to the locals, including poisoning and pre-cancerous growths. Principle 2 of the Rio Declaration provides that States have, in accordance with the Charter of the United Nations and the principles of international law, the sovereign right to exploit their own resources pursuant to their own environmental and developmental policies, and their responsibility to ensure that activities within their jurisdiction or control do not cause damage to the environment of other States or of areas beyond the limits of national jurisdiction. The complaints alleged that Texaco's activities in Ecuador were 'designed, controlled, conceived and directed ... through its operations in the United States.' In a preliminary decision, the District Court appeared responsive

---

[1425]   Restatement (Third) of Foreign Relations Law § 602(2) (1972) provides that: '[w]here pollution originating in a state has caused significant injury to persons outside that state, or has created a significant risk of such injury, the state of origin is obligated to accord to the person injured or exposed to such risk access to the same judicial or administrative remedies as are available in similar circumstances within the state.'

[1426]   Natalie L. Bridgeman, *op. cit.* at 19; Kathleen Jaeger, *op. cit.* at 527.

[1427]   Armin Rosencranz and Richard Campbell, Foreign Environmental and Human Rights Suits Against U.S. Corporations in U.S. Courts, 18 *Stan. Envtl. L.J.* 145–208 at 156 (1999).

[1428]   *Ibid.*

[1429]   142 F. Supp. 2d 534 (S.D.N.Y. 2001).

to claims premised on Principle 2 of the Rio Declaration.[1430] Judge Broderick went
so far as to speculate that the plaintiffs could contend that '[t]he Rio Declaration
may be declaratory of what it treated as pre-existing principles just as was the
Declaration of Independence.'[1431] The court even went further, to point out the
U.S. international and domestic commitments to controlling hazardous waste,
and suggesting that the plaintiffs could have their claim sustained under ATS if
they were able to establish 'misuse of hazardous waste of sufficient magnitude to
amount to a violation of international law.'[1432] However, following the death of
Judge Broderick in March 1995, the case was assigned to Judge Rakoff. The latter
granted Texaco's motion to dismiss the suit on grounds of *forum non conveniens*
(FNC), international comity, and for failure to have joined two indispensable
parties – PetroEcuador and the Republic of Ecuador (which were exempt from
suit under the Foreign Sovereign Immunities Act).[1433] The suit was dismissed
without reaching a final decision on the merits of the environmental issues raised.

However, subsequently in *Jota v. Texaco, Inc.*,[1434] *Aguinda* was consolidated
with *Jota* and its dismissal reversed and remanded for reconsideration by the
Second Circuit. Following the consent of Texaco to the jurisdiction of Ecuadorian
courts, the district court in *Aguinda* rejected each of plaintiffs' objections to the
adequacy of an Ecuadorian forum, and dismissed the case on the basis of FNC,
on the ground that the cases had 'everything to do with Ecuador and nothing
to do with the United States.'[1435] As regards the fact that the activities of Texaco
'violated evolving environmental norms of customary international law,' the
judge reasoned that these lacked 'any meaningful precedential support.'[1436]

It is unfortunate that these cases ended prematurely without allowing them
to be determined on their merits.

4.10.3.3 Sarei v. Rio Tinto PLC[1437]

The plaintiffs, residents of the island of Bougainville in Papua New Guinea (PNG),
filed suit against the defendants under the ATCA, alleging that the defendant's

---

[1430] Principle 2 of Rio Declaration grants the States the sovereign right to exploit their own
resources and the responsibility to ensure that activities within their jurisdiction or control do
not cause damage to the environment of other States or of areas beyond the limits of national
jurisdiction.
[1431] *Aguinda* v. *Texaco, Inc.*, 1994 U.S. Dist. LEXIS 4718.
[1432] *Ibid.*
[1433] 28 U.S.C. §§ 1603(b) and 1604.
[1434] The court ruled that FNC dismissal was inappropriate, 'at least absent a commitment by
Texaco to submit to the jurisdiction of the Ecuadorian courts ...' *Jota v. Texaco, Inc.*, 157 F.3d
153, 155, (2d Cir. 1998) (consolidated with *Aguinda* v. *Texaco, Inc.*, 1994 U.S. Dist. (S.D.N.Y., 13
August 1997).
[1435] *Aguinda* v. *Texaco, Inc.* 142 F. Supp. 2d 534 S.D.N.Y., 2001. This decision was affirmed by the
Second Circuit in *Aguinda*, 303 F. 3D 470 (2d Cir. 2002).
[1436] *Aguinda*, 303 F. 3D at 552.
[1437] 221 F. Supp. 2d 1116 (C.D. Cal. 2002).

mining activities had destroyed their island's environment, harmed the health of its residents in violation of their rights to life and health, and had led to ten-years (1989–1999) of war crimes. Specifically, the plaintiffs alleged that improperly dumped waste rock and tailings from the Panguna mining operations had harmed the island's environment and the health of its residents. The protests that resulted from the defendant's labour and hiring practices, as well as the environmental harm caused by the mines, had escalated and became violent. The plaintiffs alleged that the defendant was complicit in war crimes and crimes against humanity by the PNG army, having assisted the Government, through blockage of medical supplies, and leading to numerous deaths of civilians. The court rejected the plaintiffs' rights to life and health claims on the grounds that these rights are not sufficiently specific to support an ATCA claim. The court was not persuaded that 'nations universally recognize [that such rights] can be violated by perpetrating environmental harm.'[1438] To support their claims based solely on environmental harm, the plaintiffs relied on the principle of sustainable development and the United Nations Convention on the Law of the Sea (UNCLOS).[1439] As regards the principle of sustainable development, the court found that it did not constitute a specific, universal, and obligatory norm that could form part of the law of nations.

On the plaintiffs' claim under UNCLOS that the marine pollution caused by the defendant violated the UNCLOS provisions, the court, after noting that the U.S. was not a party to the treaty, nevertheless found that the 'plaintiffs have adequately stated a claim for violation of the customary international law reflected in UNCLOS.'[1440] According to the court, UNCLOS having received 166 ratifications (excluding the U.S., which is only a signatory), had become part of customary international law. The court therefore came to conclusion that the plaintiffs had a cognizable claim under ATCA. However, as the activities of the defendant were intertwined with the acts of a foreign sovereign (indeed, Rio Tinto conducted its mining activity pursuant to an agreement between its subsidiary and the PNG Government), the court used its discretion to dismiss the entire case, based on the Act of State doctrine.[1441] The court alternatively invoked the "political questions" doctrine as well as the doctrine of international comity[1442] as reasons for dismissal of the plaintiffs' complaint. On appeal, a three-judge panel (with one dissenting) affirmed the decision of the District Court that UNCLOS was applicable.[1443] The court agreed that the plaintiffs' claims for violations of

---

[1438]   *Ibid*, 1158.
[1439]   *Ibid*, 1160–1161. UNCLOS requires states to take 'all measures … necessary to prevent, reduce and control pollution of the marine environment that involves hazards to human health, living resources and marine life through the introduction of substances into the marine environment' and to 'adopt laws and regulations to prevent, reduce, and control pollution of the marine environment caused by land-based sources.'
[1440]   *Ibid*, 1161.
[1441]   *Ibid*, 1193.
[1442]   *Ibid*, 1198, 1199, 1207.
[1443]   *Sarei II*, 456 f. 3d at 1078.

UNCLOS implicated 'specific, universal and obligatory norm[s] of international
law' that properly form the basis for ATCA claims. It further noted that '*Sosa*'s
gloss on this standard does not undermine the District Court's reasoning. All of
the plaintiffs' remaining claims, with the exception of the UNCLOS claim, assert
jus cogens violations that form the least controversial core of modern day ATCA
jurisdiction.'[1444] Following a petition for rehearing and for rehearing *en banc*, the
three judges withdrew their earlier opinion and issued a new opinion overriding
the earlier one.[1445] However, the court was unable to decide whether the UNCLOS
claims fell under the 'law of nations' due to the invocation of the Act of State
doctrine which put a stop to the hearing.

Sarei is important because the District Court's opinion that UNCLOS reflects
customary international law, notwithstanding its subsequent dismissal of the
claim, would serve as a useful precedent for future litigants in their claims against
corporations for environmental harm.

4.10.3.4 Beanal v. Freeport-McMoran[1446]

This case involved alleged violations of international law committed by U.S.
corporations conducting mining activities abroad in the Pacific Rim. Beanal, a
resident of Tamika, Irian Jaya (Indonesia), alleged that Freeport, a multinational
mining corporation, had engaged in environmental abuses, human rights
violations, and cultural genocide. Specifically, he alleged that Freeport's mining
operations had caused destruction, pollution, alteration, and contamination of
natural waterways, as well as surface and ground water sources; deforestation;
and the destruction and alteration of physical surroundings.[1447] The plaintiff had
alleged that Freeport engaged in cultural genocide by destroying the Amungme's
habitat and religious symbols, thus forcing the Amungme to relocate. Beanal and
the *amici*[1448] referred the District Court to three international environmental law
principles to show that the alleged environmental abuses caused by Freeport's
mining activities were cognizable under international law. They are (1) the
Polluter Pays Principle, (2) the Precautionary Principle, and (3) the Proximity
Principle.[1449] Rejecting Beanal's claims, the District Court held that Beanal had

---

[1444] *Ibid*, at 1210. *Jus cogens* means, a set of rules, which are peremptory in nature from which no
derogation is permitted.

[1445] *Sarei III*, 487 f. 3d at 119–1197, *en banc* hearing granted, 499 F. 3d 923 (9th Cir. 2007); See
Kathleen Jaeger, *op. cit.*, 534.

[1446] *Beanal* v. *Freeport-McMoran, Inc. (Beanal I)*, 969 f. Supp. 362b(E.D. La. 1997), affirmed in 197
F. 3d. 161 (5th Cir. 1999).

[1447] *Beanal I, Ibid*, 369.

[1448] *Amici Curiae* included the Earth Rights International, the Sierra Club, the Center for
Constitutional Rights, Center for Justice and Accountability, and the Four Directions Council.

[1449] *Beanal I, op. cit.*, 383–384. The 'Polluter pay principle' provides that the costs of pollution are
to be paid by the party responsible for causing the pollution; the 'Precautionary Principle provides that '[w]here there are threats of serious or irreversible damage, lack of full scientific
certainty shall not be used a reason for postponing cost-effective measures to prevent envi-

failed to articulate environmental torts that were cognizable under international law. The court stated that the principles invoked 'apply to "members of the international community" rather than to non-state corporations ... A non-state corporation could be bound to such principles by treaty, but not as a matter of international customary law.'[1450]

On appeal, the Fifth Circuit,[1451] affirming the lower court's decision, found that the 'sources of international law cited by Beanal and the *amici* merely refer to a general sense of environmental responsibility and state abstract rights and liberties devoid of articulable or discernable standards and regulations to identify practices that constitute international environmental abuses or torts.'[1452] The court went further, saying that the 'federal courts should exercise extreme caution when adjudicating environmental claims under international law to insure that environmental policies of the United States do not displace environmental policies of other governments ... especially when the alleged environmental torts and abuses occur within the sovereign's borders and do not affect neighboring countries.'[1453] Although Beanal and the *amici* had urged the court to recognize cultural genocide as a discrete violation of international law, the court refused to merge what it termed the amorphous right to 'enjoy culture,' or the right to 'freely pursue' culture, or the right to cultural development with the concept of cultural genocide. In the opinion of the court, it would be 'imprudent for a United States tribunal to declare an amorphous cause of action under international law that has failed to garner universal acceptance.'[1454]

Although Beanal's environmental tort claim under ATCA failed, the court did not, however, preclude such claims from eventually becoming customary international law and thus actionable under the ATCA.[1455] And '[g]iven the fluid nature of customary international law, it is possible that rules proscribing environmental degradation could one day emerge as an international consensus, meet the *Filartiga* requirements, and become susceptible to this sort [environmental claims] of litigation.'[1456] While hoping for this day to come, it is submitted that national Governments of all countries need to work on their laws

---

ronmental degradation,' while the 'Proximity Principle' requires that waste be disposed of as close to the originating source as possible and by the fastest means. See Elizabeth Pinckard, Indonesian Tribe Loses in its Latest Battle Against Freeport-McMoran, Inc., Operator of the World's Largest Gold and Copper Mine, 9 *Colo. J. Int.l Envtl L. & Pol'y* 141–145 at 142 (1998). For the meanings and further discussion of these principles, see Sumudu A. Atapattu (2006), *Emerging Principles of International Environmental Law*, Inc., Transnational Publishers, Ardsley, NY.

[1450]   *Beanal I, Ibid.*
[1451]   *Beanal II,* 197 f. 3d at 161.
[1452]   *Ibid,* 167.
[1453]   *Ibid.*
[1454]   *Ibid.*
[1455]   Natalie L. Bridgeman, *op. cit.,* 21.
[1456]   Jason W. Brant, *Flores v. Southern Peru Copper, Corporation:* The Second Circuit Closes the CourtHouse Door on Environmental Claims Brought Under the ATCA, 35 *U. Miami Inter-Am. L. Rev.* 131–151 at 151 (2003–2004).

regulating the environment, with domestic courts adequately equipped to handle environmental claims.

4.10.3.5 *Flores v. Southern Peru Copper*[1457]

The plaintiffs in this case were residents of Ilo, Peru and brought this action against Southern Peru Copper Corporation ('SPCC'), a U.S. company, alleging that pollution from SPCC's copper mining, refining, and smelting operations in and around Ilo had caused the plaintiffs severe lung disease. In particular, they alleged that the defendant infringed upon their customary international law 'right to life,' 'right to health,' and right to 'sustainable development.' The District Court found that the plaintiffs had failed to state a claim under ATCA because they had not alleged a violation of customary international law, that is, that they had not 'demonstrated that high levels of environmental pollution within a nation's borders, causing harm to human life, health, and development,' violated 'well-established, universally recognized norms of international law.'[1458]

Affirming the decision of the lower court, the Second Circuit found that the 'right to life' and 'right to health' relied on by the plaintiffs were 'insufficiently definite to constitute rules of customary international law,'[1459] as they failed the 'clear and unambiguous' *Filartiga* rule. The court reviewed the principles – UDHR; ICESCR; Rio Declaration on Environment and Development ('Rio Declaration') –, relied on by the plaintiffs, and came to the conclusion that the principles expressed therein were 'boundless and indeterminate.' It found that such 'vague,' 'amorphous,' 'nebulous' and 'infinitely malleable' notions do not form part of customary international law.[1460] The court then construed the plaintiffs' complaint under a more narrowly-defined customary international law rule against intra-national pollution which involved a careful examination of the evidence[1461] the plaintiffs had submitted to demonstrate the existence of such a norm of customary international law. The plaintiffs in *Flores* appeared to base their claims on human rights law, by dwelling on the rights to life, health and right to sustainable development. However, the District Court rejected the distinction made between *Flores* and *Aguinda*, *Amlon* and *Beanal* stating that 'the labels

---

[1457] *Flores* v. *Southern Peru Copper, Corp.* (*Flores I*), 253 f. Supp. 2d 510, 514 (S.D.N.Y. 2002), affirmed in *Flores* v. *Southern Peru Copper, Corp.* (*Flores II*) 342 F. 3d 140 (2d Cir. 2003).

[1458] *Flores I, Ibid*, 525.

[1459] *Flores II, op. cit.*, 160.

[1460] *Flores II, Ibid*, 161.

[1461] The plaintiffs had submitted: (1) treaties, conventions and covenants; (2) non-binding declarations of the United Nations General Assembly; (3) other non-binding multinational declarations of Principles; (4) decisions of multinational tribunals, and (5) affidavits of international scholars. The court was not swayed by the reliance on treaties because the U.S. had only ratified one (ICCPR) out of the several treaties, and also, they do not profess to govern the conduct of private actors. It came to the conclusion that the treaties, conventions or covenants relied on by the plaintiffs do not support the existence of a customary international law rule against intra-national pollution.

plaintiffs affix to their claims cannot be determinative.'[1462] More importantly, *Flores* demonstrates that environmental ATCA claims brought using a human rights approach will not be successful, unless such rights are well-established as part of the 'law of nations.'[1463]

4.10.4 PURSUING ENVIRONMENTAL CLAIMS UNDER ATCA: THE NIGER DELTA PEOPLE

The environmental claims brought under ATCA by the Niger Delta people reveal a wide range of human rights abuses and massive environmental degradation suffered by the weak and ecologically dispossessed local population, and the legal and practical barriers they face in accessing a judicial remedy before the U.S. courts.

4.10.4.1 Kiobel v. Royal Dutch Petroleum[1464]

The plaintiffs, who were residents of Ogoni in the Niger Delta region of Nigeria, claimed that the defendants had engaged in oil exploration and production, and aided and abetted the Nigerian Government in committing human rights abuses directed at them. The plaintiffs alleged that the defendants had, *inter alia*, (1) provided transportation to Nigerian forces, (2) allowed their property to be utilized as a staging ground for attacks, (3) provided food for soldiers involved in the attacks, and (4) provided compensation to those soldiers. They sought damages against the defendants under ATCA for aiding and abetting the Nigerian Government in alleged violations of the law of nations.

The outcome of this decision was a clear departure from the other recent ATCA claims against corporations. Even though actions can be filed against corporations in the U.S. because U.S. law recognizes corporate personhood, the 2nd Circuit Court of Appeals in *Kiobel* held that it is customary international law which governs the scope of liability under the ATCA. In a 2–1 panel decision, the Second Circuit court held, on September 17, 2010, that: 'Because corporate liability is not recognized as a "specific, universal, and obligatory" norm, it is not a rule of customary international law that we may apply under the ATS. Accordingly, insofar as plaintiffs in this action seek to hold only corporations liable for their conduct in Nigeria (as opposed to individuals within those corporations), and only under the ATS, their claims must be dismissed for lack of subject matter jurisdiction.'[1465] The court held further that '[No] corporation has ever been subject to *any* form of liability (whether civil, criminal, or otherwise)

[1462]   *Flores I*, 253 F. Supp. 2d 510, 519.
[1463]   Natalie L. Bridgeman, *op. cit.*, 24; Kathleen Jaeger, *op. cit.*, 532.
[1464]   Docket Nos. 06–4800-cv, 06–4876-cv (decided 17 September 2010); 621 F.3d 111 (2d Cir. 2010).
[1465]   *Ibid*, 43.

under the customary international law of human rights. Rather, sources of
customary international law have, on several occasions, explicitly rejected the
idea of corporate liability. Thus, corporate liability has not attained a discernable,
much less universal, acceptance among nations of the world in their relations
inter se, and it cannot, as a result, form the basis of a suit under the ATS.'[1466]
The court cited the Nuremberg trials, and other international criminal tribunals,
in support of its decision that international law has *never* extended the scope of
liability to a corporation. The court by this decision threw into doubt the use of
ATCA against corporations. Indeed, 'where *Sosa* narrowed the potential class of
claims under the ATS, the 2nd Circuit's decision in *Kiobel* narrows the class of
potential defendants to States, Governments and individuals.'[1467] Certainly, no
international tribunal has ever had jurisdiction over corporations. But equally,
before the 2nd Circuit decided *Filartiga*, no one has ever been prosecuted by the
international system for torture.[1468] In the words of Ralph Steinhardt, 'Filartiga
itself, the fountainhead of ATS litigation, would have been impossible if Judge
[Irving] Kaufman had looked to other examples of torturers being held civilly
liable. *Filartiga* understood that the law of nations had changed.'[1469]

However, Judge Pierre Laval, in his dissenting opinion, strongly criticised
the majority opinion's finding on corporate liability as '[w]ithout any support
in either the precedents or the scholarship of international law[.]'[1470] Analysing
the potential impact which the majority rulings might have, Judge Laval stated
that: '[A]ccording to the rule my colleagues have created, one who earns profits by
commercial exploitation or abuse of fundamental human rights can successfully
shield those profits from victims' claims for compensation simply by taking the
precaution of conducting the heinous operation in the corporate form... By
protecting profits earned through abuse of fundamental human rights protected
by international law, the rule my colleagues have created operates in opposition
to the objective of international law to protect those rights.'[1471] The argument of
Judge Laval is similar to the 2005 opinion in *In re Agent Orange Prod. Liab. Litig.*
in which the District Court for the Eastern District of New York found that '[l]
imiting civil liability to individuals while exonerating the corporation directing
the individual's action through its complex operations and changing personnel

---

[1466]   *Ibid*, 48.

[1467]   Melissa Maleske, *Court Decision Could Block Alien Tort Statute Against Corporations*, Inside
         Counsel, 11/1/2010, at www.insidecounsel.com/Issues/2010/November-2010/Pages/Court-
         Decision-Could-Block-Alien-Tort-Statute-Claims-Against-Corporations.aspx?PrintPreview
         [accessed 18 June 2011].

[1468]   Marco Simons, Quoted in Melissa Maleske, *Ibid*.

[1469]   Ralph Steinhardt , quoted in John Donovan, *2nd Circuit Rejects Corporate Liability in Alien
         Tort Act Cases*, 18 September 2010, at http://royaldutchshellplc.com/2010/09/18/2nd-circuit-
         rejects-corporate-liability-in-alien-tort-act-cases/ [accessed 5 November 2010].

[1470]   *Kiobel* v. *Royal Dutch Petroleum*, Docket Nos. 06–4800-cv, 06–4876-cv, at p.1.

[1471]   *Kiobel* v. *Royal Dutch Petroleum*, U.S. Circuit Court of Appeals for the Second Circuit, Docket
         Nos. 06–4800-cv, 06–4876-cv, at pp.1 -2.

makes little sense in today's world.'[1472] The decision appears to give immunity to corporations for their corporate wrongs, an immunity which would not extend to foreign States, thereby elevating corporations to a status superior to States under international law and thus violating the general principles of legality and of sovereign equality under international law.[1473]

On 4 February 2011, the Second Circuit Court of Appeals denied the plaintiffs their petition filed for a rehearing *en banc*. A full panel of the New York-based appellate court later refused to hear the case by a 5–5 vote. The tie leaves intact the original 2–1 panel ruling from September 2010,[1474] thus providing a justification for a petition to the U.S. Supreme Court[1475] for the final resolution of the question of corporate liability under the ATS. The Supreme Court was only asked to rule on whether corporations can be held liable for international human rights violations under the ATS. The Court however broadened the scope of its judgment to answer the question whether and under what circumstances the ATS allows courts to recognize a cause of action for violations of the law of nations occurring within the territory of a sovereign other than the United States. Chief Justice Roberts, who delivered the opinion of the Supreme Court ruled that the ATS is not applicable to actions committed on foreign territory. He stated that: 'On these facts, all the relevant conduct took place outside the United States. And even where the claims touch and concern the territory of the United States, they must do so with sufficient force to displace the presumption against extraterritorial application … Corporations are often present in many countries, and it would reach too far to say that mere corporate presence suffices. If Congress were to determine otherwise, a statute more specific than the ATS would be required.' The implication of the ruling is that ATS claims for human rights violations against a corporation in the U.S. cannot be filed merely because they are present in the U.S. There is a need for additional connection to the U.S. This decision will seriously change the

---

[1472] Quoted in Gwendolyn Wilber Jaramillo, *Second Circuit Holds that Corporations are not proper Defendants Under the Alien Tort Statute*, Corporate Social Responsibility and the Law, Foley Hoag LLP Publication, 19 September 2010, at www.csrandthelaw.com/2010/09/articles/litigation/alien-tort-statute/second-circuit-holds-that-corporations-are-not-proper-defendants-under-the-alien-tort-statute/ [accessed 3 April 2010]. A scholar once noted that '[I] am not aware of any legal system in which corporations cannot be sued for damages when they commit legal wrongs that would be actionable if committed by an individual.' See Doug Cassel, Corporate Aiding and Abetting of Human Rights Violations: Confusion in the Courts, 6 *Nw. J. Int'l Human Rights* 304–326 at 322 (2008).

[1473] Eric Engle, *Kiobel v. Royal Dutch Petroleum Co.: Corporate Liability Under the Alien Torts Statute*, December 17, 2010, at http://papers.ssrn.com/sol3/papers.cfm?abstract_id=1727331 [accessed 7 April 2011]. The principle of sovereign equality recognises the equality of all States, and so, States are deemed equal and should be given equal respect by the other Nation-States or international organisations.

[1474] WestLaw News and Insight, *U.S. appeals court declines to rehear case re Shell in Nigeria*, 4 February 2011, at http://westlawnews.thomson.com/National_Litigation/News/2011/02_-_February/U_S__appeals_court_declines_to_rehear_case_re_Shell_in_Nigeria/ [accessed 13 May 2011].

[1475] *Kiobel et al. v. Royal Dutch Petroleum Co. et al.* 569 U. S. (2013), delivered on 17 April 2013.

current face of ATS litigation today,[1476] reduce significantly international human
rights litigations in U.S. courts and undermine the progress achieved so far in
preventing human rights abuse by corporations. In essence, the decision would
allow the Nigerian Government to abdicate its duty to protect human rights; with
the result that companies like Shell, Chevron, Texaco/Agip, etc will continue
to trample on the human rights of millions of people in the Niger Delta region
for profit. It would promote a culture of impunity and a lack of accountability,
which will gravely affect the human rights of the people, not only in Nigeria but
around the world. However, as noted by Requejo, '[E]ven though the *Kiobel* case
turned out to be a substantial victory for the defendant corporations, they did not
get their most favorable outcome. When it comes to the first question regarding
the interpretation of the ATS, the Supreme Court has not closed the door to all
cases of human rights violations committed by corporations. The Court did not
decide that corporations are immune from the ATS.'[1477] The Court has not totally
shut the door against foreign victims to file ATS claims in the U.S. as there are
possibilities to set aside the presumption against extraterritoriality where such
cases have sufficient connection with U.S. territory. Indeed, foreign victims of
human rights violations by corporations may apply some passages from Justice
Anthony Kennedy's concurring opinion in the case that provides some ray of
hope for victims. According to him: '… Other cases may arise with allegations of
serious violations of international law principles protecting persons, cases covered
neither by the TVPA nor by the reasoning and holding of today's case; and in those
disputes the proper implementation of the presumption against extraterritorial
application may require some further elaboration and explanation.' Plaintiffs can
still bring an action under these situations.

4.10.4.2 Bowoto v. Chevron Texaco[1478]

The plaintiffs, who were victims of Chevron Texaco's human rights abuses in the
Niger Delta filed a lawsuit in May 1999 at the Federal Court in the United States
against Chevron Texaco, an American based company. They alleged that they
had suffered human rights violations, including torture and summary execution,
at the hands of the Nigerian military and police, acting in concert with Chevron
to suppress the plaintiffs' protests against Chevron's environmental practices
in the Niger Delta.The case cites two incidents of human rights abuses by the
defendants, specifically: the shooting of peaceful protestors at Chevron's Parabe
off-shore platform; and the destruction of two villages by soldiers in Chevron

---

[1476]   Russell Jackson, quoted in Melissa Maleske, *op. cit.*
[1477]   Marta Requejo, 'Kiobel: No Role for the United States as World Police,' *Conflict of Law.net*,
         19 April 2013, at http://conflictoflaws.net/2013/kiobel-no-role-for-the-united-states-as-world-
         police [accessed 18 May 2013].
[1478]   No. 09–15641 D.C. No. 3:99-cv-02506-SI; See Earthrights International, *Bowoto* v. *Chevron
         Texaco*, at www.earthrights.org/chevron/index.shtml [accessed 16 April 2011].

helicopters and boats. A series of pre-trial rulings, which took over a decade, reduced the number of claims. The District Court issued three pre-trial rulings that were challenged on appeal, among which the District Court held that the plaintiffs could not bring claims against Chevron under the Torture Victim Protection Act (TVPA).[1479] The District Court observed that the statute permitted claims to be brought only against 'an individual' who had committed torture. It reasoned that because Congress used the term 'individual,' it did not intend the TVPA to apply to corporations. The jury found in favour of Chevron on all claims. On appeal by the plaintiffs, the U.S. Court of Appeals for the 9th Circuit, on 10 September 2010, held that the plain language of the TVPA does not allow for suits against a corporation but only against individuals, and that the legislative history demonstrates that Congress rejected the notion of corporate liability.[1480] The plaintiffs offered an alternative theory of 'aiding and abetting' under the TVPA. But the 9th Circuit stated that: 'Even assuming the TVPA permits some form of vicarious liability, the text limits such liability to individuals, meaning in this statute, natural persons. The language of the statute thus does not permit corporate liability under any theory.'[1481] In the words of William Jeffress,[1482] the combination of this decision and *Kiobel* is going to cut back dramatically on claims against multinational companies.

It is disheartening to note that following the verdict of the jury, Chevron Corp. (whose record profits in 2008 hit U.S.$23.8 billion) filed a motion in December 2010 seeking reimbursement of the sum of U.S.$485,000 for the litigation costs from the Nigerian Plaintiffs. Even though Chevron claimed that it is merely exercising its legal right to recoup costs, the plaintiffs' counsel believes Chevron's action is primarily meant as a warning to future would-be plaintiffs.[1483] This no doubt illustrates the attitude of oil MNCs towards the poor local inhabitants of the Niger Delta who do not have access to clean drinking water or means of livelihood. The legal costs claimed by Chevron have, however, been rejected by U.S. District Judge Susan Illston, citing the 'stark' economic disparity between destitute Nigerian villagers and an international oil company.[1484] On 24 September 2010,

---

[1479] *Bowoto* v. *Chevron Corp.*, No. C 99–02506 SI, 2006 WL 2604591 (N.D. Cal. 22 August 2006).

[1480] *Bowoto* v. *Chevron Corp.*, No. 09–15641 D.C. No. 3:99-cv-02506-SI, at 13906.

[1481] *Ibid*, 13907.

[1482] Quoted in Melissa Maleske, *op. cit.*

[1483] EarthRights International, *Chevron Seeks $485,000 From Nigerian Protesters*, Friday 20 February 2009, at www.earthrights.org/legal/chevron-seeks-485000-nigerian-protesters [accessed 16 February 2010].

[1484] Pamela A. MacLean, *Judge Denies Chevron's $485,000 Claim in Human Rights Case*, *The National Law Journal*, 24 April 2009, at www.law.com/jsp/article.jsp?id=1202430172170&slret urn=1&hbxlogin=1. [accessed 3 March 2010]. In *Stanley v. USC*, 178 F.3d 1069 (9th Cir. 1999), the Appeals Court found that imposition of 'high costs on losing civil rights plaintiffs of modest means may chill civil rights litigation in this area.' The Court further noted, 'Without civil rights litigants who are willing to test the boundaries of our laws, we would not have made much of the progress that has occurred in this nation since *Brown v. Board of Educ.*, 347 U.S. 483 (1954).'

EarthRights International (ERI) and its co-counsel filed a petition for rehearing
of the case to a Federal Appeals Court. It asked a three-judge panel to reconsider
its own decision, and also asked the entire court to examine the case 'en banc,'
before a larger panel of eleven judges.[1485] The plaintiff's petition for rehearing was
rejected on February 2011. Also, the U.S. Supreme Court, in April 2012 denied
the plaintiffs' petition for certiorari that the trial court and the Ninth Circuit
incorrectly ruled that Chevron could not be sued under the Torture Victim
Protection Act (TVPA) when it ruled in *Mohamad, et al. v. Palestinian Authority,
et al.*[1486] that only human beings, and not corporations and organizations, could
be sued under the TVPA.[1487]

Even though the plaintiffs suffered a defeat in this case, it did help to bring
some publicity to egregious human rights violations and the problems in the
Nigeria oil sector.

4.10.4.3 *Wiwa et al v. Royal Dutch Petroleum et al*[1488]

This case accused the Royal Dutch Petroleum Company and Shell Transport
and Trading Company (Royal Dutch/Shell)[1489] with complicity, on November
10, 1995, in the hangings of Ken Saro-Wiwa and John Kpuinen, two leaders of
MOSOP (Movement for the Survival of the Ogoni People), and the torture and
detention of Owens Wiwa, among others. The plaintiffs brought claims against
the defendants for aiding and abetting the Nigerian Government in alleged
violations of the law of nations. The plaintiffs sought to hold Shell vicariously
responsible for a number of offences committed by the Nigerian security forces,
allegedly on its behalf and with its support and assent.[1490] The plaintiffs' action
was brought under ATCA and the TVPA. The plaintiffs also alleged violations of
the Racketeer Influenced and Corrupt Organizations Act (RICO),[1491] because the

---

[1485] EarthRights International, *ERI Files Petition for Rehearing in Bowoto v. Chevron*, Monday 27
September, 2010, at www.earthrights.org/legal/eri-files-petition-rehearing-bowoto-v-chevron
[accessed 10 March 2011].

[1486] 566 U.S. 2012 (decided 18 April 2012).

[1487] EarthRights International, *As Expected, Bowoto v. Chevron Petition is Denied after Mohamad
Decision*, 24 April 2012, at www.earthrights.org/blog/expected-bowoto-v-chevron-petition-
denied-after-mohamad-decision [accessed 2 May 2013].

[1488] The case was filed on 8 November 1996 on behalf of a relative of the murdered environmental
and human rights campaigners from Ogoniland, Nigeria, by the Centre for Constitutional
Rights (CCR) along with co-counsel from EarthRights International against Royal Dutch
Petroleum Company and Shell Transport and Trading Company. The cases are *Wiwa* v. *Royal
Dutch Petroleum* No. 96 Civ. 8386 (Wiwa I), *Wiwa* v. *Anderson* No. 01 Civ. 1909 (Wiwa II), and
Wiwa v. *Shell Petroleum Development Company* No. 4 Civ. 2665 (Wiwa III), settled on 8 June
2009.

[1489] Royal Dutch and Shell are holding companies incorporated respectively in the Netherlands
and the United Kingdom, while SPDC is incorporated in Nigeria.

[1490] Christen Broecker, *Alien Tort Statute Litigation and Transnational Business Activity:
Investigating the Potential for a Bottom-Up Global Regulatory Regime*, Institute for International
Law and Justice (IILJ) Emerging Scholars Paper 16 (2010), 1–89 at p.3.

[1491] 18 U.S.C. §§ 1961–1968.

defendants, and their Nigerian subsidiary, allegedly bribed witnesses to give false witnesses. The defendants, however, filed a motion to dismiss the matter on 21 May 1997 on the grounds of *forum non conveniens* (FNC). On 25 September 1998, Judge Kimba Wood confirmed the personal jurisdiction of the court, but still granted the defendants' motion to dismiss on grounds of FNC, in that England was a more convenient forum to hear the matter.[1492] On appeal, the Second Circuit Court of Appeals and the Court of Appeal on 14 September 2000 reversed the lower court decision, confirming the U.S. as a proper forum on the basis of personal jurisdiction over the defendants who have an office in New York. The case was remanded back to the District Court.

In March 2001, the plaintiffs also sued Brian Anderson, the former Managing Director of Royal Dutch/Shell's Nigerian subsidiary. Royal Dutch/ Shell and Mr. Anderson brought motions to dismiss the case, contending that the claim did not have a legal basis. On 22 February 2002, in the U.S. District Court, Judge Kimba Wood denied the defendant's motions and found that the plaintiffs were entitled to bring their actions under ATCA, TVPA, and RICO, and that plaintiffs had sufficiently set forth their case which was that defendants knew what its Nigerian subsidiary was doing. In April 2004, an additional case was brought against Shell Petroleum Development Company (SPDC),[1493] but the claim was dismissed by the District Court for the Southern District of New York (SDNY) on March 2008 for lack of personal jurisdiction. Judge Wood denied the plaintiffs additional jurisdictional discovery and thereby dismissed the case. On 3 June 2009, the Second Circuit Court of Appeals in New York issued a Summary Order vacating the District Court's decision in an appeal brought by plaintiffs and ordered jurisdictional discovery against SPDC of Nigeria.[1494] On June 8, 2009, that is, five days later, the three Wiwa actions were settled, thus bringing to an end the cases without proceeding to the merits. Admitting no wrongdoing, Shell agreed to pay U.S.$15.5 million in damages, for the creation of a trust to benefit the Ogoni people in terms of education and regional development, and the reimbursement of certain costs of litigation.[1495] This was in settlement of the lawsuits which had lasted 13 years. One may ask why it took Shell 13 years to make this 'humanitarian gesture.' The significance of the settlement will be discussed later in this work.

[1492] Order of Judge Wood on 96 Civ. 8386 (KMW) (HBP), 25 September 1998.

[1493] *Wiwa etc. v. Shell Petroleum Development Company of Nigeria Limited*, 04 CV 2665, SDNY, 5 April 2004 (ccrjustice.org/files/04.05.04%20spdc%20complaint.pdf).

[1494] *Wiwa v. Shell Petroleum Development Corp.*, No. 08 Civ. 1803, 2009 WL 1560197 (2d Cir. June 3, 2009). Jurisdictional discovery relates to 'any preliminary discovery to establish whether a United States federal court has jurisdiction over the person, the *res*, or the subject matter of the dispute' that normally takes place prior to discovery on the merits. See Strong, S.I., Jurisdictional Discovery in United States Federal Courts, 67 *Wash. & Lee L. Rev.* 489–587 at 491 (2010).

[1495] International Federation for Human Rights (FIDH), *Corporate Accountability for Human Rights Abuses: A Guide for Victims and NGOs on Recourse Mechanisms, op. cit.*, p.187.

4.10.5 VARIOUS PROCEDURAL HURDLES IN ATCA
LITIGATION

A number of obstacles lie in the way of claimants in ATCA cases, be they
environmental claims or otherwise. Some of these will be briefly considered in
this subsection. First is the doctrine of *forum non conveniens*. This is a common
law doctrine which allows courts a discretion to refuse to exercise jurisdiction over
certain matters on the grounds that an adequate alternative forum is available.
Once a defendant is able to establish this ground, his next task is to convince the
court that dismissing the suit would be in the best interests of the parties and
the forums.[1496] The court takes several factors into consideration when faced with
a motion to dismiss as FNC. The court does confer a measure of deference to
the forum choice of a resident plaintiff rather than a non-resident plaintiff,[1497] as
shown in *Wiwa v. Royal Dutch Petroleum*.[1498] Some of the alien plaintiffs in this
case were U.S. residents, even though they were not resident in New York, where
the action was instituted. An adequate alternative forum which the defendant is
subject to, and which would permit litigation on the subject matter of the dispute,
must also exist. The court also takes into account relevant public interests, which
include U.S. policy interests in favour of or against the hearing of the case in
the U.S., and administrative burdens such as court congestion.[1499] The court also
weighs the relevant private interests such as the convenience of the plaintiffs and
defendants, and the availability of witnesses and evidence.[1500] FNC has proved to
be an effective weapon in the hands of defendants to frustrate plaintiffs' claims
under ATCA, thereby hindering them from getting justice against MNCs. It
has almost become 'a trump card' for MNCs to 'defeat-delay-frustrate'[1501] suits
brought against them for alleged violations of environmental human rights.
Almost all the cases that have been dismissed on the ground of FNC are not in
fact pursued again by the plaintiffs. Little wonder that 'not one corporation has,'
as of 2011, 'lost an ATCA suit on the merits.'[1502]

Questioning the applicability of this doctrine in the present globalised world,
Justice Doggett of the Texas Supreme Court has stated that:

[1496] For detail discussions of *forum non conveniens* in alien tort litigation, see E. Helen Mardirosian,
Forum Non Conveniens, 37 *Loy. L.A. L. Rev.* 1643 (2004); Matthew R. Skolnik, The Forum Non
Conveniens Doctrine in Alien Tort Claims Act Cases: A *Shell* of Its Former Self After *Wiwa*, 16
Emory Int'l L. Rev. 187 (2002).

[1497] Sarah Joseph (2004), *Corporations and Transnational Human Rights Litigation*, Hart
Publishing, Oxford-Portland Oregon, pp.88–89.

[1498] 226 F 3d 88 (2d Cir 2000) 101.

[1499] Sarah Joseph, *op. cit.*, p.92.

[1500] Examples of cases that were rejected on the ground of the doctrine of *forum non conveniens*
include: *Flores, Aguinda, Sarei, Wiwa*. See Sarah Joseph, *Ibid*, pp.94–95.

[1501] Surya Deva, Corporate Code of Conduct Bill 2000: Overcoming Hurdles in Enforcing Human
Rights Obligations Against Overseas Corporate Hands of Local Corporations, *Newc L.R.* Vol.
8 No. 1 87–116 at 91–92 (2004).

[1502] Matthew R. Skolnik, *op. cit.*, 224.

"The doctrine of forum non conveniens is obsolete in a world in which markets are global and in which ecologists have documented the delicate balance of all life on this planet. The parochial perspective embodied in the doctrine of forum non conveniens enables corporations to evade legal control merely because they are transnational... In the absence of meaningful tort liability in the United States for their actions, some multinational corporations will continue to operate without adequate regard for the human and environmental costs of their actions. This result cannot be allowed to repeat itself for decades to come. As a matter of law and of public policy, the doctrine of forum non conveniens should be abolished."[1503]

In order to enhance a victim's access to a remedy in its jurisdiction, Belgium has inserted a *forum-conveniens* clause in its new Code of Private International Law in 2004.[1504] Article 11 of the Code states that '[i]rrespective of the other provisions of the present Code, Belgian judges have jurisdiction when the case has narrow links with Belgium and when proceedings abroad seem to be impossible or when it would be unreasonable to request that the proceedings are initiated abroad.' Although, this law requires 'narrow links with Belgium' (which phrase is not defined) and does not set forth universal tort jurisdiction, such a clause may raise some hopes for foreign victims of environmental and human rights related abuses committed by foreign MNCs.[1505]

A second obstacle to an ATCA claim is the Act of State doctrine, which provides that a U.S. court should abstain from adjudicating claims when it is required to invalidate or judge the acts of foreign sovereign Governments made within their own sovereign territory,[1506] unless the official acts form a violation of *ius cogens* or an international treaty.[1507]

A third hurdle is the "political question" doctrine. This provides that a court may dismiss a case, or refuse to adjudicate on a dispute despite, having jurisdiction when it finds that it raises issues which should be addressed by the political rather than the judicial branches of Government within the constitutional framework.[1508] The doctrine arises when a case raises issues that are just 'too political' for an appointed judge to handle.[1509]

[1503]   *Dow Chemical Company* v. *Castro Alfaro*, 786 SW2d 674 (Tex 1990), cert. denied, 498 U.S. 1024 (1991).

[1504]   See C. De Droit International Prive art. 11 (Belgium), quoted in Jan Wouters and Cedric Ryngaert, Litigation for Overseas Corporate Human Rights Abuses in the European Union: The Challenge of Jurisdiction, *The Geo. Wash. Int'l L. Rev.* Vol. 40, 939–975 at 963–964 (2009).

[1505]   Jan Wouters and Cedric Ryngaert, *Ibid*, 964.

[1506]   Michael Koebele (2009), *Corporate Responsibility under the Alien Tort Statute: Enforcement of International Law through US Torts Law*, Martinus Nijhoff Publishers, Leiden, Boston, p.348. In *Banco Nacional de Cuba* v. *Sabbatino* 376 U.S. 398, 401–402 (1964), the Supreme Court based the concept on the constitutional separation of powers doctrine.

[1507]   Kathleen Jaeger, Environmental Claims Under the Alien Tort Statute, 28 *Berkeley J. Int'l L.* 519–536 at 525 (2010).

[1508]   Michael Koebele, *op. cit.*, pp.349–350. *See* Baker v. *Carr*, 369 U.S. 186, 228 (1962) where the court established a six-factor test for applying this doctrine.

[1509]   Lea Brilmayer, International Law in American Courts: A Modest Proposal, 100 *Yale Law Journal* 2277–2314 at 2305 (1991); For more discussion on the doctrine of political question,

Fourth is the "international comity" doctrine, designed to avoid placing a country's judiciary in the position of giving a legal judgment that may be contrary to, or impinge upon the sovereignty of other states.[1510] In *Hilton* v. *Guyot,* the Supreme Court explained the doctrine as 'neither a matter of absolute obligation, on the one hand, nor of mere courtesy and good will, upon the other. But it is the recognition which one nation allows within its territory to the legislative, executive or judicial acts of another nation, having due regard both to international duty and convenience …'[1511] This doctrine is a matter for the court's discretion in deciding whether to refrain from adjudicating a claim that touches the laws and interests of other sovereign states. In this regard, reasonableness is an essential element the court uses in coming to decisions. The U.S. Federal Courts must always take into consideration that the compelling interests in adjudicating cases that border on human rights violations by MNCs, like those from the indigenous peoples,' including the Niger Delta local inhabitants, should override the comity and sovereignty interests.[1512] If "convenience" is to be taken into consideration in environmental claims brought under ATCA, it should be weighed in favour of the plaintiffs who bring valid environmental and human rights claims.

4.10.6 SIGNIFICANCE OF ATCA IN ENVIRONMENTAL AND HUMAN RIGHTS CLAIMS TO THE NIGER DELTA PEOPLE

Differences between the levels of regulation of MNCs, and the remedies available against them, between the developing countries and developed countries, are quite wide. While the level of regulation in most developed countries is stringent, that of many developing countries is more inconsistent and patchy, with remedies quite inadequate for victims. Some of the problems faced by victims include accessibility of courts abroad, most especially in developing countries like Nigeria where legal aid is inadequate or unknown, inadequate environmental legislation, insignificant environmental remedies and limited tort law.[1513] Others include weak enforcement capacity to impose effective regulation; ineffective judicial systems for resolving human rights claims; corruption in Government, thereby allowing

---

see Amy Endicott, The Judicial Answer? Treatment of the Political Question Doctrine in Alien Tort Claims, 28 *Berkeley J. Int'l L.* 537 (2010).

[1510] Joanna E. Arlow, The Utility of ATCA and the "Law of Nations" in Environmental Torts Litigation: *Jota v. Texaco, Inc.* and Large Scale Environmental Destruction, 7 *Wis. Envtl. L.J.* 93–138 at 111 (2000).

[1511] 159 U.S. 113, 164 (1895).

[1512] Kathryn Lee Boyd, The Inconvenience of Victims: Abolishing Forum Non Conveniens in U.S. Human Rights Litigation, 39 *Va. J. Int'l L.* 41–87 at 48 (1998).

[1513] Joanna Arlow, *op. cit.*, p. 105; John Alan Cohan, Environmental Rights of Indigenous Peoples Under the Alien Tort Claims Act, the Public Trust Doctrine and Corporate Ethics, and Environmental Dispute Resolution, 20 *UCLA J. Envtl. L. & Pol'y* 133–185 at 147 (2002); Anita Ramasastry, *op. cit.*, 92.

entities with significant resources to prevent the enforcement of the regulations that do exist or obstruct judicial or prosecutorial inquiries into their conduct, etc[1514] For these reasons, plaintiffs seeking compensation for human rights and environmental harm by MNCs, and the NGOs and civil society who support them, prefer not only to take advantage of the broad jurisdictional reach of ATCA but also to enjoy other benefits which the U.S. courts offer. As observed by two scholars, '[T]he jury system, the class action mechanism, and the availability of punitive damages all enhance the chances of winning large judgments. Perhaps most important, a lawsuit in the U.S. provides a forum for the exposure of human rights violations abroad which might otherwise attract little attention.'[1515] This is in addition to the absence of the loser-pays system (where lawsuit losers are made to pay the legal fees and expenses of litigation winners) which applies in some other countries; and the large network of public interest lawyers who may provide *pro bono* assistance.[1516]

The ongoing pollution of the Niger Delta environment by oil MNCs, and the indifferent posture of the Nigerian Government to the plight of the local inhabitants of the region, perpetuates the powerlessness felt by these people, as they lose control of their environment and their health. One of the ways the local inhabitants have felt they can change this feeling of powerlessness is by finding a way to hold accountable both the corporations that operate in the community and the Government responsible for enforcing environmental laws and regulations.[1517]

The fact that they were able to institute actions against these powerful MNCs is an important victory for these communities. In particular, it helped to remove the sense of many in the oil rich region that they were powerless to address ongoing environmental degradation and the attendant human rights abuses in their community. The outcome of these instances of litigation against these corporations, though with some losses and settlements, broke the cycle of powerlessness and transformed the community's mood from hopeless to one of empowerment.[1518] This also put the corporations and the Government on notice that they must act responsibly to avoid court actions. Advising its members to

---

[1514]   Christen Broecker, *Alien Tort Statute Litigation and Transnational Business Activity: Investigating the Potential for a Bottom-Up Global Regulatory Regime*, Institute for International Law and Justice (IILJ) Emerging Scholars Paper 16, 1–89 at pp.12–15 (2010).

[1515]   Anne-Marie Slaughter and David Bosco, Alternative Justice, *Crimes of War Magazine: The Tribunal*, May 2001, at www.crimesofwar.org/tribun-mag/relate_alternative_print.html [accessed 6 May 2010].

[1516]   Emeka Duruigbo, The Economic Cost of Alien Tort Litigation: A Response to *Awakening Monster: The Alien Tort Statute of 1789*, 14 *Minn. J. Global Trade* 1–41 at 32–34 (2004); See also Audrey Koecher, Corporate Accountability for Environmental Human Rights Abuse in Developing Nations: Making the Case for Punitive Damages Under the Alien Tort Claims Act, 17 *J. Transnat'l L. Pol'y* 151–170 at 160 (2007).

[1517]   Sheila Foster, The Challenge of Environmental Justice, *Rutgers University Journal of Law and Urban Policy*, Vol. 1, Issue 1, p.11 at www.rutgerspolicyjournal.org/1-1.html [accessed 3 March 2010].

[1518]   *Ibid*, p.12.

be more community conscious, William Divine, the President of the Petroleum
Foundation of America said that: 'some oil companies developed oilfields with
little regard to the environment because there were no regulations. Now we
are suffering the backlash. Many of us have gone overseas in reaction to these
problems. This is a mistake … The writing is on the wall. Look at the growing
opposition to oil developments and the lawsuits such as in Ecuador with Texaco
… [W]e need to take measures to regulate ourselves.'[1519]

The fact that plaintiffs have not been able to obtain an outright judicial
victory in ATCA cases because of the apparent dearth of binding international
agreements on corporate environmental responsibility does not mean that the
litigation is entirely devoid of legal significance. The settlement in *Wiwa*'s case
confirms this. For example, though the *Wiwa* case did not proceed to the merits
stage, nor rule on the illegality of Shell's activities before settlement,[1520] yet the
case is significant for relatively powerless foreign victims of environmental and
human rights abuses in the hands of the MNCs, such as the Niger Delta people, as
it demonstrates that they can find meaningful redress through the U.S. courts.[1521]
Both sides derive benefits by avoiding further litigation-[1522] moral vindication,
financial benefits or psychological relief.

Wiwa's settlement has set important precedents for the use of innovative legal
mechanisms based on extraterritorial jurisdiction as seen in its pleadings and
rulings, which may help pave the way for the creation of new forums such as an
'International Criminal Court' that would provide legally binding remedies for

---

[1519]   William Divine, Where Does the Revenue Go?, *Offshore*, December 1, 1998, at www.offshore-mag.com/index/article-display/24798/articles/offshore/volume-58/issue-12/news/general-interest/where-does-the-revenue-go.html [accessed 8 June 2010].

[1520]   Xiuli Han, The Wiwa Cases,' *Chinese Journal of International Law* 433–449 at 448–449 (2010).

[1521]   Xiuli Han, *Ibid*.

[1522]   Anthony J. Sebok, *Unocal Announces It Will Settle A Human Rights Suit: What Is the Real Story Behind Its Decision?*, FindLaw, January 10, 2005, at http://writ.news.findlaw.com/sebok/20050110.html. [accessed 3 March 2010]. Note the *Doe v. Unocal*, 395 F.3d 932 (9th Cir. 2002) settlement- a suit where Unocal was accused of human rights violations, including forced labour, in the construction of the Yadana gas pipeline project in Myanmar, formerly Burma. The settlement was agreed in December, 2004, a day before the Ninth Circuit was due to hear an appeal *en banc* from the 2002 decision (*Doe I v. Unocal*, 403 F.3d 708 [9 Cir. 2005]). Unocal noted: 'Although the terms are confidential, the settlement will compensate plaintiffs and provide funds enabling plaintiffs and their representatives to develop programs to improve living conditions, health care and education and protect the rights of people from the pipeline region. Unocal reaffirms its principle that the company respects human rights in all of its activities and commits to enhance its educational programs to further this principle.' In the words of Earthrights, the NGO that instituted the case on behalf of the Burmese villagers, the settlement would 'reverberate in corporate board rooms around the world and [would] have a deterrent effect on the worst forms of corporate behavior.' Quoted in Foreign Direct Investment (fDi) Magazine, *Under the Shadow of ATCA*, June 5, 2006, at www.fdimagazine.com/news/printpage.php/aid/. [accessed 3 March 2010]. Other confidential settlements on ATCA include *Doe v. Gap* (D.N. Mar. I. 2002), *Doe v. Reddy* (N.D. Cal. 2004), and *Xiaoning v. Yahoo!* (N.D. Cal. 2007).

victims of human rights abuse in the hands of business enterprises.[1523] The call for international Criminal Court is premised on the fact that international legal mechanisms for perpetrators of human rights abuses should not be limited to civil liability but be made to extend to criminal liability. Currently, there is no established international criminal mechanism to address corporate human rights abuses, thus necessitating the need to establish an International Criminal Court where corporate executives can be subject to liability for violation of human rights.[1524] The U.S. courts' repeated rejections of Shell's efforts to dismiss the *Wiwa* case sets important legal precedents for the continued trial of corporations in breach of international law, thus reinforcing the plaintiffs' demands that corporations have a duty to human rights and the environment.[1525] Plaintiffs' counsel are getting smarter as they learn from both negative and positive rulings and from settlements. The body of law is gradually developing and the world is getting closer and closer to a corporate alien tort jury verdict.[1526]

Also important is the fact that the publicity which normally accompanies cases brought under ATCA is not always palatable to corporations,[1527] and this may also help to prevent the MNCs from further damaging the environment and violating the rights of the people. The reputational harm that resulted from the negative publicity surrounding the *Wiwa* trial no doubt played a significant role in the move taken by the Shell in settling on the eve of the trial.

Also, the length of time and the high costs involved in defending ATCA suits will play a significant role in pushing corporations to seek out of court resolution of disputes and also to protect human rights and the environment where they operate. The *Wiwa* cases and the ATCA will encourage all the stakeholders involved in the ongoing Niger Delta crisis, in particular, the MNCs, to take the environment and the human rights of the people more seriously in their pursuit of profit. Though the settlements in both *Wiwa* and *Unocal* make clear that the MNCs are 'not admitting to any wrongdoing, the fact of the settlement and the amount of the compensation suggest at a minimum that corporations are ... sensitive to the possibility of human rights-related liability, and determined to

---

[1523] Jana Silverman and Alvaro Orsatti (2009), *Holding Transnational Corporations Accountable for Human Rights Obligations: The Role of Civil Society*, Social Watch Thematic Report, p.32.

[1524] See De la Vega Connie, Mehra Amol & Wong Alexandra, *Holding Businesses Accountable for Human Rights Violations: Recent Developments and Next Steps*, Friedrich-Ebert-Stiftung/Global Policy and Development, Germany, 2011, p.9.

[1525] Marco Simons, being an opinion expressed following Settlement Reached in Human Rights Cases Against Royal Dutch/Shell, at www.earthrights.org/sites/default/files/documents/Wiwa-v-Shell-Settlement-Press-Release.pdf [accessed 3 March 2010].

[1526] Steptoe Drimmer, quoted in Michael D. Goldhaber, *A Win for Wiwa, A Win for Shell, A Win for Corporate Human Rights*, The AM Daily Law, June 10, 2009, at http://amlawdaily.type-pad.com/amlawdaily/2009/06/a-win-for-wiwa-a-win-for-shell-a-win-for-corporate-human-rights.html [accessed 14 July 2010].

[1527] See Jonathan Drimmer, Human Rights and the Extractive Industries: Litigation and Compliance Trends, *Journal of World Energy Law & Business*, Vol. 3, No. 2, pp.121–139 at 131 (2010).

make sure that such cases are resolved prior to any final judgment which might be cited as a formal precedent in the future.'[1528]

Even where the plaintiffs have lost ATCA environmental and human rights claims, they have exposed to the public the alleged environmental sharp practices of MNCs in developing countries as compared to their conduct in developed countries. It has brought symbolic victories that bring international attention to the environmental and human rights abuses in the Niger Delta region. In support of the need for the continued use of the ATCA as a means of promoting corporate accountability, the International Commission of Jurists Expert Legal Panel on Corporate Complicity has stated that:

> "ATS litigation has reverberated around the world. It has motivated lawyers in other jurisdictions to explore the feasibility in their own countries of seeking the civil liability of actors involved in gross human rights abuses … [T]hese developments are creating a network of avenues to accountability and justice that is slowly establishing opportunities for victims to obtain civil redress when companies are involved in human rights abuses … [G]overnments must take steps necessary to ensure that the law of civil remedies is able to respond in an effective manner when it is called upon to address claims for a remedy in respect of gross human rights abuses."[1529]

ATCA has become a promising means of redress, and an effective weapon for human rights groups to force changes in the behavior of MNCs. As argued by Bridgeman, 'plaintiffs should benefit from a globalization of justice, just as corporations have benefited from a globalization of resources.'[1530] For example, by the late 1990s, Shell's global image and profits had been seriously dented by the globalisation of the Niger Delta protests, the furore over the executions of Ken Saro-Wiwa and the 'Ogoni Nine,'[1531] and the ensuing ATCA litigation. This forced the company to review its corporate responsibilities, both in Nigeria and elsewhere. It started on a worldwide review of its policies by publishing, in 1997, a 'General Statement of Business Principles.' Its Nigerian subsidiary, SPDC, embarked on the publication of its annual 'People and the Environment' reports, expanded its community development programmes and reviewed its

---

[1528]   Ronald Slye, *Wiwa v. Shell Settlement a Victory for Corporate Accountability*, Seattle University School of Law Faculty, Cases and Controversies, at http://lawfacultyblog.seattleu.edu/2009/06/09/wiwa-v-shell-settlement-a-victory-for-corporate-accountability/ [accessed 5 June 2011].

[1529]   International Commission of Jurists (ICJ), *Report of the ICJ Expert Legal Panel on Corporate Complicity in International Crimes: Corporate Complicity & Legal Accountability. Volume 1: Facing the Facts and Charting a Legal Path*, 2008, Vol. 1, at 6, available at www.refworld.org/docid/4a78418c2.html [accessed 3 May 2013].

[1530]   Natalie Bridgeman, *op. cit.* at 1–2 (2003).

[1531]   Okey Ibeanu and Robin Luckham, "Nigeria: political violence, governance and corporate responsibility in a petro-state", in Mary Kaldor *et al.* (eds) (2007), *Oil Wars*, Pluto Press, London, p.58.

environmental monitoring.[1532] This was followed by other oil multinationals in the industry.

In addition to making some MNCs modify their overseas operations, occasionally through divestment from hazardous projects, ATCA litigation has further encouraged MNCs to carefully reassess their relationships with subsidiaries, business partners and host Governments, thus helping to build corporate accountability. This they do by insisting on certain standards of conduct which significantly lower the risk of human rights abuses capable of giving rise to ATCA liability.[1533] For example, the sudden adoption of the Voluntary Principles on Security and Human Rights, and other voluntary initiatives by some extractive industries, including Shell in Nigeria, is partly due to the threats of ATCA litigation.

Of course, ATCA can be a part of the solution to the problem of providing redress to victims of gross human rights violations. Justice Ian Binnie of the Supreme Court of Canada urged the Canadian Parliamentarians to consider enacting ATCA:

> "[Y]ou cannot have a functioning global economy with a dysfunctional global legal system: there has to be somewhere, somehow, that people who feel that their rights have been trampled on can attempt redress – and if the complaints turn out to be unfounded, so be it … if [the ATCA] were replicated in more countries, there would be more avenues whereby companies could clear their names of allegations made against them, or complainants could obtain redress, depending on what the evidence shows."[1534]

And in the wake of the *Wiwa* settlement, some well-known Dutch citizens, including former Prime Minister Ruud Lubbers, criticized the absence of legal avenues in Europe for *Wiwa* plaintiffs to pursue their claims against Shell. Lubbers and his colleagues noted that:

> "We should be ashamed, as Dutch and Europeans, that there was no place in the Netherlands for Saro-Wiwa's relatives to take their grievances. There is work to be done here for Dutch and European lawmakers … Society has the right to expect

---

[1532] *Ibid*, p.71. It was reported that following the execution of Ken-Saro-Wiwa and the other eight Ogoni leaders and the subsequent suit by their families, Shell publicly threatened to pull out of a billion dollar joint venture in Nigeria if the nation failed to improve its human rights record. See, Shell Threat to Nigeria Deal, *The Express*, February 12, 1999, p.63, quoted in Armin Rosencranz and Richard Campbell, Foreign Environmental and Human Rights Suits Against U.S. Corporations in U.S. Courts, 18 *Stan. Envtl. L.J.* 145–208 at 207 (1999).
[1533] Christen Broecker, *op. cit.* at pp.27–28.
[1534] Cristin Schmitz, Binnie Calls for Corporate Accountability, *The Lawyers Weekly*, August 29, 2008, at www.lawyersweekly.ca/index.php?section=article&articleid=745 [accessed 3 March 2010].

corporations to act in a social responsible manner, especially so in the case of multi-national corporations because of the great power and influence they have."[1535]

It is therefore crucial that other countries, particularly those where there are headquarters of MNCs, should consider the enactment of laws covering the scope of ATCA or TVPA or wider, to enable their courts to offer redress against human rights abusers found within their jurisdiction.[1536] It is suggested that the use of ATCA, together with judicial mechanisms that exists in the host States, would go a long way in providing access to judicial remedies for individuals who are harmed by the activities of MNCs, particularly the Niger Delta people, and ensure that they are protected and unexploited.

4.11 ACTION AGAINST MNCs IN OTHER JURISDICTIONS

Apart from the U.S., transnational human rights litigation has also arisen in other countries like England, the Netherlands, Canada and Australia. We shall briefly look at the situation in England, Netherlands and Canada.

In England, the courts can exercise jurisdiction over the extraterritorial acts of English companies, and the foreign companies that carry on business 'to a definite and, to some extent, permanent place' within jurisdiction.[1537] The foreign corporation must have 'premises in England from which or at which its business is carried out.'[1538] A Foreign corporation may also be subjected to English jurisdiction if its agent, including a subsidiary, is present within jurisdiction.[1539] Even though the UK has no statute which equates with ATCA or the TVPA,[1540]

[1535] Ruud Lubbers *et al.*, Ken Saro-Wiwa Jr. was let down by the Netherlands, NRC Handelsblad (June 10, 2009), at www.scribd.com/doc/16315596/The-Netherlands-Let-Down-Ken-SaroWiwaJr [accessed 3 March 2010].

[1536] Richard B. Lillich, Damages for Gross Violations of International Human Rights Awarded by US Courts, 15 *Hum. Rts. Q.* 207–229 (1993).

[1537] *Littauer Glove Corp* v. *F W Millington* (1920) Ltd (1928) 44 TLR 746 (KB Div) 747, quoted in Sarah Joseph, *op. cit.*, p.113.

[1538] *Adams* v. *Cape Industries* [1990] Ch 433 (CA) 468.

[1539] Sarah Joseph, *op. cit.*, p.114.

[1540] Torture Victim Protection Act of 1991 (TVPA), Pub. L. No. 102–256, 106 Stat. 73 (1992) (codified as amended at 28 U.S.C. $ 1350 (2002) differs from the ATCA, according to Skolnik, in four ways: 'it extends the coverage of section 1350 from solely alien or U.S. (non-citizen) resident plaintiffs to include U.S. citizen plaintiffs... Second, it contains an explicit state actor requirement. Third, it only provides a cause of action for torture and extrajudicial killings. Fourth, it establishes an exhaustion of local remedies requirement "in the [state] in which the conduct giving rise to the claim occurred."' See Matthew R. Skolnik, The Forum Non Conveniens Doctrine in Alien Tort Claims Act Cases: A *Shell* of its Former Self After *Wiwa*, 16 *Emory Int'l L. Rev.* 187–225 at 194–195 (2002).

civil human rights claims may be brought under customary international law, which is accepted as being part of English common law.[1541]

Just as in the U.S.A., the English courts consider preliminary issues as well as the actual merits of cases. In *Spiliada Maritime Corporation* v. *Consulex Ltd.*,[1542] the House of Lords noted that dismissal for *forum non conveniens* (FNC) will be appropriate where the defendant is able 'to establish that there is another available forum which is clearly or distinctly more appropriate than the English forum.'[1543] Where the defendant is able to establish this, the court will ordinarily grant the stay unless there are circumstances by reason of which justice requires that a stay should be refused. It is this introduction of the element of justice that distinguishes the English test from the U.S. test, where justice is not an explicit part of the FNC principle,[1544] and this has opened a new road for bringing foreign tort claims in English courts.[1545] This is well demonstrated in *Connelly* v. *R.T.Z.*[1546] In *Connelly*, the plaintiffs, former employees of RTZ's subsidiary, Rossing Uranium Ltd., operating in Namibia, sued R.T.Z. Corporation Plc, an English corporation, alleging that they had suffered asbestos-related injuries as a result of one of its South African mine's activities. The plaintiffs alleged that the British parent company had failed in its duty to ensure that its subsidiary provided an adequate work safety system to afford the miners protection, failure of which the plaintiffs claimed had led to their contracting cancer. The defendants applied to have the claim dismissed for FNC. This was reviewed by several courts, and was eventually rejected by the House of Lords. According to that court: [f]aced with a stark choice between one jurisdiction, albeit not the most appropriate in which there could in fact be a trial, and another jurisdiction, the most appropriate in which there never could, in my judgment, the interest of justice would tend to weigh, and weigh strongly in favour of that forum in which the plaintiff could assert his rights.'[1547]

In *Lubbe et al* v. *Cape Plc.*,[1548] a class action case was filed by over 3000 claimants. They claimed damages for personal injuries (and in some cases death) allegedly suffered as a result of exposure to asbestos and other related products, which had occurred in the course of their employment, or as a result of living, in a contaminated area. The plaintiffs claimed that the defendant, Cape Plc was negligent in failing to ensure that its South African subsidiary had adopted safe working practices resulting in personal injury to them. Rejecting the defendants application for a stay on the basis of FNC, the House of Lords found that: 'if

---

[1541]   Sarah Joseph, *op. cit.*, p.115.
[1542]   [1987] AC 460.
[1543]   *Ibid*, 477.
[1544]   Sarah Joseph, *op. cit.*, p.116.
[1545]   Oren Pezez (2004), *Ecological Sensitivity and Global Legal Pluralism: Rethinking the Trade and Environment Conflict*, Hart Publishing, Oxford & Portland Oregon, at p.204.
[1546]   [1998] AC 854.
[1547]   *Ibid*, p.866.
[1548]   [2000] 4 All ER 268.

these proceedings were stayed in favour of the more appropriate forum in South
Africa, the probability is that the plaintiffs would have no means of obtaining the
professional representation and the expert evidence [they need] … This would
amount to a denial of justice … [L]ack of the means, in South Africa, to prosecute
these claims to a conclusion provides a compelling ground, at the second stage
of the *Spiliada* [*Spiliada Maritime Corp v Cansulex Ltd* [1987] A.C. 460] test, for
refusing to stay the proceedings here.'[1549] This case reemphasises the importance
of justice in the determination of such issues as regards the appropriate forum for
transnational litigation.

The more recent decision of the European Court of Justice (ECJ) in *Owusu*
v. *Jackson & Others*[1550] has further curtailed the ability of defendants in the
English Courts from invoking the doctrine of FNC. This decision concerned the
Brussels Convention on Jurisdiction and Enforcement of Judgments in Civil and
Commercial Matters,[1551] Article 2 of which provides that courts of States members
of the European Union (EU) must exercise jurisdiction over persons domiciled
within their jurisdiction, regardless of the domicile of the claimants. Owusu,
the plaintiff, a British national domiciled in England, suffered a serious injury
while on holiday in Jamaica, when he struck his head when swimming against
a submerged sandbank. The holiday villa was rented to Owusu by Jackson, the
first defendant, who was also domiciled in the England. Owusu sued Jackson in
England for breach of an implied term that the private beach where the accident
occurred would be reasonably safe. In the same action, Owusu also sued various
Jamaican companies, which had an interest in the holiday resort and were
responsible for the maintenance of the beach facilities. The defendants applied
for a stay of proceedings on the ground that Jamaica (a non-contracting state to
the Brussels Convention) was the appropriate forum for trial. The motion was
refused by the judge of first instance because Article 2 of the Brussels Regulation
was mandatory, thus implying that it was open to Owusu to sue Jackson in his
place of domicile.

On appeal, the Court of Appeal granted a stay pending the outcome of the
submission of the case to the European Court of Justice. The ECJ found, *inter
alia*, that the FNC doctrine was incompatible with the Brussels Convention
as Article 2 is mandatory in nature and can only be derogated from in ways
expressly provided for by the Convention. The implication of the ECJ's ruling
was that Owusu was entitled to bring the proceedings in England, even though
England had no connection with the accident and Jamaica was the more suitable

---

[1549]   *Lubbe et al* v. *Cape Plc* [2000] 4 All ER 268 at 279–280.
[1550]   ECJ, *Owusu* v *Jackson* C-281/02 (2005).
[1551]   Jurisdiction and recognition and enforcement of judgments in civil and commercial matters
("Brussels Regulation"), Brussels Regulation No 44/2001 of 22 December 2000 (Brussels I) and
entered into force on 1 March 2002. It replaces the Brussels Convention of 27 September 1968.

forum for the trial.[1552] This decision has finally shut the door completely upon the doctrine of FNC. As stated by Ulrich Magnus, the 'doctrine of *forum non conveniens* so well known in Common Law jurisdictions is not allowed under the Regulation.'[1553] This is a welcome development given the time spent focusing on this issue in cases such as *Lubbe* v. *Cape PLC* where: '[h]earings on this aspect [i.e. jurisdiction/ *forum non conveniens*] in *Cape Plc* took three High Court, two Court of Appeal and two House of Lords hearings over a period of four years, during which time approximately 1,000 out of the 7,500 claimants died.'[1554] It is expected that this decision will encourage poorly resourced litigants from developing countries, like Nigeria, to launch legal claims against multinationals in the European courts.[1555] Article 2 of the Brussels Regulation is therefore significant for victims of European MNCs' overseas abusive practices because it

---

[1552]   Herbert Smith, *Regulating jurisdiction: English courts discretion to stay proceedings curtailed*, November 2005, at www.herbertsmith.com/NR/rdonlyres/3F7524EE-9AB8-4B6A-9993-285934A7EF14/1605/Regjuris.pdf [accessed 3 March 2010].

[1553]   Ulrich Magnus, "Introduction", in Ulrich Magnus and Peter Mankowski (eds) (2007), *European Commentaries on Private International Law, Brussels I Regulation*, Sellier, European Law Publishers, p.8.

[1554]   Corporate Responsibility (CORE), Leigh Day & Co, The TUC, Amnesty International, Rights & Accountability in Development (RAID), One World Action, Global Witness and The Cornerhouse, *Submission to the European Commission regarding Brussels I Regulation (EC 44/2001)*, at http://corporate-responsibility.org/submission-to-europeancommission-regarding-brussels-1-regulation-ec-442001/ [accessed 8 June 2009], quoted in International Law Association Interim Report, *Private International Law Aspects of Civil Litigation for Human Rights Violations*, The Hague Conference (2010), available at www.ila.hq.org/download [accessed 14 August 2011]. See also *Rio Tinto, Sithole* v. *Thor Chemicals TLR* February, 1999.

[1555]   See the *Trafigura case* concerning events in Côte d'Ivoire. This is a suit filed in the United Kingdom by some Ivorians against Trafigura, a corporation registered in the United Kingdom, for compensation for injury suffered from toxic waste allegedly dumped in Ivory Coast by Trafigura, resulting in 10 people dead and 100,000 people injured. In September 2009, the parties reached a settlement agreement in which Trafigura agreed to pay each of the 30,000 claimants a certain amount, approximately U.S.$1500. For a summary, see the Business & Human Rights, Site *Case profile: Trafigura Lawsuits (re Côte d'Ivoire)*, at www.business-humanrights.org. [accessed 3 August 2011]. Mr. Day, who represented the plaintiffs, said he was 'able to bring the case in London thanks to the 2005 European ruling, which gave any claimant an automatic right to sue in the defendant's home country. That meant Leigh Day could sue Trafigura's British arm, rather than going to court in Ivory Coast.' See Michael Peel, 'European Lawyers in Hunt for Big Game,' Financial Times, January 30, 2008, at www.ft.com/cms/s/0/927bab82-cf57-11dc-854a-0000779fd2ac.html#axzz1Es1Nqguk [accessed 3 August 2011]. In criminal charges brought against Trafugura, a Dutch court has found Trafigura guilty of illegally exporting toxic waste from Amsterdam and concealing the nature of the cargo and the company was fined 1m euros (£836,894). A Trafigura employee Naeem Ahmed, who was involved in the ship's operation in Amsterdam, was fined 25,000 euros and the captain of the Probo Koala, Sergiy Chertov, was sentenced to a five-year suspended jail term. The firm was however acquitted of the charge of forgery. In a further application brought by the environmental group Greenpeace Netherlands requesting the court to force the Dutch Public Prosecutor to prosecute Trafigura for the dumping of illegal waste in Ivory Coast, an appeal court in The Hague, in April 2011 refused to grant the application. See BBC News Africa, 23 July 2010, at www.bbc.co.uk/news/world-africa-10735255 [accessed 3 August 2011]; Case profile: Trafigura lawsuits (re Côte d'Ivoire), at www.business-humanrights.org/Categories/Lawlawsuits/Lawsuitsregulatoryaction/LawsuitsSelectedcases/TrafiguralawsuitsreCtedIvoire [accessed 3 August 2011].

allows the defendant European MNC to be brought to the court in its home state
regardless of where the harm occurred or who the victims are.[1556]

In the recent Canadian case of *Choc v. Hudbay Minerals Inc.*,[1557] the
indigenous Mayan Q'eqchi' from El Estor, Guatemala brought three related
actions against Canadian mining company, Hudbay Minerals, and its wholly
controlled subsidiaries. The plaintiffs alleged that security personnel working for
Hudbay's subsidiaries, who were allegedly under the control and supervision of
Hudbay, the parent company, committed human rights abuses. The allegations of
abuse include a shooting, a killing and gang-rapes committed in the vicinity of
the former Fenix mining project, a proposed open-pit nickel mining operation
located in eastern Guatemala. The plaintiffs claim was that Hudbay was itself
negligent in failing to prevent the harms that its subsidiaries have committed, in
particular, the management of relevant security personnel. It further observed
that Hudbay made statements publicly that they were committed to adhering to
certain standards of conduct, including adherence to Guatemalan international
law and the *Voluntary Principles on Security and Human Rights.* On the other
hand, the defendants contended, among others, that there is no recognized duty
of care owed by a parent company to ensure that the commercial activities carried
on by its subsidiary in a foreign country are conducted in a manner designed
to protect those people with whom the subsidiary interacts. Dismissing the
defendants' preliminary motion to strike out claims by indigenous Guatemalans
for the human rights abuses alleged against security staff employed by the
defendant's Guatemalan subsidiary, the Ontario's Superior Court of Justice found
that the plaintiffs have pled all material facts required to establish the constituent
elements of their claim of direct negligence as against Hudbay, separate and
distinct from any claims framed in vicarious liability against it, namely: (1) that
the harm complained of is a reasonably foreseeable consequence of the alleged
breach; (2) that there is sufficient proximity between the parties that it would not
be unjust or unfair to impose a duty of care on the defendants; and, (3) that there
exist no policy reasons to negative or otherwise restrict that duty. According to
the court, it is not plain and obvious that the statement of claim discloses no
cause of action in negligence as the plaintiffs have properly pleaded the elements
necessary to recognize a novel duty of care. The plaintiffs have also pleaded that
the defendants breached the duty of care and that the breach caused the plaintiffs'
losses. The court therefore ruled that the case may proceed to trial even though
the plaintiffs are from another country.

This decision is not only a stunning victory for the Mayan plaintiffs as it paves
the way for future lawsuits against Canadian mining companies for human rights
and environmental harms committed through their foreign operations but also

---

[1556] Jan Wouters and Cedric Ryngaert, Litigation for Overseas Corporate Human Rights Abuses
in the European Union: The Challenge of Jurisdiction, 40 *The Geo. Wash. Int'l Rev.* 939–975 at
948 (2009).
[1557] 2013 ONSC 1414.

for all the indigenous people in the world, including the Niger Delta people. The case supports the existence of a duty of care where a parent company's subsidiary is alleged to be involved in gross human rights abuses.[1558] While the court's decision did not rule on the merits of the case, it however sends a signal to the Canadian mining corporations of the changing landscape of liability for their foreign operations, including subsidiaries, that they 'can no longer hide behind their legal corporate structure to abdicate responsibility for human rights abuses that take place at foreign mines under their control at various locations throughout the world … and Canadian companies [may] not be able to take advantage of broken-down or extremely weak legal systems in other countries to get away with them there."[1559] If successful at the trial, *Choc v. Hudbay* could create the pathway for Canada to become the new jurisdiction for extraterritorial human rights suits and open the door for stricter corporate accountability regulations in the natural resources sector.

Turning our focus to the Netherlands, in May 2008, four Nigerian farmers and fishermen, from the villages of Goi, Oruma and Ikot Ada Udo, in conjunction with Friends of the Earth Netherlands, filed a suit against Royal Dutch Shell Plc (the parent company) and Shell Petroleum Development Company of Nigeria (SPDC) in a Dutch court for damages suffered from oil spills, alleging Shell's negligence in allowing them to happen.[1560] The plaintiffs claim that the oil spills have prevented them from being able to fish or farm their land, which is their only source of livelihood. They allege that the oil spill has affected the environment in a large area near Oruma and that their health may be damaged as a result of the pollution. In response to the filing of the suit, Shell has denied any wrongdoing and denied that the parent company had authority and control to ensure that the oil spills in Nigeria were prevented and cleaned up. In May 2009, additional summonses were served calling for more information on the leaks. Shell further claimed that SPDC is a Nigerian company and thus is not required to appear before a Dutch court. However, on 30 December 2009, the court held that the

---

[1558] See Manning Environmental Law, Human Rights Claims Against Canadian Corp for Acts of its Overseas Subsidiary may Proceed, 2 August 2013, at http://manningenvironmentallaw. com/2013/08/02/july-22-2013-human-rights-claim-against-canadian-corp-for-acts-of-its-overseas-subsidiary-may-proceed/ [accessed 10 August 2013].

[1559] Murray Klippenstein, of Toronto's Klippensteins, Barristers & Solicitors, who's representing 13 Maya Qeqchi from El Estor, Izabal, Guatemala, in *Choc v. Hudbay Minerals Inc. & Caal v. Hudbay Minerals Inc.*, at www.chocversushudbay.com/ [10 August 2013].

[1560] *Oguru et al v. Royal Dutch Shell Plc. & Anor*, Court of the Hague, Civil law section, Case No./ Docket No.: 330891 / HA ZA 09–579. Three cases concerning oil pollution in three different villages are being brought before the Dutch court in the Hague in three separate legal cases: the cases of Oruma, Goi and Ikot Ada Udo. Of these, Oruma case was the first of three civil suits to be brought. The other two cases were introduced in May 2009. Shell contested the jurisdiction of the Dutch court in the Goi and Ikot Ada Udo cases, and a '*lis pendis*' (suit pending) question in Ikot Ada Udo (disposal of Nigerian cases filed concerning the same leak). See Milieudefensie Factsheet, 'The people of Nigeria versus Shell: The case: step by step, Milieudefensie, February 2010, at www.milieudefensie.nl/publicaties/alle-publicaties/Timeline%20Shell%20courtcase. pdf/view [accessed 3 August 2011].

Dutch court had international jurisdiction over the case and can rule on the actions of both Shell Plc and SPDC.[1561]

On 30 January 2013, the Dutch District Court in The Hague (The Netherlands) held that SPDC committed a specific tort of negligence against Akpan by insufficiently securing the IBIBIO-I well at Ikot Ada Udo, in Akwa Ibom State, to prevent the sabotage that was committed in a simple manner prior to the two oil spills in 2006 and 2007, thus liable for the damage that Akpan suffered as a result.[1562] According to the Court: 'SPDC had a specific duty of care in respect of the people living in the vicinity of the IBIBIO-I well and especially fishermen and farmers like Akpan, to take security measures against sabotage that can be reasonably demanded.'[1563] It ordered SPDC to compensate Akpan for the damage he suffered as a result, to be assessed by the court. It is however disappointing that only the subsidiary (Nigerian Shell) was held liable for violations that occurred in Nigeria, not the parent company [Royal Dutch Shell Plc). It held that under Nigerian law, parent companies generally have no legal duty to prevent (overseas') damage to third parties by their subsidiaries. Thus, the parent companies are allowed to reap the profits from their foreign subsidiaries without any corresponding burden by being made liable for the damage caused by the operations of their subsidiaries abroad while making the profits. Though, considered not a clear victory for the NGO and the Nigerian farmers, who are desirous of holding the parent companies responsible for the damages,[1564] *Akpan's* case will no doubt empower victims of overseas corporate abuse, particularly, in countries with weak and ineffective legal systems, like Nigeria, and offer them the protection of the law, even in faraway courts.[1565] Being the first time a Dutch multinational has been brought before the court in its home State for environmental harm caused abroad, this, according to Rowell, '… could open the flood gates for litigation against Shell or other multinationals in other countries. The court may have ruled that sabotage was to blame for some of the spills, but … the court has ruled that Shell also has a duty to prevent sabotage of its pipelines. This fact could also open the legal floodgates too.'[1566]

[1561] *Oguru et al v. Royal Dutch Shell Plc. & Anor, Ibid*; Stichting Onderzoek Multinationale Ondernemingen (SOMO), *Royal Dutch Shell Overview of controversial business practices in 2009*, SOMO, May 2010 pp.7–8.

[1562] *Akpan & Anor. v. Royal Dutch Shell Plc & Anor.*, Case No. / Docket No: C/09/337050 / HA ZA 09–1580, delivered 30 January 2013.

[1563] *Ibid*, paras. 4.44.

[1564] Marie-José van der Heijden, 'Unique Case against Shell – The first Dutch Foreign Direct Libility Case,' *Invisible College Blog, Weblog of the Netherlands School of Human Rights Research*, at http://invisiblecollege.weblog.leidenuniv.nl/2013/02/08/%EF%BB%BFunique-case-against-shell-the-first-dutch-foreign-direct-liability-case/ [accessed 23 May 2013].

[1565] Cedric Ryngaert, *Editorial: The Case of Kiobel v. Royal Dutch Dutch Petroleum before the U.S. Supreme Court*, Newsletter, School of Human Rights Reaserach, Vol. 17, Issue 1, March 2013.

[1566] Andy Rowell, Legal Precedent Set as Shell found Guilty in the Hague, *The Price of Oil: Exposing the True Costs of Fossil Fuels*, 30 January 2013, at http://priceofoil.org/2013/01/30/legal-prece-dent-set-as-shell-found-guilty-in-the-hague/ [accessed 20 May 2013].

The court however dismissed the other claims filed against the Dutch parent company as it concluded, *inter alia*, that there are insufficient evidence that the spills at Goi in Ogoni,[1567] Rivers State and Oruma[1568] communities in Bayelsa State were not cleaned up.

4.12 HUMAN RIGHTS APPROACH TO ENVIRONMENTAL PROTECTION

Most of the ATCA cases filed in the U.S. and other jurisdictions discussed above arose out of human rights abuse allegedly committed by corporations.[1569] It is sad that up till now, no U.S. court has recognized purely environmental harm as being within the ambit of the Alien Tort Statute.[1570] This is partly because of the lack of precedents showing judicial recognition of international environmental laws as binding, customary law.[1571] As shown above, the court dismissed the environmental claims in *Beanal*, *Amlon*, *Aguinda*, *Flores*, and *Sarei*, either substantially or owing to procedural defects. In *Amlon* and *Flores*, the environmental claims alleged were dismissed for failure to have established a violation of the law of nations; *Aguinda* was dismissed on the grounds of FNC and comity, *Beanal* for failure to have alleged violation of a universal, definable and obligatory international norm and *Sarei* was dismissed on the political question doctrine.[1572]

Only a small category of norms, prohibiting the most serious human rights abuses, such as torture, genocide, slavery, crimes against humanity and

---

[1567] *Barizaa Manson Tete Dooh & Anor. v. Royal Dutch Shell Plc. & Anor*, Case No. / Docket No. C/09/337058 / HA ZA 09–1581 and another proceeding in *Barizaa Manson Tete Dooh & Anor. v. Shell Petroleum N.V. & Anor*, Case No. / Docket No. C/09/365482 / HA ZA 10–1665. This concerns two cases on the same oil spill and the same parties; both cases are essentially the same claims and the defenses in the two cases are closely related. For this reason, the District Court assessed the two cases collectively. In a ruling delivered on 30th January 2013, the District Court dismissed the two legal proceedings, as it ruled that no tort of negligece of SPDC against Dooh, a Nigerian farmer and fisherman in Ogoniland, is involved. It further held that the oil spill from the underground oil pipeline in 2004 near Goi was, in fact, caused by sabotage by third parties.

[1568] *Oguru et al v. Royal Dutch Shell Plc. & Anor*, Case No. / Docket No. C/09/330891 / HA ZA 09–0579 and another proceeding in *Oguru et al v. Shell Petroleum N.V. & Anor.*, Case No. / Docket No.: C/09/365498 / HA ZA 10–1677, delivered on 30 January 2013. The District Court, while dismissing the two legal proceedings, ruled that under Nigerian law, Shell *et al.* did not commit any tort against the applicants, Nigerian farmers from Oruma community in Bayelsa State, as contained in their main claims. It further held that the pollutions were caused by sabotage by third parties and, that under Nigerian law, oil companies are not responsible unless they breach their duty of care.

[1569] See *Shell v. Wiwa (supra)*; *Unocal v. Doe (supra)*.

[1570] Ronald Slye, *op. cit.*

[1571] Joanna E. Arlow, *op. cit.*, p.95.

[1572] Natalie L. Bridgeman, *op. cit.*, p.35.

war crimes[1573] have been recognised by the U.S. Federal Courts. Of these, only genocide[1574] appears likely to be closely related to environmental abuses, so as to help establish a cognisable environmental claim. It has been argued by advocates that in circumstances where partial or full extinction of a group of people is likely, deliberate Government destruction of the environment or cultural heritage of such group is a form of genocide.[1575] In support of the genocidal intent of Shell in Ogoniland [Niger Delta], Ken Saro-Wiwa alleged that the destruction of the ecosystem on which the Niger Delta people rely for survival through gas flaring and the frequency of oil spills,[1576] with their attendants health effects on the people, were all done with the intent to wipe out the entire Ogoni people. Also, the forced displacement of the people as a result of the exploitation of oil has led to a breakdown in the historic social structure of Niger Delta people and to the disintegration of their cultural identity and unity.[1577] It is not likely, however, that the Federal Courts will categorize the horrendous environmental damage and human rights abuses which the oil MNCs have caused in the Niger Delta as genocide.[1578] This is because the plaintiff has to prove that there was an intention on the part of the MNC 'to destroy the group, in whole or in part' as required by the Genocide Convention. This will likely be the most difficult element of genocide to prove as the MNC may contend that environmental harm merely resulted from their oil exploratory activities, and not from ill-will towards a particular group [Niger Delta people].[1579]

Be that as it may, scholars must not relent in their efforts at pushing for the development of international environmental law until environmental law norms becomes recognised as part of the law of nation for ATCA purposes. Examples can be seen from the recent entrance of human rights law into the law of nations.[1580] In *Sarei*, Judge Morrow would have sustained the plaintiffs' claim based on

---

[1573] *Sosa*, 542 U.S. 762.

[1574] Convention on the Prevention and Punishment of the Crime of Genocide, 78 U.N.T.S. 277, entered into force 12 January 1951. Art. 2 prohibits any of the following acts committed with intent to destroy, in whole or in part, a national, ethnical, racial or religious group, as such: (a) Killing members of the group; (b) Causing serious bodily or mental harm to members of the group; (c) Deliberately inflicting on the group conditions of life calculated to bring about its physical destruction in whole or in part; (d) Imposing measures intended to prevent births within the group; (e) Forcibly transferring children of the group to another group. Genocide is contrary to the spirit and intendment of the UN and it is outrightly condemned by the civilised world.

[1575] Schwartz, Michelle Leighton, International Legal Protection for Victims of Environmental Abuse, 18 *Yale J. Int'l L.* 355–387 at 367 (1993).

[1576] Ken Saro-Wiwa, *Genocide in Nigeria: The Ogoni Tragedy, op. cit.*, pp.80–82.

[1577] Schwartz, Michelle Leighton, International Legal Protection for Victims of Environmental Abuse, *op. cit.* 367.

[1578] James Donelly-Saalfield, Irreparable Harms: How the Devastating Effects of Oil Extraction in Nigeria Have not been Remedied by Nigerian Courts, the African Commission, or U.S. Courts, 15(2) *Hastings W. Nw. J. Envtl. L. & Pol'y* 371–429 at 398 (2009).

[1579] Lauren A. Mowery, Earth Rights, Human Rights: Can International Environmental Human Rights Affect Corporate Accountability?, 13 *Fordham Envl. L.J.* 343–372 at 368–369 (2002).

[1580] Natalie L. Bridgeman, *op. cit.*, p.40.

UNCLOS were it not for the dismissal of the entire case on doctrine of political question. Nigerian plaintiffs bringing an action under ATCA may rely upon the reasoning of the court in *Sarei* by alleging that the massive environmental degradation caused by the regular oil spills through the activities of the oil MNCs operating in the Niger Delta region have transnational implications, namely the pollution of the high seas, thus violating the UNCLOS.[1581] To overcome the problem of proving which particular MNC was responsible for the harm caused, the plaintiffs may bring in all the oil MNCs operating in the region as defendants. Such succeed in their UNCLOS claim if they were able to prove that the fishing grounds of neighbouring countries were damaged by oil spillage and leakage from the Niger Delta.[1582] Plaintiffs could also establish that the effects of continual gas flaring in the Niger Delta in the form of acid rain, contributing to global warming, and pollution of the air are transnational. If they can establish the health implications and the harm to infrastructure caused by the gas flaring to neighbouring countries, it may be possible for them to convincing a court that gas flaring violates customary international law.[1583] This is not without its problems as it may be difficult for the plaintiffs to establish causation – a correlation between gas flaring and health problems. In addition, the plaintiffs may also find it difficult to convince the U.S. courts that gas flaring violates customary international law because 'it does not have specificity comparable to the 18th century ATS paradigms such as offences against ambassadors and piracy.'[1584] This is because the steps been taken by some states to prohibit gas flaring are based on self initiatives, as the international community is yet to reach a consensus on the specific measures states must take to reduce greenhouse gas emissions.

With the continuous consolidation of environmental principles into the formal body of public international law and a broadening recognition of non-State corporations as rights and obligations bearers under international law, ATCA claims in environmental suits may become easier to invoke.[1585] And when the U.S. courts start to declare environmental torts, even when committed by MNC's as violations of law of nations, foreign poorly resourced plaintiffs, like the Niger Delta people, will be able to get a proper remedy for the environmental and human rights abuses suffered at the hands of the powerful MNCs. While waiting for this day, we agree with scholars who suggest a human rights proxy approach:[1586] that 'plaintiffs should attempt to bring environmental law claims under the ATCA

[1581] James Donnelly-Saalfield, *op. cit.*, p.416.
[1582] *Ibid*, p.417.
[1583] *Ibid*, p.417.
[1584] *Ibid*, pp.417–418.
[1585] Oren Perez, *op. cit.*, p.219.
[1586] This approach however has its own problem such as the difficulty of determining 'what environmental harms are of sufficient magnitude to be considered violations of international human rights,' and the 'lack of jurisprudence on the rights implicated by environmental problems or the standards that should be used to measure such violations.' See James Boeving, *op. cit.*, p.136.

only in coordination with human rights claims arising from the same case or controversy.'[1587] Bridgeman continued that even if the environmental claims are dismissed, the plaintiffs can seek carefully craft remedies for the human rights claims in order also to redress the environmental harms.[1588] Plaintiffs in the Niger Delta region, proposing to bring an action for environmental claims under ATCA could adopt this approach. Among human rights claims, it is the civil and political rights that are most likely to pass the *Sosa* standard of universal recognition among nations.[1589] As seen in the previous environmental ATCA cases, such as *Beanal* and *Flores*, courts are not yet inclined to accept human rights claims that are based on second and third generation human rights.[1590]

It is also important to stress that monetary relief for human rights abuses in the Niger Delta would probably not be adequate because the violations are ongoing, including those from a complex source such as suppression of opposing views regarding a development project.[1591] Plaintiffs might additionally seek an injunction to restrain MNCs from carrying on the underlying developmental projects which are found to be a major source of the human rights violations. The Ninth Court in the U.S. has held that for such a remedy, plaintiffs must demonstrate 'irreparable harm and inadequacy of [other] legal remedies.'[1592] Irreparable damage may be easy to demonstrate in Nigeria because the environmental harms from exploratory activities are grave and catastrophic. Inadequacy of legal remedies should also not pose a problem to the plaintiffs because money damages – the other principal legal remedy – are inadequate to halt or repair the severe environmental damage caused by the activities of the oil MNCs in the region. Nor can money compensate them for the elimination of their rights to life, health and other rights caused by ongoing development projects.[1593]

It is further submitted that in addition to monetary damages, future ATCA environmental and human rights claims should include other terms of settlement. For example, in Nigeria, such could include steps to be taken by parties towards the phasing out of gas flaring in the oil rich region. This term of settlement will

---

[1587] L. Bridgeman, *op. cit.*, p.42; See generally Hari M. Osofsky, Environmental Human Rights Under the Alien Tort Statute: Redress for Indigenous Victims of Multinational Corporations, 20 *Suffolk Transnat'l L. Rev.* 335, 372 (1997) where he states that '[i]f the connection between these rights [to life, health, livelihood, culture and privacy] and the environment is accepted, then derived human environmental rights also can be considered part of the law of nations.'; Caroline Dommen, Claiming Environmental Rights: Some Possibilities Offered by the United Nation's Human Rights Mechanisms, 11 *Geo. Int'l Envt'l L. Rev.* 1 (1998); Armin Rosencranz and Richard Campbell, *op. cit.*; James Boeving, *op. cit.*, pp.134–135, 138.

[1588] *Ibid.*

[1589] Kathleen Jaeger, *op. cit.*, p.536.

[1590] Kathleen Jaeger, *Ibid.*

[1591] Natalie L. Bridgeman, *op. cit.*, p.37.

[1592] *Los Angeles Memorial Coliseum Comm'n v. National Football League*, 634 F.2d 1197, 1202 (9th Cir. 1980).

[1593] Natalie L. Bridgeman, *op. cit.*, pp. 37–38; See also James Donnelly-Saalfield, *op. cit.*, pp.418–419.

help to bring an end to the bureaucratic rhetoric of cessation of gas flaring in Nigeria and contribute to solving the problems of global warming.

4.13 ATTEMPTS BY SOME JURISDICTIONS TO ENACT LAWS TO REGULATE MNCs

Attempts had been made in some countries to adopt laws which impose extraterritorial liability on transnational corporations for breach of specified human rights standards. These are the Australian Corporate Code of Conduct Bill 2000,[1594] a Belgian proposal in 1999 (amended in 2003), and the UK Corporate Responsibility Bills. None of these bills has been enacted. The Australian Corporate Code of Conduct Bill 2000 was aimed at introducing a home State model of extraterritorial regulation. It aimed at imposing environmental, employment (including the core International Labour Organisation Conventions), health and safety and human rights standards on the conduct of Australian corporations, or related corporations, which employ more than 100 persons in a foreign country.[1595] It expressly allowed non-Australian residents the right to bring an action before the Australian Federal Courts in order to seek redress for human rights abuses by Australian corporations committed abroad.[1596] This Bill applied to companies established in Australia, to their holding companies or subsidiaries, or to a subsidiary of a holding company of such a company, but was declared unworkable, impracticable, unwarranted and unnecessary by the majority of the members of the Australian Parliamentary Joint Statutory Committee on Corporations.[1597]

In Belgium, a socialist parliamentarian came up with a proposal in 1999 to give universal civil jurisdiction to Belgian courts in relation to human rights obligations of companies with assets in Belgium. The scope of the human rights protection of the Bill was limited to the core International Labour Organisation Conventions. This Bill was opposed by the Belgian Government, on the ground that it took jurisdiction beyond that allowed under international law.[1598] The original Bill was amended to insert a link to Belgian jurisdiction so that it would apply to companies incorporated in Belgium or with their central administration

---

[1594] Australian Corporate Code of Conduct Bill 2000, at www.austlii.edu.au/au/legis/cth/bill/ ccocb2000248/ [accessed 3 March 2010]. This Bill was introduced in the Senate on 6 September 2000.

[1595] *Ibid*, cl. 3(1)(a).

[1596] *Ibid*, cl. 17(1)(5).

[1597] Chatham House Report, *Human Rights and Transnational Corporations: Legislation and Government Regulation*, being a Note of a meeting held at Chatham House on 15 June 2006, available at www.chathamhouse.org.uk/files/3337_il150606.pdf [accessed 5 March 2010].

[1598] *Ibid*.

or company headquarters in Belgium, but the proposal failed, because, *inter alia*, of concerns about the possible adverse effects on the Belgian economy.[1599]

In the UK, the 2003 NGO-led Corporate Responsibility Bill[1600] sought to impose mandatory reporting requirements, a duty to consult extraterritorially with affected stakeholders beyond the company's shareholders, the extension of the director's duties to take into account the social and environmental impact of overseas operations, and statutory obligations to pay damages to those harmed overseas.[1601] The Bill envisaged a parent company-based system of regulation, whereby the parent company should ensure the compliance of its subsidiaries with human rights standards.[1602] It made provisions for a wide range of penalties,[1603] ranging from fines to delisting the company, but this Bill lacked political and business support and was dropped.[1604] As part of efforts to ensure that UK companies adhere to international human rights and environment standards when they operate abroad, the Corporate Responsibility Coalition (CORE) proposes the establishment of a UK Commission for Business, Human Rights and the Environment.[1605] The main objectives of the Commission would include to: (1) provide redress for overseas victims of human rights abuses involving UK companies (2) promote appropriate environmental and human rights standards for UK companies operating overseas and promulgate best practice, (3) work with other human rights commissions and relevant bodies to share learning and build their collective capacity to strengthen the effectiveness of redress in developing countries.[1606]

Also, in April 2010, the Dutch Parliament approved a motion requesting the Government to consider the creation of a fund to assist foreign victims seeking justice in Dutch courts for harm caused by Dutch multinational corporations.[1607] This followed proposals tabled by Friends of the Earth Netherlands and the motion was approved in the midst of a court case in the Netherlands against Shell

---

[1599]   *Ibid.*

[1600]   Corporate Responsibility Bill, Bill 129, at www.publications.parliament.uk/pa/cm200203/cmbills/129/2003129.pdf [accessed 3 March 2010].

[1601]   *Ibid*, cl. 3, 4, 5, 7, 8, 10; See Chatham House Report, Human rights and Transnational corporations: Legislation and Government Regulation, *op. cit.*

[1602]   Chatham House Report, *Ibid.*

[1603]   Corporate Responsibility Bill, *op. cit.*, cl. 11.

[1604]   *Ibid.*

[1605]   International Federation for Human Rights (FIDH) & European Coalition for Corporate Justice (ECCJ) Report, *CSR at a turning point: time for the EU to move forward for true accountability*, being a contribution to the European Multi-stakeholder Forum on CSR, 29–30 November 2010, at www.fidh.org/IMG/pdf/FIDH_Contribution_to_the_European_Multistakeholder_Forum_on_CSR_2010.pdf [accessed 13 May 2011].

[1606]   Corporate Responsibility (CORE), *UK Commission Proposal: A New Commission for Business, Human Rights and the Environment*, at http://corporate-responsibility.org/campaigns/uk-commissions-proposal/ [accessed 8 June 2010].

[1607]   International Federation for Human Rights (FIDH) & European Coalition for Corporate Justice (ECCJ) Report, *op. cit.*

and its subsidiary for the harm caused by oil spills in the Niger delta region of Nigeria.[1608]

What can be inferred from the current approach to business and human rights by these countries is the failure of their Governments to take a positive stand on measures to provide guidance to companies on how to avoid abuse of human rights violations where they operate. This has led to the absence of authoritative guidance for MNCs to avoid such negative impacts, as well as the absence of solutions and accountability in the event of breaches taking place.[1609] Developed countries must recognize the growing social, economic and human rights impacts of corporate activities on the lives of the people in the developing countries, in the name of profit. They should also appreciate the harm likely to be done to the reputation of the developed countries as a whole.

4.14 CONCLUSION

States, including the Nigerian Government are seeking to exploit and develop their natural resources, the MNCs are busy pursuing the business of making profits, and technology is daily advancing and transforming the world. Unfortunately, the environment and the ecosystems of the communities in which resources are exploited for such 'progress' and 'growth' are daily been destroyed, with people's human rights being violated by the activities of the MNCs. Most importantly, international law appears to be lagging behind as the MNCs are neither within the reach of international law nor do any real mechanisms exists to hold the MNCs accountable for the destruction of the environment and violation of human rights.[1610] Given the failure of the national Government to regulate the activities of the oil MNCs in the Niger Delta, it is not unlikely that the spate of protests, kidnappings, car bombings, sabotage of oil installations, extortion that have characterised the region as a result of environmental and human rights abuse will continue.

As shown in this chapter, environmental degradation is one of the underlying causes of human rights violation in the Niger Delta. The chapter has contended that although self regulation and other voluntary initiatives play vital roles in encouraging MNCs to behave responsibly, they may not be sufficient to prevent environmental-related human rights violations by MNCs in the Niger Delta region. While hoping for the adoption of an international legally binding instrument for corporate accountability, the foreign victims of corporate harm such as the Niger Delta people can continue in the U.S. to use ATCA to hold MNCs accountable for the environmental human rights abuse. Oil MNCs should refrain from the

---

[1608]   *Ibid.*
[1609]   Corporate Responsibility (CORE), *UK Commission Proposal: A New Commission for Business, Human Rights and the Environment, op. cit.*
[1610]   Lauren A. Mowery, *op. cit.* at 373.

exploitation of natural resources in Nigeria and other developing countries, in ways that directly or indirectly contribute to the violation of the human rights of the local inhabitants. Rather, they should make human rights central to their business and ensure that their conduct contributes to the protection of the human rights and a healthy environment for the local communities where they operate. MNCs should serve as 'agents of justice' by pursuing policies that go 'beyond compliance' with host (and even home) State laws governing environmental and human rights standards.[1611]

[1611] David Kinley, *Civilising Globalisation. Human Rights and the Global Economy, op. cit.*, pp.158–159.

CHAPTER FIVE

OIL AND CORRUPTION IN
THE NIGER DELTA, NIGERIA:
THE HUMAN RIGHTS IMPLICATIONS

5.1 INTRODUCTION

Corruption is one of the major challenges for the regulation of the activities of the oil MNCs in Nigeria. This chapter addresses the linkage between corruption and violations of human rights. Most importantly, it addresses corruption from the natural resource perspective and how this perspective undermines the Niger Delta people's chances of enjoyment of basic rights of access to essential services. It argues that corruption is one of the real reasons for human rights abuse in the Niger Delta region, and stresses that addressing the human rights violations in the region should entail tackling the pervading corruption in the oil sector, involving Government officials and the oil MNCs collaborators who cheat the nation on oil revenue. This chapter discusses the factors that contribute to corruption in the oil sector, the consequences of corruption on the human rights of the people, particularly, those living in the oil rich region of the Niger Delta, the various national and international attempts to curtail the ubiquitous presence of corruption in the sector, and the challenges and prospects faced in this regard. True access to justice for the Niger Delta people can be better addressed only after transparency and accountability of Government and its agencies to citizens, as well as the inequities embedded in the oil industry in Nigeria, have been justly addressed.[1612]

5.2 MEANING OF CORRUPTION

The term 'corruption' is not capable of any precise definition. However, it has been generally defined by the World Bank and the non-governmental organization Transparency International as 'the abuse of public office for private gain.' According to the World Bank, this definition includes situations where a public

---

[1612] Engobo Emeseh, 'The Niger Delta Crisis and the Question of Access to Justice,' in Cyril Obi and Siri Aas Rustad (eds) (2011), *op. cit.*, p.70.

official 'accepts, solicits, or extorts a bribe,' and where private actors or agents 'offer bribes to circumvent public policies and processes for competitive advantage and profit.'[1613] The World Bank also noted that corruption in public office can also occur, even if no bribery occurs, in the form of patronage and nepotism, the theft of State assets, or the diversion of State revenues.[1614] Corruption and lack of transparency are major problems in Nigeria. While a World Bank report observes that 80% of Nigeria's oil wealth benefits only 1% of the population,[1615] the United Nations currently ranks Nigeria as among the world's worst performing countries in terms of life expectancy and infant mortality.[1616] Nigeria, one of the top 10 oil producing and exporting countries, ranked 156 out of 187 countries in the 2011 UNDP's Human Development Index,[1617] placing it below every other top ten oil producing countries in the world. The Harmonized Nigeria Living Standard Survey (HNLSS) 2009/2010 revealed that Nigeria's relative poverty measurement in 2004 stood at 54.4%, but increased to 69% (or 112,518,507 Nigerians) in 2010; whilst the proportion of those living on less than the US$1 per day poverty line increased from 51.6% in 2004 to 61.2% in 2010.[1618] Almost 90% of the local inhabitants of the Niger Delta fall below the poverty line of $1 per day and they depend on aquatic resources for their livelihoods.[1619] A situation typified as a 'resource curse,'[1620] (paradox of plenty), meaning, a situation where resource-rich countries tends to have less economic growth and worse development outcomes than countries with fewer natural resources.[1621] Corruption is rampant in Nigeria, as can be seen in daily newspaper reports. The 2011 Transparency International Corruption Perception Index ranked Nigeria 143 out of 183 countries with

---

[1613] The World Bank (1997), *Helping Countries Combat Corruption: The Role of the World Bank*, The World Bank, Washington, DC, p.8; Human Rights Watch (2007), *Chop Fine: The Human Rights Impact of Local Government Corruption and Mismanagement in Rivers State, Nigeria*, Volume 19, No. 2(A), p.17.

[1614] *Ibid*, pp.8–9.

[1615] Frontline (PBS), 'Nigeria: *The Hidden Cost of Corruption*, April 24, 2009, at www.pbs.org/frontlineworld/stories/bribe/2009/04/nigeria-the-hidden-cost-of-corruption.html [accessed 3 March 2010].

[1616] The United Nations World Population Prospects: The 2008 Revision, quoted in United States Senate Permanent Subcommittee on Investigations, Committee on Homeland Security and Governmental Affairs, *Keeping Foreign Corruption out of the United States: Four Case Histories*, February 4, 2010 Hearing Washington, DC. p.175.

[1617] Human Development Report, *Sustainability and Equity: A Better Future for All*, UNDP, New York, 2011 at http://hdr.undp.org/en/ [accessed 13 June 2012].

[1618] National Bureau of Statistics (NBS), Nigeria Poverty Profile 2010, January 2012; Yemi Kale, *The Nigeria Poverty Profile 2010 Report*, being Press Briefing by the Statistician-General of the Federation/Chief Executive Officer, National Bureau of Statistics (NBS), held at the NBS Headquarters, Abuja on Monday 13 February 2012.

[1619] Michael Watts, "Sweet and Sour", in Michael Watts (ed) (2008), *Curse of the Black Gold: 50 Years of Oil in the Niger Delta*, powerhouse Books, New York, p.40.

[1620] *Ibid*, p.39.

[1621] Ying Wang, *The Natural Resource Curse*, at www.neaef.org/public/neaef/files/documents/publications_pdf/young_leaders/5th/Wang%20Ying.pdf [accessed 30 March 2013].

an index score of 2.4 on a scale from 10 (very clean) to 0 (highly corrupt),[1622] indicating rampant and acute corruption.

In the oil sector, corruption is very prevalent in the award of oil licences and contracts. But the most prevalent is bribery and the embezzlement of oil rent. Jeffrey Sachs and Andrew Warner, in a comparative analysis of 97 countries, based on evidence from 1970–1989, found that 'resource-poor countries often vastly outperform resource-rich economies in economic growth.'[1623] They observed in the past thirty years, 'the world's star performers have been the resource-poor Newly Industrializing Economies of East Asia – Korea, Taiwan, Hong Kong, Singapore – while many resource-rich economies such as the oil-rich countries of Mexico, Nigeria, and Venezuela, have gone bankrupt.'[1624] Looting of oil wealth has been documented in many resource rich countries, including Angola, Kazakhstan, Sao Tome, Congo, and Equatorial Guinea. However, the economic growth in the UK and Norway, both major oil exporting countries, reveal that this resource "curse" is avoidable provided there are functioning institutions and good governance in place. The benefits from natural resources for corrupt Government officials can be enormous. The corrupt Government officials live in opulence by diverting billions of dollars generated by the sale of natural resources into their own pockets or for their own purposes.[1625] It was estimated that in the late 1970s, U.S.$25 million per day was transferred abroad on behalf of Nigeria's corrupt officials.[1626]

Corruption is one of the major causes of the laxity and inadequacy of environmental protection regime in Nigeria, involving weak regulatory systems and poor enforcement of national laws. Corruption has meant that Government officials are quick to turn a blind eye to gross violations of environmental laws or regulations,[1627] thus creating room to pollute with impunity on the part of the MNCs. Partly because of corruption, the Nigerian Government has failed to address the inadequacy inherent in the domestic regulation of oil MNCs so as to ensure protection of human rights in Nigeria. The enforcement of various laws introduced to protect the environment, including regulations to outlaw

---

[1622] See Transparency International, *2011 Corruption Perceptions Index*, at http://cpi.transparency. org/cpi2011/results/ [accessed 3 June 2012].

[1623] Jeffrey D. Sachs and Andrew M. Warner, *Natural Resource Abundance and Economic Growth*, November 1997, p.2 at www.cid.harvard.edu/ciddata/warner_files/natresf5.pdf [accessed 3 March 2010].

[1624] *Ibid*, pp.2–3.

[1625] See James C. Owens, Government Failure in Sub-Saharan Africa: The International Community's Options, 43 *Virginia Journal of International Law*, 1003–1049 at 1011(2003); Jennifer M. Hartman, Government by Thieves: Revealing the Monsters Behind the Kleptocratic Masks, 24 *Syracuse Journal of International Law & Commerce*, 157–175 at 158 (1997) (arguing that indigenous spoilation 'destroys the essential foundation of the economic lives of societies').

[1626] James C. Owens, *Ibid*, 1012.

[1627] Uwafiokun Idemudia, *Corporate Partnerships and Community Development in the Nigerian Oil Industry: Strengths and Limitations, op. cit.*, p.21.

the flaring of gas, has been thwarted by bribery and corruption on the part of the special agencies created to enforce these laws and the Government officials saddled with responsibility for ensuring accurate documentation. U.S. President Obama, on 27 May 2010, on the U.S. Government's relationship with BP and other oil companies stated: 'the oil industry's cosy and sometimes corrupt relationship with Government regulators mean[s] little or no regulation at all.'[1628] This aptly captures the situation between the Nigerian Government and the multinational oil companies. Corruption not only undermines accountability but also privilege those with power and money over the citizens, 'allowing them to profit at the expense not only of the rest of us – but of the planet itself.'[1629] The environmental and human rights costs of corruption in Nigeria, particularly in the Niger Delta region, take the form of pollution – land, air and water, climate change and threats to the civil, political, social, economic and cultural rights of the local population, as it gives the oil MNCs an unrestricted freedom to exploit the natural resources irresponsibly.

The oil MNCs give bribes to secure licences. In this way, they can reduce the cost of acquiring the natural resources by bribing the Government officials to get concessions. This is because it is far cheaper to pay a large amount of bribe to Government officials than to pay the market price for concessions for oil or some other natural resources.[1630] Bribes can also be used to reduce the amount of taxes or other fees payable; can be offered to speed up the Government's granting of permission to carry out legal activities; and can be used to change the outcome of legal processes.[1631] The result of the bribe – is a loss to the nation, and gain to the MNCs. For example, Halliburton has acknowledged that it paid bribes worth $2.4 billion to some Nigerian government officials for tax breaks related to its operations in Nigeria.[1632] Royal Dutch Shell, after settling with U.S. authorities in November 2010, agreed to pay U.S.$10 million in fines to the Nigerian Government over alleged bribes paid on its behalf by Panalpina.[1633] Also, in 2008, Albert Jackson Stanley of Kellogg, Brown and Root, a US oil service company, pleaded guilty to paying around U.S.$180 million in bribes to NNPC, the Petroleum Ministry, and other government officials from 1994 to 2004, to secure four contracts worth

---

[1628] Quoted in Bianca Jagger, *Crimes Against Present and Future Generations*, being a paper delivered at the Council of Europe Fifth Summer University for Democracy on 2 July 2010, at Strasbourg, at www.coe.int/t/dgap/sps/Source/Speech%20Bianca%20Jagger.pdf [accessed 5 July 2011].

[1629] Kumi Naidoo, 'Foreword,' in Transparency International, "Global Corruption Report: Climate Change," Earthscan Publishing, London, Washington, DC, 2011, p. xiv.

[1630] Joseph E. Stiglitz (2006), *Making Globalization Work*, op. cit., p.191.

[1631] The World Bank, *Helping Countries Combat Corruption: The Role of the World Bank*, op. cit., p.9.

[1632] Jim Cason (2003), *US firm Halliburton acknowledges bribes to Nigerian Official*, News. http://allAfrica.com/stories/200305090511.html [accessed 3 March 2010]; See also Uwafiokun Idemudia, *Corporate Partnerships and Community Development in the Nigerian Oil Industry: Strengths and Limitations*, op. cit., p.21.

[1633] Chika Amanze-Nwachuku, Firm to pay $2.5m for Bribery Case, *This Day*, 8 February 2011.

over U.S.$ 6 billion, to build liquefied natural gas facilities[1634] in Bonny Island in the Niger Delta. While Stanley was sentenced to 30 months in prison, and three years' probation following his release, two British men, attorney Jeffrey Tesler and businessman Wojciech Chodan, were also sentenced on criminal charges to 21 months in prison and one year on probation respectively.[1635] Etete, Nigeria's former Petroleum Minister, 1993–1998, was convicted by a Paris Criminal Court on 7 November 2007, fined a total of €250 million and sentenced to three years imprisonment for using – €15 million 'in funds obtained fraudulently' to purchase a string of expensive properties in France between 1999 and 2000.[1636] The money laundered was reportedly part of bribes received from Kellogg, Brown, and Root, a Halliburton subsidiary.[1637] On appeal, the Appeals court on 18 March 2009, lifted the three year prison sentence on Etete and reduced the fine to eight million Euros (U.S.$10.5m).[1638] Meanwhile, the Nigerian Federal Ministry of Justice had written to French Government saying that they did not have any evidence against Etete of corrupt practices.

The above evidences how the oil MNCs in Nigeria sponsor official corruption, and this undermines democracy, stifles economic growth and furthers the abuse of the human rights of Nigerian citizens. It raises concerns about the high level of official corruption in Nigeria despite avowed Government claims to fight corruption. It is submitted that the poor enforcement of environmental laws and policies, the inadequate provision of public infrastructure and services to the people, and the slow development in the country's policy reforms in the oil industry, are largely caused by this endemic corruption. This is not only bad for sustainable development but also for human rights.

5.3 IMPACT OF CORRUPTION IN THE OIL SECTOR ON HUMAN RIGHTS IN NIGERIA

The widespread violence and human rights abuse in the Niger Delta region is one of the symptoms of rampant corruption. While corruption is generally seen as a crime against the State, little attention is paid to its impact on individual citizens, especially those in the most vulnerable sectors of the population (the Niger Delta people, the poor, women and children) who continue to bear the brunt of the consequences, without any direct access to effective remedies, in the

---

[1634] Alexandra Gillies, *Reforming Corruption out of Nigerian Oil? Part one: Mapping corruption risks in oil sector governance*, Chr. Michelsen Institute, Bergen (U4 Brief 2009:2), p.4.

[1635] The FCPA Blog, *Stanley Jailed for 30 Months*, 23 February 2012, at www.fcpablog.com/blog/tag/albert-jack-stanley [accessed 24 February 2012].

[1636] Davidson Iriekpen, French Court Fines Etete $10.5m, *ThisDay*, 19 March 2009.

[1637] Idris Akinbajo, France Slams $10.5m fine on Etete, *Next* 19 March 2009, at http://234next.com/csp/cms/sites/Next/Home/5394254-146/France_slams_$10.5m_fine_on_Etete.csp [accessed 23 May 2010].

[1638] Punch Newspaper, French Court Fines Etete $10.5m, *Punch*, 19 March 2009.

form of compensation or the guarantee of non-repetition.[1639] Most worrisome is
the fact that most of these corrupt practices are 'justified'by the perpetrators,
using 'grand utterances' which include seeing corruption as a way of recovery of
'one's due,' referring to notions of good manners, 'perks of office' or 'privileges',
meeting social pressures, or 'doing as everyone else does,' or as mere 'borrowing'
with the intention to repay.[1640] In other words, using the concepts of 'privilege,'
'social pressure,' 'redistribution,' to show that the actor is motivated by need,
thereby ostensibly legitimizing practices that are illegal; while at the same time,
using euphemisms such as 'recovery,' 'good manners,' 'borrowing' to neutralize
the negative connotations of corrupt acts.[1641] Corruption undermines good
governance and has grave implications for the enjoyment of civil and political
as well as socio-economic and cultural rights as guaranteed under the various
regional and international human rights instruments. This fact was well noted
by Chaskalson P. in the Constitutional Court of South Africa in *South African
Association of Personal Injury Lawyers v. Heath &Ors*:

> "*Corruption and maladministration are inconsistent with the rule of law and the
> fundamental values of our Constitution. They undermine the constitutional com-
> mitment to human dignity, the achievement of equality and the advancement of
> human rights and freedoms. They are the antithesis of the open, accountable, demo-
> cratic government required by the Constitution. If allowed to go unchecked and
> unpunished they will pose a serious threat to our democratic State.*"[1642]

With the increase in world oil prices, Nigerian Government coffers collect
windfall oil revenues, while ordinary Nigerians derive little benefit from this
super wealth. The former Chair of the Nigerian Economic and Financial Crimes
Commission (EFCC), Nuhu Ribadu, in an interview, estimated that since Nigeria's
Independence in 1960, more than U.S.$380 billion dollars had been wasted or
lost to corruption,[1643] while standards of living have plummeted. The regimes of
General Ibrahim Babangida and Abacha (1985–1993 and 1993–1998 respectively)
were noted for their reckless looting of the nation's treasury. For example, as
much as U.S.$12.2 billion dollars in oil revenues are alleged to have 'disappeared'

[1639]   Adetokunbo Mumuni, *Legal Redress for Victims of Corruption: Enhancing the role of civil
society to bring and to represent victims in legal proceedings*, being a paper presented at the
International Anti-Corruption Conference, Bangkok, Thailand, November 2010, at www.
serap-nigeria.org/campaign/seraps-paper-the-international-anti-corruption-conference-
bangkok-thailand/ [accessed 18 August 2011].

[1640]   G. Blundo and J-P. Olivier de Sardan, The Popular Semiology of Corruption, in G. Blundo and
J-P. Olivier de Sardan (eds.), *Everyday Corruption and the State: Citizens and Public Officials in
Africa*, David Philip, Cape Town & Zed Books, London and New York, 2006, pp.112–120.

[1641]   *Ibid*, p. 120.

[1642]   [2000] ZACC 22; 2001 (1) BCLR 77, para. 4 (28 November 2000).

[1643]   *BBC News*, Nigerian Leaders 'Stole' $380bn, 20 October 2006, at http://news.bbc.co.uk/2/hi/
africa/6069230.stm. [accessed 8 July 2010].

during the Babangida administration.[1644] In 2005, Nigeria recovered U.S.$458m dollars found in Swiss bank accounts linked to Nigeria's late military ruler Sani Abacha, during his four year reign in which he stole between one and three billion U.S. dollars.[1645]

Corruption serves as a major barrier against the State fulfilling its obligations to respect, protect and fulfil the human rights of individuals. Corruption of the Nigerian political elite endangers the right to life when it allows the oil MNCs to exploit oil with little or no regard to the negative impacts on the health, water, food, employment, housing, electricity, good schools, etc of the people. These basic infrastructural facilities are not available to Nigerians, particularly the Niger Delta people, as a result of endemic corruption.

Abject poverty in some states in the Niger Delta ranks amongst the worst in the world. Oil revenues that could have been spent on improving the infrastructural facilities and providing jobs for Nigerian citizens have instead been squandered and embezzled by the governing elite.[1646] The result is that the higher the oil prices, the more widespread the human rights abuse in the region. While these oil-producing States have budgets that are larger than some other African Countries, unfortunately, this money ends up in foreign accounts through money laundering. For example, in 2007, a British court froze some U.S.$35m (£21m) in assets, including a private jet, belonging to former Delta State Governor James Ibori, whose annual salary while in office was around U.S.$25,000.[1647] The Economic and Financial Crimes Commission (EFCC) commenced the prosecution of former Governor of Abia State, Orji Kalu, for allegedly laundering an estimated 5 billion naira (approximately U.S.$31.6 million) of Abia State funds. The Court of Appeal, Abuja Division, on 27 April 2012, held that Orji Kalu, had a case to answer over his alleged theft of public funds while in office between 1999 and 2007,[1648] thus clearing the coast for the continuation of his trial at the Federal High Court, Abuja. In July 2007, the former Bayelsa State Governor, Diepreye Alamieyeseigha, who was arrested in 2005 on charges of money laundering, pleaded guilty to six of the charges preferred against him, and was sentenced to 12 years in prison, but was released a day after his conviction due to time already served.[1649] The court also ordered the confiscation and forfeiture of some of his assets located in several countries, and funds in excess of 2.4 billion naira

---

[1644] Human Rights Watch (2007), *Chop Fine: The Human Rights Impact of Local Government Corruption and Mismanagement in Rivers State, Nigeria, op. cit.*, p.16.

[1645] *BBC News*, Nigerian Leaders 'Stole' $380bn, *op. cit.*

[1646] Eric Guttschuss, 'Nigeria's Delta blues,' guardian.co.uk, 17 July 2008, at www.guardian.co.uk/commentisfree/2008/jul/17/nigeria.gordonbrown [accessed 8 July 2010].

[1647] *Ibid.*

[1648] Lanre Adewole, 'Alleged N5b Fraud: Orji Kalu Has Case To Answer – Appeal Court,' *Saturday Tribune*, 28 April 2012, at www.tribune.com.ng/sat/index.php/news/7234-alleged-n5b-fraud-orji-kalu-has-case-to-answer-appeal-court.html [accessed 30 April 2013].

[1649] U.S. State Department, *2008 Human Rights Report: Nigeria*, 25 February 2009, at www.state.gov/g/drl/rls/hrrpt/2008/af/119018.htm. [accessed 3 March 2010].

(approximately U.S.$20.4 million).[1650] He was, however, granted a State pardon along with eight others by President Goodluck Jonathan on 12 March 2013, the action which has been described as a setback in the fight against corruption.[1651]

The State and Local Governments in the Niger Delta have failed to utilize the oil wealth – 13 per cent derivation fund accruable to their States from the Federal allocation – to combat poverty or meet the human rights obligations in the form of access to good water, health, education, and infrastructural development for their people. Rather, this money is spent on opaque, phantom and questionable projects such as security votes (money set aside under the guise of enhancing State security), and miscellaneous expenses (entertainment and hospitality) which always total more than double that on health, education and other essential services. In 2007, the Delta State, one of the richest states in Nigeria, prepared a budget of U.S.$1.27bn. Out of this, it 'allocated only 5.1% to education (1.5 per cent to primary and secondary education), 3.8 per cent to health, and 2.6% to water and sanitation.[1652] Security issues are often manipulated by the executives for personal and economic gains. According to the Human Rights Watch Report on Rivers State, the amount allocated to security for both Khana (N60 million (U.S.$461,000)) and Tai (N40 million (U.S.$300,000)) Local Government chair persons in their 2006 budgets exceeded the total capital budgets for either health or education.[1653] Even the funds allocated often end up in private pockets, as the politicians see this as free money to be shared among members of their political parties and family members.

A recent report of the Center for Reproductive Rights (CRR) has shown a link between widespread corruption and the high Maternal Mortality Rate (MMR) in Nigeria.[1654] As shown in the 2010 Millennium Development Goals (MDG) Report, Nigeria's maternal mortality ratio (the number of women who die during pregnancy and childbirth, per 100,000 live births) declined from 800 per 100,000 live births in 2004 to 545 in 2008. Notwithstanding this decline, the MMR in Nigeria is still one of the highest in the world.[1655] Data obtained from

---

[1650]   *Ibid.*

[1651]   Vanguard, 'US Denounces Pardon for Alamieyeseigha, Others,' 16 March 2013, at www.van-guardngr.com/2013/03/us-denounces-pardon-for-alamieyeseigha-others/ [accessed 30 April 2013].

[1652]   State Government of Nigeria (2007) Ministry of Planning, Delta State, Nigeria, quoted in Oxfam International Briefing Paper, *Lifting the Resource Curse: How Poor People can and should benefit from the revenues of extractive industries*, December 2009, p.29, at www.oxfam. org/sites/www.oxfam.org/files/bp134-lifting-the-resource-curse-011209.pdf [accessed 18 August 2011].

[1653]   Human Rights Watch (2007), *Chop Fine: The Human Rights Impact of Local Government Corruption and Mismanagement in Rivers State, Nigeria, op. cit.*, pp.32–33.

[1654]   Center for Reproductive Rights (CRR) (2008), *Broken Promises: Human Rights, Accountability and Maternal Death in Nigeria*, CRR, New York; Ebenezer Durojaye, "Corruption as a Threat to Human Security in Africa", in Ademola Abass (ed) (2010), *Protecting Human Security in Africa*, Oxford University Press, New York, p.228.

[1655]   Nigeria Millennium Development Goals Report 2010, p.31 at www.mdgs.gov.ng [accessed 18 June 2012].

the 2008 Nigeria Demographic and Health Survey Reports (1990, 1999, 2003 and 2008) reveals that under-five mortality increased to 201 per 1000 live births in 2003 but decreased to 157 in 2008, suggesting that Nigeria is still not on track to achieve the MDG.[1656] This is because the Millennium Development Goal 5 on Maternal Health calls for countries to reduce their maternal mortality rate by three quarters (75% drop) by 2015. Many of these children die from diseases that are either preventable or treatable at low cost.[1657] The few available health centres, particularly in the Niger Delta region, are in a dilapidated state, lack trained medical personnel, and have a poor supply of drugs and other essential facilities. The only medicines some of the health centres have are those donated by foreign donors and UN agencies.[1658] According to the UN Committee on Economic, Social, and Cultural Rights, 'violation of the obligation to fulfil' regarding the right to health can occur through 'insufficient expenditure or misallocation of public resources which results in the non-enjoyment of the right to health by individuals or groups, particularly the vulnerable or marginalized.'[1659] Also, the Maastricht Guidelines on Violations of Economic, Social, and Cultural Rights, which interpret the ICESCR, provides that violations of economic, social and cultural rights can occur when the State or other entity engages directly in the 'reduction or diversion of specific public expenditure, when such reduction or diversion results in the non-enjoyment of such rights and is not accompanied by adequate measures to ensure minimum subsistence rights for everyone.'[1660] The pervasive corruption in Nigeria has continued to render the Government incapable of sufficiently protecting the rights of its citizens, particularly the Niger Delta people, to food, shelter, education and work. Unless there is a determined effort to address the high rate of corruption that exists within the oil sector, the violence and the widespread human rights abuse in the Niger Delta will continue unabated, with disastrous effects on the lives of ordinary Nigerians, particularly the local inhabitants of the Niger Delta, and it will inevitably endanger also the needs and well-being of future generations.

Recently, it was revealed that many of the witnesses that testified against Ken Saro-Wiwa and the eight Ogoni leaders before the Military tribunal had later admitted that they had been bribed by the Nigerian Government to support the

[1656] Ibid, pp.27–28.
[1657] Human Rights Watch (2007), Chop Fine: The Human Rights Impact of Local Government Corruption and Mismanagement in Rivers State, Nigeria, op. cit., p.40.
[1658] Ibid, p.69.
[1659] UN Committee on Economic, Social and Cultural Rights, 'Substantive Issues Arising in the Implementation of the International Covenant on Economic, Social and Cultural Rights,' General Comment No. 14, The Right to the Highest Attainable Standard of Health, General Comment No. 14, E/C.12/2000/4 (2000), para. 52(a).
[1660] The Maastricht Guidelines on Violations of Economic, Social, and Cultural Rights, January 1997, para. 14(g) at www1.umn.edu/humanrts/instree/Maastrichtguidelines_.html [accessed 10 June 2009].

criminal allegations.[1661] The threats to the rule of law and the massive incidents of violence as it's particularly present in the Niger Delta region today can be linked to the high rate of corruption in Nigeria.[1662] This is because nearly all the violence and inter-communal rivalry in the region has its roots in the struggle for access to the benefits from the natural resources located in the region. This fact was much attested to recently by the immediate past Economic and Financial Crimes Commission (EFCC) Chairman, Mrs. Farida Waziri, at the 8th Anniversary of the Anti-Corruption Agency and launch of the Economic and Financial Crimes Law Reports, in Abuja in June 2011. She said that: '[T]he various cases of militancy and terrorism that we currently experience across the country [Nigeria] are as a result of corruption. People who perpetrate these violent acts tend to draw their motivation from the unimaginable corruption they see going on around them.'[1663] The people, being dissatisfied with the level of environmental degradation, the culture of impunity and the inequitable distribution of oil wealth, felt they had to resort to violence against both the Government and oil MNCs.

Corruption is not limited to Nigeria. From 1997 to 2002, some US$4.22 billion in funds disappeared from Government accounts in Angola, nearly equal to all foreign and domestic social and humanitarian spending in that country over that same period.[1664] As noted by Human Rights Watch, the diversion and mismanagement of oil resources that should have been used to provide for essential social services seriously undermines the Angolans' ability to enjoy their economic, social, and cultural rights, and so involves a violation of the country's obligations under international human rights law.[1665] In 2009, Angola improved from 159th out of 179 countries in 2007 to 148th in 2011 out of 187 countries in the United Nations Development Programme's Human Development Index (HDI); but it still ranked 168 out of 183 countries in Transparency International's 2009 Corruption Perceptions Index.[1666] The situation is the same in Equatorial Guinea, where money generated from oil exploitation activities is concentrated in the hands of the few top Government officials. The diversion of the oil revenue

---

[1661] Jon Entine, *Seeds of NGO Activism: Shell Capitulates in Saro-Wiwa Case: Accountability & Transparency Trends*, NGO Watch, 18 June 2009, at www.globalgovernancewatch.org/ngo_watch/seeds-of-ngo-activism-shell-capitulates-in-sarowiwa-case [accessed 3 March 2010].

[1662] Kanokkan Anukansai, Corruption: The Catalyst for Violation of Human Rights, *National Anti-Corruption Commission (NACC) Journal*, Special Issue, Vol. 3 No. 2, July 2010, pp.6–15 at 11.

[1663] Quoted in Oscarline Onwuemenyi, EFCC boss blames crime, militancy on corruption, *Vanguard*, 14 June 2011.

[1664] Human Rights Watch, *Transparency and Accountability in Angola: An Update,* New York, April 2010, p.1.

[1665] Human Rights Watch, *Some Transparency, No Accountability: The Use of Oil Revenue in Angola and Its Impact on Human Rights,* January 2004, pp.5, 28, 31.

[1666] Human Rights Watch, *Transparency and Accountability in Angola: An Update, op. cit.,* p.2; Transparency International, 2011 Corruption Perceptions Index, *op. cit.*; UNDP, Human Development Index 2009, http://hdr.undp.org/en/media/HDR_2009_EN_Indicators.pdf [accessed 3 March 2010]; Human Development Report (2011), *Sustainability and Equity: A Better Future for All, op. cit.*

away from the local communities in these countries has resulted in the massive violence that is prevalent in these countries.

5.4 ROLE OF THE INTERNATIONAL COMMUNITY IN COMBATING CORRUPTION IN NIGERIA

The international community can contribute more than at present to the elimination of corruption in Nigeria. Prosecutions as presently witnessed under the US Foreign Corrupt Practices Act (FCPA) are a promising development, and could serve as a serious deterrent for companies listed on US exchanges.[1667] For example, in 2013, the U.S. Securities and Exchange Commission (SEC) announced a non-prosecution agreement (NPA) with Ralph Lauren Corporation in which the company is expected to disgorge more than U.S.$700,000 in illicit profits and interest obtained in connection with bribes paid by a subsidiary to Government officials in Argentina from 2005 to 2009.[1668] SEC charged the worldwide drilling services and project management firm, Parker Drilling Company, with violating the FCPA by authorizing improper payments to a third-party intermediary in order to entertain Nigerian officials involved in resolving the company's customs disputes. The company has agreed to pay U.S.$4 million to settle the SEC's charges.[1669] Also, as a way of improving accountability and transparency in the financial system, the US Government, in July 2010, enacted a law requiring oil, gas and mining companies which file Annual Reports with the US Securities and Exchange Commission to disclose tax and revenue payments made to host Governments for the extraction of oil, natural gas and minerals.[1670] It is important to note that 'twenty-nine of the world's 32 largest international oil companies and eight of the world's 10 largest mining companies are registered and file annual reports with the SEC.'[1671] This should help to improve transparency in Nigeria's oil industry and avoid the failures in governance that have worsened the human rights abuses in the country, particularly, in the oil-producing communities.

The UK Government has also shown great zeal in combating money-laundering by corrupt Nigerian officials. This was demonstrated, in May 2010, by the arrest in Dubai of the former Delta State Governor (1999–2007), James Ibori, on an Interpol warrant from the UK; and by the conviction and sentence of six of

---

[1667]   Alexandra Gillies, *Reforming Corruption out of Nigerian Oil? Part two: Progress and Prospects,* Chr. Michelsen Institute, Bergen (U4 Brief 2009:6) p.4.

[1668]   U.S. Securities and Exchange Commission Spotlight, SEC Enforcement Actions: FCPA Cases, at www.sec.gov/spotlight/fcpa/fcpa-cases.shtml [accessed 30 April 2013].

[1669]   *Ibid.*

[1670]   See Dodd-Frank Wall Street Reform and Consumer Protection Act, HR 4173, US Congress, section 1504.

[1671]   Veit, Peter *et al.* (2011). "Avoiding the Resource Curse: Spotlight on Oil in Uganda," WRI Working Paper. World Resources Institute, Washington DC, p.2, available at www.wri.org/project/equity-poverty-environment.

Ibori's associates in June 2010 to prison terms ranging from 30 months to 10 years
– his sister, Christine Ibori-Ibie, his wife, Theresa Ibori, his mistress, Udoamaka
Okoronkwo Onuigbo to five years imprisonment each, his London-based solicitor,
Bhadresh Gohil to ten years imprisonment, Daniel Benedict McCann, a fiduciary
agent to 30 months imprisonment, and Lambertus De Boer, a corporate financier
to 30 months imprisonment.[1672] James Ibori, who had on 27 February 2012
pleaded guilty to the charges of money laundering and fraud, was on 17 April
2012 sentenced to 13 years by the United Kingdom Court sitting in Southwark,
London for money laundering of over $79 million.[1673] As noted by Daniel
Bekele, the Africa Director, Human Rights Watch (HRW), Ibori's conviction is
a 'landmark in the global fight against corruption' and an acknowledgement of
'global responsibility for helping to stop the devastating human cost of corruption
in Nigeria.'[1674] These efforts are gradually yielding positive results as the corrupt
leaders are now finding certain countries difficult places in which to keep their
stolen and ill-gotten wealth.

The cooperation of developed countries in fighting corruption in Nigeria is
important because the 'resource curse' affects not only the producing countries
but also the developed nations. In the words of Senator Richard Lugar, '[I]t
exacerbates global poverty which can be a seedbed for terrorism, it empowers
autocrats and dictators, and it can crimp world petroleum supplies by breeding
instability'.[1675] The enforcement of anti-corruption laws and codes by OECD
countries in a determined manner, as it is being done by the U.S., could help to
stem the tide of corruption in Nigeria. The OECD Convention on Combating
Bribery of Foreign Public Officials in International Business Transactions[1676] was
adopted in 1997 and came into force on 15 February 1999. It has been ratified
by 34 OECD member countries and six non-member countries – Argentina,
Brazil, Bulgaria, Colombia, Russia, and South Africa. It obliges each State
Party to adopt national legislation making it a crime to bribe foreign public
officials in international business transactions. Transparency International's
(TI's) annual progress reports on the status of OECD enforcement show steady
progress in the enforcement of the Convention since it came into effect a decade

---

[1672] Human Rights Watch, *World Report 2011 – Nigeria*, 24 January 2011, at www.unhcr.org/ref-world/docid/4d3e80220.html [accessed 26 May 2011]; West London today, 'Nigerian politician who stole $250m was Ruislip cashier,' at www.westlondontoday.co.uk/content/nigerian-politi-cian-who-stole-250m-was-ruislip-cashier [accessed 18 April 2012].

[1673] Abiodun Oluwarotimi, 'Nigeria: UK Court Jails Ibori for 13 Years', *All Africa*, 17 April 2012, at http://allafrica.com/stories/201204180067.html [accessed 18 April 2012].

[1674] Daniel Bekele, 'Nigeria: UK Conviction a Blow Against Corruption', *Human Rights Watch News*, 17 April 2012, at www.hrw.org/news/2012/04/17/nigeria-uk-conviction-blow-against-corruption [accessed 18 June 2012].

[1675] Oxfam International, *US Congress Passes Law to End Secrecy in Oil, Gas, and Mining Industry*, 15 July, 2010 at www.oxfam.org/en/pressroom/pressrelease/2010-07-15/us-congress-passes-law-end-secrecy-oil-gas-mining-industry [accessed 18 August 2011].

[1676] OECD Convention on Combating Bribery of Foreign Public Officials in International Business Transactions (17 December 1997) 37 ILM 1.

ago. It reveals active enforcement in seven countries (representing 30% of world exports), moderate enforcement in nine countries (representing 20% of world exports) and little or no enforcement in 21 countries (representing 15% of world exports).[1677] Until recently, offering bribes to public officials in Africa as a way of getting contracts 'was a perfectly normal way of doing business in many OECD countries.'[1678] As at 1997 when the OECD Convention was signed, nearly half of the OECD countries allowed bribes aid to foreign officials to be deducted from taxes.[1679] With the emerging economies like China coming into play in the oil industry sector in countries like Nigeria, much needs to be done to ensure that they also adopt international anti-corruption standards. For instance, China has no law making foreign bribery a criminal offence.[1680] Efforts must therefore be made to encourage these emerging economies to commit themselves to signing and enforcing anti-corruption conventions.[1681]

Finally, active collaboration between the Nigerian law enforcement and anti-corruption agencies and their foreign counterparts is vital. This form of partnership will help in the capacity building of Nigerian officials as they identify and prosecute corrupt activities and follow up on money-tracing.

5.5 NIGERIA'S EFFORTS AT FIGHTING CORRUPTION

5.5.1 THE ECONOMIC AND FINANCIAL CRIMES COMMISSION (EFCC) AND THE INDEPENDENT CORRUPT PRACTICES AND OTHER RELATED OFFENCES COMMISSION (ICPC)

Former President Olusegun Obasanjo (1999–2007) created the Economic and Financial Crimes Commission (EFCC) in 2002 to complement the efforts of the Independent Corrupt Practices and Other Related Offences Commission

---

[1677] Transparency International, *Progress Report 2011: Enforcement of the OECD Anti-Bribery Convention*, at www.transparency.org [accessed 5 November 2011].

[1678] Martine Milliet-Einbinder, *Writing off Tax Deductibility*, 220 OECD Observer, April 2000, at www.oecdobserver.org/news/fullstory.php/aid/245/Writing_off_tax_deductibility_.html. [accessed 3 March 2010]. She notes that while Czech Republic classified all bribes as gifts, which were mostly not deductible; bribes were categorised as entertainment expenses in Japan, which by definition made them non-deductible anyway.

[1679] Reagan R. Demas, Moment of Truth: Development in Sub-Saharan Africa and Critical Alterations Needed in Application of the Foreign Corrupt Practices Act and Other Anti-Corruption Initiatives, 26 *Am. U. Int'l L. Rev.* 315–369 at 338 (2011).

[1680] Stefan Bringezu and Raimund Bleischwitz, 'Preventing a resource curse fuelled by the green economy,' in Transparency International, "Global Corruption Report: Climate Change," Earthscan Publishing, London, Washington, DC, 2011, p. 201.

[1681] *Ibid*, p. 203.

(ICPC) which had been in existence since September 2000.[1682] The EFCC is empowered under section 6 of the Economic and Financial Crimes Commission (Establishment, Etc) Act 2004 to investigate and prosecute all offences connected with or related to economic and financial crimes including those perpetrated either by individuals, corporate bodies or groups, be it in the private or public sector. The Act, in section 46, defines 'economic and financial crimes' to include any form of fraud, narcotic drug trafficking, money-laundering, embezzlement, bribery, looting, and any form of corrupt malpractices, illegal arms dealing, smuggling, human trafficking and child labour, illegal oil bunkering, and illegal mining, tax evasion, and foreign exchange malpractices.

These two bodies (ICPC and EFCC) have different mandates but have overlapping functions in the investigation and prosecution of corruption. This has led to the recent calls, from several quarters, that the two bodies be merged together as one. Both institutions, but particularly the EFCC, have been able to prosecute successfully a few high profile corruption and other fraud-related cases against public officials, and recovered billions of dollars. However, in spite of these developments, not much significant success had been achieved by the Nigerian Government in reducing the high levels of corruption in the country. Several factors account for the failure, which include the dysfunctional judicial system, the weak Government institutions, and most importantly, the insincerity among the Nigerian leaders in truly addressing corruption. The insincerity among Nigerian leaders partly accounted for why no Chief Executive of the Nigeria's EFCC has been allowed to complete his or her term of office. Benjamin Chuka Osisioma notes that, 'the anti-corruption agencies are allowed to operate, to the extent that they do not cross invisible boundaries imposed by the Government of the day… They have all been applauded when they hound the real or perceived enemies of the Government of the day, and removed from office when they step on sacred toes.'[1683]

[1682] Economic and Financial Crimes Commission (Establishment, Etc) Act, 2004 (which repealed the Economic and Financial Crimes Commission (Establishment) Act No. 5 2002, Cap E1 Laws of the Federation 2004) and the Independent Corrupt Practices and (Other Related Offences) Commission Act (ICPC Act) 2000. Prior to these two enactments, there were already in existence the Nigerian Criminal Code Act, Cap. 77 LFN 1990 (as applicable to the Southern part of Nigeria), the Penal Code, Cap. 89 Laws of Northern Nigeria 1963 (as applicable to the Northern part of Nigeria), and the Public Conduct Code as contained in the fifth Schedule to the Constitution of the FRN 1999, all aimed at curbing corruption, particularly in the public sector. There is also in place the Money Laundering (Prohibition) Act, 2011 signed into law on 3 June, 2011 which seeks to prohibit the laundering of the proceeds of a crime or an illegal act. It repealed the Money Laundering (Prohibition) Act, 2004 by expanding the scope of the supervisory and regulatory authorities in order to be able to address the challenges faced in the implementation of the anti-money laundering regime in the country. See Daniel Idonoh, Jonathan signs terrorism, money laundering bills into law, *Vanguard*, 6 June 2011.

[1683] Benjamin Chuka Osisioma, *Combating Fraud and White Collar Crimes: Lessons from Nigeria*, being a Paper Presented at the 2nd Annual Fraud & Corruption Africa Summit, held at Zanzibar Beach Resort, Zanzibar Republic of Tanzania, at www.managementnigeria.org/index.php/81-

5.5.2 EXTRACTIVE INDUSTRIES TRANSPARENCY INITIATIVE (EITI)

On 2 September 2002, the EITI was launched by British Prime Minister, Tony Blair, at the World Summit on Sustainable Development in Johannesburg, South Africa. EITI was a coalition of Governments, companies, civil society groups, investors and international organisations and presently has about thirty-five implementing countries (compliant and candidate countries).[1684] EITI was a voluntary initiative meant for Governments of countries like Nigeria and Angola that are resource-rich and aims to strengthen governance by ensuring that these countries get the benefits due to them from the extractive industries, in accordance with the principles of transparency, accountability, sustainable development and poverty reduction.[1685] As part of its criteria, EITI participating countries are required to ensure the regular publication, to a wide audience in a publicly accessible, comprehensive and comprehensible manner, of all material oil, gas and mining payments by companies to Governments ("payments") and all material revenues received by Governments from oil, gas and mining companies ("revenues").[1686]

In fulfillment of his commitment to EITI, former President Olusegun Obasanjo launched the Nigeria Extractive Industries Transparency Initiative (NEITI) in February 2004, and a Bill was introduced to the National Assembly in December 2004 to give legal backing to the work of NEITI. The NEITI Act[1687] was passed into law on 28 May 2007, thus making the country the first EITI-implementing country.[1688] Nigeria was accepted as an EITI candidate country on 27 September 2007 and was designated as EITI Compliant on 1 March 2011.[1689] The primary objectives of NEITI include: ensuring due process and transparency in the payments made by all extractive industry companies to the Federal Government and statutory recipients; monitoring and ensuring accountability

---

highlights/59-combatting-fraud-and-white-collar-crimes-lessons-from-nigeria [accessed 30 April 2013].

[1684] EITI, *History of EITI*, at http://eiti.org/eiti/history [accessed 13 March 2011]. A country is deemed 'compliant' once it has been assessed through the validation process; and a Candidate country is one that has fully and to the satisfaction of the EITI Board met the requirements of membership. A country that has obtained the Candidate status, has two and a half years to be validated as a Compliant country. See EITI, *Candidate Country*, at http://eiti.org/candidate-countries [accessed 30 April 2013].

[1685] EITI, *Nigeria, Compliant Country*, at http://eiti.org/Nigeria [accessed 13 March 2011].

[1686] EITI, *The EITI Principles and Criteria*, at http://eiti.org/eiti/principles [accessed 13 March 2011].

[1687] Nigeria Extractive Industries Transparency Initiative, (NEITI) Act, 2007. For the purpose of realizing its objectives under this Act, the NEITI shall, *inter alia*, 'develop a framework for transparency and accountability in the reporting and disclosure by all extractive industry companies of revenue due to or paid to the Federal Government.' See generally section 3 of NEITI Act.

[1688] EITI, *Nigeria, Compliant Country, op. cit.*

[1689] *Ibid.*

in the revenue receipts of the Federal Government from extractive industry
companies; eliminating all forms of corrupt practices in the determination,
payment, receipt and posting of revenue accruing to the Federal Government
from extractive industry companies; ensuring transparency and accountability
of government in the use of resources from payment received from extractive
industry companies, and ensuring conformity with the principles of EITI.[1690]

NEITI has no doubt brought about positive developments in revenue
transparency in the oil industry. The first set of financial, physical and process
audits[1691] for the period 1999–2004 undertaken by a consortium led by the
London-based Hart Group, was published in 2006; and a second Report covering
2005 was released on 11 August 2009, which identified unprecedented financial
discrepancies, under-payments, errors of computation, mispaid taxes, and system
inefficiencies. The Report revealed that Nigeria does not actually know how
much oil it is producing. It was found out that: 'Over US$800m of unresolved
differences between what companies said that they paid in taxes, royalties and
signature bonuses, and what the Government said it received was identified. Of
this amount, US$560m was identified as shortfalls in taxes and royalties owed
to the Government, and around US$300m [was] payment discrepancies relating
to signature bonuses, payments of dividends, interest and loan repayments.'[1692]
On 1 February 2011, NEITI published the 2006–2008 EITI Reconciliation Report
showing that total revenues for 2006, 2007 and 2008 were U.S.$45bn, U.S.$43bn
and U.S.$59bn respectively.[1693] As noted by a NEITI spokesperson: 'We know how
much the industry sells, but we don't know how much they produce [...] [T]here
is a dark hole between the oil field and the terminal.'[1694] Lack of transparency is
the order of the day in the oil industry, as the Nigerian Government is kept in
the dark by the oil MNCs regarding how much oil they are daily extracting from
the country. The Report includes useful observations and recommendations for
improving the management of revenues from the extractive sector. The positive
impacts of NEITI have led to the inclusion of a fundamental clause in the proposed
Petroleum Industry Bill (PIB) on compliance of all industry operations with the

---

[1690]   NEITI Act 2007, section 2.
[1691]   Physical Audit report delineate the physical flows of oil, gas and refined products to ensure
that the volumes extracted are accurately reported and that each company's reported production tallies with the numbers the Government uses for the calculation of tax and royalty.
The Process Audit reports, on the other hand, outline how key agencies in the oil and gas
manage the sector, including how the Government's interest in joint ventures is managed and
how refineries are run and oil is imported. See Zainab Ahmed, NEITI: The Prospects, Issues
and Challenges, being a paper presentation to the IMF Mission, at www.imf.org/external/np/
seminars/eng/2012/kinshasa/pdf/za.pdf [accessed 5 May 2013].
[1692]   EITI, *Nigeria, Compliant Country, op. cit.*
[1693]   NEITI 2006–2008 EITI Reconciliation Final Report, Issued 3 February, 2011, p.6, at www.
neiti.org.ng/files-pdf/NEITI2006-2008Reconciliation-FinalReport-010211.pdf [accessed 13
March 2011].
[1694]   Wasiri Adio, Reuters/International Herald Tribune, 25 February 2008, quoted in Oxfam
International Briefing Paper, *Lifting the Resource Curse: How Poor People can and should benefit from the revenues of extractive industries, op. cit.,* p.18.

NEITI 2007 principles.[1695] In an interview with an academic, former Special Assistant to the Hon. Attorney-General of Federation and Minister of Justice of Nigeria and human rights expert, Prof. 'Yemi Akinseye-George, the researcher asked for the interviewee's view on why the Nigerian State has failed to stand by its people in spite of the wanton destruction of the environment and the abuse of the human rights of the Niger Delta people by the multinational oil companies. In his response, he contended that there is a lack of transparency in the extractive industry and an over-dependence on oil. He added that, 'nobody knows how much oil is being taken and how much is being paid. Most of the figures are cooked up. The oil companies are not subject to Nigeria's anti-corruption laws. They are treated like sacred cows. They often get away with serious crimes to individuals, communities and the environment. Corruption plays an important role in all these. The people are poor and lack proper legal representation. Civil society is weak.'[1696] As a way forward, he suggested the need for greater transparency and accountability. According to him, 'there is need for a Marshall Plan that would prioritise human security and development. The plan should be funded by the Government and the MNCs. It should restore the environment and empower the people and set up accountable mechanisms. The passage of the Petroleum Industry Bill is partly aimed at overhauling the oil and gas industry and ensuring a better regulatory regime. It should be passed into law speedily.'[1697] All this confirms the place of corruption in human rights violations of the people in the oil-producing communities of Nigeria and the need for accountability and transparency for human rights protection.

5.5.3 THE UNITED NATIONS CONVENTION AGAINST CORRUPTION (UNCAC)

As part of the effort aimed at combating corruption, the Nigerian Government ratified the United Nations Convention Against Corruption (UNCAC)[1698] in December 2004. The UNCAC, which was adopted by the UN General Assembly on 31st October 2003, came into force on 14 December 2005, signed by 140 countries. It is the only legally binding universal anti-corruption instrument.[1699] It requires countries to criminalize a wide range of acts, including bribery, embezzlement,

---

[1695] Section 5 of PIB Bill. See Uche Igwe, Africa: In Search of Good Governance: Essays and Analysis, at www.wilsoncenter.org/sites/default/files/UcheCompilation.pdf.

[1696] Interview with Prof. 'Yemi Akinseye-George in Abuja, Nigeria in January 2011.

[1697] Ibid.

[1698] United Nations Convention Against Corruption (CAC), adopted October 31, 2003, G.A. Res 58/34, entered into force December 14, 2005, at www.unodc.org/pdf/crime/convention_corruption/signing/Convention-e.pdf [accessed 13 March 2011].

[1699] United Nations Office on Drugs and Crime (UNODC), UNODC's Action against Corruption and Economic Crime, at www.unodc.org/unodc/en/corruption/index.html?ref=menuside [accessed 5 March 2010].

misappropriation or other diversion of public funds, abuse of functions, trading
in influence, illicit enrichment, money laundering, concealment of illegal
proceeds and obstruction of justice and various acts of corruption in the private
sector.[1700] Appreciating the importance of the independence of the judiciary in
combating corruption, Article 11(1) of the Convention requires each State Party
to take measures to strengthen the integrity of, and to prevent opportunities for
corruption among members of the judiciary. Such measures may include rules
with respect to the conduct of members of the judiciary. Even though Nigeria has
ratified the UN Convention, it is yet to implement it domestically as required by
section 12 of the Nigerian Constitution. For the Convention to become enforceable
in Nigeria, it needs to be domesticated as part of Nigerian law and such a step
would show the genuineness of Nigeria's commitment to combating corruption.

5.5.4 THE AFRICAN UNION (AU) ANTI-CORRUPTION CONVENTION

Nigeria is also a party to the African Union Convention on Preventing and
Combating Corruption and Related Offences.[1701] The AU Anti-Corruption
Convention was adopted on 11 July 2003 by the AU Assembly of Heads of State
and Government. It criminalizes corruption both in the public and *private
sector*, by enjoining State Parties to adopt legislative, administrative and other
measures to address corruption. Article 1 defines 'Private Sector' as 'the sector
of a national economy under private ownership in which the allocation of
productive resources is controlled by market forces, rather than public authorities
and other sectors of the economy not under the public sector or Government.'
This definition covers all kinds of private entities, including partnerships, small/
medium enterprises and MNCs.[1702] For instance, Article 11 enjoins State Parties
to undertake to adopt legislative and other measures to prevent and combat
acts of corruption committed in, and by agents, of the *private sector*; establish
mechanisms to encourage participation by the *private sector* in the fight against
unfair competition, in respect of the tender procedures and property rights; and
to adopt such other measures as may be necessary to prevent *companies* from
paying bribes to win tenders.[1703]

[1700] United Nations Convention Against Corruption (CAC), Arts 15–25.
[1701] African Union Convention on Preventing and Combating Corruption, adopted July 11, 2003,
entered into force August 4, 2006, at www.africa-union.org/root/au/Documents/Treaties/
Text/Convention%20on%20Combating%20Corruption.pdf [accessed 5 March 2010]. This was
signed by Nigeria on 16 December, 2003 and ratified on 26 September 2006.
[1702] Olufemi O. Amao, The African Regional Human Rights System and Multinational
Corporations: Strengthening Host State Responsibility for the Control of Multinational
Corporations, 12(5) *The International Journal of Human Rights*, 761–788 at 779 (2008).
[1703] Italics mine.

The Convention has the following objectives: to promote and strengthen the development in Africa of anti-corruption mechanisms; to promote, facilitate and regulate cooperation among the State Parties to ensure the effectiveness of measures and actions to address corruption; to coordinate and harmonize the policies and legislation between State Parties for the purposes of eradicating corruption; to remove obstacles to the enjoyment of economic, social and cultural rights as well as civil and political rights; and establish the necessary conditions to foster transparency and accountability in the management of public affairs.[1704]

Article 9 of the AU Anti-Corruption Convention requires each State Party to adopt legislative and other measures to give effect to the right of access to any information that is required to assist in the fight against corruption and related offences. The recent passage of the Freedom of Information Act into law is in compliance with this provision. The Convention also recognises the role of civil society groups and the media in monitoring and implementing the principles of the Convention at the domestic level, and the need to create an enabling environment that will enable them to hold Governments to the highest levels of transparency and accountability in the management of public affairs.[1705]

The AU Convention has been criticized for its excessive use of claw-back clauses as contained in several of its provisions, granting supremacy to domestic laws of state parties. For example, Article 7(5) provides that any immunity granted to public officials shall not be an obstacle to the investigation of allegations against, or the prosecution of, such officials, *subject to the provisions of domestic legislation*. Also, Article 8(1) requires that State Parties undertake to adopt necessary measures to establish under their laws an offence of illicit enrichment, *subject to the provisions of their domestic law*. As stated by Olaniyan, all these claw-back clauses, like those contained in the African Charter, undermine or defeat the objectives of the Convention – the eradication of corruption and the promotion of internationally recognised human rights, including economic, social and cultural rights – and emasculate its uniform application within member states.[1706] The AU Convention on Corruption has also been criticised for lack of provisions on the liability of corporations. While it recognises the need to control MNCs, it focuses on State responsibility without making provision for the direct liability of MNCs.[1707] Addressing these challenges will no doubt help to strengthen the Convention's capacity to tackle corruption in Africa and complement the efforts taken at the domestic levels.

[1704] African Union Anti-Corruption Convention, Art. 2.
[1705] African Union Anti-Corruption Convention, Art. 12.
[1706] Kolawole Olaniyan, The African Union Convention on Preventing and Combating Corruption: A Critical Appraisal, 4 *Afr. Hum. Rts. L. J.* 74–92 at 86 (2004).
[1707] Olufemi O. Amao, The African Regional Human Rights System and Multinational Corporations: Strengthening Host State Responsibility for the Control of Multinational Corporations, *op. cit.*, p.781.

5.6   CRITICISMS OF EITI AND THE PROSPECTS OF COMBATING CORRUPTION IN NIGERIA

Some of the major criticisms of EITI are that it only enhances the transparency of Government income, and does little to enhance the transparency of Government expenditure in Nigeria, and the fact that the initiative was not extended to State and Local levels.[1708] This is against the background of the 'looting' of treasuries, and the money-laundering activities, of State Governors and Local Government Chairmen. Information regarding how the nation allocates and spends the oil wealth is important for accountability purposes as it will enable citizens to hold their Government accountable for using revenue from the oil, gas and minerals to address essential services like health, education, and job creation.

There is also a need for public disclosure of extraction agreements so as to ensure a sound and proper legal framework for the extractive sector. Unfortunately, Governments, and most of the extractive industries, are still very reluctant to disclose the nature of payments and the details of their Memorandum of Understanding (MoU), citing agreed confidentiality clauses or possible damage to the sector due to loss of comparative advantage.[1709] 'Opacity is the glue holding together the patterns of revenue extraction and distribution that characterize petro-states as well as the entire international petroleum sector. Companies do not publish what they pay to States, and States do not disclose what they earn and spend.'[1710] As a result, 'huge amounts of money are virtually untraceable and not subject to any oversight.'[1711] All this goes to promote corruption in resource rich countries, like Nigeria.

Also, the dependence of NEITI on the public administration hinders it from performing its monitoring and sanctioning role. The close Government oversight of NEITI seriously damages its image as a public sector 'watchdog' agency as it cannot effectively sanction illicit behaviour by public officials.[1712] For effective

---

[1708] Human Rights Watch (2007), *Chop Fine: The Human Rights Impact of Local Government Corruption and Mismanagement in Rivers State, Nigeria, op. cit.*, p.103; See also Uwafiokun Idemudia, 'Corporate Social Responsibility and the Niger Delta Conflict: Issues and Prospects,' in Cyril Obi and Siri Aas Rustad (eds.), *Oil and Insurgency in the Niger Delta: Managing the complex politics of petro-violence*, Zed Books, London/New York, 2011, p.180.

[1709] Oxfam International Briefing Paper, *Lifting the Resource Curse: How Poor People can and should benefit from the revenues of extractive industries, op. cit.*, p.18; Michael J. Watts, Righteous Oil? Human Rights, the Oil Complex, and Corporate Social Responsibility, 30 *Annu. Rev. Environ. Resour.* 373–407 at 389 (2005).

[1710] Karl Terry Lynn, "Ensuring Fairness: The Case for a Transparent Fiscal Social Contract", in M. Humphreys *et al.* (eds) (2007), *Escaping the Resource Curse*, University Press, Columbia, quoted in Thorsten Benner and Ricardo Soares de Oliveira, "The Good/Bad Nexus in Global Energy Governance", in Andreas Goldthau and Jan Martin Witte (eds) (2010), *Global Energy Governance: The New Rules of the Game*, Global Public Policy Institute, Berlin, p.292.

[1711] Thorsten Benner and Ricardo Soares de Oliveira, *Ibid.*

[1712] Madeline R. Young, *Energy, Development and EITI: Improving coherence of EU policies towards Nigeria*, European Development Co-operation (EDC) 2020 Policy Brief, No. 4, November 2009.

performance, efforts should be made to ensure the independence of NEITI so as to promote its objectivity and increase its accountability. Increase in international funding to promote greater civil society oversight of NEITI may help to improve its objectivity and enhance its independence from the Government.[1713] Civil society groups must continue to demand greater transparency and accountability from the Government and MNCs as '[g]reater transparency in all areas of Government practice is probably the most effective single instrument against corruption.'[1714]

The Nigeria Freedom of Information Act 2011[1715] will help to ensure transparency and accountability in Government spending, and gives every Nigerian the right to demand from the Government information on, *inter alia*, the amount of revenue generated from the oil exploration and how this has been spent. The U.S. Freedom of Information Act ("FOIA") provides a cause of action for non-state actors against any Government agency which fails to respond to information requested for within the time provided by the law, or which improperly withholds information.[1716] The agency has the responsibility to show that it has produced the document as requested, or it is unidentifiable or is one exempted by the Act.[1717] The Nigeria FOI Act will provide access to information on various activities of Government and the oil MNCs which in the past have been shrouded in secrecy, breeding corruption. It will help to remove the veil of secrecy that engulfs corrupt activities in the Nigerian oil industry and improve efforts aimed at disclosing corruption in both the public and private sectors. In South Africa, an Expert Panel survey was constituted to evaluate the various measures needed to fight corruption. The anti-corruption experts and practitioners when asked to rate on a scale of one to four, promoting access to information and transparency and measures promoting transparency in government tender procedures, were viewed as the most effective in this category, as the majority (93%) of the experts felt that such a measure would be either effective or very effective in combating

---

[1713] *Ibid.*

[1714] Peter Eigen, *Introducing the Global Corruption Report 2001*, p.4 at www.mekonginfo.org/ HDP/Lib.nsf/0/3F1E4D5F8F211ABB47256DC0002850A9/$FILE/Q%203.5%20-%20T.I.%20 -%20Global%20Corruption%20Report%202001.pdf [accessed 9 June 2009].

[1715] The Swedish Parliament was the first to legislate on freedom of information in 1776, followed by Colombia which enacted the law in 1888, with Finland being the third country. Sweden and Finland are considered today as the least-corrupt countries in the world. See Anders Chydenius, His Majesty's Gracious Ordinance Relating to Freedom of Writing and of the Press (Peter Hogg, trans.) (1766), in Juha Mustonen (ed) (2006), *The World's First Freedom of Information Act: Anders Chydenius' Legacy Today*, Art-Print Ltd., Kokkola, pp.8–9; Dave Banisar (2002), *Freedom of Information and Access to Government* 11, at www.article19.org/ work/regions/latin-america/FOI/pdf/DbanisarFOI2002.pdf. [accessed 23 November 2009]; Roy Peled and Yoram Rabin, The Constitutional Right to Information, 42 *Columbia Human Rights Law Review*, 357–401 at 368–369 (2011).

[1716] Linda A. Malone, "Enforcing International Environmental Law through Domestic Law Mechanisms in the United States: Civil Society Initiatives Against Global Warming," in LeRoy Paddock *et al.* (2011), *Compliance and Enforcement in Environmental Law: Towards More Effective Implementation*, The IUCN Academy of Environmental Series, Edward Elgar Publishing, Cheltenham, UK & Northampton, USA, p.116.

[1717] *Ibid.*

corruption.[1718] With this law, Nigeria has joined the rest of the world in complying with international obligations to promote and respect the right to freedom of expression.[1719] This greater access will make the Government and the oil MNCs more responsive to the interests of the local inhabitants of Niger Delta in making decisions concerning oil exploitation.

However, following the signing into law of the Freedom of Information Bill, there has been argument that the law only applies to the Federal Government. Suffice it to say that Nigeria operates a Federal system of Government and information is listed under the concurrent legislative list.[1720] The Freedom of Information Act only applies to the Federal Government and its institutions and so cannot apply to the States unless and until the Act is replicated in the States of the Federation by the State Houses of Assembly as State law.[1721] It is hoped that the States in Nigeria, particularly the Niger Delta States, will in the interest of transparency and accountability in governance ensure the quick replication of this Act in their States.

Civil society has a role to play in the education of people, particularly the Niger Delta people, about the existence of the Act, its provisions, its application and their rights under the Act in order for them to be able to use it to stem the tide of corruption and its negative consequences on their human rights. They must continue to mobilize the people to demand greater transparency from the Government and MNCs by using the Act, and hold them accountable for their actions, and where possible, subject government actions to judicial review. At the Government level, Government must enlighten its officials through lectures, seminars, and workshops about the provisions of the law and the duties imposed on them.

[1718] Lala Camerer (2001), *Corruption in South Africa: Results of an Expert Panel Survey*, Monograph 65, at www.iss.co.za/Pubs/Monographs/No65/Chap7.html [accessed 7 March 2010].

[1719] See Article 19(2) of the International Covenant on Civil and Political Rights which provides that '[e]veryone shall have the right to freedom of expression; this right shall include freedom to seek, receive and impart information and ideas of all kinds.' Similarly, the African Charter on Human and People's Rights provides under Article 9, that '[e]very individual shall have the right to receive information.' Also, the African Union's African Commission on Human and Peoples' Rights adopted at the 32nd Ordinary Session, held from 17–23 October 2002, in Banjul, a Declaration of Principles on Freedom of Expression in Africa, which provides in Part IV on 'Freedom of Information' that '[p]ublic bodies hold information not for themselves but as custodians of the public good …' Part I(1) of the Declaration provides that 'Freedom of expression and information, including the right to seek, receive and impart information and ideas, either orally, in writing or in print, in the form of art, or through any other form of communication, including across frontiers, is a fundamental and inalienable human right and an indispensable component of democracy.'

[1720] Section 318 of the Constitution of the Federal Republic of Nigeria 1999 (as amended) defines "Concurrent Legislative List" to mean the list of matters set out in the first column in Part II of the second schedule to the Constitution with respect to which the National Assembly and a House of Assembly may make laws to the extent prescribed, respectively, opposite thereto in the second column thereof.

[1721] Itse Sagay (SAN), quoted in Davidson Iriekpen, FoI Act: One More Hurdle to Cross, Say Top Lawyers, *This Day*, 2 June 2011.

Another major challenge in eradicating corruption in Nigeria is the lack of political will. Political will in this regard have been referred to as 'the demonstrated credible intent of political actors (elected or appointed leaders), civil society watchdogs, and stakeholder groups, to attack perceived causes of corruption at a systemic level.'[1722] It refers to the sincerity, or the level of commitment, of these leaders towards enacting and implementing the various measures and initiatives necessary for fighting corruption. Lack of political will, not only robs citizens of their basic needs, but threatens the rule of law and human rights, which are pillars of democracy. As discussed earlier, Nigeria has done a lot in prosecuting high-profile corruption cases, but there are still many of the leaders who have been indicted on offences of money-laundering and the looting of State treasuries, particularly State Governors of the oil rich regions, who are not only moving about freely, but still "calling the shots" in Government. Many of them today are members of the National Assembly, ministers, special advisers, board/commission members, with their relatives also appointed to revered offices. In 1994, the Federal Government under the administration of late General Sani Abacha set up the Pius Okigbo Panel to investigate the activities of the Central Bank of Nigeria (CBN), and recommend measures for the re-organization of the apex bank. The Panel reportedly discovered that about U.S.$12.4 billion which accrued to the country during the Gulf War and was reserved in the 'Dedicated and Special Accounts,' of the CBN had been depleted to U.S.$200 million by June 1994.[1723] Notwithstanding the revelation that the alleged mismanagement of the money occurred during the administration of the then Military President, General Ibrahim Babangida, Government is yet to prefer any charges against him. However, six civil society groups, led by the Socio-Economic Rights and Accountability Project (SERAP), brought an action[1724] before an Abuja High Court against the Attorney-General of the Federation (AGF) and the Central Bank of Nigeria (CBN) over the much publicised $12.4 billion oil windfall. The applicants sought for orders to compel the Federal Government to release a Report of a Probe Panel headed by Pius Okigbo which probed the spending of the money by the Government. They also sought for orders directing the respondents to diligently bring to justice anyone suspected of corruption and mismanagement of the money and to return to the Federation account any money which was the subject matter of corruption. The court, on 29 November 2012, dismissed the suit on the ground that the applicants

[1722] Sahr J. Kpundeh, *Political Will in Fighting Corruption,* in Corruption and Integrity Improvement Initiatives in Developing Countries, p.92 at http://mirror.undp.org/magnet/Docs/efa/corruption/Chapter06.pdf [accessed 3 March 2010].
[1723] *Ikechukwu Nnochiri,* Nigeria: U.S$12.4 Billion Oil Windfall – AGF Asks Court to Hands Off Suit, *Vanguard,* 24 November 2012, at http://allafrica.com/stories/201211240152.html?viewall=1.
[1724] Suit No FHC/ABJ/CS/640/10.

lack the *locus standi* to institute the case.[1725] All this give the impression that the
Government is not sincere in its avowed commitment to fight corruption.

In some cases, while the Government of the home countries of corporations
(U.S. and European countries) have convicted some of the corporations and their
top managers, it is surprising that the situation has not, until recently, raised any
serious reactions from the appropriate Nigerian authorities, which have often
claimed 'zero-tolerance' for corruption.[1726] For instance, it was not until December
2010 that Nigeria's EFCC filed an indictment against nine people and entities,
including the former US Vice-President Dick Cheney, involved in the Halliburton
bribe-for-contract scandals. Halliburton has however agreed to pay U.S.32.5
million dollars to the Nigerian government, plus U.S.2.5 million dollars in costs,
so as to have the lawsuits and charges withdrawn.[1727] The Nigerian Government
is yet to take any serious action against some of the Government officials or the
MNCs involved or linked to these high profile corruption cases.

Another example involved the former Vice-President Atiku Abubakar (1999–
2007), who was alleged to be involved in financial scams in several countries,
including the US; but no steps have been taken to investigate him. Not even the
trial and conviction of Jefferson, Atiku's business crony, could spur the Nigerian
Government into action.[1728] One begins to wonder how if Jefferson could be tried
in his country, the U.S., and jailed for scams involving Nigerian public officials,
the Nigerian Government could not take any action in bringing its own officials
to justice.[1729] This gives the impression that some are "sacred cows" when it comes
to prosecution and this has continued to frustrate efforts to rid the country of
corruption. A nation that engages in discrimination and selective prosecution
cannot succeed in the fight against corruption.

The anti-corruption agencies are frequently hindered from performing
their statutory duties, independently and effectively, by the executive arm of
Government. There have been situations when the Attorney-General of the
Federation and Minister of Justice has stepped in to stop the prosecution of
corruption cases. Some have portrayed the former Attorney-General of the
Federation of Nigeria, Aondoakaa (2007–2010), as one who seriously relegated
the anti-corruption efforts within and outside the country, and defended 'those
charged with corrupt practices by refusing to provide countries like France,

---

[1725]   Socio-Economic Rights and Accountability Project (SERAP), *Missing $12.4bn oil wind-
fall ruling a setback in the fight against corruption, says SERAP*, at http://serap-nigeria.org/
missing-12-4bn-oil-windfall-ruling-a-setback-in-the-fight-against-corruption-says-serap/.

[1726]   Dauda Garuba, *Halliburton, Bribes and the Deceit of 'Zero-Tolerance' for Corruption in Nigeria*,
CoP-MfDR-Africa, at www.cop-mfdr-africa.org/profiles/blogs/halliburton-bribes-and-the
[accessed 3 June 2011].

[1727]   Public Intelligence, *Halliburton to Pay $35 Million to Settle Nigeria Bribery Charges*, 22
December, 2010, at http://publicintelligence.net/halliburton-to-pay-35-million-to-settle-
nigeria-bribery-charges/ [accessed 3 March 2010].

[1728]   Adeniran, Plea Bargain will make Corruption Pervasive in Nigeria, *The Economy*, available at
www.theeconomyng.com/interview30.html [accessed 6 May 2010].

[1729]   *Ibid.*

Britain and the United States of America with the necessary information to nail the criminals and institutions under the Mutual Legal Assistance Treaty (MLAT).'[1730] All this reveals that there has not been a strong political will by the Government to fight corruption, resulting in impediment to the full enjoyment of economic, social and cultural rights. Government must be prepared to support the anti-graft agencies and the courts by ensuring that they enjoy adequate physical, human and financial resources to be able to discharge their responsibilities effectively. It must ensure that appropriate laws are enacted and adequately implemented by the authorities concerned no matter who the defendants may be found to be.

Independence of Judiciary: As a result of corruption in the Nigerian judiciary, courts have not been effective in punishing corrupt officials. Corruption destroys the independence and impartiality of the judiciary which are requirements needed to provide remedies for violations of human rights. While the Nigerian judiciary have been able to secure convictions in some few corruption cases,[1731] they have however not lived up to expectations in many of the cases. Long adjournments are given in cases involving high profile corrupt individuals, who are often given liberal bail conditions, thus letting them take their trial lightly. Trials thus turn into charades where powerful litigants, assisted by unscrupulous lawyers and faithless judges, manipulate the judicial process to achieve preordained outcomes.[1732] Some judges give unnecessary injunctions, including *ex-parte* and perpetual injunctions, to shield indicted political leaders, senior public officials and corporate bodies from investigation or prosecution.[1733] For example, the

---

[1730] *Ibid.*

[1731] The Nigerian courts have been able to secure convictions in some few high profile corruption cases. For example, the former Nigerian Inspector-General of Police, Chief Tafa Balogun, was convicted of corruption in 2005 and sentenced to six months in prison. The court also ordered him to pay a fine of 4m naira ($30,000), while some U.S.$150m worth of cash and property was confiscated. BBC News, *Nigerian ex-police chief jailed*, 22 November 2005, at www. nigeriavillagesquare.com/articles/nvs/tafa-jailed-for-6-months-13.html. [accessed 6 May 2010]. Also noteworthy is the conviction of the former Vice-Chairman of the ruling political party (Peoples' Democratic Party (PDP)), Chief Bode George, with five others on 26 October 2009 by Hon. Justice Joseph Oyewole of the Lagos High Court in *Federal Republic of Nigeria v. Olabode George & Ors*, Unreported Suit No. ID/71/2008. They were sentenced to two years each on corruption related matters (contract inflation to the tune of N84 billion naira between 2000–2003) during his tenure as the board Chairman of the Nigerian Ports Authority. The Court of Appeal dismissed the appeal filed by Olabode George against the High Court judgment.

[1732] Okechukwu Oko, Seeking Justice in Transitional Societies: An Analysis of the Problems and Failures of the Judiciary in Nigeria, 31(1) *Brook. J. Int'l L.* 9–82 at 16 (2005).

[1733] In *Attorney-General for Rivers State v. The Economic and Financial Crimes Commission & 3 Ors*, Unreported Suit No. FHC/PHC/CSI78/2007, a Federal High Court Judge sitting in Port-Harcourt, Hon. Justice Ibrahim Buba granted an injunction, in a manner rather suspicious, forbidding the EFCC from investigating, arresting, or prosecuting the former Governor of Rivers State (Niger Delta), Dr. Odili, for any acts of corruption. In essence, the judge granted a perpetual injunction against the investigation and prosecution of the said governor concerning the corrupt allegations. Also, a judge in the Abia State (Niger Delta) High Court curiously granted a similar injunction to the former Governor of the State, Dr. Orji Kalu. See Ebenezer Durojaye, *op. cit.*, p.239. This unwholesome development has led the National Judicial

former governor of Edo State, Lucky Igbinedion, who stole many billions of naira
was only fined U.S.$25,000 (£16,700) for embezzling U.S.$21m (£14m), which he
spitefully paid immediately and was released. He also has to repay U.S.$3.5m
(£2.3m) and surrender three of his properties.[1734] Also disturbing is the judgment
of the Federal High Court, Asaba, in *Federal Republic of Nigeria v. James Onanefe
Ibori & Ors*[1735] where the court quashed all the 170 charges against James Ibori,
the former Governor of Delta State, currently standing trial in the UK for money
laundering, on the ground that the prosecution's proof of evidence did not disclose
a prima face case against the accused person. While the judgment had been hailed
as well-reasoned in some quarters, some civil society groups have described it as
'a travesty and let down.'[1736] These kinds of rulings and decisions have not only
eroded public trust and confidence in the courts and the democratic process,
but have led to calls for other alternatives to getting justice. Judicial corruption
represents one of the most damaging of all types of corruption. When the
judicial arm becomes hampered by corrupt practices, biased interpretation and
application of the laws impairs the courts in serving as an effective tool to fight
against corruption.[1737] Judicial accountability is therefore vital to the protection
of the human rights of the economically dispossessed local inhabitants of the
Niger Delta who are often the most affected victims of corruption in Nigeria. In
addition to judicial accountability, other criteria for the success of the courts in
fighting corruption include: the existence of and compliance with a well planned
national strategy; presence of political will; existence of adequate legal framework

---

Commission (NJC) – the body charged with the appointment and discipline of judicial officers
in Nigeria- to start looking into some of these cases. Some of the judges found to have com-
promised their positions in the discharge of their responsibilities have either been removed or
suspended. The Kayode Eso Panel set up in 1994 to look into corruption within the judiciary
came out with startling revelations of corruption among judicial officers and recommended
the dismissal of 47 judges. Disappointingly, only six of these were eventually dismissed. Justice
Wilson Egbo-Egbo, formerly of Federal High Court, Abuja, was compulsorily retired in 2004
following the Federal Government's approval of a recommendation for his removal by the NJC
over his indiscriminate issuance of *ex-parte* injunctions under questionable circumstances.
Also, Justice Selong of the Federal High Court was dismissed in 2004 after being implicated in
a bribery scandal. Justice M.M. Adamu of the Plateau State High Court was also dismissed for
receiving a bribe. See Okechukwu Oko, *Ibid*, p.27.

[1734] BBC News, 'Nigeria graft fine 'no deterrent',' *BBC News*, 19 December 2008, at http://news.bbc.
co.uk/2/hi/8418302.stm [accessed 5 May 2013]; Adeniran, Plea Bargain will make Corruption
Pervasive in Nigeria, *op. cit.*

[1735] Charge No.: FHC/ASB/IC/09, judgment delivered on 17 December 2009 (Honourable Justice
Marcel I. Awokulehin).

[1736] Socio-Economic Rights and Accountability Project (SERAP), quoted in Bernard Imarhiagbe
and Akintokunbo A Adejumo, *'Does Ibori Own the Nigerian Judiciary?: A statement from
Champions for Nigeria*, Transparency for Nigeria, 22 December, 2009, at www.transparen-
cyng.com/index [accessed 3 March 2010].

[1737] Petter Langseth and Edgardo Buscaglia, *Empowering the Victims of Corruption through
Social Control Mechanisms*, Global Programme against Corruption, Centre for International
Crime Prevention (CICP-17), Research and Scientific Series, Office of Drug Control and
Crime Prevention, United Nations Office, Prague, 2001, p.23 at www.unodc.org/pdf/crime/
gpacpublications/cicp17.pdf [accessed 3 March 2010].

with inclusive offence definitions and enforcement provisions; impartiality and independence from political influences; existence of transparency and effective accountability mechanisms; credibility and public trust; appropriate expertise and specialization; full computerisation of the court's operations, high level of ethics and codes of conduct and adequate resources and funding.[1738]

Another problem with the judiciary in Nigeria, as discussed earlier, are delays in the administration of justice. Generally, cases, including those on corruption brought by the anti-graft agencies, drag on in court for a long time thus making the public lose trust in the courts as a sure means of getting justice. In view of the negative impact of corruption on governance and on the human rights of the people, it is suggested that a special court, manned by competent and honest personnel, be set up to handle cases on corruption. Such courts should be given a time limit of six months maximum within which to begin the trial and conclude cases filed before them. Section 26(3) of the ICPC Establishment Act does provide for a time limit for the commencement and disposal of corruption cases. It states that '[A] prosecution for an offence shall be concluded and judgment delivered within ninety (90) working days of its commencement save that the jurisdiction of the court to continue to hear and determine the case shall not be affected where good grounds exists for a delay.' Sadly, this provision has been invalidated by the Supreme Court in *Attorney-General of Ondo State v. Attorney-General of the Federation and Ors*,[1739] on the ground that it is contrary to the principle of separation of powers. However, vindicating the time limit of six months, the former Chief Justice of Nigeria (CJN), Justice Dahiru Musdapher, has recently gave a directive to all Nigerian judges: '... to accelerate the hearing of such cases [corruption] and ensure that they are dispensed with within six months of filing. If for any reason the prosecution is not ready to proceed with the case, then the matter should be struck out rather than leaving the public with the impression that the judiciary is not performing its necessary role in curbing corrupt practices in Nigeria. These delays cannot be tolerated any longer.'[1740]

Special courts to try corruption cases will not only enhance the speedy trial of corruption cases, increase the recovery of stolen funds, improve the performance of the anti-graft agencies, and reduce the rate of corruption in the country, but will also help to strengthen the trust of the people in the judicial system. The call for special courts is not to pass a vote of no confidence on the judiciary or an attempt to create yet another malfunctioning institution, especially in countries like Nigeria with systemic corruption and weak institutions,[1741] or one that

---

[1738] U4 Anti-Corruption Resource Centre, *Special courts for corruption cases*, at www.u4.no/helpdesk/helpdesk/query.cfm?id=19 [accessed 3 August 2011].
[1739] (2002) 9 NWLR (Pt. 772) 222.
[1740] Justice Dahiru Musdapher, *The Nigerian Judiciary: Towards Reform of the Bastion of Constitutional Democracy*, being a paper delivered in Abuja at a lecture organised by the Nigerian Institute of Advanced Legal Studies (NIALS), quoted in Kamarudeen Ogundele, 'Judges get six months deadline to dispose of corruption cases,' *The Nation*, 11 November 2011.
[1741] U4 Anti-Corruption Resource Centre, *Special courts for corruption cases, op. cit.*

could be misused for political purposes, as some critics perceive. Rather it is a call to avoid the long delays presently witnessed in the trial of corrupt officials and individuals in the regular courts, giving the impression that the country is not serious in its fight against corruption. Nigeria can learn from countries like France, Philippines, Pakistan, Kenya, Ghana and South Africa that have resorted to the creation of special courts to try corruption cases. The South African Expert Panel Survey, evaluating the various measures used to fight corruption (on a scale of one to four), with one considered the least effective and four the most, assessed special anti-corruption courts as very effective receiving 3.27.[1742] Special courts will help to prevent the current practice in the regular courts where the accused persons manipulate the rigid and technical processes in Nigeria's laws and criminal justice system to frustrate and prolong their trials.[1743] In fulfillment of their law-making function under section 4 of the CFRN 1999 (as amended), the National Assembly should as a matter of urgency begin the process of enacting a law to create a special court to try offences of corruption.

There is a need for more awareness, through educating the public. Uninformed people are easy to deceive by their corrupt leaders. This is true of Nigeria where the leaders deceive their people, making them to believe that their investigation and prosecution on corruption cases are politically motivated by the government. For example, when Dr Edmund Daukoru, who hails from Bayelsa State, former group managing director of the NNPC was arraigned in court in 1994 on charges of corrupt enrichment, involving approximately U.S.$47 million belonging to the NNPC, his kinsmen carried out regular protests at the court premises asking that he be released.[1744] The protest was not based on the fact that he was innocent, but the fact that the money allegedly stolen formed part of the proceeds of oil found in their region. The Nigerian Government later abandoned the charges, and Daukoru was in 2003 appointed Presidential Adviser on petroleum and energy matters and in July 2005 as the Minister of State, Petroleum Resources by President Obasanjo.[1745] Similarly, in April 2010, Oghara youths and women organised a series of protests for days against the arrests of the former Governor of Delta State, Chief James Onanefe Ibori, on corruption and money-laundering allegations, at Oghara his home town, alleging that the arrest and investigation were being politically carried out by the EFCC and government to victimise their son.[1746] Citizens need to be informed about the effects of corruption on service delivery and Governance. Once they are made to understand that they have a stake in the abuse of public funds, they will be able to appreciate that poor

---

[1742]   Lala Camerer, *op. cit.*; U4 Anti-Corruption Resource Centre, *Ibid.*

[1743]   Farida Waziri, quoted in Sam Nzeh and Leonard Okachie, Nigeria: Corruption – Desirability of Special Courts, *Daily Champion*, 27 February 2010.

[1744]   Transparency International, *National Integrity Systems TI Country Study Report Nigeria 2004*, Berlin, 2004, p.11 at http://info.worldbank.org/etools/ANTIC/docs/Resources/Country%20 Profiles/Nigeria/TransparencyInternational_NIS_Nigeria.pdf [accessed 3 March 2010].

[1745]   *Ibid.*

[1746]   Emma Amaize, IBORI: Oghara calm, awaits EFCC's fresh move, *Vanguard*, 23 April 2010.

service delivery, poor health facilities, few and ill-equipped schools, poor access to housing, food and water, bad roads, unemployment, the incessant conflicts in the Niger Delta region, and the spate of kidnappings and bombings in the country are the results of pervasive corruption. The educational system, particularly at the primary and secondary levels should be totally overhauled to incorporate ethical and moral teachings, and the curricula made to reflect values such as integrity, honour and discipline. Article 5(8) of the AU Convention enjoins States Parties to '[a]dopt and strengthen mechanisms for promoting the education of populations to respect the public good and public interest, and awareness in the fight against corruption and related offences, including school educational programmes and sensitization of the media, and the promotion of an enabling environment for the respect of ethics.' The law can only achieve its ultimate objective of making Government work for the people when the people are properly enlightened.

Human rights litigation could also be used to challenge cases of official corruption. This is being presently used by the Socio-Economic Rights & Accountability Project (SERAP), a NGO in Nigeria, to fight against large scale official corruption. It instituted an action filed in 2008, *SERAP v. President of Nigeria, the Power Holding Company of Nigeria, the Minister of Energy (Petroleum, Gas & Power) and the Attorney-General of the Federation and Minister of Justice*[1747] seeking (i) a declaration, *inter alia*, that the failure and complicity of the defendants to address effectively the systemic and official corruption in the power sector, and the resulting haphazard and unreliable electricity services, is unlawful and violates the right to the best attainable state of physical and mental health of majority of Nigerians, and constitutes bad faith on the part of the defendants to meet Nigeria's international legal obligations to achieve the minimum core contents of the right to health; (ii) a declaration that the failure and complicity of the defendants to develop and implement a coherent action plan to ensure reliability of electricity services to millions of Nigerians constitutes a lack of due diligence and violates their right to safe drinking water and the right to health recognized and guaranteed by the African Charter on Human and Peoples' Rights; (iii) an order directing the defendants to recover the stolen U.S.$16 billion budgeted for the power projects, and to use the same to provide reliable electricity services for Nigerians; and (iv) to arrest and prosecute those suspected to have committed these thefts of Nigeria's resources.[1748] The case is presently pending in the court. This kind of initiatives should be supported by the international community as part of the effort to fight corruption in developing countries, particularly Nigeria. This can be done through the training of human rights NGOs, civil society and lawyers so that they are able to provide legal advice and assistance to victims of corruption and associated human rights violations.[1749]

[1747] Suit No. FHC/L/CS/281/2008.
[1748] *Ibid.*
[1749] Adetokunbo Mumuni, *op. cit.*

In addition, steps should be taken to amend the UN Convention against
Corruption and the AU Convention on Preventing and Combating Corruption
to include the possibility for victims of corruption and human rights violations,
such as the Niger Delta people, to directly file cases in the courts for remedies.[1750]
The AU Convention on Corruption is at present devoid of human rights content
as it largely focuses on the criminal aspects of corruption. It fails to provide for
the human rights dimension by excluding the possibility of remedies for victims
of official corruption, in a manner inconsistent with human rights obligations
under the Africa Charter.[1751] The EFCC and ICPC laws should be reformed along
these lines by providing means of redress to persons or groups alleging violations
of their human rights, including economic, social and cultural rights, as a result
of corruption. Help can be taken by African Governments from the Council of
Europe Civil Law Convention against Corruption which states that '[e]ach state
party shall provide in its internal law for effective remedies for persons who
have suffered damage as a result of acts of corruption, to enable them to defend
their rights and interests, including the possibility of obtaining compensation
for damage.'[1752] Article 5 of the Convention enjoins each Party to 'provide in its
internal law for appropriate procedures for persons who have suffered damage as a
result of an act of corruption by its public officials in the exercise of their functions
to claim for compensation from the State or in the case of a non-State Party, from
that Party's appropriate authorities'. Amending the AU Convention and the UN
Convention on Corruption along these lines will help to guarantee the rights of
individuals affected by acts of corruption, and serve as a further legal framework
to combat the menace of corruption. These provisions under the Nigerian laws
would help to vindicate the human rights of victims of corruption, particularly
the local inhabitants of Niger Delta, as it would serve as an instrument through
which they could seek compensation when their rights are violated as a result of
corruption. What is clear from the above in the fight against corruption in Nigeria
is that corruption is now '... attracting more public scrutiny ... than in the past;
the secretive web that once shrouded it is fast disentangling ... There is now a
growing tide of awareness ... that combating the plague is integral to achieving a
more effective, fair and efficient Government.'[1753] Strengthening institutions such
as the ICPC and EFCC will help Nigerian citizens, particularly the Niger Delta
people, in ensuring that their leaders, various agencies and bodies and the oil
MNCs act responsibly, and are accountable for their activities which violate the

---

[1750]   *Ibid.*
[1751]   Kolawole Olaniyan, The African Union Convention on Preventing and Combating Corruption:
        A Critical Appraisal, *op. cit.*, p.91.
[1752]   Civil Law Convention on Corruption Strasbourg, 4 November 1999. This Convention, which
        opened to signature in 1999, and entered into force on 1 November 2003, serves to complement
        the Council's Criminal Law Convention on Corruption aimed at criminalizing corruption in
        the both the public and private sector.
[1753]   Nsongurua J. Udombana, Fighting Corruption Seriously? Africa's Anti-Corruption
        Convention, 7 *Singapore Journal of International & Comparative Law*, 447–488 at 488 (2003).

rights of the people. It is only by addressing the root causes of endemic corruption in Nigeria that Government can begin to meet its constitutional and international human rights obligations in the areas of health, housing, food, education and employment.

5.7 CONCLUSION

Oil exploitation and resources extraction in the Niger Delta should stimulate economic growth, reduce poverty, and promote infrastructural developments like access roads, pipe-borne water and electricity. They should lead to the promotion of the economic, social and cultural rights of the people in the region. As revealed in this Chapter, the reverse is the case in Nigeria, where the lot of the inhabitants of the oil region has been to suffer hardship in the form of environmental degradation, poverty, ill-health and loss of their livelihoods, largely as a result of corruption by corrupt leaders and Government officials in collaboration with the oil MNCs. This is unlike the situations in Canada, Norway, and Australia where the people have benefitted from the extractive industries in those countries. Only by addressing corruption, which has contributed to the deprivation of the social, economic and cultural rights of the inhabitants in the Niger-Delta, through effective policies and legislative reforms can peace and stability be restored in the region. With the proper management of oil wealth, the Nigerian Government could use the revenues from the oil sector to provide basic infrastructural facilities and create jobs – which are conditions for ensuring long-term development, eradicating poverty and facilitating the full enjoyment of human rights by the people. The enjoyment of the rights guaranteed under the Nigerian Constitution and other regional and international human rights Conventions, by ordinary Nigerians, particularly the Niger Delta people, to a large extent depends on the presence of political will on the part of the Government; and the entrenchment of good governance – accountability, openness and transparency, predictability and the rule of law.[1754] Effective control of corruption in Nigeria will enable public agencies, institutions and even the judiciary to hold the MNCs to account for their activities resulting in human rights violations to the local population. And given the fact that corruption is a global problem, this Chapter has canvassed the need for international assistance in strengthening Nigeria's judicial system. There is a need for developed nations to 'establish more stringent oversight of the activities of their transnational enterprises in resource-rich countries, and punitive policies to prosecute those enterprises whose international business

---

[1754] Kempe Ronald Hope, Sr, Corruption and Development in Africa, in Kempe Ronald Hope, Sr, and Bornwell C. Chikulo (eds.) (2000), *Corruption and Development in Africa: Lessons from Country Case-Studies*, Macmillan Press Ltd., Great Britain, p.35.

practices are corrupt.'[1755] This is because "[B]ad actors in the resource industry
that are involved in corruption or make a mess environmentally, socially or
from a safety perspective, not only drag their own reputation down, they taint
the entire industry,'[1756] and that of their countries of origin. So both the industry
and the developed nations need to do more as regards 'outing' the bad actors.
Also, the elimination of corruptive practices and mismanagement of oil resources
will help in the socio-economic development of the Niger Delta region, protect
the socio-economic rights of the people in the region and help to promote
the rule of law through which the Government will be able to hold the MNCs
accountable. An increase in revenue allocation to the Niger Delta States, without
accountability and transparency regarding the use of public funds by the State
and Local Governments, will neither bring about remediation/restoration of the
environment nor improve the living conditions and human rights of the people
in the region.

[1755] Janelle Melissa Lewis, The Resource Curse: Examining Corruption in the Extractive Industries,
       Perspectives on Global Issues, Vol.2, Issue 1, New York University (2007), p.10, at www.perspec-
       tivesonglobalissues.com/0201/articles0201/TheResourceCurse.pdf [accessed 18 August 2011].
[1756] Tom Albanese, Rio Tinto's CEO, talks to Critical Resource, Q & A with Rio Tinto CEO: indus-
       try needs to 'out' bad actors, *Critical Resource*, September 2011, at www.c-resource.com/view_
       article.php?aid=179 [accessed 18 August 2011].

CHAPTER SIX

STRENGTHENING THE NATIONAL AND REGIONAL INSTITUTIONS TO ADDRESS HUMAN RIGHTS CONCERNS IN THE NIGER DELTA REGION

6.1 INTRODUCTION

The current international gap in corporate accountability requires new ways and measures that will genuinely create a future where development/domestic economic growth and environmental considerations can harmoniously coexist, and where, in particular, human rights abuse and environmental harm caused by oil exploitation will be eliminated. In Chapter Four of this book, lack of access to justice, environmental information or public participation were mentioned, without elaborate discussion, as parts of the challenge to effective regulation of the practices of oil MNCs in Nigeria. This Chapter argues that ensuring corporate accountability and addressing the human rights concerns in the Niger Delta region, requires that these challenges be addressed through the strengthening of national and regional institutions. It contends that strengthening those procedural rights: the right of the public to access environmental information, public participation in decision-making in environmental matters, and the public's access to courts in environmental matters, are vital to the protection of the rights of the Niger Delta people and their environment. Apart from this, the Chapter calls for the strengthening of civil society groups, who play a complementary role in regulating the activities of the oil MNCs in Nigeria. All this will send a message to oil MNCs and other stakeholders in the industry that oil exploitation in the Niger Delta, with its attendant environmental and human rights consequences, must be taken seriously. '[W]ithout good governance, strong institutions and a clear commitment to rooting out corruption and mismanagement'[1757] particularly in the oil industry and wherever it is found in Nigeria, regulating the oil MNCs and

---

[1757] Kofi Annan, *In larger Freedom: Towards Development, Security and Human Rights for All*, Report of the Secretary-General, UN General Assembly Document A/59/2005 of 21 March 2005, para. 36, at www2.ohchr.org/english/bodies/hrcouncil/do`cs/gaA.59.2005_En.pdf [accessed 23 November 2009].

protecting the rights of the local inhabitants of the Niger Delta will prove difficult
to achieve.

6.1 ACCESS TO JUSTICE AS A PANACEA TO THE NIGER DELTA CRISIS

6.1.1 ACCESS TO JUDICIAL REDRESS FOR ENVIRONMENTAL GRIEVANCES

The term 'access to justice' is not closely defined in legal instruments but it has been
variously defined by scholars, in different contexts to refer to a bundle of rights
that have been accorded recognition under various national and international
legal instruments. According to Francioni, the term can be used in three ways:
i.) in a general manner, to signify the possibility of the individual bringing an
action before a court and have it adjudicated upon, ii.) in a more qualified sense,
to signify the right of an individual not only to enter a court of law, but to have
his or her case adjudicated in accordance with substantive standards of fairness
and justice, and iii.) in a narrower sense to describe the existence of legal aid for
the needy, in the absence of which judicial remedies will be unavailable to them
as a result of the prohibitive cost of legal representation and the administration of
justice.[1758] Real access to justice connotes the absence of significant impediments
to an individual or group seeking redress for perceived wrongs through lawful
means.[1759] The term does not only mean the right of individuals to bring an action
to seek redress before a court of law or tribunal established by law, it also extends
to the possibility of having those decisions enforced.

As regard environmental matters, access to environmental justice is said to be
located at the interstices of procedural human rights, environmental law, and good
governance.[1760] It refers to judicial and administrative procedures and remedies
available to a person aggrieved, or likely to be aggrieved, by an environmental
issue, and the existence of a fair and equitable legal framework that protects
environmental rights and ensures delivery of environmental justice.[1761] This is

---

[1758] Francesco Francioni, "The Rights of Access to Justice under Customary International Law", in
Francesco Francioni (ed) (2007), *Access to Justice as a Human Right*, Oxford University Press,
Oxford, p.1.

[1759] Engobo Emeseh, "The Niger Delta Crisis and the Question of Access to Justice", in Cyril Obi
and Siri Aas Rustad (eds) (2011), *Oil and Insurgency in the Niger Delta: Managing the Complex
Politics of Petro-violence* Zed Books, London/New York, p.57.

[1760] Catherine Redgwell, "Access to Environmental Justice", in Francesco Francioni (ed), *Access to
Justice as a Human Right, op. cit.*, p.153.

[1761] Muhammed T. Ladan, *Enhancing Access to Justice on Environmental Matters: Public
Participation in Decision-Making and Access to Information*, being a paper presented at a
Judicial Training Workshop on Environmental Law in Nigeria, organized by the National
Judicial Institute, Abuja, in Collaboration with the United Nations Environment Programme
(UNEP), held at the National Judicial Institute, Abuja 6–10 February 2006, p.7.

evident in the Aarhus Convention.[1762] Even though this Convention primarily applies currently to Europe, it is significant to the entire world, including Nigeria, in terms of environmental governance, particularly its three pillars: the right of the public to access environmental information, public participation in decision-making in environmental matters and the public's right of access to courts in environmental matters.

The right of access to justice has been also recognized in Principle 10 of the Rio Declaration. As earlier discussed, in Chapter Four, the rights to information, to participation, and to suitable remedies are generally guaranteed under the various universal and regional instruments for the protection of human rights. Victims of human rights abuses in the hands of the oil MNCs in Niger Delta are entitled to an effective remedy that offers redress for the harm suffered. However, the inability of the local inhabitants to obtain redress (either due to the absence of requisite legislation or the non-enforcement of existing law or regulations) compounds the original violation and itself constitutes a violation of their rights. This reinforces the need to promote access to justice for victims of corporate-related abuses in Nigeria.[1763] In his 2008 Report, Ruggie initiated the ideas of 'protect, respect and remedy' as a framework for addressing these challenges. The framework rests on three pillars: the State's duty to protect against human rights abuses by third parties, including business, through appropriate policies, regulation, and adjudication; the corporate responsibility to respect human rights, which means to act with due diligence to avoid infringing the rights of others; and *greater access by victims to an effective remedy, judicial and non-judicial.*[1764]

This subsection argues that where access to justice is denied to many of the victims of human rights abuse, securing corporate accountability for their actions will be extremely difficult.

6.1.2 RIGHT TO INFORMATION

Access to environmental information is important for ensuring effective public participation in decision-making and in monitoring the activities of the Government and the private sector, including the non-state actors. '[I]ndeed the whole system for the protection of human rights, cannot function properly without freedom of information. In that sense, it is a foundational human right,

---

[1762] *Op. cit.* See Chapter Four for discussion.

[1763] Human Rights Watch and Center for Human Rights & Global Justice (2008), *On the Margins of Profit: Rights at Risk in the Global Economy*, pp.48–49 at www.chrgj.org/publications/docs/bhr.pdf [accessed 3 March 2010].

[1764] John Ruggie, *Protect Respect and Remedy: A Framework for Business and Human Rights, op. cit.* This framework was endorsed by the Human Rights Council on 18 June 2008, which further extended the mandate of the SRSG until June 2011 with a request that he elaborate on the framework with a view to operationalizing and promoting it through coordination with relevant international and regional organizations and other stakeholders.

upon which other rights depend.'[1765] Effective access to information laws should
include, *inter alia*, 'obligations on agencies to collect and maintain relevant
information, to meet information requests in a timely manner, and to keep
information application fees low and within the means of all people.'[1766] Such
information would include relevant standards, permits conditions, emissions or
enforcement, monitoring reports, spill reports and EIAs.

It is important for Government to always release information about its own
projects so as to increase public knowledge. The State must also give notice to
individuals likely to be affected by any situation or event, which could produce
effects deleterious to their environment[1767] and human health. Even though the
Nigerian Constitution contains no explicit right to information, the applicants
in *Gbemre v. Shell Petroleum Development Co.*,[1768] sought to derive such a right
from the right to life.[1769] The applicants claimed in their pleadings that Shell
and NNPC's failure to carry out environmental impact assessments in their
community concerning gas flaring violated Nigeria's Environmental Impact
Assessment Act and 'contributed to the violation of the applicant's fundamental
rights to life and dignity' under the Nigerian constitution. The court ruled in
favour of the applicants.

Sometimes, Government and the oil companies invoke national security,
trade secrets or other grounds to counter reasonable requests by citizens and local
inhabitants for information about the hazardous materials and effluents resulting
from crude oil production and refining.[1770] Lack of information in environmental
matters, as depicted by the situation in Niger Delta, does amount to a 'violation
of informed consent and procedural justice.'[1771] The information which must
be made publicly available must also be repeated and updated at appropriate
intervals.

The environmental protection laws of countries like South Africa and Thailand
provide specific provisions for environmental information to complement

---

[1765] Toby Mendel, Freedom of Information: An Internationally Protected Human Right, 1 *Comp.
Media L.J.* 1 (2003).

[1766] Benjamin J. Richardson and Jona Razzaque, "Public Participation in Environmental Decision-
making", in Benjamin J. Richardson and Stepan Wood (eds) (2006), *Environmental Law for
Sustainability: A Reader*, Hart Publishing, Oxford & Portland, Oregon, p.181.

[1767] Ayesha Dias, *Human Rights, Environment and Development: With Special Emphasis on
Corporate Accountability*, Human Development Report 2000, Background Paper, at http://hdr.
undp.org/en/reports/global/hdr2000/papers/ayesha%20dias%20.pdf [accessed 3 March 2010].

[1768] Suit No. FHC/CS/B/153/2005.

[1769] See Amy Sinden, *An Emerging Human Right to Security from Climate Change: The Case against
Gas Flaring in Nigeria*, Temple University Beasley School of Law, Research Paper No. 2008–77,
pp.14–15.

[1770] Okechukwu Ibeanu, "Two Rights Make a Wrong: Bringing Human Rights Back into the Niger
Delta Discourse", in *International Conference on the Nigerian State, Oil Industry and the Niger
Delta*, *op. cit.*, p.105.

[1771] David Schlosberg (2007), *Defining Environmental Justice: Theories, Movements, and Nature*,
Oxford University Press, Oxford, p.69.

access to information laws.[1772] Happily, the Freedom of Information (FoI) bill first introduced to the National Assembly in 1999 was finally signed into law by President Goodluck Jonathan on 28 May 2011, thus 'heralding the conclusion of arguably the most exciting legislative odyssey in post-colonial Nigeria.'[1773] Section 1 of the Act guarantees the right of all persons to access or request information, whether or not contained in written form, which is in the custody or possession of any public official, agency or institution howsoever described. It further provides that an applicant needs not demonstrate any specific interest in the information being applied for; and in case of refusal, such person shall have the right to institute proceedings in the Court to compel any public institution to comply with the provisions of the Act.[1774] Section 2(7) of the Act defines public institutions as 'all authorities whether executive, legislative or judicial agencies, ministries, and extra-ministerial departments of the government, together with all corporations established by law and all companies in which government has a controlling interest, and private companies utilizing public funds, providing public services or performing public functions.' Even though environmental information is not specifically mentioned in the Act, it can be presumed that it forms part of the information within the custody of any public official, agency or institution which any interested person can request. The Act also tries to clarify its relationship with other pieces of legislation like the Criminal Code, Penal Code and Official Secrets Act, which prescribe criminal sanctions for actions regarding the disclosure of information. Section 27 provides that notwithstanding anything contained in the Criminal Code,[1775] Penal Code,[1776] the Official Secrets Act,[1777] or any other enactment, no civil or criminal proceedings shall lie against an officer of any public institution, or against anyone acting on behalf of a public institution in respect of the disclosure in good faith of any information, or any part thereof pursuant to the Act. This should help to overcome the fears expressed by public officials about violation of the provisions of the Official Secrets Act when formal requests for information in their custody are made by local communities on issues relating, for example, to compensation, revenue, accountability, environmental hazards and other major decisions concerning oil exploitation

With this, Nigeria has joined the few African countries that have adopted Freedom of Information laws. In all, there are now ten countries – South Africa (2000), Liberia (2010), Uganda (2005), Ethiopia (2008), Tunisia (2011), Guinea-Conakry (2010), Niger (2011), Nigeria (2011), Angola (2005) and Zimbabwe (2002 as amended in 2007). With the enactment of the Freedom of Information Act in

---

[1772] Benjamin J. Richardson and Jona Razzaque, "Public Participation in Environmental Decision-making", in Benjamin J. Richardson and Stepan Wood (eds), *Environmental Law for Sustainability: A Reader, op. cit.*, p.181.
[1773] Chidi Odinkalu, FOI Act: A Tale of Friends, *This Day*, 3 June 2011.
[1774] Section 1(1), (2) & (3) of the Freedom of Information Act 2011.
[1775] Cap. C38 LFN, 2004 (applicable in Southern Nigeria).
[1776] Cap. P3 LFN, 2004 (as applicable in Northern Nigeria).
[1777] Cap O3 LFN, 2004.

Nigeria, the Niger Delta people can now avail themselves of its provisions to seek access to information concerning environmental problems affecting or likely to affect their environment. It will assist the citizens, particularly the Niger Delta people to understand the extent of compliance with environmental law by both the regulatory agencies and the MNCs.[1778]

6.1.3 PARTICIPATION IN DECISION-MAKING

Public participation (PP) concerns the right of those affected by an activity to have a say in the determination of their environmental future,[1779] and it is an important component of a human rights approach to development projects. In addition to its inclusion in the Aarhus Convention, the principle of public participation was also included in the Rio Conference Documents (Agenda 21) of which chapter 8 is entirely devoted to this issue. In contemporary international law, indigenous peoples have the right to take part in decision-making processes and to give, or withhold, their consent to activities affecting their lands and resources or rights in general. The legal status of this right has been strengthened through the adoption of the United Nations Declaration on the Rights of Indigenous Peoples (2008).[1780] As noted by Shrader-Frechette, in medical ethics, the four conditions to be met to satisfy informed consent are: those creating the risk must disclose full information, the potential victims must be competent to evaluate the information, they must understand the danger involved, and they must voluntarily accept the risk.[1781] This consent must be 'freely given, obtained prior to [the] implementation of activities and be founded upon an understanding of the full range of issues implicated by the activity or decision in question; hence the formulation, free, prior and informed consent.'[1782] Dan Magraw and Lauren Baker define prior informed consent as 'a consultative process whereby a potentially affected community engages in an open and informed dialogue with individuals

[1778] Oludayo Amokaye, Human Rights and Environmental Protection: The Necessary Connection, 1 (1) *UNILAG Journal of Human Right Law*, pp. 89–120 at 114 (2007).

[1779] Muhammed T. Ladan (2007), *Biodiversity, Environmental Litigation, Human Rights and Access to Justice: A Case Study of Nigeria*, Faith Printers and Publishers, Zaria, p.160.

[1780] United Nations Declaration on the Rights of Indigenous Peoples 2008, 61/295, at www.un.org/esa/socdev/unpfii/documents/DRIPS_en.pdf [accessed 5 May 2013]; The Center for People and Forests, *Free, Prior, and Informed Consent in REDD+: Principles and Approaches for Policy and Project Development*, Bangkok, February 2011, at www.recoftc.org/site/uploads/content/pdf/FPICinREDDManual_127.pdf [accessed 5 May 2013].

[1781] Kristin Shrader-Frechette (2002), *Environmental Justice: Creating Equality, Reclaiming Democracy*, Oxford University Press, Oxford, p.77, quoted in David Schlosberg, *Defining Environmental Justice: Theories, Movements, and Nature, op. cit.*, p.69.

[1782] International Network for Economic, Social & Cultural Rights (ESCR-Net) Corporate Accountability Working Group, *Joint NGO Submission Consultation on Human Rights and the Extractive Industry*, Geneva, 10–11 November 2005, p.18 at www.earthrights.org/sites/default/files/documents/escr-joint-ngo-submission.pdf [accessed 3 March 2010].

or other persons interested in pursuing activities in the area or areas occupied or traditionally used by the affected community.'[1783]

Much of the violence and human rights abuse in natural resource countries like Ecuador (Sarayaku Kichwa people), Columbia (Uwa People), and Nigeria (Niger Delta people) would have been avoided if free, prior and informed consent have been obtained. Even now, the feelings of alienation among the Niger Delta people, and the frosty relationship between the community leaders and members on one hand, and the oil MNCs and the Government on the other hand, would become a thing of the past if public participation in decision making is allowed. Discussions with the people should take place prior to, and continue throughout, the period the activity is to be carried out, with the community having the right to withhold their consent during the life cycle of the project. The community should be afforded a clear understanding of how the proposed project is going to benefit or harm them, and the project should take into account cultural valuations of impacts or benefits and traditional modes of decision making[1784] according to the customary laws and practices of the affected community. Giving voices to the voiceless will promote environmental justice, satisfy the fair-hearing aspects of human rights, enhance the accountability of decisions concerning resource use, and help in the integration of ecological, social and human rights considerations in Governmental decisions.[1785]

6.1.3.1 Public Participation, Recognition and Environmental Justice in the Niger Delta

As discussed in the previous chapters of this book, the legal framework regulating the oil industry in Nigeria 'mis-recognizes'[1786] the host communities; disempowers them from democratic and participatory decision-making process as it concerns the oil industry, with the result that conflicts are bound to occur and re-occur in the region irrespective of the on-going developmental initiatives, such as the Niger Delta Development Commission (NDCC), the creation of the Ministry of Niger Delta, as discussed in Chapter Three of this Book, embarked upon by

---

[1783]   Dan Magraw and Lauren Baker, Globalization, Communities and Human Rights: Community-Based Property Rights and Prior Informed Consent, 35 *Denv. J. Int'l L. & Pol'y* 413–428, 421 (2007).

[1784]   Dan Magraw and Lauren Baker, *Ibid.*

[1785]   See Jona Razzaque, "Participatory Rights in Natural Resource Management: The Role of Communities in South Asia", in Jonas Ebbesson and Phoebe Okowa (eds) (2009), *Environmental Law and Justice in Context,* Cambridge University Press, Cambridge, p.123.

[1786]   Mis-recognition in this context implies want of recognition in the form of neglect, unjustifiable curtailment of freedom, domination and oppression. Recognition according to Shutkin means 'having democratic institutions that convey a communal acknowledgment of equal individual worth,' the absence of which results in exclusion, unfair and unequal treatment of individuals in matters concerning them. See William A. Shutkin, The Concept of Environmental Justice and a Reconception of Democracy, 14 *Virginia Environmental Law Journal*, 579–588 at 585 (1995).

the Federal Government.[1787] Where the rules of society misrecognize a group, the latter is deprived of participatory rights thereby contributing to conflicts.[1788] John Rawls, in developing a theory of justice, posited that we should step into an hypothetical 'original position,' behind what he calls a veil of ignorance, to a place where no one knows his strengths and weaknesses or his place in society, his class, position or social status; his intelligence, the generation to which he belongs, his economic or political situation,or his fortune in the distribution of natural assets and abilities.[1789] From this impartial position, Rawls argues that an individual would come up with a notion of justice that could be appreciated by everyone. Central to Rawls' principles of justice, conceived first as fairness, are: first, that everyone would have an equal right to the most extensive scheme of equal basic liberties, and secondly, that the social and economic inequalities are to be arranged so that they are to benefit everyone, and in particular, the least-advantaged members of society.[1790] This second principle implies that social and economic inequalities 'should be evaluated in terms of how well off they leave the worst off.'[1791] However, Rawls' notion of 'justice as fairness', with its particular emphasis on distribution, has been criticised by theorists like Young,[1792] Fraser and Boucher;[1793] Honneth,[1794] and contending that there is more to injustice than maldistribution. For example, Young and Fraser, along with other theorists like Honneth have argued that a lack of recognition in the social and political realms, evidenced in the forms of insults, degradation, cultural injustice, infliction of pain, and damage to marginalised individuals and communities, are essential to understanding and addressing these injustices and inequities.[1795] Young stresses that part of the reason for injustice and unjust distribution is lack of recognition of group difference, and that 'where social group differences exist and some groups are privileged while others are oppressed, social justice requires explicitly

---

[1787] Rhuks T. Ako, *Substantive injustice: oil-related regulations and environmental injustice in Nigeria*, being a paper prepared for the joint-workshop organized by the IUCN Academy of Environmental Law, Environmental Law Centre and Commission on Environmental Law, entitled "Linking Human Rights and the Environment: A Comparative Review," held at the University of Ghent, Belgium, September 2010, at https://community.iucn.org/rba1/resources/Documents/Rhuks%20Temitope.pdf [accessed 23 December 2010].

[1788] *Ibid.*

[1789] John Rawls (1999), *A Theory of Justice*, Revised ed., Belknap Press of Harvard University, Harvard, p.118; David Schlosberg, *op. cit.*, 12–13.

[1790] John Rawls, *Ibid*, p.53; David Schlosberg, *Ibid.*

[1791] Philippe Van Parijs, Difference Principles, p.1 at http://members.internettrash.com/shev/dochX71XXpvpX.pdf [accessed 2 February 2012].

[1792] Iris Young (1990), *Justice and the Politics of Difference*, Princeton University Press, Princeton NJ, p.1.

[1793] Nancy Fraser, "Social Justice in the Age of Identity Politics: Redistribution, Recognition and Participation", in Nancy Fraser and Axel Honneth (eds) (2003), *Redistribution or Recognition? A Political-Philosophical Exchange*, Verso, London, New York, p.9.

[1794] Axel Honneth, "Redistribution as Recognition: A Response to Nancy Fraser", in Nancy Fraser and Axel Honneth (eds) (2003), *Ibid*, pp.135–136.

[1795] David Schlosberg, *op. cit.*, pp.14–15.

acknowledging and attending to those group differences in order to undermine oppression.'[1796]

Rawls's notion of justice, and the ideas of his critics like Young and Fraser, are very germane to the question of environmental injustice[1797] in the Niger Delta. According to Ako, the legal framework regulating Nigeria's oil industry, presently skewed in favour of the Federal Government, would have certainly be different (fairer) had the Federal Government made the rules from 'behind a veil of ignorance' while in occupation of the 'original position' as posited by Rawls.[1798] The Government would have made the laws fairer to all, including the marginalized indigenous people of the Niger Delta communities. Young's concept of "justice as recognition" arguably also fits well into the situation in the Niger Delta in view of the neglect, domination and oppression the region has been made to suffer largely based on lack of 'recognition.' Recognition is fundamental to ensuring that all members of society have an equal participation in social life and have a voice. This is because 'a society whose institutionalized norms impede parity of participation is morally indefensible ...'[1799] Lack of recognition of the Niger Delta people has definitely resulted in their lack of participation in environmental issues that affect them. Hence, the insistence of Young on 'democratic decision-making procedures as an element and condition of social justice'[1800] to rescue the oppressed, marginalized and those suffering from distributional inequity. In his words: '[T]he idea of justice here shifts ... to procedural issues of participation in deliberation and decision-making. For a norm to be just, everyone who follows it must in principle have an effective voice in its consideration and be able to agree to it without coercion. For a social condition to be just, it must enable all to meet their needs and exercise their freedom; thus justice requires that all be able to express their needs.'[1801] There is therefore a need for emphasis to be placed on the elimination of institutionalized domination and oppression[1802] represented by the various laws and institutional rules that disrespect or unjustifiably disadvantage the Niger Delta people and which are in conflict with their well-founded claims to recognition.[1803] Justice for the Niger Delta people requires both redistribution and recognition. This goes to confirm Fraser's contention that 'neither redistribution alone nor recognition alone can suffice to overcome injustice today; ... they need

---

[1796] Iris Young, *Justice and the Politics of Difference* (Princeton, NJ: Princeton University Press, 1990), p.3, quoted in David Schlosberg, *Ibid*, pp.14–15.

[1797] Environmental injustice is seen by Schlosberg as 'a process that takes away the ability of individuals and their communities to fully function, through poor health, destruction of economic livelihoods, and general and widespread environmental threats.' David Schlosberg, *Ibid*, p.80.

[1798] Rhuks T. Ako, *Substantive injustice: oil-related regulations and environmental injustice in Nigeria, op. cit.*

[1799] Nancy Fraser, *op. cit.*, p.32; Paddy McQueen, Social and Political Recognition, *Internet Encyclopedia of Philosophy*, 2011, at www.iep.utm.edu/recog_sp/ [accessed 5 May 2013].

[1800] Iris Young, *op. cit.*, p.23.

[1801] *Ibid*, p.34.

[1802] Iris Young, quoted in David Schlosberg, *op. cit.*, p.15.

[1803] See *Ibid*.

somehow to be reconciled and combined.'[1804] In virtually all the 'Bills of Rights', of the various groups, communities, and other actors in the Niger Delta region, such as the Ogoni Bill of Rights, the Urhobo Bill of Rights, the Kaiama (Ijaw) Declaration, the Bill of Rights of the Oron People, the Ikwerre Rescue Charter, the call for active public participation in natural resources have dominated their agitations, that no amount of infrastructural development in the region can assuage their feelings of want of recognition and participation in the oil industry.

6.1.3.2   Environmental Impact Assessment (EIA) in the Niger Delta Region

The EIA Act No. 86, 1992[1805] is the first Nigerian law formally to give rights of participation in decision-making processes concerning development to parties other than the Government and private entities concerned.[1806] As observed by Wawryk, a thorough and well-conducted EIA offers a number of benefits, including:

> "[i]t provides a procedure for identification of likely adverse environmental impacts, including cultural impacts, before a decision to proceed with a development activity is made; it provides opportunities to the public and affected people, such as indigenous peoples, to present comments and recommendations to the decision-maker and participate in the development process; it precludes secrecy in official decision-making, and opens the process of development to scrutiny; it provides an opportunity to identify and take alternative development options; it presents an opportunity to identify and incorporate mitigation measures into a development activity; and conditions of approval may ensure monitoring of environmental (including cultural) impacts, annual reporting by the proponent, post-project analyses and independent environmental auditing."[1807]

Section 2(2) of the Nigeria's EIA Act requires that an EIA survey be carried out before any project or activity whose extent, nature or location is such that it is likely to significantly affect the environment. Section 22 provides that before the commencement of activities described in the mandatory study list, which includes oil activities, the Nigerian Environmental Protection Agency shall,

---

[1804]   Nancy Fraser, *op. cit.*, p.9.

[1805]   Formerly 'Decree' under the Military regime. See discussion in Chapter III of this work.

[1806]   Yinka Omorogbe, "The Legal Framework for Public Participation in Decision-Making on Mining and Energy Development in Nigeria: Giving Voices to the Voiceless", in Donald Zillman *et al.* (2002), *Human Rights in Natural Resource Development: Public Participation in the Sustainable Development of Mining and Energy Resources*, Oxford University Press, Oxford, p.565.

[1807]   Alexandra S Wawryk, *International Environmental Standards in the Oil Industry: Improving the Operations of Transnational Oil Companies in Emerging Economies*, at http://ugandapetroleum.com/linked/international_environmental_standards_in_the_oil_industry.pdf [accessed 9 August 2011].

(a) ensure that a mandatory study is conducted, and a mandatory study report is prepared and submitted to the Agency, in accordance with the provisions of this Act; or

(b) refer the project to the Council for a referral to mediation or a review panel in accordance with section 25 of this Act.

Also, the Agency is required to give opportunities for public participation before it takes any decision on the activity. Thus section 7 of the Act provides that:

> "Before the Agency gives a decision on an activity to which an environmental assessment has been produced, the Agency shall give opportunity to government agencies, members of the public, experts in any relevant discipline and interested groups to make comment on environmental impact assessment of the activity."

The provisions of the EIA Act do not appear to provide real participation in environmental issues. Section 4 prescribes the minimum content of an EIA and this forms the basis for the mandatory study report and yet, it does not provide a role for the public at this stage.[1808] Section 37 of the Act provides that where the report of the assessment is sent for a review, the public should be given an opportunity to participate in the assessment and a summary of any comments received from the public should be made part of the report to be submitted to the Council and the Agency. Also, section 25(2) of the Act provides that any person may only file comments with the Agency on the conclusions and recommendations of the mandatory study report. Public involvement and input at this stage is rather late and minimal as it becomes difficult to accommodate the interests and concerns of the stakeholders, especially with regards to environmental rights and protection, thus making the EIA process in Nigeria one undertaken merely to 'legitimize' participation,[1809] that is, one done to superficially satisfy the requirement of the law. The Gbaran Deep Oil Field Landlords Association had this to say concerning the *Gbarain Oil fields Phase 1 Field Development by SPDC (Well Drilling Campaign)*:

> "Whereas Section 7 of the EIA Decree empowers government agencies, the public and other interest groups to make input in EIA reports, no copy of the said EIA was displayed either at Yenagoa Local Government Council Office, nor Okolobiri, headquarters of Gbarain/Ekpetiama LGA. Therefore, the interested groups in the main host local government areas were denied the opportunity to have access to and comment on the EIA report. No health risk analysis in the Gbarain Oil Field

---

[1808] Rhuks T. Ako, *Substantive Injustice: Oil Related Regulations and Environmental Injustice in Nigeria, op. cit.*

[1809] Rhuks T. Ako *et al.*, Resolving Legislative Lapses through Contemporary Environmental Protection Paradigms- A Case Study of Nigeria's Niger Delta Region, 47 (3) *Indian Journal of International Law*, 432–450 at 442 (2007).

*communities and therefore no mitigation measures. There was no consultation with
communities..."[1810]*

Thus, it has become a common occurrence in the Niger Delta that in carrying
out projects, it is either there is a lack of proper consultation with regards
to the proposed project or such consultation is not performed adequately. A
situation where the affected individuals are not allowed to have a say in the
early (scoping) process which defines the scope and methodology of the study
but are only included just before the take off of the project is a far cry from
what true environmental governance should be as it can lead to grave injustice
for the communities. The communities become aware of any shortcomings in
projects undertaken in the region only when they have reached an advance
stage.[1811] Participation, to be meaningful, should be considered right from the
beginning, from concept development and planning, through implementation,
to monitoring and the evaluation of outcomes.[1812] The involvement of the public
at the early stage of a development project would enhance the credibility of the
decision-making process, ensure that a consensus is built, and enhance a public
sense of 'ownership'[1813] thereby helping to avoid the incessant conflicts in the
Niger Delta region.

6.1.3.3   Constraints to Public Participation

In practice, the application of prior informed consent (PIC) may encounter some
difficulties. As noted by Magraw and Baker:

> *"Despite some initial efforts and successes at applying PIC, in practice there have
> also been difficulties in the application of this right. States and businesses have
> sometimes had difficulty determining who to ask for consent, how to do it (especially
> in the light of cultural differences), how much information is necessary, and what
> constitutes consent. For example, communities may not have set processes for PIC,
> or may have procedures that are not clear, transparent or broadly representative.
> Also, different people within a community may have different or incompatible inte-
> rests and expectations for a proposed project. Dialogue between communities and
> outside interests may also be impeded by language, cultural barriers, or distrust.
> Finally, those seeking access to community land or resources may believe that PIC*

[1810]   Quoted in Tari Dadiowei, *Environmental Impact Assessment and Sustainable Development in
the Niger Delta: The Gbarain Oil Field Experience*, Niger Delta Economies of Violence Working
Paper No. 24, 2009.

[1811]   Yinka Omorogbe, "The Legal Framework for Public Participation in Decision-Making on
Mining and Energy Development in Nigeria: Giving Voices to the Voiceless", *op. cit.*, p.572.

[1812]   Mark S. Reed, Stakeholder Participation for Environmental Management: A Literature Review,
141 *Biological Conservation* 2417–2431 at 2422 (2008).

[1813]   Christoph Schwarte, *Public Participation and Oil Exploitation in Uganda*, International
Institute for Environment and Development (IIED), Gatekeeper Series 138, December 2008,
p.4.

procedures are unnecessary, too costly or time-consuming, and thus may resist or engage only minimally in the process."[1814]

Other criticisms levied against PP by critics include the following: it is expensive and time consuming; community members often allow their emotional attachments to guide them, and so, are not in the best position to make important decisions; the problem of knowing the right parties, and whose interests, to recognise; the communities are often represented by elites, and their views cannot be taken to be those of the majority of the people.[1815] These difficulties are surmountable. The Niger Delta region is the hub of oil and gas production in Nigeria, and bears the nation's wealth. Since the entire process of oil production negatively affects the people of the region and their environment, it is therefore important that the Government ensure the involvement of the people in decision making processes in matters concerning oil and gas exploitation.[1816] They are the people most affected by the activities of the oil MNCs and so best to appreciate the impact of oil exploitation on their lives and are able to monitor and report on the human rights abuses relating to oil exploration activities. They could be assisted and supported by the civil society and NGOs in monitoring the activities of the MNCs and their compliance with national and international standards on best practices in the oil industry.

6.1.3.4 Justifying the Niger Delta Communities Involvement in Environmental Matters

Public participation (PP) is vital to the effectiveness of law and can improve the legitimacy of Government regulations, and legitimacy in turn affects compliance[1817] with regulations. Legitimacy itself depends on participation:[1818] the people being given the opportunity to have a say in matters that affects them. As stated by Duruigbo, PP 'engenders a sense of empowerment in those who participate, strengthens local communities and other groups, promotes conflict reduction among competing interests, facilitates the accountability of public officials, and imbues the decisions reached with greater legitimacy. In addition, the decisions have chances of better substantive quality ... Involving

---

[1814]   Dan Magraw and Lauren Baker, Globalization, Communities and Human Rights: Community-Based Property Rights and Prior Informed Consent, 35 *Denv. J. Int'l L. & Pol'y* 413–428, 423 (2007).

[1815]   Emeka Duruigbo, Managing Oil Revenues for Socio-Economic Development in Nigeria: The Case for Community-Based Trust Funds, *op. cit.*, p.166; Benjamin J. Richardson and Jona Razzaque, *op. cit.*, p.193.

[1816]   Yinka Omorogbe and Peter Oniemola, "Property Rights in Oil and Gas Under Domanial Regimes", in Aileen McHard *et al.* (eds) (2010), *Property and the Law in Energy and Natural Resources*, Oxford University Press, New York, p.132.

[1817]   Donald K. Anton and Dinah L. Shelton (2011), *Environmental Protection and Human Rights*, Cambridge University Press, New York, p.381.

[1818]   *Ibid.*

local communities, including both the leadership and the ordinary citizens, in development activities will comport with the right to development.'[1819] The Niger Delta people are entitled to the right to development. Article 2 of the UN Declaration on the Right to Development[1820] states that human persons must be the central subject of development and should be the active participants and beneficiaries of the right to development. It further calls on States to formulate appropriate national development policies that would constantly improve the well-being of the people through 'their active, free and meaningful participation in development and in the fair distribution of the benefits resulting therefrom.' It connotes a developmental process in an accountable and transparent manner, participatory and non-discriminatory, equitable and just; and the right to a process of development in which all human rights and fundamental freedoms can be fully realized.[1821] For any meaningful change in the lives of the local inhabitants of Niger Delta, the Nigerian Government must ensure their full participation by allowing their voices to be heard and taken into account in matters of oil exploration and production. When people to be affected are allowed to participate in development projects, they will feel a sense of ownership, leading to less litigation in the long run, and fewer delays, which may lead the way for genuine development in the communities.

Participation must be informed in order to lead to higher quality decisions and high quality natural resource management. Participation must therefore be accompanied by access to information, and open to specialized actors that can offer technical expertise on relevant issues.[1822] Aaron Sachs of the Sierra Club describes the impact public participation can have in this way: '[o]f course, the human-rights approach to environmentalism is most effective when it is integrated directly into development projects, allowing those affected to voice their concerns from the very beginning. Local people who get to participate in relevant decisions and who have access to ecological information are well positioned to act as stewards of the local environment.'[1823] This may be referred to as a bottom-up corporate community relationship. By providing sufficient community participation in social investment projects, it could serve to empower

---

[1819]   Emeka Duruigbo, Managing Oil Revenues for Socio-Economic Development in Nigeria: The Case for Community-Based Trust Funds, *op. cit.*, p.167.

[1820]   Declaration on the Right to Development A/RES/41/128, 4 December 1986.

[1821]   Preliminary study of the independent expert on the right to development, Mr. Arjun Sengupta, on the impact of international economic and financial issues on the enjoyment of human rights, submitted in accordance with Commission resolutions 2001/9 and 2002/69, UN Economic and Social Council, E/CN.4/2003/WG.18/2, 12 December 2002, para. 38.

[1822]   Jorge Daniel Taillant, *Environmental Discrimination*, Center for Human Rights and Development (CEDHA) November 2000, at www.cedha.org.ar/en/documents. [accessed 3 March 2010].

[1823]   Aaron Sachs, *A Planet Unfree*, at www.sierraclub.org/sierra/199711/humanrights.html [accessed 3 March 2010].

the Niger Delta communities, stimulate their growth and serve as a formal or informal institution for conflict resolution.[1824]

In addition to the required 'Environmental Impact Assessment,' MNCs may also be enjoined to carry out a Human Rights Impact Assessment (HR Impact Assessment), which may include environmental and other human rights, and furnish a Human Rights Management Plan (HR Management Plan). The HR Management Plan, for instance, will have to show what preparations or provisions the business will be making to prevent, correct, or compensate for the environmental and other human rights impacts of their proposed activities.[1825] HR Impact Assessment in the Niger Delta will help to reveal in advance the effects that oil exploration activities can have on the local communities and dictate an HR Management Plan that will tackle the problem. In the words of Minkah-Premo, J.K:

> "A comprehensive HR Management Plan ... will achieve a harmonious relationship between the community and ... business. It will also be a source of co-operation between the State and big business in providing social amenities for the people. It may also serve as [a] ready source of ascertainable rights enforceable by the community in which the business is operating. Without such an effort, Cipo rights (civil and political rights) will mean nothing to the mass of people in the third world."[1826]

6.2 STRENGTHENING DOMESTIC ENVIRON-MENTAL ADJUDICATION IN NIGERIA

In the absence of any binding international regimes on corporate accountability for infringement of human rights, or any favoured method of addressing the regulatory gap,[1827] it becomes necessary to adopt the next best alternative, which is regulation by domestic regimes.[1828] Environmental regulation of the MNCs by the host country appears ideal in curbing the corporate abuses like those in the Niger

---

[1824]   Uwafiokun Idemudia (2007), *Corporate Partnerships and Community Development in the Nigerian Oil Industry: Strengths and Limitations*, United Nations Research Institute for Social Development, Markets, Business and Regulation Programme Paper Number 2, p.22, at www. unrisd.org/ [accessed 4 June 2009].

[1825]   J.K. Minkah-Premo, The Role of Judicial Enforcement of ECOSOC Rights in National Development: The Case of Ghana, *African Society of International and Comparative Law*, Proc. 11, p.77 (1999).

[1826]   *Ibid* at 80.

[1827]   Regulatory gaps arise where there are transnational problems- environmental problems such as pollution, acid rain- but inadequate or few international regulatory bodies, thus leading to under-regulation or no regulation. See Robert Wai, Transnational Liftoff and Juridical Touchdown: The Regulatory Function of Private International Law in an Era of Globalization, 40 *Colum. J. Transnat'l L.* 209–274 at 251 (2002).

[1828]   Robert Wai, *Ibid*, p.250.

Delta region because 'it respects the universal concept of state sovereignty.'[1829]
And as the judicial systems in developing countries are developed and upgraded,
it will help bring to an end a situation where the dismissal of a case brought in
a MNCs home State on the ground of *forum non conveniens* signals the death of
that case, no matter how meritorious.[1830] Indeed, the importance of the domestic
state courts as a source of regulating MNCs was pointed out by Ruggie, when he
stated that:

> "States should strengthen judicial capacity to hear complaints and enforce remedies
> against all corporations operating or based in their territory, while also protecting
> against frivolous claims ... [and] should address obstacles to access to justice, inclu-
> ding for foreign plaintiffs – especially where alleged abuses reach the level of wide-
> spread and systematic human rights violations."[1831]

The judiciary has a major role to play in the interpretation, enhancement,
implementation and enforcement of laws and regulations. Courts have a great
role to play in the protection of the environment. In *Fuel Retailers Association of
Southern Africa v. Director-General Environmental Management, Department of
Agriculture, Conservation and Environment, Mpumalanga Province & Others,*[1832]
Ngcobo J. held that 'the importance of the protection of the environment cannot
be gainsaid. Its protection is vital to the enjoyment of the other rights contained
in the Bill of Rights; indeed, it is vital to life itself. It must therefore be protected
for the benefit of the present and future generations. The present generation holds
the earth in trust for the next generation. This trusteeship position carries with
it the responsibility to look after the environment. It is the duty of the court to
ensure that this responsibility is carried out.' In view of the various challenges
facing the Niger Delta people today – concerning, *inter alia*, loss of food and
means of sustenance, pollution, loss of species and ecosystems, land degradation
and climate change, it becomes imperative for the judiciary which is the ultimate
arbiter in human affairs and the rule of law, to rise to the occasion by making the
'law an effective instrument of environmental and social justice.'[1833]

As discussed in Chapter Three, the present environmental laws, coupled with
poor enforcement machinery, are inadequate to regulate the activities of the oil

---

[1829] Alison L. Shinsato, Increasing the Accountability of Transnational Corporations for
Environmental Harms: The Petroleum Industry in Nigeria, 4(1) *Northwestern Journal of
International Human Rights* 186–209 at 194 (2005).

[1830] Robert V. Percival, Liability for Environmental Harm and Emerging Global Environmental
Law, 25 *Maryland Journal of International Law* 37–63 at 63 (2010).

[1831] John Ruggie, *Protect, Respect and Remedy: a Framework for Business and Human Rights, op.
cit.*, para. 91.

[1832] Case No. CCT 67/06; ILDC 783 (ZA 2007), para. 102.

[1833] Sarah L. Timpson, *Creating a Just Future- The Role of the Judiciary and the Law on Sustainable
Development*, Southeast Asian Justices Symposium: The Law on Sustainable Development,
UNEP/UNDP/Hanns Seidel Foundation/Supreme Court of the Philippines, Manila,
Philippines, 4–7, 1999, p.10.

MNCs causing environmental damage in the Niger Delta region. The Nigerian judiciary must be willing to intervene to confront any environmental predators, whether in the form of the State itself or the non-state actors. Hence, there is need for an activist court for the development and promotion of environmental rights in Nigeria. Judicial activism or judicial creativity is a concept where judges move away from strictly following the law to developing progressive and sound policies to meet the needs of the society. It requires the judiciary to be absolutely current in recent developments in the field, equipped with relevant literature and be well trained in the modern environmental jurisprudence.[1834]

6.2.1 REFLECTIONS ON ENVIRONMENTAL HUMAN RIGHTS LITIGATION ORIGINATING FROM THE NIGER DELTA

The human rights approach serves as an avenue for individuals whose rights have been affected by oil-related activities to seek redress, particularly in Nigeria's Delta region, where the Federal Government has failed to protect its citizens against foreseeable threats to human rights caused and/or exacerbated by oil exploration activities. Environmental human rights litigation provides a potent weapon for holding polluters, including the oil MNCs, responsible for activities that constitute harm to the environment and result in human rights abuse to the local inhabitants. Unfortunately, in spite of the negative impacts of oil exploitation, and its attendant consequences for the human rights of the local communities, there have been relatively few cases filed in Nigeria in which human rights law has been extensively invoked for oil-related harms.

The first case was *Jonah Gbemre v. Shell Petroleum Development Company Nig. Ltd. and 2 others*,[1835] filed at the Federal High Court Benin City, Nigeria in July, 2005 by Jonah Gbemre in a representative capacity for himself and the Iwherekan community in Delta State. The claim alleged that the activities (gas flaring) of the respondents (Shell and NNPC) violated his constitutional right to life and the dignity of his person in that they adversely affected his health, his life and the immediate natural environment. Referring to the applicant's evidence, linking gas flaring to greenhouse gas emissions and climate change, the court held, *inter alia*, that the actions of the 1st and 2nd respondents in continuing to flare gas in the course of their oil exploration activities in the applicant's community was a violation of his fundamental rights to life (including healthy environment) and dignity of human person guaranteed by sections 33(1) and 34(1) of the 1999 Constitution of Nigeria and reinforced by Articles 4 (respect for life and the

---

[1834] A.V. Narsimha Rao, "Environmental Jurisprudence and Judicial Activism", in Areti Krishna Kumari (ed) (2007), *Environmental Jurisprudence: Country Perspectives*, The Icfai University Press, India, p.221.

[1835] Suit No: FHC/B/CS/53/05.

integrity of person), 16 (right to enjoy the best attainable state of physical and
mental health), and 24 (right to a general satisfactory environment favourable to
their development) of the African Charter. Most importantly, the court declared
the provisions of section 3(2)(a), (b) of the Associated Gas Reinjection Act 1979[1836]
and section 1 of the Associated Gas Re-injection (continued flaring of gas)
Regulations of 1984 under which the continued flaring of gas in Nigeria may be
allowed, to be inconsistent with the applicant's right to life and/or dignity of his
human person and therefore unconstitutional, null and void. It restrained the
respondents from further flaring of gas in the applicant's community. It ordered
the Attorney-General to meet with President, and other responsible arms of
Government, to set in motion the necessary processes for the enactment of new
gas flaring legislation that would be consistent with the Constitution.

This case is important as it emphasizes the often ignored fact that
environmental degradation affects human life, and recognizes the linkages between
the environment and human rights. It affirms the existence and justiciability
of environmental rights in Nigeria and revolutionalised understanding of the
nature of the fundamental objectives and directive principles of State policy in
the Constitution of Nigeria. It affirmed the enforceability of the provisions of
the African Charter in Nigeria and adopted a liberal interpretation to the rights
to life and dignity of human persons in the absence of any express provision in
the domestic laws providing for the existence of the right to environment. This
is a new development in Nigeria, even though it has gained global acceptance
elsewhere, particularly in countries that does not have express provision for
the right to a clean environment. The trial court's ruling 'is a classic, triumphal
human rights story, in which the politically powerless communities of the Niger
Delta use human rights to beat back the Goliath of corporate-backed Government
power.'[1837] Domestically, *Gbemre* has made the constitutional and health effects
of gas flaring a matter of national public debate, and in the international realm
it has become something of a *cause célèbre* in the environmental and human
rights community of scholars, activists, and practitioners.[1838] Also, the explicit
recognition of the duties of non-state actors (MNCs) *vis-à-vis* human rights shows
that there is a prospect of the horizontal application of human rights provision
to non-state actors in Nigeria.[1839] Despite this laudable pronouncement by the
learned trial judge in *Gbemre*, nothing has been done in terms of submitting to
the court a detailed, phase-by-phase, technical scheme of arrangement to achieve
a total end to gas flaring in Nigeria. Rather than the Attorney-General meet with

---

[1836] Cap 26 LFN, now Cap A25 LFN 2004.
[1837] Amy Sinden, *op. cit.*, p.12.
[1838] Navraj Singh Ghaleigh, "Six honest serving-men": Climate change litigation as legal mobilization and the utility of typologies, 1(1) *Climate Law* 31–61 at 47 (2010).
[1839] Olufemi Amao, Human Rights, Ethics and International Business: The Case of Nigeria, in
Aurora Voiculescu and Helen Yanacopulos (eds) (2011), *The Business of Human Rights: An
Evolving Agenda for Corporate Responsibility*, Zed Books Ltd., London, p.204.

the relevant executive bodies and present a Bill to the National Assembly for the enactment of a new gas flaring law to end gas flaring, the Federal Government shifted the flare-out date from 31 December 2008 till 31 December 2012.[1840] This deadline was however not met as the oil companies had again suggested 2013 as the new deadline for prohibition of gas flaring. Gas flaring has persisted while the case has been on appeal since 2006 when Shell lodged it.

In *Shell v. Ijaw Aborigines of Bayelsa State*,[1841] voted the 'most important international law case of the month'[1842] when it was delivered, a group of local Ijaws filed a suit at the Federal High Court, Yenagoa (sitting in Port-Harcourt) against Shell to enforce the payment of the sum of U.S.$1.5 billion after it failed to abide by an order from the Nigerian Senate to pay the sum as compensation to local Ijaw communities for environmental pollution caused by its exploratory activities. The court ruled that since both sides had earlier agreed to go before the National Assembly, the order was binding on both sides. The Court of Appeal[1843] sitting at Abuja has, however, granted Shell an unconditional stay of execution of the judgement pending the hearing and final determination of Shell's substantive appeal.

Even though this case involved the implementation of a disputed arbitral award, it is important as it represents compensation for severe health hazards, economic hardship, injurious affection, and avoidable deaths that have been suffered as a direct or indirect consequence of the oil exploratory activities of Shell in Bayelsa State since 1956 when its operations commenced in the area.[1844] In other words, the award constitutes formal recognition of the right to a clean and pollution-free environment.[1845] Little wonder the ruling of the trial court was described as an 'unusual example of communitarian international rights being enforced at the national level.'[1846]

However, in *Ikechukwu Opara & Others v. Shell Petroleum Development Company Nig. Ltd. and 5 others*,[1847] where the facts were similar to *Gbemre's* case, the High Court struck out the case due to procedural defects. It held that the

---

[1840] Adeola Yusuf, Gas Flare – Oil majors in race to beat 2012 deadline, *Daily Independent (Nigeria) Newspaper*, 24 May 2010.

[1841] Suit No. FHC/YNG/CS/03/05, judgment on 24 February 2006.

[1842] Roger Alford, *Case of the Month: Shell v. Ijaw Aborigines of Bayelsa State* (Opinio Juris), at http://opiniojuris.org/2006/02/28/case-of-the-month-shell-v-ijaw-aborigines-of-bayelsa-state/ [accessed 23 March 2009].

[1843] Appeal No. CA/A/209/06, judgment delivered on 10 May 2007.

[1844] A Motion to cause the Enforcement of the Recommendation of the Legal Advisory Panel on the Investigative Hearing of Petition by the Ijaw Aborigines of Bayelsa State Against Shell Petroleum Development Company Limited (SPDC) as Presented to the House of Representatives through the House Committee on Public Petitions dated 24 February 2003, at www.senatorleemaeba.com/MOTIONS/MOTION%20ON%20THE%20IJAW%20 ABORIGINES%20OF%20BAYELSA.pdf [accessed 23 March 2009].

[1845] Hakeem O. Yusuf, Oil on troubled waters: Multinational corporations and realising human rights in the developing world, with specific reference to Nigeria, 8 *African Human Rights Law Journal* 79–107 at 95 (2008).

[1846] Roger Alford, *op. cit.*

[1847] Suit No. FHC/PH/CS/518/2005.

rights created by the African Charter were beyond the definition ascribed to
'fundamental rights' as contemplated by section 46 of the Nigerian Constitution
and so cannot be enforced by means of the Fundamental Rights (Enforcement
Procedure) Rules. This case is also on appeal.

This case raises questions about the 'judicial attitude' of Nigerian judges
in matters relating to environmental hazards created by oil companies which
disadvantage their host-communities. With all due respect to the Court, the
applicants' claims were for the protection of their rights – life and dignity of
the human person – which are expressly listed under chapter IV of Nigeria's
Constitution and therefore enforceable by means of the Fundamental Rights
(Enforcement Procedure) Rules. To strike out the case on the ground that the
applicants' reinforced their claims by citing Articles 4, 16 and 24 of African
Charter, suggests that the Court's reasoning was faulty. The Court should have
taken account of the fact that Nigeria has incorporated these rights by virtue of the
ratification and subsequent domestication of the African Charter into its domestic
law. Although the learned trial judge conceded to the applicants' counsel's
argument that 'issues bordering on whether there is a right to pollute free air
or whether the same is right to life (sic) requires interpretation of constitutional
provisions under Chapter IV and [are] not a matter[s] to be determined at this
interlocutory stage but during the substantive stage,' he still struck out the case
notwithstanding the continued negative environmental impacts the continuation
of the activities would have. It is hoped that the Appeal Court will be bold and
courageous in this case and uphold the existence of environmental rights in
Nigeria as did by the trial courts in *Gbemre* and *Ijaw Aborigines*. This will enable
victims of climate change and other environmental harm to ventilate their rights
in court against the actors responsible.

From the decisions of the Nigerian courts in environmental issues that have
been discussed, it can be argued that while Frynas's opinion that the recent
decisions (including *Shell Petroleum Development Company Ltd. v. F. Farah and 7
others*,[1848] *Edise & Others v. William International Limited*,[1849] *Elf (Nigeria) Limited
v. Sillo*,[1850] *Shell Petroleum Development Company Ltd. v. Tiebo VII*[1851] and *Agbara
& Others v. Shell Petroleum Development Company Ltd. & 2 Others*[1852]) indicate
that the 'judicial posture' of Nigerian judges has changed,[1853] it can be asserted
that these decisions border more on increasing the hitherto poor compensation

---

[1848] (1995) 3NWLR (Pt. 382) 148.
[1849] (1986) 11 CA 187.
[1850] (1994) 6 NWLR (Pt. 350) 258.
[1851] (1996) 4 NWLR (Pt. 445) 657.
[1852] Suit No: FHC/ASB/CS/231/2001, judgment delivered on 14 June 2010 (the court awarded the sum of N15.4 billion damages against Shell for a 1970 oil spill, which Shell had appealed to the Court of Appeal).
[1853] Jedrzej George Frynas, Legal Change in Africa: Evidence from Oil-related Litigation in Nigeria, 43(2) *Journal of African Law*, 121–150 (1999).

paid to claimants than the recognition of their right to healthy environment.[1854] In all, only the *Gbemre* case has explicitly made reference to the existence of a right to a healthy environment in Nigeria.[1855]

6.2.2 USING THE HUMAN RIGHTS APPROACH TO SOLVING OIL-RELATED LITIGATION IN THE NIGER DELTA

6.2.2.1 *Liberal and Creative Interpretation by Courts*

The Nigerian judiciary as the custodian of the Constitution and the final arbiter on constitutionality has an important role to play in the realization of the right to clean environment through liberal and creative interpretation of the provisions of the Constitution and other human rights instruments to which Nigeria is a party. Human rights exist for the purpose of promoting human dignity and meaningful existence. Happily, the Fundamental Rights (Enforcement Procedure) (FREP) Rules, 2009[1856] which came into force on 1 December 2009, promulgated by the Chief Justice of Nigeria (CJN) in exercise of the powers under section 46(3) of the Nigerian Constitution, have done a lot to improve access to judicial remedies where such rights are threatened or about to be infringed. By the inclusion of the African Charter in the Rules, the CJN has taken a giant step in complying with Article 1 of the Charter, which imposes on member states, including Nigeria, an obligation to 'adopt legislative and other measures to give effect to the [charter]' at the national level. Therefore, the reference to the African Charter Ratification Act[1857] not only distinguishes the Rules from the 1979 Rules, but also, reinforces the applicability in Nigeria of the rights and freedoms contained under that Act including the socio-economic rights.[1858] In the words of Amechi, 'the Rules laid to rest any lingering doubt regarding the justiciability of the socio-economic provisions of the Act including the right to a healthy environment, by expressly defining fundamental rights as including 'any of the rights stipulated in the African Charter on Human and Peoples' Rights (Ratification and Enforcement) Act.'[1859] It can be submitted that the individual rights contained in the Charter

---

[1854] Rhuks T. Ako, The Judicial Recognition and Enforcement of the Right to Environment: Differing Perspectives from Nigeria and India, 3 *NUJS Law Review* 423–445 at 436, 443 (2010).

[1855] *Ibid.*

[1856] The Fundamental Rights (Enforcement Procedure) Rules, 2009. This rule replaced the Fundamental Rights (Enforcement Procedure) Rules, 1979.

[1857] Cap. 10 LFN 1990, now Cap A9 LFN 2004.

[1858] Emeka Polycarp Amechi, Litigating Right to Healthy Environment in Nigeria: An Examination of the Impacts of the Fundamental Rights (Enforcement Procedure) Rules 2009, in Ensuring Access to Justice for Victims of Environmental Degradation, 6/3 *Law, Environment and Development Journal*, pp.320–334 at 329 (2010).

[1859] *Ibid.*; Order 1(2), FREP 2009.

are also justiciable, having been defined as fundamental rights by the FREP. The case of *Ikechukwu Opara & Others v. Shell Petroleum Development Company Nig. Ltd. and 5 others* would be therefore decided otherwise today based on the new Rules. Thus, an individual whose socio-economic rights have been or are likely to be violated can rely on the provisions of the African Charter, including the right to a satisfactory environment under Article 24 of the Charter to advance the protection of such rights.

The interconnection between all human rights makes it imperative for the courts to rise up to the challenge of giving meaningful interpretation to section 20 of the Constitution, as there can be no dignified life for the people in the oil-producing areas facing environmental degradation without its fulfillment. The courts, in interpreting and applying the provisions of the Constitution, should therefore, like the Indian courts have done, interpret them in such a way as to make socio-economic rights, including the right to environment, enforceable and justiciable. Article 37 of the Indian Constitution 1950 expressly declared the directive principles not to be enforceable by any court. In a series of cases, the Indian Supreme Court has elevated the right to environment to the status of a fundamental right, making its violation actionable under the Constitution.[1860] The Supreme Court in India has enlarged the right to life in Article 21, to include various economic and social rights such as the right to a livelihood,[1861] and the rights to shelter,[1862] health[1863] and education.[1864] In the Indian case of *Subhash Kumar v. State of Bihar*,[1865] the Supreme Court stated that: 'The right to life is a fundamental right under article 21 of the Constitution and it includes the right of enjoyment of pollution-free water and air for the full enjoyment of life. If anything endangers or impairs that quality of life in derogation of laws, a citizen has the right to have recourse to article 32 of the Constitution for removing the pollution of water or air which may be detrimental to the quality of life.'

India is not alone in this progressive development. The concept of social justice is well-entrenched in Philippine jurisprudence. It is understood in terms of the principle that 'those who have less in life should have more in law' and commands a legal bias in favour of the underprivileged.[1866] The Supreme Court

---

[1860] Sumudu Atapattu, The Right to a Healthy Life or the Right to Die Polluted?: The Emergence of a Human Right to a Healthy Environment Under International Law, *op. cit.*, p.104.

[1861] *Tellis & other v. Bombay Municipal Corporation & others* (1987) LRC (Const.) 351.

[1862] *Ahmedabad Municipal Corporation v. Nawab Khan Gulab Khan & others* (1997) AIR SC 152.

[1863] *Paschim Banga Khet Mazdoor Samity v. State of West Bengal* (1996) AIR SC 2426 (right to emergency medical treatment).

[1864] *Jain v. State of Karnataka* (1992) 3 SCC 666; *Unnikrishnan J.P v. State of Andhra Pradesh* (1993) 1 SCC 645.

[1865] A.I.R. 1991 SC 420 at 424 (India).

[1866] Fr. Joaquin G. Bernas, S.J. (2003), *The 1987 Constitution of the Federal Republic of the Philippines: A Commentary*, Rex Publishing, Manila, p.61, quoted in Gilbert Sembrano, "Mechanisms and Avenues for Judicial and Quasi-Judicial Implementation of ESC Rights: The Philippine Experience", in Fons Coomans (ed) (2006), *Justiciability of Economic and Social*

of Philippine, in the landmark case of *Oposa v. Factoran*,[1867] (which involved the right to health and the right to a balanced and healthful ecology) held, *inter alia*, that:

> *"While the right to a balanced and healthful ecology is to be found under the Declaration of Principles and State Policies and not under the Bill of Rights, it does not follow that it is less important than any of the civil and political rights enumerated in the latter. Such a right belongs to a different category of rights altogether for it concerns nothing less than self-preservation and self-perpetuation – aptly and fittingly stressed by the petitioners – the advancement of which may even be said to predate all governments and Constitutions. As a matter of fact, these basic rights need not even be written in the Constitution for they are assumed to exist from the inception of humankind…"*

This pronouncement, it has been contended, can be used and be invoked in litigating economic, social and cultural (ESC) rights in two ways: (1) since most of these rights concern 'self-preservation' and 'self-perpetuation', such as the rights to food and adequate housing, then *Oposa* can be used to argue in favour of their justiciability; and (2) those jurisdictions whose Constitutions do not explicitly contain a provision on the right to a balanced and healthful ecology or right to health, may argue that 'these basic rights need not even be written in the Constitution for they are assumed to exist from the inception of humankind'.[1868] It therefore implies that the provisions on environmental protection, as contained in the normally not binding Fundamental Objectives and Directive Principles of State Policy under the Nigerian Constitution, can nevertheless be invoked in relation to environmental matters. The Pakistan case of *Shehla Zia & others v. Water and Power Development Authority*[1869] is also important. A group of citizens sued and obtained a Supreme Court judgment, stating that the right to life included a right to live in a clean environment. The court noted that: 'Where [the] life of citizens is degraded, the quality of life is adversely affected and health hazards are created affecting a large number of people, the Supreme Court in exercise of its jurisdiction under Article 184(3) of the Constitution of Pakistan may grant relief to the extent of stopping such activities which create pollution and environmental degradation.'[1870] Also in Bangladesh, where the Constitution does not provide for the right to clean environment, the Supreme Court has been adopting this liberal approach to determine that the right to life in the Constitution includes the right to a clean and healthy environment.[1871]

[1867] *Rights. Experiences from Domestic Systems,* Intersentia, Antwerpen-Oxford, pp. 269–307 at 292.

224 SCRA 792, at 809 (1993).

[1868] Gilbert Sembrano, *op. cit.,* p.288.

[1869] PLD 1994 SC 693.

[1870] *Ibid*, at 715.

[1871] *Dr. M. Farooque v. Secretary, Ministry of Communication, Government of the Peoples' Republic of Bangladesh & 12 Ors* (Unreported); see, Jona Razzaque, *Human Rights and the Environment:*

Decisions of the European Court on Human Rights are also relevant. The court in *López Ostra v. Spain*[1872] held that severe environmental pollution from a waste treatment plant built close to the applicant's house was a breach of the applicant's right to private and family life, guaranteed under Article 8 of the ECHR. And in *Öneryıldız v. Turkey*,[1873] the court held that there had been a violation of the right to life enshrined in Article 2; violation of the right to peaceful enjoyment of possessions as protected by Article 1 of the Protocol No. 1 and violation of the right to a domestic remedy as provided in Article 13 of the Convention, as a result of negligence on the part of the relevant authorities that led to the applicant losing of nine members of his family. The Court has by these decisions 'opened the door for the protection of human rights against *nearly all sources of environmental pollution*, as opposed to just noise emissions and radiation, as was the case in the 1970s and 1980s.'[1874]

From the above, it is submitted that the decision of the court in *Okogie v. Lagos State Government*[1875] should no longer be good law, particularly as it relates to environmental matters.[1876] It is submitted further that the Nigerian courts could borrow a leaf from the practice of other jurisdictions shown above to infer the right to a clean and healthy environment from the Chapter IV of the Constitution dealing with civil and political rights. Environmental pollution in the form of gas flaring and oil spills and their attendant health effects could be held to be a violation of the right to life as guaranteed under the Chapter IV of the Constitution. In the same vein, the gas flaring resulting in air pollution and serious health hazards, and the frequent use of explosives causing sound pollution and damages in the peoples' homes could be held to constitute a deprivation of the residents' right to privacy and family life under Chapter IV of the Constitution.[1877] Besides, section 13 of the 1999 Constitution provides that 'it shall be the duty and responsibility of all organs of government, and of all authorities and persons,

---

The National Experience in South-Asia and Africa, Joint UNEP-OHCHR Expert Seminar on Human Rights and the Environment 14–16 January 2002, Geneva: Background Paper No. 4, at http://www2.ohchr.org/english/issues/environment/environ/bp4.htm [accessed 8 May 2010].

[1872] (Appl. no. 16798/90 ECtHR 9) December 1994.

[1873] (Appl. No. 48939/99) *[2004] ECHR 657 (30 November 2004)*.

[1874] Alfred Rest, Enhanced Implementation of International Environmental Treaties by Judiciary – Access to Justice in International Environmental Law for Individuals and NGOs: Efficacious Enforcement by the Permanent Court of Arbitration, 1(1) *Macquarie Journal of International and Comparative Environmental Law* 1–28 at 15 (2004).

[1875] *Supra* (See the discussion in Chapter Four). This decision was greatly influenced by the Indian case of *State of Mandras v. Champakam* AIR 1951 SC 226 which Indian Courts have since superceded by blazing the trail in the field of environmental litigation through judicial activism.

[1876] Oludayo Amokaye, Human Rights and Environmental Protection: The Necessary Connection, *op. cit.*, p.109.

[1877] Edwin Egede, Human Rights and the Environment: Is there a Legally Enforceable Right of a Clean and Healthy Environment for the "Peoples" of the Niger Delta Under the Framework of the 1999 Constitution of the Federal Republic of Nigeria?, 19(1) *Sri Lanka Journal of International Law* 51–83 at 70 (2007).

exercising legislative, executive or *judicial powers, to conform to, observe and apply* the provisions of this Chapter [Chapter II] of this Constitution.'[1878] When this section is read together with the contingent modifier 'except as otherwise provided by this Constitution' in Section 6(6)(c) of the Nigerian Constitution, the conclusion that can be drawn is that 'Nigeria's Constitution expressly requires the application of judicial powers to Chapter Two.'[1879] Thus, section 6(6)(c) should no longer serve as a barrier to the realization by the Nigerian judges in the realization of the socio-economic rights, which of all the human rights are the human rights of the Niger Delta people mostly violated. Assuming, however, that the socio-economic rights as contained in the Chapter II of the Constitution, are not justiciable, the domestication of the African Charter on Human and Peoples' Rights into Nigerian domestic law has helped to overcome the problem of non-justiciability. The African Charter contains provisions on socio-economic rights that can be used to serve the interests of Nigerian citizens, including the Niger Delta people. Nigeria is bound to apply the provisions of this Charter, including the right to a satisfactory environment, for the protection of its citizens as a nation cannot use its domestic laws to contract out its international obligations. This is important in view of section 19(d) of the Constitution, which provides that the foreign policy of the Nigerian State shall include 'respect for international law and treaty obligations.' International law and treaty obligations would include the African Charter. In his argument in support of the justiciability of socio-economic rights, Ogowewo avers, and rightly so, that the Supreme Court could overcome this barrier by 'simply recognizing that the programmatic aspirations set out in Chapter II were rendered justiciable the moment the legislature took the socio-economic inchoate rights in the African Charter and made them law in Nigeria when the Charter was domesticated.'[1880] It can therefore be submitted that there is more than one route by which the Nigerian courts can enforce socio-economic rights for the benefit of the Niger Delta people – by the combined reading of sections 6(6)(c) and 13 of the 1999 Constitution of Nigeria, or through the use of the provisions of African Charter as done in *Gbemre's* case, or through the provision of the Fundamental Enforcement Procedure Rules 2009, or by inferring the right to a clean and healthy environment from Chapter IV of the Constitution dealing with the civil and political rights.

[1878] Italics mine.

[1879] Chidi Anselm Odinkalu, *Do Our People Matter to Our Courts?: The Case for Justiciable Socio-Economic Rights in Nigeria*, being a keynote paper to the 1st Annual Human Rights Conference of the Nigerian Bar Association, held between 6–8 December 2009 at the Rockview Hotel, Abuja, p.12.

[1880] Tunde Ogowewo, *Wealth (Dis)creation through Corporate (Mis)governance and Banking (Mis) supervision: The Outlines of a Reform Agenda*, being a paper presented in Honour of Hon. Justice E.O. Ayoola on 25 November 2009 at the Nigerian Institute of International Affairs, p.3.

6.2.2.2 Implementation of International Environmental Law Treaties

Another way to overcome the non-justiciability of the environmental commitments
provided in the Nigerian Constitution, in order to ensure the protection of
environmental rights, is by the effective implementation of the environmental
treaties entered into by the Government. Nigeria has been actively involved in the
development of various international environmental law frameworks. It has not
only been an ardent participant in several international conferences[1881] relating to
the preservation of the environment, including the 1972 Stockholm Declaration
of the United Nations Conference on the Human Rights, but has also ratified
most of the international environmental treaties. The National Policy on the
Environment affirms this as it states in Article 7.0 that:

> *"In order to ensure effective implementation of international treaties to which
> Nigeria has acceded and will accede to in future, national laws, consistent with those
> treaties will be promulgated promptly. Legislative action will be taken to implement
> Conventions and Treaties already ratified by Nigeria. Nigeria will continue to par-
> ticipate actively in the progressive development and codification of international
> laws, instruments and guidelines on environmental protection and facilitate their
> adoption and inclusion in national laws and procedures."*[1882]

Governments that ratify human rights treaties are expected to take measures to
respect, protect and fulfill the rights in the treaties, and one of the ways this can
be done is through their domestic laws.

Thus, international treaties protecting the right to a safe and clean environment
which we discussed in Chapter Four of this book may be incorporated into the
domestic law of Nigeria through national legislation. Such international treaties
like the ICESCR, CEDAW, and other international instruments touching on
the right to a clean environment, and to which Nigeria is a signatory, should be
enacted into law, in the same manner as the African Charter is incorporated. No
treaty between the Nigerian Government and any other State can have the force of
domestic law except where such a treaty has been enacted into law by the National
Assembly.[1883] This makes the provision of these treaties enforceable in Nigerian
Courts.

These international treaties containing environmental principles may, even
if not domesticated, be used by the courts to interpret domestic legislation where

---

[1881] Nigeria participated in the UN Conference on Environment and Development 1992, the UN
Conference on Climate Change 1997, the Vienna Convention for the Protection of the Ozone
Layer, 1985, Montreal Protocol on Substances that Deplete Ozone Layer, 1987, etc.

[1882] See National Policy on Environment, launched on 27 November 1989, FEPA Special Publication
No. 3, quoted in P.T. Akper, "Consumer Protection and the Protection of the Environment", in
I.A. Ayua and D.A. Guobadia (eds), *op. cit.*, p.439.

[1883] See Section 12(1) of the 1999 Constitution of the Federal Republic of Nigeria; *Abacha v.
Fawehinmi* (2000) FWLR (pt. 4) 533.

the latter is ambiguous.[1884] Only very few of the international environmental principles are reflected explicitly in Nigeria's domestic law. Some of these principles include those that are more substantive in nature like the precautionary principle, the polluter pays principle and the prevention principle. The explicit (principles explicitly incorporated in the national legislation) or implicit (environmental principles of customary international law without them being laid down as principles)[1885] introduction of these important substantive principles of environmental law in the Nigerian environmental laws could easily serve as reference and guidelines for the Judges and administrative bodies when applying the norms or reviewing their applications. It can help them to provide a clear meaning to any vague provisions in the law.

Furthermore, codification of the principles of international environmental law into domestic law would enable the judges, administrative bodies and citizens to have a better understanding of the motive behind specific rules, thus assisting in the interpretation of those rules.[1886] In addition to providing direction in situations where a great number of rules apply as is often the case in environmental decisions, it may also assist in helping Nigeria meet its international obligations.[1887] While it is true that international environmental documents are not always legally binding, the principles laid down in them, for example, the Rio Declaration, are important guiding norms, which should be taken seriously by State parties.[1888] Nigeria has not been forthcoming in meeting its international obligations on the environment, and this has contributed a lot to the violations of the rights of the local inhabitants of the oil-producing regions.

The judiciary rarely refers to international principles in their decisions on environmental matters, whether through lack of knowledge on the part of the lawyers and the judges or the failure of Nigeria to have adopted detailed provisions of the international agreement into relevant laws (or both).[1889] This is unlike the position in the Indian courts where references are often made to international principles that touch on the right to a healthy environment, or refer to the growing jurisprudence on environmental issues, thereby enriching the quality of their decisions. Also, the Indian courts do not shy away from consulting widely with relevant authorities before arriving at their decisions. They are also noted

---

[1884] See *R v. Secretary of State for the Home Department, ex Parte Brind* [1991] 1 AC 696 at 747–748.
[1885] Piet Gilhuis, "The Consequences of Introducing Environmental Law Principles in National Law", in M. Sheridan and Lavrysen L. (eds) (2002), *Environmental Law Principles in Practice*, Bruylant, Bruxelles, p.55.
[1886] *Ibid.*, 52.
[1887] *Ibid.*
[1888] *Ibid.* For example, the Rio Declaration adopted the precautionary principle in its Principle 15, polluter pay principle in its Principle 16, Intergenerational Principle in Principle 3.
[1889] International Development Law Organization (IDLO) Report, *Strengthening Environmental Law Compliance and Enforcement in Indonesia: Towards Improved Environmental Stringency and Environmental Performance*, IDLO Development Law Update, Issue 6, 2006, p.4 at www.idlo.int/publications/30.pdf [accessed 3 March 2010].

for the enforcement of their judgments on polluters.[1890] Nigerian courts must as
a matter of necessity find ways of recognizing and breathing life into Nigeria's
international commitments on the environment, even, as is usually the case,
in the absence of implementing legislation.[1891] The Judges must pay heed to the
international environmental treaties which Nigeria has ratified over the years. As
noted by Robinson:

> "The courts serve a crucial role in ensuring that the systems recommended in Agenda
> 21 [1992] may become widespread … Clear articulation of the basic legal principles
> underlying environmental law can guide society in shunning conduct that breaches
> the strictures of those principles. With careful delineation of those principles in judi-
> cial opinions, the Ministries of Government can guide the affairs of State accor-
> dingly. The bar can counsel clients in the private sector to follow the clear delineated
> path. Similarly, the legislatures can formulate new policies and statutes to give more
> effective implementation to those principles. In short, as the courts advance the
> remedial objectives of Environmental Law, they advance the rule of law itself."[1892]

The Indian courts, through judicial activism and public interest environmental
litigation, have in a number of cases successfully invoked principles from
international environmental law jurisprudence to ensure the protection of the
rights of victims of environmental harm. They have, through an extensive and
innovative jurisprudence, held that the principles of precaution, polluter-pays
and intergenerational equity, as well as the public trust doctrine are part of
environmental law in India.[1893] Evidence abounds that the orders of the Indian
Supreme Court on environmental issues have led to a substantial reduction in
the pollution levels, and an increase in environmental quality, in the country,
for example in Delhi.[1894] The success of Indian courts is premised on its dogged
determination to fill the gaps in domestic law by applying, where necessary,
international instruments governing human rights and environment. In the
Indian case of *Andhra Pradesh Pollution Control Board-II v. Prof. M.V. Nayudu &*

[1890] Rhuks T. Ako, The Judicial Recognition and Enforcement of the Right to Environment:
Differing Perspectives from Nigeria and India, *op. cit.*, pp.443–444.

[1891] See Flerida Ruth P. Romero, *The Role of the Judiciary in Promoting the Rule of Law in the Area
of Environmental Protection in the Philippines*, Southeast Asian Justices Symposium: The Law
on Sustainable Development, UNEP/UNDP/Hanns Seidel Foundation/Supreme Court of the
Philippines, Manila, Philippines, 4–7, 1999, p.62.

[1892] Nicholas A. Robinson, *Principles of Environmental Justice: A Foundation for Dispute
Prevention and Resolution*, in Report of the Regional Symposium on the Role of the Judiciary
in Promoting the Rule of Law in the Area of Sustainable Development, Colombo, Sri Lanka,
4–6 July 1997, p.181.

[1893] *Vellore Citizens' Forum v. Union of India* (1996) 5 SCC 647. See Lavanya Rajamani, The Right to
Environmental Protection in India: Many a Slip Between the Cup and the Lip?, 16(3) *RECIEL*
274–286 at 274 (2007).

[1894] Michael G. Faure and A.V. Raja, Effectiveness of Environmental Public Interest Litigation in
India: Determining the Key Variables, 21 *Fordham Environmental Law Review* 239–294 at 288
(2010).

Others,[1895] the court referred to the Declaration of the UN Water Conference; the ICCPR and ICESCR; and the Rio Declaration on Environment and Development, as well as the jurisprudence of the ECJ; ECHR, and the Inter-American Commission on Human Rights, as well as decisions of the national courts of the Philippines, Columbia and South Africa, as persuasive authorities in implying a right of access to drinking water as part of the right to life in the Indian Constitution. Also, in the Sri Lanka's case of *Bulankulama and Others v. Secretary, Ministry of Industrial Development and (Eppawela Case)*,[1896] the Supreme Court noted that though, 'the principles set out in the Stockholm and Rio De Janeiro Declarations are not legally binding in the way in which an Act of our Parliament would be … [n]evertheless, as a Member of the United Nations, they could hardly be ignored by Sri Lanka. Moreover, they would, in my view, be binding if they have been either expressly enacted or become a part of the domestic law by adoption by the superior Courts of record and by the Supreme Court in particular, in their decisions.'

Furthermore, in a review of Belgian environmental case law, it was noted that in over 100 Belgian cases, there is reference to one or more of the environmental principles that are enshrined in the EC Treaty.[1897] According to Lavrysen, the relatively intense use of these principles in recent times in Belgium may be explained by the fact that these principles are incorporated into national law, both at the Federal level and at the Flemish Regional level. He concludes that this is a positive development to Belgian jurisprudence and that the reference to those principles has given a decisive turn in the cases.[1898] Nigerian judges stand to gain a lot from these various jurisdictions in aid of the protection of the environment and human rights of Nigerian citizens, particularly in environmental matters.

6.2.2.3   *Accessibility of Courts to the People*

The Constitution of the Federal Republic of Nigeria 1999 (as amended) (CFRN) confers exclusive jurisdiction on the Federal High Court with regard to 'Mines and Minerals (including oil fields, oil mining, geological surveys and natural gas).'[1899] This is coupled with the fact that most of the national laws regulating the environment confers jurisdiction on the Federal High Court. For instance, section 13 of the Harmful Waste (Special Criminal Provisions, etc) Act of 1988 provides that the Federal High Court shall have exclusive jurisdiction to try the crimes specified in that Act. Unfortunately, these courts are not located in every

---

[1895]   [2001] 4 LRI 657 (Sup. Ct. India); *Narmada Bachao Andolan v. Union of India* AIR 2000 SC 3751. See Donald K. Anton and Dinah L. Shelton (2011), *Environmental Protection and Human Rights*, Cambridge University Press, New York, p.66.

[1896]   SLR – 243, Vol. 3 of 2000 [2000] LKSC 18; (2000) 3 Sri LR 243 (2 June 2000), per Amerasinghe, J.

[1897]   Luc Lavrysen, *European Environmental Law Principles in Belgian Jurisprudence*, at http://www-user.uni-bremen.de/~avosetta/lavrysenrep03.pdf [accessed 9 March 2011].

[1898]   *Ibid.*

[1899]   Section 251 (1) (e) & (n) of the 1999 Constitution of the Federal Republic of Nigeria.

State in Nigeria, but are sited at capital cities of some of the States representing the
different regions of the country. Victims of oil pollution who are mostly the poor
and marginalized people of the Niger Delta, farmers and fishermen, have to travel
from their local communities (usually a distance from the city) in order to be
able to file their actions. In addition to this, the huge amount of money to be paid
as filing fees by the victim in order to commence an action in the Federal High
Court is enough to deter some indigent victims from seeking judicial redress.[1900]
Aside from the professional fees and the potential costs for expert witnesses and
scientific evidence to prove the pollution and its effects on them, lawyers in Nigeria
now charges additional fees called 'transportation fees' each time they go to court
for their clients. When this is considered against the background that a case could
last for more than five to seven years even at the court of first instance, one begins
to see the effect on the indigent litigant. Thus, victims of human rights violations,
especially those from the Niger Delta region, find it extremely difficult to exercise
their legal rights when oil-related activities adversely affect their rights and means
of livelihood.[1901] In the *Gbemre's* case, the applicants, who resided in Iwherekan,
a rural community in Delta State, had to travel to the judicial division of the
Federal High Court sitting in Edo State, some kilometres away, to institute their
action for the enforcement of their fundamental human rights. This they may not
have been able to do without the support of the environmental NGOs who were
responsible for the institution and prosecution of the case. This is coupled with
the absence of legal aid for civil claims. The inability to easily access justice often
forces victims to resort to self help.

The Nigerian judiciary has an important role to play in ensuring that every
Nigerian, particularly the Niger Delta people, have access to justice. Therefore,
steps should be taken to ensure that jurisdiction is granted to courts that are
more easily accessible to the people, and that the court rules and procedures
that inhibit access of people to justice are adequately addressed. In this regard,
the Federal High Court rules – prohibitive filing fees and technical procedure –
which preclude a large proportion of the people of the Niger Delta from enforcing
their environmental rights should be reviewed and the filing fees drastically
reduced.[1902]

[1900]   S. Gozie Ogbodo, *The Role of the Nigerian Judiciary in the Environmental Protection Against
Oil Pollution: Is it Active Enough?*, at www.nigerianlawguru.com/articles/environmental%20
law/ [accessed 3 March 2010].

[1901]   Nlerum S. Okogbule, Access to Justice and Human Rights Protection in Nigeria: Problems and
Prospects, 2 (3) *SUR – International Journal on Human Rights*, 95–113 at 101 (2005).

[1902]   Nlerum S. Okogbule, *Ibid*, p.107.

6.2.2.4 Legal Aid and Victims of Environmental Harm

There is a need to extend the provision of legal aid[1903] to cover victims of environmental injustice. Availability of legal aid to citizens is necessary to guarantee their access to the courts and for the pursuit of their environmental rights. However, as an extension of the legal aid concept, victims of environmental harm in Nigeria can also avail themselves of the often ignored section 46(4)(b) of the 1999 Constitution[1904] on financial aid to indigent citizens to access justice. As earlier discussed, this can be done using the fundamental rights provisions of the Constitution, such as rights to life, and dignity of the human person to make a case for free legal assistance in the form of legal representation or advice for the purpose of realising the environmental objectives of the Constitution as contained in section 20. This is because Constitutional goals and state policies for human rights, environment and development will be meaningless if there is no easy access for the people to seek their enforcement when breached[1905] or about to be breached. Nigeria can borrow a leaf here from New South Wales in Australia[1906] and the Legal Services Commission in Britain that offer legal aid specifically for environmental litigation.[1907] This should be complemented with the establishment of legal aid clinics solely focusing on environmental matters. This can be enhanced by building the capacity of the public interest clinics at Faculties of Law in Nigerian Universities and linking them with well established law firms.[1908] Since the number of Law Faculties having law clinics is quite few, it is suggested that a law clinic should be made compulsory for all Law Faculties in Nigeria, and the lecturers provided with adequate training for effective delivery. This would help to enhance public interest litigation and promote access to justice for victims of environmental damage, which would lead to a reduction in the current spate of violence and agitations in the Niger Delta region.

[1903] Notwithstanding the fact that the Nigerian Legal Aid Scheme was started in 1976, it was only made to cover criminal cases. Further amendment in 1986 merely extended it to cover civil claims in respect of accidents. See Section 7 of the Legal Aid Act, Cap. L9 LFN 2004. See also Engobo Emeseh, "The Niger Delta Crisis and the Question of Access to Justice", in Cyril Obi & Siri Aas Rustad (eds), *Oil and Insurgency in the Niger Delta: Managing the Complex Politics of Petro-Violence, op. cit.*, pp.65, 214.

[1904] Section 46(4)(b) of the Constitution provides that the 'The National Assembly ... (b) shall make provisions – (i) for the rendering of financial assistance to any indigent citizen of Nigeria where his right under this Chapter has been infringed or with a view to enabling him to engage the services of a legal practitioner to prosecute his claim, and (ii) for ensuring that allegations of infringement of such rights are substantial and the requirement or need for finaincial or legal aid is real.'

[1905] Muhammed T. Ladan, Towards an Effective African System for Access to Justice in Environmental Matters, 23–24 *Ahmadu Bello University Law Journal*, pp.10–40 at 24 (2005–2006).

[1906] Legal Aid Commission Act 1979 (NSW) s 47l.

[1907] Benjamin J. Richardson and Jona Razzaque, *op. cit.*, pp.189–190.

[1908] Patricia Cameri-Mbote, *Towards Greater Access to Justice in Environmental Disputes in Kenya: Opportunities for Intervention*, International Environmental Law Research Centre (IELRC) Working Paper 2005, p.11 at www.ielrc.org/content/w0501.pdf [accessed 7 March 2009].

6.2.2.5 Addressing the Delay in Justice System

A situation where a poor farmer or fisherman from the Niger Delta region has to wait for more than seven years before having his case disposed of speaks volumes about injustice in Nigeria. As pointed out by Justice Adolphus Karibi-Whyte: 'The aphorism justice delayed is justice denied is as accurate as the saying that quick justice inevitably results in injustice. The imperfection of human memory in recollecting the events, identifying the main participants and assessing impressions long after the event is as risky as the impression when the freshness of the event leads to exaggeration, [and] when mistaken identity is without further reflection assumed to be the real thing. Hence, both inordinate delay and hasty dispensation of justice are not conducive to the proper administration of justice.'[1909]

6.2.2.6 Relaxing the Locus Standi Rule (standing to sue)

The Nigerian courts have always held *locus standi* to be a condition precedent to the commencement of any proceeding.[1910] The term implies the legal capacity of a person or group of persons to initiate an action in court. The basis for filing a citizen's suit can be found in section 46(1) of the CFRN, 1999 which provides that: 'Any person who alleges that any of the provisions of this Chapter has been, is being or likely to be contravened in any State in relation to him may apply to a High Court in that State for redress.' The emphasis here is the phrase 'in relation to him.' It means that any community or NGOs, group or persons seeking remediation for the violation of environmental rights, or non-compliance with environmental laws, must show that they have an interest in the violation which is over and above the interests of others before they can have the right to sue. This has restrained the ability of individuals, including NGOs, who are interested in the protection of environment, or assisting in the protection of the rights of the local inhabitants affected by environmental harms, from taking proceeding when not themselves affected. In *Douglas* v. *Shell Petroleum Dev. Co. Ltd.*,[1911] the plaintiff filed an action at the Federal High Court, challenging the failure of the defendant to comply with the Environmental Impact Assessment Decree of 1992 regarding the Nigeria Liquefied Natural Gas project whose multi-billion dollar investment was about to be commissioned. The plaintiff sought to restrain the defendants from carrying out or commissioning the afore-mentioned project until an EIA was carried out with the active public participation of those to be affected.

[1909] See A.G. Karibi-Whyte, "An Examination of the Criminal Justice System", in Y. Osinbajo and Kalu A.U. (eds) (1990), *Law Development and Administration in Nigeria*, Federal Ministry of Justice, Lagos, pp.55–77.

[1910] *Adesanya* v. *President of Nigeria* (1982) 3 NCLR 306; *Owodunni* v. *Registered Trustees of Celestial Church of Christ* (2000) 10 NWLR (pt. 675) 315.

[1911] (1999) 2 NWLR (pt. 591) 466.

Notwithstanding the fact that the plaintiff was a renowned environmentalist, and a native of one of the host communities of the project, the court dismissed his application on the ground that he had no *locus standi*, and for his failure to show *prima facie* evidence that his personal right was affected by the failure of the defendant in complying with the environmental law. On appeal, the court remitted the case back for retrial on the technical ground that it was wrong for the court to conclude that the appellant had no *locus standi* without looking at the statement of claims or in the absence of any evidence. A fall-out from this case is the practice of environmental NGOs sponsoring actual victims of environmental harm to litigate against those responsible for such harm.[1912] This practice obviously depends on the determination of the victims to prosecute the suit to a conclusion as they may be tempted financially to abandon the case halfway by the polluters,[1913] who are usually the oil MNCs. Nigerian courts should move away from the strict interpretation of this technical procedural rule about standing and borrow a leaf from countries like Portugal and Spain whose Constitutions allow open standing to sue, or citizens suits, without the need to show any special legal interest;[1914] or the South Asian countries that have achieved tremendous success in using public interest litigation to address environmental concerns.[1915]

In order to ensure a healthier, cleaner and safer environment for present and future generations, Nigerian environmental laws need to be modified to encourage private actions to remedy environmental wrongs.[1916] Australia (New South Wales) has pioneered 'open' standing provisions that permit any person to have standing to enforce compliance with many environmental laws.[1917] Section 123 of the

---

[1912] Emeka Polycarp Amechi, Litigating Right to Healthy Environment in Nigeria: An Examination of the Impacts of the Fundamental Rights (Enforcement Procedure) Rules 2009, in Ensuring Access to Justice for Victims of Environmental Degradation, *op. cit.*, p.330.

[1913] *Ibid.*

[1914] Rose Nwebaza, "Improving Environmental Procedural Rights in Uganda", in Marianela Cedeño *et al.* (eds) (2004), *Environmental Law in Developing Countries*, IUCN Environmental Policy and Law, Paper No. 43, Vol. II, IUCN, Gland, Switzerland and Cambridge, p.42.

[1915] The Supreme Court of India has recently relaxed the *locus standi* rule. This development has not only increased the number of public interests cases brought under Article 21 of the Constitution of India, but has created the opportunity for its judiciary to play an active role in addressing environmental issues. Chief Justice Kirpal endorses the relaxation of standing requirements as a means to '[t]ake care of the many interests that went unrepresented- for example, that of the common people who normally had no access to the high judiciary.' He noted that in addition to addressing the perceived short-comings of the other branches of government, public interest litigation, 'is usually more efficient in dealing with environmental cases, for the reason that these cases are concerned with rights of the community rather than the individual,' and so 'the court [is] able to look at the matter from the point of view of an environmental problem to be solved, rather than a dispute between two parties.' B.N. Kirpal, *Environmental Justice in India*, at www.ebc-india.com/lawyer/default.htm [accessed 3 April 2010]. For more discussion, see J Razzaque, Linking Human Rights, Development, and Environment: Experiences from Litigation in South Asia, *op. cit.*, pp.587–608.

[1916] Oludayo Amokaye, Human Rights and Environmental Protection: The Necessary Connection, *op. cit.*, pp.119–120.

[1917] Donna Craig and Michael Jeffrey, QC, "Non-Lawyers and Legal Regimes: Public Participation for Ecologically Sustainable Development", in David Leary and Balakrishna Pisupati (eds)

Environmental Planning and Assessment Act 1979 (NSW) provides open standing
provisions which permit 'any person' to approach the court to enforce any breach
or apprehended breach of the law. The application of open standing provisions has
been extended, at the Commonwealth level, to non-governmental organisations
(NGOs) under the *Environment Protection and Biodiversity Conservation Act
1999* (Cth).[1918]

The 2009 Fundamental Rights (Enforcement Procedure) (FREP) Rules[1919]
specifically mandate the Court to 'proactively pursue enhanced access to justice
for all classes of litigants, especially the poor, the illiterate, the uninformed, the
vulnerable, the incarcerated, and the unrepresented.'[1920] The rule further requires
the court to 'encourage and welcome public interest litigation in the human
rights field and no human rights case may be dismissed or struck out for want of
locus standi. In particular, human rights activists, advocates, groups, or any non-
governmental organisations, may institute human rights application on behalf
of any potential applicant.'[1921] The rule has not only consigned the doctrine of
locus standi to the dustbin of history, but also enlarged the category or class of
persons who can bring an action in cases of violation of human rights under the
Constitution to include anyone acting in his own interest; anyone acting on behalf
of another person; anyone acting as a member of, or in the interest of a group or
class of persons; anyone acting in the public interest, and associations acting in
the interest of their members or other individuals or groups.[1922] Based on these
provisions, private environmental litigants, such as NGOs, communities and
other public spirited individuals can now initiate private proceedings to enforce
the fundamental rights of persons affected or threatened either by environmental
degradation or by any act, neglect or default of the Nigerian Government in the
execution of environmental law resulting in the infringement of human rights,[1923]
without having their case dismissed or struck out for want of *locus standi*. Private
suits of this nature are vital for the effective enforcement of environmental laws
and regulations, particularly, in cases of State inaction, or under-regulation
by the regulatory agencies concerned. Empowering private citizens to initiate
environmental suits against the erring MNCs operating in the Niger Delta,

---

(2010), *The Future of International Environmental Law,* United Nations University Press,
Tokyo, p.118.

[1918] *Environment Protection and Biodiversity Conservation Act 1999* (Cth), section 475; See Michael
I. Jeffery QC, Environmental Governance: A Comparative Analysis of Public Participation
and Access to Justice, 9 (2) *Journal of South Pacific Law* (2005), at www.paclii.org/journals/
fJSPL/vol09no2/2.shtml [accessed 13 April 2010].

[1919] The Fundamental Rights (Enforcement Procedure) Rules, 2009. This rule replaced the
Fundamental Rights (Enforcement Procedure) Rules, 1979.

[1920] FREP Rules, 2009, Para 3(d).

[1921] *Ibid.,* Para 3(e).

[1922] *Ibid.,* Para 3(e)(i)-(v).

[1923] Emeka Polycarp Amechi, Litigating Right to Healthy Environment in Nigeria: An Examination
of the Impacts of the Fundamental Rights (Enforcement Procedure) Rules 2009, in Ensuring
Access to Justice for Victims of Environmental Degradation, *op. cit.,* p.331.

where the State refuses to act, will go a long way in curbing the activities of these corporations that continue to violate the rights of the people. This will also serve as a check and balance to the current paternalistic[1924] approach to environmental protection in Nigeria.[1925] What is required on the part of the environmental and human rights NGOs is to begin to take advantage of the FREP Rules to vindicate the rights of victims of environmental and human rights abuse in Nigeria. The Nigerian judiciary on their part must begin to emulate the practice of courts in other jurisdictions, like India, by encouraging and welcoming public interest litigation in the environmental and human rights field.

6.2.2.7   Recognition of Class Action Suits

Another major challenge is the non-recognition of the class action in Nigeria. This is unlike other jurisdictions where civil right groups are allowed to institute actions and claim damages, on behalf of a class. What is allowed in Nigeria is a representative action, where a person represents a group as opposed to everyone in a class that is represented by one group and a judgment for one is a judgment for all.[1926] A single injured individual – say a poor farmer in Niger Delta – may not be able to bring an action in court for damage to his health due to gas flaring. But by acting collectively with other individual members of the community who have suffered the same fate, the victims have more hope of bringing an action and even getting redress. For example, those injured in Bhopal, India may have received little compared to the injury suffered, but they were able to get as much as they did because of a class action.[1927] Victims should have an opportunity to

---

[1924]   According to Matthew Thomas and Luke Buckmaster, Paternalism refers to 'the interference of a Government or State with a person without their consent and defended or motivated by a claim that the person interfered with will be better off or protected from harm.' See Matthew Thomas and Luke Buckmaster, *Paternalism in social policy when is it justifiable?*, Parliament of Australia, Research Paper no. 8 2010–11 (2010), at www.aph.gov.au/About_Parliament/Parliamentary_Departments/Parliamentary_Library/pubs/rp/rp1011/11rp08. Paternalist policies of Nigerian Government in environmental matters cover situations where the authority makes environmental laws and policies without the involvement of the people to be affected, thereby depriving the people of their autonomy and freedom.

[1925]   Oludayo Amokaye, Human Rights and Environmental Protection: The Necessary Connection, *op. cit.*, p.120.

[1926]   Odein Ajumogobia, Minister of State for Energy (Petroleum) being an interview granted Tell, *Tell, Nigeria's Independent Weekly*, 18 February 2008, p.120. The difference between class actions and representative actions has been identified as "on the one hand, actions [are] being maintained by persons who have the 'same interest' in the proceedings, and on the other, actions being maintained by persons where there is a 'common issue of law or fact' at stake." That is, the difference is whether the commonality is on the nature of the parties or the nature of the issues. See Maggie Doyle, "The Nature of Representative or Class Actions in the Context of Compensation Claims against Resource and Utilities Companies" (1999) Australian Mining and Petroleum Law Yearbook, at www.ampla.org/publications/yearbk99_sum1.htm, quoted in Jeffrey F. Harris, *Re: Impact of Class Action Rules on Lawsuits by Aboriginal Nations in Federal Court*, being a letter to Secretary to the Rules Committee, Federal Court of Appeal, Ottawa, 10 August 2004 at www.cba.org/cba/submissions/pdf/04-30-eng.pdf.

[1927]   Joseph E. Stiglitz (2006), *Making Globalization Work*, Penguin Books Ltd., London, p.207.

join their claims and to act collectively against corporate abuse. The class action is imperative for victims of environmental harm, which may affect a widely spread group, and are often complex and expensive to litigate. Such an action could help to improve access to the courts by reducing the costs for individual claimants[1928] and may save the courts' time and reduce delays.

6.2.2.8 Establishment of Special National Environmental Courts

There is need for the setting up of special national environmental courts to be staffed by judges trained in environmental law and assisted or advised by environmental scientists/experts. The need for special environment courts, as in New South Wales in Australia and in New Zealand, is premised on the fact that many environmental issues are highly complex and technical and so require specialised institutions for the evaluation of the claims and the evidence. It would also enhance the development of a more consistent environmental jurisprudence by specialist judges.[1929] This specialised court could develop its own unique procedures to ease the investigation of environmental claims. The courts would benefit from increased social legitimacy, and have power to issue broader, more creative orders to remedy environmental violations[1930] particularly needed in the Niger Delta region. This would help to overcome the present problems described by Justice Feliciano, in *Minors Oposa*:

> "[T]he result will be, it is respectfully submitted, to propel courts into the unchar-
> ted ocean of social and economic policy making. At least in respect of the vast area
> of environmental protection and management, our courts have no claim to spe-
> cial technical competence and experience and professional qualification. Where no
> specific, operable norms and standards are shown to exist, then the policy making
> departments – the legislative and executive departments – must be given a real and
> effective opportunity to fashion and promulgate those norms and standards, and to
> implement them before the courts should intervene."[1931]

Realising the need for Environmental Courts in India, the court in *Andhra Pradesh Pollution Control Board-II v. Prof. M.V. Nayudu & Others*,[1932] recommended that

---

[1928] Filip Gregor, *Principles and Pathways: Legal Opportunities to Improve Europe's Corporate Accountability Framework*, European Coalition for Corporate Justice (ECCJ), November 2010, at www.corporatejustice.org/IMG/pdf/eccj_principles_pathways_webuseblack.pdf [accessed 3 June 2011].

[1929] Benjamin J. Richardson and Jona Razzaque, *op. cit.*, p.187; See generally, George (Rock) Pring and Catherine (Kitty) Pring, *Greening Justice: Creating and Improving Environmental Courts and Tribunals*, The Access Initiative, 2009, at www.accessinitiative.org/sites/default/files/Greening%20Justice%20FInal_31399_WRI.pdf [accessed 3 March 2010].

[1930] James R. May and Erin Daly, Vindicating Fundamental Environmental Rights Worldwide, 11 *Oregon Review of International Law*, 365–439 at 437 (2009).

[1931] *Supra* at 205 (Feliciano, J., concurring); See James R. May and Erin Daly, *Ibid*.

[1932] [2001] 4 LRI 657, para. 74 (Sup. Ct. India).

the Law Commission should review Indian environmental laws and consider the need for environmental courts consisting of experts in environmental law, and judicial members, in the light of experience in other countries.

Nigerian courts will also do well to take judicial notice of studies carried out by international organisations such as UNEP, Amnesty International and others which demonstrate environmental pollution and degradation in the Niger Delta region. An example of these Reports is the 2011 UN Environmental Programme, Environmental Assessment of Ogoniland (Niger Delta): a study commissioned by both the UN and the Nigerian Government. In the Chilean case of *Pedro Flores et al. v. Corporación del Cobre (CODELCO)*,[1933] the Chilean Court of Appeals explicitly referred to a UNEP study in finding that the Chanaral coastline was one of the most polluted around the Pacific Ocean due to mining activities. This was affirmed by the Supreme Court of Chile in *Pedro Flores v. Corporación del Cobre, Codelco*,[1934] in stopping a mining company from further depositing copper tailing wastes onto Chilean beaches to protect marine life. This approach is also being adopted in a recent suit filed by the people of Ogale, in Eleme Local Government, Rivers State, Nigeria, against Shell asking a US court to order Shell to pay the sum of U.S.$1 billion as damages for over 50 years of pollution and environmental degradation suffered by the community. The case, which was filed by the plaintiffs on 18 October 2011 in a US District Court in Detroit is premised on the US Alien Tort and Oil Pollution Acts, with the plaintiffs' asserting that they will be relying on the Final Report and the Executive Summary of UNEP findings on the Environmental Assessment of Ogoniland, of which Ogale community belongs.[1935] While waiting for the outcome of this decision in the US Court, it is hoped that Nigerian lawyers and judges will borrow a leaf from these developments so as to be able to secure justice for the victims of environmental harms.

6.2.2.9 Building a Strong and Virile Judiciary

There is an urgent need to strengthen the capacity of judges, prosecutors and legislators, in the process of implementation, development, and enforcement of environmental law, including multilateral environmental agreements (MEAs).[1936] The MNCs can also be involved in such efforts to tackle the considerable capacity challenges in the Nigerian judiciary, and so improving the administration of justice so that the courts can offer effective remedies. Building an independent

---

[1933] Quoted in Donald K. Anton and Dinah L. Shelton, *op. cit.*, p.67.
[1934] Rol 12.753.FS641 (23 June 1988).
[1935] Laolu Akande, Oil Pollution: Eleme People Sue Shell in US Court, Seek $1 Billion, *The Guardian*, 23 October 2011, at http://ngrguardiannews.com/index.php? [accessed 8 November 2011].
[1936] Lal Kurukulasuriya, *The Role of the Judiciary in Promoting Environmental Governance and the Rule of Law*, being a paper prepared for Global Environmental Governance: the Post-Johannesburg Agenda, Yale Center for Environmental Law and Policy New Haven, CT, 23–25 October 2003, at www.environmentalgovernance.org/cms/wp-content/uploads/docs/dialogue/oct03/papers/Kurukulasuriya%20final.pdf [accessed 7 July 2010].

judiciary will help to protect the business and financial interests of non-state actors in the country. In recognition of such benefits, some companies, like the Norwegian oil company Statoil, have joined with the Amnesty International, the UN Development Program, and the local judiciary, in the training of Venezuelan judges in human rights.[1937] In addition to the training of judges and court workers, the judiciary can further be strengthened through enhanced remuneration; recruitment of the most qualified people, not only in learning but also in character; and funding a watchdog to monitor activities in the judiciary.[1938] Developing the domestic courts will serve as a valuable tool in the hands of human rights victims to vindicate their rights, empower citizens and enhance citizenship education. According to Schrage: 'First, local adjudication provides the plaintiffs with an opportunity to have their day in court, an important act of participation in the political and civil development of their society. Second, it promotes the development of an active and vibrant legal community, willing and able to represent the interests of all citizens and protect their rights. Finally, it grants local courts an important opportunity to demonstrate their independence and professionalism. It may even prove to be a victory for the defendants, since they too may someday find themselves in need of a strong, independent and respected court system.'[1939]

Suffice it to say that '[E]nvironmental degradation and exploitation are transported globally by transnational corporations … It is the poor and minority groups that bear the biggest burden of pollution. Dirty extraction industries (ie oil, timber and minerals) that devastate the ecosystem and destroy lives are located in communities that are powerless and represent the path of least resistance for corporations.'[1940] Responsibility lies on African States to ensure the protection of human rights of their citizens through the adoption of forward looking and innovative approaches. As a result, domestic institutions, including National Human Rights Commissions and courts, have a major role to play. The existence of an independent judiciary in Nigeria, and respect for their decisions by all governmental bodies and organizations, is vital for the protection of the rights of the citizen, particularly the Niger Delta people. It will help to provide hope, for victims of environmental harm, and recognition for the hearing of their complaints and getting justice from the abusers of their rights. This will further help to overcome some of the challenges that have made victims of the environmental harm in the Niger Delta region prefer to litigate abroad.

[1937] See Sarah Murray, When Exploration Rights Meet Human Rights, *Fin. Times*, Mar. 15, 2002, at 12; Elliot J. Schrage, Judging Corporate Accountability in the Global Economy, 42 *Columbia J. Transnat'l L.* 153–176 at 169 (2003).

[1938] Emeka Duruigbo, Exhaustion of Local Remedies in Alien Tort Litigation: Implications for International Human Rights Protection, 29 *Fordham Int'l L.J.* 1245–1311 at 1297 (2006).

[1939] Elliot J. Schrage, *op. cit.* 167.

[1940] Beverly Wright, "Race, Politics and Pollution: Environmental Justice in the Mississippi River Chemical Corridor", in Julian Agyeman *et al.* (eds) (2003), *Just Sustainabilities in an Unequal World,* Earthscan Publications Ltd., London, p.136.

The observations of Naagbaton following the admission of liability by Shell on 3 August 2011 to a class action lawsuit filed at the High Court in London, for two massive oil spills in Bodo village in Ogoni between 2008 and 2009[1941] is very instructive. Naagbanton stated that: 'I helped the Bodo community file a case against Shell in the High Court in London because it is easy for Shell to abuse the judicial system in Nigeria. The oil giant spent decades fighting lengthy appeals that bled the victims dry in legal costs. Shell is appealing against a 2006 order to pay U.S.$1.5bn in damages to the Ijaw communities of Bayelsa State. Since 2005, Shell has refused to comply with a court order to end gas flaring in the Iwherekan community ... Rural communities impacted by pollution in the Niger Delta are routinely denied access to justice. Taking the Bodo case to London, the seat of one of Shell's corporate headquarters and a European oil capital, was a last resort.'[1942]

The existence of adequate and efficient institutions in the host country would help to build the trust and confidence of its citizens in the domestic legal system thereby reducing the rush for legal redress abroad by victims of human rights violations. This approach was adopted recently in the Ecuadorean case of *Aguinda v. Texaco, Inc.*[1943] This was a class action brought on behalf of 30,000 Ecuadoreans in 1993 by the Amazon Defense Coalition against oil giant Chevron (formerly Texaco, as Chevron purchased Texaco in 2001) for widespread environmental devastation in the Ecuadorian Amazon, and demanding cleanup and compensation in damages. They alleged that Texaco had dumped over 18 billion gallons of toxic materials into their rivers and water sources relied upon by the local residents between 1972 and 1992. However, Chevron contended that Texaco had spent U.S.$40m in cleaning the area in the 1990s, and had signed an agreement with Ecuador in 1998 absolving it of any further responsibility. After more than 17 years of litigation in Federal Courts in New York, the cases were dismissed by the Court of Appeals, subject to Chevron Texaco accepting the jurisdictions of Ecuador's courts. The plaintiffs re-filed the case in Ecuador in 2003,[1944] after Texaco agreed to submit to jurisdiction in Ecuador. In February 2011, a Provincial Court in Ecuador ruled that Chevron should pay U.S.$8.6 billion in damages and clean up costs, with the damages increasing to U.S.$18 billion if Chevron failed to tender a public apology within 15 days after the end of

---

[1941]   Platform Report (2011), *'Counting the Cost: Corporations and Human Rights Abuses in the Niger Delta,'* p.8, at http://platformlondon.org/nigeria/Counting_the_Cost.pdf. [accessed 11 November 2011]. Shell in the case faces a compensation claim of U.S.$410 million and could be forced to clean up extensive environmental damage.

[1942]   Patrick Naagbanton, Shell has admitted liability but has a long way to go to make amends, *the guardian*, 4 August 2011, at www.guardian.co.uk/commentisfree/2011/aug/04/shell-nigeria-oil-spills [accessed 11 November 2011].

[1943]   *Aguinda v. Texaco, Inc.*, 142 F. Supp. 534, 545 (S.D.N.Y. 2001), *aff'd*, 303 F.3d 470 (2d Cir. 2002).

[1944]   *Aguinda v. ChevronTexaco Corp.*, Superior Court of Justice of Nueva Loja (Lago Agrio), Ecuador (No. 002–2003); *See* Judith Kimerling, Indigenous Peoples and the Oil Frontier in Amazonia: The Case of Ecuador, ChevronTexaco, and Aguinda v. Texaco, 38 *New York University Journal of International Law and Politics* 413–664, at 629, 631 (2006) (for the history of Ecuadorian litigation).

the first appeal in the case. ChevronTexaco made damaging fraud and conspiracy allegations against the Ecuadorian judges and their lawyers, presumably to try to make foreign-country judgment recognition in the United States unavailable in relation to the Ecuadorian judgment. This is because since Chevron has no assets in Ecuador, the plaintiffs' chances of recovery ultimately depend on whether a court in a country where Chevron has assets, such as the United States, will recognize and enforce the judgment.[1945] In doing this, Chevron will be relying on one of the exceptions (fraud) to judgment enforcement in the United States.[1946] On 19 September 2011, the 2nd Circuit Court of Appeals in New York lifted US District Court Judge Lewis Kaplan's injunction issued on 7 March 2011, which had prohibited the Ecuadorian plaintiffs from enforcing the U.S.$18 billion judgment against Chevron. What has been likened to a biblical David and Goliath struggle for justice in Ecuador's rainforest represents an 'historic precedent for human rights, environmental justice, and corporate accountability,'[1947] which developing countries like Nigeria can benefit from. This is historic as the MNCs were sued by the indigenous people in Ecuador for the crime committed in the country and won. It also represents the highest award of damages ever issued in an environmental lawsuit: bigger than Bhopal, the 1989 Exxon Valdez disaster and the recent emergency in the Gulf of Mexico.[1948]

Likewise, the High Court of South Africa in *Minister of Water Affairs and Forestry v. Stilfontein Gold Mining Co. Ltd. & Others*,[1949] while granting an order holding the respondent company and its four directors guilty of contempt of court for failing to abide by the court's previous order compelling them to comply with directives relating to the pumping of underground water issued by the Regional Director of Water Affairs and Forestry for the Free State, stated that: 'The object of the directives is to prevent pollution of valuable water resources. To permit mining companies and their directors to flout environmental obligations is contrary to the Constitution, the Mineral Petroleum Development Act and to the National Environmental Management Act. Unless courts are prepared to

---

[1945] Christina Weston, The Enforcement Loophole: Judgment-Recognition Defenses as a Loophole to Corporate Accountability for Conduct Abroad, 25 *Emory International Law Review*, 731–770 at 736 (2011).

[1946] See Uniform Foreign Money-Judgments Recognition Act (UFMJRA), Prefatory Note, 13 U.L.A. 391 (1962) adopted by a majority of the states in the United States, revised in 2005 under the title 'Uniform Foreign-Country Money Judgments Recognition Act,' at www.law.upenn. edu/bll/archives/ulc/ufmjra/2005final.htm. [accessed 1 November 2010]. While section 4(a) of the Act provided three mandatory grounds (impartial tribunals or procedures; the foreign court did not have personal jurisdiction over the defendant; and over the subject matter) for non-recognition of foreign judgments, section 4(b) listed six discretionary grounds for non-recognition, including fraud.

[1947] Amazon Watch, *Understanding Recent Developments in the Landmark Chevron-Ecuador Case*, Clean Up Ecuador Campaign Briefing Paper, Winter 2011, at http://amazonwatch.org/assets/files/Chevron-Ecuador-Briefing-Winter-2011.pdf [accessed 23 November 2011].

[1948] *The Independent*, Ecuador: Finally, the Polluter is Commanded to Pay, 16 February 2011, at www.independent.co.uk/opinion/leading-articles/ [accessed 11 November 2011].

[1949] 2006 JOL 17516 (W) (Stilfontein).

assist the State by providing suitable mechanisms for the enforcement of statutory obligations, an impression will be created that mining companies are free to exploit the mineral resources of the country for profit, over the lifetime of the mine; thereafter they may simply walk away from their environmental obligations. This simply cannot be permitted in a constitutional democracy which recognises the right of all of its citizens to be protected from the effects of pollution and degradation.'[1950] The court therefore held that the directors could not ignore the environmental obligations, and so were held accountable for the companies' failure to have complied with the court's order. Oil exploration activities are responsible for serious environmental damage in the oil-producing communities in Nigeria, and so, it behoves the legislature, executive and the judiciary to ensure that MNCs comply with the legal framework regulating the oil industry. As noted by Kotzé, 'Ensuring enforcement and compliance with environmental laws arguably requires a concerted and mutually-supportive effort from all branches of government, namely the executive, legislative and judicial authority. Whilst the legislative authority is responsible for drafting environmental laws and policies, the executive has as its primary function the duty to enforce these laws. Both these authorities can be assisted… by the judiciary in interpreting the existing laws and applying it to instances where enforcement becomes problematic due to, sometimes, the "cavalier and off-handed approach" of industry.'[1951]

Strengthening the legal institutions in host countries will assist thousands of litigants who cannot afford the cost of litigating in U.S. forums to have their day in court; and serve as opportunities for local laws and national legal systems to develop and function more effectively for justice delivery.[1952] Thus, all effort must be made by the USA, European countries and the business community to support the host countries where the MNCs are operating by assisting them to reform their legal institutions for effective justice delivery.

[1950]   *Ibid,* para 16. 9.
[1951]   Louis J. Kotzé, 'Judicial Enforcement of Liabilities and Responsibilities for Pollution Prevention and Remediation: No more "Business as Usual" for South African Mines,' in LeRoy Paddock *et al.* (2011), *Compliance and Enforcement in Environmental Law: Towards More Effective Implementation,* IUCN Law Series, Edward Elgar, Cheltenham, UK & Northampton, MA, USA, pp.475–499 at 489.
[1952]   Emeka Duruigbo, The Economic Cost of Alien Tort Litigation: A Response to *Awakening Monster: The Alien Tort Statute of 1789,* 14 (1) *Minn. J. Global Trade* 1–41 at 34–35 (2004).

6.3 THE NATIONAL HUMAN RIGHTS COMMISSION AND THE PROMOTION OF HUMAN RIGHTS IN THE NIGER DELTA

6.3.1 INTRODUCTION

In line with the Resolution of the General Assembly of the UN which enjoins all member states to establish Human Rights Institutions for the promotion and protection of human rights, the National Human Rights Commission (NHRC) was established in Nigeria by the National Human Rights Act, 1995[1953] and it is headed by an Executive Secretary. The establishment of the Commission came as a result of serious human rights violations witnessed in Nigeria during the military regime,[1954] particularly against the rights of people living in the Niger Delta region. The climax was the execution of Ken Saro-Wiwa and eight other Ogoni environmental activists by the Military head of State, General Abacha, in November 1995. It was following these egregious human rights violations that the Commission was established, not only to protect and promote human rights but also to advise the Government on the need to meet its international obligations in the various treaties to which the country is a signatory. The Commission aims at creating an enabling environment for the extra-judicial recognition, promotion, protection and enforcement of human rights. The functions of the Commission are provided in section 5 of its enabling Act, and these include to:

a. deal with all matters relating to the protection of human rights as guaranteed by the Constitution of the Federal Republic of Nigeria, the African Charter, the United Nations Charter and the Universal Declaration on Human Rights and other international treaties on human rights to which Nigeria is a signatory;

b. monitor and investigate all alleged cases of human rights violation in Nigeria and make appropriate recommendation to the President for the prosecution and such other actions as it may deem expedient in each circumstance;

c. assist victims of human rights violations and seek appropriate redress and remedies on their behalf;

d. undertake studies on all matters relating to human rights and assist the Federal Government in the formulation of appropriate policies on the guarantee of human rights;

e. publish regularly reports on the state of human rights protection in Nigeria.
   …

[1953] Now National Human Rights Commission Act, Cap N. 46, LFN, 2004.

[1954] Nigeria was under the military dictatorship for nearly thirty years between January 1966 and May 1999, with just the four year 'interruption' of civilian rule of Alh. Shehu Shagari (1979–1983).

In order to be able effectively and efficiently to carry out its mandate, the Commission has identified 15 thematic areas of focus, with each area having a Special Reporter and Programme Officer. One of these thematic areas is 'Environment and the Niger Delta,' that is, addressing environmental and human rights problems arising out of oil exploration and production activities of the oil MNCs in the Niger Delta. The Commission has put in place a complaint treatment mechanism at its Headquarters in Abuja and all the six zonal offices, to handle complaints of human rights violations. Complaints (stating the facts and the relief sought) may be in writing or it may be oral, addressed to the National Office of the Commission or to a representative of the Commission at a Zonal office or other offices of the Commission. Such written complaints have to be signed.[1955] Where made orally, they are to be reduced into writing by the office of the Commission where the complaint was made and signed or thumb-printed by the complainant or his agent. The fact that the complaint is lodged free of charge makes the Commission accessible to the people, particularly the poor and vulnerable people of Niger Delta. The need to address the environmental and human rights issues in the Niger Delta region may be what led to the opening of a zonal office in Port Harcourt to take care of the South-South geo-political zone, comprising the Niger Delta.

It is noteworthy that the Commission, through mediation, has been able to provide assistance to some of the communities in the Niger Delta. For example, following receipt by the commission of a complaint from the people of Ekerekana community in Rivers State against the Port Harcourt Refinery Company alleging environmental pollution, the Commission intervened by arranging a meeting involving the Commission, the communities and the management of the Port Harcourt Refinery.[1956] After long deliberations, the parties were able to come to an agreement in which the refinery promised to curtail the activities which were resorting in the discharge of untreated effluents into the community. The Commission has also visited other communities like Ogbodo in Ikwerre LGA, and Ayama, Obunuku I & II in Oyigbo LGA.

However, the Commission has not been effective in the area of protecting minority rights in Nigeria, as these were not adequately included within its mandate.

[1955] National Human Rights Commission of Nigeria, at www.nigeriarights.gov.ng/index.php? [accessed 5 March 2011].

[1956] Jennifer S. Aga, The Role Played by the National Human Rights Commission in Enhancing Access of Individuals, Groups and Communities to Effective Remedies from Oil Corporations and other Multinationals when Violation Occurs, in Social and Economic Rights Action Center (SERAC) (2005), *Perpetuating Poverty, Consolidating Powerlessness: Oil and the Niger Delta*, SERAC, Lagos, p.124.

6.3.2 CHALLENGES FACING THE NHRC FROM DISCHARGING ITS HUMAN RIGHTS OBLIGATIONS

One of the major challenges of the Commission in this regard is lack of independence in the discharge of its responsibilities. There has been undue interference and control of the Commission by the Government. This was confirmed in a 2005 Report by the then UN Special Representative of the Secretary-General on Human Rights Defenders, which noted that the 1999 Constitution does not guarantee the existence of the Commission and that the commission's statutes do not adequately guarantee its independence.[1957] The Commission was established in 1995 by the Military Government of Gen. Sanni Abacha by a fiat under a Decree. Moreover, the Constitution of Nigeria which came into effect in 1999, after the creation of the Commission, did not take into cognizance the Commission as it did in the case of other Commissions.[1958] The lack of constitutional backing for its enabling Act contributes to the ineffectiveness of the Commission. The body is still to a great extent under the Minister of Justice and the Attorney-General of the Federation, and is regarded almost as a branch of the Federal Ministry of Justice. The Governing Council of the Commission, its Chair and Executive Secretary, who are appointed by the Head of State on the recommendation of the Attorney-General and Minister of Justice of the Federation, can be removed by the Head of State, if [s]he is 'satisfied that it *is not in the interest of the public that the member should remain in office.*'[1959] A situation where any of its members can be removed on the nebulous and vague phrase that his/her occupation of the office is not in the public interest may not augur well for the efficient performance of Commission members as the power of removal could be abused by the President to victimize the members. The members therefore lack security of tenure. In June 2006, Bukhari Bello, the Executive Secretary of the Commission at the time, was relieved of his job four years before the end of his term on the order of the Minister of Justice for ostensibly criticising the authorities for the harassment and intimidation of media men by national security agencies, and for his strong comments on the attempt by the President to modify the Constitution to secure a third term mandate.[1960]

[1957] Report of the Special Representative of the Secretary-General on Human Rights Defenders on her Visit to Nigeria (3–12 May 2005), para. 17, E/CN.4/2006/95/Add.2.

[1958] Section 153 of the Constitution of the Federal Republic of Nigeria 1999 (as amended) provides for the establishment of 14 Commissions with the exclusion of only the Nigerian NHRC. This is unlike the position in South Africa, Ghana, Tanzania, Malaysia where the enabling Act of their NHRC received parliamentary approval.

[1959] National Human Rights Commission Act, Cap N. 46, LFN, 2004, Section 4(2).

[1960] Corlett Letjolane *et al.*, *NIGERIA: Defending Human Rights: Not Everywhere, Not every Right*, International Fact-Finding Mission Report of World Organisation Against Torture (OMCT), FIDH and Front Line, 2010, at www.omct.org/files/2010/05/20688/nigeria_mission_report. pdf [accessed 1 August 2011].

426

In the same vein, Mrs Kehinde Ajoni, the Executive Secretary of the NHRC, appointed for the statutory period of five years and by which her contract was expected to end in 2011, was dismissed on 18 March 2009 by a letter from the Attorney-General of the Federation and Minister of Justice. The statement by the Federal Ministry of Justice merely stated that Mrs. Ajoni was 'recalled to the ministry'.[1961] In November 2007, the Government dissolved the Governing Council of the NHRC before their mandate ended and has only just inaugurated a new Governing Council in November 2012 under the chairmanship of Chidi Odinkalu that would be meeting at least once a month to discharge the functions of the Commission.

All these are clear indications of the Government's lack of political will to maintain an independent and effective NHRC. An NHRC perceived by civil society as lacking independence will always find it difficult to build strong and constructive relationships with human rights organisations on the ground, and so will have great difficulties working to effectively tackle human rights violations.[1962] Appalled by the lack of independence of the Commission and the 'irregular removal' of its members, the UN International Coordinating Committee of National Institutions for the Promotion and Protection of Human Rights downgraded Nigeria's membership to 'B' status in 2008.[1963] This has led to passivity and inaction by the leadership of the Commission on sensitive matters, including human rights abuses, as are presently being seen in the Niger Delta.

Also important is the Commission's lack of financial autonomy. Section 15 of the Act requires the Governing Council of the Commission to submit its budget, through the Attorney-General of the Federation, to the Federal Executive Council for approval. The Commission is more or less a government body rather than independent body it ought to be, and this has continued to weaken the effective performance of its role as protectors of victims of human rights abuse in the hands of the oil MNCs and the Government.

The UN Special Representative of the Secretary-General on Human Rights Defenders also expressed concerns over the Commission's lack of investigative powers or authority to compel authorities to respond to its queries;[1964] and its inability to enforce its own decisions. For example, during the visit to the Odi community in Bayelsa State after its invasion by armed soldiers on 20 November

---

[1961] Amnesty International, *Nigeria: Independence of National Human Rights Commission Under Threat*, 20 March 2008, London, at www.amnesty.org/en/library/asset/AFR44/009/2009/en/ [accessed 23 November 2009].

[1962] Emerlynne Gil, "An Unwavering Struggle for Independent and Effective NHRIs", in Emerlynne Gil *et al.* (eds) (2010), *2010 ANNI Report on the Performance and Establishment of National Human Rights Institutions in Asia*, The Asian NGOs Network on National Human Rights Institutions (ANNI). Asian Forum for Human Rights and Development (FORUM-ASIA) Publications, Bangkok, Thailand, p.16.

[1963] Amnesty International, *Nigerian President Signs Landmark Human Rights Bill, 2011*, at www. amnestyusa.org/category/country/nigeria [accessed 1 November 2011].

[1964] Report of the Special Representative of the Secretary-General on Human Rights Defenders on her Visit to Nigeria (3–12 May 2005), paras. 17 and 18, *op. cit.*

1999, the Commission assessed the level of damage. It pointed out the grave human rights violations that occurred through the Federal Government action; and the latter agreed to rebuild the community. Following the failure of the Federal Government to effectuate its promise, the people of the area in Bayelsa State filed an action against the Federal Government before a Federal High Court in Port Harcourt,[1965] demanding N100 billion as damages for gross violation of their rights. Ruling on the matter on 18 February 2013, Hon. Justice Lambi Akanbi held that the Federal Government violated the fundamental human rights of the victims to movement, life and to own property and live peacefully in their ancestral home. It ordered the Federal Government to pay N37.6 billion (special damage of N17.6 billion and a general damage of N20 billion) as compensation to victims of the military invasion. It is worthy of note that while the proceeding lasted, the counsel to the Federal Government and the military did not make any formal appearance as they alleged they did not receive any invitation from the court. However, court records show they actually received invitations but ignored them. The Federal Government has however applied for stay of execution of the judgement pending its appeal at the Court of Appeal.

The Commission is also hampered by lack of capacity and resources. For example, it was reported that while its activities cover the entire country, the central investigative team has only one vehicle available.[1966] The NHRC is not adequately connected as it should be to the yearnings of the most vulnerable, like the indigenous people of Niger Delta, who can be described using Upendra Baxi words as the 'voices of suffering.'[1967] A close examination of the enabling Act of the Commission reveals that the human rights concerns of these groups were not adequately reflected in the design of the operations of the Commission. When the author visited the office of the NHRC in Abuja, in January 2011, he was informed by an officer of the Commission, who demanded not to be named, that the Commission has not done much in the area of 'Environment and Niger Delta.' To ensure adequate protection of the rights of the Niger Delta people there is a need for the Commission to pay much closer attention to the human rights impacts of oil exploration by the MNCs.[1968] It is disappointing to note that after 15 years existence the Commission can only boast of six zonal offices in a country with over 140 million people. For example, the one office located at Port Harcourt to cover the Niger Delta states of Akwa Ibom, Bayelsa, Cross River, Delta, Edo, and Rivers is grossly inadequate to take care of the environmental and human

---

[1965] Suit No.FHC/PH/CP/11/2000. See Chukwudi Akasike, 'FG to Pay N37bn Compensation for Odi's Invasion,' *The Punch*, 20 February, 2013, at www.punchng.com/news/fg-to-pay-n37bn-compensation-for-odis-invasion/ [accessed 13 May 2013].

[1966] Jennifer S. Aga, *op. cit.*, p.125.

[1967] Upendra Baxi, Voices of Suffering and the Future of Human Rights, 8 *Transn'l L. Contemp. Prob.* 15 (1998).

[1968] Obiora Chinedu Okafor and Shedrack C. Agbakwa, On Legalism, Popular Agency and "Voices of Suffering": The Nigerian National Human Rights Commission in Context, 24 *Human Rights Quarterly*, 662–720 at 693–694 (2002).

rights violations that daily occur in that region. This is in sharp contrast with Ghana's NHRC, which had over 120 offices outside its headquarters as far back as 1999, and was establishing an average of five offices a year as against less than one office a year for the Nigerian NHRC.[1969] By 2007, Ghana's NHRC had ten regional offices and 100 local offices in the 138 district capitals of the country apart from its headquarters.[1970] Even though the argument may be made that Ghana's NHRC was created years before that of Nigeria, the fact is that Nigeria's population (over 140 million people) far outweighs Ghana's (about 30 million people), and there are many more human rights abuses in Nigeria, particularly in the natural resources extraction communities, than Ghana. The few offices of the Commission in the Niger Delta region accounted for the few complaints been filed by the Niger Delta people on the abuse of their rights. It can therefore be argued that one of the major reasons why the impact of the NHRC has not been felt in the Niger Delta area is the lack of accessibility of the Commission's offices by the victims of the human rights abuses, who are mostly poor farmers and fishermen in the rural communities who can scarcely afford to transport themselves to the capital city to seek redress. This has led to the gap that exists between the commission and the voiceless people of the region.

6.3.3 NHRC: PROTECTING THE HUMAN RIGHTS OF THE NIGER DELTA PEOPLE

6.3.3.1 *Accessibility*

For the Commission to be able to address the human rights abuse suffered by the local inhabitants of the region from the activities of the oil MNCs, it must be changed from being an 'urban-based elitist-oriented institution'[1971] to a rural-based people-oriented institution, working closely with the local people of the region, who are the voices of the suffering. In the course of my visit to the Commission in January 2011 to see what the Commission is doing in the matter of environment and Niger Delta, it was a surprise to know that not much has been done in this area. A look at the Commission's annual statutory reports reveals this despite this matter being a thematic area of the Commission. For instance, out of the 1,061 complaints received in 2009, only 12 were on environmental issues (1.32%)[1972] (not limited to Niger Delta). Such a low level of complaints in

---

[1969] *Ibid*, p.707.
[1970] Anna Bossman, Acting Chairman Commission on Human Rights and Administrative Justice (CHRAJ) Ghana, *Promoting and Protecting Human Right, Ensuring Administrative Justice and Fighting Corruption in Ghana,* being a paper delivered at the Commonwealth Conference of National Human Rights Institutions, Malborough House, London, 26–28 February 2007, p.2.
[1971] Obiora Chinedu Okafor and Shedrack C. Agbakwa, *op. cit.,* p.716.
[1972] National Human Rights Commission Nigeria Annual Report (2009), at www.nigeriarights. gov.ng/images/articles/2009%20Annual%20Report.pdf [accessed 5 May 2010].

comparison with the magnitude and the frequency of human rights abuse in the
oil-producing communities in Nigeria may not be unconnected with the lack of
awareness about the Commission and its functions by the Niger Delta people,
and the problem of accessibility. According to an expert group convened by the
Commonwealth Secretariat in March 2001 to consider the establishment and
operation of national human rights institutions, they stated in their Report that
the complaint procedures of an National Human Rights Institutions (NHRI)
'should be simple, accessible, inexpensive and expeditious. Where necessary for
the protection of witnesses or victims, confidentiality should be guaranteed.'[1973]
The inaccessibility of NHRC offices and the cost to complainants of lodging
complaints are matters of grave concern which must be urgently addressed.
Efforts should also be made to establish an NHRC office in each of the local
governments that make up the Federation of Nigeria, particularly in each of
the local governments in all the states in the Niger Delta region, with a view to
enhancing early detection of violations of environmental and human rights in the
region by the oil MNCs, and allowing timely response in protecting these rights.

6.3.3.2 Monitoring Role

The Commission should be deeply involved in monitoring the impact on
minorities of development plans and programmes, including oil exploitation
activities, to ensure, *inter alia*, that such activities do not impact negatively
on them, nor violate their rights.[1974] The Nigerian NHRC has a moral duty to
protect the rights of minorities, including the Niger Delta people, even where
such a mandate has not specifically been incorporated in the enabling legislation
setting it up. This is because it is uniquely placed to address human rights issues,
coupled with its special interactive relationship with State institutions and non-
governmental organizations.[1975]

6.3.3.3 Independence

To further strengthen the power of the NHRC to protect the rights of the people
in the oil communities in Nigeria, there is a need to ensure its independence in
line with the Paris principles;[1976] to ensure its financial autonomy; to empower it

---

[1973] Commonwealth Secretariat Report, *National Human Rights Institutions: Best Practice*, Legal
and Constitutional Affairs Division, London, 2001, p.20.
[1974] UN Economic and Social Council, Commission on Human Rights, *Report of the International
Seminar on Cooperation for the Better Protection of the Rights of Minorities,* Fifty-eight Session,
Item 14(b) of the Provisional Agenda, E/CN.4/2002/92, 30 January 2002, para. 75.
[1975] Justice Emile Short, quoted in *Ibid*, para. 74.
[1976] National Institutions for the Promotion and Protection of Human Rights, adopted on 4 March
1994, G.A. Res. 48/134, UN GAOR, 48th Sess., UN Doc. A/Res/48/134 (1994). Principle 3(a)(iv)
of the Paris Principles requires the establishment of National Human Rights Commissions
for the purpose of '[d]rawing the attention of the government to situations in any part of the

to bring legal actions in court on behalf of victims of human rights abuse, such as the Niger Delta people; to confer on it exclusive power to compel the cooperation of any person, to secure any information or document, and to enter and search any premises.[1977] Happily, President Goodluck Jonathan, on 25 February 2011, signed into law the National Human Rights Commission (NHRC) (Amendment) Act 2010, which had been pending approval since 2005. This new law amends the NHRC Act of 1995 to provide among other things for independence in the conduct of the Commission's affairs,[1978] for the funds of the Commission becoming a direct charge on the Consolidated Revenue Fund of the Federation,[1979] for the establishment of a Human Rights Fund for the conduct of research on human rights issues,[1980] and the recognition and enforcement of the awards and recommendations of the Commission as decisions of the High Court.[1981] More importantly, section 5 of the principal Act was amended by introducing a new paragraph, which now empowers the Commission to 'deal with all matters relating to the promotion and protection of human rights guaranteed by the Constitution of the Federal Republic of Nigeria, the United Nations Charter and the Universal Declaration on Human Rights, the International Convention on Civil and Political Rights, the International Convention on the Elimination of

---

country where human rights are violated and making proposals to it for initiatives to put an end to such situations and, where necessary, expressing an opinion on the positions and reactions of the government.' Part II para. III of the Principle requires governments to 'ensure a stable mandate for the members of the national institution, without which there can be no real independence.' By article 26 of the African Charter on Human and Peoples' Rights, Nigeria is obligated to 'allow the establishment and improvement of appropriate national institutions entrusted with the promotion and protection of the rights and freedoms guaranteed by the present Charter.'

[1977] Obiora Chinedu Okafor and Shedrack C. Agbakwa, *op. cit.*, pp.717–718.

[1978] See section 7 of the Act which subjects the appointment of the Executive Secretary of the Commission by the President to Senate confirmation. Section 6(1) of the new Act now empowers the Commission to institute any civil action on any matter it deems fit in relation to the exercise of its functions and also gives it authority to become a party in a case. It further empowers the Commission to make determinations as to the damages or compensation payable in relation to any violation of human rights where it deems this necessary in the circumstances of the case. The Commission, by section 6(2) of the new Act, now has power to issue a warrant to compel the attendance of any person and compel the attendance of witnesses, to produce evidence. With the authority to summon suspects of human rights abuse, the Commission will now have access to information which is vital for the effective discharge of its mandate. This could serve as a powerful agent to regulate the activities of the MNCs and ensure they comply with international standards and practices on natural resource extraction.

[1979] See new section 12(2) of the Act. This is similar to the practice in Uganda where NHRC's administrative expenses are charged directly to the Consolidated Revenue Fund, that is, a special fund, to reflect their independence. The Constitution of the Federal Republic of Nigeria 1999 (as amended) provides in Section 80(1) that 'All revenues or other moneys raised or received by the Federation (not being revenues or other moneys payable under this Constitution or any Act of the National Assembly into any other public fund of the Federation established for a specific purpose) shall be paid into and form one Consolidated Revenue Fund of the Federation.' This will help to insulate the Commission from executive and legislative interference. See Obiora Chinedu Okafor and Shedrack C. Agbakwa, *op. cit.*, p.702.

[1980] *Ibid* section 15 of the Act

[1981] *Ibid* section 22 of the Act.

all forms of Racial Discrimination, the International Convention on Economic, Social and Cultural Rights, the Convention on the Elimination of all forms of Discrimination Against Women, the Convention on the Rights of the Child, the African Charter on Human and Peoples' Rights and other International and regional Instruments on human rights to which Nigeria is a party.'

It is salutary to note that the new Act has widened the scope of the Commission's power to cover the ICCPR, ICESCR, and other international human rights instruments previously not covered by the principal Act. The Committee on Economic, Social and Cultural Rights (CESR) adopted in December 1998 General Comment 10,[1982] which covers the role of NHRIs in the protection of human rights, including 'examining complaints alleging violations of applicable economic, social and cultural rights standards within the state.' It emphasized the need for NHRCs to give full attention to economic, social and cultural rights (ESCRs) in the discharge of its mandate. This provision will help to remove the confusion on whether or not the mandate of the commission extends to social, economic and cultural rights (some of the rights negatively impacted by the oil MNCs in the Niger Delta), which has often made the Commission decline issues that border on social, economic and cultural rights. This confusion can be inferred from Bukhari Bello's, (a former Executive Secretary of the Commission) opinion that social, economic and cultural rights are not justiciable until pronounced otherwise by the Supreme Court.[1983]

The Act specifically mandates the NHRC to carry out research on human rights. In pursuance of this objective, section 15(2) allows the commission to receive contributions to the 'Human Rights Fund' from national and multinational, public and private companies and institutions carrying on business in Nigeria. Despite the good intent of this provision, it is doubtful if the Commission can be fully objective in its reports on human rights and oil exploitation given the fact that the funds for the research come from the oil MNCs being monitored. This will no doubt make it difficult for the Commission to offer protection to victims of corporate human rights abuse in the Niger Delta 'who are unable to seek justice in

---

[1982] UN Economic and Social Council, *The Role of National Human Rights Institutions in the Protection of Economic, Social and Cultural Rights*, General Comment No. 10, 19 Sess., UN Doc. E/C.12/1998/25 (1998).

[1983] Bukhari Bello, *Welcome Statement by Bukhari Bello, Executive Secretary, National Human Rights Commission of Nigeria at the 5th Conference of African National Human Rights Institutions (ANHRIs)*, held in Abuja, Nigeria 8–10 November 2005, quoted in Raheem Kolawole Salman, *The Effectiveness of Nigerian National Human Rights Commission in Human Rights Protection*, being a thesis submitted in fulfillment of requirement for the degree of Doctor of Philosophy, Ahmad Ibrahim Kulliyyah of Laws, International Islamic University Malaysia, 2011. See also the Nigerian NHRC Annual Reports for the years 2002, 2003 and 2004 which stated the civil and political rights (justiciable rights) promoted and protected by the Commission. The focus of the Commission had always been on the promotion and protection of civil and political rights, as if it was created to respond only to violations of CPRs. It was not until 2006 that the Commission took a bold and courageous step to include economic, social and cultural rights like education, environment, labour, food and shelter, health etc as part of its thematic areas.

the over-crowded, time-consuming judicial system.'[1984] Nigeria greatly needs an effective, independent, transparent and accountable NHRC capable of ensuring that the oil MNCs are accountable for their human rights abuses and that the rights of the local inhabitants are adequately guaranteed. It is therefore suggested that this provision be reviewed. The Commission must be properly funded by the Government through an increase in its budgetary allocation and with the legislature exercising its power of budgetary oversight. It is hoped that this will help to improve the human rights situation in Nigeria, in particular, the egregious human rights abuses by the oil MNCs in the Niger Delta region.

6.3.3.4 Appropriate Policy

The NHRCs must develop proper policies within its institutional mandate. This is necessary in order to respond to human rights abuses that take place because of some policies adopted by the Nigerian Government on account of the functioning of the oil MNCs in the country, most especially when issues relating to the ESCRs are at stake.[1985] To further ensure the protection of the Niger Delta people, the NHRC may in accordance with section 5 of its mandate 'monitor and investigate all alleged cases of human rights violation in Nigeria' and undertake studies on all matters pertaining to human rights.' It may also require the oil MNCs to submit annual reports to its Governing Council on their efforts to ensure that their conduct conforms with the Constitution and human rights obligations that have been entered into by Nigerian Government.[1986] By so doing, they will be able to monitor the extent to which the oil MNCs have been able to ensure the protection of the rights of the local inhabitants at every stage of the oil exploration and production processes and help reduce the frequency of abuse of the human rights of the people by the corporations. Indeed, the adverse human rights impacts of business operations on the indigenous and marginalized people, including the Niger Delta people, call for increased attention on the corporate sector by the NHRCs as part of their mandate. The Nigerian NHRC can monitor and report on the human rights situation in the exploitation of natural resources; contribute to the reform of laws and administrative procedures that protect human rights in the corporate sector, such as environmental regulation or laws about bribery and corruption; and can hear and resolve individual grievances related to allegations of corporate sector human rights abuses.[1987]

[1984]   People's Watch-India (PW) 1, *The NHRC in India – Another Department of the Govt. of India?*, in Emerlynne Gil *et al.* (eds.), *op. cit.*, p.74.

[1985]   Raj C. Kumar, National Human Rights Institutions and Economic, Social, and Cultural Rights: Towards the Institutionalization and Developmentalization of Human Rights, 28 *Human Rights Quarterly* 755–779 at 777 (2006).

[1986]   Obiora Chinedu Okafor and Shedrack C. Agbakwa, *op. cit.*, p.719.

[1987]   Report from the Roundtable of National Human Rights Institutions on the Issue of Business and Human Rights, Copenhagen, 1–2 July 2008, hosted by the Danish Institute for Human Rights in Collaboration with the Swiss Federal Department of Foreign Affairs, at www.nhri.

6.3.3.5 Enforcement of NHRC Recommendations through the Court

The Nigerian NHRC could contribute to the protection of the human rights of the voiceless and environmentally susceptible people of the oil-producing communities in Nigeria by adopting a proactive approach, including raising awareness on the part of the Niger Delta communities and oil MNCs of the complaint mechanisms of the Commission, identifying and targeting incessant environmental and human rights abuses and violations, and conducting investigations of 'systemic complaints' using litigation and legal aid.[1988] The NHRC will be able to achieve a lot in the protection of the human rights of the Niger Delta people having been empowered by section 6 of the Act to bring action in court. This section could be used by the Commission to seek remedy as may be appropriate against the oil MNCs and the Government for the enforcement of its recommendations, as is done in Ghana,[1989] Uganda,[1990] India,[1991] and Kenya.[1992] Recommendations without means of implementation will only make the Commission 'a toothless tiger,' but what Nigeria needs now is a tiger-like human rights body with all of its teeth. It can also resort to settling the case through conciliation and mediation, and adoption of memoranda of understanding to reflect the agreement made, in order to reduce the case-load of the courts.

6.3.3.6 Advocacy Role

The NHRC also needs to do more in the area of encouraging the Government to implement the international human rights standards to which it is a party. NHRC has a role in seeking to persuade the Nigerian Government to introduce and implement legislation and regulations that meet international best practice in the prevention of human rights violations by oil MNCs and ensure the creation of laws that clearly identify the obligations of corporations to respect human rights.[1993] The Commission could help in advocating human rights impact assessment reports by oil MNCs to be a mandatory requirement in their annual

---

[1988] net/2009/report_from_the_round_table_of_national_human_rights_institutions_on_the_issue_of_business_and_human_rights.pdf [accessed 3 March 2010].

[1988] Danish Institute of Human Rights 2008, *Report from the round table on Business institutions and human rights,* in collaboration with the Swiss Federal Department of Foreign Affairs, Copenhagen, 1–2 July 2008; Med S.K Kaggwa, *Access to remedy for corporate human rights abuses,* at http://nhri.net/2010/Access%20to%20remedy%20for%20corporate%20human%20rights%20abuses-Uganda.pdf [accessed 4 March 2011].

[1989] See Art. 18(2) Ghana's Commission on Human Rights and Administrative Justice Act, 1993, Act 456.

[1990] See section 7(2) Uganda Human Rights Commission Act, 1997.

[1991] See section 13 of the Protection of Human Rights Act, 1993 [As amended by the Protection of Human Rights (Amendment) Act, 2006 – No. 43 of 2006].

[1992] See section 19 Kenya National Commission on Human Rights Act, 2002, No. 9 of 2002.

[1993] Asia Pacific Forum of National Human Rights Institutions (APF), *ACJ Report on Human Rights, Corporate Accountability and Government Responsibility,* Part 2: Supplementary Paper, the 13th Annual meeting of the APF, Kuala Lumpur, Malaysia, 27–31 July 2008.

reports; engaging with government and relevant Departments of State to promote a greater awareness of the impact of oil MNCs on the realisation of human rights; and utilising existing National Human Rights Institution (NHRI) tools, such as the human rights compliance assessment tools developed by the Danish Institute of Human Rights, to assist corporations comply with their human rights obligations.[1994]

6.3.3.7 *Effective Partnership*

To be able to protect the rights of the people in the oil-producing communities of the Niger Delta, the Nigerian NHRC must in accordance with the Paris Principles[1995] develop a strong partnership with the civil society and NGOs working in the area of the environmental and human rights. This kind of relationship will not only help to enhance the legitimacy and credibility of the NHRC, but reciprocally, it will create another line of accountability that enables civil society to see if the NHRC is executing its mandate effectively and efficiently.[1996] The NHRC occupies a unique position in the society which gives them a distinctive role in the society – between the government on one hand, and civil society and NGOs, on the other hand.[1997]

National Human Rights Institutions, including the Nigerian NHRC, are in a good position to deal with 'the challenges raised under the framework developed by the [Special Representative of the Secretary-General] SRSG ['Protect, Respect and Remedy'] and to facilitate dialogue and collaboration among key stakeholders from business, Government and civil society. They can, amongst other things, engage directly with business enterprises to promote good human rights practices; build the capacity of Government departments and civil society organizations on issues of business and human rights; convene and facilitate human rights dialogue between businesses, civil society and Government; handle human rights complaints relating to businesses; monitor the human rights practices of business enterprises; and provide information and advice to victims about available grievance resolution mechanisms.'[1998] Its flexible procedures, ability to investigate and adjudicate complaints at minimal costs (if any at all) and its educational and preventive orientation, commend it to the poor, the marginalised and the

---

[1994] *Ibid.* Danish Institute for Human Rights established a Human Rights and Business Project and this provides an example for the types of activities that can be carried out by NHRC in Nigeria.

[1995] Paris Principle, *op. cit.* states in para. 3(g) that: 'In view of the fundamental role played by the non-governmental organizations in expanding the work of the national institutions, develop relations with the non-governmental organizations devoted to promoting and protecting human rights, to economic and social development, to combating racism, to protecting particularly vulnerable groups (especially children, migrant workers, refugees, physically and mentally disabled persons) or to specialized areas.'

[1996] Anne Smith, The Unique Position of National Human Rights Institutions: A Mixed Blessings?, 28 *Human Rights Quarterly*, 904–946 at 945 (2006).

[1997] Anne Smith, *Ibid*, p.905.

[1998] Med S.K Kaggwa, *op. cit.*

oppressed (such as the Niger Delta people) as a credible and effective substitute
to the regular courts (with their highly technical and expensive procedures).[1999]
In an interview with R.K. Salman, a human rights expert, on his views regarding
what the NHRC could do to improve the human rights situation in the Niger Delta
region, he stated that: 'the NHRC, among others, should continue to intervene
between the Niger Delta people and the MNCs to ensure adequate protection of
their rights; should visit the region from time to time to assess the level of human
rights violations with a view to ensuring that the Government perform its role of
protecting them; and it should continue to sensitise the Niger Delta people of their
rights so that they will know how to enforce these rights when violated or about
to be violated by the MNCs and the Government. The people should be sensitised
of the dangers in resorting to violence in settling the conflicts in the region.'[2000]
If the NHRC is strengthened in line with the above recommendations, it will
be able to prevent or reduce the frequency of the incidences of abuse of human
rights not only by the Government but also by other non-state actors like the oil
MNCs operating in the Niger Delta. In other words, to become an effective means
of promoting and protecting the human rights of the people, which is the main,
core and exclusive mandate of any Human Rights Commission. With the huge
success it has recorded in the protection of the rights of prisoners and detainees,
the NHRC has the potential of recording similar or even greater success in the
field of human rights and environment, in particular, as it affects the Niger Delta
people.

6.4 THE ROLE OF NGOs IN THE PROTECTION OF THE RIGHTS OF THE NIGER DELTA PEOPLE

6.4.1 INTRODUCTION

There has been a proliferation of civil society groups, such as environmental and
human rights NGOs in Nigeria, who are deeply concerned with the Niger Delta
struggle. Civil society organizations (CSO) have been defined as the 'vast array of
public-oriented associations that are not formal parts of the governing institutions
of the State: everything from community associations to religious institutions,
trade unions, [and] non-governmental organizations... [operating] to promote
the interests and perspectives of a particular sector of society, but not all issues for
all sectors...'[2001] Environmental and human rights NGOs form an important part
of civil society. Philippe Schmitter, sees NGOs as 'intermediary organizations ...
that lie between the primary units of society – individuals, families, clans, ethnic

---

[1999]   Obiora Chinedu Okafor and Shedrack C. Agbakwa, *op. cit.*, p.718.
[2000]   Interview with Dr. R.K. Salman, human rights expert on 16 January 2011 in Lagos, Nigeria.
[2001]   Anthony Wanis-St. John and Darren Kew, Civil Society and Peace Negotiations: Confronting
      Exclusion, 13 *International Negotiation*, 11–36 at 15 (2008).

groups of various kinds, village units – and the ruling collective institutions and agencies of the society.'[2002] Civil society can contribute a great deal in the regulation of corporations, and the promotion of the rights of the Niger Delta people. Civil society is 'independent of both Government and business and is in fact too diverse to be susceptible to capture by business ... suffers the ill effects of corporate irresponsibility, it is likely to continue to have the impetus to protect itself from corporate excesses as well as seek the effective enforcement of laws and regulatory policies.'[2003]

The emergence of a grass-roots environmental justice movement in the Niger Delta has been attributed to oil extraction-induced environmental injustice, marginalization, neglect, frustration and selective victimization of the Niger Delta region, all of which has largely contributed to the violation of fundamental human rights, including environmental rights, of the local inhabitants.[2004] Three types of environmental and civil rights groups that have played key roles as rights advocates and monitors in the Niger Delta struggle have been identified: those based in the Niger Delta such as Environmental Rights Action, Social Action, Niger Delta Human and Environmental Rescue Organization, Oil Watch Group, Ijaw Council for Human Rights; national civil rights and pro-democracy organizations that have been active on Niger Delta issues, such as Ethnic Minorities Rights Organization of Nigeria, Civil Liberties Organization, Social and Economic Rights Action Center (SERAC), Socio-Economic Rights and Accountability Project (SERAP), Campaign for Democracy, Constitutional Rights Projects; and international civil society groups, including Human Rights Watch, World Council of Churches, Sierra Club, Greenpeace, Project Underground and Amnesty International.[2005] Other notable ethnic groups in the region include the Movement for the Survival of the Ogoni People (MOSOP), which may be seen as the harbinger of civil society involvement in the region,[2006] Movement for the Survival of Ijaw Ethnic Nationality (MOSIEN), Community Rights Initiative (CORI), Niger Delta Women for Justice (NDWJ), Chiccoco Movement, Ijaw National Congress and Egbema National Congress.

[2002] Quoted in Claude E. Welch, Jr. (1995), *Protecting Human Rights in Africa: Strategies and Roles of Nongovernmental Organizations,* University of Pennsylvania Press, Philadelphia, p.44.

[2003] Evaristus Oshionebo (2009), *Regulating Transnational Corporations in Domestic and International Regimes: An African Case Study,* University of Toronto Press, Toronto, Buffalo, London, p.214.

[2004] Tunde Agboola and Moruf Alabi, "Political Economy of Petroleum Resource Development, Environmental Injustice and Selective Victimization: A Case Study of the Niger Delta Region of Nigeria", in Julian Agyeman *et al.* (2003), *Just Sustainabilities in an Unequal World,* Earthscan Publications Ltd., London, pp.282–283.

[2005] See Eghosa E. Osaghae, Social Movements and Rights Claims: The Case of Action Groups in the Niger Delta of Nigeria, 19 *Voluntas* 189–210 at 205 (2008); Augustine Ikelegbe, Civil Society, Oil and Conflict in the Niger Delta Region of Nigeria: Ramifications of Civil Society for a Regional Resource Struggle, *J. of Modern African Studies* 39(3) 437–469 at 450 (2001).

[2006] Augustine Ikelegbe, *Ibid*, 443.

These movements and rights organizations have continued to help in
internationalizing the Niger Delta struggle such that the whole world is now
aware of the environmental injustice taking place in the region. They were
able to achieve a lot in this regard through advocacy campaigns regarding the
environmental and human rights conditions in the region, peaceful protests and
demonstrations, supporting litigation against companies accused of involvement
in human rights violations, issuing reports highlighting complicity of MNCs in
human rights abuses and publication of facts and figures on perceived injustices.
It is sad to note that, since around 2005, the pattern of unarmed peaceful protest
and demonstrations used by the Civil Society groups against the unwholesome
activities of the MNCs operating in the Niger Delta region has shifted to a violent
one by the armed militant groups, like the Movement for the Emancipation of
the Niger Delta (MEND), Egbesu Boys, the Niger Delta People's Volunteer Force
(NDPVF), and others, to the extent that the whole region has become highly
militarised. This has led to a spate of kidnappings and hostage taking, bombings,
oil-facility sabotage, destruction of properties and even killings. The rise of
groups like the MEND is said to be traceable to the lack of opportunities for
peaceful opposition movements and the failure of the Government and the MNCs
in ensuring that the Niger Delta people enjoy the benefits of oil production.[2007]
Suffice it to say that the adoption of armed struggle can never be the best means of
forcing the MNCs and the government to behave in a desired manner. This action
has consistently been condemned by the various human rights and environmental
groups, including ERA/Friends of the Earth Nigeria, as it harms not only the
environment but also the people.

6.4.2 REGULATING THE OIL MNCs IN THE NIGER
DELTA: THE ROLES OF THE NGOs

6.4.2.1 NGOs as Watchdog and Whistle-Blower

NGOs can help a lot in ensuring that corporations comply with human rights
standards in their operations, thus helping to fill the regulatory gap that exists
under international law. They also ensure that governmental agencies abide
by their own rules and regulations. This they can do in several ways including
causing damage to corporate reputation, encouraging shareholders to act to
ensure that companies comply with human rights standards, and dialogue
and partnership with companies. The environmental and human rights NGOs
in Nigeria are daily engaging the oil MNCs operating in the Niger Delta over

---

[2007]   Nnimmo Bassey, *The Oil Industry and Human Rights in the Niger Delta*, being his Testimony
before the United States Senate Judiciary Subcommittee on Human Rights and the
Law, 24 September 2008, at www.earthrights.org/sites/default/files/documents/Nnimo-
testimony-9-24-08.pdf [accessed 23 November 2009].

their irresponsible behaviour in the region, and uncovering the failures of the Government in fulfilling its international commitments, thus increasing the prospect of Government and MNCs accountability. Following the execution of Ken Saro-Wiwa and other eight Ogonis in 1995 by Abacha's Government, there was an international outcry against Shell, by NGOs, Civil Society, and other well-meaning individuals, for not speaking out against the decision of the Government to execute the environmentalists. This public outcry of human rights complicity, coupled with the international outcry that greeted the company's decision to jettison the Brent Spar oil platform in the deep ocean, was extremely damaging to what was then one of the most respected companies in the world.[2008] This consequently led to dialogue between Shell and its shareholders on how best to guard against the re-occurrences. Following this discussion, Shell revised its Statement of General Business Principles to include respect for the human rights of employees and 'support for fundamental human rights in line with the legitimate role of business.'[2009] Even though it does not seem that Shell has significantly altered its conduct, its explicit adoption of human rights principles shows that the company realizes that it is no longer 'business as usual', and this also provides the basis upon which the company can be held accountable by the public in the future.[2010]

6.4.2.2 NGOs as Experts and Lobbyists

Environmental and human rights NGOs campaigns can and do have effects on both national and international law and policies. Based on their specialized knowledge, the NGOs are more and more successful in helping to change, or re-orient, policies taken by State decision-makers on environmental and social justice issues. Since international environmental matters are highly complex, decision-makers often turn to NGOs to use their well-established and wide experience, expertise and capacity to help them in understanding the nature of the problems and the implications of various policy alternatives.[2011] Sometimes, civil society organisations (CSOs) do lobby parliamentarians, testify before law-makers and engage in letter-writing campaigns to the executives to apply human rights obligations to corporations. At the regional and international forums, the NGOs are also involved in lobbying at international conferences where new rule-making on environmental issues are agreed and where final trades-off

---

[2008] Rory Sullivan, NGO Influence on the Human Rights Performance of Companies, 24(3) *Netherlands Quarterly of Human Rights*, 405–432 at 415 (2006).

[2009] Royal Dutch/Shell, *Revised Statement of General Business Principles*, March 1997, Royal Dutch/Shell, The Hague, 1997; Rory Sullivan, *Ibid.*

[2010] Evaristus Oshionebo (2009), *Regulating Transnational Corporations in Domestic and International Regimes: An African Case Study, op. cit.*, p.100.

[2011] M. Betsill and Elisabeth Corell, NGO Influence in International Environmental Negotiations: A Framework for Analysis, 1(4) *Global Environmental Politics*, 65–85 at 74 (2001).

are made.[2012] The recently passed Freedom of Information (FOI) Act in Nigeria
that guarantees the right of access of individuals to information held by public
institutions would not have been possible but for an NGO called Media Rights
Agenda (MRA), alongside the Civil Liberties Organisation (CLO) and the Nigeria
Union of Journalists (NUJ) who sponsored a private bill in 1993 before the
National Assembly.

6.4.2.3 Public Awareness of Environmental Issues

Civil society and NGOs in Nigeria have contributed largely to the bringing of
the Niger Delta issue to global attention. The late Ken Saro-Wiwa was able to use
his writings, and participation at an international event through the Movement
for the Survival of the Ogoni People (MOSOP), as an opportunity to bring to
world attention the unholy alliance between the Nigerian Government and oil
MNCs operating in the Niger Delta, to seek support from International Non-
governmental Organizations (INGOs) concerned with indigenous rights as well
as from other world bodies and sympathetic Governments in support of the cause.
This global campaign, coupled with the non-violent protest of MOSOP placed
the Nigerian Government and Shell under serious pressure for their roles in the
human rights violations and environmental degradation of Ogoniland, which
eventually forced Shell to stop its operations in the community in 1993.[2013] As
noted by the late Wangari Maathai, leader of the Kenyan Green Belt Movement:
... if Governments lack political will to apply laws, regulations and agreements
to which they have subscribed, only an informed and involved community can
stand for the environment and demand development that is sustainable ...[2014]

INGOs such as Human Rights Watch, Amnesty International, Greenpeace,
Platform Forum have also contributed a lot in exposing the high rate of corruption
and other venal acts that exist in some States and local government in the Niger
Delta region.[2015] When the host State refuses to heed the calls for change made
by local NGOs, the latter often engage the INGOs which then exert pressure that

---

[2012] Farhana Yamin, NGOs and International Environmental Law: A Critical Evaluation of their
Roles and Responsibilities, 10(2) RECIEL, 149–162 at 156–157 (2001).

[2013] Cyril Obi and Siri Aas Rustad, "Introduction: Petro-violence in the Niger Delta- the Complex
Politics of an Insurgency", in Cyril Obi and Siri Aas Rustad (eds), Oil and Insurgency in the
Niger Delta: Managing the Complex Politics of Petro-violence, op. cit., p.8.

[2014] Wangari Maathai, being a speech delivered to the World Bank in 1993, quoted in Riva Krut,
Globalization and Civil Society: NGO Influence in International Decision-Making, United
Nations Research Institute for Social Development (UNRISD) Discussion Paper No. 83, April
1997, p.38, at www.unrisd.org/ (accessed 3 March 2010).

[2015] See the Human Rights Watch (2007), Chop Fine; The Human Rights Impact of Local
Government Corruption and Mismanagement in Rivers State, Nigeria, op. cit.; Platform Report
(2011), 'Counting the Cost: Corporations and Human Rights Abuses in the Niger Delta,' at http://
platformlondon.org/nigeria/Counting_the_Cost.pdf. [accessed 11 November 2011], which
implicates Shell concerning cases of serious violence in the Niger Delta region from 2000 to
2010.

'curves around local State indifference and repression to put foreign pressure on local policy elites. Thus international contacts amplify voices to which domestic Governments are deaf, while the local work of target country activists legitimizes the efforts of activists abroad.'[2016] These INGOs, with others like the World Wildlife Fund-UK, the International Union for the Conservation of Nature (World Conservation Union), have helped to publicize the ecological damage and human rights violations that have characterized the entire region. They have also continued to put pressure on the Nigerian Government at all levels to address the situation through changes in existing environmental regulatory policies as well as resource distribution formulas, and have called on international organizations and the developed countries, like the U.S., the UK, and some European countries that are home to many of the MNCs, to influence them to change their pollution-contributing practices in the region.[2017]

6.4.2.4 NGOs as Enforcers

The failure of Government to hold the non-State actors such as corporations to account for their actions resulting in environmental damage, and the inability of the Government to take decisions that could help to protect the citizens, has led to the increase in the use of litigation by the NGOs and civil society at both the domestic and international levels. Around the world, environmental and human rights NGOs, acting as the legal guardians of human rights and environmental issues, have taken to the use of court proceedings in a pro-active manner to draw the attention of the public to specific instances of corporate abuse of the environment and/or social injustices.[2018] For example, the *Minors Oposa case* was brought by a group of children, including Antonio Oposa, a renowned environmental activist, in conjunction with the Philippine Ecological Network, Inc., an NGO, to stop the destruction of the rain forests in Philippine, raising questions of intergenerational responsibility. In Nigeria, the case of *SERAC v. Nigeria*,[2019] brought before the African Commission was filed by SERAC, an NGO, and the US-based Center for Economic and Social Rights, on behalf of the Ogoni people, for the violation of their social and economic rights as a result of the oil exploration activities of MNCs in the Niger Delta region. By using the African Commission as a platform to underscore the environmental and human rights

---

[2016]   Margaret Keck and Kathryn Sikkink (1998), *Activists Beyond Borders: Advocacy Networks in International Politics* Cornell University Press, Ithaca, NY, quoted in David Naguib Pellow, "Politics by Other Greens: The Importance of Transnational Environmental Justice Movement Networks", in JoAnn Carmin and Julian Agyeman (eds) (2011), *Environmental Inequalities Beyond Borders: Local Perspectives on Global Injustices*, MIT Press, Cambridge, p.252.

[2017]   Max Stephenson Jr. and Lisa A. Schweitzer, Learning from the Quest for Environmental Justice in the Niger Delta, in JoAnn Carmin and Julian Agyeman (eds) (2011), *Ibid*, pp.60–61.

[2018]   Farhana Yamin, NGOs and International Environmental Law: A Critical Evaluation of their Roles and Responsibilities, *op. cit.*, pp.159–160.

[2019]   *Supra.*

impacts of those oil exploitation activities, the African Commission has been
sensitized by these NGOs toward the goal of positively affecting governmental
action in Nigeria.[2020]

The efforts of these INGOs and NGOs, in addition to community protests,
coupled with the advent of a civilian regime have created some changes in the
programmes and attitudes of the MNCs, particularly in the area of consultation
with the local communities, and have also resulted in some efforts by the State
to address corrupt practices, and the arrogance and environmental recklessness
of the MNCs.[2021] Summing up the impact that civil society in Nigeria has had on
corporate responsibility and accountability in the extractive sector, Augustine
Ikelegbe has stated that:

> "Civil Society ... has constituted in the last few years, a solid formation of intense
> ethnic and regional resistance against perceived corporate and state abuses in res-
> pect of the costs and benefits of oil production and the distribution and utilisation
> of oil revenues. Civil society has re-constructed the old agitation of oil producing
> communities by broadening [their] grievances and demands, raising mobilisation
> and participation, intensifying the conflict, redirecting it to political objectives, and
> turning it into a civil, environmental and human rights issue. As a result, the Niger
> Delta conflict has become a broad, participatory, highly mobilised and coordinated
> platform of civil groups in a struggle for self-determination, equity, civil rights, and
> the reformation and restructuring of the Nigerian state and social responsibility of
> MNOCs ... The civil society group activities have heightened awareness and con-
> sciousness, enhanced education, information and interest about the Niger Delta
> problem and compelled the entrance of the problem into the national agenda..."[2022]

The activities of the civil groups in the Niger Delta has not only made the State
'more concerned today about environmental issues, [about] MNC relations
with host communities and [about] the development of the region,' it has also
led to consistent calls by the Government on the MNCs to 'negotiate and reach
memoranda of understanding with host communities, honour agreements, and
be more responsive to Niger Delta problems.'[2023] It has also led to some positive
changes to the policies and actions of the Government to matters concerning the
development and well-being of the people in the region. For example, the creation
of the Oil Mineral Producing Areas Development Commission (OMPADEC)
(now defunct) in 1992 and the eventual setting up of the NDDC in 2000 by the
government to accelerate the development of the region. Also important is the

---

[2020] Obiora Chinedu Okafor, Modest Harvests: On the Significant (But Limited) Impact of Human
Rights NGOs on Legislature and Executive in Nigeria, 48(1) *Journal of African Law*, 23–49 at
44 (2004).
[2021] Max Stephenson Jr. and Lisa A. Schweitzer, *op. cit.*, pp.61–62.
[2022] Augustine Ikelegbe, Civil Society, Oil and Conflict in the Niger Delta Region of Nigeria:
Ramifications of Civil Society for a Regional Resource Struggle, *op. cit.*, pp.464–465.
[2023] *Ibid*, pp.464, 460.

steep rise in the special share of oil revenues allocated to the oil-producing States from 1.5% to 3% in 1992, and again to 13% in 1999 (though still poor), can be partly attributed to the efforts of the civil society and NGOs in Nigeria.[2024]

Also, the activities of civil society in the Niger Delta, in addition to other factors, appear to have impacted tremendously on the Nigerian judiciary. Unlike what existed prior to the Ogoni crisis, when Nigerian courts lacked the necessary courage to give a decision against the MNCs or Government even in the face of widespread allegations of environmental damage,[2025] the situation now appears to be improving. The Ogoni crisis has led to a lot of positive changes, particularly regarding the attitudes of Nigerian judges to oil-related litigation, with more concern being shown to the plight of the oil-producing communities. For example, in *Shell v. Isaiah*,[2026] the court awarded compensation for environmental damage in the sum of N22 million naira. Likewise, it awarded about N245 million naira in favour of the plaintiffs in *Edamkue & Ors v. Shell*;[2027] and in the *Ijaw Aborigines* case ordered Shell to pay US$1.5 billion to local communities affected by oil pollution;[2028] and in *Gbemre v. Shell*,[2029] for the first time, the court declared gas flaring illegal.[2030]

Yet, despite the significant efforts the NGOs have made in promoting the cause of the Niger Delta people, particularly those touching on human rights, they have not been able to participate effectively in the promotion of corporate accountability and regulatory effectiveness in Nigeria. The reasons for this include lack of expertise; lack of access to corporate information; poor funding; divergent interests and lack of cooperation among the grassroots NGOs and ethnic community associations; the proliferation of NGOs, especially in the Niger Delta oil rich region, with no good intention to pursue social goals but operating for personal enrichment; the emergence of youth armies and ethnic militias who now resort to violence and other illegal/destructive methods in turning civil society into 'uncivil' society in the name of fighting for justice; internal conflicts and maladministration in some NGOs; the urban-centric nature of civil society groups who are not able to integrate the local communities where their services are most needed; poor networking ability; and the absence of a right of private

---

[2024] Obiora Chinedu Okafor, Modest Harvests: On the Significant (But Limited) Impact of Human Rights NGOs on Legislature and Executive in Nigeria, *op. cit.*, p.37.

[2025] Injunctions are rarely granted against oil MNCs, presumably because of the perceived importance of oil to the Nigerian economy. Even where damages are awarded, they are paltry. See the discussion in Chapter Three above.

[2026] (1997)6 NWLR (pt. 508)236.

[2027] Suit No. FHC/PH/84 & 85/94 (Unreported), judgment dated 28 June 1999.

[2028] *Shell v. Ijaw Aborigines of Bayelsa State, Supra.*

[2029] *Supra.*

[2030] Evaristus Oshionebo (2009), *Regulating Transnational Corporations in Domestic and International Regimes: An African Case Study, op. cit.*, p.101.

enforcement of regulatory laws,[2031] etc. In an interview with Chima Williams[2032] of Environmental Rights Action and Friends of the Earth Nigeria during the fieldwork carried out during the course of this reearch, Williams analysed some of the challenges facing the NGOs in effectively fulfilling their mandates. Most importantly, he stressed that the problem of funding often leads to derailment of NGOs from fulfilling their mandate to the people, as the NGOs have to satisfy the interests of their funders, which sometimes may not be in tandem with the vision of the NGO. He also mentioned the problem of the insecurity of civil society groups, particularly in the hands of an autocratic Government when such NGO is perceived to be working against the economic interest of the Government in the oil industry. He cited the recent gruesome murder of Chidi Nwosu, Human Rights Activist and founder of Human Rights and Justice Foundation, in Abia State on 29 December 2010, believed to be politically motivated.

6.4.3 STRENGTHENING THE ENVIRONMENTAL AND HUMAN RIGHTS NGOs FOR EFFECTIVE PERFORMANCE

In the absence of mandatory international legal instruments to rein in the activities of the MNCs and so protect the rights of the citizens where they operate, the strengthening of NGOs will go a long way in monitoring the MNCs and Government against actions and policies that are capable of violating the human rights of the people. In line with Agenda 21, Chapter 27, the United Nations and other intergovernmental organizations and forums, bilateral programmes and the private sector, as appropriate, must continue to provide increased financial and administrative support to the NGOs and provide them with necessary training at the international and regional levels to enhance their partnership role in programme design and implementation. Agenda 21 also calls on Governments to 'promulgate or strengthen, subject to country-specific conditions, any legislative measures necessary to enable the establishment by non-governmental organizations of consultative groups, and to ensure the right of non-governmental organizations to protect the public interest through legal action.'[2033] Also, the 2000 Malmö Ministerial Declaration, adopted at the First Global Ministerial Environment Forum, stressed the important role been played by civil society 'in bringing emerging environmental issues to the attention of policy makers, raising

---

[2031] *Ibid*, pp.119–124; Okechukwu Ibeanu, *Civil Society and Conflict Management in the Niger Delta: Scoping Gaps for Policy and Advocacy*, CLEEN Foundation Monograph Series, No. 2, August 2006, pp.45–46.
[2032] Interview with Chima Williams, ERA's Head of Legal Resources, conducted on 10 January 2011 at the head office of ERA, in Uselu, Benin City, Nigeria.
[2033] Agenda 21, Chapter 27 (12 & 13), at www.un.org/esa/sustdev/documents/agenda21/english/Agenda21.pdf [accessed 23 November 2009].

public awareness, promoting innovative ideas and approaches, and promoting transparency as well as non-corrupt activities in environmental decision-making.'[2034] It declared in para. 16 that '[t]he role of civil society at all levels should be strengthened through freedom of access to environmental information to all, broad participation in environmental decision-making, as well as access to justice on environmental issues.'

There is a need to empower the civil society groups. This could take the form of the inclusion of empowerment programmes in those Nigerian regulatory instruments and policies which will allow the inclusion of civil society groups and individuals in the formulation, enforcement and monitoring of laws and policies concerning environmental matters. The involvement of civil society groups, particularly those with expertise in the specific area of the regulations, will significantly help to improve the democratic character of decision making in environmental matters, enhance the capacity and effectiveness of the regulatory agencies, and lessen the regulatory burdens placed on these agencies.[2035] The Nigerian Freedom of Information Act 2011 is a step in the right direction as it will assist civil society in overcoming the barrier of accessing corporate and governmental information relating to resource extraction. The NGOs are now better positioned to monitor closely the income from the extractive industry, and how it is spent for the benefit of citizens and the environment.

There is also a need for constant training to strengthen the capacity of the NGOs and staff. Where NGO capacity is weak and ill-trained, it becomes difficult for it to function effectively, and may end up 'taking instructions' from the MNCs that it is supposed to regulate. NGOs in Nigeria have a great role to play in ensuring that the regulatory agencies for environment and the oil industry live up to expectations in regulating the MNCs. With proper funding and adequate support from international NGOs, it is possible for them to 'keep up with every scientific development relevant to the regulations that they try to follow.'[2036] There is also a need for continued cooperation between the local NGOs and the INGOs as the latter rely on the local NGOs for first-hand information on local issues which connect to global. Cooperation is also necessary in view of the fact that most NGOs rely on the INGOs for funds and capacity building. As discussed above, the international awareness of Ogoni's plight in the hands of Shell and other oil MNCs was made possible owing largely to the cooperation between the Movement for the Survival of Ogoni People (MOSOP) members and the INGOs. This cooperation is significant in that it increases the pressures on the MNCs

---

[2034]   Malmö Ministerial Declaration, First Global Ministerial Environment Forum- Sixth Special Session of the Governing Council of the United Nations Environment Programme, Fifth plenary meeting, 31 May 2000, Para. 15, at www.unep.org/malmo/malmo_ministerial.htm [accessed 23 November 2009].

[2035]   Evaristus Oshionebo (2009), *Regulating Transnational Corporations in Domestic and International Regimes: An African Case Study, op. cit.*, p.217.

[2036]   Thomas O. McGarity, 'Regulation and Litigation: Complementary Tools for Environmental Protection,' 30(2) *Columbia Journal of Environmental Law* 371–402 at 389 (2005).

to behave, and also helps in the transformation of local issues into international
problems, thus broadening the avenues for resolving the problem, including
exerting international pressure on both the oil MNCs and the Government.[2037]

We may note here also that the rules of *locus standi*, that have been liberalized
by FREP Rules 2009, will help NGOs to perform effectively their role of protecting
the people and the environment from policies and actions that could negatively
affect them.

The international and local NGOs have thus been contributing to the
protection of the local inhabitants of the Niger Delta with regard to environmental
and human rights issues. It was largely as a result of their efforts that the
international initiatives on the regulation of MNCs discussed in Chapter Four of
this Book emerged.

6.5 THE AFRICAN COMMISSION, AFRICAN COURT ON HUMAN AND PEOPLES' RIGHTS, AFRICAN COURT OF JUSTICE AND THE ENVIRONMENT: THE CASE OF THE NIGER DELTA PEOPLE IN NIGERIA

6.5.1 INTRODUCTION

This sub-section examines the role the regional African systems could play in the
protection of human rights of the local communities of the Niger Delta people.
Is there a solution in the African Charter? What lessons can the national courts
learn from the decisions of the African Commission and the African Court that
could assist in the regulation of the activities of the MNCs thereby guaranteeing
the protection of the rights of the people? These are some of the questions that will
be examined under this heading.

The African Charter on Human and People's Rights was adopted by the
African Heads of States and Government during their 18th ordinary Assembly
in Nairobi, Kenya in June 1981. The Charter became part of Nigerian law by
virtue of the African Charter on Human and Peoples' Rights (Application and
Enforcement) Act[2038] of 1983. Even though the Organization of African Unity
(OAU), within which the Charter is designed to function, had been replaced by the
African Union (AU), the new AU recognises the African Charter as the primary
instrument for the protection and promotion of human rights in Africa.[2039] One

---

2037   Evaristus Oshionebo, *op cit.*, pp.214–215.
2038   Chapter A9 Laws of Federation of Nigeria (LFN) 2004.
2039   John C. Mubangizi, Some reflections on recent and current trends in the promotion and
        protection of human rights in Africa: The pains and the gains, 6 *African Human Rights Law
        Journal*, pp.146–165 at 147 (2006). See Art. 3(h) of the Constitutive Act of the AU.

unique attribute of the Charter is that it does not only provide for the traditional individual civil and political rights, it further seeks to promote economic, social and cultural rights and the so-called third generation rights, thus making it the first international human rights convention to guarantee all the categories of human rights in one document.[2040] The enumerated and protected socio-economic rights in the Charter include equitable and satisfactory conditions of work,[2041] right to health,[2042] right to education,[2043] protection of the family,[2044] right to self-determination,[2045] right to dispose of wealth and natural resources,[2046] right to economic, social and cultural development,[2047] right to peace,[2048] and right to a satisfactory and favourable environment.[2049] The African Commission on Human and Peoples' Rights (Commission) is a quasi-judicial body established within the AU, by virtue of Article 30 of the Charter, to promote human and peoples' rights and ensure their protection. Article 24 of the Charter specifically provides: 'All peoples shall have the right to a general satisfactory environment favourable to their development.'

The Commission has promotional and protective functions. The promotional mandate of the African Commission includes, *inter alia*, human rights education, sensitization, and raising awareness of the African Charter. The Commission exercises its protective mandate, through its decisions or recommendations following the consideration of communications or complaints brought before it. It has continued to use the communication procedure to progressively and generously interpret the African Charter, resulting in a rich jurisprudence.[2050]

[2040]   *Ibid*, p. 148.
[2041]   Art. 15.
[2042]   Art. 16.
[2043]   Art. 17.
[2044]   Art. 18.
[2045]   Art. 20.
[2046]   Art. 21.
[2047]   Art. 22.
[2048]   Art. 23.
[2049]   Art. 24.
[2050]   Japhet Biegon and Magnus Killander, Human rights developments in the African Union during 2009, 10 *African Human Rights Law Journal*, pp.212–232 at 224 (2010). The Commission is empowered, *inter alia*, to receive and consider communications. Communications may be submitted by one State claiming that another State party to the Charter has violated one or more of the provisions in the Charter. It may involve communications from individuals and organisations alleging that a State party to the Charter has violated one or more of the rights guaranteed in the Charter. Upon the receipt of a communication, it is registered under a file number in the Commission's Official Register of Communications kept at the Secretariat of the Commission. The Secretariat acknowledges receipt of the letter of complaint. See The African Commission on Human and Peoples' Rights Information Sheet No. 3, at www1.umn. edu/humanrts/africa/achpr-infosheet3.html [accessed 13 May 2013].

With the incorporation of the Charter as part of Nigerian law, it has become part of Nigerian legal system with the full force of law and enforcement machinery.[2051] Section 1 of the Act provides that:

> "As from the commencement of this Act, the provisions of the African Charter on Human and Peoples' Rights which are set out in the Schedule to the Act shall, subject as thereunder provided have force of law in Nigeria and shall be given full recognition and effect and be applied by all authorities and persons exercising legislative, executive or judicial powers in Nigeria."

The import of the ratification of the Charter is that it is now possible to canvass alleged violations of the Charter before Nigerian courts, including the right to a general satisfactory environment

6.5.2 STATUS OF THE AFRICAN CHARTER ACT *VIS-À-VIS* THE NIGERIAN CONSTITUTION

Whether, and to what extent, a domestic court will apply international human rights treaties depends on whether domestic law adopts a monist (international law automatically forms part of domestic law) or a dualist (international law needs to be domesticated) approach concerning its relationship with the international law.[2052] Nigeria adopts a dualist approach with respect to the domestic effect of international treaties. This means that international treaties in Nigeria are not self-executing, but rather, they must be incorporated into domestic legislation to have the force of law.[2053] As discussed earlier in this work, the non-justiciability of the Chapter II provisions as a result of section 6(6)(c) of the Constitution has led to the refusal of the Nigerian courts to adjudicate directly on any of its provisions, except where they are incorporated in legislative or executive action.[2054] However, the Charter goes beyond civil and political rights to include socio-economic, cultural and solidarity rights. While it can be argued that the 'African Charter generally supplements and does not necessarily derogate from the Constitution, there are certain rights under the African Charter which are enforceable but are expressly identified by the Constitution as unenforceable.'[2055] The status of the

---

[2051]   See Lawrence Atsegbua, A Critical Appraisal of Environmental Rights Under the Nigerian Courts, 2(1) *Benin Journal of Public Law* p.55 (2004).

[2052]   See generally, A.O. Enabulele, Implementation of Treaties in Nigeria and the Status Question: Whither Nigerian Courts?, 17 *African Journal of International and Comparative Law*, pp.326–341 (2009); See also Ademola Abass (2012), *International Law: Text, Cases, and Materials*, Oxford University Press, Oxford, pp.160–187.

[2053]   See section 12 of the Constitution of Nigeria, 1999.

[2054]   *Attorney-General, Ondo State v. Attorney-General, Federation* (2002) FWLR 1972.

[2055]   Edwin Egede, Bringing Human Rights Home: An Examination of the Domestication of Human Rights Treaties in Nigeria, 51(2) *Journal of African Law*, 249–284 at 255 (2007).

African Charter was considered in *Abacha v. Fawehinmi*.[2056] The Supreme Court held that the Charter is part of Nigerian law and possesses 'a greater vigour and strength' than any domestic statute. However, the Charter was held not to be superior to the Constitution because its international flavour does not prevent the National Assembly or Federal Military Government (as the case may be) from repealing it.

It is clear from the above decision that even though the African Charter is a statute with international flavour, it is not superior to the Constitution. Therefore, any conflict between any sections of the 1999 Constitution of Nigeria and Article 24 of the African Charter will be resolved in favour of the Constitution. As such, some scholars have expressed doubts whether the Charter can be used to elevate environmental rights from non-justiciable rights to justiciable rights.[2057]

6.5.3 JURISPRUDENCE OF THE AFRICAN COMMISSION ON SOCIO-ECONOMIC RIGHTS AND ENVIRONMENT

The most prominent case on socio-economic rights, and which borders on environmental issues, handled by the Commission is *Social and Economic Rights Action Center (SERAC) and Anor v. Nigeria*,[2058] which was a communication filed by a socio-economic rights' Non-Governmental Organization (NGO) against the Federal Government of Nigeria. It alleged that the Government of Nigeria was directly involved in oil production through the State Oil Company, the NNPC, which is the majority shareholder in a consortium with Shell. It also alleged that the widespread contamination of soil, water and air and the destruction of homes in the Ogoni communities constituted a violation of rights to health, a healthy environment, housing and food. They also complained that the Government had condoned and facilitated violation of international standards by placing the legal and military powers of the State at the disposal of the oil companies; withholding information from the communities about the dangers of oil activities, and ignoring the concerns of the communities. The African Commission, briefly, considered the right to a satisfactory environment as a right that requires a Government to: take reasonable measures to prevent pollution and ecological degradation;[2059] promote conservation and ensure ecologically sustainable development and use of natural resources;[2060] permit independent scientific monitoring of threatened environments;[2061] undertake environmental and social impact assessments prior

---

[2056]   *Supra*.
[2057]   See Lawrence Atsegbua, *op. cit.*, 143.
[2058]   Communication 155/96.
[2059]   Para 52 of the Communication.
[2060]   *Ibid*.
[2061]   Para. 53 of the Communication.

to industrial development;[2062] provide access to information to communities
involved;[2063] and grant those affected an opportunity to be heard and to participate
in the development process.[2064]

The Commission found that the Nigerian Government had violated
Articles 2 (non-discriminatory enjoyment of rights), 4 (right to life), 14 (right
to property), 16 (right to health), 18 (family right), 21 (right of peoples to freely
dispose of their wealth and natural resources) and 24 (right of peoples to a
satisfactory environment). The Commission further commented on the impact
of globalization in developing countries that '[T]he intervention of multinational
corporations may be a potentially positive force for development if the State
and the people concerned are ever mindful of the common good and the sacred
rights of individuals and communities.'[2065] Even though the right to housing
was not explicitly mentioned in the Charter, the complainants argued, and the
Commission accepted, that the right to housing and shelter could be found in
the combined reading of articles 16, 14 and 18 of the Charter. The Commission
held that the right to shelter 'embod[ies] the individual's right to be let alone and
to live in peace – whether under a roof or not,'[2066] and the right to housing covers
protection against forced evictions.[2067] It concluded that Nigerian Government,
which has a duty to ensure that all human rights in the African Charter are
guaranteed, did not live up to that expectation. It appealed to the Government
to ensure the protection of the environment, health and livelihood of the Ogoni
people and the entire Niger Delta, *inter alia* by: (i) stopping all attacks on Ogoni
[Niger Delta] communities by the Rivers State Internal Securities Task Force;
(ii) conducting an investigation into the said human rights violations and
prosecuting officials of the security forces, NNPC and relevant agencies involved
in the human rights violations; (iii) ensuring adequate compensation to victims
of human rights violations, and undertaking a comprehensive cleanup of lands
and rivers damaged by oil operations; (iv) ensuring appropriate environmental
and social impact assessments for any future oil development, and the safe
operation of any further oil development; (v) providing information on health
and environmental risks and meaningful access to regulatory and decision-
making bodies to communities likely to be affected by oil operations.[2068]

These obligations, as spelt out by the African Commission, clearly contain
both procedural – right to access environmental information and the opportunity

---

[2062]   *Ibid.*
[2063]   *Ibid.*
[2064]   *Ibid.*
[2065]   Communication 155/96.
[2066]   Para. 61.
[2067]   Para. 62.
[2068]   Para 69 of the Communication. See Morné van der Linde and Lirette Louw, Considering
the Interpretation and Implementation of Article 24 of the African Charter on Human and
Peoples' Rights in Light of the SERAC Communication, 3 *African Human Rights Law Journal*
167–187 at 178 (2003).

to be heard in the event that one's environmental rights are impaired or run the risk of being impaired; and substantive aspects – the duty of the Government to prevent pollution and ecological degradation and the obligation to promote conservation and sustainable development.[2069] This decision mirrors the virtues contained in international environmental principles such as the preventative principle and the duty of care principle.[2070]

However, this decision has been criticized on the ground that, rather than recognizing the inequalities of power that exist between MNCs and the developing countries like Nigeria, the African Commission in *SERAC* case laid responsibility for the violations that had been committed by the MNCs wholly on the State. This may be due to the fact that there is no mechanism provided by the regional human rights system of Africa where private parties can be held directly accountable for human rights violations.[2071] But while it is true under the international law that the State has the primary responsibility for protecting human rights, the Commission should have gone further to consider the accountability of the non-state actor, particularly where the criminal law, or the regulatory framework of the host State, are too weak to tackle the problem.[2072] All the elements to find Shell liable were present in the case: Shell knew that their business ventures were involved in State-sponsored violations; and Shell itself committed several violations including calling for security force intervention during protest by the oil communities, raising grievances against the company.[2073] Oloka-Onyango has argued that as a result of the difficulty involved in using domestic institutions in dealing with issues like those in the *SERAC* case, there is need for the Commission and international human rights bodies to confront the abuses. And in doing this, the Commission needs to consider those provisions within the Charter that articulate the issue of responsibility and duty, and seek an appropriate balance between state responsibility and that of the non-State actor.[2074] In view of the challenges posed by the MNCs operating in developing countries like Nigeria, the Commission should have been more pro-active by going further in finding against Shell rather than limiting the liability to the State. Taking this approach would, however, mean a total departure from the current position under the international law on state responsibility discussed in Chapter IV of this work. Adopting this position would help to curb the reckless conduct

---

[2069] Morné van der Linde and Lirette Louw, *Ibid*.

[2070] M. Kidd, *Environmental Law: A South African Perspective* (1997) 8, quoted in Morné van der Linde and Lirette Louw, *Ibid*, 178–179.

[2071] Tineke Lambooy and Marie-Eve Rancourt, *Shell* in Nigeria: From Human Rights Abuse to Corporate Social Responsibility, 2(2) *Human Rights and International Legal Discourse*, pp.229–275 at 249 (2008); Nicola Jägers (2002), *Corporate Human Rights Obligations: In Search of Accountability*, Intersentia, Antwerpen, p.219.

[2072] J. Oloka-Onyango, Reinforcing Marginalized Rights in an Age of Globalization: International Mechanisms, Non-State Actors, and the Struggle for Peoples' Rights in Africa, 18 *Am. U. Int'l L. Rev.* 851–913 at 903 (2003).

[2073] J. Oloka-Onyango, *Ibid*, pp.904–905.

[2074] J. Oloka-Onyango, *Ibid*, p.911.

of the multinational corporations, promote responsible conduct and further help to protect the rights of the people. In the alternative, rather than embarking on 'a strained interpretation' of the existing provisions of the African Charter, the AU could embark on an amendment or revision of the Charter by extending the Charter obligations to private persons (including corporations) for the purpose of protecting and promoting all aspects of human rights within the region.[2075] The decision has therefore exposed some of the gaps that need to be filled if the Charter is to be able to afford better protection for the poor and marginalized people of Africa against private non-State actors like corporations. This is more important as the Commission has boldly, innovatively and creatively declared that all rights under the Charter are to 'be made effective.'[2076]

Notwithstanding the above, this decision, described by Heyns as 'extraordinary'[2077] represents a giant stride towards the realisation of economic and social rights. The Commission has effectively shown that economic and social rights are capable of judicial enforcement as it unequivocally stated that 'there is no right in the African Charter that cannot be made effective.'[2078] It has further shown how the Charter can be interpreted generously to guarantee the effective enjoyment of the rights contained therein.[2079] This case is also important as it articulates the duties of African Governments to monitor and control the activities of MNCs operating in their countries to ensure respect for economic, social and cultural rights.[2080] The decision serves as a platform through which victims of human rights violations and civil society groups can put pressure on the Government to regulate the activities of private non-State actors to stop them from violating the rights provided under the Charter. Also, by recognizing that non-State actors are capable of violating the Charter rights of others, this decision increases the prospect of holding private entities liable for rights violations under the Charter.[2081] The decision of the Commission has far-reaching implications for Nigerian Government which has, over the years, excused its abrogation of the rights of the Niger Delta people to their land and natural resources by relying on the domanial theory of ownership, which vests all the natural resources in

---

[2075]   Evaristus Oshionebo (2009), *Regulating Transnational Corporations in Domestic and International Regimes: An African Case Study, op. cit.*, pp.111–112.

[2076]   *SERAC & CESR v. Nigeria, Supra*, para. 68.

[2077]   Christof Heyns, The African Regional Human Rights System: The African Charter, 108(3) *Penn State Law Review* 679–702 at 691 (2004).

[2078]   See para. 68.

[2079]   Justice C. Nwobike, The African Commission on Human and Peoples' Rights and the Demystification of Second and Third Generation Rights under the African Charter: Social Economic Rights Action Center (SERAC) and the Center for Economic and Social Rights (CESR) v. Nigeria, 1 *Africa J. Legal Stud.* 2 (2005) 129–146 at 145.

[2080]   Dinah Shelton, Decision Regarding Communication 155/96 (Social and Economic Action Center/Center for Economic, Social Rights v. Nigeria), Case No. ACHPR/COMM/A044/1, 96 *Am. J. Int'l L.* 937–942 at 941 (2002).

[2081]   Evaristus Oshionebo, *Regulating Transnational Corporations in Domestic and International Regimes: An African Case Study, op. cit.*, p.112.

the Federal Government, to the exclusion of all others.[2082] The Commission's recommendations, if enforced, would not only have helped in vindicating the rights that had been violated but would also have deterred future violations and established a relationship of trust between the Nigerian Government and the Niger Delta people.[2083]

In *Centre for Minority Rights Development (Kenya) and Anor v Kenya*,[2084] a complaint was filed by the Centre for Minority Rights Development (CEMIRIDE) and Minority Rights Group International (MRG), on behalf of the Endorois Community. The complainants alleged that the Government of Kenya, in violation of the African Charter on Human and Peoples, had violated their rights following their displacement from their ancestral lands, with the failure to have adequately compensated them for the loss of their property, the disruption of the community's pastoral enterprise and violations of the right to practise their religion and culture, as well as the overall process of development of their community. The complainants alleged that the Endorois have no say in the management of their ancestral land as the failure to register the Endorois Welfare Committee, which is the representative body of the Endorois community, often led to illegitimate consultations taking place, with the authorities selecting particular individuals to lend their consent 'on behalf' of the community.' The Commission held that the complainants, who had been evicted from their ancestral land with minimal compensation, had had their rights to freedom of religion, property, cultural life, free disposal of natural resources, and development as guaranteed in the Charter, violated. The Commission recommended that Kenya should restore the Endorois to their ancestral land, pay adequate compensation for losses suffered and pay royalties to the community for economic activities on their land. In terms of consultation and compensation, the Commission noted that the conditions of the consultation failed to fulfill its own standard of consultations,[2085] as the community members were informed of the impending project as a *fait accompli*, and not given an opportunity to shape either the policies or their role in the Game Reserve. It held that 'no effective participation was allowed for the Endorois, nor has there been any reasonable benefit enjoyed by the community. Moreover, a prior Environment and Social Impact Assessment was not carried out. The absence of these three elements is tantamount to a violation of Article 14, the right to property, under the Charter. The failure to guarantee effective participation and to guarantee a reasonable share in the profits of the Game Reserve … also

---

[2082] Nsongurua J. Udombana, Between Promise and Performance: Revising States' Obligations under the African Human Rights Charter, 40 *Stan. J. Int'l L.* 105–142 at 133 (2004).

[2083] Christopher Mbazira, Enforcing the economic, social and cultural rights in the African Charter on Human and Peoples' Rights: Twenty years of redundancy, progression and significant strides, 6 *African Human Rights Law Journal*, 333–357 at 351 (2006).

[2084] Afr. Comm'n HPR, Case 276/2003 (4 February 2010).

[2085] Report of the African Commission's Working Group of Experts on Indigenous Populations/ Communities (Twenty-eighth session, 2003).

extends to a violation of the right to development.'[2086] This is a great contribution
to jurisprudence on the rights of indigenous peoples as it is the first decision to
determine who indigenous peoples in Africa are, and what their rights are, and it
sets a major precedent that is likely to have major spill-over effects, particularly
regarding potentially similar minorities and indigenous communities in Africa,
including the Niger Delta communities in Nigeria.[2087] It is also the first decision in
which the Commission has found a violation of the right to development in article
22 of the African Charter, the only international treaty that includes that right.[2088]

So much development has taken place in the views and communications
of the Commission that one can fairly assert that the Commission is no longer
what a scholar once referred to as 'a yoke that African leaders have put around
our necks.'[2089] Since 1996, its decisions on complaints filed before it, have been
well-reasoned and elaborate on the issues of law and fact,[2090] thus contributing
meaningfully to the development of international human rights law reflecting the
African experience.

6.5.4 APPLICATION OF THE JURISPRUDENCE OF AFRICAN COMMISSION ON SOCIO-ECONOMIC RIGHTS AND ENVIRONMENT BY NIGERIAN COURTS

Despite the landmark decisions like *SERAC*, few African courts, including those
in Nigeria, cite the jurisprudence of the Commission when deciding cases that
touch on the violation of rights guaranteed under the Charter. For example,
even though the decision of the court in *Gbemre's* case[2091] has been applauded
in some quarters, it was bereft of any application of international law principles
and appropriate legal authorities. Whilst the applicant premised its complaints
on Articles 4, 16 and 24 of the Charter, the lack of reference to domestic African
jurisprudence, particularly the *SERAC* case that had exhaustively dealt with
these ESC rights, left much to be desired. The court fails to expressly consider
whether the rights in the Charter could be applied by virtue of the Constitutional

---

[2086]   *Centre for Minority Rights Development (Kenya) and Another v Kenya, op. cit.*, para 228.
[2087]   Victor Mosoti, *Endorois Welfare Council v. Kenya*, The World Bank (Law and Development),
          December 2010, at http://web.worldbank.org/ [accessed 18 August 2011].
[2088]   Japhet Biegon and Magnus Killander, Human rights developments in the African Union dur-
          ing 2009, 10 *African Human Rights Law Journal*, 212–232 at 225–226 (2010).
[2089]   Makau wa Mutua, The African Human Rights System in a Comparative Perspective, 3 *Rev. Afr.
          Comm'n Hum. Peoples' Rts.* 5, 11 (1993).
[2090]   Chidi Anselm Odinkalu and Camilla Christensen, The African Commission on Human and
          Peoples' Rights: The Development of its Non-State Communication Procedures, 20 *Human
          Rights Quarterly*, 235–280 at 278 (1998).
[2091]   *Supra.*

provisions enjoining legislative measures to implement the principles in the Charter.[2092]

Also in *Ikechukwu Opara v. Shell*,[2093] no reference was made by the Judge to any international or African human rights instruments on socio-economic rights. Had the judge had recourse to the Commission's jurisprudence on socio-economic rights, he would have known that the indivisibility and interdependency of all human rights calls for equal attention to be given to both the civil and political rights and the socio-economic rights. The fact that the local communities of the Niger Delta live in abject poverty, and do not enjoy the minimum standard of living, calls for an expansive and creative interpretation of Chapter II of the Constitution of Nigeria dealing with socio-economic rights so as to make them justiciable. *Gbemre* and *Opara* cases are on appeal in the Court of Appeal and it is only hoped that the appellate court will be able to pronounce on the justiciability of socio-economic rights involved in these cases, relying on the Commission's decisions.

Nigerian judges will do well to avail themselves of these decisions, using them creatively and liberally either as applicable authoritative laws or as persuasive authorities to interpret constitutional and legislative provisions[2094] on socio-economic rights issues. This is because domestic courts are better positioned than the international tribunals to 'provide binding and enforceable relief, whether injunctive … or compensatory,' and to 'enforce international law because of their authority over the assets of the most common polluters, corporations and individuals.'[2095] At the same time, States are more likely to obey judgments and decisions of their own courts than those of a far-away international institution which they may treat with suspicion.[2096] The current conservative judicial posture may have led to reluctance of litigants from the Niger Delta region in basing their lawsuits on alleged infringements of their socio-economic rights, despite acknowledgement of the existence of these rights in the Charter[2097] and the Commission's decisions. The result is the resort to extra-judicial means of getting justice and increase in lawlessness. By relying on the Commission's jurisprudence,

---

[2092] Deji Adekunle, Domestic protection of socio-economic rights: Case studies on the implementation of socio-economic rights in the domestic systems of three West African countries, 11(3) *ESR Review*, 15–16 at 16 (2010). See Article 1 of the African Charter on Human and Peoples' Rights, *op. cit.*

[2093] *Supra.*

[2094] See Nsongurua J. Udombana, Between Promise and Performance: Revisiting States' Obligations Under the African Human Rights Charter, 40 *Stan. J. Int'l L.* 105–142 at 140 (2004).

[2095] Linda A. Malone, "Enforcing International Environmental Law through Domestic Law Mechanisms in the United States: Civil Society Initiatives Against Global Warming", in LeRoy Paddock *et al.*, *op. cit.*, p.118.

[2096] Nsongurua J. Udombana, Between Promise and Performance: Revisiting States' Obligations Under the African Human Rights Charter, *op. cit.*, pp.140, 142.

[2097] Rhuks T. Ako, The Judicial Recognition and Enforcement of the Right to Environment: Differing Perspectives from Nigeria and India, *op. cit.*, p.436.

Nigerian courts will not only be furthering the purpose of the Charter but will also be providing victims of human rights abuse in Nigeria with actual redress for the wrongs suffered at the hands of the Government and private non-state actors, rather than the court's relying on the non-justiciability provision of the Constitution to deny the victims a remedy.

6.5.5 BENEFITS OF THE APPLICATION OF THE AFRICAN COMMISSION JURISPRUDENCE BY NIGERIAN COURTS

A liberal interpretation of the Charter's provisions on socio-economic rights will aid the Nigerian Government in its efforts to enact legislation to improving the status of human rights, while also providing a rich body of jurisprudence for the national courts, daily grappling with the interpretation and application of socio-economic rights.[2098] This will further encourage individuals, particularly the Niger Delta people and non-State entities to lodge more complaints before the Commission, which, in turn, will further develop the Charter's provisions.[2099] The African Commission on Human and Peoples' Rights (ACHPRs), at its 19th Ordinary Session held in April 1996 at Ouagadougou, called upon lawyers always to place much reliance on the Charter and other international and regional human rights instruments in their legal advocacy. It also urged the judges to 'play a greater role in incorporating the Charter and future jurisprudence of the Commission in their judgments thereby promoting and protecting the rights and freedoms guaranteed by the Charter.'[2100] It called on the judges 'to base their reasoning and judgments on all relevant human rights instruments, either as applicable authoritative laws or as persuasive aids to interpretation of constitutional and legislative provisions on fundamental rights, freedoms and duties.'[2101] Thus, even where the lawyers fail to cite the Charter and the Commission's decisions in support of their cases, Nigerian judges can learn from Ngcobo J. of the Constitutional Court of South Africa, who has distinguished himself from the rest of other judges by using the Charter to creatively strengthen his decisions.[2102]

[2098] Nsongurua J. Udombana, The African Commission on Human and Peoples' Rights and the development of fair trial norms in Africa, 6 *African Human Rights Law Journal*, 299–332 at 330 (2006).

[2099] *Ibid.*

[2100] Ninth Annual Activity Report of the African Commission on Human and Peoples' Rights-1995/96, AHG/207 (XXXII), at www.achpr.org/english/activity_reports/9th%20Activity%20Report.pdf [accessed 17 March 2009].

[2101] *Ibid.*

[2102] See his decisions in *Richard Gordon Volks No v. Ethel Robinson & Ors.* (2005) 5 BCLR 446; *Bhe v. Magistrate Khayelitsha & Ors*, (2004) AHRLR 212 (SACC 2004); Obiora C. Okafor (2007), *The African Human Rights System, Activist Forces, and International Institutions*, Cambridge University Press, Cambridge, p.171.

The application of the Commission's decisions by domestic courts in Nigeria will help to overcome the problem of enforcement of the Commission's decision. This is because the domestic courts are closer to the people and domestic mechanisms for the enforcement of their decisions is quite easy. Their decisions on socio-economic rights and the environment are likely to have a bigger and meaningful impact in comparison with the African Commission and the African Court – whose enforcement mechanism may be somewhere in Gambia and Addis Ababa respectively.[2103]

6.5.6 THE AFRICAN COURT ON HUMAN AND PEOPLES' RIGHTS

The proposal for the establishment of this court was first made in 1961 at the Africa Conference on the Rule of Law.[2104] The Protocol establishing the African Court on Human and Peoples' Rights (the African Court) was adopted on 10 June 1998, and finally entered into force in January 2004, after ratification by the required 15 States. On 2 July 2006, 11 Judges were sworn in. It is hoped that this court will adequately 'complement the protective mandate of the African Commission',[2105] which was set up in 1987, and will help in ensuring the realisation of the rights contained in the Charter, particularly the right to a clean and satisfactory environment by taking a cue from its American and European counterparts. Viljoen describes the complementary role of the African Court as a move from a quasi-judicial to judicial institution, thus resulting in a change from recommendatory to a binding findings; from uncertainty in remedies to clear and appropriate remedies; from an *ad hoc* to a comprehensive implementation and compliance system; from excessive confidentiality or secrecy in handling proceedings to a more open system; from delays in reaching a finding to more immediate justice; from an inadequate to an adequate and efficient way of handling matters of urgency; from an obscure (African Commission) to a more visible (African Court) institution.[2106] In other words, Viljoen looked forward to a court that would help to overcome some of the challenges facing the Commission in terms of effective performance.

The African Court appears set to remedy some of these problems besetting the African Commission. The African Court will deliver conclusive decisions, and

---

[2103]   See Christopher Mbazira, *op. cit.*, p.356.
[2104]   International Commission of Jurists, African Conference on the Rule of Law, Lagos, Nigeria, 1961.
[2105]   See Protocol to the African Charter on Human and Peoples' Rights on the Establishment of the African Court on Human and Peoples' Rights, Art. 2, Doc. OAU/LEG/MIN/AFCHPR/PROT/III (1998), www.achpr.org/english/_info/court_en.html [accessed 6 June 2009]; See Frans Viljoen, A Human Rights Court for Africa, and Africans, 30 *Brook. J. Int'l L.* 1–66 at 2 (2004).
[2106]   See Frans Viljoen, *Ibid*, pp.13–22 (2004).

the protocol establishing it provides that States parties to the Protocol undertake
to comply with the judgment in any case to which they are parties within the
time stipulated by the Court and to guarantee its execution.[2107] Borrowing a
leaf from the experience of other international human rights oversight bodies
such as the Inter-American and European Courts of Human Rights, Article 27
of the Protocol provides that if the Court finds that there has been violation
of a human or peoples' right, it shall make 'appropriate' orders to remedy the
violation, including the payment of fair compensation and reparations. It further
states that in cases of extreme gravity and urgency, and when necessary to avoid
irreparable harm to persons, the Court shall adopt such provisional measures
as it deems necessary. Article 29(2) provides that the AU Council of Ministers
shall be notified of the judgment and shall monitor its execution on behalf of the
AU Assembly, and Article 30 provides that States are bound to execute decisions.
Article 31 provides that the Court shall submit a Report on its work at each regular
session of the AU Assembly, and the Report shall specify, in particular, the cases
in which a State has not complied with the Court's judgment.

These legal provisions are quite encouraging and should greatly assist
victims of human rights violations, including the Niger Delta people, to access
the court and get adequate remedies where violations are proved. However, the
legal structure is one thing, compliance with same is another. The question that
remains is whether Nigeria and other African States will change their behaviour,
and abide by the judgments of the Court.[2108] In order to ensure the enforcement
of decisions of the Inter-American Court on Human Rights, the Inter-American
Convention on Human Rights provides in its Article 68(2) that that part of
Court's judgment 'may be executed in the country concerned in accordance with
domestic procedure governing the execution of judgments against the State.' This
approach has also been adopted by the Economic Community of West African
States (ECOWAS) Court of Justice, whose judgments can be enforced in the
highest domestic court of member States.[2109] The victims of human rights abuse
in Nigeria, particularly the Niger Delta people, would be able to have their rights
adequately protected if this approach could be emulated. Efforts should be made
to uproot the pervasive culture of non-compliance in matters of human rights
abuse that has permeated the entire region by ensuring that State parties accepts,
respect and abide by the provisions of the Protocol. After all, they all agreed to be
bound by the court's decisions and so have an obligation to implement them in

---

[2107] Protocol to the African Charter on Human and People's Rights on the Establishment of an
African Court on Human and People's Rights, *op. cit.*, Article 30.

[2108] Muna Ndulo, "African Commission and Court Under the African Human Rights System",
in John Akokpari and Daniel Shea Zimbler (eds) (2008), *Africa's Human Rights Architecture*,
Fanele, South Africa, p.198.

[2109] George Mukundi Wachira, African Court on Human and Peoples' Rights: Ten Years on and
Still no Justice, *Minority Rights Group International Report*, p.23 (2008).

accordance with the principle *pacta sunt servanda*, and by virtue of the provisions of Article 1 of the African Charter.[2110] As observed by the Commission itself:

> *"The Nigerian Government itself recognises that human rights are no longer solely a matter of domestic concern. The African Charter was drafted and acceded to voluntarily by African States wishing to ensure the respect of human rights on this continent. Once ratified, States Parties to the Charter are legally bound to its provisions. A state not wishing to abide by the African Charter might have refrained from ratification. Once legally bound, however, a State must abide by the law in the same way an individual must."*[2111]

One of the major problems faced by the African Commission is that of enforcement of its recommendations and this has rendered the Commission's findings remote, if not virtually meaningless, to the victims.[2112] For instance, in the case of *International Pen, Constitutional Rights Project, Interights on behalf of Ken Saro-Wiwa Jr and Civil Liberties Organisation v Nigeria*,[2113] the Nigerian Government, under the leadership of the military dictator, the late Gen. Sani Abacha, even disputed the mandate of the Commission to consider cases, not to mention to make recommendations. In this case, following the Commission's findings that Nigeria had violated its human rights obligations, the Government contended that the Commission lacked judicial capacity to make the recommendations.[2114] Thus, notwithstanding the interim measures given by the Commission requesting that the death sentences on Ken Saro-Wiwa and other eight Ogoni's environmentalists be suspended until the Commission had discussed the case with the Nigerian Government, Gen. Sani Abacha ignored the Commission and carried out the execution. Also, since 2001, when the communication was made in *SERAC* case, the Nigerian Government has not taken any serious step towards implementing the decisions of the Commission,[2115] knowing well that the Commission is incapable of enforcing its own decision. The Government not only disregards

---

[2110] Article 1 of the African Charter provides that member states shall recognize the rights, duties and freedoms enshrined in the Charter and shall undertake to adopt legislative *or other measures* to give effect to them. See also, George Mukundi Wachira, *op. cit.*, p.474; see also Ademola Abass (2012), *International Law: Text, Cases, and Materials*, Oxford University Press, Oxford, p.167.

[2111] *International Pen, Constitutional Rights Project, Interights on behalf of Ken Saro-Wiwa Jr and Civil Liberties Organisation v Nigeria*, Communications 137/94, 139/94, 154/96 and161/97, African Commission on Human and Peoples' Rights, 31 October 1998, paras. 116, at www.unhcr.org/refworld/docid/3ae6b6123.html [accessed 6 June 2009].

[2112] Makau Mutua, "The Construction of the African Human Rights System: Prospects and Pitfalls", in Samantha Power and Graham Allison (eds) (2006), *Realizing Human Rights: Moving from Inspiration to Impact*, Palgrave Macmillan, New York, p.151.

[2113] *Supra*, paras. 8, 19, 103, 114–115.

[2114] George Mukundi Wachira, African Court on Human and Peoples' Rights: Ten years on and still no justice, *op. cit.*, p.11.

[2115] The setting up of agencies such as the NDDC, creation of the Niger Delta Ministry subsequent to the decision of the African Commission can be partly attributed to the decision as well as

the recommendations but continues with the violation of human rights of the local inhabitants of the Niger Delta in conjunction with the oil MNCs operating in the region. Oil exploitation in the Niger Delta region is still characterized by oil pollution with detrimental effects on the people. As noted by Justice C. Nwobike,[2116] the conduct of the Nigerian Government in the Ogoni case ran contrary to international human rights law and was tantamount to withdrawing support for the Convention. Having already adopted legislative measures as a way of fulfilling the obligation 'to take steps' towards the progressive realization of these rights, it has by its decision in this matter taken retrogressive steps.

Thus, notwithstanding the ratification of the African Charter by all members of the AU, including Nigeria, thereby evincing their intention to be bound by its provisions, the African Commission's findings of a violation on the part of a State party does not necessarily provide a remedy to the victim.[2117] At present, there is no mechanism that can compel States to abide by its recommendations and so much depends on the good will of States.[2118] All this perpetuates a culture of impunity for violations and may deter victims of human rights violations from submitting their cases to the African Human Rights organs.

Remarkably, rule 118 of the new Rules of Procedure of the Commission provides that pursuant to Article 5(1)(a) of the Protocol, it may submit cases of non-compliance to the African Court where it 'considers that the State has not complied or is unwilling to comply with its recommendations in respect of the communication within the period stated in Rule 112(2) [180 days of being informed of the decision].'[2119] This means that the Commission may refer to the African Court its unenforced decisions by member states who are parties to the African Court Protocol for legal enforcement. This is a good provision provided the African Court will be willing to enforce these recommendations timeously and effectively. In view of the likelihood of delay in having to wait for the African Court to enforce the Commission's decisions, it is suggested that the Commission be empowered to have its own enforcement mechanism.[2120] This will enhance the work of the Commission and help provide relief to the majority of victims of human rights violations, including the Niger Delta people.

---

the agitations in various quarters in the country to address the economic and social deprivations in the Niger Delta region.

[2116]   Justice C. Nwobike, *op. cit.*, 145.

[2117]   George Mukundi Wachira, Twenty Years of Elusive Enforcement of the Recommendations
of the African Commission on Human and Peoples' Rights: A possible Remedy, 6 *African
Human Rights Law Journal* 465–492 at 470 (2006).

[2118]   The African Commission on Human and Peoples' Rights, *Information sheet No. 3,
Communication Procedure, Organisation of African Unity*, p.9.

[2119]   The Rules of Procedure of the African Commission on Human and Peoples' Rights was
approved by the African Commission on Human and Peoples' Rights during its 47th ordinary
session held in Banjul (The Gambia) 12–26 May 2010.

[2120]   George Mukundi Wachira, Twenty Years of Elusive Enforcement of the Recommendations of
the African Commission on Human and Peoples' Rights: A possible Remedy, *op. cit.*, p.489.

However, one of the important areas that needs to be addressed concerning the African Court is in the area of access to the court. There are two categories of people that can take cases before the court. The first comprises States, organs of the AU, the African Commission, and Inter-Governmental organizations, and these have direct and unfettered access to the court. The second category are the individuals and NGOs with observer status at the Commission, and they can only take cases before the court where a State has made a declaration under article 34(6) allowing such direct access, and, in any event, the Court has the discretion to grant or refuse such access.[2121] As at October 2012, only 26 states, including Nigeria had ratified the Protocol and only 5 of the State parties (Burkina Faso, Ghana, Malawi, Mali and Tanzania) had made a declaration allowing individuals and NGOs to have direct access to the court.[2122] In other words, only individuals from these countries in Africa can take their cases before this Court, while the rest have to rely on the African Commission to bring their cases to the African Court. This implies that the Commission will both be acting as a clearinghouse (a place to determine which NGOs are eligible) for NGOs seeking to bring cases before the Court themselves, and also assist in filtering meritorious cases from the Commission to the Court for further review.[2123] This provision will no doubt limit the right of individuals and NGOs – the main users and beneficiaries – to access the court to seek a remedy. This limited direct access of individuals and NGOs before the Court may likely reduce its effectiveness, giving the fact that States are not likely to submit complaints against each other.[2124] This is also coupled with the fact that, in most cases, these abuses may be attributable to or linked, to the States themselves, as in the human rights abuses in the Niger Delta region of Nigeria which has been linked to the Nigerian Government in complicity with the oil MNCs. This, in effect, means that the majority of the victims of human rights violations, particularly the Niger Delta people, will be denied justice as they will only be able to access the court through the African Commission.[2125]

[2121] Article 5 of the Protocol to the African Charter on Human and Peoples' Rights on the Establishment of an African Court on Human and Peoples' Rights; Nobuntu Mbelle, "Civil Society and the Promotion of Human Rights in Africa", in John Akokpari and Daniel Shea Zimbler (eds), *Africa's Human Rights Architecture, op. cit.*, p.171.

[2122] Devota A. Mwachang, *Ratify African Court's Charter, AU members told*, IPP Media, 27 May 2011, at www.ippmedia.com/frontend/index.php?l=29520 [accessed 18 August 2011]; Southern Africa Litigation Centre (SALC) Blogger, *A Human Rights Court for Africa*, 16 March 2011, at http://salcbloggers.wordpress.com/2011/03/16/a-human-rights-court-for-africa-2/ [accessed 3 July 2011].

[2123] Sybil Sakle Thompson, "The African Human Rights System: Comparison, Context, and Opportunities for Future Growth", in Michael Wodzicki (ed) (2008), *The Fight for Human Rights in Africa Perspectives on the African Commission on Human and Peoples' Rights, Rights & Democracy,* International Centre for Human Rights and Democratic Development, Canada, p.41.

[2124] Since the coming into force of the Charter over two decades ago, only one inter-state complaint (*Democratic Republic of Congo v. Burundi, Rwanda and Uganda*, Communication 277/99) had been submitted before the African Commission.

[2125] Nobuntu Mbelle, *op. cit.*, p.171.

If the avowed commitment of the Nigerian Government to the implementation
of international and regional instruments aimed at promoting and protecting
human rights is not to become mere rhetoric, it is important that it complies with
Article 34(6) of the Protocol through its declaration permitting individuals and
NGOs with observer status, direct access to the court. Such a declaration will
assist the victims of environmental and human rights abuses in the Niger Delta
to bring actions directly before this Court. It should be noted that regional and
international human rights bodies are meant to provide complementary roles
to the domestic courts/tribunals – 'the main *situs* and *locus* for the enforcement
of human rights.'[2126] They are meant to provide remedies to alleged victims of
human rights abuse after they have exhausted local remedies. Hence, access to
these international and regional human rights bodies should not be fettered.
The success or otherwise of the African Court will depend on its accessibility to
individuals and NGOs, and how far it would be able to tackle the problems that
have rendered the African Commission ineffective.

There is also a need for more awareness to be created by the AU of the
existence of the African Court, as citizens of member states still lack knowledge
and information about the Court and what it can offer in terms of human rights
protection. Since it started its work in 2006, it has only handled very few cases,
with the first delivered in December 2009.[2127] As noted by Pityana:

> "It is unfortunate that judges of the African Court on Human and Peoples' Rights
> and indeed the Court itself has not provided much information, if any, to the public
> it is expected to serve on progress made, which is a cause for concern. It is essential
> that the African Court on Human and Peoples' Rights provides sufficient informa-
> tion on its progress if it hopes to receive requisite support and cases from individuals
> and the peoples it is created to protect."[2128]

Hence, the need to create awareness of the existence and mandate of the Court
should be given a priority. There is also a need to develop the capacity of lawyers
in member states, including Nigeria, on how to file and conduct proceedings
before the Court and monitor the implementation of the court's judgment.[2129]
In fulfillment of their commitment to promote the effectiveness of the Court

---

[2126] Dan Juma, Access to the African Court on Human and Peoples' Rights: A Case of the Poacher
turned Gamekeeper, 4(2) *Essex Human Rights Review* 1–21 at 6 (2007); Bilder R., "An Overview
of International Human Rights Law", in H. Hannum (ed) (1999), *Guide to International
Human Rights Practice,* 3rd ed., Transnational Publishers, New York, p.3.

[2127] *Michelot Yogogombaye v. The Republic of Senegal,* AfCHPR, Application No. 001/2008, judgment on 15 December 2009. For the decisions and Judgments of the Court, see African Court
on Human and Peoples' Rights, *Judgments and Orders,* at www.african-court.org/en/cases/
judgments-and-orders/ [accessed 2 February 2012].

[2128] Interview with BarneyPityana, quoted in George Mukundi Wachira, African Court on Human
and Peoples' Rights: Ten years on and still no justice, *op. cit.,* p.25.

[2129] Southern Africa Litigation Centre (SALC) Blogger, *op. cit.*

and campaign for the universal ratification of its Protocol, the civil society organisations have a great role to play in educating the people about the Court, encouraging litigation before it, lobbying member states to ratify the courts' Protocol and helping to build the capacity of lawyers across the continent.[2130]

Taking into consideration the fact that the African Court has been given the powers to issue legally binding judgments, and high calibre of the persons elected as the first judges of the court – in terms of experience in human rights and international law, it is hoped that the Court will help to complement the somewhat limited protective role of the Commission, particularly as it concerns socio-economic rights. Nonetheless, the success of the Court will not only depend on the quality of the judicial personnel that man it, but also on the will of States to adhere to the Protocol by respecting, honouring and executing the decisions of the Court when they are made,[2131] and will depend on domestic courts relying on the Courts' decisions in ESRs issues before them.

6.5.7 THE AFRICAN COURT OF JUSTICE AND HUMAN RIGHTS

A new development has emerged in the African regional judicial landscape with the merger of the African Court on Human and Peoples' Rights and the African Court of Justice (ACJ)[2132] through the adoption of an instrument merging the courts.[2133] They were merged into a single Court and established as 'The African Court of Justice and Human Rights.'[2134] As at August 2010, only three States, namely Libya, Mali and Burkina Faso, had ratified the protocol.[2135] The new Court, the African Court of Justice and Human Rights, comprises two sections, *viz.*, a General Affairs section and a Human Rights section,[2136] and it provides for

---

[2130] *Ibid.*

[2131] John C. Mubangizi, Some reflections on recent and current trends in the promotion and protection of human rights in Africa: The pains and the gains, 6 *African Human Rights Law Journal*, 146–165 at 151 (2006).

[2132] The African Court Justice (ACJ) was established by the Constitutive Act of the African Union, 2002, and it's designed to operate as separate court different from the African Court on Human and Peoples' Rights. A Protocol to set up the Court of Justice of the African Union was adopted on 11 July 2003, and entered into force on 11 February 2009, AU Doc. Assembly/AU/Dec. 25 (II). Article 2 of the Protocol establishes the ACJ. Although the Protocol has been ratified by the required 15 AU State parties, this Court was never operationalised by the AU.

[2133] Protocol on the Statute of the African Court of Justice and Human Rights, EX CL/253 (IX), Annex II Rev, Art. 1.

[2134] *Ibid*, Art. 2.

[2135] Coalition for an Effective African Court on Human and Peoples' Rights, *Ratification Status: Protocol on the Statute of the African Court of Justice and Human Rights*, at www.african-courtcoalition.org/ [accessed 3 March 2010]. The reasoning for the merging was attributed to problem of funding for the two courts and to avoid having two courts having competence over matters regarding human rights.

[2136] Draft Protocol on the Statute of the African Court of Justice and Human Rights, EX CL/253 (IX), Annex II Rev, Arts. 5, 16 and 19.

a transitional period not exceeding one year or any other period determined by
the Assembly, after entry into force of the Protocol, to enable the African Court
on Human and Peoples' Rights to take the necessary measures for the transfer of
its prerogatives, assets, rights and obligations to the new African Court of Justice
and Human Rights.[2137]

The African Court of Justice and Human Rights also expanded the categories
of people who can access the court so as to include individuals, and relevant Non-
Governmental Organizations accredited to the African Union or to its organs.[2138]
By dispensing with the old requirement of an additional declaration to allow
individuals and NGOs to bring petitions, it will prevent the potential by States
to frustrate individuals and NGOs from accessing the court.[2139] It will enable
the victims of human rights abuse, such as the Niger Delta people to approach
the court directly.[2140] This is similar to what obtains under the European Court
of Human Rights, as Article 34 of the Convention for the Protection of Human
Rights and Fundamental Freedoms imposes an obligation on State parties not to
hinder in any way the exercise of the right guaranteed.[2141]

Article 43(6) empowers the Executive Council to monitor the execution of
Court judgment on behalf of the Assembly. This will go a long way to overcome
the frustrations experienced, particularly by victims of human rights violations,
concerning the non-implementation of the decisions of the African Commission.
This provision is similar to what exists under the European Convention on
Human Rights.[2142]

African Court of Justice and Human Rights decisions are final and binding
on the parties. Where a party has failed to comply with a judgment, the Court
refers the matter to the AU Assembly, which decides upon measures to be taken
to give effect to that judgment.[2143] In this regard, the AU Assembly may impose
sanctions, by virtue of paragraph 2 of Article 23 of the Constitutive Act.[2144] This
provision shows the importance of the AU Assembly – a political body, in the
enforcement of the decisions of the human rights bodies, be it in the African

---

[2137]   *Ibid*, Art. 7.

[2138]   *Ibid*, Art. 30.

[2139]   Abdelsalam A. Mohamed, Individual and NGO Participation in Human Rights Litigation
Before the African Court of Human and Peoples' Rights: Lessons from the European and
Inter-American Courts of Human Rights, 43 *Journal of African Law*, 201–213 at 204 (1999).

[2140]   George Mukundi Wachira, *op. cit.*, p.490.

[2141]   Convention for the Protection of Human Rights and Fundamental Freedoms, Rome, as
amended by Protocol Nos. 11 and 14. Article 34, relating to individual applications, provides
that: 'The Court may receive applications from any person, non-governmental organisation or
group of individuals claiming to be the victim of a violation by one of the High Contracting
Parties of the rights set forth in the Convention or the Protocols thereto. The High Contracting
Parties undertake not to hinder in any way the effective exercise of this right.'

[2142]   See Article 54 of the European Convention on Human Rights, Rome, 4 November 1950 and its
Five Protocols, www.hri.org/docs/ECHR50.html [accessed 5 July 2010].

[2143]   Draft Protocol on the Statute of the African Court of Justice and Human Rights, *op. cit.*, Art.
46.

[2144]   *Ibid*, Art. 46 (5).

Court on Human and Peoples' Rights or the African Court of Justice and Human Rights or the recommendations of the African Commission. Notwithstanding the binding nature of decision of African Court of Justice and Human Rights, if there is absence of the requisite political will on the part of the member States to enforce the decisions of the court, those decisions will be meaningless and the entire regional system will be an empty façade. Thus, in addition to the use of sanctions to ensure compliance with decisions of the Court, its member states are urged voluntarily to respect their human rights obligations, the decisions of the Commission and the Court.[2145] It is by doing this that the majority of the victims of human rights violations, particularly the Niger Delta people, would be able to utilize the Court and the Commission for better protection from the Nigerian Government and the oil MNCs. The African regional judicial system, if well reformed and monitored could help to complement the ability of the host state and the efforts being taken at the international level to hold the MNCs accountable for their human rights violations.

The Court of Justice of the Economic Community of West African States (ECOWAS) has also dealt with cases relating to the status and enforceability of the provisions of the African Charter in Nigeria. In the *Registered Trustees of the Socio-Economic Rights and Accountability Project (SERAP) v. President of the Federal Republic of Nigeria & 8 Ors*,[2146] the plaintiff, a human rights non-governmental organisation (NGO), alleged that the devastating activities of the oil industry in the Niger Delta constitutes a 'violation of the right to adequate standard of living, including the right to food, to work, to health, to water, to life and human dignity, to a clean and healthy environment; and to economic and social development.' It further alleged that the 4th (SPDC), 5th (Elf), 6th (Agip), 7th (Chevron), 8th (Total) and the 9th (ExxonMobil) defendants were active participants in the human rights violations of the Niger Delta people. Parts of the objections raised by the defendants included that the plaintiff did not have *locus standi* to institute the action for and on behalf of the people of Niger Delta. They contended that the plaintiff is not a legal person under Nigerian law and so lacks the capacity to institute proceedings before the Court. They further alleged that the Court lacks jurisdiction to adjudicate the dispute brought to it because they were neither a member of ECOWAS nor a Community Institution. In a ruling delivered on 10 December 2010, the Court held that the plaintiff is a legal entity duly constituted having been registered under the Nigerian laws as a human rights non-governmental organisation. On the issue of *locus standi*, the Court, relying on various international human rights law treaties like the Aarhus Convention, the American Convention on Human Rights, Rules of Procedure of African Court of Justice and Human Rights, and the doctrine of *action popularis*, held that the plaintiff, being duly constituted and enjoying observer status before

---

[2145]   George Mukundi Wachira, *op. cit*, p.491 (2006).
[2146]   Suit No. ECW/CCJ/APP/08/09; Rul. No: ECW/CCJ/APP/07/10.

ECOWAS institutions, did not need any specific mandate from the people of Niger
Delta to bring the action for the alleged violation of human rights that affect the
people of that region. On the Court's competence, it held that the Supplementary
Protocol, which modified the ECOWAS Treaty, conferred on it competence to
determine cases of human rights violations that occur in any Member State of
the Community. However, on the contention of the 4th-9th defendants that not
being parties to the Treaty or other ECOWAS legal instruments, they cannot be
sued before the ECOWAS Court, the court based itself on the current situation in
international law and held that it did not have jurisdiction to entertain disputes for
alleged violation of human rights perpetrated by the defendants as only Member
States and Community Institutions can be sued before it. Relying on its earlier
decision in *Peter David v. Ambassador Ralph Uwechue,*[2147] the court held that:

> "As an International Court with jurisdiction over human rights violation, the Court
> cannot disregard the basic principles and the practice that guided the adjudication
> of the disputes on human rights at international level. Viewed from this angle, the
> Court recalls that the international regime of human rights protection before inter-
> national bodies relies essentially on treaties to which States are parties as the prin-
> cipal subjects of International Law. As a matter of fact, the international regime
> of human rights imposes obligations on States. All mechanisms established thereof
> are directed to the engagement of State Responsibility for its commitment or failure
> toward those international instruments. From what has been said, the conclusion to
> be drawn is that for the dispute between individuals on alleged violation of human
> rights as enshrined in the African Charters on Human and Peoples' Rights, the
> natural and proper venue before which the case may be pleaded is the domestic court
> of the State party where the violation occurred. It is only when at the national level,
> there is no appropriate and effective forum for seeking redress against individuals,
> that the victim of such offences may bring an action before an international court,
> not against the individuals, rather against the signatory State for failure to ensure
> the protection and respect for the human rights allegedly violated. Within ECOWAS
> Community, apart from Member States, other entities that can be brought to this
> court for alleged violation of human rights are the institutions of the community
> because, since they cannot, as a rule, be sued before domestic jurisdiction, the only
> avenue left to the victims for seeking redress for grievance against those institutions
> is the Community Court of Justice."

While the ECOWAS Court, by its liberal and dynamic interpretation of relevant
treaties, has recognised the rights of Nigerians to enjoy a healthy environment,
it failed to take the bold step to assert jurisdiction over non-State actors such
as corporations for the human rights violations allegedly committed by them,
following *Kiobel v. Royal Dutch Petroleum Co.*[2148]

[2147]   Delivered on 11 June 2010.
[2148]   *Supra.* See the discussion in Chapter Four of this book.

6.6 CONCLUSION

This chapter has argued that since the regulation of MNCs under international law and under the voluntary initiatives has not been successful, those efforts should be supported by the strengthening of national and regional institutions, including civil society. Although this chapter has contended that weak institutions largely contribute to the problems of human rights abuses by MNCs in Nigeria, it has suggested that institutions, if effectively strengthened, have the potential to be part of the way out of the present quagmire. Strengthening the institutions that ensure rights protection, the rule of law, recognition, participation procedures, transparency and accountability will no doubt empower the Niger Delta people to resort to law to protect their rights. Identifying ways in which the domestic courts and local institutions can be strengthened and reformed, as discussed above, will serve to enhance the protection of the rights of citizens against human rights abuse in the hands of the Government and MNCs and help to enhance the capabilities of the domestic courts and local institutions/agencies. Given the quality of Nigerian crude, the profitability of the region's oil operations, the reliance of the MNCs State Governments on the region's oil, and the fact that it is impracticable for the multinationals engaged in resource extraction to move their capital to wherever labour is more accommodating since the resources are immovable,[2149] States like Nigeria should take advantage of these things to negotiate better and more sustainable exploratory practices with the MNCs.

Strengthening State institutions will result in more efficient law enforcement not only through the improvement of the State's capacity to implement laws and environmental standards but also through the enhancement of its public image. A restored public image will enable the State to gain the citizens' trust, and their participation in the decision making process. This will finally ensure that, in addition to being fair, just and equitable, environmental legislation and policies are implemented more efficiently.[2150]

[2149] Max Stephenson Jr. and Lisa A. Schweitzer, *op. cit.*, pp.61–62.
[2150] Alberto Costi, "Environmental Protection, Economic Growth and Environmental Justice: Are they Compatible in Central and Eastern Europe?", in Julian Agyeman *et al.* (eds), *Just Sustainabilities in an Unequal World, op. cit.*, p.303.

CHAPTER SEVEN
GENERAL CONCLUSIONS

7.1 OVERVIEW

This book has examined the question of 'Oil Exploitation and Human Rights Violations in Nigeria's Oil Producing Communities.' It has dealt with the human rights impacts of oil exploitation in the oil-rich Niger Delta region of Nigeria, the adequacy or otherwise of the legal framework in place to ensure the protection of the human rights of the local inhabitants and the local and international responses to these violations. It has proposed solutions to the problems identified, using the human rights approach and the process of institution building.

Chapter One examined who the oil producing communities (Niger Delta region) are, the history and development of oil exploitation in Nigeria, and the oil MNCs that are involved in the oil exploitation activities in the Niger Delta region. It argued that notwithstanding the State ownership of oil and its share in oil profit, the managerial and technical skills are completely in the hands of the oil MNCs. As a result, the oil MNCs usually take the important decisions relating to the operation of the business which have direct or indirect impact on the human rights of the people. In view of the relevance of technology in the oil sector, the book has argued that as obtained in countries like Norway and Brazil, the Nigerian Government should place more emphasis on the development of its manpower and technical resources as against primarily maximizing returns from oil. In addition to this, the book contends that since the State is in alliance with the oil MNCs under the joint venture and production sharing contracts, the State finds it difficult to regulate the oil MNCs as regards the human and environmental consequences of their reckless activities. Being partners under the joint venture agreements, tight regulation means less profit and less money for Government. As both equity partner and regulator of joint venture agreements, the State is unable to ensure that the oil MNCs comply with the relevant Nigerian laws, court decisions, the companies own environmental and business standards, and with internationally recognised best practice. Consequently, a lot of practices employed by operators in the oil industry, which result in the violation of the rights of the local inhabitants, are not monitored or regulated by the Department of Petroleum Resources or other agencies under the Nigerian National Petroleum Corporation, because of their status as Government agencies. To overcome

these challenges, the regulatory agencies should be granted more autonomy and
independence.

Chapter Two of this book examined the status of the indigenes of Nigeria's
oil-rich Niger Delta region under international law, to determine whether they
may be classified as indigenous peoples and/or minorities within the Federation,
and so entitled to benefit from the rights ascribed to these groups by international
law with regards to the use of land and natural resources. Identification as one
or the other (or possibly, both) has implications for the 'local' ownership of land
and natural resources with which this Chapter particularly engaged. The Chapter
concluded that the indigenes of the Niger Delta region qualify both as Indigenous
Peoples and minorities under international law and ought to benefit from the
international laws that promote the recognition of these groups to own, control
and benefit from their ancestral lands and the natural resources exploited from
such lands. However, the national laws that regulate the ownership of land and
oil in Nigeria grant the Federal Government exclusive rights of ownership and
control, while recognizing the indigenes as mere occupiers of the land, which may
be appropriated (without due notice and/or compensation) subject to the will of
the Government. Furthermore, the exploitation of oil resources and the allocation
of oil-revenues remains the exclusive preserve of the Federal Government without
due recognition of the rights of the indigenes of the region under international
law. The book finds that the ownership of land and oil in Nigeria takes little or no
cognizance of the indigenes' rights.

The Chapter also argued that the 'subverted' Federalism found in Nigeria
has given rise to the present agitation for resource control. The restiveness in the
region largely revolves around the central issue of the allocation of oil revenues,
which is itself determined by the ownership structure of the resource, which is
legally vested in the Federal Government. Therefore, the clamour for resource
control appears to be one for adequate compensation, amendment of the revenue
allocation formula, control of resources and development, and a fair, just and
equitable treatment of all people. The formula in the derivative principle based
on 13% derivation under section 162(2) of the 1999 Constitution is inadequate
and should be reviewed, as it completely ignores the environmental or ecological
damage done to the oil-producing States. It should be increased to 25% in favour
of the States where the natural resources are located. In addition to providing just
and fair revenue to the oil-producing states, this increase may propel the non-oil
producing states in Nigeria to look inward to begin to exploit the natural resources
in their own domain, rather than relying solely on oil as source of revenue,
thereby paving the way for diversification of the economy. A look into the history
of Nigeria shows that during the pre-oil economy, each of the regions that made
up of Nigeria was blessed with diverse agricultural and natural resources – West
(cocoa, etc), East (oil palm, etc) and North (cotton, groundnut, etc). The country
depends on these as major sources of income and foreign exchange earnings.
But with the oil economy (found mainly in the territory of ethnic minorities of

the Niger Delta), the regions have abandoned these natural resources to depend primarily on the 'cheap money' from oil. However, rather than yielding to the clamour of the Niger Delta states for resource control, this chapter supports the Federal Government's recent plan to give 10 per cent of oil revenues to host-communities to enhance their participation in the oil industry and to use the fund for socio-economic development of these communities. This will require that the Government should cede some of its equity to the host communities and not just to the State where the host communities are located, so giving them a stake in the oil and gas industry. To avoid the situation where the money (10% oil equity share) will end up in the pockets of local politicians and leaders of these communities, it is suggested that rather than paying the money into the State or Local Government accounts, a trust account could be opened for this purpose, to be managed by an independent institution or body. If this initiative is properly planned and well implemented, it will go a long way in reducing the violence and conflicts in the region.

Also, in line with the practice in U.S., section 44(3) of the 1999 Constitution should be amended to make the continental shelf a part of the seaward States, in addition to the territorial waters and Exclusive Economic Zone. But this must be with a qualification that the Federal Government has exclusive legislative powers over all matters relating to territorial waters, Exclusive Economic Zone and the Continental Shelf.[2151] This will enable the seaward States to benefit from the derivative principles in the Constitution and be compensated for the environmental pollution caused to their land, rivers, streams and creeks arising from exploitation of oil in the continental shelf of Nigeria.

Chapter Three examined the existing legal framework governing oil exploitation in Nigeria and pointed out some of the inadequacies in these laws and regulations. It contends, *inter alia*, that most of the environmental laws in Nigeria are inadequate to protect the human rights of the oil-producing communities. For example, the Land Use Act (LUA) 1978 changed the structure of land ownership that was hitherto vested in the family/community in the southern parts of the country including the Niger Delta region. The oil-communities consider the LUA, which divested them of their interest in the land, as a primary reason for the restiveness in the region. By reason of the Act, the Niger Delta people were deprived of their right to participate in the exploitation of natural resources (oil) from their ancestral lands. The Associated Gas Re-Injection Act[2152] on the other hand has allowed the continued flaring of gas, to the detriment of the local inhabitants of the oil-producing communities. As argued in Chapter Three, even the proposed Petroleum Industry Bill (PIB) 2012, which is currently before the National Assembly, and which is aimed at setting out a new legal and regulatory

---

[2151] Emmanuel Okon, "The Legal Aspect of Ownership and Control of Natural Resources in Nigeria", in *Contemporary Issues in the Administration of Justice, Essays in Honour of Justice Atinuke Ige*, Treasure Hall Konsult, Lagos, 2002) p.206.
[2152] Cap. A25, LFN 2004.

framework for the organisation and operation of the entire oil industry in Nigeria, does not provide adequate protection for the environment and the human rights of the people in the oil-producing areas. Hence, several of these laws appear to run counter to the indigenous peoples' rights under the international law. The result is continuous degradation of the environment, and human rights abuse of the people, contrary to the rights guaranteed under national, regional and international legal instruments. The chapter suggests a need for active participation of the Niger Delta people in the extraction of oil and gas in their region, thus creating an avenue for their voices to be heard. By giving the Niger Delta people the right to take part in the decision-making process, and the right to give or withhold their consent to activities affecting their lands and resources or rights in general, Nigeria will be complying with its obligations under the various regional and international instruments, as discussed in Chapters Two, Four and Six. There is also a need to ensure the entrenchment in the Petroleum Industry Bill provisions which promote human rights and protection of the environment of the oil-producing communities.

Chapter Three also examined some of the developmental agencies, such as the NDDB, OMPADEC, NDDC, COSEND, and the Niger Delta Ministry that have been put in place by the Government to address the Niger Delta issues and considered how effective they are in addressing the environmental and human rights challenges of the region. Despite the massive environmental degradation, and human rights violations, with which the people in this region are daily faced, the enabling statutes of these agencies are silent on important issues of social and economic rights. Making these institutions focus instead mainly on the provision of infrastructural facilities (which they rarely do as a result of corruption, among others) makes them inadequate in protecting the rights of the Niger Delta inhabitants.

In view of the above, the Government should embark on the immediate repeal/amendment of all laws which have failed to protect the rights of the local inhabitants of the Niger Delta region as a result of the oil exploration activities. It is suggested that the LUA, together with the Constitutional provisions backing it up, be repealed to ameliorate the impacts of oil exploration activities and reduce the basis for agitation and restiveness in the oil-rich region. Also, to be repealed and or amended in line with the suggestions made in Chapter Three are the Petroleum Act 1990, the Oil Pipelines Act 1990 and other subsidiary legislation. One major challenge is the cumbersome process of amendment of the LUA. A significant characteristic of the LUA is that it was made part of the previous 1979 Constitution of Nigeria by virtue of section 274(5) and later re-enacted in the 1999 Constitution of the Federal Republic of Nigeria under section 315(5). Thus, any proposed amendment to rectify its inadequacies must satisfy the formal requirements for the amendment of the Constitution which are onerous, if not impossible, when considered against the backdrop of political and economic interests that must be satisfied.[2153] Constitutional innovations alone cannot solve the problems of the minority in Nigeria. However, these innovations can 'compensate for some of the weaknesses in the social structure and political environment. Even the most imaginative Constitutions may be ... abused. But a shrewdly crafted Constitution may reduce the scope for abuse...'[2154] The LUA is one of Nigeria's most controversial pieces of legislation, and is in need of review. It is doubtful whether there can be peace in the Niger Delta region if the quest of the people for the abrogation/repeal of the various laws, including the LUA, that have dispossessed them of their right to manage their land and natural resources is not met. Taking that step could help to transform the present mode of oil production in ways that are beneficial to the Niger Delta. This requires a visionary and committed leadership backed by progressive social movements, willing to face the challenges of the equitable restructuring of the Nigerian Federal State and reverse the 'asymmetries and injustices embedded in "fossil fuel capitalism".'[2155] What is urgently required is a strong political will to commence the process of the repeal/ amendment of the LUA. The same goes for the Petroleum Act and all other related laws in order to 'bring the laws within the context of contemporary legal norms, based on international practice.'[2156] This complex amendment process should not be a barrier to the taking of steps, at the same time, to redress perceived issues of environmental injustice against the minorities. Every legal framework and institutional policy depriving the local inhabitants from benefiting from and participating in the oil industry, and which are at the root of the crises in the region, must be urgently addressed. Happily, appreciating the need to amend the LUA, the Federal Government under the late President Yar'Adua, and in fulfilment of his land reform agenda, sent a bill in March 2009 to the National Assembly entitled the Land Use Act (Amendment) Act 2009 or the Constitution (First Amendment) Act 2009), which proposed amendments to the Act to include the vesting of ownership of land in the hands of those with customary rights of ownership.[2157] This Bill is presently before the National Assembly. The National Assembly, as the peoples' representative, has the responsibility to amend laws that are obsolete, contrary to justice, equity, or capable of bringing about disunity in

---

[2153] For example, section 9(2) provides that a proposal for the alteration of the Constitution, not being an Act to which section 8 applies, shall not be passed by the National Assembly 'unless the proposal is supported by the votes of not less than two-thirds majority of all the members of that House and approved by resolution of the Houses of Assembly of not less than two-thirds of all the States.'

[2154] Larry Diamond, Issues in the Constitutional Design of a Third Nigerian Republic, 86(343) *African Affairs* 209–226 at 226 (1987).

[2155] Cyril I. Obi, Oil Extraction, Dispossession, Resistance, and Conflict in Nigeria's Oil-Rich Niger Delta, 30 (1–2) *Canadian Journal of Development Studies* 219–236 at 234 (2010).

[2156] New Nation, *Niger Delta Technical Committee's Report 'Create More States and Local Governments in the Region,* at www.condidia.com/notes [accessed 5 July 2010].

[2157] Dipo Peters, Review of the Land Use Act, *Business World*, 15 March 2009, at http://business-worldng.com/web/articles/135/1/Review-of-the-Land-Use-Act/Page1.htm l[accessed 5 July 2010].

the country. With the high calibre of legislators now in the National Assembly, in terms of their education and experience, lots could be achieved notwithstanding the 'minority status' of the Niger Delta people. It is hoped that the National Assembly will expedite action on this Bill. Amending/repealing these laws will help to ensure good relationship between the local inhabitants, the oil MNCs and the Government, which could bring about enduring peace to the region.

In addition, the chapter found that there is poor enforcement by the Government agencies and bodies responsible for the laws that are meant to protect the environment and the local inhabitants of the region. The unenforceability of these laws, coupled with some of their inadequacies, tends to diminish the faith of the oil-producing communities in the ability of laws to protect their rights to enjoy a clean and healthy environment, and to some extent, weakens their hope of getting justice. The non-enforcement of the laws perpetuates the deprivation, alienation, exclusion, and insecurity of the local inhabitants and this breeds their contempt and hatred against the oil MNCs and Government. The Nigerian Government should therefore, ensure enforcement and compliance with these laws and regulations, particularly halting illegal gas flaring so as to guarantee the protection of the rights of the local inhabitants of the region. Indeed, new environmental legislation in developing countries like Nigeria, no matter how well crafted, will amount to nothing if it is not accompanied by the development of the country's capabilities for policy development, the training of management, monitoring, and enforcement personnel, and improvement of institutional structures and administrative competence.[2158] The enforcement of these laws requires adequate monitoring equipment, staff and proper funding, as well as an absolute commitment to the enforcement of environmental protection laws and regulations by all categories of people charged with the responsibility of enforcing them.

Further, the chapter found that the compensation regime is inadequate. There is need for adequate compensation of victims of environmental harm. As long as harms are inflicted on the people and environment, compensation remains indispensable and should be legally obligatory. There must be adequate statutory compensation provisions both for the land acquired for oil exploration purposes and for damage resulting from the oil exploration activities. The current laws concerning the determination of the value and process of compensation are deficient and must be reviewed to make it easier for adequate and meaningful compensation to be received by victims of environmental harm. A new compensation regime that will engage the use of independent consultants/ valuers must be put in place to avoid the current oppressive regime where the oil communities are left at the mercy of the all-powerful oil MNCs. The Niger Delta

---

[2158] W. Onzivu, Tackling the Public Health Impact of Climate Change: The Role of Domestic Environmental Health Governance in Developing Countries, *International Lawyer*, Vol. 43, No. 3, pp.1311–1335 at 1331 (2009); J. Mayda, Environmental Legislation in Developing Countries: Some Parameters and Constraints, 12 *Ecology L.Q.* 997, 1013, 1023 (1985).

people themselves should be involved in any proposal for the construction of standard compensation scales for environmental damages because being directly affected by the losses they are best able to fully address the extent of their losses. Until the Nigerian Government starts to develop laws and policies that enshrine the principles of participatory democracy in environmental matters, the poor and the voiceless people of the Niger Delta will continue to pay the supreme sacrifice in the relentless rush towards globalization. Also needing to be addressed is the poor, or absence of, monetary compensation in some of the environmental court cases in the Nigerian courts, as seen in *Gbemre's* case, thus making the Nigerian courts less attractive than the US and European courts by litigants for filing their claims. In addition, laws prohibiting the payment of compensation for damages arising from sabotage should be repealed as this works against innocent individuals in the community who may not have been involved in the sabotage and yet suffer considerable loss as a result. While culprits caught should be treated as saboteurs, innocent victims should be compensated and the laws against their being compensated repealed.

Also important is the issue of cleaning-up of the environment. The Government must ensure that the oil MNCs embark on prompt and adequate clean-up of the environment and its restoration to the position it was in before the harm, in the true spirit of inter-generational responsibility. This is the great challenge that the region is presently facing. The present legal regime primarily focuses on providing a remedy (generally inadequate) for the individual victims affected by the environmental harm without considering the need for the degraded environment to be cleaned-up and restored to its natural state. Several communities in the region, including the Bodo and Ejama Ebubu that have been affected by the oil-related activities are waiting for clean-up and remediation of their land, damaged by oil pollution from the activities of the oil MNCs. In many other communities like Oruma, the clean-up purportedly carried out by the oil MNCs was not properly done.[2159] There is a need for the taking of a comprehensive inventory of oil spill sites, estimated as of April 2008 to number approximately 2,000,[2160] with a view to embarking on a massive clean-up and remediation of the impacted sites. For example, the U.S. environmental laws such as the CERCLA, or the 'Superfund' and the Oil Pollution Act (OPA), require *inter alia*, the polluters to cover the cost of restoring publicly owned natural resources damaged by their activities, while also compensating the public for irreparable damages and for the services lost during the process of ecosystem recovery.[2161] Such legislation is

---

[2159] Friends of the Earth Netherlands, *The Case of Oruma: Spills from a High Pressure Pipeline*, at http://milieudefensie.nl/publicaties/factsheets/factsheet-oruma [accessed 3 March 2010]; See also Amnesty International Report, *Nigeria: Petroleum, pollution and poverty in the Niger Delta, op. cit.*, pp.19–13, 33.
[2160] Amnesty International Report, *Ibid.*, p.16.
[2161] K.D. Holl and R.B. Howarth, Paying for Restoration, 8(3) *Restoration Ecology*, 260–267 at 261 (2000).

lacking in Nigeria. However, the Ministry of Environment, in collaboration with
some stakeholders, has developed a draft Bill termed Response Compensation and
Liability for Environmental Damage in Nigeria (RECLED), similar to CERCLA.
RECLED is aimed at putting in place a legal framework capable of ensuring that
the polluted environment is adequately compensated by way of remediation and
restoration; the victim is equitably compensated; and the offender or saboteur
is made to bear full liability.[2162] The proposed law is also expected to set up a
fund similar to Superfund in the U.S., to be used to remedy and respond to
environmental damages, rehabilitate impacted areas and pursue conservation
programmes, particularly in the oil industry.[2163] Efforts should be made by the
National Assembly to fast track the passage of this draft Bill into law.

At the European level, the European Parliament adopted on 21 April 2004, the
EU Directive[2164] with regard to the prevention and remedying of environmental
damage, and gave Member States till 30 April 2007 to transpose it. The Directive
is based on the 'polluter pays' principle, that is, the operator who causes the
damage should be held financially responsible. The goal is to make the polluter
pay for the cost of remediation/restoration of the environment. The Directive
makes provision for the taking of preventive measures where environmental
damage has not occurred but is imminent, and for remediation measures where
the damage has occurred.[2165] The Directive further enjoins Member States to
take measures to encourage the use by operators of any appropriate insurance
or other forms of financial security, and encourages the development of financial
security instruments and markets in order to provide effective cover for financial
obligations.[2166] These laws may guide the Nigerian legislators in enacting laws
to prevent and remedy environmental damage. By so doing, Nigeria will be
complying with principle 13 of the 1992 Rio Declaration that says that 'States
shall develop national law regarding liability and compensation for the victims
of pollution and other environmental damage. States shall also cooperate in
an expeditious and more determined manner to develop further international
law regarding liability and compensation for adverse effects of environmental
damage ...' Laws must ensure that polluters are made to restore the impacted
environment to contemporary international standards in the developed
countries. As signatory to the Convention on Biological Diversity, 1992, Nigeria

---

[2162] K. Nnadozie, "Environmental Regulation of the Oil and Gas Industry in Nigeria", in Beatrice
Chaytor B. and K.R. Gray (eds) (2003), *International Environmental Law and Policy in Africa*,
36 Environment and Policy Kluwer Academic Publishers, Dordrecht Netherlands, p.124.
[2163] *Ibid.*
[2164] 2004/35/EC (EC Environmental Liability Directive).
[2165] Annex II to the Directive, *Ibid;* Environmental Damage (Prevention and Remediation)
Regulations 2009, England, 2009 No. 153, Schedule 4, Part I, which came into force on 1 March
2009 to implement Directive 2004/35/EC; Tullio Scovazzi, "Implementation of Environmental
Legal Regimes at Regional Level: The Case of the Mediterranean Sea", in David Leary and
Balakrishna Pisupati (eds) (2010), *The Future of International Environmental Law*, United
Nations University Press, Tokyo, Japan, p.95.
[2166] Para. 27, *Ibid.*

should respect its obligations as contained in Article 8 (f) of the Convention by embarking on massive rehabilitation and restoration of the degraded ecosystems of the Niger Delta, and by taking necessary steps to promote the recovery of threatened species in the region. Provision must be made for the remediation of the environment and where restoration is not humanly feasible, or it is grossly disproportionate to the lost resource value, the polluter should be obligated to make monetary compensation. The oil MNCs should also be made to take out compulsory liability insurance for environmental damage, which would, in effect, entitle victims of pollution damage to claim compensation directly from the insurer of the oil MNCs.

The chapter also discussed the amnesty programme of the Federal Government of Nigeria. This is one of the initiatives of the Government aimed at ensuring durable peace in the Niger Delta region. It involves the grant of amnesty to some militant leaders who are willing to give up all illegal arms in their possession and completely renounce militancy unconditionally. The chapter argued that in addition to amnesty, the underlying economic, social, environmental and human rights problems, which triggered militancy in the Niger Delta must be holistically addressed, as without this, it is doubtful whether the amnesty programme alone could bring any durable peace to the volatile region. The amnesty will only bring a temporary peace to the region. Sooner or later, new and more dangerous groups may emerge in the region if nothing is done to adequately address the root causes of the Niger Delta crisis.

The Nigerian Government should also take urgent steps to begin the full implementation of the UNEP Report on Environmental Assessment of Ogoniland.[2167] In the two-year study, UNEP revealed the severe environmental damage caused by the MNCs to Ogoniland (Niger Delta), and called for the setting up of an Environmental Restoration Fund, *inter alia*, to address the widespread and extensive damage that has been done to Ogoniland, which it believed may take 25–30 years to remediate even after the ongoing pollution has been brought to an end. The Report proposed that a fund to be used only for activities concerning the environmental restoration of Ogoniland should start with an initial capital of USD1 billion, with financial inputs from the oil MNCs/NNPC. It is hoped that the Federal Government will act on this Report soon and ensure that its implementation is made to cover the entire Niger Delta region which is facing similar challenges. Government must also take the necessary steps to implement in full the findings and recommendations of the African Commission on Human and Human Peoples' Rights in *SERAC v. Nigeria*,[2168] to wit: stopping all attacks on Ogoni communities (Niger Delta); conducting an investigation into the human rights violations in the region and prosecuting officials of the security forces, NNPC and relevant agencies involved; ensuring

---

[2167]   UNEP Report (2011), *Environmental Assessment of Ogoniland, UNEP, Kenya*, pp.202–231.
[2168]   *Supra.*

adequate compensation to victims of the human rights violations, undertaking a comprehensive cleanup of lands and rivers damaged by oil operations; ensuring that appropriate environmental and social impact assessments are prepared before any future oil development; and providing information on health and environmental risks, and meaningful access to regulatory and decision-making bodies, to communities likely to be affected by oil operations, including making appropriate laws to protect the rights of citizens.

In fulfilment of one of its primary objectives, Chapter Four examined the general trend of the environmental and human rights abuses arising *via* the environment. It argued that environmental degradation is one of the underlying causes of human rights violation in the Niger Delta. It discussed how the activities of the MNCs affect the health, life, property, food, water, private lives and homes, housing, culture of the local communities. It examined the responsibilities of States for acts by non-State actors such as corporations, the responsibilities of non-State actors themselves, and the place of voluntary codes of conducts and similar initiatives in regulating the activities of MNCs. The chapter contends that self regulation, and other voluntary initiatives, play vital roles in encouraging MNCs to behave responsibly, but that the events in the Niger Delta have clearly shown that they are not sufficient to prevent environmental-related human rights violations. While hoping for the adoption of an international legally binding instrument for corporate accountability, foreign victims of corporate harm such as the Niger Delta people can continue to use the Alien Tort Claims Act to hold the MNCs accountable in the U.S. for environmental human rights abuses.

Also, if, the 'environment is man's first right,' without which 'man cannot exist to claim other rights be they social, political or economic,'[2169] the right to a healthy environment should be entrenched in Chapter IV of the Constitution of Nigeria as a fundamental human right. This will provide individuals and communities with judicial remedies and processes through which they may seek redress where their environment has been degraded, or their human rights violated, or for any potential threat to either their environment or human rights. There is no better time towards advancing a human rights argument for the provision of the right to environment in the Nigerian Constitution than now when the National Assembly is considering amendment of the 1999 Constitution.

In addition, the oil MNCs must also ensure that the security personnel comply with human rights standards. The engagement by the oil MNCs of military personnel (whom they have no control over) and local youths (particularly ex-militants apparently to pacify them) to protect their infrastructural facilities, and to ensure access of their staff to oil infrastructure, contributes to the gross human rights violations in the region. While the Voluntary Principles on

---

[2169] Ken Saro-Wiwa, "My Life, My Struggle. Being Text of Ken-Saro-Wiwa's unaccepted Address to the Ogoni Civil Disturbances Tribunal", in Omotoye Olorode *et al.*, (eds) (1998), *Ken Saro-Wiwa and the Crises of the Nigerian State,* CDHR, Lagos, p.351.

Security and Human Rights implicitly approve of corporate engagement with 'paramilitaries,' it requires oil MNCs to assess the risk of engaging actors with poor human rights records.[2170] As stated by the International Commission of Jurists: "… no prudent company would seek to protect itself from legal liability by a "don't ask, don't tell" approach to certain risks … [S]uch a strategy will not be rewarded by the law, and instead of minimising a company's chances of legal accountability, will increase the zone of legal risk."[2171]

Peace can only be ensured in the Niger Delta region when the oil MNCs and their Nigerian counterparts begin to prioritise the human rights of local communities over the company's level of oil exploitation and profit margins. Hence, the oil MNCs must take all necessary steps to screen hired security personnel for previous human rights violations or excessive use of force, and prevent such persons involved from providing company security; stop hiring private military and security companies (PMSCs) that are known for their human rights abuses; ensure that all allegations of human rights abuses by security staff and contractors are properly investigated, and where such investigation is being conducted by the Nigerian authorities, monitor the process and push for adequate and transparent resolution within a reasonable time; do away with the hiring of local youths to protect oil facilities; work in partnership with the Nigerian Government in ensuring a transition to professional, community-focused policing under a shared security model; ensure strict compliance with the Nigeria's guidelines on the use of force and the United Nations Code of Conduct for Law Enforcement Officials.[2172]

Chapter Five discussed the need to address the effects of corruption on human rights, particularly, those of the local inhabitants of the Niger Delta. The inability of the Government to meet its socio-economic and political responsibilities because of such corruption makes the people resort to self help, often manifested in violent, extra-legal and criminal practices. There is also a need for public awareness and regular training programmes for all public officials at all levels of government in Nigeria, on the nexus between corruption, human rights, development and good governance. A well informed citizen will be able to play an active role in the elimination or control of corruption and in the demand for

---

[2170] Platform Report (2011), *Counting the Cost: corporations and human rights abuses in the Niger Delta, op. cit.*, p.27. The report also detailed the various forms of repression and high-handed-ness the local inhabitants of Niger Delta have suffered at the hands of the security forces and the hired 'security contractors.'

[2171] Report of the International Commission of Jurists Expert Legal Panel on Corporate Complicity in International Crimes, *Corporate Complicity & Legal Accountability: Facing the Facts and Charting a Legal Path*, Volume 1 (Geneva: International Commission of Jurists, 2008), p.23 at http://icj.org/IMG/Volume_1.pdf [accessed 3 March 2010].

[2172] Platform Report (2011), *Counting the Cost: corporations and human rights abuses in the Niger Delta, op. cit.*, pp.55–56.

accountability from the leadership.[2173] Hence, anti-corruption agencies must make corruption a public issue among the citizens in Nigeria. In this way, they will be able to gain the confidence and support of the people, and the people will in turn feel free to bring information on corrupt practices to the appropriate agencies, without which help the country cannot succeed in the fight against corruption. The social, economic and cultural rights of the people of Niger Delta will be secured if the Government musters the needed political will to fight corruption aggressively, enact proper laws and ensure they are faithfully implemented and guarantee independence of the judiciary and other anti-graft agencies. Fighting corruption in Nigeria, particularly in the oil industry, implies a fight against one of the greatest barriers standing in the way of the Niger Delta people's enjoyment of their human rights. It is a strategy for the promotion of rule of law and human rights in Nigeria generally.

Chapter six argued that the strengthening of the scope of the procedural rights: the right of the public to access environmental information, public participation in decision-making in environmental matters and the public's access to courts for environmental matters, are vital to the protection of the rights of the Niger Delta people in the hands of both the Government and the oil MNCs. In virtually all the 'Bills of Rights' of the various groups, communities, militias, and other actors in the Niger Delta struggle, the call for active public participation in natural resources has dominated their agitations. For durable peace in the Niger Delta, there is a need to embrace a rights-based approach to economic growth, which emphasizes development that is consistent with, and quite helpful to the realisation of human rights. This should be achieved through adequate and prior consultation.[2174] Hence, in using a human rights approach to solve oil-related litigation in the Niger Delta, there is need for liberal, creative and realistic interpretation of the provisions of the Constitution and other human rights instruments to which Nigeria is a party; effective implementation of environmental treaties entered into by the Government; accessibility of courts to the people; extension of the provision of legal aid to cover environmental victims; relaxation of the *locus standi* rule, reduction in the delays in the Nigerian judicial system; recognition of class suits; a strong and independent judiciary, and the establishment of special national environmental courts.

Furthermore, judgments made in foreign courts should be enforceable in developed countries, as is the case today in most international commercial arbitrations – aimed at protecting the investors.[2175] For example, if a court in Nigeria realized that an American oil company has caused a billion dollars' worth of damage in Nigeria but with no substantial assets in Nigeria to cover the same,

[2173] Sahr J. Kpundeh, "Political Will in Fighting Corruption", in Sahr J. Kpundeh and Irene Hors (eds) (1998), *Corruption and Integrity Improvement Initiatives in Developing Countries,* United Nations Development Programme, New York, p.103.
[2174] *Centre for Minority Rights Development (Kenya) and Another v. Kenya, op. cit.,* para. 135.
[2175] Joseph E. Stiglitz (2006), *Making Globalization Work, op. cit.,* pp.205–206.

the successful litigant should be able to engage the U.S. courts to help secure the judgment sum. This should be extended to protect the developing countries from the harmful effects of the activities of the MNCs, who in order to limit their liability, limit their assets in host countries. Once this is done, unscrupulous MNCs will no longer have a safe haven for any of their activities that cause environmental harm, as they may be proceeded against in other jurisdictions where they have assets to account for their actions.

In addition, the NHRC has an important role to play in the protection of the rights of the Niger Delta people against the activities of oil MNCs and the Government. This book argues that for NHRC effectively to protect the rights of marginalised people, particularly the Niger Delta people, it must have powers to investigate alleged violation of rights, summon witnesses, sue, and enforce its decisions through courts of law. It must also have power to mediate between the parties (between the communities themselves; between the oil MNCs and the communities; and between Government and the communities) through the processes of negotiation, conciliation, or mediation. It agrees with Ruggie's recommendations that 'States should take appropriate steps to ensure the effectiveness of domestic judicial mechanisms when addressing business-related human rights abuses, including considering ways to reduce legal, practical and other relevant barriers that could lead to a denial of access to remedy;' and that 'States should provide effective and appropriate non-judicial grievance mechanisms, alongside judicial mechanisms, as part of a comprehensive State-based system for the remedy of business-related human rights abuse.[2176] In other words, in addition to effective judicial mechanisms, the State should also promote non-judicial mechanisms for resolving cases between the oil MNCs/Government and the victims of human and environmental harm. With the present degree of independence and legitimacy given to the Nigerian NHRC under the NHRC (Amendment) Act 2010, it is hoped that it will be able to function effectively as a domestic enforcement mechanism to monitor Government policies on human rights and environment, the activities of the MNCs, monitor Government compliance with international treaty obligations on human rights, educate the people on human rights, initiate investigations on its own or on complaint by any party, on matters relating to violation of human rights of the people, particularly the Niger Delta people. Also, since most of the oil communities in the Niger Delta region have little or no access to the oil MNCs and the State, the accessibility of the NHRC to the people, the flexibility of its procedure, adequate funding, well-

---

[2176] John Ruggie, *Guiding Principles on Business and Human Rights: Implementing the United Nations "Protect, Respect and Remedy" Framework*, Report of the Special Representative of the Secretary-General on the issue of human rights and transnational corporations and other business enterprises, Human Rights Council, 17th Session, A/HRC/17/31, 21 March 2011, paras. 26 and 27, at www.business-humanrights.org/media/documents/ruggie/ruggie-guiding-principles-21-mar-2011.pdf [accessed 23 July 2011].

trained and experienced staff help to make the Commission a peaceful avenue for
the Niger Delta people to lodge their complaints for the ventilation of their rights.

Further, the NGOs have a great role to play in ensuring that regulatory
agencies live up to their expectations in regulating the MNCs through the
regulatory process. The Freedom of Information Act 2011 is a vital weapon that
could be used by the NGOs and individuals to demand from the Government and
the oil MNCs information concerning environmental and human rights impacts
of the oil exploration activities and the measures put in place to mitigate any
adverse effects of these activities. When the civil society groups are strengthened,
they will be well equipped to educate the citizens, particularly the Niger Delta
people on how to use the human rights legal framework to protect themselves
against the conduct of the State and that of the MNCs that infringe or are likely to
infringe the realization of their fundamental human rights and freedoms. Also,
it will through its monitoring capabilities be able to promote transparency in the
Nigerian oil industry and ensure compliance of the oil MNCs with the domestic
laws and international standards of the industry. Therefore, given enough
financial support and resources, proper and dynamic networking with credible
environmental NGOs, the existence of democratic governance, adequate training
and capacity building and cooperation of the Government and other international
NGOs, NGOs in Nigeria have the potential for improved performance in the area
of transformation of environmental and human rights protection in the Niger
Delta region.

Also, independence of the judiciary is essential to the promotion and
protection of the human rights contained in the Constitution and other
international human rights instruments. In this regard, the National Judicial
Council (NJC),[2177] the body saddled with the responsibility of recommending
to the appropriate authorities (President – federal courts and Governors – state
courts) the appointment, discipline and removal of the Federal and State judicial
officers, should be more alert to its responsibility to ensure the independence of
judiciary. Notwithstanding section 14(3) of the Constitution of Nigeria 1999[2178]
on federal character, the NJC must ensure that due process and guidelines on
appointment of judicial officers is strictly followed no matter the 'political'
pressure. The current politicisation of the appointment of judicial officers by the

---

[2177] See Sections 153(1)(i) and 162(9) and Third Schedule Part 1 Paras. 20 and 21 of the Constitution
of the Federal Republic of Nigeria, 1999.

[2178] Section 14(3) provides that '[T]he composition of the Government of the Federation or any
of its agencies and the conduct of its affairs shall be carried out in such a manner as to reflect
the Federal character of Nigeria and the need to promote national unity, and also to command national loyalty, thereby ensuring that there shall be no predominance of persons from
a few State or from a few ethnic or other sectional groups in that Government or in any of its
agencies.' The federal character principle was defined by the Political Bureau as 'fair and effective representation of the various components of the Federation in the country's positions of
power, status and security.' See Government's Views on Bureau's Report, p. 67, cited in Rotimi
T. Suberu, 'Federalism and Nigeria's Political Future: A Comment', 87 *African Affairs*, 348
(1988), pp. 431–439, 432.

executive makes some of the judges feel that they owe obligations to the President or Governors who appointed them, rather than acting strictly in accordance with their oaths of office. The NJC must embark on tight and rigorous screening for those aspiring to come to the bench, to guard against the appointment of incompetent and unqualified persons. This will serve as a check on the power of the executives in the appointment of judicial officers. They must ensure that a prospective judicial officer has a high sense of duty and discipline, integrity, moral probity, courage, honesty, transparency, and above all, is above-board in character and learning. In order to avoid undue political interference in the judicial appointments, the composition of the NJC itself must be devoid of partisan politics. Independence of judiciary will help to guarantee the protection of the rights of the people, including the Niger Delta people and bolster their confidence in the domestic judicial system for effective remedies.

The non-entrenchment of socio-economic rights, including the right to environment, in Chapter IV of the Nigerian Constitution should not be a barrier to the Nigerian judges in promoting such rights. The courts can draw guidance from the landmark decisions of the African Commission on socio-economic rights regarding the indivisibility and interdependence of rights in the African Charter to breathe life into these rights through the civil and political rights protected under the Constitution, thereby making them justiciable. As shown in this work, the decisions of the African Commission leave no room for doubt about the enforceability of socio-economic rights and if applied by the Nigerian judges could help to change the Constitutional provisions on socio-economic rights, including the right to environment. Importantly, the Charter has been incorporated into the national laws of Nigeria. Considering the contribution of the decisions of the European Commission on Human Rights and the ECHR Court to the legal jurisprudence of some Member States, Donnelly states that:

> "The decisions of the European Commission and the Court, and the general guidance provided by the European Convention, have had a considerable impact in a number of states. For example, detention practices have been altered in Belgium, Germany, Greece and Italy. The treatment of aliens has been changed in the Netherlands and Switzerland. Press freedom legislation was altered in Britain. Wiretapping regulations have been changed in Switzerland. Legal aid practices have been revised in Italy and Denmark. Procedures to speedy trials have been implemented in Italy, the Netherlands, and Sweden."[2179]

The decisions of the African Commission can yield much better results than this only if the Nigerian courts were willing to apply such decisions and draw out a well-reasoned jurisprudence on socio-economic rights, including the right to environment. In view of the fact that the African Court had been given the

---

[2179]   Jack Donnelly (1993), *International Human Rights,* Westview Press, Boulder, p.83.

powers to issue legally binding judgments and the high calibre of persons elected
as the judges of the court, it is hoped that the court will help to complement the
somewhat limited protective role of the Commission, particularly on socio-
economic rights, which could be applied by domestic courts. In addition, there
must be willingness on the part of member States to comply with the African
Court Protocol by honouring and implementing the Court's decisions, so as
to avoid the current state of impunity with which the State members treat the
decisions of the African Commission as exemplified in the *SERAC* case. This
would go a long way in encouraging the victims of human rights violations,
including the Niger Delta people, to submit their cases to the African Human
Rights organs for the protection of their rights.

There is a need also for diversification of the economy. The overdependence
on oil in Nigeria as a major source of revenue generation is largely responsible
for the gross violation of human rights in the Niger Delta region. The business of
oil exploration is a major devourer of land, forest and water, and unfortunately,
the natural environment and the world's poor, such as the Niger Delta people,
are the ones made to pay the price in the form displacements, environmental
degradation, loss of biodiversity, loss of daily livelihood, poverty, disease and
death. Oil is the mainstay of Nigeria's economy and any inhibition to its flow
is seen by the Government as a breach of security. The response of the Nigerian
Government to the Ogoni struggle, which led to the killing of Ken Saro-Wiwa
and other eight Ogoni leaders as well as a brutal military repression that saw some
2,000 Ogoni killed, indicate how quickly civil and political rights can be eroded
where Government solely depends on just one resource.[2180] Nigeria needs to reduce
its heavy dependence on oil as its sole foreign exchange earner by diversifying its
economy into other alternative areas like agriculture and industrialization. Prior
to the oil boom era, Nigeria thrived in both mining and agriculture. Indeed, up
till the late 1970s, Nigeria was a major exporter of products like groundnut and
palm oil. This giant step will not only help to stabilise the Nigerian economy and
generate employment opportunities, but will help to reduce the rate of corruption
that has pervaded the entire polity, bring an end to environmental problems related
to oil exploration, and help to guarantee the rights of the local inhabitants of the
Niger Delta. Nigeria needs to put in place a diversification plan like countries such
as Brazil, Malaysia, Indonesia and Mexico, which have through diversification
stabilised their economies. For example, in the 1960s and late 1970s, Nigeria and
Indonesia received large windfalls from oil revenue, which they both squandered.
However, the difference between the two countries is the strong commitment
of the Indonesian Government to developing the non-oil sector, by promoting
manufactured exports and supporting agricultural development.[2181] With this

---

[2180] Ledum Mitee, quoted in Kelvin Ebiri, Nigeria's Dependence on Oil Caused Murder of Saro-
Wiwa, Others, says Mitee, *The Guardian*, 8 June 2011.
[2181] Oxfam International Briefing Paper, *Lifting the Resource Curse: How Poor People can and
should benefit from the revenues of extractive industries*, op. cit., p.21.

development, Indonesia's exports of manufactured products increased from 1.2% of total exports to 54.4% in 1999 (almost double the proportion of oil), whilst Nigeria on the other hand, continued to depend on crude oil, with the exports representing 41% of the country's total exports in 1999. Between, 1962 to 1984, real value added[2182] per agricultural worker rose by over 65 per cent in Indonesia, but dropped in Nigeria by about 15%.[2183] Nigeria neglected agriculture and solid mineral mining by concentrating on oil and gas, leading to the control of oil wealth by the few elites in the country, and to the detriment of the environment and the human rights of the people in the local communities of the Niger Delta. More importantly, oil is an exhaustible and non-renewable commodity which experts, according to President Goodluck Jonathan, have predicted may dry up in Nigeria in 35 years time on the current rate of depletion.[2184]

Finally, this book has examined the Niger Delta people's attempts to use the rights-based approach to promote and achieve environmental justice. An examination of the demands of several associations on the heels of the Ogoni crisis in the Niger Delta region showed that 'rights' is at the heart of the environmental struggle. For instance, the Ogoni Declaration, which was the first of the ethnic Bills of Rights (BoRs) asserts in para. 1 of the Addendum that the Government of Nigeria 'has…since independence in 1960 till [now], denied us our political rights to self determination, economic rights to our resources, cultural rights to the development of our languages and culture, and social rights …' In paras. 9 and 10 of the BoR, the Ogonis highlight their state of environmental, social and economic deprivation thus: in 'over 30 years of oil mining, the Ogoni nationality have provided the Nigerian nation with a total revenue estimated at over 40 billion Naira (N40 billion) or [U.S.]30 billion dollars … That in return for the above contribution, the Ogoni people have received NOTHING.' Paragraph 11 of the Ogoni BoR lists 'nothing' at the time to include: no representation whatsoever in all institutions of the Federal Government of Nigeria; no pipe-borne water, electricity, job opportunities for the citizens in Federal, State, public sector or private sector companies; and no social or economic projects undertaken by the Federal Government in the area. It alleged in paras. 15 and 16, that the search for oil has caused severe land and food shortages in Ogoni and the neglectful environmental pollution laws and sub-standard inspection by the Federal authorities has led to the ecological disaster witnessed in Ogoni. While reaffirming their wish to remain part of Nigeria, the Ogonis further asserted in para. 7 of the Addendum that 'the Ogoni … demand political autonomy as a distinct and separate unit within the Nigerian nation with the full right to (i) control Ogoni political affairs; (ii) use at least fifty per cent of Ogoni economic resources for

---

2182   Value added shows the contribution of labour and capital to production.
2183   Oxfam International Briefing Paper, *Lifting the Resource Curse: How Poor People can and should benefit from the revenues of extractive industries, op. cit.*, p.21.
2184   Quoted in Ahamefula *et al.*, Jonathan- Oil Reserve May Dry Up in 35 Years, *ThisDay*, 21 December 2011, at http://allafrica.com/stories/201112210791.html [accessed 2 February 2012].

Ogoni development; (iii) protect the Ogoni environment and ecology from further degradation; and (iv) ensure the full restitution of the harm done to the health of our people by the flaring of gas, oil spillages, oil blow-outs, etc. ...'.

From this, it appears that the Niger Delta people have attempted to use the rights-based option to articulate their struggle for environmental justice. The Ogoni BoR is clearly framed in rights-based language; the title and much of the contents explicitly refer to rights; the structure of the Bill is patterned along that of the UDHRs, and the seven points demanded in the Bill deal with right to self determination, development, political participation, language and religion, and environmental rights.[2185] Even if the claims are not framed in human rights language, they could well be human rights claims.[2186] It can therefore be asserted that achieving enduring peace in the Niger Delta requires the acknowledgment and appreciation of the human rights issues involved in the exploitation of its natural resources by the Government and the oil MNCs, and to recognize and respect the human rights of those likely to be affected by environmental related decisions, policies and programmes. This presupposes that a human rights approach must be adopted in environmental related activities, including oil exploitation activities, commencing from the grant of the permit/licence, the exploration, to the production and transportation stage. It also implies the stakeholders, including the oil MNCs, take into consideration and address the likely human rights implications of environmental decisions, procedures, plans and programmes and make human rights an integral part of those environmental policies and programmes, including their design, implementation, monitoring and evaluation. Thus, human rights and environmental protection must be clearly incorporated into the bilateral investment agreements signed between Nigeria and the oil MNCs as it will help to avoid the current situation where economic interest and profit margins are prioritised over social, developmental, environmental and human rights concerns. In other words, human rights must take precedence over the economic desires of private corporations.[2187] The Petroleum Industry Bill (PIB) currently provides an opportunity for the Nigerian Government to review the oil industry laws by making its terms more favourable to the State, ensure that it promotes and guarantees human rights and affords better protection for the people of Niger Delta. The National Assembly will do well to speed up the process of the passage of this Bill into law.

[2185] Richard Boele et al., Shell, Nigeria and the Ogoni. A study in Unsustainable Development: II. Corporate Social Responsibility and 'Stakeholder Management' Versus a Rights-Based Approach to Sustainable Development, 9 *Sustainable Development* 121–135, at 128 (2001).

[2186] Koen De Feyter, *Human Rights: Social Justice in the Age of the Market, op. cit.*, p.216.

[2187] *Ross Eventon,* "Alternatives to the BIT Framework", in Ross Eventon (ed) (2010), *Reclaiming Public Interest in Europe's International Investment Policy, EU Investment Agreements in the Lisbon Treaty Era: A Reader,* the Transnational Institute on behalf of the Investment Working Group of the Seattle to Brussels Network, Amsterdam, p.45.

7.2   DIRECTIONS FOR FUTURE RESEARCH

Further research may need to be carried out on the use of Alternative Dispute Resolution (ADR), including negotiation, conciliation, mediation and arbitration, for redressing human rights abuses caused by State and non-State actors, including the MNCs. This is with a view to overcoming the problem of access to justice by victims of environmental and human rights violations under the traditional methods of litigation. ADR, an informal justice system for resolution of legal disputes, is an alternative to litigation, and has been adjudged to be 'simpler, less expensive, faster and more efficient' and can be used as a parallel mode 'without blocking the path to the litigation and without competing with it.'[2188] It has also been associated with helping to reduce courts' caseloads, improving access for the people to get justice and preserving the parties' relationship. These are vital in ensuring harmonious relationship between the local inhabitants of Niger Delta and the oil MNCs. As noted by Ruggie,[2189] '[G]aps in the provision of remed[ies] for business-related human rights abuses could be filled, where appropriate, by expanding the mandates of existing non-judicial mechanisms and/or by adding new mechanisms. These may be mediation-based …'. The future research work may need to examine the use of ADR in developed countries, like in the EU and the U.S., consider its development in Nigeria in resolving environmental and human rights disputes, and looking at the role of the various NHRCs in this regard.

It will also be necessary for future researchers to consider the role that criminal law can play in the protection of victims of environmental harm in Nigeria, through the criminalisation of serious corporate violations of human rights. This can be done by taking a look at the United Kingdom Corporate Manslaughter Act 2007 (Chapter 19) which aims at protecting the right to life of individuals enshrined in Article 2 of the European Convention on Human Rights. The 2007 Act provides that organisations can be found culpable of corporate manslaughter as a result of serious management or organizational failure which causes a person's death, and amounts to a gross breach of a relevant duty of care owed by the organisation to the deceased. The Act which, is targeted at corporations, therefore seeks to protect the right to life of individuals enshrined in Article 2 of the Convention.

Further research should also examine the gender dimension to human rights violations in Niger Delta. No doubt, the environmental and human rights impacts of oil exploitation in the Niger Delta are often considerable, horrible and negative and affect both men and women, including children. Such a proposed study would consider whether women are the most affected.

[2188]   Elena Nosyreva, Alternative Dispute Resolution in the United States and Russia: A Comparative Evaluation, 7 *Ann. Surv. Int'l & Comp. L.* 7–19 at 7–8, 19 (2001).

[2189]   John Ruggie, *Guiding Principles on Business and Human Rights: Implementing the United Nations "Protect, Respect and Remedy" Framework, op. cit.*, see Commentary to para. 27.

There is also a need to examine in the future the involvement of local oil companies in Nigeria's oil industry (such as Atlas, Amni International Consolidated Oil, and others) to see if there are differences in their involvement in human rights abuse in the Niger Delta. The research may have a look into the indigenisation programme embarked upon by the Government and how it has helped in the growth of the indigenous oil and gas companies. It would examine their compliance with the domestic laws governing oil exploitation and the international standards in the industry. Most importantly, it would consider whether there are any differences between these indigenous companies and the oil MNCs in their manner of operation that could lead to different human rights abuses of the people in the region

7.3 IMPLICATIONS OF THE RESEARCH FOR LEGISLATION, POLICY AND PRACTICE

This book has a lot of implications for Nigerian legislators, policy makers, judiciary and the African regional system.

In the first place, the suggestions proposed in this book regarding the inadequacies in some of the legal frameworks regulating the environment may help the legislators and policy-makers in reforming these laws and policies in order to ensure the better protection of the environment and the human rights of people in the oil-producing communities. They will also help them in taking urgent steps in the domestication of some important treaties on the environment and human rights which have been entered into by the Government to guarantee its enforceability. They will also assist the legislators to put in place adequate machinery for the strengthening of the various institutions and agencies responsible for the implementation of the environmental laws and policies. They will further assist the Government in taking steps to make the right to environment justiciable like civil and political rights or in deleting the provisions of section 6(6)(c) of the Constitution of Nigeria 1999 (as amended) which hinder the implementation of the right to environment and other socio-economic rights in Nigeria.

Also, with regards to the judiciary, the custodian of the Constitution and the final arbiter on constitutionality, the book may serve as an important tool in their hands in addressing the challenges in making the right to a clean environment in Nigeria a reality, through the creative interpretation of the Constitution and other international human rights instruments relating to environment and human rights. This book may also spur the judiciary into taking steps to build the capacity of judicial officers and other court personnel for effective delivery of justice in Nigeria.

To the MNCs and other non-private actors, this book will help them to be community conscious and always to consider the human rights implications of any of their activities/strategies/policies, and to take adequate measures to protect the people and the environment. This will help them to enjoy cordial and harmonious relationships with the host communities and avoid litigation and damage to their reputations.

To the regional system, it will help the African Union in taking steps to strengthen its Court and Commission for effective justice delivery to the marginalised people of Africa, particularly the Niger Delta people, and to embark on an amendment or revision of the Charter to make its obligations cover private persons (including corporations) for the purpose of protecting and promoting all aspects of human rights within the region.[2190]

The research is also significant because a number of recommendations and ameliorative strategies proffered for the benefit of the oil-producing communities in Nigeria may be useful also to other oil-rich African countries like Cameroon, Chad, Southern Sudan, Gabon, Angola, Algeria, Côte d'Ivoire, Mauritania, Ghana, and Uganda, notwithstanding the differences in the socio-cultural, political, legal regimes and type of oil extraction [onshore and offshore] between these countries and Nigeria. The human rights abuses, corruption, environmental degradation, conflicts and other ills in the Niger Delta offer vital lessons not only for these countries but also to other oil producing communities all over the world. This book will help those countries to plan against factors that militate against the effective regulation of the activities of the oil MNCs and causing human rights abuses.

Finally, it will help the entire human rights community in creating and stimulating an appropriate legal framework to improve environmental protection and human rights.

7.4   LIMITATIONS OF THE RESEARCH

One of the limitations of this book has been an inability to cover all the nine oil-producing States, because of the instability of, and the militancy in, the Niger Delta Region. The region has been engulfed in oil-related conflicts since the early 1990s. While acknowledging that violence in the region is reducing as a result of the amnesty policy introduced in June 2009 a non-violent measure, introduced by the Nigerian Government to bring about peace in the region – the region till date is still enmeshed with violence. While the focus of this study is made up of nine States, the fieldwork was limited to three States. The communities visited were Ubeji and Iwherekhan (Delta), Awoye in Ilaje (Ondo) and Bodo in Ogoniland (Rivers). Based on the situation in the communities visited, and the views of the people interviewed, it is believed that the situation would not have been different

---

[2190]   Evaristus Oshionebo (2009), *op. cit.*, pp.111–112.

in the places not covered.[2191] However, the author was able to access some recent
works and reports that helped to bridge some of these gaps. These include the
Human Rights Watch Report titled: *The Price of Oil: Corporate Responsibility and
Human Rights Violations in Nigeria's Oil Producing Communities 1999*; Amnesty
International Reports such as *Nigeria: Are human rights in the pipeline? 2004*;
Nigeria: Ten years on: injustice and violence haunt the oil Delta 2005; *Nigeria:
Petroleum, Pollution and Poverty in the Niger Delta 2009*; Platform Reform
entitled: *Counting the Cost: corporations and human rights abuses in the Niger
Delta 2011*; and the UNEP Report 2011 titled: *Environmental Assessment of
Ogoniland*. These reports revealed similar situations in all the oil-producing
communities concerning the impacts of oil exploration activities.

Coupled with the above is the current volatile nature of Nigeria, including
the Federal Capital Territory, Abuja, which is the headquarters of most of the
Federal Government agencies. Nigeria has been under violent attack, since 2009,
by a dreaded religious sect called 'Boko Haram' – 'Western education is a sin.' The
waves of bomb and gun attacks has been targeted against Federal Government
institutions, churches, military formations, prisons, and International Institutions,
and this has led to the loss of many lives and destruction of properties worth
millions of dollars. As a result, the author was unable to conduct interviews with
some of the agencies responsible for environmental protection. At the time of
writing, these militant groups are daily carrying out sophisticated suicide bomb
attacks, including the attack on the UN building on 26 August 2011 in Abuja
which claimed twenty three lives.

Another limitation on the research was the inability to get responses from
the MNCs about the environmental damage, and the human rights impacts, of
their activities in these communities. This is as a result of the volatile nature of
the region and the reluctance of these MNCs to grant requests for interviews.
However, the book is able to rely on various reports from the MNCs, their
responses to some of the reports on their activities by civil society groups and
other international organisations, interviews given by MNCs on their activities,
and other important documents.

7.5   CONCLUDING REMARKS

This book does not pretend to offer a permanent solution to the problem of
human rights abuse in the Niger Delta caused by the reckless and irresponsible
exploration activities of the oil MNCs. It has found that the continuous violations

---

[2191]   For instance, in Iwherekhan community, all the people that were interviewed attested to the
destruction of their farmland and damage to the health of the local inhabitants due to the gas
flaring emanating from the Shell facilities. The situation is similar in Awoye community of
Ondo State, very close to the ocean where the inhabitants complained of the effects of gas flaring from the Chevron's Opuekeba Flow Station.

of human rights of the people, and the poor regulation of the oil MNCs in Nigeria, are caused by a combination of several factors including: the inadequate legal framework which robs the people of their rights to land and natural resources; poor regard for environmental considerations; poor enforcement of the relevant environmental laws; over-reliance on oil by the Nigerian State; prolonged military rule; high rate of corruption in the oil industry and the entire body polity of Nigeria; the non-justiciability of the right to environment; weak institutions such as the judiciary and the National Human Rights Commission. All of these continue today. Therefore, securing an adequate remedy for individuals whose rights are violated by the non-State actors like MNCs is vital to the current debate on business and human rights. The strengthening of the national/regional institutions, and promotion of a rights-based approach to environmental justice in the Niger Delta region, deserve concentrated attention and effort from all actors in the industry. Increased commitment by the oil MNCs to the protection and promotion of the human rights of the people in the communities will not only benefit their businesses but will bring about enduring peace in the region. Any proposed solution to the Niger Delta conflict that fails to take into consideration the rights of the host communities and their environment is bound to fail. It is only by shifting the current focus to a rights-based approach that some hope for sustainability and environmental justice can be offered to the people in the oil producing communities in the Niger Delta. In the words of Wolfgang Sachs:

> "The reference to rights – even human rights – strengthens the position of the poor, since rights can be claimed before courts ... Rights generate duties, needs and – in the best cases – active solidarity. Anyone who speaks of rights asserts that certain institutions and authorities have an obligation to give an account of themselves; the language of rights strengthens the power of the marginalized. Besides, rights cannot be so easily suspended, whereas the needs of some can always be thrown into the balance with the needs of others. Human rights, in particular, are inalienable; they cannot be set off against the greatest utility for the greatest number. In an age when the poor are often casually sacrificed for tomorrow's hypothetical utility, a rights-centred approach definitely strikes a nerve. In fact, it is the only approach that allows us to derive the claim to a dignified life here and now – and not only in the future."[2192]

Consequently, all the relevant actors in the industry must be involved in ensuring corporate accountability and human rights protection for victims of environmental harm. This is in line with De Feyter's suggestion that 'an ideal regulatory system for TNCs would be hybrid in nature, requiring the participation in the standard-setting exercise of all relevant actors, including TNCs, home

---

[2192] Wolfgang Sachs, *Environment and Human Rights*, Wuppertal Institute for Climate, Environment, and Energy, Wuppertal, p.31 at www.wupperinst.org/globalisierung/pdf_global/human_rights.pdf [accessed 3 March 2010].

and host States, intergovernmental organizations, professional associations, and non-governmental and, where relevant, indigenous organizations ... with each of the actors taking on commitments in ensuring corporate responsibility for development, according to their own specific mandates'[2193] No one derives benefit from the present situation except the irresponsible MNCs, and so maintaining the status quo leaves the voiceless, the impoverished and the marginalised people of the Niger Delta badly off. It would mean more deaths like that of Ken Saro-wiwa and the eight Ogoni patriots and increase in the restiveness in the region. The costs of Government inaction as regards the regulation of the oil MNCs in Nigeria are not only borne locally but have global repercussions, including contributions to global warming and climate change (one of the world's greatest challenge) as a result of the continuous gas flaring. Therefore, the States (home and host States), MNCs, NGOs and INGOs, the Niger Delta people, and indeed, the whole international community have an important and urgent role to play. They must act now to introduce solutions that will ensure benefit to millions of poor citizens in the Niger Delta region, and other like-communities in the world, or watch passively as the situation regarding their fundamental human rights deteriorates still further in the face of environmental injustice.

[2193]   Koen De Feyter (2001), *World Development Law: Sharing Responsibility for Development*, Antwerp-Groningen-Oxford, p.191.

SELECTED BIBLIOGRAPHY

1.   LEGISLATIONS AND QUASI-LEGISLATION

1.1 International mechanisms and Declarations

- Berne Convention on the Conservation of European Wildlife and Natural Habitats UKTS 56 (1982)
- Civil Law Convention on Corruption Strasbourg, 4.XI.1999.
- Convention on International Trade in Endangered Species 993 UNTS 243
- Convention on Biological Diversity, UN Conference on Environment and Development, UNEP.Bio.Div./CONF. L2.1992 (1992).
- Convention Concerning Indigenous and Tribal Peoples in Independent Countries, June 27, 1989, 169 I.L.O. 1989
- Convention on the Prevention and Punishment of the Crime of Genocide, 78 U.N.T.S. 277, entered into force Jan. 12, 1951.
- Convention for the Protection of Human Rights and Fundamental Freedoms, Rome, as amended by Protocol Nos. 11 and 14.
- Convention on the Rights of the Child (1989)
- Copenhagen Declaration, UN Doc A/CONF.166/7/Annex (1995)
- European Convention on Human Rights 1950
- International Convention Against Torture and Other Cruel, Inhuman, or Degrading Treatment or Punishment
- International Covenant on Civil and Political Rights (ICCPR)
- International Covenant on Economic, Social and Cultural Rights (ICESR)
- Declaration on Sustainable Development and the Plan of Implementation (UN, Report of the WSSD, UN Doc A/Conf 199/20 (2002))
- Declaration on Granting Independence to Colonial Countries and Peoples 1960
- Declaration of the Hague on the Environment, 11 March 1989, 28 I. L. M (1989)
- Declaration of the World Conference to Combat Racism and Racial Discrimination 1983
- Declaration on Principles of International Law Concerning the Friendly Relations and Co- operation Among States in Accordance with the Charter of the UN 1970
- Declaration on the Right to Development A/RES/41/128, 4 December 1986

- ILO, Convention Concerning the Protection and Integration of Indigenous and Other Tribal and Semi-Tribal Populations in Independent Countries (ILO No. 107), June 26, 1957.
- ILO Convention Concerning Indigenous and Tribal Persons in Independent Countries (ILO No. 169), June 27, 1989
- ILO Declaration on Fundamental Principles and Rights at Work 1998
- Geneva Convention on the Continental Shelf
- OECD Convention on Combating Bribery of Foreign Public Officials in International Business Transactions (17 December 1997) 37 ILM 1
- Rio Declaration on Environment and Development, adopted at the United Nations Conference on Environment and Development in 1992
- United Nations Convention Against Corruption (CAC), adopted October 31, 2003, G.A. Res 58/34, entered into force December 14, 2005
- United Nations Declaration on the Elimination of All Forms of Racial Discrimination, Adopted on 20 November 1963
- U.N Convention on Law of the Sea (UNCLOS) 1982
- United Nations Declaration on the Rights of Indigenous Peoples, General Assembly, A/RES/61/295, 13 September 2007
- World Charter for Nature, UN General Assembly Res. No. 37/7, adopted on 28 October 1982
- World Heritage Convention 11 ILM (1972)

1.2 Regional Instruments

- African Charter on Human and Peoples' Rights (Ratification and Enforcement) Act, Cap. A9, Laws of the Federation 2004
- African Union Convention on Preventing and Combating Corruption, adopted July 11, 2003, entered into force August 4, 2006
- American Convention on Human Rights 1988
- Constitutive Act of the African Union.
- Draft Protocol on the Statute of the African Court of Justice and Human Rights, EX CL/253 (IX)
- Protocol to the African Charter on Human and Peoples' Rights on the Establishment of the African Court on Human and Peoples' Rights, Doc. OAU/LEG/MIN/AFCHPR/PROT/III (1998).
- UN Economic Commission for Europe, Convention on Access to Information, Public Participation in Decision-Making and Access to Justice in Environmental Matters (June 25, 1998) (Aarhus Convention).

1.3 National legislations

- Allocation of Revenue (Federation Account etc) (Amendment) Decree 1992, No.106 of 1992

– Associated Gas Re-Injection Act, Cap. A25 LFN 2004 and the Regulations
– Independence Constitution of Nigeria, 1960
– Republican Constitution of Nigeria, 1963
– Constitution of the Federal Republic of Nigeria, 1979
– Constitution of the Federal Republic of Nigeria, 1999
– Criminal Code, Cap. C38 LFN, 2004
– Economic and Financial Crimes Commission (Establishment, Etc) Act, 2004
– Endangered Species (Control of International Trade and Traffic) Act 1985, Cap. E9, LFN 2004
– Environmental Guidelines and Standards (EGASPIN) 1991
– Environmental Impact Assessment Decree of 1992, Cap. E12, LFN 2004
– Environmental Planning and Assessment Act 1979 (NSW)
– Exclusive Economic Zone Act of 1978, Cap. E17, LFN 2004
– Federal Environmental Protection Agency Act (Decree No. 58 of 1988), Cap. F10 LFN, 2004
– Federal Republic of Nigeria Official Gazette, Government Notice No. 61, Act No. 25
– Forestry Law (Western Region) 1958 as applicable to Delta State.
– Freedom of Information Act 2011
– Fundamental Rights (Enforcement Procedure) Rules, 2009
– Guidelines and Standards for Environmental Pollution Control in Nigeria 1991
– Harmful Waste (Special Criminal Provisions etc) Act 1988, now Cap. H1, LFN 2004
– Independent Corrupt Practices and (Other Related Offences) Commission Act (ICPC Act) 2000.
– Interpretation Act, Cap I23, LFN 2004
– Land Tenure Law 1962.
– Land and Native Rights Proclamation 1910
– Land Use Act, 1978, Cap. L5, LFN 2004
– Legal Aid Act, Cap. L9, LFN 2004
– Minerals Oil Ordinance No. 17 of 1914 (amended in 1925, 1950 and 1958)
– Minerals Ordinance 1916
– Minerals Ordinance of 1945
– Money Laundering Act 1995 (amended in 2003)
– Money Laundering (Prohibition) Act, 2011
– National Environmental Protection (Effluent Limitation) Regulations 1991
– National Environmental Protection (Pollution Abatement in Industries and Facilities Generating Wastes) Regulations 1991
– National Environmental Protection (Management of Solid and Hazardous Wastes) Regulations 1991
– National Environmental Standards and Regulations Enforcement Agency (NESREA) Act 2007
– National Human Rights Commission Act, Cap N. 46, LFN 2004
– National Oil Spill Detection and Response Agency (Establishment) Act 2006
– National Parks Decree 1991

- National Policy on the Environment (1989)
- Niger Delta Development Commission Act No. 2 of 1999, now Cap. N86, LFN 2004
- Nigeria Extractive Industries Transparency Initiative, (NEITI) Act, 2007
- Nigerian Oil and Gas Industry Content Development Act, 2010
- Official Secrets Act, Cap. O3, LFN 2004
- Offshore Revenue Act of 1971
- Offshore/Onshore Oil Dichotomy Abolition Act, 2004
- Oil in Navigable Waters Act, Cap. O6, LFN 2004
- Oil Minerals Producing Areas Development Commission Decree No. 23 of 1992 (as amended in 1996).
- Oil Pipelines Act, Cap. O7, LFN 2004
- Penal Code, Cap. P3 LFN, 2004
- Petroleum Act 1969, Cap. P.10, LFN 2004 and the Petroleum (Drilling and Production) Regulations
- Petroleum Industry Bill 2012
- Sea Fisheries Decree 1992, now Cap. S4, LFN 2004
- Wild Animals Preservation Law (Western Region) 1959 as applicable to Delta State.

1.4 Other legislations

- Angola Constitution adopted by the People's Assembly on 25 August 1992
- Australian Corporate Code of Conduct Bill 2000
- Ghana's Commission on Human Rights and Administrative Justice Act, 1993
- Indian Constitution 1950
- Kenya National Commission on Human Rights Act, 2002
- Legal Aid Commission Act 1979 (New South Wales)
- Uganda Human Rights Commission Act, 1997

2. OFFICIAL PUBLICATIONS

2.1 United Nations and its agencies

- DAES, E.I. (1996) Working Paper by the Chairperson-Rapporteur, Mrs. Erica-Irene A. Daes. On the Concept of 'Indigenous People', UN Doc. E/CN.4/Sub.2/AC.4/1996/2
- EIDE, A., Possible Ways and Means of Facilitating the Peaceful and Constructive Solution of Problems Involving Minorities, E/CN.4/Sub.2/1993/34.
- Human Development Report, *Sustainability and Equity: A Better Future for All*, UNDP, New York, 2011, available at http://hdr.undp.org/en/ [accessed 13 June 2012].
- International Chamber of Commerce, *Joint views of the IOE and ICC on the draft norms on the responsibilities of transnational corporations and other business enterprises with regard to human rights* UN ESCOR, 55th Sess. UN Doc E/CN.4/Sub.2/2003/NGO/44 (2003)

–   KI-MOON, Ban, "Protect, Promote, Endangered Languages, Secretary-General Urges in Message for International Day of World's Indigenous People", SG/SM/11715, HR/4957, OBV/711 (23 July 2008)

–   MARTINEZ COBO, Jose R., *Study of the Problem of Discrimination Against Indigenous Populations,* UN Doc. E/CN.4/Sub.2/1986/7/Add.4, UN Sales No. E.86.XIV3 (1986).

–   RUGGIE, John, *Protect, Respect and Remedy: A Framework for Business and Human Rights*, Report of the Special Representative of the Secretary General on the issue of human rights and transnational corporations and other business enterprises (7 April 2008) UN Doc A/HRC/8/5

–   RUGGIE, John, *Business and human rights: Towards operationalizing the 'protect, respect and remedy' framework*, report of the Special Representative of the Secretary-General, UN Human Rights Council, A/HRC/11/13, April 2009.

–   RUGGIE, John, *Business and Human Rights: Further steps toward the operationalization of the 'protect, respect and remedy' framework*, report of the Special Representative of the Secretary-General, UN Human Rights Council, A/HRC/14/27, April 2010

–   RUGGIE, John, *Guiding Principles on Business and Human Rights: Implementing the United Nations "Protect, Respect and Remedy" Framework*, Report of the Special Representative of the Secretary-General on the issue of human rights and transnational corporations and other business enterprises, Human Rights Council, 17th Session, A/HRC/17/31, 21 March, 2011.

–   Special Rapporteur Mrs. Daes, in her final report to the Sub-Commission on the Promotion and Protection of Human Rights, Indigenous Peoples' Permanent Sovereignty over Natural Resources. Final Report of the Special Rapporteur, Erica-Irene A. Daes, E/CN.4/Sub.2/2004/30, 13 July 2004

–   Traditional Knowledge and Biological Diversity, UNEP/CBD/TKBD/1/2, 18 October 1997.

–   UNEP/UNICEF/WHO, *Children in the New Millennium: Environmental Impact on Health*, Nairobi/New York/ Geneva, 2002

–   United Nations Centre for Human Settlements (Habitat), Cities in a Globalizing World- Global Report on Human Settlements 2001, Earthscan Publications, London, 2001

–   UN Centre on Transnational Corporations and Economic and Social Commission for Asia and the Pacific, *Environmental Aspects of Transnational Corporations Activities in Pollution-Intensive Industries in Selected Asian and Pacific Developing Countries*, ESCAP/UNCTC Publications Series B, no. 15 (1990)

–   UN Committee on Economic, Social and Cultural Rights, '*Substantive Issues Arising in the Implementation of the International Covenant on Economic, Social and Cultural Rights,*' General Comment No. 14, The Right to the Highest Attainable Standard of Health, General Comment No. 14, E/C.12/2000/4 (2000)

–   United Nations Conference on Trade and Development UNCTAD/CALAG African Oil and Gas Services Sector Survey Volume 1- Nigeria Creating Local Linkages by

Empowering Indigenous Entrepreneurs UNCTAD/DITC/COM/2005/6, United
Nations Publications, New York and Geneva, 2006.

– UN Economic and Social Council, Commission on Human Rights, *Report of the
International Seminar on Cooperation for the Better Protection of the Rights of Minorities,* Fifty-eighth Session, Item 14 (b) of the Provisional Agenda, E/CN.4/2002/92,
30 January 2002

– United Nations Office on Drugs and Crime (UNODC), *UNODC's Action against
Corruption and Economic Crime,* available at www.unodc.org/unodc/en/corruption/
index.html?ref=menuside [accessed 5 March 2010]

– UN Economic and Social Council, *The Role of National Human Rights Institutions in
the Protection of Economic, Social and Cultural Rights,* General Comment No. 10, 19
Sess., UN Doc. E/C.12/1998/25 (1998)

– UN Committee on Economic, Social and Cultural Rights (CESCR), *UN Committee
on Economic, Social and Cultural Rights: Concluding observations: Nigeria,* 16 June
1998, E/C.12/1/Add.23

– UNDP, Human Development Index 2009, available at http://hdr.undp.org/en/media/
HDR_2009_EN_Indicators.pdf [accessed 5 March 2010]

– UNDP, 'Human Development Index,' 2007, 2008, available at http://hdr.undp.org/en/
media/HDI_2008_EN_Tables.pdf [accessed 5 March 2010]

– UN Economic and Social Council, Commission on Human Rights, Norms on the
Responsibilities of Transnational Corporations and other Business Enterprises with
Regard to Human Rights, E/CN.4/Sub.2/2003/12/Rev. 2, 26 August 2003

2.2 Multilateral and other institutions

– International Labour Organization, *The Labour Principles of the United Nations Global Compact: A Guide for Business,* International Labour Office, Geneva: ILO, 2008

– SWARTZ, John and UQUILLAS, Jorge: *Aplicación de la Política del Banco sobre
Poblaciones Indígenas (OD 4.20) en América Latina (1992–1997),* World Bank, Regional Office for Latin America and the Caribbean (1999).

– The World Bank, *Helping Countries Combat Corruption: The Role of the World Bank*
(Washington, DC: The World Bank, 1997).

– The World Bank, *Nigeria Rapid Country Environmental Assessment, Final Report,* 30
November 2006.

– World Bank, *Niger Delta Social and Conflict Analysis,* Washington, DC, 2008.

– World Bank World Development Report 1996 and Fortune's Global 500 of 1994, Fortune, August 7, 1995

– World Bank, *Defining an Environmental Development Strategy for the Niger Delta,*
25 May 1995, Vol. II, Industry and Energy Operations Division West Central Africa
Department

– World Bank, Operational Policies: Indigenous Peoples (OP 4.10, July 2005).

3. BOOKS, MONOGRAPHS AND REPORTS

3.1 Books

- ABASS, Ademola (2012), *International Law: Text, Cases, and Materials*, Oxford University Press, Oxford.
- ANTON, Donald K. and SHELTON, Dinah L. (2011), *Environmental Protection and Human Rights*, Cambridge University Press, New York.
- ARIWERIOKUMA, Soala (2009), The Political Economy of Oil and Gas in Africa: The Case of Nigeria, Routledge, London & New York.
- ATAPATTU, Sumudu A. (2006), *Emerging Principles of International Environmental Law*, Inc., Transnational Publishers, Ardsley, NY.
- AZAIKI, Steve (2006), *Oil, Politics and Blood: The Niger Delta Story*, Y-Books.
- AZAIKI, Steve (2007), *Inequities in Nigerian Politics: The Niger Delta, Resource Control, Under Development and Youth Restiveness*, Y-Books.
- AZAIKI, Steve (2007), *Oil, Gas and Life in Nigeria*, Y-Books.
- BAUGHEN, Simon (2007), *International Trade and the Protection of the Environment*, Routledge-Cavendish, London & New York.
- BERLIN, Isaiah (1969), Four Essays on Liberty XIII.
- BERNAS, Joaquin G. (2003), *The 1987 Constitution of the Federal Republic of the Philippines: A Commentary,* Rex Publishing, Manila.
- BIRNIE, Patricia *et al.* (2009), *International Law and the Environment*, 3rd Edition, Oxford University Press, Oxford New York.
- BISONG, Kekong (2009), *Restorative Justice for Niger Delta*, Maklu Publishers, Antwerpen.
- BOND, P. and REHANA, D. (2005), *Trouble in the Air, Global Warming in the Privatised Atmosphere*, Civil Society Reader, Durban.
- BOSSELMANN, Klaus (2008), *The Principle of Sustainability: Transforming Law and Governance*, Ashgate, Aldershot, Hampshire.
- BROWNLIE, Ian (1990), *Principles of Public International Law,* 4th ed., Oxford.
- CASSESE, A. (1998), *Self-Determination of Peoples: A Legal Reappraisal*, Cambridge University Press, Cambridge.
- CHURCHILL, R.R. and Lowe A.V. (1999), *The Law of the Sea*, 3rd ed., Manchester University Press, Manchester.
- CLAPHAM, Andrew (2006), *Human Rights Obligations of Non-State Actors,* Oxford University Press, Oxford.
- COKER, G. (1966), *Family Property Among the Yorubas*, Sweet & Maxwell, London.
- CURTIN, Philip, FEIERMAN, Steve, THOMPSON, Leonard and VANSINA, Jan (1981), *African History,* Longman Group Limited, London.
- CURTIS, M. (2001), *Trade for Life: Making Trade Work for the Poor*, Christian Aid, London.
- DONNELLY, Jack (1993), *International Human Rights,* Westview Press, Boulder.

- DOUGLAS, Oronto and Okonta I. (2001), *Where Vultures Feast*, Sierra Club San Francisco
- DREWER, John D. (2000), *Ethnography*, Open University Press, Buckingham
- EBEKU, Kaniye (2006), *Oil and the Niger Delta in International Law. Resource Rights, Environmental and Equity Issues*, Rudiger Koppe Verlag, Germany.
- EKPO, U. (2004), *The Niger Delta and Oil Politics*, International Energy Communications Limited Publications, Lagos.
- ELIAS, T.O. (1971), *Nigerian Land Law*, 4ᵗʰ Ed., Sweet & Maxwell, London.
- ENAHORO, Anthony *et al.* (1992), *"Position Paper, Movement for National Reformation." A General Brief*, Saros International Publishers, Port Harcourt.
- ETIKERENTSE, G. (1985), *Nigerian Petroleum Law*, 1ˢᵗ ed., Macmillan, London.
- FEYTER, Koen De (2001), *World Development Law: Sharing Responsibility for Development*, Intersentia, Antwerp-Groningen-Oxford.
- FEYTER, Koen De (2005), *Human Rights: Social Justice in the Age of the Market*, Zed Books Ltd., London & New York.
- GLESNE, Corrine (1999), *Becoming Qualitative Researchers: An Introduction*, Longman Inc., New York.
- HAYWARD, T. (2005), *Constitutional Environmental Rights*, Oxford University Press, Oxford.
- HUGO, Victor (1877), *Histoire D' Un Crime* (1877).
- IKEIN, Augustine (1991), *The Impact of Oil on a Developing Country: The Case of Nigeria*, Evans Brothers Nigeria Ltd., Ibadan.
- JAGERS, Nicola (2002), *Corporate Human Rights Obligations: In Search of Accountability*, Intersentia, Antwerpen.
- JOSEPH, Sarah (2004), *Corporations and Transnational Human Rights Litigation*, Hart Publishing, Oxford-Portland Oregon.
- KECK, Margaret and SIKKINK, Kathryn (1998), *Activists Beyond Borders: Advocacy Networks in International Politics*, Cornell University Press, Ithaca, NY.
- KHAN, Sarah Ahmad (1994), *Nigeria: The Political Economy of Oil*, Oxford University Press, USA.
- KINLEY, David (2009), *Civilising Globalisation. Human Rights and the Global Economy*, Cambridge University Press, United Kingdom.
- KISS, Alexandre and SHELTON, Dinah (1995), *International Environmental Law*, Transnational Publishers, Ardseley, New York.
- KOEBELE, Michael (2009), *Corporate Responsibility under the Alien Tort Statute: Enforcement of International Law through US Torts Law*, Martinus Nijhoff Publishers, Leiden, Boston.
- LADAN, Muhammed T. (2007), *Biodiversity, Environmental Litigation, Human Rights and Access to Justice: A Case Study of Nigeria*, Faith Printers and Publishers, Zaria.
- LAPONCE, J.A. (1960), *The Protection of Minorities*, University of California Press, Berkeley & Los Angeles.

- MALANCCZUK, P. (1997), *Akehurst's Modern Introduction to International Law*, 7th ed., Routledge, London.
- MASON, Jennifer (2002), *Qualitative Researching*, Sage Publications Ltd., London, Thousand Oaks, New Delhi
- MOORE, William A. (1970), *History of Itsekiri*, Frank Cass & Co. Ltd., London.
- MUSGRAVE, Thomas (1997), *Self Determination and National Minorities*, Clarendon Press, Oxford.
- NWABUEZE, B.O. (1982), *Nigerian Land Law*, Nwamife Publishers, Enugu.
- NWOKEDI, R. Chiemeka (2003), *Revenue Allocation and Resource Control in Nigerian Federation*, 2nd ed., Snaap Press Ltd., Enugu, 2003.
- OKABA, B.O. (2005), *Petroleum Industry and the Paradox of Rural Poverty in the Niger Delta*, Ethiope Publishers, Benin City.
- OKAFOR, Obiora C. (2007), *The African Human Rights System, Activist Forces, and International Institutions,* Cambridge University Press, Cambridge.
- OKIGBO, P.C.N. (1965), *The Nigerian Public Finance*, Longman, London.
- OKORODUDU-FUBARA, M.T. (1998), *Law of Environmental Protection: Materials and Text*, Caltop Publications Ltd., Lagos.
- OLISA, M.M. (1987), *Nigerian Petroleum Law and Practice*, Fountain Press, Ibadan.
- OMEJE, Kenneth (2006), *High Stakes and Stakeholders: Oil Conflict and Security in Nigeria*, Ashgate Publishing Ltd., England.
- OMOWEH, Daniel A. (2005), *Shell Petroleum Development Company, the State and Underdevelopment of Nigeria's Niger Delta: A Study in Environmental Degradation*, Africa World Press, Inc., Trenton, NJ and Asmara, Eritrea.
- OMOROGBE, Yinka (2001), *Oil and Gas in Nigeria*, Malthouse Press Ltd., Lagos.
- Oshionebo, Evaristus (2009), *Regulating Transnational Corporations in Domestic and International Regimes: An African Case Study,* University of Toronto Press, Toronto, Buffalo, London.
- PATTON, M. (1990), *Qualitative evaluation and research methods,* Sage Publications, Newbury Park, CA.
- PEZEZ, Oren (2004), *Ecological Sensitivity and Global Legal Pluralism: Rethinking the Trade and Environment Conflict*, Hart Publishing, Oxford & Portland Oregon.
- PIDDINGTON, Ralph (1950), *An Introduction to Social Anthropology*, Oliver and Boyd, London.
- PLANT, R. (1994), *Land Rights and Minorities*, Minority Rights Group, London.
- RAWLS, John (1999), *A Theory of Justice,* Revised ed., Belknap Press of Harvard University, Harvard.
- REHMAN, Javaid (2000), *The Weaknesses in the International Protection of Minority Rights*, Kluwer Law International, Netherlands.
- ROWELL, A. *et al.* (2005), *The Next Gulf: London, Washington and Oil Conflict in Nigeria*, Constable and Robinson, London.
- SARO-WIWA, Ken (1992), *Genocide in Nigeria: The Ogoni Tragedy*, Saros International Publishers, London, Lagos & Port Harcourt.

- SARO-WIWA, Ken (1995), *A Month and a Day: A Detention Diary,* Penguin Books, New York.
- SCHÄTZL, L.H. (1969), *Petroleum in Nigeria,* Oxford University Press.
- SCHLOSBERG, David (2007), *Defining Environmental Justice: Theories, Movements, and Nature,* Oxford University Press, Oxford.
- SHRADER-FRECHETTE, Kristin (2002), *Environmental Justice: Creating Equality, Reclaiming Democracy,* Oxford University Press, Oxford.
- STEINER, H.J. *et al.* (2008), *International Human Rights in Context. Law, Politics, Moral. Text and Materials,* Third Edition, Oxford University Press, Oxford.
- STIGLITZ, Joseph E. (2006), *Making Globalization Work,* Allen Lane, an imprint of Penguin Books Ltd., London.
- SUBERU, R.T. (1996), *Ethnic Minority Conflicts and Governance in Nigeria,* Spectrum Books Ltd., Ibadan.
- TAYLOR, Prue (1998), *An Ecological Approach to International Law. Responding to Challenges of Climate Change,* Routledge, London and New York.
- THORNBERRY, P. (1991), *International Law and the Rights of Minorities,* Clarendon Press, Oxford.
- THORNTON, J. and BECKWITH, S. (2004), *Environmental Law,* 2nd edition, Sweet & Maxwell, London.
- UDOMA, U. (1994), *The History and the Law of the Constitution of Nigeria,* Spectrum Books Ltd., Ibadan.
- UTUAMA, A.A. (1989), *Nigerian Law of Real Property,* Shaneson, Ibadan.
- VILLIGER, M.E. (1985), *Customary International Law and Treaties,* Martinus Nijhoff Publishers, Dordrecht.
- WELCH, Claude E. Jr. (1995), *Protecting Human Rights in Africa: Strategies and Roles of Nongovernmental Organizations,* University of Pennsylvania Press, Philadelphia.
- WHEARE, K.C. (1963), *Federal Government,* 4th ed., Oxford University Press, London.
- YOUNG, Iris (1990), *Justice and the Politics of Difference,* Princeton University Press, Princeton NJ.
- ZHIGUO, Gao (1994), *International Petroleum Contracts: Current Trends and New Directions,* Graham & Trotman/M. Nijhoff, London.

3.2 Monographs

- Adewale, O. (1990), *Sabotage in the Nigerian Petroleum Industry: Some Socio-Legal Perspective,* Nigerian Institute of Advanced Legal Studies Occasional Paper.
- Center for Reproductive Rights (CRR) (2008), *Broken Promises: Human Rights, Accountability and Maternal Death in Nigeria,* CRR, New York.
- Constitutional Rights Project (CRP) (1999), *Land, Oil and Human Rights in Nigeria's Delta Region,* CRP, Lagos.

- Environmental Law Institute (2007), *Constitutional Environmental Law: Giving Force to Fundamental Principles in Africa*, 2nd ed., Environmental Law Institute, Washington DC.
- IBEANU, Okechukwu (2006), *Civil Society and Conflict Management in the Niger Delta: Scoping Gaps for Policy and Advocacy*, CLEEN Foundation Monograph Series, No. 2 August.
- IBEANU, Okechukwu (2008), *Affluence and Affliction: The Niger Delta as a Critique of Political Science in Nigeria*, being 27th Inaugural Lecture of the University of Nigeria delivered on 20 February, University of Nigeria Press Ltd., Nsukka.
- International Institute for Democracy and Electoral Assistance (IDEA) (2002), *Democracy in Nigeria: Continuing Dialogue for Nation Building*, Lagos/Nigeria.
- IJALAYE, D.A. (2001), *The Imperatives of Federal/State Relations in a Fledgling Democracy: Implication for Nigeria*, NIALS publication, Lagos.
- IKELEGBE, A. (2010), *Oil, Resource Conflicts and the Post Conflict Transition in the Niger Delta Region: Beyond the Amnesty*, Centre for Population and Environmental Development (CPED) Monograph Series No. 3, Ambik Press, Benin City.
- OKORODUDU-FUBARA, M.T. (1999), *Dynamics of a New World Environmental Legal Order*, An Inaugural Lecture delivered at Oduduwa Hall, Obafemi Awolowo University, Ile-Ife, Nigeria on Tuesday, 13 April, Inaugural Lecture Series 133, Obafemi Awolowo University Press Ltd., Ile-Ife.
- Open Society Justice Institute (2005), *Legal Remedies for the Resources Curse: A Digest of Experience in Using Law to Combat Natural Resource Corruption*, Legal Policy Series.
- Programme on Ethnic and Federal Studies (PEFS) (2004), *The Niger Delta Question: Background to Constitutional Reform*, Monograph New Series No. 8, Department of Political Science, University of Ibadan, Ibadan.
- Social and Economic Rights Action Center (SERAC) (2005), *Perpetuating Poverty, Consolidating Powerlessness: Oil and the Niger Delta*, SERAC, Lagos.

3.3 Reports focusing on Nigeria

- Amnesty International Report (1995), *Nigeria: The Ogoni Trial and Detentions*, AI Index: AFR 44/020/95.
- Amnesty International Report (1996), *Nigeria: A Travesty of Justice: The Secret Treason Trial and Other Concerns*, AI Index: 44/03/96
- Amnesty International Report (2004), *Nigeria: Are Human Rights in the Pipeline?* AI Index: AFR 44/020/2004.
- Amnesty International Report (2005), *Nigeria: Claiming Rights and Resources Injustice, Oil and Violence in Nigeria*, available at www.amnesty.org. [accessed 5 March 2010]
- Amnesty International Report (2006), *Nigeria: Rape – the Silent Weapon*, Amnesty International 28 November.

– Amnesty International Report (2009), *Nigeria: Petroleum, Pollution and Poverty in the Niger Delta*, available at www.amnesty.org/en/library/asset/AFR44/017/2009/en/e2415061-da5c-44f8-a73c-a7a4766ee21d/afr440172009en.pdf [accessed 5 March 2010]

– Ashton-Jones, N. J. and Oronto N. D. (1994), *Report to Statoil (Nigeria) Ltd.: Baseline Ecological Survey of the Niger Delta,* Pro-Natura International, Lagos.

– Christian Aid, *Behind the mask, Sustained Misery: Shell in the Niger Delta*, available at www.evb.ch/cm_data/public/Shell%20Award%20Nominierung_Behind%20the%20mask_0.pdf [accessed 7 March 2010]

– Environmental Resource Manager Limited (1998), *Niger Delta Environmental Survey Final Report*, Phase 1, Vol. 1, Niger Delta Environmental Survey, Lagos.

– Environmental Rights Action/Friends of the Earth Nigeria/Climate Justice Programme Report (2005), *Gas Flaring in Nigeria: A Human Rights, Environmental and Economic Monstrosity,* available at www.climatelaw.org/cases/case-documents/nigeria/report/section9 [accessed 26 February 2010]

– Human Rights Watch/Africa (1995), *Nigeria: The Ogoni Crisis: A Case Study of Military Repression in Southeastern Nigeria*, available at www.unhcr.org/refworld/docid/3ae6a7d8c.html [accessed 26 September 2010]

– Human Rights Watch (HRW) (1999), *The Price of Oil: Corporate Responsibility and Human Rights Violations in Nigeria's Oil Producing Communities*, New York.

– Human Rights Watch (2002), *The Niger Delta: No Democratic Dividend*, Vol. 14 No. 6 (A), available at www.hrw.org/reports/2002/nigeria3/nigerdelta.pdf

– Human Rights Watch (2007), *Chop Fine: The Human Rights Impact of Local Government Corruption and Mismanagement in Rivers State, Nigeria,* Volume 19, No. 2(A).

– Human Rights Watch, *World Report 2011 – Nigeria*, 24 January 2011, available at www.unhcr.org/refworld/docid/4d3e80220.html [accessed 26 May 2011]

– International Crisis Group Africa Report (2006), *Fuelling the Niger Delta Crisis*, Africa Report No. 118.

– International Crisis Group Policy Briefing (2008), *Nigeria: Ogoni Land after Shell*, Crisis Group Africa Briefing No. 54.

– Joint UNDP/World Bank Energy Sector Management Assistance Programme (ESMAP) Report (2004), *Taxation and State Participation in Nigeria's Oil and Gas Sector.*

– National Human Rights Commission Nigeria Annual Report (2009), available at www.nigeriarights.gov.ng/images/articles/2009%20Annual%20Report.pdf [accessed 5 May 2010].

– Niger Delta Environmental Survey (1997), *Environmental and Socio-economic Characteristics, second phase of field report*, Vol. 1, Environmental Resource Manager Limited.

– Niger Delta Human Development Report (2006), UNDP Publication

– Niger Delta Regional Development Master Plan: Summary of Draft Report.

– Nigerian Environment Study/Action Team (1991), *Nigeria's Threatened Environment. A National Profile.*

– Nigeria Extractive Industries Transparency Initiative Report on the Physical Audit 1999- 2004 Appendix C: Gas System (2006), prepared by Hart Resources Ltd., available at www.neiti.org.ng/FinalAuditReports-Sept07/PhysicalReports/Appendicies/AppCGasSystemBinder.pdf [accessed 22 April 2010].

– NWOKEJI, Ugo G. (2007), *The Nigerian National Petroleum Corporation and the Development of the Nigerian Oil and Gas Industry: History, Strategies and Current Directions*, Prepared in Conjunction with an Energy Study sponsored by the James A. Baker III Institute for Public Policy and Japan Petroleum Energy Center, Rice University, available at www.rice.edu/energy/publications/docs/NOCs/Papers/NOC_NNPC_Ugo.pdf [accessed 22 April 2010].

– Oputa Report, Vol. 3, available at www.nigerianmuse.com/nigeriawatch/oputa/OputaVolumeThree.pdf [accessed 22 April 2010].

– Platform Report (2011), '*Counting the Cost: Corporations and Human Rights Abuses in the Niger Delta*,' available at http://platformlondon.org/nigeria/Counting_the_Cost.pdf. [accessed 11 November 2011].

– POWELL, C.B. (1993), *Sites and species of Conservation Interest in Central Axis of the Niger Delta (Section C)*, report submitted to the Natural Resources Conservation Council of Nigeria, Biodiversity Unit, Rivers State University of Science and Technology, Port Harcourt, Nigeria

– Report of the Special Representative of the Secretary-General on Human Rights Defenders on her Visit to Nigeria (3–12 May 2005).

– Report of the Technical Committee on the Niger Delta (2008), available at www.mosop.org/Nigeria_Niger_Delta_Technical_Committee_Report_2008.pdf [accessed 6 May 2010].

– SPDC Nigerian Annual Report (1998), *People and the Environment*

– Social Development Integrated Centre (Social Action) (2009), *Carry Go*, Citizens Report on State and Local Government Budgets in the Niger Delta 2008, Published by Niger Delta Citizens and Budget Platform, available at http://saction.org/ebook/carry%20go-full%20report.pdf [accessed 5 May 2010].

– Social Development Integrated Centre (Social Action) (2009), *Communities and the Petroleum Industry Bill (PIB)*, being Report of Communities and Civil Society Consultation Forum on the Petroleum Industry Bill 2009, organized by Social Action, Stakeholder Democracy Network (SDN) in collaboration with the Bayelsa State NGO Forum (BANGOF), Yenagoa, Bayelsa State, 27–28 November 2009.

– UNEP Report (2011), *Environmental Assessment of Ogoniland*, UNEP, Kenya.

– Willink Commission, *Report of the Willink Commission Appointed to Enquire into the Fears of Minorities and the Means of Allaying them*, C.O.957/4, Colonial Office, July 1958, London.

– World Bank (1995), *Defining an Environmental Development Strategy for the Niger Delta*, World Bank, Washington DC.

– World Bank Report, *Niger Delta Social and Conflict Analysis*, Sustainable Development Department Africa Region, May, 2008, available at http://siteresources.worldbank.org/EXTSOCIALDEV/Resources/ [accessed 3 March 2010].

4   ARTICLES IN BOOKS AND JOURNALS

4.1 Articles in books

–   ADAM, S.M., "Human Rights and Environmental Protection in Nigeria", in J.M. Nasir *et al* (eds) (2008), *Contemporary Readings in Governance, Law and Security: Essays in Honour of (Sir.) Mike Mbama Okiro, Inspector-General of Police,* Constellation (Nig.) Publishers, Ibadan, Abuja.

–   ADEWALE, Bola, "An Overview of Biological Biodiversity Laws in Nigeria", in I.A. Ayua (ed) (1995), *Law, Justice and the Nigerian Society: Essays in Honour of Hon. Justice Mohammed Bello,* NIALS, Lagos.

–   ADIGUN, Olayide, "An Egalitarian Land Policy for Nigeria", in J.A. Omotola (ed) (1991), *Issues in Nigerian Law,* Faculty of Law, University of Lagos, Lagos.

–   AGA, Jennifer S., "The Role Played by the National Human Rights Commission in Enhancing Access of Individuals, Groups and Communities to Effective Remedies from Oil Corporations and other Multinationals when Violation Occurs", in Social and Economic Rights Action Center (SERAC) (2005), *Perpetuating Poverty, Consolidating Powerlessness: Oil and the Niger Delta,* SERAC, Lagos.

–   AGBOOLA, Tunde and ALABI, Moruf, "Political Economy of Petroleum Resource Development, Environmental Injustice and Selective Victimization: A Case Study of the Niger Delta Region of Nigeria", in Julian Agyeman, *et al.* (eds) (2003), *Just Sustainabilities in an Unequal World,* Earthscan Publications Ltd., London.

–   AHMAD, Ali, "Policing industrial Pollution in Nigeria", in Beatrice Chaytor and Kevin R. Gray (eds) (2003), *International Environmental Law and Policy in Africa,* Environmental and Policy Vol. 36, Kluwer Academic Publishers, Dordrecht Netherlands.

–   AJOMO, M.A., "An Examination of Federal Environmental Laws in Nigeria", in M.A. Ajomo and O. Adewale (eds) (1994), *Environmental Law and Sustainable Development in Nigeria,* Lagos.

–   AKINSEYE-GEORGE, Y. "Niger Delta Development Commission (NDDC) Act: Human Rights Dimension", *Nigerian Law: Contemporary Issues. Essays in Honour of Sir, Chief (Dr.) Gabriel Osawaru Igbinedion,* in M.O. Ogungbe (ed) (2003), College of Law, Igbinedion University, Okada.

–   AKO, Rhuks Temitope, "Resource Control or Revenue Allocation: A Path to Sustainable Peace in Nigeria's Oil Producing Communities", in Ademola O. Popoola (eds) (2008), *Proceedings of the 35ᵗʰ and 36ᵗʰ Annual Conferences of the Nigerian Society of International Law 2005 & 2006,* Nigerian Society of International Law, Lagos.

–   AKPER, Peter Terkaa, "Socio-Political Issues in Oil and Gas Exploitation in Political and Economic Reform in Nigeria", in I.A Ayua and D.A. Guobadia (eds.) (2001), *Political Reform and Economic Recovery in Nigeria,* NIALS Publication, Lagos.

–   AKPER, Peter Terkaa, "Consumer Protection and the Protection of the Environment", in I.A. Ayua and D.A. Guobadia (eds) (2001), *Political Reform and Economic Recovery in Nigeria,* NIALS Publication, Lagos.

- ALAGOA, E.J., "The Niger Delta States and their Neighbours to 1800", in J.F.A. Ajayi and Michael Crowder (eds) (1976), *History of West Africa*, Volume One, Longman Group Limited, London

- ALAGOA, E.J., "The Eastern Niger Delta and the Hinterland in the 19th Century", in O. Ikime (ed), *Ground Work of Nigerian History*, Heinemann Educational Books Ltd., Ibadan

- Odiase-ALEGIMENLEN, O.A., "Oil and Nigerian Development: An Overview", in I.A. Ayua and D.A. Guobadia (eds) (2001), *Political Reform and Economic Recovery in Nigeria*, NIALS Publication, Lagos.

- ALSTON, Philip, "International Law and the Right to Food", in Asbjon Eide *et al.* (eds) (1984), *Food as a Human Right*, United Nations University, Tokyo.

- AMAO, Olufemi, "Human Rights, Ethics and International Business: The Case of Nigeria", in Aurora Voiculescu and Helen Yanacopulos (eds) (2011), *The Business of Human Rights: An Evolving Agenda for Corporate Responsibility*, Zed Books Ltd., London.

- AWOSIKA, L.F., "Impacts of global climate change and sea level rise on coastal resources and energy development in Nigeria", in Umolu, J.C. (ed) (1995), *Global Climate Change: Impact on Energy Development*, DAMTECH Nigeria Limited, Nigeria.

- AYUA, I.A, "Constitutional Scheme on the Sharing of Revenue Resources and its Implementation: An Assessment", in I.A. Ayua *et al.* (eds) (2001), *NIGERIA: Issues in the 1999 Constitution*, NIALS Publication, Lagos.

- BENNER, Thorsten and DE OLIVEIRA, Ricardo Soares, "The Good/Bad Nexus in Global Energy Governance", in Andreas Goldthau and Jan Martin Witte (eds) (2010), *Global Energy Governance: The New Rules of the Game,* Global Public Policy Institute, Berlin.

- BENTSI-ENCHILL, Kwamena, "Do African Systems of Land Tenure Require a Special Terminology?", in Gordon R. Woodman and A.O. Obilade (eds) (1995), *African Law and Legal Theory*, Dartmouth Publishing Co. Ltd., England.

- BILDER, R., "An Overview of International Human Rights Law", in H. Hannum (ed) (1999), *Guide to International Human Rights Practice,* 3rd ed., Transnational Publishers, New York.

- BOYLE, Alan, "The Role of International Human Rights Law in the Protection of the Environment", in Alan E. Boyle and Michael R. Anderson (eds) (1996), *Human Rights Approaches to Environmental Protection,* Clarendon Press, Oxford.

- CHANDLER, Geoffrey, "The Responsibilities of Oil Companies", in Asbjorn Eide *et al.* (eds) (2000), *Human Rights and the Oil Industry*, Intersentia, Groningen-Oxford.

- CHYDENIUS, Anders, "His Majesty's Gracious Ordinance Relating to Freedom of Writing and of the Press (Peter Hogg, trans.) (1766)", in Juha Mustonen (ed) (2006), *The World's First Freedom of Information Act: Anders Chydenius' Legacy Today,* Art-Print Ltd., Kokkola.

- COOMANS, F., "Some Remarks on the Extraterritorial Application of the International Covenant on Economic, Social and Cultural Rights", in F. Coomans and

M.T. Kamminga (eds) (2004), *Extraterritorial Application of Human Rights Treaties,* (Intersentia, Antwerp and Oxford).

– COSTI, Alberto, "Environmental Protection, Economic Growth and Environmental Justice: Are they Compatible in Central and Eastern Europe?", in Julian Agyeman, *et al.* (eds) (2003), *Just Sustainabilities in an Unequal World,* Earthscan Publications Ltd., London.

– CRAGG, Wesley, "Multinational Corporations, Globalisation, and the Challenge of Self Regulation", in John J. Kirton and Michael J. Trebilcock (eds) (2004), *Hard Choices, Soft Law: Voluntary Standards in Global Trade, Environment and Social Governance*, Ashgate Publishing Co. Ltd, England.

– CRAIG, Donna and JEFFREY, Michael QC, "Non-Lawyers and Legal Regimes: Public Participation for Ecologically Sustainable Development", in David Leary and Balakrishna Pisupati (eds) (2010), *The Future of International Environmental Law,* United Nations University Press, Tokyo.

– CRUZ, Branca Martins da, "The constitutional right to an ecologically balanced environment in Portugal", in Isabelle Larmuseau (ed) (2007), *Constitutional rights to an ecologically balanced environment,* V.V.O.R. Report 2007/2, Gent, Belgium.

– DEJEANT-PONS, M., "The Right to Environment in Regional Human Rights Systems", in Mahoney K.E. and Mahoney P. (eds) (1993), *Human Rights in the Twenty-First Century,* Kluwer Academic Publishers, Dordrecht.

– DEVA, Surya, "'Protect, Respect and Remedy': A Critique of the SRSG's Framework for Business and Human Rights", in Karin Buhmann *et al.* (eds) (2011), *Corporate Social and Human Rights Responsibilities: Global Legal and Management Perspectives*, Palgrave Macmillan, New York.

– DUPUY, Pierre, "Due Diligence in the International Law of Liability", in OECD (ed) (1977), *Legal Aspects of Transfrontier Pollution,* OECD, Paris.

– DUROJAYE, Ebenezer, "Corruption as a Threat to Human Security in Africa", in Ademola Abass (ed) (2010), *Protecting Human Security in Africa,* Oxford University Press, New York.

– ECKERSLEY, Robyn, "Greening Liberal Democracy: The Rights Discourse revisited", in Brian Doherty and Marius de Geus (eds) (1996), *Democracy and Green Political Thought: Sustainability, Rights and Citizenship*, Routledge, London.

– EMESEH, Engobo, "The Niger Delta Crisis and the Question of Access to Justice", in Cyril Obi and Siri Aas Rustad (eds) (2011), *Oil and Insurgency in the Niger Delta: Managing the Complex Politics of Petro-violence,* Zed Books, London/New York.

– ERHUN, Mercy O., "A Comparative Evaluation of Resource Exploitation and Management in Global Deltas: A Case for the Niger Delta Region in Nigeria", in *International Conference on The Nigerian State, Oil Industry and the Niger Delta*, Conference Proceedings, organized by the Department of Political Science, Niger Delta University, Wilberforce Island, Bayelsa State, Nigeria, Harey Publications Co., Port Harcourt, 2008.

- ETIKERENTSE, Godfrey, "Oil and Gas Exploration in Nigeria: Challenges for the 21st Century", in I.A Ayua and D.A. Guobadia (eds.) (2001), *Political Reform and Economic Recovery in Nigeria*, NIALS Publication, Lagos.
- EVENTON, Ross, "Alternatives to the BIT Framework", in Ross Eventon (ed) (2010), *Reclaiming Public Interest in Europe's International Investment Policy, EU Investment Agreements in the Lisbon Treaty Era: A Reader*, the Transnational Institute on behalf of the Investment Working Group of the Seattle to Brussels Network, Amsterdam.
- FONTANA, Andrea and FREY, James H., "The Interview: From Structured Questions to Negotiated Text", in Norman K. Denzin and Yvonna S. Lincoln (eds) (2003), *Collecting and Interpreting Qualitative Materials*, Sage Publications, Inc., California.
- FRANCIONI, Francesco, "The Rights of Access to Justice under Customary International Law", in Francesco Francioni (ed) (2007), *Access to Justice as a Human Right*, Oxford University Press, Oxford.
- FRASER, Nancy, "Social Justice in the Age of Identity Politics: Redistribution, Recognition and Participation", in Nancy Fraser and Axel Honneth (eds) (2003), *Redistribution or Recognition? A Political-Philosophical Exchange*, Verso, London, New York.
- FREGENCE, P., "Oil Exploration and Production Activities: The Socio-Economic and Environmental Problems in Warri-Itsekiri Homeland", in Funmi Adewunmi (ed) (1997), *Oil Exploitation, The State and Crises in Nigeria's Oil Bearing Enclave*, Friedrich Ebert foundation, Lagos.
- FRYNAS, Jedrzej George, "The Oil Industry in Nigeria: Conflict Between Oil Companies and Local People", in Jedrzej George Frynas and Scott Pegg (eds) (2003), *Transnational Corporations and Human Rights*, Palgrave Macmillan, New York.
- GANESAN, Arvind, "Human Rights, the Energy Industry, and the Relationship with Home Governments", in Asbjørn Eide, *et al.* (eds) (2000), *Human Rights and the Oil Industry*, Intersentia-Groningen-Oxford.
- GENUGTEN, Willem J.M. van, "The Status of Transnational Corporations in International Public Law with Special Reference to the Case of Shell", in Asbjørn Eide *et al.* (eds) (2000), *Human Rights and the Oil Industry, Ibid.*
- GIL, Emerlynne, "An Unwavering Struggle for Independent and Effective NHRIs", in Emerlynne Gil *et al.* (eds) (2010), *2010 ANNI Report on the Performance and Establishment of National Human Rights Institutions in Asia*, The Asian NGOs Network on National Human Rights Institutions (ANNI). Asian Forum for Human Rights and Development (FORUM-ASIA) Publications, Bangkok, Thailand.
- GILHUIS, Piet, "The Consequences of Introducing Environmental Law Principles in National Law", in M. Sheridan and L. Lavrysen (eds) (2002), *Environmental Law Principles in Practice*, Emile Bruylant , Bruxelles.
- GUNNINGHAM, Neil, "Corporate Environmental Responsibility: Law and Limits of Voluntarism", in Doreen McBarnet *et al.* (eds) (2007), *The New Corporate Accountability: Corporate Social Responsibility and the Law*, University Press, Cambridge.
- HANDL, Gunther, "Human Rights and Protection of the Environment: A Mildly 'Revisionist' View", in Antonio Trindade (ed) (1992), *Human Rights, Sustainable*

Development and the Environment, Instituto Interamericano de Derechos Humanos,
San Jose, Costa Rica.

– HAYWARD, Tim, "Constitutional Environmental Rights: A Case for Political Analysis", in Andrew Light and Avner de-Shalit (eds.) (2003), *Moral and Political Reasoning in Environmental Practice,* The MIT Press, Cambridge, England.

– HONNETH, Axel, "Redistribution as Recognition: A Response to Nancy Fraser", in
Nancy Fraser and Axel Honneth (eds) (2003), *Redistribution or Recognition? A Politi-
cal- Philosophical Exchange,* Verso, London and New York.

– HOPE, Kempe Ronald, Sr, "Corruption and Development in Africa", in Kempe
Ronald Hope, Sr, and Bornwell C. Chikulo (eds.) (2000), *Corruption and Develop-
ment in Africa: Lessons from Country Case-Studies,* Macmillan Press Ltd., Great
Britain.

– IBABA, Ibaba S., "State Intervention in the Niger Delta: A Critical Appraisal of the
Ideology of Developmental Commission", in *International Conference on The Nigerian State, Oil Industry and the Niger Delta.*

– IBEANU, Okechukwu, 'Two Rights Make a Wrong: Bringing Human Rights Back
into the Niger Delta Discourse,' in *International Conference on The Nigerian State, Oil
Industry and the Niger Delta.*

– IBEANU, Okey and LUCKHAM, Robin, "Nigeria: political violence, governance and
corporate responsibility in a petro-state", in Mary Kaldor *et al.* (eds) (2007), *Oil Wars,*
Pluto Press, London.

– IBIDAPO-OBE, Akin, "Criminal Liability for Damages Caused by Oil Pollution", in
J.A. Omotola (ed) (1990), *Environmental Laws in Nigeria Including Compensation,*
Faculty of Law, University of Lagos, Lagos.

– IKELEGBE, Augustine, "Interrogating a Crisis of Corporate Governance and the
Interface with Conflict: The Case of Multinational Oil Companies and the Conflicts
in the Niger Delta", in *International Conference on The Nigerian State, Oil Industry
and the Niger Delta.*

– ILENRE, Alfred, "The Case of Shell-Nigeria", in Oil Policy in the Gulf of Guinea.
Security and Conflict, Economic Growth, Social Development, Rudolf Traub-Merz/
Douglas Yates, International Conference Friedrich-Ebert-Stiftung Proceedings,
2004.

– IRUONAGBE, T. Charles, "The Niger Delta Crisis: Challenges and Prospects for
Peace and Stability", in *International Conference on The Nigerian State, Oil Industry
and the Niger Delta.*

– IYAYI, Festus, "Oil Companies and the Politics of Community Relations in Nigeria",
in Wumi Raji, Ayodele Ale and Eni Akinsola (eds) (2000), *Boiling Point. A CDHR
Publication on the Crises in the Oil Producing Communities in Nigeria.*

– JIKE, V., "The Political Sociology of Resource Control in the Niger Delta", in Hassan
A. Saliu (ed) (2005), *Nigeria Under Democratic Rule, 1999–2003,* Vol. 2, University
Press, Ibadan.

– KARIBI-WHYTE, A.G., "An Examination of the Criminal Justice System", in Y. Osinbajo and A.U. Kalu (eds) (1990), *Law Development and Administration in Nigeria,* Federal Ministry of Justice, Lagos.

– KELLER, Helen, Codes of Conduct and their Implementation: the Question of Legitimacy, in Rüdiger Wolfrum and Volker Röben (eds) (2008), *Legitimacy in International Law,* Vol. 194, 219–298.

– KINLEY, David *et al.,* "'The Norms are Dead! Long Live the Norms!' The Politics behind the UN Human Rights Norms for Corporations", in Doreen McBarnet *et al.* (eds) (2007), *The New Corporate Accountability: Corporate Social Responsibility and the Law,* Cambridge University Press.

– KIRSCH, Stuart, Mining and Environmental Human Rights in Papua New Guinea, in Jedrzej George Frynas & Scott Pegg (eds.) (2003), *Transnational Corporations and Human Rights,* Palgrave Macmillan, New York.

– KOTZÉ, Louis J., 'Judicial Enforcement of Liabilities and Responsibilities for Pollution Prevention and Remediation: No more "Business as Usual" for South African Mines,' in LeRoy Paddock, *et al.* (2011), *Compliance and Enforcement in Environmental Law: Towards More Effective Implementation,* IUCN Law Series, Edward Elgar, Cheltenham, UK & Northampton, MA, USA.

– KPUNDEH, Sahr J., "Political Will in Fighting Corruption", in Sahr J. Kpundeh and Irene Hors (eds) (1998), *Corruption and Integrity Improvement Initiatives in Developing Countries,* United Nations Development Programme, New York.

– LADAN, M.T., "Human Rights and Environmental Protection", in Constitutional Rights Project (CRP) (1999), *Text for Human Rights Teaching in Schools,* CRP, Lagos.

– LAVRYSEN, Luc and THEUNIS, Jan, "The right to the protection of a healthy environment in the Belgian Constitution: retrospect and international perspective", in Isabelle Larmuseau (ed) (2007), *Constitutional rights to an ecologically balanced environment,* V.V.O.R. Report 2007/2, Gent, Belgium.

– LERNER, N., "The Evolution of Minority Rights in International Law", in Catherine Brolmann *et al* (eds) (1993), *Peoples and Minorities in International Law,* Martinus Nijhoff Publishers Dordrecht, The Netherlands.

– LOWE, Vaughan and STAKER, Christopher, Jurisdiction, in Malcolm D. Evans (ed) (2010), *International Law,* Third Edition, Oxford University Press, Oxford.

– LYNN, Karl Terry, "Ensuring Fairness: The Case for a Transparent Fiscal Social Contract", in M. Humphreys *et al.* (2007), *Escaping the Resource Curse,* University Press, Columbia.

– MACKAY, Fergus, "The Rights of Indigenous Peoples in International Law, in Human Rights and the Environment: Conflicts and Norms in a Globalizing World", Lyuba Zarky (ed) (2002), Earthscan Publications Ltd.

– MACLEOD, Sorcha, "The United Nations, human rights and transnational corporations: challenging the international legal order", in Nina Boeger *et al.* (2008), *Perspectives on Corporate Social Responsibility,* Edward Elgar Publishing Ltd., Cheltenham UK.

– MAES, F., "Environmental Law Principles, their Nature and the Law of the Sea: A Challenge for Legislators", in M. Sheridan and L. Lavrysen (eds) (2002), *Environmental Law Principles in Practice*, Bruylant Brussels.

– MAGNUS, Ulrich, "Introduction", in Ulrich Magnus and Peter Mankowski (eds) (2007), *European Commentaries on Private International Law, Brussels I Regulation*, Sellier, European Law Publishers.

– MALONE, Linda A., "Enforcing International Environmental Law through Domestic Law Mechanisms in the United States: Civil Society Initiatives Against Global Warming", in LeRoy Paddock, *et al.* (2011), *Compliance and Enforcement in Environmental Law: Towards More Effective Implementation*, The IUCN Academy of Environmental Series, Edward Elgar Publishing, Cheltenham, UK & Northampton, USA.

– MBELLE, Nobuntu, "Civil Society and the Promotion of Human Rights in Africa", in John Akokpari and Daniel Shea Zimbler (eds) (2008), *Africa's Human Rights Architecture,* Fanele, South Africa.

– MORSE, Bradford, "Indigenous Rights as a Mechanism to Promote Environmental Sustainability", *Reconciling Human Existence with Ecological Integrity: Science, Ethics, Economics and the Law*, Laura Westra *et al.* (eds) (2008), Earthscan U.K.

– MUCHLINSKI, Peter T., "Corporate Social Responsibility and International Law: The Case of Human Rights and Multinational Enterprises", in Doreen McBarnet *et al.* (eds) (2007), *The New Corporate Accountability: Corporate Social Responsibility and the Law*, Cambridge University Press.

– MUTUA, Makau, "The Construction of the African Human Rights System: Prospects and Pitfalls", in Samantha Power and Graham Allison (eds) (2006), *Realizing Human Rights: Moving from Inspiration to Impact,* Palgrave Macmillan, New York.

– NDULO, Muna, "African Commission and Court Under the African Human Rights System", in John Akokpari and Daniel Shea Zimbler (eds) (2008), *Africa's Human Rights Architecture* Fanele, South Africa.

– NNADOZIE, K., "Environmental Regulation of the Oil and Gas Industry in Nigeria", in Beatrice Chaytor B. and Gray, K.R., (eds) (2003), *International Environmental Law and Policy in Africa*, 36 Environment and Policy, Kluwer Academic Publishers, Dordrecht Netherlands.

– NWEBAZA, Rose, "Improving Environmental Procedural Rights in Uganda", in Marianela Cedeño *et al.* (eds) (2004), *Environmental Law in Developing Countries*, IUCN Environmental Policy and Law, Paper No. 43, Vol. II, IUCN, Gland, Switzerland and Cambridge.

– OBI, Cyril and RUSTAD, Siri Aas, "Introduction: Petro-violence in the Niger Delta-the Complex Politics of an Insurgency", in Cyril Obi and Siri Aas Rustad (eds) (2011), *Oil and Insurgency in the Niger Delta: Managing the Complex Politics of Petro-violence,* Zed Books, London/New York.

– OBI, Cyril and RUSTAD, Siri Aas, "Conclusion: amnesty and post-amnesty peace, is the window of opportunity closing for the Niger Delta?.", in Cyril Obi and Siri Aas Rustad, (eds.) (2011), *Oil and Insurgency in the Niger Delta: Managing the complex politics of petro- violence,* Zed Books, London/New York.

– OBI, Cyril and SOREMEKUN, Kayode, "Oil and the Nigerian state: an overview", in Kayode Soremekun (ed) (1995), *Perspectives on the Nigerian Oil Industry*, Amkra Books, Lagos.

– OKON, Emmanuel, "The Legal Aspect of Ownership and Control of Natural Resources in Nigeria", in *Contemporary Issues in the Administration of Justice, Essays in Honour of Justice Atinuke Ige* (2002), Treasure Hall Konsult Rehoboth Publishing, Lagos.

– OMOROGBE, Yinka, "Regulation of Oil Industry Pollution in Nigeria", in E. Azinge (ed) (1993), *New Frontiers in Law*, Oliz Publishers, Benin City.

– OMOROGBE, Yinka, "The Legal Framework for Public Participation in Decision-Making on Mining and Energy Development in Nigeria: Giving Voices to the Voiceless", in Donald Zillman *et al.* (eds) (2002), *Human Rights in Natural Resource Development: Public Participation in the Sustainable Development of Mining and Energy Resources*, Oxford University Press, Oxford.

– OMOROGBE, Yinka and ONIEMOLA, Peter, "Property Rights in Oil and Gas Under Domanial Regimes", in Aileen McHard *et al.* (eds) (2010), *Property and the Law in Energy and Natural Resources*, Oxford University Press, New York.

– OMOWEH, Daniel A., "Oil Exploration and Production in Nigeria: A Theoretical Overview", in Wumi Raji, Ayodele Ale and Eni Akinsola (eds) (2000), *Boiling Point, A CDHR Publication on the Crises in the Oil Producing Communities in Nigeria*.

– ONOSODE, G., "Environmental Management and Sustainable Development in the Niger Delta", in Osuntokun A. (ed) (2000), *Environmental Problems of the Niger Delta*, Friedrich Ebert Foundation, Lagos.

– ORFORD, A., "Globalization and the Right to Development", in P. Alston (ed) (2001), *Peoples' Rights*, Oxford.

– ORLUWENE, Ozioma B., "Elite Networks and Conflicts in the Niger Delta Region", in *International Conference on The Nigerian State, Oil Industry and the Niger Delta*.

– OWARIETA, G., "Sustaining Industrial Harmony in Nigeria's Petroleum Industry", in Nigerian Petroleum Business: A Handbook (1997), Advent Communications Limited, Lagos.

– PATHAK, R.S., "The Human Rights System as a Conceptual Framework for Environmental Law", in E.B. Weiss (ed) (1992), *Environmental Change and International Law*, United Nations University Press.

– PEDIADITAKI, Tonia, "The right to the protection of the environment in the Greek Constitution", in Isabelle Larmuseau (ed) (2007), *Constitutional rights to an ecologically balanced environment*.

– PELLOW, David Naguib, "Politics by Other Greens: The Importance of Transnational Environmental Justice Movement Networks", in JoAnn Carmin and Julian Agyeman (eds) (2011), *Environmental Inequalities Beyond Borders: Local Perspectives on Global Injustices*, The MIT Press, Cambridge.

– PRITCHARD, Sarah, "Working Group on Indigenous Populations: Mandate, Standard-Setting Activities and Future Perspectives", in Sarah Pritchard (ed) (1998), *Indigenous Peoples, United Nations and Human Rights*, Zed Books, London.

– RAO, A.V. Narsimha, "Environmental Jurisprudence and Judicial Activism", in Areti Krishna Kumari (ed) (2007), *Environmental Jurisprudence: Country Perspectives,* The Icfai University Press, India.

– RAZZAQUE, Jona, "Participatory Rights in Natural Resource Management: The Role of Communities in South Asia", in Jonas Ebbesson and Phoebe Okowa (eds) (2009), *Environmental Law and Justice in Context,* Cambridge University Press, Cambridge.

– REDGWELL, Catherine, "Access to Environmental Justice", in Francesco Francioni (ed) (2007), *Access to Justice as a Human Right,* Oxford University Press, Oxford.

– RICHARDSON, Benjamin J. and RAZZAQUE, Jona, "Public Participation in Environmental Decision-making", in Benjamin J. Richardson and Stepan Wood (eds) (2006), *Environmental Law for Sustainability: A Reader,* Hart Publishing, Oxford & Portland, Oregon.

– SAGAY, I.E., "Anatomy of Federalism with Special Reference to Nigeria", in Olubayo Oluduro *et al.,* (eds) (2007), *Trends in Nigeria Law: Essays in Honour of Oba DVF Olateru-Olagbegi III,* Constellation (Nig.) Publishers, Ibadan/Abuja.

– SARO-WIWA, Ken, "My Life, My Struggle," in Omotoye Olorode *et al.* (eds) (1998), *Ken Saro-Wiwa and the Crises of the Nigerian State,* Committee for the Defence of Human Rights (CDHR) Publications, Lagos.

– SARO-WIWA, Ken, "Why I championed Ogoni Cause," in Omotoye Olorode, *et al* (eds) (1998), *Ken Saro-Wiwa and the Crises of the Nigerian State.*

– SCHRIJVER, Nico, "Unravelling State Sovereignty? The Controversy on the Right of Indigenous Peoples to Permanent Sovereignty over their Natural Wealth and Resources", in Ineke Boerefijn and Jenny Goldschmidt (eds) (2008), *Changing Perceptions of Sovereignty and Human Rights: Essays in Honour of Cees Flinterman,* Intersentia, Antwerp-Oxford- Portland.

– SCOVAZZI, Tullio, "Implementation of Environmental Legal Regimes at Regional Level: The Case of the Mediterranean Sea", in David Leary and Balakrishna Pisupati (eds) (2010), *The Future of International Environmental Law,* United Nations University Press, Tokyo, Japan.

– SEMBRANO, Gilbert, "Mechanisms and Avenues for Judicial and Quasi-Judicial Implementation of ESC Rights: The Philippine Experience", in Fons Coomans (ed) (2006), *Justiciability of Economic and Social Rights. Experiences from Domestic Systems,* Intersentia, Antwerpen-Oxford.

– SHA' ABA, Rekiya Agnes, "MOSOP and the Ogoni Struggle", in Omotoye Olorode *et al* (eds) (1998), *Ken Saro-Wiwa and the Crises of the Nigerian State,* Committee for the Defence of Human Rights (CDHR) Publications, Lagos.

– Shell Petroleum Development Company of Nigeria Limited, "Should Oil Companies Directly Finance Development Projects for Local Communities? The Case of Shell-Nigeria", in Oil Policy in the Gulf of Guinea. Security & Conflict, Economic Growth, Social Development, Rudolf Traub-Merz/Douglas Yates, International Conference Friedrich-Ebert- Stiftung Proceedings, 2004.

– SHELTON, Dinah, "Environmental rights in the State Constitutions of the United States", in Isabelle Larmuseau (ed) (2007), *Constitutional rights to an ecologically balanced environment.*

– SOREMEKUN, Kayode and OBADARE, Ebenezer, "Politics of Oil Corporations in Post Colonial Nigeria", in Omotoye Olorode *et al.* (eds) (1998), *Ken Saro-Wiwa and the Crises of the Nigerian State,* Committee for the Defence of Human Rights (CDHR) Publications, Lagos.

– STEPHENSON, Max Jr. and SCHWEITZER, Lisa A., "Learning from the Quest for Environmental Justice in the Niger Delta", in JoAnn Carmin and Julian Agyeman (eds) (2011), *Environmental Inequalities Beyond Borders: Local Perspectives on Global Injustices,* MIT Press, Cambridge, Mass.

– TAMUNO, T.T., "The Geographical Niger Delta (GND)", in *International Conference on the Nigerian State, Oil Industry and the Niger Delta.*

– THOMPSON, Sybil Sakle, "The African Human Rights System: Comparison, Context, and Opportunities for Future Growth", in Michael Wodzicki (ed) (2008), *The Fight for Human Rights in Africa Perspectives on the African Commission on Human and Peoples' Rights, Rights & Democracy,* International Centre for Human Rights and Democratic Development, Canada.

– UDOMBANA, Nsogurua J., "Weighed in the Balances and Found Wanting: Nigeria's Land Use Act and Human Rights", in I.O Smith (ed) (2003), The Land Use Act-Twenty Five Years After, Department of Private and Property Law, University of Lagos, Lagos.

– UDOMBANA, Nsogurua J., "The Right to a Healthy Environment: Foreground and Forecasts", in I.A. Ayua and D.A. Guobadia (eds) (2001), *Political Reform and Economic Recovery in Nigeria,* NIALS Publication, Lagos.

– UKAOGO, Victor, "From Injustice to Injustice: The Ethnicity of Resistance and Rebellion in the Niger Delta", *in International Conference on the Nigerian State, Oil Industry and the Niger Delta, op. cit.*

– WATTS, Michael, "Sweet and Sour", in Michael Watts (ed) (2008), *Curse of the Black Gold: 50 Years of Oil in the Niger Delta,* powerHouse Books, New York.

– WRIGHT, Beverly, "Race, Politics and Pollution: Environmental Justice in the Mississippi River Chemical Corridor", in Julian Agyeman *et al.* (eds) (2003), *Just Sustainabilities in an Unequal World,* Earthscan Publications Ltd., London.

– YATES, Douglas A., "Changing Patterns of Foreign Direct Investment in the Oil-Economies of the Gulf of Guinea", in Rudolf Traub-Merz/Douglas Yates (eds) (2004), *Oil Policy in the Gulf of Guinea. Security and Conflict, Economic Growth, Social Development,* International Conference Friedrich-Ebert-Stiftung Proceedings.

4.2 Articles in journals

– ADEDEJI, A.A. and AKO, Rhuks T., Hindrances to Effective Legal Response to the Problem of Environmental Pollution in Nigeria, *Ibadan Bar Journal* Vol. 4, 12–23 (2005).

– ADEDEJI, A.A. and AKO, Rhuks T., 'Towards achieving the United Nations' Millennium Development Goals: The Imperative of reforming water pollution control and waste management laws in Nigeria, *Desalination* 248, 642–649 (2009).

– ADEKUNLE, Deji, Domestic protection of socio-economic rights: Case studies on the implementation of socio-economic rights in the domestic systems of three West African countries, 11 (3) *ESR Review*, 15–16 (2010).

– ADEOLA, Francis O., Environmental Injustice and Human Rights Abuse: The States, MNCs and Repression of Minority Groups in the World System, *Human Ecology Review*, Vol. 8, No. 1, 39–59 (2001).

– ADEPETUN, Sola, Production Sharing Contracts- the Nigerian Experience, *J. Energy Nat. Resources L.* 21–28 (1995).

– ADESOPO, A.A. and ASAJU, A.S., Natural Resource Distribution, Agitation for Resource Control Right and the Practice of Federalism in Nigeria, *J. Hum. Ecol.* 15(4), 277–289 (2004).

– ADEWALE, O., The Right of the Individual to Environmental Protection: A Case Study of Nigeria, l2 (4) *Rivista Giuridica Dell' Ambiente* 649 (1991).

– ADEWALE, O., The Right of the Individual to Environmental Protection: A Case Study of Nigeria, *Environment and Urbanization*, Vol. 4, No. 2, 176–183 (1992).

– AGBAKWA, Shedrack C., Reclaiming Humanity: Economic, Social and Cultural Rights as the Cornerstone of African Human Rights, 5 *Yale Human Rights and Development Law Journal* 177, (2002).

– AGHALINO, S.O., The Olusegun Obasanjo Administration and the Niger Delta Question, 1999–2007, *Stud Tribes Tribals* 7 (1), 57–66 (2009).

– AGHALINO, S.O., Corporate Response to Environmental Deterioration in the Oil Bearing Area of the Niger Delta, Nigeria, 1984–2002, *Journal of Sustainable Development in Africa*, Vol. 11, No. 2, 281–294 (2009).

– AGHALINO, S.O. and EYINLA, B., Oil Exploitation and Marine Pollution: Evidence from the Niger Delta, Nigeria, *J. Hum Eco.* 28 (3), 177–182 (2009).

– AIGBEDION, I. and IYAYI, S.E., Environmental Effect of Mineral Exploitation in Nigeria, 2 (2) *International Journal of Physical Sciences*, 33–38 (2007).

– AJAI, Olawale, Environmental Impact Assessment and Sustainable Development: A Review of the Nigerian Legal Framework, *Nigerian Current Legal Problems,* Vols. 2 & 3, 16 (1998).

– AJAI, Olawale, Implementing the Biodiversity Convention in Nigeria: Some Problems and Prospects, *Nigerian Current Law Problems* (Special Volume: Essays in Honour of Prof. M.A. Ajomo), 167 (1995).

– AJOMO, M.A., Ownership of Mineral Oils and the Land Use Act, *Nigerian Current Law Review,* 330 (1982).

– AKINWALE, Akeem Ayofe, Re-Engineering the NDDC's Master Plan: An Analytical Approach, *Journal of Sustainable Development in Africa*, Vol. 11, No. 2, 142–159 (2009)

– AKINWALE, A.A., Amnesty and human capital development agenda for the Niger Delta, *Journal of African Studies and Development,* Vol. 2 (8), 201–207 (2010).

– AKO, Rhuks T., Entrenching the Right to Environment into Nigeria's Constitution, *Ikeja Bar. Journal,* Vol. 1 Part 1, 121 (2005).

– AKO, Rhuks T., Ensuring Public Participation in Environmental Impact Assessment of Development Projects in the Niger Delta Region of Nigeria: A Veritable Tool for Sustainable Development, *Environtropica, An International Journal of the Tropical Environment,* Vol. 3 Nos. 1 & 2, 1–5 (2006).

– AKO, Rhuks T. *et al.,* Resolving Legislative Lapses through Contemporary Environmental Protection Paradigms- A Case Study of Nigeria's Niger Delta Region, 47 (3) *Indian Journal of International Law,* 432–450 (2007).

– AKO, Rhuks T., Nigeria's Land Use Act: An Anti-Thesis to Environmental Justice, 53 (2) *Journal of African Law,* 296 (2009).

– AKO, Rhuks T. and OKONMAH, Patrick, Minority Rights Issues in Nigeria: A Theoretical Analysis of Historical and Contemporary Conflicts in the Oil-Rich Niger Delta Region, 16 *International Journal on Minority and Group Rights* (2009).

– AKO, Rhuks T., The Judicial Recognition and Enforcement of the Right to Environment: Differing Perspectives from Nigeria and India, 3 *NUJS Law Review* 423–445 (2010)

– ALABI, Reuben Adeolu, Comparative Analysis of Socio-Economic Constraints in Niger Delta, 10 *European Journal of Economics, Finance and Administrative Sciences,* 63–74 (2008).

– AL FARUQUE, Abdullah and HOSSAIN, MD Zakir, Regulation Vs Self Regulation in Extractive Industries: A Level Playing Field, *MqJICEL* Vol. 3, 45–64 (2006).

– ALUBO, O., Citizenship and Nation Making in Nigeria: New Challenges and Contestations Identity, *Culture and Politics,* Vol. 5, Nos. 1 & 2, 135–161 (2004).

– ALUKO, M.A.O., Sustainable Development, Environmental Degradation and the Entrenchment of Poverty in the Niger Delta of Nigeria, *J. Hum. Ecol.* 15 (1), 63–68 (2008).

– AMAO, Olufemi O., The African Regional Human Rights System and Multinational Corporations: Strengthening Host State Responsibility for the Control of Multinational Corporations, 12 (5) *The International Journal of Human Rights,* 761–788 (2008).

– AMECHI, Emeka Polycarp, Litigating Right to Healthy Environment in Nigeria: An Examination of the Impacts of the Fundamental Rights (Enforcement Procedure) Rules 2009, in Ensuring Access to Justice for Victims of Environmental Degradation, 6/3 *Law, Environment and Development Journal,* 320–334 (2010).

– AMOKAYE, Oludayo, Human Rights and Environmental Protection: The Necessary Connection, 1 (1) *UNILAG Journal of Human Right Law,* 89–120 (2007).

– ANAYA, S.J., The Capacity of International Law to Advance Ethnic or Nationality Rights Claims, 13 (3) *Hum. Rts. Q.* 403–411 (1991).

– ANAYA, S.J., International Human Rights and Indigenous Peoples: The Move Toward the Multicultural State, 21 *Ariz. J Int'l & Comp. L.* 13 (2004).

– ANAYA, S.J., The Emergence of Customary International Law Concerning the Rights of Indigenous Peoples, *Law & Anthropology,* Vol. 12, 127–139 (2005).

– ANAYA, S.J., Indigenous Peoples' Participatory Rights in Relation to Decisions about Natural Resource Extraction: The More Fundamental Issue of What Rights Indigenous Peoples Have in Lands and Resources, 22 *Ariz. J. Int'l & Comp. L.* 10 (2005).

– ANAYA, S.J., Divergent Discourses About International Law, Indigenous Peoples, and Rights Over Lands and Natural Resources: Towards a Realist Trend, 16 *Colo. J. Int'l Envtl. L. & Pol'y* 237–258 (2005).

– ANKERSEN, Thomas T., Shared Knowledge, Shared Jurisprudence: Learning to Speak Environmental Law Creole (Criollo), 16 *Tul. Envtl. L.J.* 807–830 (2003).

– ANUGWOM, Edlyne E., Oil Minorities and the Politics of Resource Control in Nigeria, *Africa Development* Vol. XXX, No. 4, 87–120 (2005).

– ANUKANSAI, Kanokkan, Corruption: The Catalyst for Violation of Human Rights, *National Anti-Corruption Commission (NACC) Journal*, Special Issue, Vol. 3 No. 2, 6–15 (2010).

– ARLOW, Joanna E., The Utility of ATCA and the "Law of Nations" in Environmental Torts Litigation: *Jota v. Texaco, Inc.* and Large Scale Environmental Destruction, 7 *Wis. Envtl. L.J.* 93–138 (2000).

– ARROW, Dennis, The Proposed Regime for the Unilateral Exploitation of Deep Seabed Mineral Resources by the United States, 21 (2) *Harv. Int'l L.J* 337–417 (1980).

– ATAPATTU, Sumudu, The Right to a Healthy Life or the Right to Die Polluted?: The Emergence of a Human Right to a Healthy Environment Under International Law, 16 *Tul. Envtl. L. J.* 65–126 (2002).

– ATSEGBUA, Lawrence, A Critical Appraisal of Environmental Rights Under the Nigerian Courts, *Benin Journal of Public Law* Vol. 2. No. 1, 46 (2004).

– BARSH, Russel Lawrence, Revision of ILO No. 107, 81 *Am. J. Int'l L.* 761 (1987).

– BAXI, Upendra, Voices of Suffering and the Future of Human Rights, 8 *Transn'l L. Contemp. Prob.* 15 (1998).

– BELLO, Akeem, Environmental Rights in Nigeria: Issues, Problems and Prospects, *Igbinedion University Law Journal*, Vol. 4, 60–95 (2006).

– BENVENISTI, Eyal, Exit and Voice in the Age of Globalization, 98 *Michigan Law Review* 167–213 (1999).

– BETSILL, M. and CORELL, Elisabeth, NGO Influence in International Environmental Negotiations: A Framework for Analysis, 1 (4) *Global Environmental Politics*,65–85 (2001).

– BIEGON, Japhet and KILLANDER, Magnus, Human rights developments in the African Union during 2009, 10 *African Human Rights Law Journal*, 212–232 (2010).

– BOELE, R. *et al.*, Shell, Nigeria and the Ogoni. A Study in Unsustainable Development: The Story of Shell, Nigeria and the Ogoni People- Environment, Economy, Relationships: Conflict and Prospects for Resolution, 9 *Sustainable Development* 79 (2001).

– BOELE, R. *et al.*, Shell, Nigeria and the Ogoni. A study in Unsustainable Development: II. Corporate Social Responsibility and 'Stakeholder Management' Versus a Rights-Based Approach to Sustainable Development, 9 *Sustainable Development* 121–135 (2001).

– BOEVING, James, Half Full...or Completely Empty?: Environmental Alien Tort Claims Post Sosa v. Alvarez-Machain, 18 *Geo. Int'l Envtl. Law Review* 109–147 (2005).

– BOJOSI, Kealeboga N. and WACHIRA, George Mukundi, Protecting Indigenous Peoples in Africa: An Analysis of the Approach of the African Commission on Human and Peoples' Rights, 6 *Afr. Hum. Rts. L.J.* 382–406 (2006).

– BOYD, Kathryn Lee, The Inconvenience of Victims: Abolishing Forum Non Conveniens in U.S. Human Rights Litigation, 39 *Va. J. Int'l L.* 41–87 (1998).

– BRADLOW, Daniel, The World Bank, the IMF and Human Rights, 6 *Transnat'l L. & Contemp. Probs.* 63 (1996).

– BRANT, Jason W., *Flores* v. *Southern Peru Copper, Corporation*: The Second Circuit Closes the Court House Door on Environmental Claims Brought Under the ATCA, 35 *U. Miami Inter-Am. L. Rev.* 131–151 (2003–2004).

– BRIDGEMAN, Natalie L., Human Rights Litigation Under the ATCA as a Proxy for Environmental Claims, 6 *Yale Hum. Rts. & Dev. L.J.* 1–43 (2003).

– BRILMAYER, Lea, International Law in American Courts: A Modest Proposal, 100 *Yale Law Journal* 2277–2314 (1991).

– BRUCH, Carl *et al.*, Constitutional Environmental Law: Giving Force to Fundamental Principles in Africa,' 26 *Colum. J. Envtl. L.* 131–211 (2001).

– BUXBAUM, Richard M. and CARON, David D., The Alien Tort Statute: An Overview of the Current Issues, 28 *Berkeley J. Int'l L.* 511–518 (2010).

– CASSEL, Douglass, Corporate Initiatives: A Second Human Rights Revolution?, 19 (5) *Fordham International Law Journal* 1963–1984 (1996).

– CASSEL, Doug, Corporate Aiding and Abetting of Human Rights Violations: Confusion in the Courts, 6 (2) *Nw. J. Int'l Human Rights* 304–326 (2008).

– CHENG, Bin, United Nations Resolutions on Outer Space: "Instant" International Customary Law? 5 *Indian J. Int'l L.* 23 (1965).

– CHOPRA, Sudhir K., Multinational Corporations in the Aftermath of Bhopal: The Need for a New Comprehensive Global Regime for Transnational Corporate Activity, 29 *Valparaiso University Law Journal* 235–284 (1994).

– COHAN, John Alan, Environmental Rights of Indigenous Peoples Under the Alien Tort Claims Act, the Public Trust Doctrine and Corporate Ethics, and Environmental Dispute Resolution, 20 *UCLA. J. Envtl. L. & Pol'y* 133, (2002).

– COLLINS, Lynda, Are We There Yet? The Right to Environment in International and European Law, 3 *McGill Int'l J. Sust. Dev. L. & Pol'y* 119–153 (2007).

– CORNTASSEL, Jeff J. and PRIMEAU, Tomas Hopkins, Indigenous "Sovereignty" and International Law: Revised Strategies for Pursuing "Self-Determination", 17 *Hum. Rts. Q.* 353 (1995).

– COUMANS, Catherine, Alternative Accountability Mechanisms and Mining: The Problems of Effective Impunity, Human Rights, and Agency, *Rethinking Extractive Industry: Regulation, Dispossession, and Emerging Claims, Canadian Journal of Development Studies*, (Special Issue), XXX (1–2), 27–48 (2010).

– CULLEN, H., Nations and its Shadows: Quebec's Non-French Speakers and the Courts, 3 (2) *Law and Critique*, 219 (1992).

– DADEM, Y.Y.D., Current Challenges for Environmental and Economic Justice in the
    Niger Delta of Nigeria, *Kogi State University Bi-Annual Journal of Public Law*, Vol. 1
    Part 1, 219–231 (2009).

– DAVIS, Megan, Indigenous Struggles in Standard-Setting: The United Nations
    Declarations on the Rights of Indigenous Peoples, 9 *Melb. J. Int'l L.* 439 (2008).

– DAES, Erica-Irene A., Some Considerations on the Right of Indigenous Peoples' to
    Self Determination, 3 *Transnat'l L. & Contemp. Probs.* 5 (1993).

– DEMAS, Reagan R., Moment of Truth: Development in Sub-Saharan Africa and Cri-
    tical Alterations Needed in Application of the Foreign Corrupt Practices Act and
    Other Anti- Corruption Initiatives, 26 *Am. U. Int'l L. Rev.* 315–369 (2011).

– DETHERIDGE, Alan and PEPPLE Noble, (Shell), A response to Frynas, *Third World
    Quarterly*, Vol. 19, No. 3, 479–486 (1998).

– DEVA, Surya, Corporate Code of Conduct Bill 2000: Overcoming Hurdles in Enfor-
    cing Human Rights Obligations Against Overseas Corporate Hands of Local Corpo-
    rations, *Newc L.R.* Vol. 8 No. 1 87–116 (2004).

– DIAMOND, Larry, Issues in the Constitutional Design of a Third Nigerian Republic,
    86 (343) *African Affairs* 209–226 (1987).

– DOMMEN, Caroline, Claiming Environmental Rights: Some Possibilities Offered by
    the United Nation's Human Rights Mechanisms, 11 *Geo. Int'l Envt'l L. Rev.* 1 (1998).

– DONELLY-SAALFIELD, James, Irreparable Harms: How the Devastating Effects of
    Oil Extraction in Nigeria Have not been Remedied by Nigerian Courts, the Afri-
    can Commission, or U.S. Courts, 15 (2) *Hastings W. Nw. J. Envtl. L. & Pol'y* 371–429
    (2009).

– DRIMMER, Jonathan, Human Rights and the Extractive Industries: Litigation and
    Compliance Trends, *Journal of World Energy Law & Business*, Vol. 3, No. 2, 121–139
    (2010).

– DUNOFF, Jeffrey L. and TRACHTMAN, Joel P., Economic Analysis of International
    Law, 24 *Yale J. Int'l L.* 1–59 (1999).

– DURUIGBO, Emeka, The Economic Cost of Alien Tort Litigation: A Response to
    Awakening Monster: The Alien Tort Statute of 1789, 14 *Minn. J. Global Trade* 1–41
    (2004).

– DURUIGBO, Emeka, Managing Oil Revenues for Socio-Economic Development in
    Nigeria: The Case for Community-Based Trust Funds, 30 *N.C.J. Int'l. & Com. Reg.*
    122–196 (2004–2005).

– DURUIGBO, Emeka, Permanent Sovereignty and Peoples' Ownership of Natural
    Resources in International Law, 38 *Geo. Wash. Int'l L. Rev.* 33–100 (2006).

– DURUIGBO, Emeka, Exhaustion of Local Remedies in Alien Tort Litigation: Impli-
    cations for International Human Rights Protection, 29 *Fordham Int'l L.J.* 1245–1311
    (2006).

– DURUIGBO, Emeka, Corporate Accountability and Liability for International
    Human Rights Abuses: Recent Changes and Recurring Challenges, 6 (2) *Northwes-
    tern Journal of Human Rights* 222–261 (2008).

– EATON, Joshua P., The Nigerian Tragedy, Environmental Regulation of Transnational Corporations, and the Human Right to a Healthy Environment, 15 *B. U. Int'l L. J.* 261–307 (1997).

– EBEKU, Kaniye, Oil and the Niger Delta People: The Injustice of the Land Use Act, *Law and Politics in Africa, Asia and Latin America, Verfassung und Recht in Übersee (VRÜ)* 35 (2002).

– EBEKU, Kaniye, Critical Appraisal of Nigeria's Niger Delta Development Act 2000, *Int'l. Energy L. & Tax'n Rev.* 203 (2003).

– EBEKU, Kaniye, Biodiversity Conservation in Nigeria: An Appraisal of the Legal Regime in Relation to the Niger Delta Area of the Country, 16 *J. Envtl. L.* 361–375 (2004).

– EBEKU, Kaniye, Constitutional Right to a Healthy Environment and Human Rights Approaches to Environmental Protection in Nigeria: *Gbemre v. Shell* Revisited, *RECIEL* 16 (3) 312–320 (2007)

– EBEKU, Kaniye, Niger Delta Oil, Development of the Niger Delta and the New Development: Some Reflections from a Socio-Legal Perspective, *Journal of Asian and African Studies* 389–425 (2008).

– EBOE, Hutchful, Building Regulatory Institutions in the Environmental Sector in the Third World: The Petroleum Inspectorate in Nigeria (1997–1987), *Africa Development*, Vol. XXIII No. 2, 121–160 (1998).

– EDINO, *et al.* Marcus O., Perceptions and attitudes towards gas flaring in the Niger Delta, Nigeria, 30 *Environmentalist* 67–75 (2010).

– EGBU, Anthony Nzodinma, Constraints to Effective Pollution Control and Management in Nigeria,' *The Environmentalist*, Vol. 20, 13–17 (2000).

– EGEDE, Edwin, Human Rights and the Environment: Is there a Legally Enforceable Right of a Clean and Healthy Environment for the "Peoples" of the Niger Delta Under the Framework of the 1999 Constitution of the Federal Republic of Nigeria?, 19 (1) *Sri Lanka Journal of International Law,* 51–83 (2007).

– EGEDE, Edwin, Bringing Human Rights Home: An Examination of the Domestication of Human Rights Treaties in Nigeria, 51 (2) *Journal of African Law,* 249–284 (2007).

– EJOBOWAH, John Boye, Who Owns the Oil? The Politics of Ethnicity in the Niger Delta of Nigeria, *Africa Today*, Vol. 47, No. 1, 28–47 (2000).

– EKINE, Sokari, Women's Responses to State Violence in the Niger Delta, 10 *Feminist Africa* 67–83 (2008).

– EKPU, A.O., Environmental Impact of Oil on Water: A Comparative Overview of the Law and Policy in the United States and Nigeria, *Denver Journal of International Law and Policy*, Vol. 24 No. 1, 89 (1995).

– EMMA-OKAFOR, Lilian Chinenye *et al.*, Biodiversity Conservation for Sustainable Agriculture in Tropical Rainforest of Nigeria, *New York Science Journal* 3(1), 81–88 (2010).

– EMOLE, C.E., Regulation of Oil and Gas Pollution, *Environmental Policy and Law,* Vol. 28 No. 2, 108 (1998).

- ENABULELE, A.O., Implementation of Treaties in Nigeria and the Status Question: Whither Nigerian Courts?, 17 *African Journal of International and Comparative Law*, 326–341 (2009).
- ENDICOTT, Amy, The Judicial Answer? Treatment of the Political Question Doctrine in Alien Tort Claims, 28 *Berkeley J. Int'l L.* 537 (2010).
- EVOH, Chijioke J., Green Crimes, Petro-violence and the Tragedy of Oil: The Case of the Niger-Delta in Nigeria, *In-Spire Journal of Law, Politics and Societies*, Vol. 4, No. 1, 40–60 (2009).
- EWEJE, Gabriel, Environmental Costs and Responsibilities Resulting from Oil Exploitation in Developing Countries: The Case of the Niger Delta of Nigeria, 69 *Journal of Business Ethics*, 27–56 (2006).
- EZETAH, Chinedu Reginald, International Law of Self Determination and the Ogoni Question: Mirroring Africa's Post-Colonial Dilemma, 19 *Loy. L.A. Int'l & Comp. L.J.* 832 (1996–1997).
- FAURE, Michael G. and RAJA, A.V., Effectiveness of Environmental Public Interest Litigation in India: Determining the Key Variables, 21 *Fordham Environmental Law Review* 239–294 (2010).
- FOWLER, Robert J., International Environmental Standards for Transnational Corporations, 25 *Environmental Law* 1–30 (1995).
- FRANCK, Thomas, Legitimacy in the International System, 82 *Am. J. Int'l L.* 705 (1988).
- FREEMAN, Bennett *et al.*, A New Approach to Corporate Responsibility: The Voluntary Principles on Security and Human Rights, 24 *Hastings Int'l & Comp. L. Rev.* 432–449 (2001).
- FROMHERZ, J. Christopher, Indigenous Peoples' Courts: Egalitarian Juridicalpluralism, Self-Determination, and the United Nations Declaration on the Rights of Indigenous Peoples, 156 *University of Pennsylvania Law Review*, 1341–1381 (2008).
- FRYNAS, Jedrzej George, Political instability and business: focus on Shell in Nigeria, *Third World Quarterly*, Vol. 19, No. 3, 457–478 (1998).
- FRYNAS, Jedrzej George, Legal Change in Africa: Evidence from Oil-related Litigation in Nigeria, 43 (2) *Journal of African Law*, 121–150 (1999).
- FRYNAS, Jedrzej George, Corporate and State Responses to Anti-Oil Protests in the Niger Delta, *African Affairs*, 100, 27–54 (2001).
- GERTZEL, C., Relations Between African and European Traders in the Niger Delta 1880- 1896, 3 *The Journal of African History* 361–366 (1962).
- GETCHES, David H., Indigenous Peoples' Rights to Water Under International Norms, 16 *Colo. J. Int'l Envtl. L. & Pol'y* 259–294 (2005).
- GHALEIGH, Navraj Singh, "Six honest serving-men": Climate change litigation as legal mobilization and the utility of typologies, 1 (1) *Climate Law* 31–61 (2010).
- GIBSON, Noralee, The Right to a Clean Environment, 54 *Sask. L. Rev.* 5–18 (1990).
- GIORGETTA, Sueli, The Right to a Healthy Environment, Human Rights and Sustainable Development, 2 *International Environmental Agreements: Politics, Law and Economics*, 173–194 (2002).

– GROSSMAN, Claudio and BRADLOW, Daniel D., Are We Being Propelled Towards a People-Centered Transnational Legal Order?, 9 *Am. U. J. Int'l L. & Pol'y* 1–25 (1993).

– HAN, Xiuli, The Wiwa Cases, *Chinese Journal of International Law* 433–449 (2010).

– HARTMAN, Jennifer M., Government by Thieves: Revealing the Monsters Behind the Kleptocratic Masks, 24 *Syracuse Journal of International Law & Commerce* 157–175 (1997).

– HENKIN, Louis, The Universal Declaration at 50 and the Challenge of Global Markets, 25 *Brooklyn J. Int'l L.* 17–25 (1999).

– HERZ, Richard L., Litigating Environmental Abuses Under the Alien Tort Claims Act: A Practical Assessment, 40 *Va. J. Int'l L.* 545 (2000).

– HEYNS, Christof, The African Regional Human Rights System: The African Charter, 108 (3) *Penn State Law Review* 679–702 (2004).

– HILL, Barry E. *et al*, Human Rights and the Environment: A Synopsis and Some Predictions, 16 *Geo. Int'l Envt'l. L. Rev.* 359–402 (2004).

– HITCHCOCK, R.K., International Human Rights, the Environment, and Indigenous Peoples', 5 *Colo. J. Int'l Env. L. & Pol'y* 10 (1994).

– HOLL, K.D. and HOWARTH, R.B., Paying for Restoration, 8(3) *Restoration Ecology*, 260–267 (2000).

– HOLZER, Boris, Framing the Corporation: Royal Dutch/Shell and Human Rights Woes in Nigeria, 30 *J. Consum. Policy*, 281–301 (2007).

– IBABA, Ibaba S., Oil and Political Consciousness in the Niger Delta, *Nigerian Journal of Oil and Politics* (Special Edition), Vol. 2, No. 1, 80 (2002).

– IBABA, Ibaba S., Amnesty and Peace-Building in the Niger Delta: Addressing the Frustration-Aggression Trap, *Africana: The Niger Delta* (Special Issue), Vol. 5 (1), 238–271 (2011).

– IBABA, Ibaba S., and OLUMATI, John C., Sabotage Induced Oil Spillages and Human Rights Violation in Nigeria's Niger Delta, *Journal of Sustainable Development in Africa*, Vol. 11 No. 4, 51–65 (2009).

– IDEMUDIA, Uwafiokun and ITE, Uwem E., Corporate-Community Relations in Nigeria's Oil Industry: Challenges and Imperatives, *Corp. Soc. Responsib. Environ. Mgmt.* 13, 194- 206 (2006).

– IDEMUDIA, Uwafiokun, and ITE, Uwem E., Demystifying the Niger Delta Conflict: Towards an Integrated Explanation, *Review of African Political Economy* 33, 109–406 (2006).

– IDEMUDIA, Uwafiokun, Assessing corporate-community involvement strategies in the Nigerian oil industry: An empirical analysis, *Resources Policy* 34 133–141 (2009).

– IDEMUDIA, Uwafiokun, Host Nation- Oil Transnational Corporation Partnership for Poverty Reduction in the Niger Delta, Nigeria- Diagnosis and Recommendations, *Exploration and Production Vol. 7 Issue 1, Touch Briefings*, 128–130 (2009).

– IDEMUDIA, Uwafiokun, Corporate Social Responsibility and the Rentier Nigerian State: Rethinking the Role of Government and the Possibility of Corporate Social Development in the Niger Delta, *Rethinking Extractive Industry: Regulation, Dispos-*

session, and Emerging Claims, Canadian Journal of Development Studies (Special Issue) XXX (1–2), 131–151 (2010).

–   IDOWU, Amos Adeoye, Human Rights, Environmental Degradation and Oil Multinational Companies in Nigeria: The Ogoniland Episode, *Netherlands Quarterly of Human Rights*, Vol. 17, No. 2, 161–184 (1999).

–   IKELEGBE, Augustine, Civil Society, Oil and Conflict in the Niger Delta Region of Nigeria: Ramifications of Civil Society for a Regional Resource Struggle, *J. of Modern African Studies* 39 (3), 437–469 (2001).

–   IKPORUKPO, C.O., The Management of Oil Pollution of Natural Resources in Nigeria, *Journal of Environmental Management*, Vol. 20, No. 3, 199–206 (1985).

–   JAEGER, Kathleen, Environmental Claims Under the Alien Tort Statute, 28 *Berkeley J. Int'l L.* 519–536 (2010).

–   JERBI, Scott, Business and Human Rights at the UN: What Might Happen Next?, 31 *Human Rights Quarterly* 299–320 (2009).

–   JOHN, Anthony Wanis-St. and KEW, Darren, Civil Society and Peace Negotiations: Confronting Exclusion, 13 *International Negotiation,* 11–36 (2008).

–   JUMA, Dan, Access to the African Court on Human and Peoples' Rights: A Case of the Poacher turned Gamekeeper, 4 (2) *Essex Human Rights Review* 1–21 (2007).

–   KAEB, C., Energy Issues of Human Rights Responsibility in the Extractive and Manufacturing Industries: Patterns and Liability Risks, 6 (2) *Northwestern Journal of International Human Rights,* 328 (2008).

–   KASIMBAZI, Emmanuel, The Environment as Human Rights: Lessons from Uganda, *African Society of International and Comparative Law*, 148 (1998).

–   KASSIM-MOMODU, Momodu, Gas Re-Injection and the Nigerian Oil Industry, *Journal of Private & Property Law* 6 & 7, 83 (1986/1987).

–   KASSIM-MOMODU, Momodu, Nigeria's Transfer of Technology, *Journal of World Trade* 22, No. 4, 58–59 (1988).

–   KIMERLING, Judith, Indigenous Peoples and the Oil Frontier in Amazonia: The Case of Ecuador, ChevronTexaco, and Aguinda v. Texaco, 38 *New York University Journal of International Law and Politics* 413–664 (2006).

–   KINGSBURY, Benedict, "Indigenous Peoples" in International Law: A Constructivist Approach to the Asian Controversy, 92 *Am. J. Int'l L.* 453 (1998).

–   KINGSBURY, Benedict, Reconciling Five Competing Conceptual Structures of Indigenous Peoples' Claims in International and Comparative Law, 34 *N.Y.U. J. Int'l. & Pol.* 189, (2001).

–   KINLEY, D. and CHAMBERS, R., The UN Human Rights Norms for Corporations: The Private Implications for Public International Law, 6 (3) *Human Rights Law Review*, 447–497 (2006).

–   KOECHER, Audrey, Corporate Accountability for Environmental Human Rights Abuse in Developing Nations: Making the Case for Punitive Damages Under the Alien Tort Claims Act, 17 *J. Transnat'l L. Pol'y* 151–170 (2007).

–   KOH, Harold Hongju, Transnational Public Law Litigation, 100 *Yale L.J.* 2347–2402 (1991).

– KOLK, Ans *et al.* International Codes of Conduct and Corporate Social Responsibility: Can Transnational Corporations Regulate Themselves?, *Transnational Corporations* 8 (1), 68 (1999).

– KUMAR, Raj C., National Human Rights Institutions and Economic, Social, and Cultural Rights: Towards the Institutionalization and Developmentalization of Human Rights, 28 *Human Rights Quarterly* 755–779 (2006).

– LADAN, Muhammed T., Towards an Effective African System for Access to Justice in Environmental Matters, 23–24 *Ahmadu Bello University Law Journal* 10–40 (2005–2006).

– LAMBOOY, Tineke and RANCOURT, Marie-Eve, *Shell* in Nigeria: From Human Rights Abuse to Corporate Social Responsibility, 2 (2) *Human Rights and International Legal Discourse* 229–275 (2008).

– LEE, John, The Underlying Legal Theory to Support a Well-Defined Human Right to a Healthy Environment as a Principle of Customary International Law, 25 *Colum. J. Envtl. L.* 283–346 (2000).

– LENNING, Emily and BRIGHTMAN, Sara, Oil, Rape and State Crime in Nigeria, 17 *Critical Criminology* 35–48 (2009).

– LINDE, Morné van der and LOUW, Lirette, Considering the Interpretation and Implementation of Article 24 of the African Charter on Human and Peoples' Rights in Light of the SERAC Communication, 3 *African Human Rights Law Journal* 167–187 (2003).

– LILLICH, Richard B., Damages for Gross Violations of International Human Rights Awarded by US Courts, 15 *Hum. Rts. Q.* 207–229 (1993).

– LIPPMAN, Mathew, Transnational Corporations and Repressive Regimes: The Ethical Dilemma, 15 *Cal. W. Int'l L.J.* 542 (1985).

– LIU, Sylvia F., The Koko Incident: Developing International Norms for the Transboundary Movement of Hazardous Waste, 8 *J. Nat. Resources & Env't. L.* 121 (1993).

– MACDONALD, Karen E., Sustaining the Environmental Rights of Children: An Exploratory Critique, 18 *Fordham Envtl. L. Rev.* 1–65 (2006–2007).

– MACKLEM, Patrick, Indigenous Recognition in International Law: Theoretical Observations, 30 *Michigan J. Int'l L.* 177–210 (2008–2009).

– MAGRAW, Dan and BAKER, Lauren, Globalization, Communities and Human Rights: Community-Based Property Rights and Prior Informed Consent, 35 *Denv. J. Int'l L. & Pol'y* 413–428 (2007).

– MALAN, Daniel, Corporate Citizens, Colonialists, Tourists or Activists? Ethical Challenges Facing South African Corporations in Africa, 18 *Journal of Corporate Citizenship* 55 (2005).

– MALUMFASHI, Garba I., Phase-Out of Gas Flaring in Nigeria by 2008: The Prospects of a Multi-Win Project (Review of the Regulatory, Environmental and Socio-Economic Issues), *Petroleum Training Journal* Vol. 4 No. 2, 102 (2007).

– MARDIROSIAN, Helen E., Forum Non Conveniens, 37 *Loy. L.A. L. Rev.* 1643 (2004).

– MARQUARDT, S., International Law and Indigenous Peoples, *International Law on Group Rights* 3, 70 (1995).

- MAY, James R., Constituting Fundamental Environmental Rights Worldwide, 23 *Pace Envtl. L. R.* 113–182 (2005–2006).
- MAY, James R. and DALY, Erin, Vindicating Fundamental Environmental Rights Worldwide, 11 *Oregon Review of International Law*, 365–439 (2009).
- MAYDA, J., Environmental Legislation in Developing Countries: Some Parameters and Constraints, 12 *Ecology L.Q.* 997 (1985).
- MBAZIRA, Christopher, Enforcing the economic, social and cultural rights in the African Charter on Human and Peoples' Rights: Twenty years of redundancy, progression and significant strides, 6 *African Human Rights Law Journal*, 333–357 (2006).
- MCCORQUODALE, Robert, Corporate Social Responsibility and International Human Rights Law, 87 *Journal of Business Ethics*, 385–400 (2009).
- MENDEL, Toby, 'Freedom of Information: An Internationally Protected Human Right, 1 *Comp. Media L.J.* 1 (2003).
- MENSAH, Nancy L., Codes, Lawsuits or International Law: How Should the Multi-national Corporation Be Regulated with Respect to Human Rights?, 14 (2) *U. Miami Int'l & Comp. L. Rev.* 243–269 (2006).
- METCALF, Cherie, Indigenous Rights and the Environment: Evolving International Law, 35 *Ottawa L. Rev.* 101–140 (2003–2004).
- MINKAH-PREMO, J.K., The Role of Judicial Enforcement of ECOSOC Rights in National Development: The Case of Ghana, *African Society of International & Comparative Law*, ASICL Proc. 11, 71 (1999).
- MOHAMED, Abdelsalam A., Individual and NGO Participation in Human Rights Litigation Before the African Court of Human and Peoples' Rights: Lessons from the European and Inter-American Courts of Human Rights, 43 *Journal of African Law*, 201–213 (1999).
- MOMOH, Hadiza Tijjani Sule, Nigerian Local Content Act: The Role of the Petroleum Training Institute, Effurun in Human Capital Development, *Petroleum Technology Development Journal: An International Journal*, Vol.3 No.1, pp.35–54 (2013)
- MORIMOTO, Tetsuya, Growing industrialization and our damaged planet: The Extraterritorial application of developed countries' domestic environmental laws to transnational corporations abroad, 1 (2) *Utrecht Law Review* 134–159 (2005).
- MOWERY, Lauren A., Earth Rights, Human Rights: Can International Environmental Human Rights Affect Corporate Accountability?, 13 *Fordham Envl. L.J.* 343–372 (2002).
- MUBANGIZI, John C., Some reflections on recent and current trends in the promotion and protection of human rights in Africa: The pains and the gains, 6 *African Human Rights Law Journal* 146–165 (2006).
- MUCHLINSKI, Peter T., Human Rights and Multinationals: Is there a Problem?, 77 *International Affairs* 31–48 (2001).
- MURPHY, Sean D., Taking Multinational Corporate Codes of Conduct to the Next Level, 43 *Colum. J. Transnat'l L.* 389–433 (2005).

– MUTUA, Makau wa, The African Human Rights System in a Comparative Perspective, 3 *Rev. Afr. Comm'n Hum. Peoples' Rts.* 5, 11 (1993).
– NEWBERY, Mark, New Indonesian Oil and Gas Law, *J. Energy Nat. Resources L.* Vol. 20 No. 4, 355–363 (2002).
– NNAMANI, A. JSC., The Land Use Act- 11 years After, 2 *GRBPL*, No. 6, 31–39 (1989)
– NOLAN, Justine, The United Nations' Compact with Business: Hindering or Helping the Protection of Human Rights, 24 *The University of Queensland Law Journal* 445–466 (2005).
– NOLAN, Justine and TAYLOR, Luke, Corporate Responsibility for Economic, Social and Cultural Rights: Rights in Search of a Remedy?, 87 *Journal of Business Ethics* 433–451 (2009).
– NOSYREVA, Elena, Alternative Dispute Resolution in the United States and Russia: A Comparative Evaluation, 7 *Ann. Surv. Int'l & Comp. L.* 7–19 (2001).
– NSIRIM-WORLU, Heoma, Oil Production and Changing Cultural Pattern in Ikwerre Ethnic Nation: A Case of Obio-Akpor, *Academic Research International*, Vol. 2 No. 1, 102–110 (2012)
– NWANKWOALA, H., Coastal Aquifers of Nigeria: An Overview of its Management and Sustainability Considerations, *Journal of Applied Technology in Environmental Sanitation*, 1 (4): 371–380 (2011)
– NWOBIKE, Justice C., The African Commission on Human and Peoples' Rights and the Demystification of Second and Third Generation Rights under the African Charter: Social Economic Rights Action Center (SERAC) and the Center for Economic and Social Rights (CESR) v. Nigeria, 1 *Africa J. Legal Stud.* 2, 129–146 (2005).
– NWOSU, E.O., Petroleum Legislation and Enforcement of Environmental Standards in Nigeria, *The Nigerian Juridical Review* Vol. 7, 80–108 (1998–1999).
– OBI, Cyril I., Oil Extraction, Dispossession, Resistance, and Conflict in Nigeria's Oil-Rich Niger Delta, 30 (1–2) *Canadian Journal of Development Studies* 219–236 (2010).
– ODINKALU, Chidi Anselm and CHRISTENSEN, Camilla, The African Commission on Human and Peoples' Rights: The Development of its Non-State Communication Procedures, 20 *Human Rights Quarterly*, 235–280 (1998).
– OGUAMANAM, Chidi, Indigenous Peoples and International Law: The Making of a Regime, 30 *Queen's L.J* 348 (2004).
– OGUINE, Ike, Nigeria's Oil Revenues and the Oil Producing Areas, 17 *J. Energy Nat. Resources L.* 112 (1999).
– O'HARA, K., Niger Delta: Peace and Co-operation Through Sustainable Development, *Environmental Policy and Law*, 31 (6), 302–308 (2001).
– OKAFOR, Obiora Chinedu and AGBAKWA, Shedrack C., On Legalism, Popular Agency and "Voices of Suffering": The Nigerian National Human Rights Commission in Context, 24 *Human Rights Quarterly*, 662–720 (2002).
– OKAFOR, Obiora Chinedu, Modest Harvests: On the Significant (But Limited) Impact of Human Rights NGOs on Legislature and Executive in Nigeria, 48 (1) *Journal of African Law*, 23–49 (2004).

- OKEAGU, Jonas E. *et al.*, The Environmental and Social Impact of Petroleum and Natural Gas Exploitation in Nigeria, *Journal of Third World Studies*, Vol. XXIII, No. 1, 199–218 (2006).
- OKO, Okechukwu, Seeking Justice in Transitional Societies: An Analysis of the Problems and Failures of the Judiciary in Nigeria, 31 (1) *Brook. J. Int'l L.* 9–82 (2005).
- OKOGBULE, Nlerum S., Access to Justice and Human Rights Protection in Nigeria: Problems and Prospects, 2 (3) *SUR–International Journal on Human Rights*, 95–113 (2005).
- OKONMAH, Patrick D., Right to a Clean Environment: The Case for the People of Oil-Producing Communities in the Nigerian Delta, *Journal of African Law*, Vol. 41, No. 1, 44 (1997).
- OKORODUDU-FUBARA, M.T., Statutory Scheme for Environmental Protection in the Nigerian Context: Some Reflections of Legal Significance for the Energy Sector, *Nigerian Current Law Review* 1–39 (1996).
- OLANIYAN, Kolawole, The African Union Convention on Preventing and Combating Corruption: A Critical Appraisal, 4 *Afr. Hum. Rts. L. J.* 74–92 (2004).
- OLOKESUSI, Femi, Legal and Institutional Framework of Environmental Impact Assessment in Nigeria: An Initial Assessment, *Environ Impact Asses. Rev.* 18, 159–174 (1998).
- OKWU-OKAFOR, Obiora, Self determination and the Struggle for Ethno-Cultural Autonomy in Nigeria: The Zangon Kataf and Ogoni Problems, 6 *African Society of International & Comparative Law, ASICL Proc.* 114 (1994).
- OLOKA-ONYANGO, J., Reinforcing Marginalized Rights in an Age of Globalization: International Mechanisms, Non-State Actors, and the Struggle for Peoples' Rights in Africa, 18 *Am. U. Int'l L. Rev.* 851–913 (2003).
- OLORUNFEMI, M.S., Managing Nigeria's Petroleum Resources, *OPEC Bulletin* 24 (1986).
- OLUWANIYI, O.O., Post-Amnesty Programme in the Niger Delta: Challenges and Prospects, *Conflict Trends*, Issue 4, 46–54 (2011).
- OMEJE, Kenneth, Development Securitisation in Nigeria's Niger Delta: An Appraisal of the Niger Delta Development Commission (NDDC), *African Renaissance*, Vol. 1 No. 1, 124–133 (2004).
- OMEJE, Kenneth, The Rentier State: Oil-Related Legislation and Conflict in the Niger Delta, Nigeria, 6 (2) *Conflict, Security and Development*, 211–230 (2006).
- OMOROGBE, Yinka, The Legal Framework for the Production of Petroleum in Nigeria, 5 *J. Energy Nat. Resources L.* 273–291 (1987).
- OMOROGBE, Yinka, Law and Investor Protection in the Nigerian Natural Gas Industry, 14 *J. Energy Nat. Resources L.* 179–192 (1996).
- OMOTOLA, Shola, From the OMPADEC to the NDDC: An Assessment of State Responses to Environmental Insecurity in the Niger Delta, Nigeria, *Africa Today*, Vol. 54 No. 1, 73–89 (2007).
- ONYEKPERE, E., The Right to Adequate Housing- The Concept of Legal Security of Tenure, 5 (2) *J. Hum. Rts. L. & Prac.* 44 (1997).

- ONZIVU, W., Tackling the Public Health Impact of Climate Change: The Role of Domestic Environmental Health Governance in Developing Countries, *International Lawyer*, Vol. 43 No. 3, 1311–1335 (2009).
- OSAGHAE, Eghosa E., The Ogoni Uprising: Oil Politics, Minority Agitation and the Future of the Nigerian State, *African Affairs* 94 (1995).
- OSAGHAE, Eghosa E., Human Rights and Ethnic Conflict Management: The Case of Nigeria, *Journal of Peace Research*, Vol. 33 No. 2, 181 (1996).
- OSAGHAE, Eghosa E., Social Movements and Rights Claims: The Case of Action Groups in the Niger Delta of Nigeria, *Voluntas* 19, 189–210 (2008).
- OSOFSKY, Hari M., Environmental Human Rights Under the Alien Tort Statute: Redress for Indigenous Victims of Multinational Corporations, 20 *Suffolk Transnat'l L. Rev.* 335- 396 (1997).
- OSUNTOKUN, Jide, Oil and Nigerian Development, *Development Outlook* 1, No. 3, 40 (1986).
- OTILLAR, Steven P. *et al.,* Recent Developments in Brazil's Oil & Gas Industry: Brazil Appears to be Stemming the Tide of Resource Nationalism, 30 *Hous. J. Int'l L.* 259–287 (2007–2008)
- OTTINGER, Richard L., Legislation and the Environment: Individual Rights and Government Accountability, 55 *Cornell L. Rev.* 666–673 (1970).
- OVIASUYI, P. O. and Jim Uwadiae, The Dilemma of Niger-Delta Region as Oil Producing States of Nigeria, *Journal of Peace, Conflict and Development*, Issue 16, pp.110-126 (2010).
- OWENS, James C., Government Failure in Sub-Saharan Africa: The International Community's Options, 43 *Virginia Journal of International Law,* 1003–1049 (2003).
- OWOLABI, Olayiwola and OKWECHIME, Iwebunor, Oil and Security in Nigeria: The Niger Delta Crisis, *Africa Development*, Vol. XXXII, No. 1, 1–40 (2007).
- PALLEMAERTS, Marc, International Environmental Law in the Age of Sustainable Development: A Critical Assessment of the UNCED Process, 15 *Journal of Law & Commerce* 623–676 (1996).
- PALLEMAERTS, Marc, A Human Rights Perspective on Current Environmental Issues and their Management: Evolving International Legal and Political Discourse on the Human Environment, the Individual and the State, *Human Rights and International Legal Discourse*, Vol. 2 No. 2, 149–178 (2008).
- PEDERSEN, Ole W., European Environmental Human Rights and Environmental Rights: A Long Time Coming?, 21 *Georgetown Int'l Envtl. Law Review* 73–111 (2008).
- PELED, Roy and RABIN, Yoram, The Constitutional Right to Information, 42 *Columbia Human Rights Law Review,* 357–401 (2011)
- PERCIVAL, Robert V., Liability for Environmental Harm and Emerging Global Environmental Law, 25 *Maryland Journal of International Law* 37–63 (2010).
- PEVATO, Paula M., A Right to Environment in International Law: Current Status and Future Outlook, 8 (3) *Rev. Eur. Cmty. &Int'l Envt'l L. (RECIEL)* 309–321 (1999).

– PINCKARD, Elizabeth, Indonesian Tribe Loses in its Latest Battle Against Freeport-McMoran, Inc., Operator of the World's Largest Gold and Copper Mine, 9 *Colo. J. Int.l Envtl L. & Pol'y* 141–145 (1998).

– POPOVIC, Neil A.F., Pursuing Environmental Justice with International Human Rights and State Constitutions, 15 *Stan. Env'l L.J.* 338–374 (1996).

– RAJAMANI, Lavanya, The Right to Environmental Protection in India: Many a Slip Between the Cup and the Lip?, 16 (3) *RECIEL* 274–286 (2007).

– RAMASASTRY, Anita, Corporate Complicity: From Nuremberg to Rangoon- An Explanation of Forced Labour Cases and their Impact on the Liability of Multinational Corporations, 20 *Berkeley Journal of International Law* 91–159 (2002).

– RATNER, Steven R., Corporations and Human Rights: A Theory of Legal Responsibility, 111 *Yale L.J.* 443–545 (2001).

– RAZZAQUE, J., Linking Human Rights, Development, and Environment: Experiences from Litigation in South Asia, 18 *Fordham Envtl. L. Rev.* 587–608 (2006–2007).

– REED, Mark S., Stakeholder Participation for Environmental Management: A Literature Review, 141 *Biological Conservation* 2417–2431 (2008).

– REST, Alfred, Enhanced Implementation of International Environmental Treaties by Judiciary- Access to Justice in International Environmental Law for Individuals and NGOs: Efficacious Enforcement by the Permanent Court of Arbitration, 1 (1) *MqJICEL* 1–28 (2004).

– RIBEIRO, Marilda Rosado De Sa, The New Oil and Gas Industry in Brazil: An Overview of the Main Legal Aspects, *Tex. Int'l L. J.* Vol. 36, 141–166 (2001).

– RODRIGUEZ-RIVERA, Luis E., Is the Human Right to Environment Recognized Under International Law? It Depends on the Source, 12 *Colo. J. Int'l Envtl. L & Pol.'y* 1- 46 (2001).

– ROSENCRANZ, Armin and CAMPBELL, Richard, Foreign Environmental and Human Rights Suits Against U.S. Corporations in U.S. Courts, 18 *Stan. Envtl. L.J.* 145–208 (1999).

– RUTHERFORD, Murray B. *et al.*, Assessing Environmental Losses: Judgements of Importance and Damage Schedules, 22 *Harv. Envtl. L. Rev.* 51–101 at 58 (1998)

– SACHAROFF, Ariadne K., Multinationals in Host Countries: Can they be Held Liable Under the Alien Tort Claims Act for Human Rights Violations?, 23 *Brook. J. Int'l L.* 927- 964 (1998).

– SALU, Abimbola, Can Laws Protect the Environment in Nigeria?, *Modern Practice Journal of Finance and Investment Law*, Vol. 2 No. 2, 140–154 (1998).

– SALU, Abimbola, Securing Environmental Protection in the Nigeria Oil Industry, *Modern Practice Journal of Finance and Investment Law*, Vol. 3 No. 2, 337–356 (1999).

– SASEGBON, Fola, Current Developments in Oil and Gas Law in Nigeria- with Comparative Analysis with other African Oil Producing Countries, *International Bar Association Energy Law*, Vol. 1, 371 (1981).

– SEPPALA, Nina, Business and the International Human Rights Regime: A Comparison of UN Initiatives, 87 *Journal of Business Ethics*, 401–417 (2009).

- SCHRAGE, Elliot J., Judging Corporate Accountability in the Global Economy, 42 *Columbia J. Transnat'l L.* 153–176 (2003).
- SCHWARTZ, Michelle Leighton, International Legal Protection for Victims of Environmental Abuse, 18 *Yale J. Int'l L.* 355–387 (1993).
- SHELTON, Dinah, Human Rights, Environmental Rights and the Right to Environment, 28 *Stanford J. Int'l L.* 103–138 (1991).
- SHELTON, Dinah, Decision Regarding Communication 155/96 (Social and Economic Action Center/Center for Economic, Social Rights v. Nigeria), Case No. ACHPR/COMM/A044/1, 96 *Am. J. Int'l L.* 937–942 (2002).
- SHELTON, Dinah, Human Rights and the Environment: What Specific Environmental Rights Have Been Recognized?, 35 *Denv. J. Int'l L. & Pol'y* 129–171 (2006).
- SHELTON, Dinah, Developing Substantive Environmental Rights, *Journal of Human Rights and the Environment*, Vol. 1 No. 1, 89–120 (2010).
- SHINSATO, Alison L., Increasing the Accountability of Transnational Corporations for Environmental Harms: The Petroleum Industry in Nigeria, 4(1) *Northwestern Journal of International Human Rights* 186–209 (2005).
- SHUTKIN, William A., The Concept of Environmental Justice and a Reconception of Democracy, 14 *Virginia Environmental Law Journal*, 579–588 (1995).
- SKOGLY, Sigrun I., Complexities in Human Rights Protection: Actors and Rights Involved in the Ogoni Conflict in Nigeria, 15(1) *Netherlands Quarterly of Human Rights*, 47–60 (1997).
- SKOLNIK, Matthew R., The Forum Non Conveniens Doctrine in Alien Tort Claims Act Cases: A *Shell* of Its Former Self After *Wiwa*, 16 *Emory Int'l L. Rev.* 187–225 (2002).
- SLAMA, Jo Lynn, *Opinio Juris* in Customary International Law, 15 *Okla. City U. L. Rev.* 603 (1990).
- SMITH, Anne, The Unique Position of National Human Rights Institutions: A Mixed Blessings?, 28 *Human Rights Quarterly* 904–946 (2006).
- STEIN, Ted L., The Approach of the Different Drummer: The Principle of the Persistent Objector in International Law, 26 *Harv. Int'l L.J* 457 (1985).
- STEPHENS, Beth, The Amorality of Profit: Transnational Corporations and Human Rights, 20 *Berkeley Journal of International Law* 45–90 (2002).
- STEVENSON, Sarah M., Indigenous Land Rights and the Declaration on the Rights of Indigenous Peoples: Implications for Maori Land Claims in New Zealand, 32 *Fordham Int'l L.J.* 298–343 (2008–2009).
- STRONG, S.I., Jurisdictional Discovery in United States Federal Courts, 67 *Wash. & Lee L. Rev.* 489–587 (2010)
- SUBERU, Rotimi, Federalism and Nigeria's Political Future: A Comment, 87 *African Affairs*, 348 (1988)
- SULLIVAN, Rory, NGO Influence on the Human Rights Performance of Companies, 24 (3) *Netherlands Quarterly of Human Rights*, 405–432 (2006).

- TAYLOR, Prudence E., From Environmental to Ecological Human Rights: A New Dynamic in International Law?, 10 *Georgetown International Environmental Law Review* 309–397 (1998).
- TUODOLO, Felix, Corporate Social Responsibility: Between Civil Society and the Oil Industry in the Developing World, *ACME: An International E-Journal for Critical Geographies* 8 (3), 530–541 (2009).
- UDOMA, U.U., Incentives for the Gas Ventures in Nigeria, *Modern Practice Journal of Finance and Investment Law* Vol. 2 No.3, (1998).
- UDOMBANA, Nsongurua J., Fighting Corruption Seriously? Africa's Anti-Corruption Convention, 7 *Singapore Journal of International & Comparative Law*, 447–488 (2003).
- UDOMBANA, Nsongurua J., Between Promise and Performance: Revisiting States' Obligations Under the African Human Rights Charter, 40 *Stan. J. Int'l L.* 105–142 (2004).
- UDOMBANA, Nsongurua J., The African Commission on Human and Peoples' Rights and the development of fair trial norms in Africa, 6 *African Human Rights Law Journal*, 299- 332 (2006).
- UGOCHUKWU, Collins N.C. and ERTEL, Jurgen, Negative Impacts of Oil Exploration on Biodiversity Management in the Niger Delta Area of Nigeria, *Impact Assessment and Project Appraisal*, 26 (2), 141–145 (2008).
- UMEZULIKE, I.A., Does the Land Use Act Expropriate? 5 *Journal of Private and Property Law* 61–69 (1986).
- VILJOEN, Frans, A Human Rights Court for Africa, and Africans, 30 *Brook. J. Int'l L.* 1–66 (2004).
- WACHIRA, George Mukundi, Twenty Years of Elusive Enforcement of the Recommendations of the African Commission on Human and Peoples' Rights: A possible Remedy, 6 *African Human Rights Law Journal* 465–492 (2006).
- WAI, Robert, Transnational Liftoff and Juridical Touchdown: The Regulatory Function of Private International Law in an Era of Globalization, 40 *Colum. J. Transnat'l L.* 209–274 (2002).
- WATTS, Michael J., Righteous Oil? Human Rights, the Oil Complex, and Corporate Social Responsibility, 30 *Annu. Rev. Environ. Resour.* 373–407 (2005).
- WAWRYK, Alexandra S., Adoption of International Environmental Standards by Transnational Oil Companies: Reducing the Impact of Oil Operations in Emerging Economies, 20 *J. Energy Nat. Resources L.* 402–434 (2002).
- WEISBURD, Arthur M., Customary International Law: The Problem of Treaties, 21 (1) *Vand. J. Transnat'l L.* 1–46 (1988).
- WEISSBRODT, David, Business and Human Rights, 74 *University of Cincinnati Law Review* 55–73 (2005).
- WESCHKA, Marion, Human Rights and Multinational Enterprises: How Can Multinational Enterprises Be Held Responsible for Human Rights Violations Committed Abroad?, 66 *ZaöRV* 625–661 (2006).

- WESTON, Christina, The Enforcement Loophole: Judgment-Recognition Defenses as a Loophole to Corporate Accountability for Conduct Abroad, 25 *Emory International Law Review*, 731–770 (2011).
- WIERSMA, Lindsey L., Indigenous Lands as Cultural Property: A New Approach to Indigenous Land Claims, *Duke Law Journal* Vol. 54, 1063–1064 (2005).
- WIESSNER, Siegfried, Rights and Status of Indigenous Peoples: A Global Comparative and International Legal Analysis, 12 *Harv. Hum. Rts. J.* 57–128 (1999).
- WILLIAMS, S., The Global Compact: Special Report on Corporate Social Responsibility, *African Business*, 40 (2007).
- WOUTERS, Jan and RYNGAERT, Cedric, Litigation for Overseas Corporate Human Rights Abuses in the European Union: The Challenge of Jurisdiction, *The Geo. Wash. Int'l L. Rev.* Vol. 40, 939–975 (2009).
- YAMIN, Farhana, NGOs and International Environmental Law: A Critical Evaluation of their Roles and Responsibilities, 10 (2) *RECIEL*, 149–162 (2001).
- YUSUF, Hakeem O., Oil in Troubled Waters: Multinational Corporations and Realising Human Rights in the Developing World, with Specific Reference to Nigeria, 8 *African Human Rights Law Journal* 79–107 (2008).

5 ARTICLES AND OTHER MATERIALS SOURCED FROM THE WORLD WIDE WEB

5.1 Articles

- ABRAMOVICH, Victor, *Courses of action in economic, social and cultural rights: Instruments and allies*, transl. by Barney Whiteoak, at www.surjournal.org/eng/conteudos/artigos2/ing/artigo_abramovich.htm [accessed 23 May 2013]
- ADENIRAN, Plea Bargain will make Corruption Pervasive in Nigeria, *The Economy*, available at www.theeconomyng.com/interview30.html [accessed 6 May 2010].
- ADUJIE, Paul I., *American Oil Spills in Gulf of Mexico: Lessons for Nigerians, Ecuadorians and Others*, New Liberian, available at http://newliberian.com/?p=1228 [accessed 23 May 2010].
- AGBO, D., Arms recovered from ex-Niger Delta militants destroyed. *Legal Oil*, 29 May 2011, available at www.legaloil.com/NewsItem.asp?DocumentIDX=1307016053 &Category=news [accessed 2 February 2012]
- AHMED, Zainab, *NEITI: The Prospects, Issues and Challenges*, being a paper presentation to the IMF Mission, at www.imf.org/external/np/seminars/eng/2012/kinshasa/pdf/za.pdf [accessed 5 May 2013]
- AJAKAIYE, Bamidele, *Role of NOSDRA in Environmental Management Protection and Enforcement in the Oil and Gas Industry*, being a paper delivered at the 2008 Manufacturers Association of Nigeria (M.A.N.), Environmental Management Seminar Theme: Preparing Businesses in Nigeria for Environmental Challenges and Opportunities, held on 4 November 2008 at the Conference Hall, M.A.N. House

77, Ikeja, Lagos, available at www.man- greencourses.com/sr.pdf [accessed 2 March
2010].

–   AKINBAJO, Idris, France Slams $10.5m fine on Etete, *Next* 19 March, 2009,
available at http://234next.com/csp/cms/sites/Next/Home/5394254-146/France_
slams_$10.5m_fine_on_Etete.csp [accessed 23 May 2010].

–   AKO, Rhuks T., *Substantive injustice: oil-related regulations and environmental injustice in Nigeria*, being a paper prepared for the joint-workshop organized by the IUCN
Academy of Environmental Law, Environmental Law Centre and Commission on
Environmental Law, entitled "Linking Human Rights and the Environment: A Comparative Review," held at the University of Ghent, Belgium, September 2010, available
at https://community.iucn.org/rba1/resources/Documents/Rhuks%20Temitope.pdf
[accessed 23 December 2010].

–   AKO, Rhuks, *Resource Control in the Niger Delta: Conceptual Issues and Legal Realities*, *e-International Relations*, 25 May 2012, available at www.e-ir.info/2012/05/25/
resource-control-in-the-niger-delta-conceptual-issues-and-legal-realities/ [accessed
23 May 2013]

–   AKPAN, Wilson, *Oil, People and the Environment: Understanding Land-Related Controversies in Nigeria's Oil Region*, available at www.codesria.org/Links/conferences/
general_assembly11/papers/akpan.pdf [accessed 3 March 2010].

–   ALBANESE, Tom, Rio Tinto's CEO, talks to Critical Resource, Q & A with Rio Tinto
CEO: industry needs to 'out' bad actors, *Critical Resource*, September 2011, available
at www.c-resource.com/view_article.php?aid=179 [accessed 18 August 2011].

–   ALFORD, Roger, *Case of the Month: Shell v. Ijaw Aborigines of Bayelsa State* (*Opinio
Juris*), available at http://opiniojuris.org/2006/02/28/case-of-the-month-shell-v-ijaw-
aborigines-of-bayelsa-state/ [accessed 23 March 2009].

–   ALLEN, Stephen, *The UN Declaration on the Rights of Indigenous Peoples: Towards
a Global Legal Order on Indigenous Rights?*, available at http://ilreports.blogspot.
com/2009/05/allen-un- declaration-on-rights-of.html [accessed 23 November 2010].

–   AMAIZE, E., 'Amnesty: Nigeria, EU to partner on Niger Delta,' *Vanguard,* 13 August,
2011, available at www.vanguardngr.com/2011/08/amnesty-nigeria-eu-to-partner-
on-niger-delta/ [accessed 2 February 2012]

–   Amazon Watch, *Understanding Recent Developments in the Landmark Chevron-
Ecuador Case*, Clean Up Ecuador Campaign Briefing Paper, Winter 2011, available
at http://amazonwatch.org/assets/files/Chevron-Ecuador-Briefing-Winter-2011.pdf
[accessed 23 November 2011].

–   American Petroleum Institute (API), *API Environmental Stewardship Pledge for
CAREFUL Operations*, available at www.api.org [accessed 23 November 2010].

–   Amnesty International, *Nigeria: Independence of National Human Rights Commission Under Threat*, 20 March 2008, London, available at www.amnesty.org/en/
library/asset/AFR44/009/2009/en/ [accessed 23 November 2009].

–   Amnesty International (Irish Section), *Our Rights, Our Future. Human Rights Based
Approaches in Ireland: Principles, Policies and Practice*, available at www.ihrnetwork.

org/files/IHRN-AI%20HRBA%20Ireland%20Sept05%20FINAL.pdf [accessed 3 March 2010].

- ANAYA, S.J. and Wiessner, S., *The UN Declaration on the Rights of Indigenous Peoples: Towards Re-empowerment*, Jurist Forum, School of Law, University of Pittsburgh, 3 October 2007, available at http://jurist.law.pitt.edu/forumy/2007/10/un-declaration-on-rights-of- indigenous.php [accessed 23 November 2009].
- ANNAN, Kofi, *In larger Freedom: Towards Development, Security and Human Rights for All*, Report of the Secretary-General, UN General Assembly Document A/59/2005 of 21 March, 2005, available at http://www2.ohchr.org/english/bodies/hrcouncil/docs/gaA.59.2005_En.pdf [accessed 23 November 2009].
- ARIEFF, Alexis, *Sexual Violence in African Conflicts*, Congressional Research Service, November 25, 2009, available at www.fas.org/sgp/crs/row/R40956.pdf [accessed 23 November 2010].
- Atlas on Regional Integration in West Africa Economy Series, *Oil and Gas*, ECOWAS-SWAC/OECD, April 2007, available at www.oecd.org/dataoecd/28/34/38798400.pdf [accessed 7 February 2012]
- ATURU, Bamidele, *Petroleum Industry Bill 2008: Combustible but Curable*, Sahara Reporters Tuesday, 28 July 2009, available at www.saharareporters.com/index.php? [accessed 23 November 2009].
- Australian Corporate Code of Conduct Bill 2000, available at www.austlii.edu.au/au/legis/cth/bill/ccocb2000248/ [accessed 23 November 2009].
- AYESHA, Dias K., *International Standard-Setting on the Rights of Indigenous Peoples: Implications for Mineral Development in Africa*, available at www.dundee.ac.uk/cepmlp/journal/html/vol7/article7-3.html [accessed 23 March 2009].
- AYESHA, Dias K., *Human Rights, Environment and Development: With Special Emphasis on Corporate Accountability*, Human Development Report 2000, Background Paper, available at http://hdr.undp.org/en/reports/global/hdr2000/papers/ayesha%20dias%20.pdf [accessed 3 March 2010].
- AYODELE-AKAAKAR, F.O., *Appraising the Oil & Gas Laws: A Search for Enduring Legislation for the Niger Delta Region*, available at www.jsd-africa.com/Jsda/Fallwinter2001/articlespdf/ARC%2020APPRAISING%20THE%20OIL%20and%20Gas.pdf [accessed 23 November 2009].
- BANISAR, Dave (2002), *Freedom of Information and Access to Government* II, available at www.article19.org/work/regions/latin-america/FOI/pdf/DbanisarFOI2002.pdf. [accessed 23 November 2009].
- BASSEY, Nnimmo, *The Oil Industry and Human Rights in the Niger Delta*, being his Testimony before the United States Senate Judiciary Subcommittee on Human Rights and the Law, 24 September, 2008, available at www.earthrights.org/sites/default/files/documents/Nnimo-testimony-9-24-08.pdf [accessed 23 November 2009].
- BAUMÜLLER, Heike, *et al.*, *The Effects of Oil Companies' Activities on the Environment, Health and Development in Africa*, being Study conducted for the Directorate-General for External Policies of the EU Parliament, August 2011, available at www.

chathamhouse.org/sites/default/files/0811ep_report_0.pdf [accessed 7 February 2012]

- BEKELE, Daniel, Nigeria: UK Conviction a Blow Against Corruption, *Human Rights Watch News*, 17 April 2012, available at www.hrw.org/news/2012/04/17/nigeria-uk-conviction-blow-against-corruption [accessed 18 June 2012].

- BRIGGS, B., *Strategic Relations Manager at Shell, talked to Shell World UK magazine about one of his hot topics: Shell in Nigeria*, available at www.shell.co.uk/home/content/gbr/aboutshell/media_centre/annual_reports_and_publications/swuk/summer_2010/nigeria.html [accessed 23 November 2010].

- BRUCH, Carl and COKER, Wole, Breathing life into Fundamental Law in Africa, available at www.eli.org/pdf/breathinglife.pdf. [accessed 3 March 2010].

- Business & Human Rights, *Case profile: Trafigura Lawsuits (re Côte d'Ivoire)*, available at www.business-humanrights.org. [accessed 3 August 2011].

- CAMERER, Lala (2001), *Corruption in South Africa: Results of an Expert Panel Survey*, Monograph 65, available at www.iss.co.za/Pubs/Monographs/No65/Chap7.html [accessed 7 March 2010].

- CAMERI-MBOTE, Patricia, *Towards Greater Access to Justice in Environmental Disputes in Kenya: Opportunities for Intervention*, International Environmental Law Research Centre (IELRC) Working Paper 2005, available at www.ielrc.org/content/w0501.pdf [accessed 7 March 2009].

- CASON, J. (2003), *US firm Halliburton acknowledges bribes to Nigerian Official*, News. http://allAfrica.com/stories/200305090511.html [accessed 3 March 2010].

- Centre for the Study of Violence and Reconciliation (CSVR), *Human Rights Violations Investigation Commission, Nigeria*, available at www.justiceinperspective.org.za/index.php?option=com_content&task=view&id=23&Itemid=57 [accessed 5 March 2010].

- Center for Constitutional Rights & EarthRights International, *Shell's Environmental Devastation in Nigeria*, available at http://wiwavshell.org/shell%E2%80%99s-environmental- devastation-in-nigeria/ (visited 21/4/10) [accessed 21 April 2010].

- Center for Human Rights and Environment, *UN Special Representative Releases Report on Human Rights and Business Calling for New UN Policy Framework to Address Corporate Abuse of Human Rights*, 18 April 2008, available at www.cedha.org.ar/en/more_information/un_special.php [accessed 3 March 2010].

- Center for International Environmental Law (CIEL), *Human Rights and Environment: Overlapping Issues*, available at www.ciel.org. [accessed 3 March 2010].

- Centre on Housing Rights and Evictions, *50 Leading Cases on Economic, Social and Cultural Rights: Summaries*, Working Paper No. 1, June 2003, available at www.cohre.org. [accessed 5 March 2010].

- Centre for the Study of Violence and Reconciliation (CSVR), *Human Rights Violations Investigation Commission, Nigeria*, available at www.justiceinperspective.org.za/index.php?option=com_content&task=view&id=23&Itemid=57[accessed 23 November 2010].

- Centre on Housing Rights and Eviction (COHRE) (2008), *A rights-based review of the legal and policy framework of the Ghanaian water and sanitation sector,* Geneva, Switzerland, at www.cohre.org/sites/default/files/rights-based_review_of_ghanaian_watsan_sector_dec_2008.pdf [accessed 3 March 2010].
- Chatham House Report, *Human Rights and Transnational Corporations: Legislation and Government Regulation,* being Note of a meeting held at Chatham House on 15 June 2006, available at www.chathamhouse.org.uk/files/3337_il150606.pdf. [accessed 5 March 2010].
- Chevron Business Conduct and Ethics Code, available at www.chevron.com/documents/pdf/chevronbusinessconductethicscode.pdf [accessed 10 March 2010].
- CHIRWA, D.M. (2002), *Obligations of Non-State Actors in Relation to Economic, Social and Cultural Rights under The South African Constitution,* Social-Economic Rights Project Community Law Centre, University of the Western Cape, available at www.community.lawcentre.org.za [accessed 10 March 2010].
- Climate Justice Programme and Environmental Rights Action/Friends of the Earth Nigeria, *Gas Flaring in Nigeria: A Human Rights, Environmental and Economic Monstrosity,* 2005, available at www.climatelaw.org/cases/case-documents/nigeria/report/section9 [accessed 26 February 2010].
- Coalition for an Effective African Court on Human and Peoples' Rights, *Ratification Status: Protocol on the Statute of the African Court of Justice and Human Rights,* available at www.africancourtcoalition.org/ [accessed 3 March 2010].
- COCKS, Tim, Nigeria Oil Bill to Outlaw Gas Flaring by end-2012, *Reuters Africa,* 28 May 2012, available at http://af.reuters.com/article/investingNews/idAF-JOE84R0A820120528 [accessed at 6 June 2010]
- Corporate Responsibility Bill, Bill 129, available at www.publications.parliament.uk/pa/cm200203/cmbills/129/2003129.pdf [accessed 3 March 2010].
- Corporate Responsibility (CORE), Leigh Day & Co, The TUC, Amnesty International, Rights & Accountability in Development (RAID), One World Action, Global Witness and The Cornerhouse, *Submission to the European Commission regarding Brussels I Regulation (EC 44/2001),* available at http://corporate-responsibility.org/submission-to-europeancommission-regarding-brussels-1-regulation-ec-442001/ [accessed 8 June 2009].
- Corporate Responsibility (CORE), *UK Commission Proposal: A New Commission for Business, Human Rights and the Environment,* available at http://corporate-responsibility.org/campaigns/uk-commissions-proposal/ [accessed 8 June 2010].
- Council of Europe Parliamentary Assembly Report, *Human Rights and Business,* Doc. 12361, 27 September 2010, available at http://assembly.coe.int/Documents/WorkingDocs/Doc10/EDOC12361.pdf [accessed 6 June 2011].
- COURSON, Elias (2006), *Odi Revisited?: Odi and State Violence in Odioma, Brass LGA, Bayelsa State,* Niger Delta Economies of Violence Working Paper No. 7-r, available at http://geography.berkeley.edu/ProjectsResources/ND%20Website/Niger-Delta/WP/7- Courson.pdf [accessed 3 March 2010].

– DAFINONE, David, *Supreme Court's Verdict on Resource Control: The Political Imperatives*, at www.nigerdeltacongress.com/sarticles/supreme_courts_verdict_on_resour.htm [accessed 4 June 2010]

– DARKWAH, Akosua K., *The Impact of Oil and Gas Discovery and Exploration on Communities with Emphasis on Women*, www.g-rap.org/docs/oil_and_gas/netright-akosua_darkwah-2010.pdf [accessed 4 March 2011].

– DIVINE, William, Where Does the Revenue Go?, *Offshore*, December 1, 1998, available at www.offshore-mag.com/index/article-display/24798/articles/offshore/volume-58/issue-12/news/general-interest/where-does-the-revenue-go.html [accessed 8 June 2010].

– DONOVAN, John, *2nd Circuit Rejects Corporate Liability in Alien Tort Act Cases*, 18 September 2010, available at http://royaldutchshellplc.com/2010/09/18/2nd-circuit-rejects-corporate-liability-in-alien-tort-act-cases/ [accessed 5 November 2010].

– Earth Rights Institute, *Niger Delta Fund Initiative: Political definition of N-Delta*, available at www.earthrights.net/nigeria/news/definition.html [accessed 10 March 2009].

– EarthRights International, *As Expected, Bowoto v. Chevron Petition is Denied after Mohamad Decision*, 24 April 2012, available at www.earthrights.org/blog/expected-bowoto-v-chevron-petition-denied-after-mohamad-decision [accessed 2 May 2013]

– Ecumenical Council for Corporate Responsibility (ECCR) Report, *Shell in the Niger Delta: A Framework for Change*, sponsored by Cordaid, February 2010, available at http://allafrica.com/download/resource/main/main/idatcs/00020052:f1951c2ce1554d231761a0196fbc9b5b.pdf [accessed 10 March 2009].

– EDEVBIE, David, *The Politics of 13 Percent Derivation Principle*, available at www.waado.org/Environment/FedGovt-NigerDelta/RevenueAllocation/13Percent/Allocation.htm [accessed 3 March 2010].

– EIGEN, Peter, *Introducing the Global Corruption Report 2001*, available at www.mekonginfo.org/HDP/Lib.nsf/0/3F1E4D5F8F211ABB47256DC0002850A9/$FILE/Q%203.5%20-%20T.I.%20-%20Global%20Corruption%20Report%202001.pdf [accessed 9 June 2009].

– EMESEH, Engobo, *The Limitations of Law in Promoting Synergy between Environmental and Development Policies in Developing Countries: A Case Study of the Petroleum Industry in Nigeria*, available at http://web.fu-berlin.de/ffu/akumwelt/bc2004/download.htm [accessed 6 March 2010].

– ENGLE, Eric, *Kiobel* v. *Royal Dutch Petroleum Co.: Corporate Liability Under the Alien Torts Statute*, December 17, 2010, available at http://papers.ssrn.com/sol3/papers.cfm?abstract_id=1727331 [accessed 7 April 2011].

– ENTINE, Jon, *Seeds of NGO Activism: Shell Capitulates in Saro-Wiwa Case: Accountability & Transparency Trends*, NGO Watch, June 18, 2009, available at www.globalgovernancewatch.org/ngo_watch/seeds-of-ngo-activism-shell-capitulates-in-sarowiwa-case [accessed 3 March 2010].

– ENTINE, Jon, *UN Global Compact: Ten Years of Greenwashing?*, Ethical Corporation, 1 November 2010, available at www.ethicalcorp.com/resources/pdfs/

content/201011154314_Last%20word_Page%2050%20ECM.pdf [accessed 3 March 2011].

– Environmental Law Institute (ELI), *Natural Resource Valuation and Damage Assessment in Nigeria: A Comparative Analysis*, Environmental Law Institute, August, 2003, available at www.elistore.org/Data/products/d13-18.pdf [accessed 18 April 2010].

– Environmental Rights Action/Friends of the Earth Nigeria, *Fact Sheet: Harmful Gas Flaring in Nigeria*, November 2008, available at www.foe.org/pdf/GasFlaringNigeria_FS.pdf [accessed 16 February 2010].

– Environmental Rights Action (ERA) Report, *When Oil Companies Volunteer*, available at www.eraction.org/media/publications/oil-politics/244-when-oil-companies-volunteer- [accessed 3 March 2010].

– EVIATAR, Daphne, *Petrol Peril: Why Iraq's Oil Wealth May Do More Harm than Good*, The Boston Globe, April 13, 2003, available at www.boston.com/news/packages/Iraq/globe_stories/041303_ideas2.htm [accessed 13 March 2009].

– FABIYI, Oluseyi, *Mapping Environmental sensitivity index of the Niger delta to oil spill: The policy, procedures and politics of oil spill response in Nigeria*, available at http://gisdevelopment.net/proceedings/mapafrica/2008/maf08_44.pdf [accessed 5 March 2010].

– FEDERICI, Silvia, *Struggles on the Nigerian Oil Rivers*, available at www.radicalpolytics.org/caffentzis/10-struggles_nigerian_oil_rivers.pdf [accessed 3 March 2010].

– FILMER-WILSON, Emilie and ANDERSON, Michael, *Integrating Human Rights into Energy and Environment Programming: A Reference Paper*, May 2005, available at http://hurilink.org/tools/Integrating_HRs_into_Energy_and_Environment_Programming.pdf. [accessed 13 March 2009].

– *Final Statement by the UK National Contact Point for OECD Guidelines for Multinational Enterprises: Afrimex (UK) Ltd*, 28 August 2008, available at www.oecd.org/dataoecd/40/29/43750590.pdf [accessed 3 March 2010].

– Food and Agricultural Organization of the United Nations report on The Federal Republic of Nigeria, FID/CP/NIR, March 2007, available at ftp://ftp.fao.org/fi/document/fcp/en/FI_CP_NG.pdf [accessed 13 May 2009].

– Foreign Direct Investment (fDi) Magazine, *Under the Shadow of ATCA*, June 5, 2006, available at www.fdimagazine.com/news/printpage.php/aid/. [accessed 3 March 2010].

– FOSTER, Sheila, The Challenge of Environmental Justice, *Rutgers University Journal of Law and Urban Policy,* Vol. 1, Issue 1, available at www.rutgerspolicyjournal.org/1-1.html [accessed 3 March 2010].

– FREEMAN, Bennett, Managing Risk and Building Trust: The Challenge of Implementing the Voluntary Principles on Security and Human Rights, *Traditional Dispute Management*, Vol. Issue 1, February 2004, available at www.transnational-dispute-management.com/samples/freearticles/tv1-1-article_30.htm [accessed 3 March 2009].

– Friends of the Earth Netherlands, *The Case of Oruma: Spills from a High Pressure Pipeline*, available at http://milieudefensie.nl/publicaties/factsheets/factsheet-oruma [accessed 3 March 2010].

– Frontline (PBS), *Nigeria: The Hidden Cost of Corruption*, April 24, 2009, available at www.pbs.org/frontlineworld/stories/bribe/2009/04/nigeria-the-hidden-cost-of-corruption.html. [accessed 3 March 2010].

– GARUBA, Dauda, *Halliburton, Bribes and the Deceit of 'Zero-Tolerance' for Corruption in Nigeria*, CoP-MfDR-Africa, available at www.cop-mfdr-africa.org/profiles/blogs/halliburton-bribes-and-the [accessed 3 June 2011].

– GILBERT, Jérémie, The United Nations Declaration on the Rights of Indigenous Peoples: Towards Partnership and Mutual Respect, available at www.liv.ac.uk/law/ielu/docs/UN_Declaration_on_the_Rights_of_Indigenous_Peoples-JG.pdf [accessed 3 March 2010].

– GOLDHABER, Michael D., *A Win for Wiwa, A Win for Shell, A Win for Corporate Human Rights*, The AM Daily Law, June 10, 2009, available at http://amlawdaily.typepad.com/amlawdaily/2009/06/a-win-for-wiwa-a-win-for-shell-a-win-for-corporate-human-rights.html [accessed 14 July 2010].

– GREGOR, Filip, *Principles and Pathways: Legal Opportunities to Improve Europe's Corporate Accountability Framework*, European Coalition for Corporate Justice (ECCJ), November 2010, available at www.corporatejustice.org/IMG/pdf/eccj_principles_pathways_webuseblack.pdf [accessed 3 June 2011].

– HARRIS, Shubha, *Establishing a Constitutional Right to Environmental Quality*, 5 May, 2008, available at http://apps.americanbar.org/environ/committees/lawstudents/writingcompetition/2008/WillMitSoL/ShubhaHarris.pdf [accessed 6 July 2009].

– HAUSFELD, Michael D., *The Importance of Corporate Accountability for Human Rights, A Commentary*, September 2008, available at www.reports-and-materials.org/Michael-Hausfeld-commentary.pdf [accessed 3 March 2010].

– HELLER, Patrick, *The Nigerian Petroleum Industry Bill: Key Upstream Questions for the National Assembly*, Revenue Watch Institute, available at www.revenuewatch.org/images/RWI_Nigeria_PIB_Analysis.pdf [accessed 13 March 2010].

– HOUPPE, Bradford, *Shell Apologises for Human Rights Violations in Niger Delta*, being Public Statement by Shell made at The Hague on 27 March 2010 http://shellapologises.com/statement.html [accessed 17 April 2010].

– Human Development Report (2010), *The Real Wealth of Nations: Pathways to Human Development* UNDP, New York, available at http://hdr.undp.org/en/media/HDR_2010_EN_Complete_reprint.pdf [accessed 13 May 2011].

– Human Rights Watch and Center for Human Rights & Global Justice (2008), *On the Margins of Profit: Rights at Risk in the Global Economy*, available at www.chrgj.org/publications/docs/bhr.pdf [accessed 3 March 2010].

– Human Rights Watch, *World Report 2011 – Nigeria*, 24 January 2011, available at www.unhcr.org/refworld/docid/4d3e80220.html [accessed 26 May 2011]

–   IBEANU, Okechukwu (2006), *Civil Society and Conflict Management in the Niger Delta: Scoping Gaps for Policy and Advocacy*, CLEEN Foundation Publication, available at www.cleen.org [accessed 3 March 2010].
–   IDEMUDIA, Uwafiokun (2007), *Corporate Partnerships and Community Development in the Nigerian Oil Industry: Strengths and Limitations*, United Nations Research Institute for Social Development, Markets, Business and Regulation Programme Paper Number 2, available at www.unrisd.org/ [accessed 4 June 2009]
–   IGWE, U., 'Is the Niger Delta Amnesty Working?', *The African Executive*, November 2010, available at www.africanexecutive.com/modules/magazine/articles.php?article=5517 [accessed 3 March 2012].
–   IMARHIAGBE, Bernard and ADEJUMO, Akintokunbo A., *Does Ibori Own the Nigerian Judiciary?: A statement from Champions for Nigeria*, Transparency for Nigeria, 22 December, 2009, available at www.transparencyng.com/index [accessed 3 March 2010].
–   Indigenous & Tribal Peoples' Rights in Practice- *A Guide to ILO Convention No. 169 Programme to Promote ILO Convention No. 169 (PRO 169)*, International Labour Standards Department, 2009, available at http://pro169.org/res/materials/en/general_resources/IPsRightsCover-english-part2-1lorez.pdf [accessed 3 March 2010].
–   Indonesia Energy Data, Statistics and Analysis – *Oil, Gas, Electricity, Coal, Energy Information Administration, Country Analysis Briefs Indonesia*, January 2007, available at www.eia.doe.gov/emeu/cabs/Indonesia/Oil.html [accessed 5 July 2009].
–   International Commission of Jurists (ICJ), *Report of the ICJ Expert Legal Panel on Corporate Complicity in International Crimes: Corporate Complicity & Legal Accountability. Volume 1: Facing the Facts and Charting a Legal Path*, 2008, Vol. 1, available at: www.refworld.org/docid/4a78418c2.html [accessed 3 May 2013]
–   International Development Law Organization (IDLO) Report, *Strengthening Environmental Law Compliance and Enforcement in Indonesia: Towards Improved Environmental Stringency and Environmental Performance*, IDLO Development Law Update, Issue 6, 2006, available at www.idlo.int/publications/30.pdf [accessed 3 March 2010].
–   International Federation for Human Rights (FIDH), *Corporate Accountability for Human Rights Abuses: A Guide for Victims and NGOs on Recourse Mechanisms*, July 2010, available at www.fidh.org/Corporate-Accountability-for-Human-Rights-Abuses [accessed 3 June 2011].
–   International Federation for Human Rights (FIDH) & European Coalition for Corporate Justice (ECCJ) Report, CSR *at a turning point: time for the EU to move forward for true accountability*, being contribution to the European Multi-stakeholder Forum on CSR, 29–30 November 2010, available at www.fidh.org/IMG/pdf/FIDH_Contribution_to_the_European_Multistakeholder_Forum_on_CSR_2010.pdf [accessed 13 May 2011].
–   International Law Association Interim Report, *Private International Law Aspects of Civil Litigation for Human Rights Violations*, The Hague Conference (2010), available at http//www.ila.hq.org/download [accessed 14 August 2011].

- International Network for Economic, Social & Cultural Rights (ESCR-Net) Corporate Accountability Working Group, *Joint NGO Submission Consultation on Human Rights and the Extractive Industry*, Geneva, 10–11 November 2005, available at www.earthrights.org/sites/default/files/documents/escr-joint-ngo-submission.pdf [accessed 3 March 2010].
- IPIECA, *Bringing together the oil and gas industry on global, environmental and social issues*, available at www.ipieca.org/ipieca_info/about.php [accessed 21 April 2010].
- James A. Baker III Institute for Public Policy, *Critical Issues in Brazil's Energy Sector*, Report of the James A. Baker III Institute for Public Policy of Rice University, March 2004, at www.rice.edu/energy/publications/docs/BrazilEnergySector_MainStudy.pdf [accessed 2 October 2011].
- JARAMILLO, Gwendolyn Wilber, *Second Circuit Holds that Corporations are not proper Defendants Under the Alien Tort Statute*, Corporate Social Responsibility and the Law, Foley Hoag LLP Publication, 19 September 2010, available at www.csrandthelaw.com/2010/09/articles/litigation/alien-tort-statute/second-circuit-holds-that-corporations-are-not-proper-defendants-under-the-alien-tort-statute/ [accessed 3 April 2010].
- JEFFERY, Michael I. QC, Environmental Governance: A Comparative Analysis of Public Participation and Access to Justice, 9 (2) *Journal of South Pacific Law* (2005), available at www.paclii.org/journals/fJSPL/vol09no2/2.shtml [accessed 13 April 2010].
- JOFFE, Paul, Global Implementation of the *UN Declaration on the Rights of Indigenous Peoples*- and Canada's Increasing Isolation, September 2009, available at http://thestar.blogs.com/files/joffe-2.doc [accessed 3 April 2010].
- JOSEPH, O., Analysis Nigeria's Delta amnesty at risk of unraveling, *Spero News*, 23 April, 2010, available at www.speroforum.com/a/31526/Analysis--Nigerias-Delta-amnesty-at-risk-of-unravelling [accessed 2 February 2012]
- KAGGWA, Med S.K., *Access to remedy for corporate human rights abuses*, available at http://nhri.net/2010/Access%20to%20remedy%20for%20corporate%20human%20rights%20abuses-Uganda.pdf [accessed 4 March 2011].
- KALDANY, Rashad, *Global Gas Flaring Reduction: A Time for Action!*, being a Keynote Speech at the Global Forum on Flaring & Gas Utilization Paris, December 13th, 2006 available at www.worldbank.org/html/fpd/ggfrforum06/kadany.pdf [accessed 16 February 2010].
- KAUFMANN, *et al.*, *Governance Matters*, available at www.worldbank.org/wbi/governance [accessed 3 April 2010].
- KEATING, Joshua E., *The World's Ongoing Ecological Disasters*, Foreign Policy, 16 July 2010, available at www.foreignpolicy.com/articles/2010/07/16/the_world_s_worst_ongoing_disasters?page=0,0 [accessed 8 June 2011].
- KHAN, Sabaha, *Transnational Corporations Liability on Environmental Harms*, Articlesbase, 27 September 2009, available at www.articlesbase.com/health-and-safety-articles/transnational-corporations-liability-for-environmental-harms-1275283.html [accessed 13 April 2010].

– Khulumani Support Group, *The Significance of the Successful Appeal Ruling*, available at www.khulumani.net/reparations/corporate/223-the-significance-of-the-successful-appeal-ruling.html [accessed 3 August 2011].

– KIRPAL, B.N., *Environmental Justice in India*, available at www.ebc-india.com/lawyer/default.htm. [accessed 3 April 2010].

– KLIPPENSTEIN, Murray, of Toronto's Klippensteins, Barristers & Solicitors, who's representing 13 Maya Qeqchi from El Estor, Izabal, Guatemala, in *Choc v. Hudbay Minerals Inc. & Caal v. Hudbay Minerals Inc.*, at www.chocversushudbay.com/ [10 August 2013]

– KOVARIK, Bill, Remembering Ken Saro-Wiwa, *SE Journal* (2005) www.radford.edu/wkovarik/misc/blog/17.wiwa.html [accessed 3 April 2010].

– KPMG, Nigerian Oil and Gas Industry Content Development Act, 2010, available at www.kpmg.com/NG/en/IssuesAndInsights/ArticlesPublications/Documents/Newsletter%20on%20Nigerian%20Oil%20and%20Gas%20Industry%20Content%20Development%20Act%20-%20June%202010.pdf

– KPUNDEH, Sahr J., *Political Will in Fighting Corruption,* in Corruption and Integrity Improvement Initiatives in Developing Countries, available at http://mirror.undp.org/magnet/Docs/efa/corruption/Chapter06.pdf [accessed 3 March 2010].

– KRUT, Riva (1997), *Globalization and Civil Society: NGO Influence in International Decision-Making*, United Nations Research Institute for Social Development (UNRISD) Discussion Paper No. 83, available at www.unrisd.org/ (accessed 3 March 2010)

– KUKU, K., being a Communiqué stating the stand of the Amnesty Office on the Issue of those Niger Delta Youths Clamouring for inclusion in the Amnesty Programme, 8 December 2011, available at www.nigerdeltaamnesty.org/index.php?option=com_content&view=article&id=251:press-statement&catid=36:news&Itemid=18 [accessed 2 February 2012]

– KURUKULASURIYA, Lal, *The Role of the Judiciary in Promoting Environmental Governance and the Rule of Law,* being a paper prepared for Global Environmental Governance: the Post-Johannesburg Agenda, Yale Center for Environmental Law and Policy New Haven, CT, 23–25 October 2003, available at www.environmentalgovernance.org/cms/wp-content/uploads/docs/dialogue/oct03/papers/Kurukulasuriya%20final.pdf [accessed 7 July 2010].

– LABA, Oghenekevwe, Appraisal of Reforms in the Oil and Gas Sector, *The Nigerian Voice*, 28 November 2012, available at www.thenigerianvoice.com/nvnews/102145/1/appraisal-of-reforms-in-the-oil-and-gas-sector.html [accessed 30 May 2013]

– LANGSETH, Petter and BUSCAGLIA, Edgardo (2001), *Empowering the Victims of Corruption through Social Control Mechanisms*, Global Programme against Corruption, Centre for International Crime Prevention (CICP-17), Research and Scientific Series, Office of Drug Control and Crime Prevention, United Nations Office, Prague, available at www.unodc.org/pdf/crime/gpacpublications/cicp17.pdf [accessed 3 March 2010].

- LAVRYSEN, Luc, *European Environmental Law Principles in Belgian Jurisprudence*, available at http://www-user.uni-bremen.de/~avosetta/lavrysenrep03.pdf [accessed 9 March 2011].
- LETJOLANE, Corlett *et al.*, *NIGERIA: Defending Human Rights: Not Everywhere, Not every Right*, International Fact-Finding Mission Report of World Organisation Against Torture (OMCT), FIDH and Front Line, 2010, available at www.omct.org/files/2010/05/20688/nigeria_mission_report.pdf [accessed 1 August 2011].
- LEWIS, Janelle Melissa, The Resource Curse: Examining Corruption in the Extractive Industries, *Perspectives on Global Issues, Vol.2, Issue 1, New York University (2007)*, available at www.perspectivesonglobalissues.com/0201/articles0201/TheResourceCurse.pdf [accessed 18 August 2011].
- MACLEAN, Pamela A., Judge Denies Chevron's $485,000 Claim in Human Rights Case, *The National Law Journal*, 24 April, 2009, available at www.law.com/jsp/article.jsp?id=1202430172170&slreturn=1&hbxlogin=1 [accessed 3 March 2010].
- MALESKE, Melissa, *Court Decision Could Block Alien Tort Statute Against Corporations*, Inside Counsel, 11/1/2010, at www.insidecounsel.com/Issues/2010/November-2010/Pages/Court-Decision-Could-Block-Alien-Tort-Statute-Claims-Against-Corporations.aspx?PrintPreview [accessed 18 June 2011].
- MAMAH, E. & AMAIZE, E., Nigeria: MEND Resumes Hostilities- Blows Up Agip Trunk Line in Bayelsa, *Vanguard,* 6 February 2012, available at http://allafrica.com/stories/201202060224.html [accessed 2 February 2012]
- MANBY, Bronwen, *Shell in Nigeria: Corporate Social Responsibility and the Ogoni Crisis*, A case study published by the Carnegie Council on Ethics and International Affairs, available at www.cceia.org/resources/publications/case_studies/20/index.html/:pf_printable [accessed 3 March 2010].
- Manning Environmental Law, Human Rights Claims Against Canadian Corp for Acts of its Overseas Subsidiary may Proceed, 2 August 2013, at http://manningenvironmentallaw.com/2013/08/02/july-22-2013-human-rights-claim-against-canadian-corp-for-acts-of-its-overseas-subsidiary-may-proceed/ [accessed 10 August 2013]
- MCKENZIE, Scott, *Oil Spills in Nigeria Highlight Lack of Accountability*, 4 September, 2010, available at www.globalpolicyjournal.com/blog/04/09/2010/oil-spills-nigeria-highlight-lack-legal-accountability [accessed 15 June 2011].
- MCQUEEN, Paddy, Social and Political Recognition, *Internet Encyclopedia of Philosophy*, 2011, available at www.iep.utm.edu/recog_sp/ [accessed 5 May 2013]
- MILLIET-EINBINDER, Martine, *Writing off Tax Deductibility*, 220 OECD Observer, April 2000, available at www.oecdobserver.org/news/fullstory.php/aid/245/Writing_off_tax_deductibility_.html. [accessed 3 March 2010].
- Misereor & Global Policy Forum Europe, *Problematic Pragmatism- The Ruggie Report 2008: Background, Analysis and Perspectives*, June 2008, available at www.wdev.eu/downloads/martensstrohscheidt.pdf [accessed 3 March 2010].
- MITEE, Ledum, *The Niger Delta: A Vision to Nigeria's Development*, being the text of a paper presented at the 5th All Nigerian Editors Conference, Kaduna, on the 3rd

April 2009, available at www.nigerianguildofeditors.com/index.php? [accessed 6 May 2010].

- MOSOTI, Victor, *Endorois Welfare Council v. Kenya*, The World Bank (Law and Development), December 2010, available at http://web.worldbank.org/ [accessed 18 August 2011].

- MUMUNI, Adetokunbo, *Legal Redress for Victims of Corruption: Enhancing the role of civil society to bring and to represent victims in legal proceedings*, being paper presented at the International Anti-Corruption Conference, Bangkok, Thailand, November 2010, available at www.serap-nigeria.org/campaign/seraps-paper-the-international-anti-corruption-conference-bangkok-thailand/ [accessed 18 August 2011].

- MWACHANG, Devota A., *Ratify African Court's Charter, AU members told*, IPP Media, 27 May 2011, available at www.ippmedia.com/frontend/index.php?l=29520 [accessed 18 August 2011].

- National Bureau of Statistics, *Review of the Nigerian Economy in 2011 & Economic Outlook for 2012–2015*, May 2012, available at www.nigerianstat.gov.ng/ [accessed 7 February 2012]

- National Oceanic and Atmospheric Administration (NOAA) Final Report to the World Bank, 'A Twelve Year Record of National and Global Gas Flaring Volumes Estimated Using Satellite Data,' 30 May 2007, available at http://siteresources.world-bank.org/INTGGFR/Resources/DMSP_flares_20070530_b-sm.pdf [accessed 3 March 2010].

- Nigeria 2006 Census Figures, Office of the National Bureau of Statistics, available at www.nigerianstat.gov.ng/Connections/pop2006.pdf [accessed 3 March 2010].

- *Niger Delta Natural Resource Damage Assessment and Restoration* Project Phase 1 – Scoping Report Federal Ministry of Environment, Abuja, Nigeria Conservation Foundation, Lagos WWF UK CEESP- IUCN Commission on Environmental, Economic, and Social Policy, 31 May, 2006, available at www.ngps.nt.ca/Upload/Interveners/World%20Wildlife%20Fund%20%20Canada/Niger_Delta_scoping_report_2006.pdf [accessed 5 March 2010].

- *Nigeria Energy Report*, Norton Rose, June 2003, available at www.nortonrose.com/knowledge/publications/pdf [accessed 3 March 2010].

- Nigeria Exchange News (2000), *Energy sector limps wearily on low funding, faulty equipment*, May 29, available at www.ngex.com/news/020600.htm [accessed 13 May 2009].

- *Nigeria First National Biodiversity Report*, July 2001, available at www.cbd.int/doc/world/ng/ng-nr-01-en.pdf [accessed 20 April 2010].

- Nigeria Millennium Development Goals Report 2010, available at www.mdgs.gov.ng [accessed 18 June 2012]

- *NIGERIA: National Biodiversity Strategy and Action Plan*, available at www.cbd.int/doc/world/ng/ng-nbsap-01-en.pdf [accessed 20 April 2010].

- Nigeria Vision 2020 Program, *Report of the Vision 2020 National Technical Working Group on Environment and Sustainable Development*, July 2009, available at www.npc.gov.ng/downloads/Environment%20&%20%20Sustainable%20Devt%20NTWG%20Report.pdf [accessed 2 March 2010].

- Ninth Annual Activity Report of the African Commission on Human and Peoples' Rights- 1995/96, AHG/207 (XXXII), available at www.achpr.org/english/activity_reports/9th%20Activity%20Report.pdf [accessed 17 March 2009].

- NORENG, Øystein, *Norway: Economic Diversification and the Petroleum Industry*, being an abridged version of a paper delivered at the 10th Annual Energy Conference of the Emirates Center for Strategic Studies and Research (ECSSR), 26–27 September, 2004 at Abu Dhabi, UAE, Middle East Economic Survey, Vol. XLVII No. 45, 8 November 2004, available at www.gasandoil.com/goc/news/nte44790.htm. [accessed 18 May 2009].

- NURAKHMET, Gulzhan, *Gas Flaring and Venting: What can Kazakhstan Learn from the Norwegian Experience?*, available at www.dundee.ac.uk/cepmlp/car/html/CAR10_ARTICLE14.PDF [accessed 16 February 2010].

- NWOKEJI, G., *The Nigerian National Petroleum Corporation and the Development of the Nigerian Oil and Gas Industry: History, Strategies and Current Directions*, being a report prepared in Conjunction with an Energy Study sponsored by the James A. Baker III Institute for Public Policy and Japan Petroleum Energy Center, Rice University, March 2007, at www.rice.edu/energy/publications/docs/NOCs/Papers/NOC_NNPC_Ugo.pdf. [accessed 3 March 2010].

- OBASI, N.K., *Foreign Participation in the Nigerian Oil and Gas Industry*, available at www.waado.org/Environment/OilExploration/oilcompanies_ history_obasi.htm [accessed 3 March 2010].

- OBASI, N., Yar'Adua Should Draw Up Roadmap to Delta Peace. *International Crisis Group*, 30 November 2009, available at www.crisisgroup.org/en/regions/africa/west-africa/nigeria/op-eds/obasi-yar-adua-should-draw-up-roadmap-to-delta-peace.aspx bid [accessed 2 February 2012]

- OCHOA, Christiana, *The 2008 Ruggie Report: A Framework for Business and Human Rights*, ASIL Insights, Vol. 12 Issue 12, June 2008, available at www.asil.org/insights080618.cfm [accessed 3 March 2010].

- ODETUNDE, Christopher, *Resource Control: Legal Action, Arbitration or Meditation?*, available at www.nigerdeltacongress.com/articles/resource_control%201.htm. [accessed 3 March 2010].

- OFEHE, S., Features on Niger Delta Amnesty. *Ex Ponto Magazine*, 11 May 2011, available at www.expontomagazine.com/nl/reportages/2279-features-on-niger-delta-amnesty [accessed 2 February 2012]

- OGBODO, Gozie S., *The Role of the Nigerian Judiciary in the Environmental Protection Against Oil Pollution: Is it Active Enough?*, available at www.nigerianlawguru.com/articles/environmental%20law/ [accessed 3 March 2010].

- OGON, Patterson, *Land and Forest Resource Use in the Niger Delta: Issues in Regulation and Sustainable Management*, available at www.globetrotter.berkeley.edu/GreenGovernance/papers/ogon2006.pdf. [accessed 18 May 2009].

- OJAKOROTU, Victor, *Oil Minorities and Politics of Exclusion in the Niger Delta of Nigeria*, available at www.sidos.ch/method/rc28/abstracts/victor%20Ojakorotu.pdf. [accessed 3 March 2010].

- OJAKOROTU, Victor, The National Question: Federalism and Oil Violence in the Niger Delta of Nigeria, in Garbutt, R. (ed) (2008), *Activating Human Rights and Peace*: *Universal Responsibility Conference 2008 Conference Proceedings*, Byron Bay, NSW, 1–4 July, Centre for Peace and Social Justice, Southern Cross University, Lismore, NSW, available at www.scu.edu.au/research/cpsj/human rights/.p.279 [accessed 3 March 2010].

- OJAMERUAYE, Emmanuel, *The Offshore/Onshore Oil Dichotomy Abolition Act-Matters Arising*, available at http://nigerdeltacongress.com/oarticles/offshore-onshore_oil_dichotomy_ab.htm [accessed 3 March 2010].

- OJAMERUAYE, Emmanuel, *Lessons from the Chadian Model for Distribution of Oil Wealth in Nigeria's Niger Delta*, available at htpp://www.waado.org/Environment/Remediation/Chadian_model_niger_ delta.htm [accessed 5 May 2010].

- OKIDI, Charles, *Environmental Rights and Duties in the Context of Management of National Resources*, Constitution of Kenya Review Commission, available at www.Kenyaconstitution.org/index.shtml. [accessed 3 March 2010].

- OKONTA, I., *The lingering crisis in Nigeria's Niger Delta and suggestions for a peaceful resolution*, available at http://nigerdeltacrises.blogspot.com/2008/09/lingering-crisis-in-nigerias-niger.html [accessed 3 March 2010].

- OLUWAROTIMI, Abiodun, Nigeria: UK Court Jails Ibori for 13 Years, *All Africa*, 17 April 2012, available at http://allafrica.com/stories/201204180067.html [accessed 18 April 2012].

- ONDUKU, Akpobibibo, *Environmental Conflicts: The Case of the Niger Delta*, being a paper presented at the One World Fortnight Programme, University of Bradford, UK, November 2001, available at www.waado.org/nigerdelta/essays/resourcecontrol/Onduku.html [accessed 3 March 2010].

- ONDUKU, Akpobibibo, The Lingering Crisis in the Niger Delta: Field Work Report, available at www.peacestudiesjournal.org.uk/docs/oilconflict.PDF [accessed 23 December 2010].

- ONWUBIKO, Emmanuel, *Environmental Friendly Oil Industry: How Feasible?*, available at www.pointblanknews.com/artopn1147.htm [accessed 3 March 2010].

- OECD Guidelines for Multinational Enterprises, submitted on 25 January 2011, available at www.business-humanrights.org/media/documents/oecd-complaint-against-shell-re-oil-pollution-in-nigeria-25-jan-2011.pdf [accessed 16 July 2011].

- QUARTERMAN, Cynthia L., *Transparency and Change Management White Paper for Nigeria's Extractive Industries Transparency Initiative ("NEITI")*, April 12 2005, available at www.neiti.org.ng/files-pdf/ChangeManagement.pdf [accessed 13 May 2010].

- OSAGHAE, Eghosa, *et al.*, *Youth Militias, Self Determination and Resource Control Struggles in the Niger-Delta Region of Nigeria*, August 2007, available at www.ascleiden.nl/Pdf/cdpnigeriaRevisedOsaghae%5B1%5D2.pdf [accessed 3 March 2010].

– OSISIOMA, Benjamin Chuka, *Combating Fraud and White Collar Crimes: Lessons from Nigeria*, being a Paper Presented at 2nd Annual Fraud & Corruption Africa Summit, Held at Zanzibar Beach Resort, Zanzibar Republic of Tanzania, available at www.managementnigeria.org/index.php/81-highlights/59-combatting-fraud-and-white-collar-crimes-lessons-from-nigeria [accessed 30 April 2013]

– OSUOKA, A.I., *Oil and Gas Revenues and Development Challenges for the Niger Delta and Nigeria*, being a paper presented at the Expert Group Meeting on the Use of Non-Renewable Resource Revenues for Sustainable Local Development, organised by the UN Department of Economic and Social Affairs, Friday 21, September 2007, UN Headquarters, New York, available at www.un.org/esa/sustdev/sdissues/institutional_arrangements/egm2007/presentations/isaacosuok.pdf [accessed 5 May 2010].

– Oxfam International Briefing Paper, *Lifting the Resource Curse: How Poor People can and should benefit from the revenues of extractive industries*, December 2009, available at www.oxfam.org/sites/www.oxfam.org/files/bp134-lifting-the-resource-curse-011209.pdf [accessed 18 August 2011].

– PARIJS, Philippe Van, *Difference Principles*, available at http://members.internet-trash.com/shev/dochX71XXpvpX.pdf [accessed 2 February 2012]

– POUDYAL, K.P., *The Protection of Socio-Economic Rights with Special Reference to the Right to Food, Right to Education and the Right to Health*, available at www.interights.org/doc/WS2_Poudyal_final.doc. [accessed 3 March 2010].

– PRING, George (Rock) and PRING, Catherine (Kitty), *Greening Justice: Creating and Improving Environmental Courts and Tribunals*, The Access Initiative, 2009, available at www.accessinitiative.org/sites/default/files/Greening%20Justice%20FInal_31399_WRI.pdf [accessed 3 March 2010].

– Public Intelligence, *Halliburton to Pay $35 Million to Settle Nigeria Bribery Charges*, 22 December, 2010, available at http://publicintelligence.net/halliburton-to-pay-35-million-to-settle-nigeria-bribery-charges/ [accessed 3 March 2010].

– QUARTERMAN, Cynthia L., *Transparency and Change Management White Paper for Nigeria's Extractive Industries Transparency Initiative ("NEITI")*, 12 April 2005, available at www.neiti.org.ng/files-pdf/ChangeManagement.pdf. [accessed 3 March 2010].

– RAZZAQUE, Jona, *Human Rights and the Environment: The National Experience in South-Asia and Africa*, Joint UNEP-OHCHR Expert Seminar on Human Rights and the Environment 14–16 January 2002, Geneva: Background Paper No. 4, available at http://www2.ohchr.org/english/issues/environment/environ/bp4.htm [accessed 8 May 2010].

– *Report of the African Commission's Working Group of Experts on Indigenous Populations/Communities*, adopted by the African Commission on Human and Peoples' Rights at its 28th ordinary session (May 2003), 2005, at www.pro169.org/res/materials/en/identification/ACHPR%20Report%20on%20indigenous%20populations-communities.pdf [accessed at 6 June 2011]

– Report from the Roundtable of National Human Rights Institutions on the Issue of Business and Human Rights Copenhagen 1–2 July 2008, hosted by the Danish Institute for Human Rights in Collaboration with the Swiss Federal Department of Foreign Affairs, available at www.nhri.net/2009/report_from_the_round_table_of_national_human_rights_institutions_on_the_issue_of_business_and_human_rights.pdf [accessed 3 March 2010].

– Report of the International Commission of Jurists Expert Legal Panel on Corporate Complicity in International Crimes, *Corporate Complicity & Legal Accountability: Facing the Facts and Charting a Legal Path*, Volume 1 (Geneva: International Commission of Jurists, 2008), available at http://icj.org/IMG/Volume_1.pdf [accessed 3 March 2010].

– REQUEJO, Martha, Kiobel: No Role for the United States as World Police, *Conflict of Law.net*, 19 April, 2013, available at http://conflictoflaws.net/2013/kiobel-no-role-for-the-united-states-as-world-police/ [accessed 18 May, 2013]

– RUGGIE, John, *Response by John Ruggie to Misereor / Global Policy Forum*, 2 June 2008, available at www.reports-and-materials.org/Ruggie-response-to-Misereor-GPF-2-Jun-2008.pdf [accessed 3 March 2010].

– RUGGIE, John, *Guiding Principles for the Implementation of the United Nations 'Protect, Respect And Remedy' Framework*, available at www.reports-and-materials.org/Ruggie-UN-draft-Guiding-Principles-22-Nov-2010.pdf [accessed 12 May 2011].

– RUGGIE, John, *Business and Human Rights- Treaty Road not Travelled*, Ethical Corporation, 6 May 2008, available at www.ethicalcorp.com/content.asp?ContentID=5887 [accessed 3 March 2010].

– SACHS, Aaron, *A Planet Unfree*, available at www.sierraclub.org/sierra/199711/humanrights.html [accessed 3 March 2010].

– SACHS, Jeffrey D. and WARNER, Andrew M., *Natural Resource Abundance and Economic Growth*, November 1997, available at www.cid.harvard.edu/ciddata/warner_files/natresf5.pdf [accessed 3 March 2010].

– SACHS, Wolfgang, *Environment and Human Rights,* Wuppertal Institute for Climate, Environment, and Energy, Wuppertal, available at www.wupperinst.org/globalisierung/pdf_global/human_rights.pdf [accessed 3 March 2010].

– SAGAY, Itse, *Federalism, the Constitution and Resource control: My Response*, available at www.nigerdeltacongress.com/farticles/federalism_the_constitution_and_html. [accessed 7 September 2009].

– SEBOK, Anthony J., *Unocal Announces It Will Settle A Human Rights Suit: What Is the Real Story Behind Its Decision?*, FindLaw, January 10, 2005, available at http://writ.news.findlaw.com/sebok/20050110.html. [accessed 3 March 2010].

– Shell Guilty Campaign: Oil Change International, Friends of the Earth (International, Europe, U.S. and The Netherlands), PLATFORM, and Greenpeace UK (2009), *Shell's Big Dirty Secret: Insight into the world's most carbon intensive oil company and the legacy of CEO Jeroen van der Veer*, available at www.foeeurope.org/corporates/Extractives/shellbigdirtysecret_June09.pdf [accessed 13 March 2011].

– Shell Petroleum Development Company (SPDC) (2007), *Shell Nigeria Annual Report 2006: People and the Environment,* available at http://narcosphere.narconews.com/userfiles/70/2006_shell_nigeria_report.pdf [accessed 21 April 2010].

– SILVERMAN, Jana and ORSATTI, Alvaro, *Holding Transnational Corporations Accountable for Human Rights Obligations: The Role of Civil Society,* Social Watch Thematic Report available at www.socialwatch.org/sites/default/files/silverman-orsatti2009_eng.pdf [accessed 21 April 2010].

– SIMONS, Marco, being an opinion expressed following Settlement Reached in Human Rights Cases Against Royal Dutch/Shell, available at www.earthrights.org/sites/default/files/documents/Wiwa-v-Shell-Settlement-Press-Release.pdf [accessed 3 March 2010].

– SLYE, Ronald, *Wiwa v. Shell Settlement a Victory for Corporate Accountability,* Seattle University School of Law Faculty, Cases and Controversies, available at http://lawfacultyblog.seattleu.edu/2009/06/09/wiwa-v-shell-settlement-a-victory-for-corporate-accountability/ [accessed 5 June 2011].

– SMITH, Herbert, *Regulating jurisdiction: English courts discretion to stay proceedings curtailed,* November 2005, available at www.herbertsmith.com/NR/rdonlyres/3F7524EE- 9AB8-4B6A-9993-285934A7EF14/1605/Regjuris.pdf [accessed 3 March 2010].

– SMOCK, David, *Crisis in the Niger Delta,* USI Peace Briefing, September 2009, available at www.usip.org/files/resources/niger_delta_crisis.pdf [accessed 6 May 2010].

– Southern Africa Litigation Centre (SALC) Blogger, *A Human Rights Court for Africa,* 16 March, 2011, available at http://salcbloggers.wordpress.com/2011/03/16/a-human-rights-court- for-africa-2/ [accessed 3 July 2011].

– SYKES, Richard, Oil and Gas Industry Efforts on Behalf of Human Rights and Sustainable Development, available at www.spe.org/twa/print/archives/2008/2008v4n2/twa2008_v4n2_Pillars.pdf [accessed 3 March 2009]

– TAILLANT, Jorge Daniel, *Environmental Discrimination,* Center for Human Rights and Development (CEDHA) November 2000, available at www.cedha.org.ar/en/documents [accessed 3 March 2010].

– The Center for People and Forests, *Free, Prior, and Informed Consent in REDD+: Principles and Approaches for Policy and Project Development,* Bangkok, February 2011, available at www.recoftc.org/site/uploads/content/pdf/FPICinREDDManual_127.pdf [accessed 5 May 2013]

– thedailygreen, *The Health Effects of Oil Spills,* available at http://dailygreen.com/environmental-news/latest/oil-spill-health-effects-0510 [accessed 3 March 2010].

– The Environment and Conservation Program, Centre for Environment, Human Rights and Development (CEHRD) Report, *Persistent oil spillage at Bodo Creek: unprecedented impacts on ecosystem stability, biodiversity and food security of Ogoni communities,* October 2008, available at www.cehrd.org/files/Press_Release_on_Persistent_Oil_Spillage_at_Bodo_Creek.pdf [accessed 3 March 2010].

–   *The International Comparative Legal Guide to: Environment Law (2008)*, Global Legal Group Ltd., London, available at www.iclg.co.uk/khadmin/Publications/pdf/2032. pdf [accessed 2 March 2010].

–   *The Maastricht Guidelines on Violations of Economic, Social, and Cultural Rights*, January 1997, available at http://www1.umn.edu/humanrts/instree/Maastrichtguidelines_.html [accessed 10 June 2009].

–   TURNER, Terisa E., being her Assessment of the Aftermath of Shell's Oil Spill Disaster at Ogbudu, Niger Delta: *Oil Companies Lie, Deceive, Play Ethnic Card to Divide Host Communities*, published by National Interest (Lagos), Vol. 221, 31 July 2001, available at www.waado.org/Environment/OilCompanies/States/Rivers/ OgbuduSpill/TerisaTurner_Interview.html, [accessed 22 April 2010].

–   Transparency International, *National Integrity Systems TI Country Study Report Nigeria 2004*, Berlin, 2004, available at http://info.worldbank.org/etools/ANTIC/ docs/Resources/Country%20Profiles/Nigeria/TransparencyInternational_NIS_ Nigeria.pdf [accessed 3 March 2010].

–   Transparency International, *2011 Corruption Perceptions Index*, available at http:// cpi.transparency.org/cpi2011/results/ [accessed 3 June 2012].

–   U4 Anti-Corruption Resource Centre, *Special courts for corruption cases*, available at www.u4.no/helpdesk/helpdesk/query.cfm?id=19 [accessed 3 August 2011].

–   United Nations Educational, Scientific and Cultural Organization (UNESCO) (2007), *A Human Rights-Based Approach to EDUCATION FOR ALL: A framework for the realization of children's right to education and rights within education* (UNICEF New York 2007), available at http://unesdoc.unesco.org/images/0015/001548/154861e.pdf [accessed 3 March 2010].

–   U.S. Securities and Exchange Commission Spotlight, SEC Enforcement Actions: FCPA Cases, available at www.sec.gov/spotlight/fcpa/fcpa-cases.shtml [accessed 30 April 2013]

–   U.S. State Department, *2008 Human Rights Report: Nigeria*, 25 February 2009, available at www.state.gov/g/drl/rls/hrrpt/2008/af/119018.htm. [accessed 3 March 2010].

–   UYIGUE, Etiosa and AGHO, Matthew, *Coping with Climate Change and Environmental Degradation in the Niger Delta of Southern Nigeria*, Community Research and Development Centre (CREDC) Nigeria (2007), available at http://priceofoil.org/ wp- content/uploads/2007/06/07.06.11%20-%20Climate_Niger_Delta.pdf [accessed 5 July 2009].

–   VAN DER HEIJDEN, Marie-José, Unique Case againstShell-The first Dutch Foreign Direct Libility Case, *Invisible College Blog, Weblog of the Netherlands School of Human Rights Research*, available at http://invisiblecollege.weblog.leidenuniv. nl/2013/02/08/%EF%BB%BFunique-case-against-shell-the-first-dutch-foreign-direct-liability-case/ [accessed 23 May 2013]

–   WANG, Ying, *The Natural Resource Curse*, available at www.neaef.org/public/neaef/ files/documents/publications_pdf/young_leaders/5th/Wang%20Ying.pdf [accessed 30 March 2013].

– WASAKI-GOODMAN, Masamii, *et al.*, *Traditional food systems of Indigenous Peoples: the Ainu in the Saru River Region, Japan*, available at ftp://ftp.fao.org/docrep/fao/012/i0370e/i0370e08.pdf [accessed 8 July 2011].

– WATTS, Michael, *Sweet and Sour*, Niger Delta Economies of Violence Working Paper No. 18, 2008, available at www.ie.ufrj.br/datacenterie/pdfs/download/seminariopped.pdf [accessed 3 March 2010].

– WATTS, Michael, *Petro-Insurgency or Criminal Syndicate? Conflict, Violence and Political Disorder in the Niger Delta*, Niger Delta Economies of Violence Working Paper No. 16, 2008, available at http://geography.berkeley.edu/ProjectsResources/ND%20Website/NigerDelta/WP/16- Watts.pdf. [accessed 3 March 2010].

– WATTS, Michael, *Has globalization failed in Nigeria?* (2009), being Interview conducted and edited by Ted O'Callahan, available at http://qn.som.yale.edu/downloads/Q5Nigeria.pdf [accessed 3 March 2010].

– WAWRYK, Alexandra S., *International Environmental Standards in the Oil Industry: Improving the Operations of Transnational Oil Companies in Emerging Economies*, available at http://ugandapetroleum.com/linked/international_environmental_standards_in_the_oil_industry.pdf [accessed 9 August 2011].

– WEILER, Todd, *Balancing Human Rights and Investor Protection: A New Approach for a Different Legal Order*, Oil, Gas and Energy Law Intelligence, Vol. 1, Issue No. 2, March 2003, available at www.dundee.ac.uk/cepmlp/journal/html/vol11/article11-5.pdf [accessed 3 March 2010].

– WestLaw News and Insight, *U.S. appeals court declines to rehear case re Shell in Nigeria*, 4 February 2011, available at http://westlawnews.thomson.com/National_Litigation/News/2011/02_-_February/U_S__appeals_court_declines_to_rehear_case_re_Shell_in_Nigeria/ [accessed 13 May 2011].

– West London today, Nigerian politician who stole $250m was Ruislip cashier, available at www.westlondontoday.co.uk/content/nigerian-politician-who-stole-250m-was-ruislip-cashier [accessed 18 April 2012].

– WIWA, Owens, *The Paradox of Poverty and Corporate Globalization*, being Speech at Ghent on 30 October 2001 at the First EU International Conference on Globalization, available at www.waado.org/environment/oilcompanies/Globalization_OwensWiwa.htm [accessed 6 September 2009].

– World Conservation Union Paper on *Human Rights and Environment: Overlapping Issues*, available at www.ciel.org. [accessed 3 March 2010].

– World Health Organization (WHO) *et al.* (2007), *Maternal Mortality in 2005: Estimates Developed by WHO, UNICEF, UNFPA, and the World Bank*, available at www.who.int/whosis/mme_2005.pdf [accessed 3 March 2010].

– Yar'Adua, Umaru, *New operator to replace Shell in Nigeria's Ogoniland*, (AFP) 4 June, 2008, available at http://afp.google.com/article/ALeqM5ilZcJKFiFVnQf_NOEa1X-JUzrjgBQ [accessed 3 March 2010].

– ZALIK, Anna and WATTS, Michael (2006), Imperial Oil: Petroleum Politics in the Nigerian Delta and the New Scramble for Africa, *Socialist Review*, available at www.socialistreview.org.uk/article.php?articlenumber=9712 [accessed 3 March 2010].

- ZERK, Jennifer (2010), *Extraterritorial Jurisdiction: Lessons for the Business and Human Rights Sphere from Six Regulatory Areas*, Corporate Social Responsibility Initiative Working Paper No. 59. 2010, at www.hks.harvard.edu/m-rcbg/CSRI/publications/workingpaper_59_zerk.pdf [acccesed 24 April 2013]

5.2 Some other unclassified materials

- ABDUL-GAFARU, Abdulai, *Are Multinational Corporations Compatible with Sustainable Development in Developing Countries?*, being a paper prepared for the conference on Multinational Corporations and Sustainable Development: Strategic Tool for Competitiveness, Atlanta, Georgia, 19–20 October 2006.
- ABULHASAN, Arwa Mohammad, *Future Relations Between Kuwait Petroleum Corporation and the International Oil Companies: Success or Failure?*, being Master of Arts in Law and Diplomacy Thesis Presented to the Fletcher School of Law and Diplomacy May 2004.
- ADEKOYA, Charles Olufemi, *Poverty: Legal and Constitutional Implications for Human Rights Enforcement in Nigeria*, being a Doctoral Dissertation in the Faculty of Law, University of Ghent, Belgium, 2008–2009.
- ADELEGAN, Joseph, *Environmental Compliance, Policy Reform and Industrial Pollution in sub-Saharan Africa: Lessons from Nigeria*, being excerpt from the Proceedings of the International Network for Environmental Compliance and Enforcement's (INECE) Eighth International Conference, Linking Concepts to Actions: Successful Strategies for Environmental Compliance and Enforcement, held 5–11 April 2008, in Cape Town, South Africa.
- Advisory Opinion of the African Commission on Human and Peoples' Rights on the United Nations Declarations on the Rights of Indigenous Peoples, adopted by the African Commission on Human and Peoples' Rights (ACHPR) at its 41st Ordinary Session held in May 2007 in Accra, Ghana, ACHPR and International Work Group for Indigenous Affairs (IWGIA), 2010.
- AGIOBENEBO, Tamunopriye J. and AZIBAOLANARI, Nelson, *Rights, Freedom, Resource Control and Politico-Economic Equilibrium of the Market for National Union*, Selected Papers presented at the 2001 Annual Conference of the Nigerian Economic Society, 2001.
- AKPAN, Wilson Ndarake, *Between the 'Sectional' and the 'National': Oil, Grassroots Discontent and Civic Discourse in Nigeria*, Unpublished Thesis Submitted in Fulfilment of the Requirements for the Degree of Doctor of Philosophy of Rhodes University, October 2005.
- Asia Pacific Forum of National Human Rights Institutions (APF), *ACJ Report on Human Rights, Corporate Accountability and Government Responsibility*, Part 2: Supplementary Paper, the 13th Annual meeting of the APF, Kuala Lumpur, Malaysia, 27–31 July 2008.

– ASIODU, P., *Improving Investment Flows: New Focus on Financing Projects*, Keynote Address at the 2nd Annual Oil and Gas Investments in Nigeria Conference, London, 27 April 2001.

– ATURU, Bamidele (1998), *Justice for Oil Communities in Oil and the Nigerian Environment*, Environmental Rights Action (ERACTION), Benin City, Nigeria.

– BASSEY, Nnimmo, *Gas Flaring: Assaulting Communities, Jeopardizing the World*, being a paper presented at the National Environmental Consultation hosted by the Environmental Rights Action in conjunction with the Federal Ministry of Environment at Reiz Hotel, Abuja between 10–11 December 2008.

– BELLO, Bukhari, *Welcome Statement by Bukhari Bello, Executive Secretary, National Human Rights Commission of Nigeria at the 5th Conference of African National Human Rights Institutions (ANHRIs)*, held in Abuja Nigeria between 8–10 November 2005.

– BOSSMAN, Anna, Acting Chairman Commission on Human Rights and Administrative Justice (CHRAJ) Ghana, *Promoting and Protecting Human Right, Ensuring Administrative Justice and Fighting Corruption in Ghana*, being a paper delivered at the Commonwealth Conference of National Human Rights Institutions, Malborough House, London, 26–28 February 2007.

– BROECKER, Christen (2010), *Alien Tort Statute Litigation and Transnational Business Activity: Investigating the Potential for a Bottom-Up Global Regulatory Regime*, Institute for International Law and Justice (IILJ) Emerging Scholars Paper 16.

– Commonwealth Secretariat Report (2001), *National Human Rights Institutions: Best Practice*, Legal and Constitutional Affairs Division, London.

– COURSON, E. (2007), *The Burden of Oil: Social Deprivation and Political Militancy in Gbaramatu Clan, Warri South West LGA, Delta State, Nigeria*, Niger Delta Economies of Violence Working Paper No. 15.

– COURSON, E. (2009), *Movement for the Emancipation of the Niger Delta (MEND): Political Marginalization, Repression and Petro-Insurgency in the Niger Delta*, Nordiska AfrikaInstitutet, Discussion paper 47, Uppsala.

– DADIOWEI, Tari (2009), *Environmental Impact Assessment and Sustainable Development in the Niger Delta: The Gbarain Oil Field Experience*, Niger Delta Economies of Violence Working Paper No. 24.

– Danish Institute of Human Rights, *Report from the round table on Business institutions and human rights,* in collaboration with the Swiss Federal Department of Foreign Affairs, Copenhagen, 1–2 July 2008.

– CONNIE, De la Vega, *et al.*, *Holding Businesses Accountable for Human Rights Violations: Recent Developments and Next Steps*, Friedrich-Ebert-Stiftung/Global Policy and Development, Germany, 2011.

– DOGO, Isuwa B., *Transnational Corporations and Environmental Pollution and Degradation*, being the text of a paper presented at the 1997 Annual Conference of the Nigerian Society of International Law in Lagos on 15 August 1997.

– EMEJURU, Chukwucheta ThankGod, *A Critical Appraisal of the Legal Framework for the Protection of the Environment Against Oil and Gas Pollution in Nigeria*, M. Phil. Thesis Submitted to Obafemi Awolowo University, Ile-Ife, Nigeria, August 2006.

– EMEKA, Chegwu, *Legal and Regulatory Challenges of Resource Control*, Proceedings of the 38th Annual Conference of the Nigerian Association of Law Teachers held at the Faculty of Law, LASU on 23–26 April 2003.

– ETENG, Inya A., *Minority Rights Under Nigeria's Federal Structure*, in M.A. Ajomo *et al* (eds), Constitutions and Federalism: Proceedings of the Conference on Constitutions and Federalism, held at the University of Lagos, Nigeria 23–25 April 1996, Friedrich Ebert Foundation, Lagos, 1997.

– European Parliament, *Business and Human Rights in EU External Relations: Making the EU a leader at home and abroad internationally*, EXPO/B/DROI/2009/2, April 2009

– EZENWE, Uka, *Revenue Allocation under the 1995 Draft Constitution: Some Comments*, being a paper presented at the 32nd Annual Conference of the Nigerian Association of Law Teachers held at the Nigerian Institute of Advanced Legal Studies, Lagos, 10–14 May 1994.

– GILLIES, Alexandra, *Reforming Corruption out of Nigerian Oil? Part one: Mapping corruption risks in oil sector governance*, Chr. Michelsen Institute (U4 Brief 2009:2), Bergen.

– GILLIES, Alexandra, *Reforming Corruption out of Nigerian Oil? Part two: Progress and Prospects*, Chr. Michelsen Institute (U4 Brief 2009:6), Bergen.

– Greenpeace U.K., *Greenpeace Oil Briefing No. 7: Human Health Impacts of Oil*, January 1993, London.

– HAGEN, K.A., Policy Dialogue between the International Labour Organization and the International Financial Institutions: The Search for Convergence, *FES Dialogue on Globalization* No. 9, October, 2003.

– Human Rights Watch, *Some Transparency, No Accountability: The Use of Oil Revenue in Angola and Its Impact on Human Rights*, January 2004.

– Human Rights Watch, *Transparency and Accountability in Angola: An Update*, April 2010, New York.

– International Commission of Jurists (1961), *African Conference on the Rule of Law*, Lagos, Nigeria.

– KALE, Yemi, *The Nigeria Poverty Profile 2010 Report*, being Press Briefing by the Statistician-General of the Federation/Chief Executive Officer, National Bureau of Statistics (NBS), held at the NBS Headquarters, Abuja on Monday, 13th February, 2012.

– KERR, Michael and SEGGER, Marie-Claire Cordonier, *Legal Strategies to Promote Corporate Social Responsibility and Accountability: A Pre-requisite for Sustainable Development*, Centre for International Sustainable Development Law (CISDL) Legal Brief, April 2004.

– KRETZMANN, S. and WRIGHT, S., *Human Rights and Environmental Information on the Royal Dutch/Shell Group of Companies, 1996–1997: An Independent Annual*

Report, Rainforest Action Network and Project Underground, San Francisco and
Berkeley, CA, 1997.

– LADAN, Muhammed T., *Enhancing Access to Justice on Environmental Matters:
Public Participation in Decision-Making and Access to Information,* being a paper
presented at a Judicial Training Workshop on Environmental Law in Nigeria, organized by the National Judicial Institute, Abuja, in Collaboration with the United Nations Environment Programme (UNEP), held at the National Judicial Institute, Abuja
between 6–10 February 2006.

– MANUEL, A., *The Dirty Four: The Case Against Letting BP Amoco, ExxonMobil, Chevron, and Philips Petroleum Drill in the Artic Refuge,* US Public Interest Research
Group Washington DC. March 2001.

– MITTEE, L., *Civil Society and Implementation of the Master Plan,* being Notes of
the Presentation at the Niger Delta Stakeholders Networks Workshop on the Implementation of the Niger Delta Regional Development Master Plan, held at the Marina
Resort, Calabar, 11- 13 November 2007.

– Multilateral Investment Guarantee Agency (MIGA) Working Paper, *The Voluntary
Principles on Security and Human Rights: An Implementation Toolkit for Major Project Sites,* July 2008.

– National Bureau of Statistics (NBS), Nigeria Poverty Profile 2010, January 2012.

– NWABUEZE, Ben, *Reflections on the 1999 Constitution: A Unitary Constitution for a
Federal System of Government,* being a paper delivered at a Seminar in Abuja, organized by the International Commission of Jurists, 4–16 February, 2000.

– NWAJIAKU-DAHOU, K., *The Politics of Amnesty in the Niger Delta. Challenges
Ahead,* Paris and Brussels: The Institut français des relations internationales (Ifri),
2010.

– NWAUCHE, E.S. *et al.,* *Legal and Regulatory Challenges of Resources Control in Nigeria,* being a paper presented at the Nigerian Association of Law Teachers, Proceedings
of the 38th Annual Conference, Faculty of Law, LASU, Ojo held between 23–26 April
2003.

– NWETE, Bede, *Soft Law and Hard Sanctions in Upstream Oil and Gas in Developing
Regions- How International Codes, Principles and Protocols Influence National Projects and Developments,* International Energy Law and Policy Research Paper Series,
Working Research Paper Series No: 2010/05, Centre for Energy, Petroleum and Mineral Law and Policy, University of Dundee.

– ODINKALU, Chidi Anselm, *Do Our People Matter to Our Courts?: The Case for Jus-
ticiable Socio-Economic Rights in Nigeria,* being a keynote paper to the 1st Annual
Human Rights Conference of the Nigerian Bar Association, held between 6–8
December 2009 at the Rockview Hotel, Abuja.

– OGOWEWO, Tunde, *Wealth (Dis)creation through Corporate (Mis)governance and
Banking (Mis)supervision: The Outlines of a Reform Agenda,* being paper presented in
Honour of Hon. Justice E.O. Ayoola on 25 November 2009 at the Nigerian Institute of
International Affairs.

- OKIGBO, Pius, *Notes on Revenue Generation and Distribution in a Federation*, (Unpublished Manuscript).
- OLUSI, O.S. (1981), *Nigerian Oil Industry and the Environment*, Proceedings of the 1981 International Seminar, NNPC, Lagos, Nigeria.
- OMOROGBE, Yinka, *Communities and the Natural Resource Industries: The Route to Survival*, being the text of a paper presented at the World Women Lawyers Conference organized by the International Bar Association, London, 1–2 March 2001.
- OMOTOLA, Shola (2006), *The Next Gulf? Oil Politics, Environmental Apocalypse and Rising Tension in the Niger Delta*, Occasional Paper Series: Vol. 1 No. 3, published by the African Centre for the Constructive Resolution of Disputes (ACCORD).
- ONIMODE, Bade, *Resources Derivation, Allocation, and Utilisation*, in M.A. Ajomo *et al* (eds), Constitutions and Federalism: Proceedings of the Conference on Constitutions and Federalism, held at the University of Lagos, Nigeria, 23–25 April 1996, Friedrich Ebert Foundation, Lagos, 1997.
- OECD (2003), *Voluntary Approaches for Environmental policy: Effectiveness, Efficiency and Usage in Policy Mixes,* OECD, Paris.
- PALLEMAERTS, Marc, Proceduralizing Environmental Rights: The Aarhus Convention on Access to Information, Public Participation in Decision-Making and Access to Justice in Environmental Matters in a Human Rights Context, in *Human Rights and the Environment* (2004), Proceedings of a Geneva Environment Network Roundtable, UNEP Publication, Geneva.
- PYAGBARA, Legborsi Saro, *The Adverse Impacts of Oil Pollution on the Environment and Wellbeing of a Local Indigenous Community: The Experience of the Ogoni People of Nigeria*, being a paper presented at the International Expert Group Meeting on Indigenous Peoples and Protection of the Environment, at Khabarovsk, Russian Federation, 27–29 August 2007.
- ROBINSON, Nicholas A., *Principles of Environmental Justice: A Foundation for Dispute Prevention and Resolution*, Report of the Regional Symposium on the Role of the Judiciary in Promoting the Rule of Law in the Area of Sustainable Development, Colombo, Sri Lanka, 4–6 July 1997.
- ROMERO, Flerida Ruth P. (1999), *The Role of the Judiciary in Promoting the Rule of Law in the Area of Environmental Protection in the Philippines*, Southeast Asian Justices Symposium: The Law on Sustainable Development, UNEP/UNDP/Hanns Seidel Foundation/Supreme Court of the Philippines, Manila, Philippines.
- ROSEMANN, N. (2005), *The U.N. Norms on Corporate Human Rights Responsibilities. An Innovating Instrument to Strengthen Business*, Human Rights Performance, Dialogue on Globalization Occasional papers, Geneva No. 20, August, Published by Geneva office of the Friedrich-Ebert-Stiftung.
- Royal Dutch/Shell, *Revised Statement of General Business Principles*, Royal Dutch/Shell, The Hague, 1997.
- SAGAY, Itse, *NIGERIA: Federalism, the Constitution and Resource Control*, being text of speech delivered at a sensitization programme organized by the Ibori Vanguard at London Restaurant, Lagos, 19 May 2001.

- SALMAN, Raheem Kolawole, *The Effectiveness of Nigerian National Human Rights Commission in Human Rights Protection*, being a thesis submitted in fulfillment of requirement for the degree of Doctor of Philosophy, Ahmad Ibrahim Kulliyyah of Laws, International Islamic University Malaysia, 2011.
- SCANLON, John, CASSAR, Angela and NEMES, Noemi, *Water as a Human Rights?*, being a paper delivered at the 7th International Conference on Environmental Law, organized Law for a Green Planet Institute, Co-sponsored by IUCN Environmental Law Programme, 'Water and the Web of Life', held at Sao Paulo Brazil between 2–5 June 2003.
- SCHWARTE, Christoph (2008), *Public Participation and Oil Exploitation in Uganda*, International Institute for Environment and Development (IIED), Gatekeeper Series 138.
- SHELTON, D., *Human Rights and the Environment: Jurisprudence of Human Rights Bodies*, Background Paper No. 2, being a paper presented at the Joint UNEP-OHCHR Expert Seminar on Human Rights and the Environment held at Geneva between 14–16 January 2002.
- SINDEN, Amy, *An Emerging Human Right to Security from Climate Change: The Case against Gas Flaring in Nigeria*, Temple University Beasley School of Law, Research Paper No. 2008-77.
- SOREMEKUN, Kayode, *Nigeria Petroleum Policy and External Relations*, Unpublished PhD Thesis Submitted to the Department of International Relations, University of Ife, 1984.
- Stichting Onderzoek Multinationale Ondernemingen (SOMO) (2010), *Royal Dutch Shell Overview of controversial business practices in 2009*, SOMO Amsterdam.
- STEINER, Richard, *Double Standards? International Standards to Prevent and Control Pipeline Oil Spills, Compared with Shell Practices in Nigeria*, published by friends of the Earth Netherlands, November 2008.
- TIMPSON, Sarah L. (1999), *Creating a Just Future- The Role of the Judiciary and the Law on Sustainable Development*, Southeast Asian Justices Symposium: The Law on Sustainable Development, UNEP/UNDP/Hanns Seidel Foundation/Supreme Court of the Philippines, Manila, Philippines.
- United States Senate Permanent Subcommittee on Investigations, Committee on Homeland Security and Governmental Affairs, *Keeping Foreign Corruption out of the United States: Four Case Histories*, 4 February 2010 Hearing, Washington, DC.
- WACHIRA, George Mukundi (2008), *African Court on Human and Peoples' Rights: Ten Years on and Still no Justice*, Minority Rights Group International Report.
- Watts, M.J., *Petro-violence: Community, Extraction, and Political Ecology*, being a paper prepared for the Workshop on Environment and Violence, University of California, Berkeley, 24–26 September, 1998.
- Women Advocates Research and Documentation Centre (WARDC), *The 11-day siege: gains and challenges of women's non-violent struggles in Niger Delta*, Lagos, December 2005.

– YOUNG, Madeline R., *Energy, Development and EITI: Improving coherence of EU policies towards Nigeria*, European Development Co-operation (EDC) 2020 Policy Brief, No. 4, November 2009.

5.3 Other websites sources

– Amnesty International USA
  www.amnestyusa.org/
– EITI
  http://eiti.org/
– Milieudefensie Factsheet
  http://www1.milieudefensie.nl/
– Nigerian National Petroleum Corporation
  www.nnpcgroup.com/
– Oxfam International
  www.oxfam.org/
– Shell Code of Conduct
  www.shell.com
– Shell Sustainability Report
  http://sustainabilityreport.shell.com
– Transparency International
  www.transparency.org/
– Voluntary Principles on Security and Human Rights
  http://voluntaryprinciples.org/

6 NEWSPAPERS AND THEIR SOURCES

– BBC News
  http://news.bbc.co.uk/
– Businessweek
  www.businessweek.com/
– Business World
  http://businessworldng.com/
– Crimes of War Magazine: The Tribunal
  www.crimesofwar.org
– Daily Champion
– Daily Independent
– Daily Times
– Daily Triumph
– Daily Trust
– Economist
  www.economist.co.uk

- Financial Times
  www.ft.com/
- Forbes
- IRIN News
  www.irinnews.org/
- National Concord
- National Mirror
- New Nation
- Newswatch
- Pambazuka News
- Radio Kudirat Nigeria.
- Sahara Reporters
  www.saharareporters.com
- Spero News
  www.speroforum.com/
- TELL
- The Corporate Examiner
- The Daily Telegraph
- The Express
- The Guardian
- The Guardian on-line
  http://ngrguardiannews.com
- The Independent
  www.independent.co.uk/
- The Lawyers Weekly
  www.lawyersweekly.ca/
- The News
- The Nation
- The Punch
- The Wall Street Journal
  http://online.wsj.com/
- This Day
- Tribune
- Vanguard

APPENDIX

MAP OF NIGERIA SHOWING STATES THAT MAKE UP THE NIGER DELTA REGION

1. Abia, 2. Akwa Ibom, 3. Bayelsa, 4. Cross River, 5. Delta, 6. Edo, 7. Imo, 8. Ondo, 9. Rivers

Source: Wikipedia, at http://en.wikipedia.org/wiki/Niger_Delta.